LIVING ECONOMIC AND SOCIAL HISTORY

LIVING ECONOMIC AND SOCIAL HISTORY

*Historians explain their interest in, and the nature of,
their subject*

Essays to mark the 75th Anniversary of the Economic History Society

Edited on behalf of the Economic History Society
by

PAT HUDSON
Cardiff University
With the assistance of Rachel Bowen

Published by the Economic History Society
Glasgow

First published in 2001 by the Economic History Society
Registered Office: Department of Economic and Social History
University of Glasgow
4, University Gardens
Glasgow G12 8QQ

http://www.ehs.org.uk

British Library Cataloguing in Publication data
A catalogue record of this book is available from the British Library

Library of Congress Cataloguing-in-publication Data
A catalogue record for this book is available from the Library of Congress

ISBN: 0-9540216-0-6 Paperback

Production editor: Pat Hudson (with the assistance of Rachel Bowen)
Cover Design: Pat Hudson

Printed by Universities Design and Print
141 St James Rd.,
Glasgow G4 OLT

Contents

Appendices

ACKNOWLEDGEMENTS

This volume could not have been produced without the dedication and commitment of the many authors who generously gave their time despite busy academic schedules. The Economic History Society would like to thank the contributors most warmly for their support for the Society and for this venture. Thanks must especially go to Negley Harte who managed to complete both his own essay and the brief history of the Society in the nick of time and against competing pressures. Douglas Farnie likewise has been a most generous friend and supporter during the long editing process. He read through the entire manuscript later than the eleventh hour identifying important errors (mistakes remaining are entirely my responsibility). His appendices to the volume are most valuable and will provide an important starting point for scholars wishing to research the history of our subject and the lives of its practitioners.

Many others have assisted, in various ways, in ensuring the successful production of the volume, in particular Maureen Galbraith, Oliver Westall, Patrick O'Brien and of course Rachel Bowen who is currently an MA student at Cardiff and who has shown organisational skills, intellectual qualities and calm good sense beyond her years during the course of our editing work.

The cover is designed from the inversion of a painting by G. H. Andrews which depicts *The Barrow Haematite Iron and Steel Company* c.1873 and is reproduced with kind permission from the Barrow Museum Service.

Pat Hudson
February 2001

INTRODUCTION

This volume celebrates the 75th anniversary of the Economic History Society founded in 1926. The aim was to produce an archive of essays, reflecting the personalities and plurality of the subject. Contributors were asked to write to the *general* theme 'What economic history means to me' or, if preferred, 'What economic and social history means to me'. The initiative was publicised in the Society's newsletter and in broadsheets circulated at conferences. Members of the Society were also approached individually. Essays of a variety of kinds were encouraged from serious academic and intellectual pieces to light hearted autobiographical or anecdotal contributions and mixes of the two. It was suggested that contributors might wish to write on the broader implications of their own specialist field, or reflect upon the nature of the subject and its links with others. Reminiscence of events, training, career paths, incidents, inspirations or personalities was encouraged.

The initiative bore extraordinarily rich fruit: a veritable melange of diverse commentaries and experiences is the result. More than 100 researchers, teachers, museum specialists, administrators, government officials, archivists and retired academics who share a commitment to economic and social history have generously spared time to write about their interest in the subject. The contributors come from very different institutional, age, gender, national and cultural perspectives: a global array and diversity which far exceeded the expectations of this editor. The project has clearly appealed most strongly to retired colleagues though most are retired in name only and remain key inspirational figures. Such writers are in a prime position to reflect upon their careers, intellectual fashions, institutional peculiarities and on early personalities in the Society. British and American academics in their 40s and 50s are also strongly represented: those benefiting from the 60s expansion of University provision and experiencing their training at a time when social science was really taking off, including econometrics, cliometrics and the new social history, and when student politics were at their height. Different cohorts with different sets of influences, perspectives and career paths can be identified. The collection also includes one or two most thoughtful essays from younger scholars just setting out on their journey in the subject. Every essay submitted is included in the collection.

Many contributors speak of important books which introduced them to economic or social history whilst still at school or in early months at University: the works of Marx, Tawney, Braudel, Hill, Bloch, Clapham, Rostow, Ashton are most often mentioned. Some authors stress the influence of family, neighbourhood and region, the economic circumstances and environment in which they were raised and the importance of economic history in making sense of such experiences. Many essays mention the ways in which important decisions and choices were made in selecting universities, courses and research topics and the importance of various mentors in assisting with those choices. The stimulus of certain lecturers and supervisors is stressed. Thus lineages of influence can be traced from one generation of historians to the next where particular individuals and institutions have clearly played a decisive role in shaping a whole generation or two of practitioners in the field. The important influence of Postan for many years at Cambridge and of Tawney, Ashton, Fisher and others at the LSE, of Unwin and his students (and Ashton) at Manchester and of the Oxford historians might be expected but the very wide impact (upon British-born historians) of the Nottingham Department under Chambers (particularly its links with Australia), of Birmingham, of Aberdeen and Belfast, amongst others, are intriguing. Similar lineages are suggested at other European centres and at key North American institutions, notably Princeton and Harvard.

The major authorities quoted by historians as influential during their training make very strange bedfellows reflecting political and methodological polarities in the subject which have contributed to its vitality: Marx, Toynbee, Postan,˙Clapham, Ashton, Tawney, Rostow, Hill, Hobsbawm, North, Fogel, Kindleberger, Kuznets, Gerschenkron, Braudel, Stone, (to capture only the most prominent). Rostow's *Stages* figure very importantly though most contributors suggest that the book was influential because it provoked their critical response. Similar views are expressed, in retrospect, about much of the cliometric revolution. Many contributors illustrate how they came to economic history via or alongside social or political history and they celebrate the broad church nature of the subject and of the Society.

Many write of the key relationship between history and economics, particularly what historical study can bring to the discipline of economics: that economics should be about understanding behaviour as well as predicting responses and that history has a key role in this respect. Several stress the need for history to go beyond gathering data to test economic theories: that historians should create their own models, theories and approaches out of the evidence and circumstances of the past. History can thus act as a reminder to economics about the temporal and cultural specificity of its ideas and of the need for dynamic and long run as well as short run analyses. Several writers argue that long-run analysis and growth theory are subjects where economic history can make a most valuable contribution. It can also highlight the difference between economic growth and rising real incomes on the one hand and human progress, in a wider moral and cultural sense, on the other. Several authors see economic history occupying a crucial position between history and economics able to combine methods from both: inductive with deductive, ideographic with nomothetic, literary with mechanical approaches. Some assess the benefits and costs of econometric approaches, others suggest the potential of increasing emphasis upon chaos and contingency in theory. Many give particular examples of work which they have done in policy-related areas or in government service.

Several writers mention the stimulus brought to the subject by new institutional approaches and Chandlerian business history. Others mention advances in economics which can bring the subject nearer to the complexities of real world situations which are the stuff of history: endogenous growth theory, new growth indicators, bounded rationality, asymmetrical information, moral hazard and time inconsistency. Some essays illustrate this very well or in other ways show the uses to which rational choice theory and marginal utility analysis can be put. Some authors are more suspicious of neoclassical and present-centred models arguing that economic history should be more open to ideas from other social sciences: anthropology, psychology, sociology. Some decry postmodernism, others assess the potential importance of post-structural approaches for economic history. Several contributors write, above all, of the need for economic history to be accessible, appealing and entertaining whilst keeping in mind and addressing big moral questions (as Tawney advocated). Barry Supple reminds us that 'Economic history is positioned at the intersection not only of disciplines but of some of the central preoccupations and moral needs of human society'. This is what makes it so important.

In addition to the personal essays, the volume benefits from Negley Harte's excellent piece on the history of the Society and from appendices researched by Douglas Farnie. Together these provide a starting point for anyone wishing further to pursue the history of the subject or the careers of those involved in the discipline more broadly.

Like history itself, the essays can be read in many ways. They can be analysed in relation to their theoretical and empirical content; prosopographically, as a (possibly unique?) exercise in the collective biography of a profession; as a series of statements about the state of economic history and its links to other subjects. But, like history, they can also be approached in another way. They can simply be enjoyed, with a smile, for what they are: stories, reflections and recollections, cool and logical in parts, musing and meandering in others: challenging, critical, speculative, satisfying, entertaining, funny, sad, personal and human. There is everything here from the technology specialist who spins wool for his own jumpers to tales about the castration of sheep using teeth. There are Klondike spaces, Damascus roads, love affairs, unintended consequences, paths, patterns, dialogues, lives and livelihoods. We meet parachutists and truffle hunters, 'big think' and 'little think' types. From Japan to Italy via Australia, France, Spain, Finland, Germany, North America and Great Britain: an intellectual odyssey, encounters with 'poseurs', giants, explorers, martyrs, saggar makers' bottom knockers and other ordinary folk.

As Patrick O'Brien writes in his essay, 'No scholar has written a history of economic history on an international or (I believe) on a national basis. There seems to be nothing on the shelves like those multi-volume magisterial histories of physics, chemistry and astronomy that help natural scientists to comprehend from where their disciplines originated, how they developed, and to point up horizons towards which they are travelling.' If the current volume is not only an enjoyable read but also provides material for such a history in the future, it will have served an important function: an excellent way to have celebrated the anniversary!

Pat Hudson
Cardiff University
February 2001

The Economic History Society, 1926-2001

Negley Harte

It is appropriate to preface the essays which follow with a short introduction to the history of the Society whose anniversary they celebrate. The Economic History Society was founded at a conference held at the Institute of Historical Research, University of London in July 1926 but the ground had been made fertile for it over the previous 50 years. It was half a century earlier, in 1876, that 'economic history' first entered the title of an examination paper. 'Political Economy and Economic History' was examined as part of the new History Tripos in Cambridge. In 1878, when the Rev. William Cunningham returned to Cambridge after four years based in Liverpool lecturing for the newly-created Cambridge extension system, he found that no-one was properly teaching for the new paper, and that what the subject needed was a text-book. In 1882 the first edition in one relatively small volume duly appeared of his *The Growth of English Industry and Commerce*, a work that was to grow into three fat volumes. Either the first exam paper in 1876 or the first textbook in 1882 can be taken to mark the beginning of what might be called the 'take-off' for economic history as a discipline in Britain.

In 1881 and 1882 Arnold Toynbee gave his famous course of lectures in Oxford, reconstructed after his early death and published as *Lectures on the Industrial Revolution of the Eighteenth Century in England* (1884). In 1882 there also appeared the second volume of Thorold Rogers's massive *History of Agriculture and Prices in England*, the first volume of which had appeared in 1866; the other five volumes were to follow in 1887 and 1902. In 1885 W. J. Ashley published the first volume of his *Introduction to English Economic History and Theory*, a book dedicated to the memory of Arnold Toynbee. In the same year Ashley left Oxford and went to Toronto as Professor of Political Economy and Constitutional History. The inaugural lecture he gave there was dedicated to Gustav Schmoller, one of the German scholars in whose hands economic history was more developed in Germany than it was in England. In 1892 Ashley moved on to Harvard, becoming the first Professor of Economic History in the English-speaking world.

From its foundation in 1895, the London School of Economics (LSE) placed economic history centrally among the Social Sciences. Cunningham was brought in from Cambridge as a part-time teacher of the subject 'to counteract Marshall', as Sidney Webb explicitly said. Economic history was also taught by the original Director, W.A.S. Hewins, whose first book, *English Trade and Finance chiefly in the Seventeenth Century* (1892) had described him on the title page as 'University Extension Lecturer on Economic History'. When Hewins resigned the Directorship of the School at the end of 1903, tempted away by Joseph Chamberlain to run the Tariff Commission, it was decided that there ought to be a full-time lectureship in economic history established in order to continue the teaching he had undertaken. Lilian Tomn, a few months later to become Mrs Knowles, was appointed and at the beginning of 1904 took up the first full-time position in the subject in a British university.

1

She had been one of the first research students at LSE, and before that a Cambridge pupil of Cunningham's. With this appointment, economic history's 'take-off' was complete and its mature growth began.

The second university appointment specifically in economic history was the lectureship held at the University of Manchester by H. O. Meredith from 1905 to 1908. The textbook he published in 1908, *Outlines of the Economic History of England* showed that the lectures he gave in Manchester were on an established rather than a pioneering discipline. In 1907 a third lectureship in the subject was established, at Oxford, and filled by L.L. Price. The fourth followed in 1908 at Edinburgh, held by George Unwin. It was Unwin who filled the first chair in the subject in Britain, that established at Manchester in 1910. Lilian Knowles had become a Reader in the subject at LSE in 1907, the first in the country, and in 1909 Price was promoted to a Readership at Oxford. But the establishment of a chair in a field marks a new stage in maturity. The second chair came in 1921, when one was established at LSE for the promotion of Mrs Knowles. By the early 1920s economic history was well established in its original quadrilateral between Cambridge, Oxford, LSE and Manchester. The Professorships at Manchester and LSE, and the Readership at Oxford had as yet no institutional equivalent in Cambridge, but J.H. Clapham was giving his lectures on economic history there from 1908, twenty years before Cambridge created a chair in the subject for him. In 1926 the first volume of Clapham's monumental *Economic History of Modern Britain*, appeared dedicated to the memory of two improbably but appropriately linked names - Cunningham and Marshall. The old Methodenstreit was over; courses of lectures and research were the order of the day.

Such was the stage economic history had grown to by 1926. Economic history was ready to accept the final accolade of recognition as an independent discipline: the founding of a professional society to bring its practitioners together and the founding of a specialist journal devoted to the subject. The first two professors of the subject both died in post, both relatively young - Unwin in 1925 and Mrs Knowles in 1926. The leading roles in founding the Society were played by a harmonious duet formed by Eileen Power and R.H. Tawney. A third part was played, crucially but less harmoniously, by E. Lipson. These three got the Economic History Society founded and the *Economic History Review* established.

Eileen Power and R.H. Tawney both taught at the London School of Economics, lived as neighbours in Mecklenburgh Square, and ran a seminar together on the social and economic history of Tudor England at the Institute of Historical Research from 1923. Power had been on the staff of LSE since 1921, the year the Institute of Historical Research was founded, becoming Reader in Economic History in 1924. She had previously taught at Girton College, Cambridge, where she had been a student, and after graduating in 1910, she had been a research student at LSE. Eileen Power was a woman of charismatic charm and beauty 'Everyone was in love with her', Nora Carus-Wilson once said to me, her eyes brightening. 'Of course we all loved Eileen; she was the only person in the department who was not a gentleman...', said Jack Fisher on another occasion. Eileen Power's biography has been engagingly written by Maxine Berg, who captures her academic and social life in the 1920s and 1930s in a fascinating manner.

Tawney had been connected with LSE since 1912. He had studied classics at Oxford and had learnt economics by lecturing on the subject at the University of Glasgow (1906-08), after which he had conducted the original pioneering tutorial classes for the Workers' Educational Association at Longton and at Rochdale. From 1917 Tawney was a Lecturer in Economic History at LSE, and a Reader from 1923. Besides his historical work, Tawney was increasingly well known in public life after 1918, when he stood as Labour Party candidate, serving on the Sankey Commission in 1919 as a representative of the Miners' Federation, and on various Church of England commissions concerned with Christianity and industrial and ethical questions. His *Acquisitive Society* (1921) made him well-known, and *Religion and the Rise of Capitalism* (1926) made him very well-known. Tawney and Power, close friends and colleagues, produced their three volumes of *Tudor Economic Documents* in 1924. Two years later - the year when Tawney's *Religion and the Rise of Capitalism* appeared - together they produced the Economic History Society.

Ephraim Lipson was a different kettle of fish. The son of a Jewish furniture dealer in Sheffield, he graduated from Cambridge with a first in history in 1910, but found no opening there and migrated to Oxford as a private tutor and independent researcher. The first volume of his *Economic History of England* appeared in 1915 and his *History of the Woollen and Worsted Industries* in 1921. He was disabled since being dropped as a small child and he was always conscious of being jeered at. He was a self-conscious outsider. He was very well-read but he did not shine like Tawney or sparkle like Power. However, he was creator of the *Economic History Review*, originally published by A. & C. Black, the publisher of his own books and for whom he was a consultant. He had first proposed an economic history equivalent of the *English Historical Review* to them in 1924.

When Eileen Power came to organise the economic history session at the second Anglo-American Historical Conference at the Institute of Historical Research in July 1926, two strands fell carefully together. Sir William Ashley - as he now was, retired from the chair of Commerce that he had occupied at the University of Birmingham from 1901 to 1925 - was to give a paper on 'the place of economic history in university studies', and there was to be discussion of, as Eileen Power put it, 'the new Economic History Society and the *Economic History Review* and other methods of promoting the subject'. The meeting, on 14th July 1926, brought the Society into existence. The Review had already been initiated by a contract between A. & C. Black and Lipson and Tawney signed on 11th May 1926 (during the General Strike). There had been preliminary meetings to discuss these matters from at least March 1926. Arthur Redford - Reader in Economic History at Manchester after Unwin's death in 1925 - came from Manchester to a couple of committee meetings, and in his diary for 23rd March he noted: 'I got the impression we were being used as camouflage for Lipson's scheming'!

Lipson was trying to move quickly at this stage, since the Royal Economic Society had decided to produce a new economic history supplement to their *Economic Journal* and the first issue of *Economic History* was speedily produced and actually appeared in January 1926. Cambridge and Keynes were trying to outwit Oxford and Lipson. Lipson, paranoid even without being persecuted, was forced into alliance with Tawney and Power, scholars enjoying the universal admiration denied to him. The first issue of the *Economic History Review* appeared in 1927, backed by the members of the new Economic History Society. (Economic History, the supplement to the *Economic Journal* continued to appear in strange rivalry until 1940; Keynes was not easily outwitted). Lipson and Tawney were the joint editors of the *Review*, but Lipson did all the editorial work in Oxford, assisted by Miss Julia Mann, then a young Vice-Principal and subsequently Principal of St Hilda's College in Oxford. She was working with A.P. Wadsworth, later editor of the *Manchester Guardian* and a student of Tawney's from the WEA class at Rochdale, on their collaborative *Cotton Trade and Industrial Lancashire,1600-1780* (1931).

Sir William Ashley duly became the first President of the Society, and his paper at the foundation meeting was published as the first article in the first number of the *Economic History Review*. He was elderly and retired (he was to die in 1927). Eileen Power became the first Secretary of the Society, and she was the driving force. The early minutes are all kept in her distinctive round hand, and all the Society's correspondence was dealt with by her aunt

Ruby (Miss Clegg). By June 1927 a membership list was printed containing 529 individual names (a slight overestimate of the real membership, since they had not all paid their subscriptions) plus 148 libraries. Of the libraries as many as 115 were overseas, 77 of them in the United States. Americans numbered 79 of the individual members, by far the largest group of foreigners, with Canada and Germany following with nine each. There was an international flavour from the start, but the great bulk of members were British, and there was always a drive to recruit as many schoolmasters and schoolmistresses as possible. F.W. Tickner, nominally joint secretary with Eileen Power at the start, was a benign and earnest schoolmaster.

It proved very hard to add to the pioneering band of 500 or so who joined the Society at the beginning. The next 20 years saw membership falling rather than rising. It did not fall very much, only once dipping below 400 to 366 in 1945, the last year of the war. But expansion would have been more heartening, and there were perpetual worries throughout the 1930s about making ends meet. In 1933 it was necessary to send out letters marked Private and Urgent to correspondents all over the provinces asking them to recruit an additional ten members each. The appeal evidently did not work, and membership in 1934 fell slightly. The perpetual membership drives brought in a few distinguished foreigners, but the domestic market could not be deepened. Many of Eileen Power's rich friends had to dig into their pockets.

The main change in the Society's struggling but stable arrangements in the 1930s came in 1934 with the resignation of Lipson as editor of the *Review*. He had already resigned the Readership in Economic History at Oxford that he had held in succession to L.L. Price since 1922 (though without being able to achieve any college affiliation). In 1931 it had been decided to establish a Chichele chair of Economic History at Oxford, and Lipson had been keen to get it. He went to great lengths to get the other two volumes of his *Economic History of England* into the publisher's hands, and at one point in 1931 A. & C. Black had 17 people working on the index. The books were published in the nick of time, but Lipson still failed to be appointed to the chair. It went to G.N. Clark (later Sir George Clark), a respectable figure though not a committed economic historian of the new style. Lipson, his paranoia confirmed, rejected Oxford in despair, and in 1934 he left the *Review* too. He travelled the world giving lectures wearing his mother's wedding ring, and writing increasingly old-fashioned text-books. Lipson lived on until 1960, but he severed his connections with economic history completely in 1934.

His successor as editor of the Review in 1934 was another outsider, but an altogether more glamorous, brilliant and quick-witted one: M.M. Postan (later Sir Michael Postan). Munia Postan (as he was known to his friends) erupted into London in 1921, when he registered as a part-time student at LSE. Accounts of where he had come from varied kaleidoscopically. Odessa figured large, but so did St Petersburg or perhaps Petrograd, Kiev, Czernowitz, Berlin and Amsterdam too. Lenin figured, and the Russian army, and the Zionist cause. At all events, he certainly took his degree at LSE in 1924 and a master's degree in medieval economic history in 1926. He was a student of Eileen Power's, and he became a collaborator in various works. From 1927 to 1931 he taught at University College London; from 1931 to 1934 he taught at the LSE; in 1934 he moved to Cambridge as a lecturer, and in 1938 he succeeded Clapham there as Professor of Economic History. In 1934 he became sole editor of the *Review* and in 1937 he became sole husband of Eileen Power (a development that astonished many at the time). The Economic History Society became a family business.

The outbreak of war in 1939 brought an era to an end, and the first period of the Economic History Society came to an abrupt end in 1940 when Eileen Power suddenly dropped dead in the Tottenham Court Road. She and Postan had made their new home in Cambridge; when the war broke out, LSE was evacuated to Cambridge, and Postan joined the Ministry of Economic Warfare, based in the LSE buildings off the Aldwych in London. There had been an odd commuting reversal. Power's death brought the Society to a full stop though various willing hands kept it going through the war. Postan also somehow managed to keep the Review going. The issues may have looked thin, but they were thin only physically. The subject was alive, and in good hands. But in 1945 the Society found itself with only 366 paid-up members (plus 228 library subscriptions), and the situation could well have been regarded as bleak as anything was in 1945.

The graph showing the membership of the Society reveals that things were about to change. The 30 years after 1946 were a different period to the first 20 years. Growth finally set in, and was most striking. Membership grew from the 400 paid-up members of 1946 to a peak of 2,576 paid-up members in the jubilee year of 1976. By an extraordinary coincidence, it was the jubilee year which was the peak. Economic history had never had it so good. It had grown beyond Eileen Power's pre-war dreams.

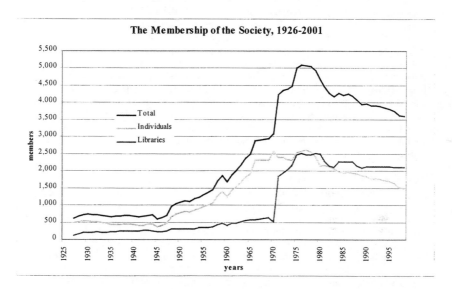

The Membership of the Society, 1926-2001

There was a 1960s boom, but the growth was pretty constant from the late 1940s to the early 1970s. The Clapham Report in the late 1940s said there should be more social science; the Robbins Report in the early 1960s said there should be more universities. The sound of the reports was heard everywhere. There was more social science. There were more universities. Economic history hit the right note to be part of this long period of expansion.

When the Society was founded, it happened that there were no professors of the subject in Britain. J.H. Clapham quite rightly filled the new Cambridge chair in 1928. G.N. Clark was the new professor in Oxford in 1931, as noted above. In 1931 both Tawney and Power were promoted to chairs at LSE, Power to the established chair vacant since Mrs Knowles's death, and Tawney to a new personal chair. Postan succeeded to Clapham's chair in Cambridge in 1938, W.K. Hancock (later Sir Keith Hancock) was an eccentric choice to succeed Clark at Oxford in 1944, and in the same year T.S. Ashton was a significant - and, as it turned out,

5

enormously influential - choice to fill the chair at LSE, vacant since Eileen Power's death. These chairs at Cambridge, Oxford and LSE remained the only ones in the country, until the quadrilateral was restored in 1945 when Arthur Redford at Manchester was promoted to occupy the chair that had been Unwin's.

In 1947 the first signs of expansion became evident on the professorial front, and W.H.B. Court became the holder of the first new chair at the University of Birmingham, where doubtless a tradition of economic history went back to Ashley and the Faculty of Commerce in the Edwardian period. The number of professors of the expanding subject more than doubled in the late 1950s: Dundee in 1957 (D.F. Macdonald), Glasgow in 1957 (S.G.Checkland), Bristol in 1958 (William Ashworth), Edinburgh (A.J. Youngson) and Nottingham (J.D. Chambers) in the same year, and Leeds in 1959 (M.W.Beresford). The expansion in the subject was becoming heady. Soon there were too many professors of the subject for them to be automatically included in *Who's Who*.

In the 1960s the number of chairs doubled again, and chairs invariably meant separate independent departments of economic history. By 1970 there were chairs at Aberdeen (P.L. Payne), Belfast (K.H. Connell), Durham (F.C.Spooner), East Anglia (R.H. Campbell), Exeter (W.E. Minchinton), Kent (T.C. Barker), Leicester (R. Davis), Sheffield (S. Pollard), Strathclyde (S.G.E. Lythe), Sussex (B.E. Supple), Swansea (A.W. Cole) and York (E.M. Sigsworth). In 1950 Hancock was succeeded at Oxford by H.J. Habakkuk(Hrothgar Habakkuk to his friends, later Sir John Habakkuk), who in his turn was succeeded in 1968 by Peter Mathias, At LSE F.J. Fisher - universally known as Jack - succeeded T.S. Ashton on his retirement in 1954. Postan retired at Cambridge in 1965 and was succeeded by David Joslin, who died young, and who was succeeded in turn in 1971 by D.C. Coleman. From 1953 E.M. Carus-Wilson was awarded a personal chair at LSE, as in 1965 was A.H. John. In 1970 Eric Hobsbawm was promoted Professor of Economic and Social History at Birkbeck College.

To trace the history of all appointments and all departments in the 1970s and up to the present period is beyond the scope of this survey. By the 1970s the subject was evidently much bigger, much more mature, and enjoying growth and all the benefits of growth. The results were all made obvious on the occasion of the burgeoning conferences that the Society held every year with such success. Before the war, there had always been an AGM held at the LSE. In the immediate post-war period, the AGM grew into a day conference held annually in May at the LSE. In 1946 it was attended by 40, declining to 25 in 1947. Extended to two days in 1948 the attendance went back up to 40 and the numbers reached 60 in 1949. It was decided in 1950 to hold a residential conference in the easter vacation, the first being held at the University of Birmingham, in acknowledgement of Court's new professorship there, recognition of the growth of the subject outside the quadrilateral.

The second conference was held at Oxford one freezing weekend in 1951, and the first weekend (or so) of the easter vacation ever since has seen the Economic History Society taking on visible and convivial form at different universities throughout the country. The locations are all listed in an appendix. By the 1970s they were being attended by over 250 people each year, almost all of them the academic staff and the research students in all the booming departments of economic (often economic and social) history in practically every university in the country, and some of the 'polytechnics' too.

The growth of the subject is reflected in the numbers of members as shown on the graph. The growth is also evident in the quantity of material published in the *Economic History Review*. In 1948 the Review began to have three issues per year, in place of the original two. This was aided by a subvention from the Royal Economic Society (in place of their failed rival

6

publication *Economic History*, which had ceased in 1940). After 1971 there were four issues per year. By 1955 the *Review* was publishing 400 gripping pages per year, 600 by 1960 and over 750 in the early 1970s. By any yardstick, economic history was bubbling and booming and so was the Economic History Society and the *Economic History Review*.

The Society was remarkably well-served by its officers over this long period of growth. All the post-war Presidents were people of remarkable distinction - first Tawney himself from 1946 to 1960, and Ashton, and then (after it was wisely decided to have a three- year term for the presidency) Postan, Carus-Wilson, Court, Sayers (a borrowing from economics - but acceptable, institutional, economics), Fisher, Checkland, Flinn. All these were scholars widely and unequivocally respected in the subject. Their successors - all listed with their dates in the appendix - have equally been highly respected and commanding and also much liked - Michael Thompson, Theo Barker, Peter Mathias, Barry Supple, Tony Wrigley and Patrick O'Brien.

In its secretaries the Society has also been extremely well-served. Eileen Power was a difficult act to follow. Sir Kenneth Berrill (as he became) and then Theo Barker ran the Society with great verve throughout the long post-war boom period, and Richard Wilson, David Jenkins and Rick Trainor have been outstandingly good and efficient in the role in more recent years. The Treasurers have been outstanding too. And the Editors of the *Review* have all been seriously central figures in the subject. All have been outstanding guardians of the direction of the subject, each of them most hard-working and some of the quickest minds of any in academic life.

At the time when I begin to sound like a glossy annual report, it is clearly time to stop. But I have to draw attention to the third period in the history of the subject as revealed in the graph. The growth in the number of members faltered in the early 1970s; a modest growth in the late 1970s was associated with the euphoria at the time of the jubilee conference in Cambridge in 1976. But by the end of the 1970s it was increasingly clear that the economic history boom was over. Numbers of individual members of the Society fell from the peak of over 2,500, at the time of the jubilee in 1976, gradually and inexorably to the level of somewhat under 1,500 as we reach the 75th anniversary in 2001. The beginnings of faltering growth in the early 1970s were disguised by a great boom in library sales of the *Review* facilitated by the enterprise of the publishers. For a time in the early 1970s over 5,000 copies of the *Review* were being read all over the world - or perhaps it would be more accurate to say, were in scholarly piles all over the world waiting to be read.

The 50th anniversary of the Society in 1976 was an occasion of happy self-congratulation. The golden jubilee issue of the *Economic History Review* in 1977 contained an interesting discussion of the Society's history by Theo Barker, and some quantitative analysis of the growth of the subject in bibliometric terms by me. It was not realised at the time that decline was about to set in. In the following year, 1977, institutional sales of the *Review* for the first time exceeded sales to individuals. In the 1950s and 1960s, 70% or more of copies of the *Review* went to individuals who actually purchased it. After the late 1970s only 40-odd% were individual purchasers or members. The institutional market through the 1980s and 1990s held up better than the individual market. Between 2,500 and 2,000 libraries continued to subscribe, while individual members seeped downwards from 2,500 to 1,500.

The Society is not yet reduced to wondering how to make ends meet. It has been remarkably well managed financially. Whether the subject has been well-managed in other ways is more open to question. Institutionally, it has certainly suffered quite a battering in the 1980s and 1990s. Many of the booming separate departments of the 1950s and 1960s have been amalgamated with other departments, usually 'history' departments. Numbers of A-level

7

candidates have fallen. Applicants for 'economic history' courses have declined, even after it was rendered more appealing through being called 'economic and social history'. After 1981 'cuts' began to hit universities, and apparently declining subjects were especially at risk. Economic history has been in a different world since the 1980s.

In intellectual terms, economic history had attained a great victory. By the 1980s, no history department was concerned with the narrow political and constitutional history that had characterised the subject when economic history was itself born institutionally. Economic and social history expanded within history, whilst social history, gender history, all sorts of cultural history became mainstream. But institutionally 'economic history' was vulnerable. The subject, as perceived in the period of post-war boom, suffered. In 1987 D.C. Coleman - a brilliantly able if powerfully unpredictable figure in the boom years - produced a book on the history of the subject with the subtitle: *An Account of the Rise and Decline of Economic History in Britain*. When the Presidency of the Society was offered to Donald Coleman he rejected it in a flurry of complexity.

The Society itself had been comfortable about the period of growth. There was a launch into publishing more than the *Review*. In 1954 the Society produced the first volume of *Essays in Economic History*, edited by E.M. Carus-Wilson, reprinting important articles largely from the *Review*. It was so successful that in 1962 two more volumes followed, reprinting articles drawn from a wider range of sources. In 1967 the Society entered into an agreement with Macmillan's to publish a series of pamphlets on various aspects of the subject, all aimed at a wider market than the narrow if scholarly 'supplements' that had been produced infrequently alongside the *Review*.

As the decline of the late 1970s and 1980s began to impinge on the consciousness of a perhaps complacent subject (a decline evident in any statistical series: A-level candidates, applications for single-subject degrees in economic history, membership of the Economic History Society, most obviously) the Society slowly began to think something should be done. At the height of the boom in the late 1960s, the Society had turned its attention from the long-established concern of ensuring the expansion of the subject in schools and universities to speaking up on behalf of a mature and expanding subject to the institutions which paid for the expansion. In particular, in 1966-67 there were long discussions with the newly-established Social Science Research Council (as it then was) in order to ensure that economic and social history was recognised as a discipline worth funding. The subject got its committee, and the subject got its research funding - for a time.

By the time of the 'cuts' after 1981, the Society was used to speaking for the subject as it existed in British universities, and it entered into ardent discussion with the then UGC about the first 'subject review' and what emerged as the first 'research assessment exercise' in the late 1980s. There was much discussion with the British Academy, with other social science subject societies, with the University Grants Committee. The Society represented a mature subject, one clearly established, and still thought to be growing. But it never lost its concern with schools and the need to ensure a supply of potential students. As the number of members began to be seen to fall in the 1980s, some of the original concerns of the 1930s began to be revived. There were various drives to refresh the teaching of economic and social history in schools including the establishment of the *ReFRESH* pamphlet series.

A major initiative came after 1987. The Council meeting at the Norwich conference in that year anguished over a proposal to establish a 'women's committee'. It was forcefully pointed out that 20% of the membership at the time of the foundation had been women, and that the proportion of the much greater total had sunk to 10%. What was the Society to do about this? Nothing, thought many. Get something going here, argued some. The activists turned out to

8

achieve a majority, carrying the vote at a dramatic Council meeting, reconvened at midnight after the conference bar closed. The Women's Committee of the Society turned out not to be a divisive influence, as had been feared. In the course of the 1990s the committee came to hold meetings both at the annual conference and in London in November, and these meetings turned out to be some of the most intellectually exciting and challenging occasions which the Society had ever organised, rivalling the Society's traditional easter residential conference in interest.

The Society finds itself on the occasion of its 75th anniversary in robust financial health. Intellectually, the subject has so overwhelmed the old narrow political history that 'history' has been transformed as a subject. Economics has retreated to narrow mathematical concerns in a way that would shock Marshall. Economics generally ignores economic history; history, by contrast, has incorporated economic history with enthusiasm. This leaves 'economic history' in an undecided position. The core of the subject itself flourishes in every way. The institutional indicators are, however, all registering decline. It is an interesting time to be celebrating an anniversary.

If Tawney were able to be with us, he would surely be fascinated by the way in which the concerns of the subject have become less dominated by the old political history, impressed by the way in which our interests have become more sociological and cultural, as well as much more international, just as he argued they should at the founding meeting in 1926. Even Lipson might lurk around and find us endlessly tolerant of the disadvantaged, the eccentric, and the antiquarian. Eileen Power would surely be thrilled to join us in Glasgow, especially since dancing was introduced as a feature of the conference, after the Saturday dinner, at Leeds in 1998 - begun, I think it should be recorded - by the current Treasurer of the Society and Pene Corfield, and in which the editor of this compilation and I were willing participants.

Bibliography

'The Beginnings of the Economic History Society' are interestingly chronicled by T.C. Barker in the golden jubilee number of the *Economic History Review*, 2nd. ser. XXX, 1 (1977), which also contains N.B.Harte, 'Trends in Publications on the Economic and Social History of Great Britain and Ireland, 1925-74' (a subject to be continued in a forthcoming article with Giorgio Riello covering the ensuing quarter-century up to2000). The origins of the subject more generally are surveyed in 'The Making of Economic History', the introduction in N.B. Harte ed., *The Study of Economic History: Collected Inaugural Lectures, 1893-1970* (1971).

The whole subject is surveyed brilliantly and quirkily in D.C. Coleman, *History and the Economic Past: An Account of the Rise and Decline of Economic History in Britain* (1987). Less exciting but more scholarly accounts of the origins of economic history as a discipline in Britain are provided in Alon Kadish, *Historians, Economists, and Economic History* (1989) and Gerard M. Koot, *English Historical Economics, 1870-1926* (1987).

Maxine Berg, *A Woman in History: Eileen Power, 1889-1940* (1996) is entrancing, and full of insights. Ross Terrill's *R.H. Tawney and his Times* (1974), and all the other general writing about Tawney, is much less interesting from an historical point of view. J.M. Winter's 'Tawney the Historian', prefaced to his edition of *History and Society: Essays by R.H. Tawney* (1978) and David Ormrod, 'R.H. Tawney and the Origins of Capitalism', *History Workshop Journal*, 18 (1984) are both clear, comprehensive and required reading. There is nothing on Lipson. .Maxine Berg, 'The First Women Economic Historians', *Economic History Review*, XLV, 2 (1992), is lively.

An interesting and comprehensive analysis of the editing and the contents of the *Economic History Review* is provided by E.A. Wrigley, 'The Review during the lat 50 Years', available on the Economic History Society's web site. http://www.ehs.org.uk R.G. Wilson and J.F. Hadwin, 'Economic and Social History at Advanced Level', *Economic History Review*, XXXVIII, 4 (1985) is a survey of the subject with wider implications than the title implies, written at a time when the implications of decline were beginning to be considered.

The archives of the Economic History Society are comprehensively catalogued and are now kept at the LSE Library. For recent times, there are more and more records generated, and we also have our memories. . .

Economic History Society Residential Conferences.

1950	Birmingham
1951	Oxford (Worcester College)
1952	Leicester
1953	Cambridge (King's College)
1954	Leeds
1955	Bristol
1956	Nottingham
1957	Cambridge (Queens' College)
1958	Swansea
1959	Wye (Agricultural College)
1960	Liverpool
1961	Exeter
1962	Sheffield
1963	Edinburgh
1964	Reading
1965	Sussex
1966	Manchester
1967	Belfast
1968	East Anglia
1969	Durham
1970	Birmingham
1971	York
1972	Kent
1973	Leicester
1974	Bristol
1975	Leeds
1976	Cambridge (Churchill College)
1977	Hull
1978	Swansea
1979	Sheffield
1980	Liverpool
1981	Loughborough
1982	Aberdeen
1983	Kent
1984	Glasgow (Strathclyde)
1985	York
1986	Cheltenham (St Paul and St Mary College)
1987	Belfast
1988	East Anglia
1989	Exeter
1990	Liverpool
1991	Manchester (Polytechnic)
1992	Leicester
1993	Hull
1994	Nottingham
1995	Edinburgh
1996	Lancaster
1997	Sussex
1998	Leeds
1999	Oxford (St Catherine's College)
2000	Bristol
2001	Glasgow

The Officers of the
Economic History Society, 1926-2001

Presidents

1926-27	Sir William Ashley
1927-40	W.R. Scott
1940-46	Sir John Clapham
1946-60	R.H. Tawney
1960-63	T.S. Ashton
1963-66	Sir Michael Postan
1966-69	E.M. Carus-Wilson
1969-72	W.H.B. Court
1972-74	R.S. Sayers
1974-77	F.J. Fisher
1977-80	S.G. Checkland
1980-83	M.W. Flinn
1983-86	F.M.L. Thompson
1986-89	T.C. Barker
1989-92	P. Mathias
1992-95	B.E. Supple
1995-98	Sir Tony Wrigley
1998-2001	P.K. O'Brien

Hon. Secretaries

1926-28	Eileen Power and F.W. Tickner
1929-32	Eileen Power and J.L. Gray
1929-40	Eileen Power
1940-42	F.J. Fisher (E. Crittall and A. Ransome, acting)
1942-44	M.G. Jones
1944-52	E.E. Rich
1952-61	Sir Kenneth Berrill
1961-86	T.C. Barker
1986-92	R.G. Wilson
1992-98	D.T. Jenkins
1998-	R.H. Trainor

Hon Treasurers

1926-35	J.A. White
1935-37	Sir Robert Birley
1937	J.F. Nichols
1937-40	M.G. Jones
1940-41	Sir John Clapham
1941-54	F.R. Salter
1954-68	Sir Kenneth Berrill
1968-88	P. Mathias
1988-96	B.W.E. Alford
1996-	O. Westall

Editors

1926-34	E. Lipson and R.H. Tawney
1934-50	Sir Michael Postan
1950-60	Sir Michael Postan and Sir John Habakkuk
1960-67	R.M. Hartwell and Charles Wilson
1967-68	R.M. Hartwell and D.C. Coleman
1968-72	D.C. Coleman and F.M.L. Thompson
1973-79	F.M.L. Thompson and B.E. Supple
1980-83	B.E. Supple and A.G. Hopkins
1983-85	A.G. Hopkins and R.A. Church

1985-90	R.A. Church and E.A. Wrigley
1990-92	C. Dyer and E.A. Wrigley
1992-95	C. Dyer and F. Capie
1995-97	F. Capie and J. Hatcher
1997-	J. Hatcher and N.F.R. Crafts

Assistant Editors

1948-50	Sir John Habakkuk
1950-52	Sir Kenneth Berrill
1952-55	D.M. Joslin
1955-57	P. Mathias
1957-60	R.M. Hartwell
1960-61	G.A. Holmes
1961-62	G.A. Holmes and N. McKendrick
1963-67	G.A. Holmes
1967-70	P. Earle
1971-75	E.H. Hunt
1975-79	P.J. Corfield
1979-84	N.B. Harte
1984-87	M.J. Daunton

Book Review Editors

1969-72	R.M. Hartwell
1973-82	M.E. Falkus
1982-86	E.H. Hunt
1986-90	F. Capie
1990-93	P. Fearon
1993-96	Nuala Zahedieh
1996-2000	Christine MacLeod
2000-	Sally Horrocks

Chairman of the Publication Committee

1973-85	J.R. Harris
1985-88	B.W.E. Alford
1988-95	P.M. Thane
1995-2000	R. Garside
2000-	P. A. Johnson

On Not Being an Economic Historian

G.E. Aylmer

I have no pretensions to be an economic historian. On the other hand I have been a member of the Economic History Society since 1951-2, and normally make an attempt to read at least some part of each issue of the *Review*. My initial interest was sparked by the 'gentry controversy'. As a graduate pupil of R.H. Tawney (and before that an undergraduate pupil of Christopher Hill), besides having heard both Lawrence Stone and H.R. Trevor-Roper (now Lord Dacre) lecture in Oxford, I could hardly not be marginally involved in that debate. In retrospect, it was J.P. Cooper's article on 'The Counting of Manors' which finally persuaded me that the original Tawney-Stone case was untenable, being fatally flawed in method if not in substance. However I was less convinced by Trevor-Roper's alternative, as advanced in his supplement to the *Review* on *The Gentry 1540-1640*; indeed my own first book, published in 1961, was thought by some to demonstrate some of the flaws in his thesis. Be that as it may, since then the interests of economic and other historians have moved on, in two related but distinct ways. First of all there has been the development of more rigorous quantitative methods and the rise of econometric history, where lacking the requisite mathematical capacity I have had to struggle to try to keep up. Secondly there has been the great burgeoning of demographic, local, social and cultural history, associated with such scholars as Hoskins, Beresford, Laslett, Wrigley, Thirsk, Thomas and many others. I hope too that it won't be thought unfair to say that fewer of the most seminal articles have appeared in the *Economic History Review*, compared with *Past & Present* and other journals, than was true at the beginning of my career.

Having been criticised by a leading Marxist historian when I was a student for 'being more of an economic determinist than I should ever dare to be' (Hill to Aylmer, 1949-59), I now have to ask myself whether what Tawney called 'the primacy of the economic factor' is still acceptable in trying to understand the human past. Plainly economic history has an enormous amount to teach us, not only about how people lived materially in earlier societies but also about their beliefs, institutions and non-economic behaviour. The model which I now prefer is an interactive, rather than a base-superstructure one; to the extent that some may think Trevor-Roper has had the best of it! On such crucial aspects as harvest fluctuation, movements of prices and earnings, the growth of national income and the distribution of wealth, the fiscal basis of the state, as well as through microcosmic studies of small groups and communities, the rest of us still have much to learn. And I am disappointed if an issue of the *Review* does not contain at least one article from which I can improve my knowledge and understanding of early modern history, primarily that of England from the sixteenth to the eighteenth centuries.

Perhaps the interactive model can be defined a little more closely. Like many others, I now see economic and technological factors as determining what can *not* happen or be achieved, limiting the range of possibilities, rather than positively determining what will happen. This

13

may well seem so shatteringly obvious as hardly to be worth saying. But the implications are a little more complex than may at first appear. Let me illustrate this from a field in which I have long been interested: American history from the earliest English settlements to the time of Independence and the U.S. Constitution. The plentifulness of land and the shortage of labour, compared to Britain or indeed to the Old World as a whole, is acceptable as a broad generalisation. But it is clearly not a sufficient explanation for the rapidity of economic and demographic growth from the 1620s to the 1770s. There have been other societies in human history where the same general conditions have obtained but where no comparably rapid growth has resulted. At a minimum we need to assess the significance of the so-called Puritan work-ethic, the familial structure of the early settlements in the northern and middle colonies, the relatively easy availability of Afro-Caribbean slave labour in the south, and the whole nature of the early English, then British, Empire with both the constraints and the incentives afforded by imperial policies and other metropolitan influences. This is by no means a definitive list of the factors requiring to be brought into consideration: relations with the native Americans and with the non-British European settlers, the effects of ecology and climate immediately occur. As someone who has taught this subject for many years but never published more than a few book reviews on it, I should like to emphasise the extraordinarily high quality of the best work on seventeenth to eighteenth century American history, published over the last 50 years or so, predominantly but by no means exclusively on the economic and social aspects. The new Constitution of 1787-8 itself provides a classic instance of earlier debates, offering a very approximate parallel with the gentry controversy in this country: from Charles A. Beard's *An Economic Interpretation of the Constitution* (1913) to the mid and later twentieth century works of authors such as Robert E. Brown, Forrest Macdonald, J.T Main and numerous others. With the triumphalism of the post-Cold War era of global market ideology, emphasis has shifted back to almost exclusively political, legal, intellectual, even philosophical interpretation. This may have been a healthy corrective, but perhaps it is a swing too far if we think of Alexander Hamilton's hidden – and open – agendas as Washington's Treasury Secretary.

Another obvious area of debate about the relative importance of economic circumstances in relation to ideas and their application is what used to be known as the Scientific Revolution (more or less from Copernicus to Newton). Although few, if any, historians would now want to argue that economic changes in late medieval-early modern Europe (the 'rise of capitalism') brought about the changes in how people thought about the natural world and sought to explain it, few would be altogether happy with an explanation formulated in terms of a self-contained world of ideas and changing intellectual paradigms to understand its nature. One could multiply examples and actual or potential case studies. Certainly there is plenty of work still to be done in applying the interactive model to particular historical problems and situations.

I am not a great conference-goer, perhaps for that very reason the few conferences of the Society which I have attended stand out in my memory the more clearly. The first was at Bristol in (?) 1955, when Eric Hobsbawm provided a remarkable, impromptu simultaneous translation of a paper by an eminent French scholar – was it Crouzet? Donald Coleman, whom I subsequently got to know and for whose work I have very great regard, read a version of what became his famous article on 'Labour in the English economy of the Seventeenth Century'. In the discussion I rashly ventured to dissent from one part of his argument; at the time I thought that he had wiped the floor with me, but afterwards T.S. Willan, that kindly mentor of his younger colleagues, said to me quietly that he thought I had made my point. The other conference was at York in the 1970s, when I was acting as a kind of unofficial host. The President was W.H.B. Court, whose book on *The Rise of the Midland Industries* Hill had urged me to read many years before. There was a plenary visiting lecture, given by Le Roy Ladurie; but this time there was no simultaneous translation. Why don't I go to more of the Society's conferences? The answer is not misanthropy (still less misogyny), but time and money. Apart from the enjoyable socialising on such occasions, virtually all the papers of any consequence will appear in print within a year or two. Maybe that is incorrect, but such is my impression. So it is not lack of interest. In fact I have very recently attended a symposium on Credit (in September 2000), but then this was held almost on my door step in Oxford. Long may the Economic History Society and its *Review* flourish. At least my executors will have a nice run of which to dispose.

Gerald E. Aylmer (b. 30. 4. 1926) was an Honorary Fellow of St. Peter's College and a member of the Modern History Faculty in the University of Oxford. From 1963 to 1978 he was Professor of History and Head of Department at the University of York, and from 1978 to 1991 Master of St. Peter's College, Oxford. He was President of the Royal Historical Society 1985-89. His first book, *The King's Servants: The Civil Servants of Charles I, 1625-42* published in 1961 was followed by his engagement in lively debate about the rise of the gentry in the seventeenth century. He authored and edited more than a dozen books and more than 40 learned articles mainly on British early-modern political and socio-economic history. Sadly, Gerald Aylmer died on 17.12.2000 as this book was being prepared for the press. An obituary by Barrie Dobson appeared in *The Independent* 30.12.2000.

What Economic History Has Meant To Me ... with an appendix, Plagiarist and Poseur Revealed?

Maurice Beresford

To the question set - what economic history has meant to me – I might have answered in one short sentence, - 'My bread and butter, and never a dull moment' – but I must say that from the earliest days it has always astonished me to be paid a salary for doing what was so pleasant, and with such a companionable gang of participants to meet at conferences, seminars, or in the pages of the *Review*. How pleasant to have been spinning words for so long, and to find that the world contained editors and publishers who were willing to turn them into galley proofs and thence to publication. Thus my collection of rejection slips numbers zero.

How flexible it has been to be able to follow one's own fancy in the choice of subject matter wherever documentary encounters in libraries and archives or the observations of field work – my chief sources of fodder – would lead me. Flexible too, in the range of subject matter that was admitted as 'economic history' and fit for the concern of a lecturer with those two words in his title – even at the risk of being thought of at different times as an archaeologist, a geographer, a travel writer: but never (I swear) as a refugee from economic theorising into cliometry.

It was History that bred me: as a schoolboy I had been first captivated by reading Tawney; and then as an undergraduate by listening to Eileen Power, to Postan and to John Saltmarsh, three lecturers of the years 1938-41 with a fatal power to captivate. Subsequently my loyalty has always been to the art of telling a good story while remembering the reader at my shoulder or the audience lined up in lecture rooms; and never forgetting the thin red line between education and entertainment.

The War intervened before I could become a research student, and the directive of a Conscientious Objectors Tribunal consigned me to labour as a social worker. An irony of fate then concealed from Sir John Clapham, the Chairman of that Tribunal, was that he, appointed 40 years earlier to be the first holder of the Chair of Economics at Leeds, was now facing a lad who, 20 years later, would become that University's first Professor of Economic History. In 1940 I was not myself dejected at the directive of the Tribunal. A life of gowns, high tables and senior common rooms as it appeared to me then was simply an ivory tower. My career ambition, in so far as anyone in that month of Dunkirk dared to have thoughts about a career, was to be a social worker, and before the end of 1947, when William Hoskins invited me over to Leicester to chat about ridge and furrow, I did not set foot in any University. My first acceptance letter as a contributor to the *Economic History Review* did not find me at a University address.

Thus the pleasures of being a University teacher of economic history came to me only when I was 28 years old and a self-taught researcher. Therefore, although when as a young lecturer at Leeds I was assigned the supervision of the doctorates of two ex-servicemen, almost my own age, in the persons of Eric Sigsworth and Peter Bowden; I had to conceal a certain amount of guilt to be revealed with no higher degree to my name. But the gamble paid off: Peter became the historian of the Tudor wool market; and in his leisure time during a career as the Canadian government's chief statistician has returned to his first love by providing the statistical material for successive volumes of the *Agrarian History*. Eric's career at York and Humberside, confirmed his status as a major historian of the Yorkshire textile industry and of Victorian society. He was a colourful personality and he and I taught each other a great deal.

Certainly, to have had at different times co-authors as varied as Herbert Finberg, John Hurst, Glan Jones, Kenneth St. Joseph and Brian Barber has given me, belatedly, something as a substitute for my lack of a formal research training. Herbert Finberg was the founding editor of the *Agrarian History*, and technically an amateur historian, coming late to our profession (as Hoskins's successor to the headship of Leicester's Department of English local history) from the business of fine book publishing at the Broadwater Press. At his retirement from Leicester he became my co-author for *English Medieval Boroughs* (1973). This seasoned controversialist could not refrain from flourishing a pistol at the University administrators by asking me to insert in the final proofs a prefatory note to explain our partnership – 'when Professor Finberg retired from his chair at Leicester under the inexorable rules of academic superannuation, which bear no relation to a scholar's capacity and inclination for continued work, it suited both of us to join forces although he adds that he is not responsible for the editorial presentation of the Gazetteer, in which the publishers have followed their house style'. The publishers David and Charles accepted this disclaimer with a good grace, coming as it did from one who had designed an Order of Service for a Coronation (despite their discovery that one of their clerks had put into an envelope and posted to Herbert a carbon copy intended for me which had a hand-written postscript growling gently about 'that awkward bugger, Finberg'). I was left to tremble in anticipation of an explosion and a flurry of writs, but Herbert's sense of humour stood the test.

I have used the word 'companionable' above for a time-remembered pleasure at the joys of being in our profession for over four decades after 1948: beginning in the Glory-Glory days of university expansion when Economic History gained so much in numbers of its recruits, both in staff and students; and when we, its practitioners, were given a self-confidence able to sustain us through the Gloomy-Gloomy days at the onset of Thatcherite philistinism. Clearly I was born at the right moment: and had it been a free choice I would not have wished it otherwise.

It was a joy to be alive
And to be young was very heaven.

Appendix: Plagiarist and Poseur revealed?

I have always enjoyed using documents to enliven the teaching of history, and I find room for what may well be my last opusculum. It documents the most recent of my un-dull moments, and may serve to illustrate the risks of engaging with an amateur. However, the happy and valuable role of the amateur in local history research I must freely and gratefully acknowledge. May their contribution continue to flourish, and may our subject always be accessible to them.

(i)   *Letter received from Dr Brian Barber, Senior Archivist, Doncaster Metropolitan Borough, 9 October 2000*, with enclosure (ii) below; reproduced here with permission, and with thanks for access to the relevant files in the Bunting papers.

The late William Bunting of Thorne deposited some photocopies of records, including some of his own, long before my time. They were never catalogued, and I came across the (enclosed) item whilst examining the records in the course of preparing a new *Guide*. Although all this has some amusement value, there is an aspect which you might not want to dismiss without some reflection; I assume that, following his usual paranoid practice he placed photocopies of this, and other documents, in various repositories. I am fairly certain that (before 1981) he deposited local material in the Brotherton Library at Leeds . . . he also gave material to York (University) (in 1988) . . .
Future users might not be in a position to know where the balance of truth lies in this matter. Perhaps you are happy to let the tone of his denunciation alert the reader to its accuracy. On the other hand you may want to write a memorandum putting the record straight. If this were so, I would be happy to send you a full copy of his 30 or so pages of closely-reasoned abuse.

(ii)   *Enclosure dated 19 April 1983, being a copy of the title page of a file, now D2/BUNT/4, put together by William Bunting of Thorne near Doncaster in 1971.*

PLAGIARISM by PROFESSOR MAURICE BERESFORD . . . DEPARTMENT OF ECONOMIC HISTORY UNIVERSITY OF LEEDS, 1971 and ongoing in respect of PLANS LISTED AS BEING OF INCLESMORE, IN THE PUBLIC RECORD OFFICE . . . GIVEN IN THE (PRO GUIDE) as having been drawn ca. 1409-10.

The revised date of c. 1407 now given by Beresford is incorrect, and Beresford's 'Paper' nonsensical it may still be, but I corrected the most obvious foolish errors in April to May 1971 for which I was thanked but have no knowledge of his paper having been published. He never had the courtesy to send me a copy . . . It is understood that Beresford frequently lectures in various places, to various gatherings and societies posing as an authority on these plans. It is now for his posing, obvious plagiarism, and failure to acknowledge that I now publish original correspondence with notes and corrections.
I sent a note to the person at (the PRO) responsible for correcting such obvious errors . . . but . . . that un-named and to me unknown official, never acknowledged my note.
With plagiarising idiots like Beresford accepting the date of 1409-10, there is no wonder that ordinary persons have been fooled into losing their lands and rights.

(iii) *Draft of a memorandum by Beresford, dated 2 December 2000, acceding to the suggestion of a memorandum to go into the Doncaster records alongside the files cited above . . .*

William Bunting was a remarkable man. He was trained as an engineer's fitter, but otherwise self-taught he became a well-known naturalist with many publications, specialising in insect embryology. His fieldwork lay principally in Thorne Moor, an area of former peatland south of the Humber on the border of Nottinghamshire and Yorkshire.
I myself was brought to this area in 1970, rather unwillingly since it lay distant from Leeds, was sparsely inhabited and devoid of public transport. My earliest letter to Bunting, written on 14 March 1971, explained that I had 'just completed a short study of two (?) fifteenth century plans of Inclesmoor in the Public Record Office, a contribution to a collective volume on early local plans to be edited by R.A. Skelton and P.D. Harvey (for the Oxford University Press)'. I asked whether he could help by locating four of the minor place-names on the plans.

18

Bunting replied at once in a friendly and helpful way and was able to identify two of the four place-names that had eluded me. He added: 'I am rather tied up with a public enquiry. I seem to have a full-time job stopping the rape of the countryside and theft of local lands. I have some good material here in my study dating from 1630 that you should find interesting. I am most thankful for the copies of the maps. I have wanted copies for many years but have never found the spare cash to buy. Old deeds did not have plans with them and rather clever persons later produced plans and used the names on the deeds to establish ownership of much more than the original deeds granted. From a very cursory glance I would say this is the case with Inclesmoor. I suggest that to establish the extent of Inclesmoor you should examine the Pipe Rolls up to the date of the plans'.

It will be seen that the hostility to me displayed in the 1971 and 1983 accusations of 'plagiarism' and 'posing' was quite missing although the references to his litigation and a suggestion that I should assist him in wresting the Snaith court rolls from private custody should have alerted me to his zeal for combat. By the time our correspondence ceased in the summer of 1971 there were ominous allusions to black dogs who I now know obsessed him: the 'bosom pals in naughtiness' and his dogmatic 'I cannot accept that the plans had any other intent or purpose than fraudulency'. He gratuitously enclosed copies of further documents, some concerning the Inclesmoor area but others extending well beyond, and all later than the period with which my own research was concerned. Most of them were related to the controversial Vermuyden project for draining the fens, the starting point for the long programme of alleged conspiracies which Bunting was sure he had uncovered.

It was also clear that Bunting was unable to read the fifteenth century documents or to understand that nature of the concessions for peat working which made the plans and the related documents that I had identified in the PRO such a unique source for the economic history of peat. At that stage I wrote what turned out to be the final letter in our correspondence (1 April 1971). It was designed simply to delimit my interest and save Bunting from sending me further material. 'I am enclosing the (typescript copy) of my manuscript but your last letter makes it necessary for me to emphasise that it is a study of the two fifteenth century maps and the events leading up to these, and deliberately says nothing about the subsequent history of the area in the period in which you are the expert'.

I must therefore send my message to posterity: Beresford had no further contact with Bunting after 1971* and thus had no intimation that offence had been caused nor that he was claiming 'plagiarism' (i.e. my use of the identification of the two minor-place names that Bunting had provided, and for which he had been thanked in my letter of 5 April 1971).

In the strict sense the accusation of 'plagiarism' made in 1983 is easy to refute, for there is no way in which Bunting could have seen what eventually appeared in Skelton and Harvey's *Local Maps and Plan from Medieval England*. The grotesque fact, which gave editor and authors no pleasure, is that Oxford University Press delayed publication from 1971 to 1985. I fear that Bunting would have got very little satisfaction, even had he seen the book. My very first footnote began with thanks to Bunting for help and information.

Should any reader of this apologia not in Oxford wish to check the accuracy of my refutation, it would not be easy: the volume was priced as if for a market of millionaire map-collectors; very few academics or libraries could afford one, and very few review copies were sent out. Had Beresford been Bunting he might have smelt a conspiracy here.

*Note: Bunting died in 1995; he always refused to divulge his age but was probably born in 1916. Much remarkable biographical detail will be found in Catherine Caufield, 'Thorne

Moor', *The New Yorker* (New York, 4 February 1991), pp. 63-72, a frank account of a remarkable life, and almost certainly based on a personal interview. His public and private combats in and out of the English lawcourts were seemingly matched by service as a courier in the Spanish Civil War and as a British agent in Yugoslavia during the Second World War.

Maurice Beresford was born in 1920 in Sutton Coldfield. He attended Jesus College, Cambridge and worked in the Birmingham University Settlement 1941-2. During the period 1948-85 he was Lecturer then Reader and Professor of Economic History at the University of Leeds. He was made FBA in 1985. His research has focused on medieval England and his many publications include the classics *Lost villages of England* (1954 and 1998); *New towns of the Middle Ages* (1967 and 1988); (with H. P. R. Finberg) *English Medieval Boroughs* (1973) and (with J.G.Hurst) *Deserted Medieval villages* (1971 and 1989).

Reflections of a Dinosaur?

Y.S. Brenner

I am an economist. Like other scientists, economists are trying to discover and formulate laws of general validity by analysing data and testing theories. For this, macroeconomists in particular need *economic history* to discover previously unrecognised regularities and for testing the validity of theories. It is their substitute for the natural scientists' laboratories.

Marshall regarded economics as part of the study of 'man's action in the ordinary business of life...'. Keynes defined economics as 'the science which treats the phenomena arising out of the economic activities of men in society.' And Lord Robbins described economics as 'the science which studies human behaviour as a relationship between ends and scarce means which have alternative uses.' All of them agree that economics is concerned with man's behaviour in society. But human beings often react to similar stimuli in different ways. Diverse cultures impose on people different modes of conduct which not only change with the passage of time, but even at the same time differ in various parts of the world. All economic prognostication is based on the study of historical events and the hope that, under similar circumstances, what happened before will yield similar results in the future. Every culture is the product of a society's history and stage of development, and this determines individuals' and societies' behaviour. By the end of the middle ages in parts of Europe people transformed from spiritual beings, who, in order to survive had to devote reasonable attention to economic interests, into what sometimes seems to be economic animals, who will be prudent nonetheless to assure their spiritual well-being.[1] When the Age of Enlightenment turned into the Age of Capital man's drives became many: 'the desire for power, the craving for acclaim, the impulsion to serve the common good and the simple urge to action. But by virtue of an inner necessity they all became subordinate to profit-making because without economic success almost none of these desires could be attained.'[2] In some parts of the earth people now take for granted that all men are created equal, in other parts they declare that women are also entitled to equal rights and pay, and again in other parts, they believe in caste systems and inequality. Ancient Rome regarded slaves as 'speaking instruments'; feudal society distinguished people with blue from red blood; early capitalism abolished slavery and 'blood' but transformed workers into a factor of production - 'labour power'; and early post-war democracy allowed workers to rise on the basis of individual competitive ability but did not provide them with equal opportunities. The liberal democratic capitalism of the *Welfare State* promoted equal rights for all irrespective of colour, religion and sex, though unfortunately they were never fully attained. In every epoch people reacted differently to economic stimuli. A farmer in America or Europe spends his savings on the acquisition of better seed or farm equipment. A Cambodian peasant uses his savings to build a new pagoda to appease the Gods because he believes that the land will also yield a crop without improved seed and better farming tools, but not without good weather and weather is in the hand of God. All this makes historical and sociological analysis an indispensable instrument for contriving meaningful economic theories and their effective practical application. Without

21

knowing how people behave, economic predictions rest on unreliable metaphysical assumptions such as the universality of *homo economicus*.

In their search for economic laws economists employ both inductive and deductive methods. Inductively they adduce historical and statistical observations to strengthen confidence in general rules. Deductively they start from these general rules and move toward the particulars by means of theory and logical conclusions. But not everything that seems logical to an economist is true, and what is true at one time under one set of circumstances need not be true forever. *Economic history* deals with empirical facts and for this reason its application to economic theory saves economics from becoming something like a new branch of scholastics. Economists are often ill equipped for the selection of relevant facts from the vast amount of information available. Many economists have brilliant sophisticated logical explanations for economic phenomena, but as they are not trained as historians they are insufficiently wary of the risk of unconsciously selecting evidence to suit their logical preconceptions. Good economic historians are alert to this pitfall and better qualified to approach data without bias. Economic history is of course a separate discipline, but like mathematics, statistics and sociology, it is a vital instrument for providing the raw material for the formulation of meaningful economic theories.

In 1958, A.W. Phillips believed he had found an inverse relationship between the rate of change of money wage-rates and the unemployment rate. His study of historical statistics seemed to justify his conclusion. But later we experienced recessions and rising unemployment with positive rates of price inflation. And since 1996 the American economy has annually grown with very little unemployment and less than 2% inflation. Some economists believe that this was, and continues to be, the result of the new information technologies which are said to stimulate productivity at a rate which is so much in excess of wages that both inflation and business cycles have become irrelevant. Perhaps this is true and perhaps it is not, but only history (time) will tell.

Since the days of Adam Smith many economists were convinced that in one way or another all ships rise with the tide - 'what is good for General Motors is good for the American people'. Vilfredo Pareto believed in a constant pyramid of income distribution. Within this pyramid individuals find their positions on the basis of competitive ability, but the shape of the pyramid as a whole always remains the same. Improvement for those at the bottom of the structure occurs when the entire pyramid is rising. But when we look at recent American statistics we discover that in spite of the rising economic tide, on average the wages of 20% of all persons employed at the bottom of the pyramid have fallen. Between 1973 and 1997 men's wages have fallen but women's wages have improved. Alas, both men's and women's wages remained too low to raise them above the widely accepted ($7.89 per hour) 'poverty line'. In other words, if one can trust the data of the American Economic Policy Institute, 20% of all Americans employed during the last decade of almost uninterrupted economic growth, were 'working poor'. In 1977 one fifth of American households had approximately $10.000 a year, in 1999 they only had $8.800. Only the top earners in the low income group, those who earned $45.100 and more, improved. But workers in the top 20% income bracket, (who earned more that $102.300 in 1999) are now 38.2% better off than they were in 1977. And the 1% of top earners, (with an income above $515.600) have increased their earnings by almost 120%. So much then for the trickle down effect, and for all ships rising with the tide.

The point is that economists tend to forget that economic laws are no more than statements of general uniformity in the relationship between two or more phenomena of economic life, and not definite and universal propositions comparable to the law of gravitation and of conservation of energy in physics. In other words, economic theory without economic history is blind.

But this is not the only meaning economic history holds for me. Like every other scientist, curiosity, the wish to know why and how, also inspires me. And not this alone. The desire to promote what I consider to be a happier, fairer and more secure future for society inspires me as well. I know that there is something called *economic growth* and something called *human progress*. But the two are not necessarily the same. They may be related, but not everything that is called economic growth engenders human progress, and not all human progress depends on economic growth.

Economic growth implies the raising of output per unit input of labour and other resources. It increases mankind's ability to satisfy its material needs more fully and with less effort. This is largely a matter of technology and the study of technology is mainly in the domain of the natural sciences. But *human progress* implies the improvement of people's well-being which involves the distribution of the fruits of economic growth. This depends on societies' modes of existence, the study of which is in the domain of history and other social sciences. In their contribution to people's welfare the domains are inextricably interrelated and interdependent. Scientific and technological achievements delimit the possible forms of social organisation, and a society's institutional framework determines the direction of its technological advancement. Science and technology govern the effort and labour-time required to satisfy man's material needs, and man's social arrangements determine the nature, diversity, extent, and all but the minimum of these needs, together with the techniques adopted and priorities allocated for their satisfaction. With the increasing efficiency of production the range of human choices widens. It becomes possible to divide more time and effort between a growing variety of purposes. Yet, as the material constraints diminish, production and distribution processes become more complex and mankind enters the bondage of an increasingly sophisticated social environment which it inherits and creates. But, as the late Ernest Gellner said, the emergence of a society without poverty, a fraternal society which incorporates everyone in a shared moral citizenship without oppression or arbitrariness, is not inscribed into any historic plan. People must desire it, and when they do, they must struggle to obtain it.[3] I want to take part in this struggle.

The constant progressive element in all of science, and not only in the social sciences, has always been the widening of the likenesses man selects among the facts. Man's observations and experiences are many, perhaps infinite; and by dividing them into what he believes matters and what does not, and into what is alike or fitting into a pattern and what is not, he passes judgment on his observations and experiences, and this judgment forms the basis of his beliefs. Newton saw the likeness between the fall of the apple and the swirling of the moon in her orbit round the earth; Einstein saw the unity of space and time, and the identity of energy and mass ($E = Mc^2$). Each of them saw unities, which no one had recognised before, and produced new conceptions of the universe. The point is that 'when we discover the wider likeness, whether between space and time or bacillus and crystal, we enlarge the order in the universe; but more than this, we enlarge its unity. And it is this conception of the unity of nature living and dead that determines progress'.[4] Early post-war democracy recognised the likeness in all men and arrived at a new conception of mankind. However, unlike Newton's and Einstein's, this conception was threatening too many of the social and economic establishment's vital vested interests to be universally accepted.

All this needs to be stated to remind people that in both the natural and the social sciences it is the shift in the judgment of things regarded alike or unlike that determines our values. *Human progress* comes when a new likeness is discovered and previously disregarded facts and events assume a new significance, or their earlier significance is reassessed, and value judgments are altered. When society discovers a new likeness, a process of re-evaluation takes place. In this context the study of economic history is essential, because failing to learn from past mistakes condemns one to repeat them.

The current inclination to regard *pure* self-interest as a unifying principle behind all behaviour as if it was a scientifically established fact, and to equate it to individualism, is nonsense and needs to be shown as such. Striving for equality is not antithetical to individuality. Equal *rights* may provide the basis for the opportunity to realise individual aims and desires, but if merely enshrined in the legal system they are insufficient to ensure them in reality. Modern science which searches for the unifying principles behind events makes the distinction between facts and values. Turning economic success into a kind of vindication of almost all the means by which it is obtained, deprives it of its progressive content even if in terms of GNP it may from time to time engender economic growth. Economic growth is necessary and desirable, but not all economic growth and not at any price. The growth fetishism offered us these days, which is oblivious to the loss of human values it engenders, and too often ignores environmental risks, can hardly lead to *human progress*. And it is the illumination of this that I see as the most important contribution economic history can make.

Alas, nowadays, macroeconomists are too busy quantifying data and constructing highly sophisticated mathematical formulae based on dubious behavioural assumptions. They simply take for granted that economic growth is *good*, but do not bother thinking about which economic growth, and good for whom? They claim to avoid normative bias, believing that this makes them into objective scientists, and forget that *good* itself is always normative. They recommend deregulation because they assume that it will promote efficiency and therefore growth, but ignore social cost, and the fact that private enterprise is also regulated though not necessarily to serve the *public good* but to serve the interests of a few successful businessmen. They turn a blind eye to the culture of egoism they promote by spreading the idea that materialistic self-interest is the only valid drive behind all human progress, and they do not worry about the moral morass into which this leads us. The study of economic history may highlight flaws in the basic assumptions upon which widely accepted erroneous economic dogmas rest, dogmas which are passed off as laws of equal validity with natural scientists' laws of nature. Economic and social historians know that economic and social systems are constantly in a process of reorganisation and that throughout this process there are points of bifurcation at which decisions are taken which influence the future. The outcome of these decisions is always unpredictable, but it is preferable to take them informed by past experience than groping in the dark.

Yehojachin Simon Brenner (born 1926) studied history, political science and economics in Jerusalem, Basel and London. From 1972 to his retirement in 1997 he held the Chair of Economics in the Faculty of Social Sciences at Utrecht University in the Netherlands. Prior to this he taught economics at the university of Maryland, the University of Ghana, the Institute of Social Science in the Netherlands and the Middle East Technical University in Turkey. Professor Y.S. Brenner is the editor of the *Journal of Income Distribution* and has written more than ten books on economics and economics-related subjects. Recently a second (revised) edition of *A Theory of Full Employment* (written together with his wife)was published by Transaction Publishers, New Brunswick and London 2000.

---

[1] Tawney R.H. [1926] *Religion and the Rise of Capitalism* Penguin, West Drayton, 1948, pp.272-3

[2] Sombart W. [1953] 'Capitalism' in *Encyclopedia of Social Sciences*, Vol.III, New York.

[3] Gellner [1988]' 'Introduction' in Baechler J. et.al (eds) *Europe and the Rise of Capitalism*, Oxford, p3.

[4] See Bronowski, J. [1951] *The Common Sense of Science*. Harmondsworth, (reprinted 1968) p.134; and concerning the political widening of unity see Ginsberg M. [1946] *Sociology* OUP.

What Economic History Means To Me

A. R. Bridbury

Teaching history for purposes of examining and hence grading students confers a measure of authenticity upon the writing of history that it does not deserve. Virtually everything that human beings have ever done either went unrecorded at the time or, if recorded, has not survived. The material with which historians have to work are irredeemably exiguous. There is nothing that we can do about that. And there is another problem to compound the difficulties of the historian. When Bismarck was asked to release his diplomatic archives for publication he commented that they could help nobody to understand the happenings of the time because only those who had participated in them could appreciate what was really going on. Participants themselves left accounts of what they witnessed; but their accounts, when they were not vitiated by the ordinary shortcomings of witness recall, were certainly compromised by the intention of their authors to vindicate themselves or denigrate others. Historians are also, in a sense, witnesses. They bear witness to the impressions left upon them by the documents they read and import into their interpretation of those documents their own experiences, conditioning and assumptions.

At some point in its development as an instrument of pedagogic discipline, history was dissolved into a congeries of separate studies in accordance with the otherwise admirable doctrine of the division of labour. Thus was economic history born having economic analysis, the most rigorous of the social studies, to provide it with its terms of reference.

Division of labour presupposes interdependence. But the interdependence of the various branches of history could never approximate to the degree of interdependence achieved by producers of goods and services who specialised their functions as markets widened or deepened. One example must suffice. By 1914, says a caustic recent observer of England's economic progress, the country had become 'a working museum of industrial archaeology'. Can we explain the undoubted truth wrapped in this calumny in economic terms? Economic analysis cannot help us. It can tell us how free markets distribute the resources of an economy so as to maximise output in terms of market demand; and it can indicate the economic ramifications of any interference with the free play of market forces. But it is powerless to tell us why England failed to take a lead in developing twentieth-century industries as it had done in developing nineteenth-century ones, despite its doctrinaire adherence to free trade and the free movement of labour and capital, its highly organised and competitive markets, its centuries of experience of trade and industry and its abundant supplies of investment funds. Explanations certainly abound; but they have to be couched in other terms than economic ones.

In short, a problem in what we have learnt to call economic history turns into a vastly more complex problem of general history as soon as we pass from the laborious and comparatively unchallenging task of assembling the facts about England's trade and industry to an attempt to explain either England's sensational rise to prosperity or its extraordinarily ineffectual response to the dramatic opportunities that later development afforded.

If a true division of labour were possible in historical studies that would be the moment when the conclusions of other historical specialisms could be summoned to combine with those of the economic historians to produce some sort of synthesis. But historical work does not lend itself to the practice of co-operative husbandry. Specialists in other branches of history go to the records with very different questions in mind; and the records will not answer questions which have not been put to them. The economic historian in quest for a comprehensive explanation of the problems he is tackling soon finds that he must himself put to the records all those questions which probe aspects of human motivation far removed from those dictated by the spur of economic gain, if he is to do more than set the scene and leave the reader to provide the answers.

The economic historian is not alone in this dilemma. Division of labour has made it a problem for all historical specialisms. And research compounds the problem because, for purposes of research, we deliberately narrow our vision in order to be able to deepen our understanding. The universities annually generate a flood of books and papers which convey precise information about historical events considered from one of any number of points of view. Laborious to compile, these works are all too often burdensome to read because they so rarely venture beyond their research briefs. In effect, they are latter-day chronicles; some of them as indispensable as bricks are to the building of a house. But the bricks, alas, are of all different sizes, shapes and consistencies. It is surely a crazy, ramshackle house that we build with them.

Division of labour rapidly loses its *raison d'etre* whatever the specialised point of view with which we embark upon our investigations of the past. The deeper we penetrate in search of explanation the more wide-ranging are the questions we find ourselves trying to answer. Only at the most superficial levels can we hope to attain truth. Below those levels all the problems of evidence and interpretation crown in upon us, not to speak of the difficulties we encounter in comprehending the range and complexity of human motivation displayed in the most ordinary interactions of social life. And overarching all are those inexplicable shifts of fashion which create the climate of opinion in which we all work, whose influence, at its most insidious, we cannot even perceive.

It is that climate of opinion which expresses society's stated values and prevailing interests. Modern western society sees itself in an historical perspective. The study of history has therefore moved to centre-stage. Economic history has probably taken a disproportionate share of the limelight ever since a powerful nation went forth and conquered in the name of a religion based upon an economic interpretation of history. But that episode is now done with; and economic history will presumably take its appropriate place henceforth as a contributory insight instead of a dominant theme in whatever contemporary judgement decides to accept as historical explanation.

A. R. Bridbury was Professor of Medieval History at the London School of Economics 1954-89 and is the author of half a dozen books on the subject. He objects to CVs even on job applications arguing that where he went to kindergarten matters far more than where he went to college.

British and International Economic History in the Twenty-First Century

Stephen Broadberry

An important challenge facing economic history at the beginning of the twenty-first century is the growing internationalisation of academic life. In the context of a British economics department, where I am based, research is increasingly assessed in terms of its international importance, growing numbers of students are coming from abroad, and all students are increasingly adopting a more outward looking viewpoint. However, it would clearly be inappropriate for each country to stop covering its own economic history because of pressures for international coverage. A more appropriate strategy, in my view, involves dealing with national economic history in an outward looking way as well as studying the international economy.

An outward looking approach to British economic history means more than simply comparing with other countries. Indeed, one highly inappropriate approach to modern British economic history has been the exaggeratedly pessimistic view derived from highly selective comparisons with other countries, focusing only on the successes of any particular country and ignoring all failures.[1] Thus the 'declinist perspective' on the British economy since the late nineteenth century often combines the most successful aspects of the economies of the United States, Germany and Japan into a unified example of 'modern best-practice' that represents some golden missed opportunity. A truly outward looking approach would note the failures as well as the successes in each country, and recognise that these countries all fit together in a world economy characterised by comparative advantage and gains from trade. It is thus not appropriate to assess the British economy simply by how closely it followed the business model of the United States, for example.[2]

A good example of the outward looking approach in practice is the work of Crafts and Harley on the British Industrial Revolution. Using the Chenery-Syrquin approach to derive 'European norms' for characteristics of the economy at particular levels of development, Crafts (1985) was able to show how Britain's development path differed substantially from that of other European countries. In particular, he noted the early release of labour from agriculture in Britain, so that by the early nineteenth century, Britain had an unusually small share of the labour force engaged in a relatively high productivity agricultural sector. Combined with the findings of Harley (1982) and Crafts (1985) on the relatively slow acceleration of industrial productivity growth during this period, this suggests that the key feature of Britain's Industrial Revolution was the structural transformation leading to the establishment of a large, but not particularly high productivity, industrial sector.

My own research on Britain's productivity performance compared with the United States and

Germany since the mid-nineteenth century, using a sectoral approach, complements the Crafts-Harley vision of the Industrial Revolution, as well as offering a reinterpretation of Britain's loss of overall productivity leadership. Working with a sectoral breakdown of GDP per employee, it is possible to show that both Germany and the United States overtook Britain in terms of aggregate labour productivity largely by shifting resources out of agriculture and improving their relative productivity performance in services rather than by improving their position in industry.[3] Despite its apparent iconoclasm, note that this view solves a number of puzzles in the literature. First, the debate on British and American technology in the nineteenth century following the work of Habakkuk (1962) makes much more sense if the US labour productivity lead in industry already existed in the nineteenth century rather than emerging in the twentieth century. Second, as I have already suggested, it sits rather well with the Crafts-Harley view of Britain's industrial sector being large rather than highly productive during the nineteenth century. And third, it makes sense of the dominance of London in international services during the late nineteenth century, and its subsequent relative decline.

Note the important change in the way that services and industry are viewed in this interpretation. Although there was a large US/UK productivity gap in industry in the late nineteenth century, it did not get any worse over time. On the other hand, although there was never a large productivity gap in services, Britain moved from a position of productivity leadership to a position of a modest productivity gap. Hence if we want to explain what changed between the late nineteenth and the late twentieth centuries, it is the loss of productivity leadership in services that really matters. And yet it is still conventional to read that Britain's relative decline has been exaggerated by excessive focus on industry, with services being neglected.[4] At first sight, this reinterpretation of Britain's productivity performance does appear to sit uneasily with the industrial orientation of much of the literature on British relative economic decline. Here, however, I would suggest that the central concern of the literature on de-industrialisation needs to be turned on its head. Given the expansion of industry during World War II, and the diminishing returns encountered, a movement of resources out of industry was inevitable during the postwar period, and the attempts to prevent this de-industrialisation were counter-productive.

I like to see this work on Britain's productivity performance as providing a bridge between macro-level research on international comparisons of productivity and the micro-level industry studies that have constituted such an important part of the British economic history tradition. Writing the case study chapters of *The Productivity Race*, I was struck by the wealth of knowledge embodied in these industry studies. It would be a shame if this type of work were to disappear.

The danger with the international economy as a topic must be superficiality. Hence it is positive to be able to report that there has been much good work on the international economy in recent years, particularly that based around the international monetary system. Books such as Eichengreen (1997) and Foreman-Peck (1995) provide excellent summaries of this work. Work on growth at the global level has perhaps been more mixed, since it is all too easy for research that covers all countries to lack the depth that comes from studies based on individual countries. Economic history has always drawn heavily on detailed local knowledge, and it would be unfortunate if this strength of earlier work were discarded in the attempt to meet the challenges of relevance in the twenty-first century. A number of recent studies of European growth have succeeded in striking the right balance between breadth and depth. In particular, I would mention Crafts and Toniolo (1996) and Feinstein et al. (1997), with the latter also covering more general macroeconomic history. These works reflect the rapid emergence of a European economic history that is grounded in national cultures but

28

also outward looking, and I would see this as one of the most positive developments of the last decade. The European Historical Economics Society has played an important role here, with the *European Review of Economic History* providing an outlet for the high quality literature that is emerging in this area.

In summary, economic history needs to internationalise. But this implies an outward orientation to British economic history as well as international economic history.

Stephen Broadberry (b. 1956) was educated at Warwick and Oxford. He has taught at Universities of Oxford, Cardiff and British Columbia, and he is currently Professor at the University of Warwick. He has published widely on the macroeconomic history of Britain, Germany and the international economy during the inter-war period. His primary research interests are now in the area of comparative growth and productivity performance, focusing in particular on Britain, Germany and the United States from the late nineteenth century to the present.

---

[1] See, for example, Levine (1967), Wiener (1981), Elbaum and Lazonick (1986).
[2] As in the work of Chandler (1990), for example.
[3] Broadberry (1998).
[4] See, for example, Rubinstein (1993).

Works cited
Broadberry, S.N. (1987), *The Productivity Race: British Manufacturing in International Perspective, 1850-1990*, Cambridge: Cambridge University Press.
 Broadberry, S.N. (1998), 'How did the United States and Germany Overtake Britain? A Sectoral Analysis of Comparative Productivity Levels, 1870-1990', *Journal of Economic History*, 58, 375-407.
Chandler, A.D. Jr. (199), *Scale and Scope: The Dynamics of Industrial Capitalism*, Cambridge, MA: Harvard University Press.
Crafts, N.F.R. (1985), *British Economic Growth during the Industrial Revolution*, Oxford: Clarendon Press.
Crafts, N.F.R. and Toniolo, G. (eds.) (1996), *Economic Growth in Europe Since 1945*, Cambridge: Cambridge University Press.
Eichengreen, B. (1997), *Globalising Capital: A History of the International Monetary System*, Princeton, NJ: Princeton University Press.
Feinstein, C.H., Temin, P. and Toniolo, G. (1997), *The European Economy Between the Wars*, Oxford: Oxford University Press.
Foreman-Peck, J. (1995), *A History of the World Economy: International Economic Relations Since 1850*, (second edition), London: Harvester Wheatsheaf.
Elbaum, B. and Lazonick, W. (eds.) (1986), The Decline of the British Economy, Oxford: Oxford University Press.
Habakkuk, H.J. (1962), *American and British Technology in the Nineteenth Century*, Cambridge: Cambridge University Press.
Harley, C.K. (1982), 'British Industrialisation before 1841: Evidence of Slower Growth during the Industrial Revolution', *Journal of Economic History*, 42, 267-289.
Levine, A.L. (1967), *Industrial Retardation in Britain, 1880-1914*, New York: Basic Books.
Rubinstein, W.D. (1993), *Capitalism, Culture and Economic Decline in Britain*, 1750-1990, London: Routledge.
Wiener, M.J. (1981), *English Culture and the Decline of the Industrial Spirit 1850-1980*, Cambridge: Cambridge University Press.

Making Economic History Accessible

Stephen Caunce

I have to start by saying that I cannot imagine a worthwhile history which does not have at least an economic component. On the other hand, I find it equally hard to believe that any specialised history based only upon an economic analysis can ever produce a meaningful explanation of any significant part of our past. Economic history is a vital subdivision of the whole human experience, but we must never forget that sooner or later all such specialisms have to be re-integrated if true generalisations are to be attempted. I remain convinced that by doing this we significantly increase our understanding of past experience, and from that we gain insight into lasting, though not directly predictable, patterns of behaviour. That in turn can help us cope with the present and prepare for the future, and history is therefore much more than the intellectually stimulating exercise I have always found it.

My fundamental interest in how things came to be as they are owes little to formal history teaching, as far as I can remember. Whether the path that events have followed was inevitable, or whether alternatives existed, are speculations I indulged in from an early age. While seeking to explain how this interest in the past always leaned towards the economic, I chanced upon a comment from 1891 that still seemed remarkably apposite:

> let the Professor of Political Economy teach what he will, even the undergraduates who seek honours in the history school, soon drop away.... Had ... these lectures [been given] in some industrial centre, hundreds of workmen would, I believe, have paid to listen to them. But in the home of learning, some dozen men of education attended lectures thrown open, free, to every member of the University.[1]

Arthur Rogers was writing a preface to the lecture notes of his father, James Thorold Rogers, which he published as *The Industrial and Commercial History of England*. I identify closely with those notional workmen, whose interest stemmed directly from their own situation, and share his bafflement at the difficulty of getting general academic acceptance of the need to consider economic matters.

Growing up in the 1950s and 60s in an industrial town of about 20,000 people in south Lancashire, the most fundamental forces that had affected my community and family seemed to be self-evidently economic, even though political structures had just as evidently modified and shaped their impact. This linkage of the personal and the historical has not diminished, even though I look at things now within a much wider context. I cannot explain my view of economic history without exploring it. The town lacked most of the social and intellectual facilities taken for granted in most urban centres of that size elsewhere, but its juxtaposition of historical elements was both unusual and (with hindsight) stimulating. It is located on the Roman road up the west coast to Scotland, at a natural communications hub. The first industrial canal ran down the south-western boundary, and over it soared the first real public railway, carried on Stephenson's first railway viaduct. It then runs through the heart of the town, before passing a memorial to Huskisson, the first railway passenger fatality. Over several decades, the East Lancashire Road, the M6 and finally the M62 boxed us in.

Newton became a factory town quite suddenly in the nineteenth century, primarily based round the railways. The environment suffered severely, but jobs, mostly manual, became plentiful. When I was a teenager, the quiet road on which we lived literally filled up twice every day with buses, bikes and pedestrians rushing into and out of the vast, proud locomotive works, originally founded by Robert Stephenson. Occasionally enormous vehicles emerged, bearing luridly coloured railway engines for some distant part of the world, too big to go by rail. People came into the town to work rather than leaving it, and the variety of different industries seemed to guarantee the future. A new colliery, the most modern in Europe, was sunk in the 1960s. Unemployment was something that parents frequently recalled, with great bitterness, but my generation believed it was dead and gone, and concentrated more on questions about how to share out the rewards of success, and cope with the damage done by the rapidity of previous changes.

Many links to its past existence as a very small market town had survived industrialisation, however. Arable farming went on between the three main settlements that now collectively made up the town. The market itself, relocated to be near the factory workers' homes, remained the biggest regular event in local life, and the High Street was so wide and lined with pubs that it instantly recalled its old role as a site for long-defunct livestock fairs. Corners of natural beauty remained and there was a gloriously half-timbered house (now demolished) and a few thatched cottages. A titled lord of the manor, resident in the south of England and never seen in the town, owned much of the land. We had ghosts and local tales and customs that seemed to link us back to times long gone, and though events like the enormous Whit Walks were more recent creations, they were just as much customary events. We were very sure of our identity, while places nearby provided fascinating contrasts between, say, Liverpool with its docks and ships, and Manchester, with its mills and warehouses, or Wigan with its mines and Warrington with its chemicals and engineering. There was no sense of any generalised, amorphous industrialisation having homogenised the area.

At the grammar school I attended, history was interesting, but said very little about this rich mix of historical issues. There was no local museum, and only an Edwardian, anecdotal local history in the library. I was part of the first cohort allowed to study A level economics, and the approach was more philosophical than scientific. My version of economics remains one that offers insight rather than certainty, and is based in social issues and concerns. It is not one where statistics and equations replace more conventional historical methodologies, though these can add a vital extra dimension. Economics to me is the interaction between socially-constructed human behaviour patterns and a world that runs to external rules we cannot influence, even though we gradually understand them better. The questions to which I seek answers today as a historian began to coalesce then: about a Lancashire industrial revolution that was not just about textiles; about the northern intertwining of industry and agriculture that is rarely acknowledged; about the importance of communications; about the role of ordinary people and their sense of themselves; and about what they got out of it all. Obviously, the scope widened, and issues took on new significance, but continuity remained. It would be impossible to understand the development of this complex local urban system without locating it within a national and international context, but it is vital not to lose the sense of difference by standing back too far.

This agenda was given a bitter twist from the 1970s as almost all the industries were closed and demolished, with the miners' strike of the 1980s followed in a few years by a hurried and seemingly spiteful blowing up of the twin towers of the colliery, which drew a symbolic line under the era of mass local employment. During this time, relatives were made redundant or failed to find work, and when I left university I soon found myself unemployed. Industrial collapse brought no clear class-based response, however. The gentry had long since left, few of the factories had had local owners, and the middle class consisted mostly of doctors, teachers, shopkeepers and lower white-collar workers like draughtsmen: hardly a rich or dominant grouping, or one to be fought for economic control. The town voted Labour by instinct, but a sizeable if ineffectual Conservative minority existed, and the majority were socially conservative and intolerant in a multitude of ways. They had a very practical attitude to life, and a wide variety of interests and beliefs that did not include high culture in any shape or form. This wasn't a town holding its breath while waiting for either a revolution or salvation through exposure to the 'finer' things of life. In the last two decades the M6/M62 motorway junction has spawned one of those mixtures of 'big shed' consumerism, mock-American leisure and eating facilities, and industrial warehousing that are almost a defining note of the late twentieth century, and which have no links with any local past. However, most people have welcomed the new jobs and leisure facilities, and today they are generally better paid and housed than ever before. While there had been a definite sense of community that was now under grave threat, it had never produced much in my lifetime that was easy to get romantic about. That, and the real nature of the English radical tradition, were added to my list of concerns.

Historians must surely aim to make sense of real patterns of change like this, which do not fit easily into any obvious category. We cannot afford to do battle over sterile ideological systems that function like faiths rather than scientific hypotheses: adequate for now but definitely not the final truth. Historians must also communicate their results outside their own ranks, thereby creating a constituency that appreciates the value of what we do. The shops are full of history books, and radio and television run frequent history programmes. The record offices are full of family historians beavering away and local histories written by amateurs abound. Few embody recent approaches and discoveries, however, especially those deriving from economic history. This now has a terrifying image among typical students as a remote, mathematical, and intensely difficult approach. Yet understanding economic issues has never been more important. Globalisation; the collapse of the state-capitalist alternative to the 'free' market; the seeming inability of the really poor countries to set in motion development that will benefit the majority of inhabitants; all these and more show that investigation of historical experience is vital. Those old local questions of mine have linked naturally to this wider agenda.

There is evidently a need to find a new way forward. Contemporary economic theory seems to have little to offer, for it is introverted and highly idealised. Indeed, it is encouraging to see Professor Crafts, for instance, acknowledging that 'the new economic history's original love affair with the invisible hand' needs to be replaced by 'a much more truly historical approach'.[2] For some, post-modernism has been a break-through, but to me it seems to lead inexorably to fragmentation and lack of general meaning. We need an economic history based around the general results of the actions and choices of conscious individuals, not a linear, mechanistic sequence of causes leading to predictable effects. Our interaction with each other and with our environment is indeed highly complex, but surely not random when judged over long periods, and when based upon the experience of large groups.

Scientists in all fields have similarly had to face the limitations of linear, mechanistic models, and long ago accepted that the real world patently is not comparable to a watch mechanism. On the other hand, in doing so they have not declared that scientific method is invalid, or that the breakthroughs of the past were just illusions. It is just that linear analysis has limits, and where they have been reached, chaos theory has allowed the evolution of coping, heuristic strategies that do produce meaningful, if not precise, results. They deal with parameters and probabilities rather than exactness. Meteorologists can now model and explain weather systems very accurately, without being able to predict actual weather for more than a few hours ahead. There is a small but growing interest in developing this approach for the humanities, and it seems to offer the chance for economic history to re-engage with understandable concerns. Chaos and complexity seem to offer the chance to re-engage with the real world and produce meaningful results. As a historian, this seems to be a goal worth pursuing.

Stephen Caunce (b. 19. 3. 1951). University College London, 1969-72 (BA). Leeds University, 1972-75, PhD, awarded 1989. Museum curator, Beamish, Kirklees, and Yorkshire Mining Museums, 1975-88. Tutor and lecturer in Economic and Social History, Leeds University, 1990-98. Senior lecturer in History, University of Central Lancashire. Interests are the industrialisation process in the north of England from c.1700, with particular emphasis on the role played by family and community structures. He is currently investigating the domestic Yorkshire woollen industry, the distinctive long-term contribution of northern agricultural systems, and the question of northern identity.

---

[1] J.E.T. Rogers, *The Industrial and Commercial History of England: Lectures delivered to the University of Oxford*, 1891, p. vii.
[2] N. F. R. Crafts, N. H. Dinsdale and R. Floud (eds), *Quantitative Economic History*, 1991, xx. He has confirmed this critique of the old 'new' economic history recently in the newsletter of the Economic History Society, 20, May 2000.

Economic and Social History

Christopher Chalklin

It is fitting to mark the 75th anniversary conference of the Economic History Society with some memories of earlier conferences. One recalls a few of the well-known economic historians who have presided at meetings, given an address or just attended. T.S. Ashton, whose books on the eighteenth-century English economy proved to be the foundation for future study of the subject, and who was thought to have declined a knighthood, presided at the first two conferences which this writer attended, at Edinburgh and Reading. It was well-known that he was Professor of Economic History at the London School of Economics when he retired in 1955; about his earlier career he reminded me personally at the Manchester conference in 1966, saying that 'I used to teach here, you know'. All succeeding Presidents have been distinguished economic and social historians, and it would be unfair to mention just two or three. Tawney, Clapham, Ashton and Postan appear as giants in the study of the subject in the early twentieth century; since the 1960s they have been succeeded by many more scholars whose output has been as large as theirs. Celebrated American economic historians and economists who have spoken at conferences from the 1960s include D.C. North, W.W. Rostow and R.Fogel. North and Fogel were Nobel Prize winners whilst Rostow was once an American assistant secretary of state. At the Edinburgh conference I recall a day outing in the Lowlands which included a tour of the New Lanark cotton mill settlement, perhaps the most impressive surviving physical remains of the Industrial Revolution. Earlier the party visited Sir Walter Scott's mansion of Abbotsford, where Professor J.D. Chambers, the great expert on the social effects of enclosures and population growth in the eighteenth-century East Midlands and Dr J.E. Williams, the historian of Derbyshire miners, were heard discussing the merits of Meredith, the late Victorian novelist. For over 20 years conferences have included new researchers' sessions where short papers by postgraduates have been presented and discussed. This author remembers chairing a meeting at Cheltenham. The audience included Sir John Habakkuk, and other well-known economic historians, but the contributor failed to appear for ten minutes!

A useful definition of economic history was written in 1962 by Professor W.H.B. Court, President of the Society at the end of the 1960s, the historian of industrialisation in the West Midlands. He wrote that economic choice was the centre of economic history: it is the history of men's allocation of resources, which are more or less limited, to chosen ends. As people are social they have made their economic choices according to the values and habits of their society. Social institutions have directed the operation of their choices, and ends have been not only economic but also social, cultural and even religious. Court's definition is more specific than some general historians, such as that of Tosh in 1984 that the subject 'embraces every aspect of economic life in the past, which is to say all those activities which have to do with production, exchange and consumption'. Court pointed to three principal themes. The first was economic change which needs to be studied not only in terms of the economic systems and wealth of one or more countries or even continents but also of factories, estates, cities, rural parishes, firms and influential people. Another theme,

34

economic welfare, concerns the distribution of wealth, that is the amount of national income and its allocation among social groups and individuals, including fluctuations in the allocation. The economic historian is also concerned with working and living conditions under which income is earned. Thirdly he studies the effect of government, including the legal system, on the use of resources and aims of the economy. To interpret these themes he draws on simple economic theories and illustrates structure and change with tables of figures and graphs. One might add that the language of the economist is often avoided.

In the early twentieth-century much economic history dealt with the detailed study of economic systems in a largely stationary state; though change and its explanation were not overlooked. *The Economic History of Modern Britain* by Clapham (1926-38), describing the whole economy between 1820 and 1914 in three volumes, and his book on France and Germany in the nineteenth century are leading examples of this approach. Since the Second World War economists have been concerned with long-run economic growth, especially its extent, causes and mechanisms, both in respect to Western countries and to the underdeveloped world. Historians have reflected this largely new study. Their work has been influenced by models explaining the growth of individual economies or showing the similarities or explaining the differences between countries. One theory interpreted economic development in terms of the balanced growth of the various sectors of the economy, and the other according to their unbalanced growth. These theories were applied by R.M. Hartwell, a former editor of the Review, to interpret the coming of the British Industrial Revolution.

Rostow argued that all countries undergo five stages of economic growth at different times, but his model was based too much on the British experience. It is arguable that it hardly fits Russia at all, and even in the British case not all the detail is acceptable. Again, the pattern of industrial growth was defined by W.G. Hoffman, who contrasted the output of consumer and capital goods in three or four chronological stages; he suggested that in this respect the development of the more advanced countries was similar to growth in the present time. This model is limited in that it considers only one important aspect of industrial growth.

Other models have been applied purely to historical settings. Gerschenkron's model of economic backwardness related to the industrialisation of the countries of Continental Europe in the nineteenth century, but was developed especially with reference to the retardation of Russia. Particularly influential among historians has been the protoindustrialisation concept. Conceived in relation to Belgian outwork textile manufacturing in the seventeenth and early eighteenth centuries, it showed that cloths made for export brought work in addition to farming, leading to population growth, which with this rural industry and capital accumulated by merchants led to the creation of workshops and machinery. This general view has of course been shown not to apply in some English regions by D.C. Coleman, a former editor of the Review.

Thus economic history may be approached in many ways. Partly because of the much greater availability of sources and the stronger links with the present industrial world, a large majority of research publications relate to the economy of the last 250 years. International studies have become more numerous, perhaps reflecting the great expansion of international trade and the spread of manufacturing since the Second World War. How may one take a general view of at least some of the important aspects of economic development since the eighteenth century, considering that industry has been at the heart of wealth creation? A comparison between countries is invited, especially related to the causes and process of industrialisation.

One may analyse first the causes of the 'Industrial Revolutions' or perhaps the 'takeoff into sustained growth' in the more important economies, such as Britain, France, Germany,

Russia, the United States and Japan. Using the approach of economists such as Dennison as well as economic historians such as the late Professor M.W. Flinn, a former President, one can compare the possible sources of capital, such as the manufacturers themselves and their relations and acquaintances, merchants, banks, the state, and foreign individuals and institutions, showing perhaps that it was plentiful in Britain, which lent to other countries, and particularly short in Russia. In addition to the French historian of the British economy, Professor F. Crouzet, the sources and structure of British capital during the Industrial Revolution were studied by the late Professor S. Pollard (who described his attendance at Conferences to me as an 'annual pilgrimage').

Next the contribution of each country to industrial technology may be discussed, pointing to the key importance of British discoveries, the work of French, German and American inventors, and their almost total absence in Russia and Japan in the nineteenth century. The causes of invention were often diverse, deriving from economic factors such as a shortage of labour or fuel, or cultural features such as the spread of technical knowledge based on a sound general education, especially among artisans. Comparisons between Britain and France have been made by the late Professor J.R. Harris, a regular participant at the Society's conferences and P. Mathias, a former Treasurer and President, among others. Enterprise, or the adoption of new techniques, is another important cause of industrial growth. One may compare the strength of entrepreneurial ability in each of the countries, and explain its emergence in terms of both economic and cultural factors, some being similar to the causes of invention.

The role of demand, or the extent of the market, is a crucial factor in industrial growth. The large size of the home market has been shown to have been particularly important in Britain and the United States, and its relative absence in France or Russia, on account of the long survival of a peasant society, helped to slow industrial development. Finally one must mention the extent of government intervention in such fields as taxation, tariffs and the protection of inventions by a patent system. Another President, Professor S.G. Checkland, wrote *British Public Policy, 1776-1939* (1983) with this in mind.

One should stress that a study of the leading countries has its limitations. In *Peaceful Conquest: the Industrialisation of Europe 1760-1970* (1981), Pollard studied regions rather than countries. In an article in the Review, 'Typologies and Evidence: has Nineteenth-Century Europe a Guide to Economic Growth?' (1977), W. Ashworth, usually to be seen at Conferences between the 1960s and 1980s, also mentioned the importance of regions, and the need to consider areas of central and eastern Europe apart from Germany and Russia. Finally, as a background to the study of industrialisation a general survey of the economic structure and development, including especially agriculture, trade and transport, banking and the standard of living is clearly needed, though these themes are studied both in relation to the causes of industrial growth and to the models of the process of growth.

Of course, one should stress that these general approaches need to be based on dozens of carefully researched monographs and papers of importance in their own right which open up new fields of study or at least novel interpretations. In manufacturing one may mention *The Glassmakers: Pilkington: The Rise of an International Company, 1826-1976* (1977) by Professor T.C. Barker, for many years Hon. Secretary and then President, and *Regions and Industries* (1989), edited by Professor P. Hudson, with its marked regional approach. For insurance there is *The Royal Exchange Assurance: A History of British Insurance 1720-1970* (1970), by Professor B. Supple, another President with an interest in economic growth among other literary research themes. This writer has published *English Counties and Public Building 1650-1830* (1998) which examined the financial aspects of the construction of bridges, prisons, shire halls and pauper lunatic asylums as a contribution to business and transport history. Such studies are based on time-consuming research largely on manuscript sources. It is on this foundation that the superstructure of general conclusions, interpretations and models are based.

Christopher Chalklin (b. 3. 4. 1933) was educated at Canterbury University College, University of New Zealand and Oxford University. From 1958-62 he was assistant archivist at Kent County Council. He was Senior Fellow of University of Wales from 1963 to 1965 and was Lecturer (1965-75) and Reader (1975-1993) at Reading University, largely teaching social and economic history. His research interests are the social and economic history of Kent since c.1600, especially 1600-1750, financial aspects of house and public building in English towns 1650-1830. His publications include *The Provincial Towns of Georgian England: A Study of the Building Process, 1740-1820* (1974).

Interesting but not Popular: Making Economic History Mean More to Others

Martin Chick

It was Christopher Hill who got me started. Rummaging through the left-overs of a church bazaar, I came across a slim book entitled *The English Revolution*. Reading it in bed that night, I had my whole view of history overturned. Previously, history was something you mugged up a few days before an exam, spewed back out on the day itself, and then forgot about as quickly as possible. What Christopher Hill wrote was entirely different. It was a driven, motivated argument, which pointed up the impact of economic forces in shaping political development.

I think from the first reading of Christopher Hill, I have seen economic history as offering a tremendous insight into the choices which people make. Both the choices which they can make (shall we drive to Stirling or Peebles?) and the choices which they are allowed to make (can we afford a car, assuming that someone's invented one?). Put more formally, what factors define the parameters within which a range of choices is available, and within that range, what are the mechanisms and preferences which influence decision-making? Of course, there are many other issues in economic history, from the sources of economic growth upwards, but it is this essentially micro-economic interest which occupies me most. However, the 'So what?' question has to be answered. The study of micro-economic decision-making in a small firm or department may be of interest, but there does have to be some sense of the quantitative importance of those decisions. One course is to concentrate on 'big issues' such as privatisation, nationalisation and economic planning which have clear national and international implications, but whose effects still have to be demonstrated out in the economy, beyond the confines of government committee rooms.

In tracing the development and outcomes of decision-making processes within government, the use of archives is essential. While it may not be cool to queue at Kew, it is difficult to think of a substitute for examining the typed record of what decision-makers perceived to be their range of options, and their reasons for, and consequences of, choosing some options and not others. Economic history is as much about rejected as selected options, and at their very least, archives probably offer the best means of discovering why alternative, 'counterfactual', routes were not pursued. This interest in the parameters and mechanisms of decision-making is potentially riven with a fundamental tension. If you view the parameters as being determined largely by economic and technological factors, and yet you also suspect that the best allocative mechanism within the parameters is probably the price mechanism, then you risk ending up as some confused form of Marxist price-loving capitalist. Yet it is precisely this tension which runs through much recent economic history, and the unpicking of which is frequently the subject of current political and public debate.

In this context, what economic history also means to me, is making it mean much more to others. While I hope that this is not borne of some vain, evangelical zeal, it does arise from a conviction that you cannot study modern economic history without thinking that economic historians have a huge amount to contribute to current debates on issues, ranging from the development of the welfare state through to the discussions of the euro. Which is not to say that economic historians should only study topics of apparent current 'relevance'. Nor is it to suggest that modern economic history is more relevant than earlier periods; the riotous debacle of the poll tax indicates the great costs of forgetting earlier history lessons. Nor should it be studied with an anachronistic imposition of current values and assumptions, not least because to do so is to diminish the sense of change over time. I do believe that all economic history is worth studying in its own right, but I also think that modern economic historians are peculiarly well placed to demonstrate the benefits of studying economic history to a wider audience.

Economic history could inform public and policy discussions, and yet current public debate seems so careless of history. Public discussions of the welfare state rarely make serious references back to Beveridge which, given that successive governments have been wandering towards reimplementing his report on social insurance, is bitterly ironic. On the few occasions when Beveridge is discussed, it is in blissful ignorance. About four years ago, when Peter Lilley suggested introducing workfare schemes, Patricia Hewitt happily informed him during a face-to-face confrontation on the Channel 4 news, that this was to fly in the face of the Beveridge Report. Her saving was that her ignorance of Beveridge's many paragraphs on this theme was shared by Lilley. Equally, it is incredible that in an economy in which sterling was devalued three times within fixed exchange rate systems during the twentieth century, and which has considerable experience of 'snake-in-the-tunnel' schemes, the Euro question should be discussed publicly as if this was some brand new idea of which we were all hitherto ignorant.

All of which begs the question of why economic history does not loom larger in the public consciousness. It is not that the public won't read history. Behind cookery and gardening in the non-fiction bestsellers' lists, there are always history books. Books on specific topics sell well, be they biographies of everyone from Alexander the Great to Winston Churchill, studies of specific events such as Stalingrad, or histories of particular plants and animals, with tulips appearing around cod pieces in bookshop windows. Indeed, there are also books by Martin Wiener, Corelli Barnett and Will Hutton which sell well and which use economic history to identify long-standing constraints to faster economic growth. Although each of them concentrates on a specific theme, they all implicitly and explicitly claim that their particular theme has far-reaching implications for our understanding of British growth performance. Yet, many academic economic historians believe the work of Wiener, Barnett and Hutton to be fundamentally flawed and misleading. So what is the answer?

Clearly, one response is to write to themes which are of current interest. Presumably publishers will continue to be interested in books on such themes as ageing, the European Community, cooking, financial crashes, and our use of natural resources and the environment. In fact, it would be good to have more books on these and other themes moving from present to past, but they will remain, by definition, only thematic studies. Indeed, it is often stated that we need more academically respectable, integrated studies which throw light on the whole picture. Commonly there is a complaint that the Research Assessment Exercise discourages the writing of textbooks which might give this broader view. Yet in fact, many of the classic economic and social history texts which did reach a broad audience were thematic studies, and not general textbooks. Both Christopher Hill's *The Century of Revolution* (1961) and E.P. Thompson's *The Making of the English Working Class* (1963) pursued themes, which nonetheless struck chords with the reading public.

Alternatively, the case of A.J.P. Taylor is often cited, as someone who reached an even wider audience. Taylor had themes, and he also had a big story to tell, notably concerning the causes and courses of world wars. The question is not therefore, how are we going to write broader economic and social histories, but rather, why don't our themes and big stories resonate as widely as they used to do.

To begin with big stories. Many of these have become blurred, less easy to tell. The English civil war is now more often civil than warlike, the local perspective encouraged by John Morrill and others having dispelled the schoolboy notion of a country rent in two, fully involved in a commercial and ideological struggle. Similarly, the heroic view of the industrial revolution in Britain, has gradually been planed away, notably in Nick Crafts' *British Economic Growth* (1985) in which it emerges as being a long drawn-out affair involving a few towns largely scattered down the west side of Britain, characterised by low productivity, low investment and the employment of vast numbers of workers who had haemorrhaged out of agriculture. This did provide a useful background for explaining the decline of the British economy in the twentieth century, but that big story is also in the process of being dismantled. Now to lament is not to complain. These reinterpretations of major events in British history have provided some of the best reading and discussions of the last decades. However, each story is more complicated and localised than it was before, and in terms of reaching a wider public, it is harder to tell the more complex, blurred story.

The problem in finding more resonant themes is in part related to the blurring of the big stories. If it is not clear to the public what is being explained, then the attraction of thematic explanations is likely to be reduced as well. In the 1960s not only were the stories clearer, but what we might very crudely dub as a quietly marxist approach to history, had a strong integrative appeal. In making their explanations, Hill and Thompson were able to integrate themes drawn from constitutional politics, political theory, English literature, and economic and social history. It all fitted together because of the force of the underlying political and economic analysis. Moreover, what both Hill and Thompson's analyses of struggle shared was their essentially Whiggish assumption of progress. This was also true of those economics texts which had the greatest impact on economic history at the time. In the 1960s, when 'Blue Peter' was collecting milk-bottle tops to buy tractors for India and Walt Rostow was sketching out the stages towards economic take-off, it must have been easy to see why you would want to study Britain's transition from an agrarian to an industrialised economy. When government policies seemed to be contributing significantly to curing unemployment and improving living standards, the value of studying policy-making must have been self-evident. Economic history was relevant, and it examined development and progress.

With the appearance of rising unemployment and stagflation during the 1970s, many of the 1960s assumptions concerning progress and policy appeared increasingly frail. The perceived divisions between Keynesian and monetarist macroeconomists, increasing references to a natural rate of unemployment, and political professions of an inability to 'buck the market', all contributed to diminishing faith in what one economist called the 'witchcraft of macroeconomics' and its related policy ambitions. Coincidentally, there was a growing interest in micro-economics, in particular in incentive structures, game theory, and information flows within and between markets and institutions. For our purposes, three particular responses of economic historians to these developments can be identified. Firstly, there was a boom in the business of decline, of identifying causes of slow growth and productivity. By definition, though often teleological, the tenor of these studies was the antithesis of a 1960s assumption of progress. Secondly, economic historians, especially the quantitative ones, increasingly emphasised how often policies, be they on industrial tariffs or employment policy, simply did not have the effects which policy makers and their historians had assumed. Thirdly, in seeking explanations of allegedly low productivity, issues of entrepreneurship and decision-making in firms attracted greater examination. The hope was that by building-up a corpus of business histories, some broader analyses of business behaviour and performance could be extracted. Symptomatically, business history was to cross-fertilise with business and management studies, more than with economics. What was unclear was whether business history and business studies could build their component parts into a bigger explanatory picture.

That each generation's interest in the past often reflects its own current interests and outlook is a cliché and, as such, probably true. It is arguable that in contrast to the big stories told by the likes of Hill and Thompson in the 1960s, the histories written since the 1970s have been more particularist, quantitative, complex and technically challenging in nature. Indeed, in their cups, some blame the complexity and technical demands for the failure of economic history to capture a wider audience. Yet, complexity and technical requirements do not prevent other subjects from capturing a wide, popular audience. Richard Dawkins's *The Selfish Gene*, and Matt Ridley's *The Red Queen*, are two bestselling science books which draw on a literature which is easily as complex, technical and quantitative as anything produced by economic historians. Why do the likes of Dawkins, Hawking, and Ridley sell so well? Because their work rests on the assumption of scientific progress; because it reflects current concerns, notably with genetics; because it tells big stories on a sweeping scale, infinitely so in Stephen Hawking's case; and because the books provide insights into fundamental factors which have a wide application and which are still working themselves out. Economic and social history does all of these things, but it keeps it a secret; it does not grab the public's attention, and this critical failure is occurring during a period when on television, radio and bookshop shelves, the evidence of an interest in history is large and growing.

And so to Lenin's question: What is to be done? Throughout this essay, I have deliberately switched between 'history' and 'economic history', and, certainly I would tend to see my own work in the post-1945 period, as belonging more to the broad study of political economy than to any narrow subset of history. Studies which emphasise breadth, which in the tired phrase are 'interdisciplinary', can then draw on the work of economists like John Kay, Nicholas Barr and John Vickers, or on that of political scientists like Des King, all of whom write accessibly and make use of history in analysing the interaction between institutions, economies, technologies and markets. They all emphasise the micro-economic perspective, from which the bigger themes concerning information, insurance, and incentive structures have emerged. In turn, these all fit into the big story persistently told by economic and social historians; that of change and uncertainty. These two issues, which are of as much concern today as they were when they formed the heart of Keynes's *General Theory*, provide just one instance of a big theme, of potentially popular appeal, which could be made to integrate and exploit much of the existing high quality research in recent economic and social history. This is one theme; I'm sure you can think of others. Having cited Lenin, why not abuse John F. Kennedy? Ask not 'what does economic history mean to me?', but rather, 'how can I make it mean more to others?'

Martin Chick (b. 16. 4. 1958) is a Senior Lecturer in Economic and Social History at the University of Edinburgh where he lectures on business history, twentieth-century economic history, and the development of the welfare state since 1945. Following his *Industrial Policy in Britain 1945-51* (Cambridge 1998), he is currently writing a book on energy policy in Britain and France since 1945.

From England to Australia to Ireland: A Cultural Odyssey

L. A. Clarkson

If I were to take the generic title of this essay collection literally, I would say that economic history has meant a satisfying career and - eventually - a comfortable income. But such a reply would, I suspect, be regarded as too flippant and too brief.

I started the study of economic and social history in 1949 at the age of 16 (Richard Pares once remarked that the right age to commence history was 25; anything learned younger was something less than history). The responsibility for this youthful folly lay with R. A. Butler who, as Minister for Education, introduced the Eleven-Plus in 1944, which I passed. This was my first step out of the London working class and a probable future as a ticket collector on the London Midland and Scottish Railway (not well paid, but a job for life). The 1944 Education Act created not only secondary modern schools to stand beside the grammar schools, but schools specialising in science, technology and English, to fit youth for the post-war world. Not many of these curious hybrids ever got under way, but there was one close to my home and the unanimous opinion of parents, relations and neighbours, whose total experience of education had been gained in London County Council Board Schools, was that my destiny should be determined in such a place. I would thus be liberated from smoky toil on the railways and qualified instead to become an electrical engineer. Nobody understood what this involved but the Battle of Britain had been won with the assistance of radar, so the prospects looked bright.

Thus, I commenced a rich menu of physics, chemistry, mathematics and English, all of which I enjoyed. But dreary hours of woodwork, metalwork and technical drawing seemed to be aimed at no future I could identify with. Two periods a week each of history, geography, French, religious education (endless maps of St Paul's missionary journeys), plus some PE, but no Latin, completed my education. An enthusiastic teacher, frustrated by the timetable, aroused an interest in history. At the age of 16 it was time to leave school. Electrical engineering had lost whatever appeal it might have had (very little), displaced by history. There were two obstacles: no Latin and the family consensus that 'there's no future in history'. My history master advised me that economic history did not require Latin, and I could enrol part-time in the local technical college and study for the intermediate BSc(Econ.) with a view to becoming an external student of London University. It was a neat resolution of the Latin lacuna and it postponed any career decision. The technical college obliged on both counts. It offered the course and also provided a part-time job as a porter-cum-office boy. I was poorly paid but also under-employed, so I spent a lot of time in the Library where I made my first acquaintance with Clapham (three volumes), Ashton's *Industrial Revolution* (brief, elegant and lucid) and Rostow (1948 vintage and pre-take-off). I was baptised into the mysteries of economics through the austere volume of Frederick Benham, which I more or less understood, and the glossy diagrams of Paul Samuelson that I largely failed to understand. Keynes was out there somewhere, but he wasn't in the Library and so I remained blissfully ignorant of the General Theory.

I decided to take the Intermediate examinations after one year to see how I was doing. To my surprise I passed and I was faced by what today would be called a Gap Year since I had not applied to go anywhere. So I stayed at the technical college reading more economic history, more economics and an *ad hoc* course in English ('read widely and indiscriminately' was the only tuition I received), but neglected my mathematics, which was a mistake. I was accepted into the LSE for October 1951 but did not wish to go since it meant commuting daily on the District Line. Instead, for no other reason than that the brother of a friend was there, I applied to Nottingham University. I was able to go because the Essex County Council awarded me an Exhibition that paid the fees and a maintenance allowance of £135 a year. (This was before the Anderson Committee in 1960 recommended mandatory grants.) I duly arrived in Nottingham equipped with a cheap new suit, two school prizes (Trevelyan's *English Social History* and Heaton's *Economic History of Europe*), and a well-thumbed copy of Ashton's *Industrial Revolution*. I was to read history, economics and, as my honours subject, economic and social history.

I had struck gold. The department consisted of three people: J. D. Chambers, an inspiring if frenetic teacher, Eric Kerridge, an intense agricultural historian who told me more about the origins of the open field system than I wanted to know; and William Woodruff, a Walter Mitty figure who appears later in my career. Kerridge left at the end of my first year. He was replaced by Robert Ashton, a student of Tawney and F. J. Fisher, and the three of them (two of them from a distance) stimulated an interest in early-modern English economic history that has remained with me. A year later Woodruff went to Illinois and in return came A. W. Coats from Johns Hopkins. He was deeply immersed in business cycles, short, long, and intermediate. My education in economic history was narrow (very little outside England except for the business cycles), but deep, intense and captivating.

I graduated in 1954 and decided I wanted to do research. I failed to win a university post-graduate award, but once more the enlightened Essex Education Committee provided me with a grant. I thought of studying the gentry in Essex (this was the time when the gentry were rising and falling like ninepins) but Jack Fisher advised against it on the reasonable grounds that there was no future in the gentry. He suggested the leather industry, a subject that nobody had thought of except himself. And so I joined the growing army of graduate students destined to write the books and articles that Fisher himself never got round to doing.

In 1958, with thesis unfinished, grant exhausted, but with a wife and two very young children, I needed a job. Through the good offices of David Chambers and Robert Ashton I was appointed senior tutor (later lecturer) in economic history at the University of Melbourne where William Woodruff was now professor. I left with Ashton's admonition, 'don't let Woodruff push you around' in my ears. I didn't understand what he meant, but I was to learn. The other members of the department were two fine Australian scholars and a Latvian refugee, who had been a professor in Riga. They were not pushable, but I was young and naïve. When Woodruff told the department that he was poised to become the Arnold J. Toynbee of economic history the prospect was so overwhelming that we resigned *en masse*. The others had taken the precaution of finding alternative employments, but I seemed to be without an academic future. Robert Ashton and David Chambers came to my rescue and found me a temporary post at Leicester where Jim Dyos was inventing urban history.

At the end of 1961 we returned to England. What had I achieved? I had finished my thesis, written two articles and learned how to lecture without being lynched to 400 extroverted

Australian students taking a compulsory course in economic history on their way to degrees in economics. I had also discovered something about the quixotic behaviour of professors.

While at Leicester I was offered a lectureship in economics at the University of Western Australia and so at the end of the year we were off again. My duties, as defined, were to teach courses in economic history, but my new head of department (another quixotic professor) adopted a literal interpretation of my title and delegated to me the task of chief (and only) examiner for the local equivalent of A-Level economics. It was a practical application of the principle of the division of labour: he got the money and played golf and I did the work. At last, I came to grips with Keynes and the multiplier. Generally, the West Australian experience was a good one. I was given a free hand to organise courses; I taught a lot, learnt a lot, wrote a bit and began to understand how universities work.

During 1964 I applied for a lectureship in University College, Bangor. Robert Ashton told me that Eric Kerridge was in for it and my chances were slim. As insurance, I sent a carbon copy of my application to Queen's Belfast that had also advertised, and forgot about it. During a period of excessively long and hot weather in January 1965, I received a one-sentence offer of appointment from Queen's. I accepted and we exchanged the blue skies and heat of Western Australia for the grey cloud and cool of Belfast.

Belfast was a culture shock. We almost took the next boat to anywhere. But my wandering days were over. The department was a joy. It was newly established, although its antecedents went back to H. O. Meredith, author of *Outlines of English Economic History* (1908), who had been Professor of Economics from 1910 to 1945. The head of department was Ken Connell, a man of enormous charm and generosity, and a very fine scholar. Cyril Erhlich (LSE educated) had arrived from Uganda a few years before and had a growing reputation as an Africanist and later as a historian of the music profession. Max Goldstrom, a pupil of W. H. B. Court, had recently come from Birmingham. Soon to follow were Eddie Hunt (LSE), Alun Davies (Aberystwyth and Princeton), K. D. Brown (Reading and Kent) and others. I gradually climbed the greasy pole of academic promotion: from lecturer to senior lecturer, to reader, and to a personal chair in 1983. There was a parallel administrative and managerial rise from adviser of studies to assistant dean, to head of department, to dean and to pro-vice chancellor. I am now peacefully parked in a lay-by labelled 'emeritus', with an office, a computer, the enjoyable task of writing the University's history of the last 50 years, but no car-parking sticker.

At Queen's I really learned what economic and social history means to me. Trevelyan wrote in *English Social History* (condemned by Eric Kerridge in the first lecture I heard as an undergraduate as a 'dull bedside book') that 'without social history, economic history is barren and political history is unintelligible'. He was right. For 10 years at Queen's I taught English economic history, but in 1975 I turned to Ireland. In 1971, I had published my *Pre-Industrial Economy*, which was my lecture course. It seemed pointless to continue in the same vein and there was a departmental need for something on Ireland before the Great Famine.

Here was a vast unexplored territory. More importantly, for the first time history became more than an intellectual game. In England, history is always important to the professionals, but for society at large it is little more than part of the heritage business, or, as Fisher put it in a lecture he gave in Queen's, part of the entertainment industry, together with the royal family and the Beatles. In Ireland, things are different. History matters. We kill one another in the name of history. The past is the present and the present is the past. In 1968, 'The Troubles' erupted and I have spent 30 years of my working life teaching economic and social history in a university located in a community tormented by mangled views of the past. My increasing involvement in university management forced me to reflect more and more on the relationship between university and society. The relationship could not be ignored, particularly in Queen's which in 1908, a decade and a half before Partition, had become an institution independent of the original Queen's University in Ireland established in 1845. For people in Northern Ireland, Queen's is woven into the fabric of society, not an accidental accretion founded by a few wandering medieval scholars, nineteenth-century civic burgers or post-Robbins civil servants. Men and women who have never entered its gates feel an ownership of the university that is deeply grounded in their sense of identity.

Would I have understood these issues better without my education in economic and social history? Perhaps. One of the benefits of having been a pro-vice chancellor was that I met scholars from other disciplines who were thinking about the social responsibilities of their subjects and of Queen's as an institution. Some have done more than merely think and have moved into areas of practical action. I am not starry-eyed about the superiority of history over other disciplines. Medicine and music, literature and law, the natural and applied sciences make greater contributions to wealth and well being, and possibly to understanding as well. Still, history is vital to all civilised societies. As for our corner of history, Sir John Clapham once wrote, 'of all varieties of history the economic is the most fundamental. Not the most important: foundations exist to carry better things'.

The subject has currently lost much of the zest that fired the founders of the Economic History Society, some of whom were still around when I became a graduate student. I attended Tawney's seminars at the Institute of Historical Research, I went to supervisions with Jack Fisher (terrifying and stimulating) I once saw Heaton at a conference and more than once heard Sir Michael Postan call for the *Review* to publish the kind of seminal articles it did when he was editor. Good things have happened since then: historical demography, women's history, and a more conscious use of social theory and statistical techniques. But the subject too often deploys its methodology on its face, like scaffolding on a building abandoned by bankrupt builders. Nevertheless it deserves to survive. If we remember the words of Trevelyan it has a good chance.

Leslie Clarkson (b. 27. 1. 1933) took both his BA and Ph.D. at the University of Nottingham. He then taught at Melbourne and Leicester Universities before spending the bulk of his career at The Queen's University of Belfast where he became a Professor in 1983. Since retiring in 1998 he is Professor-Emeritus of Belfast and became a member of the Royal Irish Academy in 1990. He is author of various books and essays on English and Irish economic and social history. Sometime General Editor of *Studies in Economic and Social History* and co-editor of *Irish Economic and Social History.* His latest book (with E.M. Crawford) is *Food in Ireland 1800-1920: a social and nutritional history* (Oxford, 2001).

What Economic History Means To Me

François Crouzet

When I try to find the origins of my interest in economic history, I have to go back to the time when I was a teenager, in the late 1930s. Both at home and at the *lycée* (grammar school), the depression, the economic policies of successive French governments (especially when the Popular Front was in power, in 1936-37), the autarky which Nazi Germany and Fascist Italy were trying to achieve, the Five-year plans in the U.S.S.R., were frequently mentioned and discussed. On the other hand, the history which I was taught at school was purely political, but geography – which then and now is associated with history in French schools and taught by the same teacher – included a good deal of information about economic problems, which greatly interested me. In the last year at school (which for me was 1938-39), when the geography syllabus was 'the world major economic powers' this was particularly so. Moreover, I then had an excellent teacher, who, though a right-winger, explained to his pupils the basic tenets of Marxism and of history's materialist interpretation. I also remember being fascinated by one lesson about Canada, in which he described the various routes through which wheat from the Prairies was exported abroad, including via the Hudson Bay in summer.

Then, for two years, I was in a *classe préparatoire* (*Khâgne* in current lingo), where candidates were coached for admission at the *Ecole Normale Supérieure*. Again, the kind of history students had to swallow was mainly political: we were expected to know what happened day by day during the crucial periods of the French Revolution, to understand Napoleon's manoeuvres at Austerlitz or Iena, to master the minutiae of the many French constitutions from 1791 to 1875. Still, some economic history crept into a number of lessons, for example about the *Zollverein* or railway policy under Napoleon III, and several lectures were devoted to the Industrial Revolution in England (they left upon me an indelible mark!).

I succeeded at the *Ecole Normale* entrance *concours* in July 1941 and, during the rest of the summer (there was not much to do in occupied Paris), I spent long hours going through the collection of *Annales d'Histoire Economique et Sociale* (this was the early appellation), from 1929 to 1939, to which my father (who was a history teacher) had subscribed. This was a revelation. I greatly enjoyed the virulent reviews, which Marc Bloch and Lucien Febvre had written about books which they did not like, as they did not conform to 'the spirit of *Annales*'. I was fascinated by Bloch's articles on agrarian history, and I then read *Les caractères originaux de l'histoire rurale française*.

Some weeks later, I entered the *Ecole Normale* and the history tutor (my best marks at the *concours* had been in history) asked me in what field I intended to specialise. My immediate answer was 'economic history', and he nearly embraced me! Jean Meuvret was one of the few French economic historians of his generation. His field was the seventeenth century, but the range of his learning was much wider, indeed immense. During the years which followed,

I was to learn a great deal from both his lectures (which included an initiation in statistics) and from his talking (he was, I must say, terribly talkative and feared therefore by many of my fellow-*normaliens*). He was also over-scrupulous, frightened to commit himself to print, and his *magnum opus* on food supply under Louis XIV was published posthumously[1]. I told Meuvret that I would like to work on agrarian medieval history, and he advised me to follow the seminar of Professor Charles-Edmond Perrin. So, for three years, I was submitted to the hard, but extremely formative discipline (because of its very rigour) of scrutinising Carolingian capitularies and polyptychs. Ch.-E. Perrin was also my supervisor for my first piece of research: a memoir for the *diplôme d'études supérieures* (roughly an M.A. dissertation), which dealt with the reconstruction and administration of the manors belonging to the Chapter of *Notre-Dame de Paris*, after the Hundred Years' War. Professor Perrin wanted me to go on along the same path and to do my PhD. on the countryside of Ile-de-France in the fifteenth century (eventually this subject was taken up by the late Guy Fourquin).

In retrospect, I sometimes wonder whether this start as a would-be medievalist was not a waste of time, and whether the right answer to my youthful interest in economic affairs would not have been to read economics. Actually, economics hardly existed as a separate subject in France at the time: it was taught as part of the curriculum leading to law degrees. Moreover, there was a watertight separation between Law Faculties – where economics were taught, and Arts (*Lettres*) Faculties, where history was taught and to which, as *normalien*, I was committed. In addition, I now know that the kind of economics I could have learned in Paris in the 1940s soon became obsolete.

However, once World War II had ended, I had a feeling that medieval history was a kind of escapism and I was attracted by more recent periods. There was at the time much discussion of the economic factors contributing to the decadence of France, which had led to the disaster of 1940, about the necessity to rebuild a modern and strong economy, and, more broadly about economic systems – socialism, communism, capitalism… Still, the study of the recent past was not considered suitable for serious research and the 50 years rule for the opening of public records was in force. I was thus led, by a sequence of circumstances, to start a doctoral thesis on the impact of the Continental Blockade upon the British economy and I spent almost four years (1946-49) in Britain, collecting materials[2].

The consequences of this expatriation were twofold. First, I did not fall – like many people of my generation – under the spell of Ernest Labrousse (who was appointed in 1945 to the Chair of Economic History at the Sorbonne, which the death of Marc Bloch had left vacant) and/or Fernand Braudel (who only returned from captivity in Germany after the war had ended). On the other hand, I came to know the English 'school' of economic history, both by reading its already abundant output, and by meeting some of its luminaries (T.S. Ashton, M.M. Postan, R.H. Tawney), as well as some younger scholars (the late Bill Chaloner became a great friend). Admittedly, this was 'old' economic history, which it was later fashionable to disparage. Still, it much impressed me, combining rigorous scholarship in the use of primary sources with the resort to economic concepts and some economic analysis – a combination which was new to me. During my own research, I also discovered various kinds of documents which were new to me, especially business records, with their huge ledgers, their bundles of in-letters and the books where out-letters had been copied.

This is enough with autobiography! It has only been intended to suggest that to me economic history was new, was relevant and therefore was exciting. It was new to me, a kind of intellectual adventure, because its development in France – despite excellent work by some pioneers – was fairly recent. Even in Britain, where it was an established and respectable subject, which had reached maturity during the inter-war period, it was clear that large tracts of land were still to be explored, and indeed economic history had in Britain, after 1945, an 'astonishing surge' (D.C. Coleman)[3]. Moreover, during the decades which followed, economic history went through a succession of 'revivals'.

There was the rise of quantitative history, which, up to mid-century, had been confined to the history of prices, but extended to building retrospective national accounts and measuring rates of economic growth[4]. Then came the invasion, from America, of the 'new economic history' – or rather cliometrics, as it was not by then very 'new'. Such novelties were received, in Britain and still more in France, with mixed feelings (to say the least) and gave rise to passionate – and enjoyable – discussions. Many scholars were horrified by the resort to counterfactual statements, to an unreal world which had never existed. Cliometricians rightly answered that traditional history also used counterfactuals, but without making these explicit and testing them... Despite some excesses, cliometrics have made and are making a significant contribution to the progress of economic history. The rise of the neo-institutionalist school and of the new theory of growth was also stimulating. As for business history, which hardly existed 50 years ago – especially in France, it has enjoyed a very fast rate of growth. I do like it, as it operates at the micro level, deals with concrete cases and is a crossroads for interdisciplinary work.

Discussions have not been confined to the ethereal level of methodology and many fascinating debates have dealt with specific, though broad problems. I shall just mention the excitement which Rostow's *Stages* created[5], the perennial controversies about Gerschenkronian backwardness and Weberian Calvinist ethics. As for the performances of the French economy during the nineteenth century, they have been for years a bone of contention at the international level, as American and British 'stagnationists' and 'revisionists' have joined Frenchmen in the fray. British economic 'decline' has been discussed for almost as long and perhaps more passionately, as the standard of living during the Industrial Revolution; in addition, the very existence of the latter deity has been disputed! Economic history has thus been in a state of constant flux and even turmoil, which has kept it refreshing and exciting[6]. Even in old age, I unwrap impatiently each new issue of *The Economic History Review*, to look at its table of contents.

However, an old man may worry about the 'decline' of economic history, which has often been mentioned for the last 20 years[7], but which – like the 'decline' of the British economy – has been 'relative' (largely a result of the rise of new subjects, like cultural history) and must not hide much vitality and diversification. There is also the basic problem of economic history's position between its two powerful neighbours: economics and history. This position has made it a meeting-ground between economists and historians, but also often a battle-ground... ; and a conflict about its very nature has developed. Presently many people are convinced that the future of the discipline lies in a closer union with economics; this rapprochement has been achieved in America and is progressing in some other countries. To take just one example the *European Review of Economic History* is proof of the fertility of such an approach. Indeed, some developments in economics open the door to interaction with history: such as the interest in institutions, in non-market activities, in path dependency (which can be called 'the legacy of history' or 'the weight of the past').

Such developments are welcome to me, but I also see dangers in an unfriendly take-over bid of economic history, by economists, as has happened de facto in the U.S.A. If economic history merges with cliometrics and is annexed by economics, it will become just a branch – and a minor one, a poor relation of the latter. On the other hand, its border with history will become an iron curtain, because historians are unable to read works in cliometrics – except their introductions and conclusions. This would be a pity for history. I sometimes say that I am one of the last Marxist historians, because I believe in the importance of economic factors in history. A complete break between economic history and history would hand over the latter to political and cultural historians, and economic factors would be ignored – as they were by nineteenth century historians. Therefore, economic history must retain its autonomy and identity, but also keep open doors to his two neighbours; it must act as go-between, interpreter, translator.

Some division of labour is also possible: macroeconomic problems might be left to cliometricians, who are the best equipped for the task. Economic historians whose training has been mainly historical could concentrate upon long-term problems and upon topics which can not be easily modelled and quantified and for which primary sources are indispensable: institutions, technological change, government policies, power, business history, the study of entrepreneurs. In a recent article, Christian Morrisson, a French economist, who also writes economic history, described the ideal 'historian-economist', an all-rounder, with a theoretical – empirical approach, who would have to be a superman/woman; so he suggested that some research might be undertaken by small teams, made up of one historian, one theorist, one econometrician[8]. The future of economic history lies in a closer relationship with both economics and history, but in interaction, not in subordination.

A last point I want to make is that economic historians are a nice lot, even though they may write furious reviews and pull to pieces either conventional wisdom or new hypotheses. They share, across national borders, interest in the same problems, they use identical methods. The international conferences, which have been held since 1960, have been convivial occasions, but also productive of much valuable work and publications. As far as I am concerned, I keep excellent memories of the conferences I attended and of the meetings of the IEHA executive committee (where I represented France for eight years). I cannot understand the attacks which were launched against this institution.

François Crouzet (b. 1922) is Emeritus Professor at the University of Paris-Sorbonne, where he taught from 1969 to 1992. He is Corresponding Fellow of the British Academy and of the Royal Historical Society and a member of the Academia Europaea. He has written on many subjects but predominantly upon aspects of British and French economic development especially in the nineteenth century.

---

[1] Meuvret, J., *Le problème des subsistances à l'époque Louis XIV* (Paris, 1977, 4 vols.).
[2] This led eventually to the publication of *L'économie britannique et le Blocus Continental, 1806-1813* (Paris, 1958, 2 vols.; 2nd edition, 1987).
[3] Coleman, D.C., *History and the Economic Past* (Oxford, 1987), p. 94.
[4] In France, attention shifted from short-term fluctuations, cycles, crises – which had been supreme under Labrousse – to the study of economic growth and the *longue durée*.
[5] Rostow, W.W., *The Stages of Economic Growth* (Cambridge, 1960).
[6] It is likely that other sectors of history have also seen change and renewal, but I am not well-informed in this respect.
[7] I was asked to organise a round table on this theme, at the Montreal Congress of 1995 : Crouzet, F., 'Y a-t-il un déclin de l'histoire économique aujourd'hui?', *18th International Congress of Historical Sciences. Actes/Proceedings* (Montreal, 1995), pp. 478-81, is an abstract of the debate.
[8] Morrisson, C., 'L'économie historique dans la Revue Economique: du programme à la réalisation', *Revue Economique*, LI (2000), pp. 1069-72.

Reminiscences and reflections of 50 years in history

Louis Cullen

An invitation towards the end of a working life to contribute to a volume on economic history brings the danger of lapsing into the unforgivable sin of anecdotage. Despite that risk, the past may merit some comment. Economic history as a subject and universities alike were buoyed up in the 1950s by prospects of a bright future, even if it would probably be stretching things far to describe the decade as a golden age. However, resources were becoming much freer; universities were expanding; they were not overcrowded. Outside the universities a sense of confidence in the future was uppermost. It is hard to convey its mood to a younger generation, but retrospectively if one had to characterise the 1950s it would be as an age of innocence and optimism.

My memories of the London School of Economics and hence of economic history in Britain reach back to 1956. An interest in the School began a year earlier. Returning from a year's research in France, among other things having worked on trade figures, prices and scraps of business records and impressed by a first acquaintance with the investigation of prices undertaken in the 1930s by Labrousse, I was given a copy of T.S. Ashton's *Economic History of England*. At that time, I was preparing for a competition for a National University of Ireland travelling studentship. Many holders of awards went to America, others to Oxford or Cambridge, and fleetingly I had thought of returning to Paris, though Labrousse had been silent in print for almost two decades and there was not therefore a siren song from Paris. Ashton's book made me want to study under him, as he wrote the type of history that one would like to imitate. I duly applied to the LSE for admission for the autumn of 1956 as a Ph.D. candidate

I did not know until I arrived that Ashton had retired. In the isolation in which students, at least those outside metropolitan centres, lived in the 1950s I was imperfectly aware of the careers of both Ashton and Labrousse. The loss was fortunately not irreparable as I had the good fortune to be supervised, for the eighteenth century, by Arthur John (Ashton's closest colleague and a man deeply attached to him) and, for the seventeenth century, by Donald Coleman. Because, my work was spread between the seventeenth and eighteenth centuries, at least if not ending up with the supervisor I had hoped for, I had the bonus of second supervisor. In going to London my intention had been to work on trade in southern Europe, but Arthur John argued that Anglo-Irish trade was important to Ireland and England alike, that he had contemplated doing it at one time, and that it should be done. After several weeks of agonising over a stint of State Papers, Spain and Portugal, on reflection I had to agree with the force of his arguments. I remained therefore not only on the books of the LSE, as was the intention, but, forays to the provinces or to Ireland apart, more or less constantly in London for three years.

The LSE itself was a rather authoritarian and hierarchical institution in drab and claustrophobic buildings of the interior period (it already had had what at the time was a great curiosity, a student revolt over the canteen), but it was very well run; the graduate school was disciplined and morale was high; supervision was very close; and the School was of course within walking distance of the Record Office and the British Museum library. London itself, still bearing many visible gaps from war time bombings, was at that time a great city for a student to live in: since then it seems to have lost something , possibly a relaxed and uncrowded atmosphere, and certainly the innocence that it, like its denizens, permanent and transient, possessed in that period.

The research students in economic history of the eighteenth century or on the fringes of the century were not many. Arthur John's seminars on Fridays, held in the Institute of Historical Research, were intimate affairs of three or four students who just about equalled and were often outnumbered by LSE staff and visitors. From the LSE, Jim Potter, Charlotte Erickson, Donald Coleman put in frequent appearances, and especially the good humoured Theo Barker and the ever buoyant Leslie Pressnell. Ashton was often there in the first year, gentle and sparing in his own comments. Walter Minchinton, very helpful to research students, often made a breathless appearance, straight off the Paddington train from Swansea. Jacob Price was sometimes seen, probably once a year, and Coates, Habakkuk, and Chambers were visitors from the provinces whose papers I well remember. I sometimes met Ashton in John's room. The first time I met him his face lighted up at meeting someone from the other side of the Irish Sea ; he had been a schoolmaster in Dublin at about the time of the first world war, and without more ado he launched into a rhapsody of the charm of balmy evenings on the crossing, made festive by music and singing aboard. Crossings, scarcely different from the ones he recalled, still existed in warm summer evenings, as I can testify from some of my own journeys across the Irish Sea.

In the 1950s, the future seemed rich with promise for Economic History. Young men whom one knew or of whom one knew, were getting newly created chairs in the subject. It was also an exciting period intellectually. The subject had marked time during the war years, because so many were taken from the universities or had had to defer or interrupt their academic career. Most teachers had war memories, as had Arthur John and Donald Coleman. Looking back from a later perspective the writing of Ashton and others in the 1930s was just beginning to bear fruit in the 1950s. It is no accident I think that the most successful and enduring text book, Peter Mathias's, is by someone whose studies began in the early 1950s. The subject was of course influenced also by longstanding discussion from the inter-war years on how to avoid recession (Beveridge *et al)* and somewhat more vaguely - W. Arthur Lewis's *Theory of Economic Growth* in 1955 was only filtering down and Rostow's all too facile *Stages of Economic Growth* was still around the corner - by recent and fashionable concepts of economic development.

Because there were by later standards relatively few teachers and students, the debate was fresh and free in direction in the 1950s. Debate on the Industrial Revolution, in terms of the factors which caused it, or why it occurred in Britain however became a jaded subject as it became protracted; somewhat like the related and long-drawn-out one on the standard of living (with its resonances of a cold war between different economic systems) or yet another polemic on the social values of businessmen (whether gentry sons entered trade or merchants exited with unseemly haste) which I have to confess were pedantic and un-illuminating debates, and still are when they erupt intermittently into life. Other debates, such as that more recently on why Japan industrialised successfully or what had Japanese management that other managements lacked, have the same characteristic. Such controversies, though made lively by the cut and thrust of argument, impose interpretations by the parameters they define in advance rather than illuminating the underlying issues. However one strength of economic history in Britain was present then, and still is: the subject was closely linked to economic theory or at least taught and written by people with some or much familiarity with economic theory.

Archivally there were changes in the air, and, much more slowly, in implementation. One, inspired by Ashton among many others was an interest in business records. Certainly a graduate student of trade or business believed from the outset that if there were business records, they were a first port of call. The Chancery Masters Exhibits, a great mass of files not withdrawn from chancery proceedings, many of them relating to firms or estates, had become available, and they provided a quarry of exceptional richness. A copy of the exchange rates abstracted from Castaing's *Course of the exchange and other things* was floating around the LSE (I think their assemblage was one of the many fruits of Ashton's interests). The exchange market and the movements in the market rates, which I had become interested in while in France, became a central feature of my research.

The local record offices were also appearing, or where they already existed, beginning to widen their brief, though they had not gone very far in the mid-1950s in bringing in papers from outside. Much research, at least in some subjects, was outside the reading room. The customs records of the out ports were located in custom houses, and talks with the collector or his officers, and coffee and biscuits made for agreeable moments in long days. I retain too memories of the Lowther papers still housed in the Estate Office in Whitehaven, and, given the key at the end of each working day, coming back after dinner, stoking up the fire in the office grate, and settling down to reading letters before getting back for a drink before the hotel shutters came down. Recollections of other not dissimilar experiences one could multiply, and I have been happy in much more recent times that, for work on the French brandy trade, the records still remained largely undisturbed in old locations. The records of the house of Hennessy were looked after by the sommelier of the firm, which had its own delights and temptations .

Franco-Irish trade and Anglo-Irish trade successively suggested (on the evidence) that in the former case a large and distorting smuggling trade was a myth and, in the latter case, the exchanges worked in a regular fashion, implying that the economy likewise was in some or many respects sound. Hence, the level of economic activity should be determined by cycles in economic activity rather than by purely structural features. Ashton was said by Arthur John in the obituary he wrote in the *Economic History Review* to have been disappointed at the lack of reaction to his *Economic fluctuations in the eighteenth century* of 1959. It seemed to me at the time an extraordinarily good book, using primary material in a concrete way, and sparing in its generalisations. When I returned to academic life after four years away from it, I was led, by an interest in fluctuations in Ireland, into an examination of investment and the building of estates and villages. One thing that became evident rather randomly was that in many areas in rural Ireland the Protestant population was much larger in the eighteenth century than in later times. That led far from trade: the pattern had implications for the rebellion of 1798. The rebellion in areas such as Wexford was not a simple jacquerie, reflecting oppressive economic conditions; there was a complex political history

It was of course in terms of my own work an aberration, but perhaps a salutary one as it involved exploring political issues. The economic history of the 1950s had much in common with Lewis Namier's approach to political history (its intellectual origins can be traced to much the same interwar years). Namier had eschewed political ideas for the study of political men in the context of family and self-interest rather than principles. Economic history similarly, in contrast to an older approach, was dismissive of politics and political thought. I now think it was a weakness of the Ashtonite approach; it was of course a wider one of the 1950s, and Ashton's appeal for me was precisely his approach. Economic history had become progressively narrower, long before econometric approaches affected it. The writing in the French journal *Annales* for instance became markedly narrower in outlook compared with the pattern of its first decade or the decade after resumption of publication at the end of the war. This weakness is one of the reasons why - together with the explosion of other historical options - the appeal of the subject for students began to decline in the 1970s.

If teaching is already in decline - think of Coleman's famous book in the late 1980s - this does not show at research level, and certainly not in the range of articles and monographs and in their quality. The best work to-day is much more sophisticated than that in the 1950s and far more assured in the use of archival sources, just as at that time consultation of theses of the 1930s revealed rather unexacting standards. In the 1950s, however, it was still literally true that one could keep abreast of most of the work in wide periods and fields. The large volume of work in later years has compounded the narrowing of interest in the subject, as teachers and students centred upon on a more circumscribed range of work. The advance of the subject can be likened rather to an explosion of detailed work on the perimeter of a large circle, with progressively less work at the centre to hold the peripheral themes together. Indeed, with the growth in taught master's courses and hence in short dissertations, there is relatively less open or novel research, and topics often grow out of well-defined perspectives, the convenient location of identifiable sources, or the focus of taught courses. Foreign trade, to take an area with which I am more familiar, has grown enormously in recent decades in the exploitation of the sources and in the examination of ports and branches of trade in Britain, France and Spain alike. Yet the progress of studies of foreign trade serves only to underline how neglected its siamese twin, domestic trade, remains; the mechanisms of payments are still neglected (there is in a British context little advance beyond David Joslin's article in the 1950s or Leslie Pressnell's book on banking and the industrial revolution, and the story is no different elsewhere); and the great metropolitan centres like London, Paris, or Madrid, admittedly vast themes, still stand like whales stranded outside their environment.

The dangers of language itself and the use of implicit models remain insidious. Thus, in western study of Japan, to take one example, the emphasis on seventeenth-century Japanese rejection of Christianity involves a reluctance to face up to the sheer scale historically of western aggression. The patronising idea of distinctive features, already in existence in what was a narrow field of western study, was later reinforced by the fact that the real growth of Japanese history in the west took place in the hands of a group which came to the language or at least to linguistic competence under war and Occupation service. In any event is foreign trade universally important or invariably a good thing? Western views of *sakoku* (national seclusion) tell us more about facile assumptions about the benefits for all circumstances of foreign trade than about the realities. There remains the danger in an intellectual sense, of parroting in research and writing the concepts and values thrown up by everyday concerns or by economic policy (think of globalisation!). In the real world, concepts when taken up by bankers and civil servants, national and international, have always acquired a deceptive but often shortlived sanction simply by a process of repetition (rather in the way that a simple error in a footnote acquires authority with repetition by every succeeding scholar) and concepts become not ways of understanding the world but actors on the stage.

History, however, should be not for today or tomorrow but for longer. There is, in any event even leaving aside the danger of concepts imported from outside, an inherent danger in academic discourse, which grows exponentially as the community increases and the quantity of publication expands. The literature is reviewed (either lovingly or critically), debates are summarised, and subjects quickly become prisoner of existing discourse or of orthodoxy, whether old or fashioned anew. Economics has lost much, indeed all, of its cranky independence. There are few antidotes to these dangers. Edmund Burke (in small doses) sometimes helps; the best medicine of all may still be a regular bed-time reading of Adam Smith's *Wealth of Nations*. Another one may be Edward Gibbon, as suggested in Negley Harte's *Independent* obituary of Donald Coleman. Perhaps too historians should retain the commitment of Tawney and others (moral commitment was close to the origins of the subject at least in England). There are real dangers in this - scarcely less serious than narrowly professional ones (think of the work and career of the brilliant E.P. Thompson) - but an approach, recognising the risks, is preferable to one predicated on desiccated or conformist thinking that can widen the gulf between a subject and the world of flesh and blood.

Louis Michael Cullen (b. 29. 11. 1932) is Professor of Modern Irish History at Trinity College, Dublin. He trained at University College, Galway, the University of Paris and the London School of Economics. He has worked for the Irish Ministry of Foreign Affairs and has held visiting posts at Paris, Oxford and Hosei University, Tokyo. His current research interests include, Choiseul's Irish circle of administrators and businessmen and changes in Japanese foreign policy and bureaucracy, 1808-1858.

Formal Estimates of Personal Income are Really Personal

Lance Davis

Between November 3, 1933 and November 3, 1939, as I aged from six to 12 years old, my total income was higher than my father's. Although he was a highly skilled bullbucker, he was employed for only a few weeks over that period; on the other hand, I had a paper route. During those years I was introduced to the importance of per capita income. Over the next dozen years, between two stints in the navy (1945-48 and 1950-52), I managed to collect a bachelors degree in economics. By that time, Keynesian and post-Keynsian developments had led most economists to believe that violent short-term fluctuations in income were a thing of the past (it was another decade before they became disabused of this idea); but my government-funded visits to such ports as Tsingtao, Manila, Pusan, and Singapore had convinced me that there were still important questions concerned with per capita income and long term growth and development.

Economics, however, had changed. Developments in micro theory during the 1930s (John R. Hicks, Joan Robinson, and their contemporaries) had provided a set of powerful theoretical tools that permitted economists effectively to examine short-run behavior and even to suggest some rational government policies. As a consequence, economists became increasingly concerned with issues that could be attacked by the 'new tools'; and, as a result, institutional economics (typified by the work of economists like Thorstein Veblen, Clarence Ayres, and John R. Commons) - a field that had been an important part of the profession's research agenda - was pushed farther and farther outside the mainstream of economics.

Instead, economists tended to focus their attention on short run issues, in part because the institutional structure - the rules that are observed or enforced that govern the ways in which economic agents can compete or cooperate - can be treated as exogenous and fixed. When those economists have been unable to avoid issues associated with institutional change, they have tended to wave their hands and mutter something about transaction costs. They have, however, seldom attempted to explore the nature of those costs, although on occasion they have mentioned the word 'institutions'. Any economist who really attempts to understand the process of long-run economic growth and development, however, must immediately confront the problem of institutional change. In the long run, the institutional structure does change, and the changes are at least partly endogenous. Any successful long-run analysis must explicitly include assumptions about the nature of institutional development, but we still know little about the relationship between the institutional structure and the more traditional economic variables, or about the way changes in the external environment – economic, political, social, and cultural – affect the institutional structure.

In the mid-1950s, modern cliometrics was born. And, while a part of the work was focused on using economic theory to explore historiographic questions (slavery, for example), some of the 'new' economic historians, following in the steps of Simon Kuznets, turned to questions of long-term growth and development. That group included Richard Easterlin, Robert Gallman, Douglass North, and William Parker. Increasingly, their work tended to focus on the role of institutions, but even these pioneers were slow to begin to think in terms of a theoretical model of institutional change. In principle, such a theory could become the basis for a model of long-term economic growth and development that would be as powerful as the present short-run microeconomic models. Much of what we do know about institutional change comes from the work of Nobel Prize winner Douglass North. To North, 'the economies of scope, complementarities, and network externalities of an institutional matrix make institutional change overwhelmingly incremental and path dependent'. Since 'the static nature of economic theory ill fits us to understand that process we need to construct a theoretical framework that models economic change'.[1] Although he clearly understands the nature of the problem, we are left with a warning, an admonishment, and a number of examples. Clearly, we are not yet ready to specify a theory of institutional change; however a taxonomy – a formal structure of classification and description – is a logical first step toward the development of any theory; and such a taxonomy is within sight.

What is needed in order to develop that taxonomy is a series of parallel case studies drawn from different times, different geographical regions, and different social and political structures. It is only recently that I have come to understand that, if there is any underlying structure to my lifetime research agenda, it has been an attempt to provide a number of such case studies in the hopes that, when combined with the work of others, it will yield such a system of classification and description. Applied micro economists, despite great gains in econometrics, still focus almost entirely on the short run. Experimental economists have produced some useful policy proposals, but almost all are based on experiments that depend critically on some form of an auction - and few laboratory auctions can be structured to cover a real time period as long as a decade, let alone a century. Only economic history provides a laboratory that permits economists to study those long-term changes in the structure of institutions and the implications of those changes for an analysis of economic growth and development.

Thus, at an intellectual level, what economic history means to me is that it is the avenue that may make it possible for me to contribute productively to a gradually emerging systematic analysis of the process of institutional change. Nor am I any longer one of a small number of voices 'crying in the wilderness' of existing micro-economic theories. The emergence in the past half decade of ISNIE (the International Society for the New Institutional Economics) and the list of distinguished economists who have joined (a group clearly not limited to economic historians) indicates that these important issues have again begun to move into the mainstream of economics.

At a personal level, economic history has, over the years, also provided the foundation for a number of friendships and intellectual partnerships that have made my life much fuller. There was (and is) the ever narrowing circle of the original cliometricians (Douglass North, Jonathan

56

Hughes, William Parker, Robert Gallman, Richard Easterlin, and Stanley Engerman), then there was the second and third generation of scholars who are currently at the forefront of research (a group that includes, but that is not limited to the likes of Claudia Goldin, Ken Sokoloff, Jeff Williamson, David Galenson, and Naomi Lamoreaux), and finally there are students that I have helped to train (Jean-Laurent Rosenthal and Robert Cull, to name only two).

Thus, to me, economic history means both intellectual and personal warmth and fulfillment.

Lance Davis (b. 3. 11. 1928) was educated at the University of Washington, Seattle and Johns Hopkins University. He has taught at the California Institute of Technology since becoming Professor of Economics there in 1968. He is currently Mary Stillman Harkness Professor of Social Science. He has published widely, mainly on American economic growth. His research interests are the evolution of international capital markets; the economic efficiency of naval blockades; and the impact of the microstructure of rules on the economic efficiency of formal markets (New York, London and Paris).

---

[1] Douglass C. North, 'Some Fundamental Puzzles in Economic History/Development'. Paper delivered at the Von Gremp Workshop in Entrepreneurial History, UCLA, February 21, 1996, pp. 7 & 30.

What Economic History Means To Me

Meghnad Desai

There is some advantage to backwardness I am sure and I benefited a lot from it. The undergraduate degree I did in Bombay was rather old fashioned. In the last two years of a four year degree we had to specialise in one discipline but not so much that we got a narrow technical education. I chose economics because it was easier to get jobs in business I thought. We had to do eight papers: two in politics and six in economics. But within those six we had to do two on economic history. This covered Britain, Japan, Russia and India. I was hooked on economic history at that very stage. Ever since I have carried on reading and occasionally 'doing' economic history.

Indian students of economics have a special reason to be interested in economic history. All through the Independence movement and even later during the first decade of Independent India, when I was studying, there was the perennial question: could India have been a developed country on its own, with its own capitalist revolution? The other half of this question was: did Britain retard or advance India's economic development? These were not academic questions. They were part of the daily diet of politics. There was also a lot of vulgar Marxism around and we bandied about terms like Bourgeois Revolution, lumpenproletariat, semi-feudalism etc. Such Marxism compels you to read a lot of economic history.

There was also the fascination of Russia and especially Russian economic development from the 1860s onwards. We had debated about the Narodniks and their quarrels with the Marxists. Then, in the period after the Revolution, the episodes of War Communism and New Economic Policy, the debate between Bukharin and Trotsky etc absorbed us. At that time, in the 1950s in India, there was the Second Five Year Plan with the Mahalanobis model which was similar to Feldman's model - itself the basis of the first Five Year Plan in Russia. In those days in India, if you mentioned the name of Preobrazhensky no one would bat an eyelid. We had read (or so we pretended) all about those 1920s battles regarding extracting surplus from the peasantry.

Thus economic history was for me central to an understanding of politics as well as economics. When I studied for my masters degree in Bombay, I did not have to do economic history anymore. Yet studying economic development and business cycles I was thrown back on much economic history. Rostow's *Stages of Economic Growth* (1960) had just come out during my final year and his sub-Marxist scheme had a basic political message that we did not buy. Yet that again took us to alternative readings of economic history.

When I got to the US for my Ph.D., I kept up my reading. Now I had access to better libraries, I quickly caught up with US economic history. Luckily for me there appeared an opening when Conrad and Meyer's book on New Economic History came out. Here at last was a marriage, I thought, of economics, econometrics and economic history. Some day I thought it may all be useful for an article or two in a learned journal.

The opportunity arose when I came to the LSE in 1965. Robert Fogel, I heard, had just passed through and there had been a stand up row between him and the old guard. So I offered to teach quantitative techniques to economic historians. I could learn more about economic history (or at least show off my meagre knowledge) and they could learn some econometrics. This led me to write my review article on cliometrics in the *Economic History Review* (Desai, 1967). But my stance was not that all was fine in the new quantitative economic history and all the old stuff was outdated. I tried to point out that not all new stuff was good economic history let alone good econometrics. Technique did not overcome some horrendous problems of causality which always hamper historians.

This was not a good career move. I was neither loved by the younger set who wanted to be triumphalist nor by the senior lot whom I only confirmed in their smugness. Soon however others took over the teaching of quantitative techniques once the Essex summer school became possible. I could get on with other things. But I did feel that in many of the cliometric models the issue was not econometrics but the use of a static neoclassical model. The idea that economic history, an inherently dynamic subject, could be packaged within static optimisation logic of neoclassical theory seemed to me then and still seems to me now absurd. It was by being econometrically simpliste yet confusing, if not threatening, to the old guard that the first generation of cliometricians got away with it.

Ideally economic history should improve economic theory by taking it beyond static or even dynamic equilibrium models. History allows one to model disequilibrium in a way that contemporary time series, no matter how long, does not. If one has to deal with dynamics in which there is structural as well as institutional change then economic history seems to me the best way forward. But then economic historians have to be tough about the theory they employ. Douglass North's success in launching neoinstitutional economics for development is a very good example of an economic historian stretching economics beyond its usual narrow confines By contrast his fellow Nobel laureate, Robert Fogel, I argued in my review article on his *Time on the Cross* (Fogel and Engerman, 1974), used the neoclassical static theory uncritically (Desai, 1976).

In turn what econometrics or even economics has to bring to economic history are the rigorous habits of model building. This allows you to set out the structure of your argument in terms of behaviour as it responds to incentives and constraints. But these latter may change as well for an economic historian and therefore a deeper model has to be built. There is no escape from theorising. All that economists do is to make their theorising explicit. A lot of economic historians, especially of the older school kept their theorising implicit and hence it was difficult to criticise. This also meant that controversies raged on and yet no dispute could be settled.

I had a first hand experience of this when quite inadvertently I found myself taking on the formidable Professor Postan. This was a result of a marvellous interdepartmental activity which the LSE Senior Common Room has - the cricket team. Malcolm Falkus who was then at the LSE told me some time in the early 1970s that a student of medieval history from Kings College wanted my advice on econometrics. It turned out that it was not so much econometrics but inference that this student needed to learn. He pointed out to me that there was a debate about the famine in medieval England and that Postan had said something about Winchester yields which was testable.

Young and innocent as I then must have been, I got hold of the book on Winchester yields by Titow and proceeded to test whether yields on the Winchester Estates were going down. Finding that they were not, I wrote a paper and sent it off to Postan and my colleague Bridbury, little realising that I had just walked into a hornet's nest! I got invited to Peterhouse for a lunch and the famous (though I did not know then) Postan inquisition. I was flattered, cajoled, threatened and told that I had got it all quite wrong. R.H. Tawney, Maurice Kendal, Karl Marx and many others were brought to bear against me. I knew then that I would never give up that topic.

To cut a long story short, I persisted with the problem. I claimed that Postan had used an a prioristic Ricardian theory to argue that yields must have been going down if there was a famine. Hence England in the early fourteenth century must have faced a Malthusian Crisis. This was simple economics of a very static variety doing a lot of work. The data, however, contradicted the hypothesis. But over the years, no one had carried out a simple test although they had disagreed with Postan about a lot of other details of his argument. I had stumbled on to this central weakness without much knowledge of either medieval economic history or its practitioners.

A negative result however was not enough. It is no good saying Ricardo does not apply to fourteenth century England. There had to be an explanation of the three successive harvest failures in 1316, 1317 and 1318 as well as the contrasting cycles of prosperity and misery in different sectors of the economy (grain versus grass) and different time periods within the half century till the Black Death. I gave up any work on this topic while I did not have the answer. Economic history, I always knew, was much more difficult to do than economics or econometrics. It was only a decade later, nearly 16 years after my fateful meeting in Peterhouse that I was able to use bits of Amartya Sen's theory of famines to be able to make sense of the data (Sen, 1981). But I had also by then read enough about fourteenth century England to know that the cattle economy was different from the wool one and both from the grain one. I did manage one long paper (Desai, 1988). But I am still hoping to write its complimentary paper which will go into regional details relying on the data from other establishments besides the Winchester one - Bolton Priory for instance.

Reading economic history is my constant pleasure but doing it, as and when I can, is the much more time consuming, much more demanding pleasure. Reading it is like soaking in a hot bath and doing it is like rock climbing. If you can do rock climbing (and I cannot) I am assured it is hard work but exhilarating. Economic history as a source of knowledge and reflection is to me absolutely vital in economics and even in politics.

Nowadays I write on poverty and human development. I am aware that the concept of poverty as a remediable phenomenon has solid Victorian roots. Thus despite much that I had read, I learnt a lot from Alan Gillie's article in the *Economic History Review* (Gillie, 1996). Much that is said about social exclusion today was at the root of Charles Booth's original inquiry about the household conditions of truant children. Economic History has this capacity for surprising us and humbling us just when we think we know everything. And being humbled is good for us all.

Meghnad Desai (b. 10. 7. 1940) has been Professor of Economics since 1983 and Director, Centre for the Study of Global Governance, since 1992, at LSE. His interests include general economic theory, econometric models and economic history.

Works cited
Conrad, A. and J. R. Meyer. *Studies in Econometric History*. London: Chapman & Hall, 1965.

Desai, M. 'Some Issues in Economic History'. *Economic History Review*, vol XX, 1968.

Idem. 'The Consolation of Slavery: A Review of R. Fogel and S. Engerman: Time on the Cross'. *Economic History Review*, vol XXIX, 1976.

Idem. Malthusian Crisis in Medieval England, *Bulletin of Economic Research*, 1991.

Fogel, R. and .S Engerman. *Time On the Cross: the Economics of American Negro Slavery*. (Boston, 1974).

Gillie, A. 'The Origin of the Poverty Line'. *Economic History Review*,vol. XLIX, 4, 1996, 715-730.

Sen, A. *Poverty and Famines*. Oxford, Clarendon Press, 1981.

Titow J.Z. *Winchester Yields*. Cambridge; Cambridge University Press, 1972.

In the Footsteps of Bertha Putnam

Marguerite Dupree

In April 1976 as a second year research student, I attended the Golden Jubilee conference of the Society at Churchill College, Cambridge. In a College classroom I heard Theo Barker give his paper on the beginnings of the Economic History Society[1] in the presence of venerable pillars of the Society, of whom Julia de Lacy Mann and M. M. Postan sitting in the front row were especially memorable as their voices came out over the tape recorder during the paper and afterwards during the discussion. In the paper Professor Barker mentioned the importance of Americans in the founding of the Society, and he listed Professor Bertha Putnam of Mount Holyoke College among the speakers recorded at the first meeting at LSE on 14 July 1926. While I had never heard of Bertha Putnam, I had first heard of economic history as an undergraduate at Mount Holyoke College. His remark gave me a sense of belonging to an academic community and tradition, including women and Americans from the outset, which has provided a coherence to my academic odyssey both previously and over the next 25 years. This essay takes what oral historians call a life history approach, yet out of it, I hope, will emerge evidence of one of the main strengths of the Society: the wide range of the historical interests its members represent and hence the broad definition of the content of economic and social history that it embodies. In short, the Society's inclusiveness in the face of pressures for narrowing and fragmentation into innumerable fields (in my case, urban history, family history, demographic history, business history, textile history, medical history, Scottish history, among others) makes it possible to move among subjects and explore links without losing a sense of 'community' and what might be called middle-range coherence.

Protests against the Vietnam War culminating in the shootings of students at Kent State dominated the spring and early summer of 1970 on American college and university campuses, and the authorities at Mount Holyoke College postponed final examinations until the end of the summer. That spring semester of 1970 I had taken Lynn Lees' European Economic History course which tested the models of Rostow and Marx against the European experience. As a result of the postponed examinations I spent more time preparing, and I discovered the *Economic History Review* as I followed up articles on the reading list. I was excited by the overarching models, the idea of testing them and the exploration of the social consequences of industrialisation, drawing on evidence ranging from price and wage series to novels. I took more courses from Lynn Lees on European urban history and on historians and historiography; she introduced me to historical demography and the work of the Cambridge Group; and having major fields in both biological sciences and history, I brought them together in a dissertation on the Irish potato famine from the perspectives of the potato population as well as the human.

Attracted by its interdisciplinary ethos and the variety of Lawrence Stone's work (initially encouraged, I later discovered, at Charterhouse by the Society's Treasurer, Robert Birley), I entered the graduate programme in History at Princeton University, completed the two years of coursework and embarked on a PhD thesis on the effects of industrialisation on family relationships in Britain. Although the topic was my choice and the period later than his main focus, Lawrence Stone supported the project from the outset, enabled me to come to Britain to work on it, and continued to take an interest and provide comments and suggestions on written work thereafter.

In the Autumn of 1974 I entered Nuffield College, Oxford as a research student with Max Hartwell as my College supervisor and I matriculated in the Modern History Faculty with Peter Mathias as my University supervisor. I attended their lectures, and a feast of other lectures and seminars not only in history but also in the social sciences on which Nuffield concentrated. At Nuffield I put my sample of the 1861 census enumerators' books for the Potteries on punch cards and explored the economic and social history of the Potteries in the mid-nineteenth century, focusing on family structure and testing Michael Anderson's conclusions based on Lancashire. In the last of my four years at Nuffield I was introduced to Sir Raymond Streat and was asked to edit his diary. Although this meant a shift to the twentieth century, to Lancashire, to the cotton industry, to its relations with Whitehall and to issues surrounding the decline of the British economy, it was a subject with which I felt equally at home as part of economic and social history and in the Economic History Society as I did with my thesis.

I continued to pursue research into these two areas when I moved to Cambridge where I was elected to a research fellowship at Emmanuel College in 1978 and from 1982 at Wolfson College. It was a stimulating environment working in close proximity to economic and social historians, including Les Hannah, Donald Coleman, Barry Supple and Geoff Eley, and to the Cambridge Group, attending seminars, using the excellent library, and benefiting from the expertise and interest of Tony Wrigley, Roger Schofield, Peter Laslett and Richard Smith, Richard Wall, Ros Davies and Jim Oeppen. Also, in Cambridge there were separate papers on British economic history and English economic and social history in Part I of the Economics Tripos and of the History Tripos respectively, and supervising undergraduates for them and giving a series of lectures gave a sense of a varied yet coherent part of history.

In 1986 I became one of the original core staff members of the Wellcome Unit for the History of Medicine at Glasgow University, and again the breadth of the economic and social history umbrella was apparent. Not least, medical history was another of the wide range of areas to which Peter Mathias has contributed as a part of economic and social history, and although the Unit has been located within the Medical Faculty for resource purposes and medical history was once the most insular of fields, members of what is now the Economic and Social History Department were instrumental in attracting the Unit to Glasgow and supporting it subsequently. Moreover, members of the Society have played important roles on the Wellcome Trust's History of Medicine Panel over the past fifteen years: Peter Mathias and now Anne Digby have chaired the Panel which has included, among others Tony Wrigley and Michael Anderson, and Richard Smith served as Director of the Oxford Wellcome Unit.

Thus, 'economic and social history', the subject of the *Review* and as embodied in the Society and its activities, means to me a tradition, from the days of Bertha Putnam, of overlapping, outward-looking networks of people and fields that eschews hard and fast distinctions and encourages investigation of a wide range of areas and approaches and of the links between them, while promoting the highest standards of scholarship. Although such an encompassing view of the nature and role of economic and social history may seem obvious, it cannot be taken for granted while there is pressure from some colleagues to draw up the sharp, exclusive, divisive categories which ultimately lead only to the parochial and antiquarian.

Marguerite Dupree (b. 1950) is a Senior Lecturer and a member of the Wellcome Unit for the History of Medicine at the University of Glasgow and a Fellow of Wolfson College Cambridge. She is editor of *Lancashire and Whitehall: the Diary of Sir Raymond Streat 1931-1957*, 2 vols. (Manchester: Manchester University Press, 1987) and the author of *Family Structure in the Staffordshire Potteries 1840-1880*, (Oxford: Clarendon Press, 1995). Currently, she is working on a book with Anne Crowther, *Lister's Men and Jex-Blake's Women: Medical Lives in the Age of Surgical Revolution.*

---

[1] T. C. Barker, 'The Beginnings of the Economic History Society' *Economic History Review*, 2nd ser, XXX (1977), 1-19.

The Medieval Economy and Society Viewed from Below

Christopher Dyer

This will express divergent and contradictory attitudes towards economic history. The subject's tendency to pull its practitioners in different directions is one of its attractions, though it is also the source of considerable frustration. I will emphasise here its capacity to entertain, and its ability to address big questions; it is both literary and scientific.

One cannot avoid agreeing with Jack Fisher's provocative opinion, quoted by Leslie Clarkson, that, 'like the Beatles and the royal family', economic history is a branch of the entertainment business. On the other hand, we would not wrestle with the subject unless we thought that it was important - that it provides the key that unlocks our understanding of fundamental processes of change, and can reveal to us great truths about the human condition. It tells us how we arrived in our present state. The significance of economic history also lies in its ability to give us an insight into the differentness of the past: it explains how people coped with problems by devising solutions which are foreign to our world, like the two field system or turnpike roads.

To begin with the 'entertainment' side of the subject, I have always believed that the end product of economic history should be a form of literature. We should write essays, articles and books that are easy to read and which interest, stimulate and even excite the reader. We will usually fall short of the ideal (this writer included) but at least we should aspire to be readable and accessible. Of course we must use methods of research which are technical and involve statistics, but these are just a means to an end, and the final stage of a piece of research is to set aside the tedious and specialised calculations, push them into a footnote or an appendix, and to express the conclusions and ideas in everyday language. If we look back to the origins of the subject between about 1890 and 1920, it attracted a huge interest among 'extra mural' and 'extension class' students. They expected to find a subject relevant to their own experiences, about working people in the past, and the subject was presented by lively and enthusiastic lecturers who also wrote lucid prose. That popular interest in the past is still there, and as well as 'continuing education' classes it is stimulated by books, magazines and television programmes. But economic history does not figure very prominently, having been supplanted by such subjects as landscape history. I have always attempted to use whatever opportunities present themselves to communicate with a non-specialist audience, and believe that we could reclaim some of the ground that we have lost in this respect.

To turn to the 'importance' of the subject, the great attraction of economic history is that it has an especially rigorous and 'scientific' approach. It uses the methods of testing hypotheses against hard evidence in a much more systematic way than other branches of history. The precision of our definitions are particularly satisfying. If an economic historian uses a term like 'town' or 'rent' or 'productivity' we can hope to know where we are, and are able to conduct discussions with a good idea that we are all talking about the same subject. There is a widespread understanding of the rules. If prices or wages rise, there are various influences and circumstances that lie behind those trends, and while we might disagree on which factors are most important, we share the same understanding of supply and demand. Again, if we use technicalities and specialist language they are only a means to an end, and the test of the success of a piece of research should be its contribution to our appreciation of large historical processes.

While I advocate the importance of economic history, and even its superiority over other subjects, it benefits enormously from its association with other disciplines. The link with the social sciences is umbilical, and gives the subject a constant stimulus. As someone with interests before 1500, I am bound to mention anthropology as a fruitful source of new ideas. In the same spirit, archaeology is capable of providing economic historians with a flood of new data, which can be said without controversy, but I also believe that archaeologists' thinking deserves our attention as well.

Many academics practise their subject because a decision in early life set them on the rails leading to particular stages and goals. In my case I have never studied economic history as a specialism - I have not passed, nor have I ever taken, an examination in economic history. My attachment to the subject has always been a matter of free choice. So why do I do it? The main attraction is the reconstruction of the lived experiences of the people of the past, in my case in the middle ages. My conviction is that peasants, artisans and other workers deserve the attention of historians, who devote far too much space to the privileged classes. This is not merely an emotional position, because the reactions and initiatives of those below the elite made decisive contributions to change. Without an input from peasants, for example, the transformations in the medieval economy could not have taken place, and their actions played an important part in bringing about the end of the traditional structure of society at the end of the middle ages. In order to explore their role, we have to use whatever sources are available, and a good deal of imagination, to visualise their attitudes and thought processes. I have found that my understanding of these people and their circumstances has been greatly helped by researching the material evidence of their houses, villages, fields and artefacts.

I have always practised my subject in a general history department, which means that I have to work hard, in a world where students choose their options, to make my subject attractive to those who regard 'economic history' with suspicion. The barriers can be removed by careful presentation, and students find themselves reading articles from the *Economic History Review* without too much pain, having signed up for courses on local history, literary sources for social history, the origins of towns, and popular rebellions.

Economic history must already be a broad church if it can accommodate someone with my interests and preoccupations as well as those who apply the most advanced statistical methods to the twentieth-century economy. Its future surely depends on maintaining that breadth, but also with recovering some of that evangelical zeal with which it preached in the early years of the twentieth century. If barriers have been erected that prevent undergraduates and the general public from appreciating its interest and importance, then we should find ways of removing them.

Christopher Dyer (b. 24. 12. 1944) was a student at the University of Birmingham, BA and Ph.D, assistant lecturer at the University of Edinburgh, then taught at the University of Birmingham where he is now Professor of Medieval Social History. He is editor of *Midland History*, and of the *Economic History Review* and Ford's lecturer in the University of Oxford. His research interests are the economic and social history of medieval England, including agrarian, urban and landscape history.

The Joy of Economic History

Stanley Engerman

Since I have spent my past 40 years as a self-described economic historian, clearly I have found this discipline to be rewarding, personally if not (based on anticipated opportunity costs) financially. I have written several articles dealing with the nature of economic history, cliometrics, quantitative history, and related concepts, so there is no need to repeat those general points about my perceptions of the nature of the discipline. Rather, I want to speculate on certain aspects of career choice, of approaches to historical questions, and of preferred means of analysis. Most academics, obviously including economists and economic historians, seem to be in violation of what many other people consider to be the fundamental premise of economic behaviour: financial profit-maximisation. Few among us actually maximise our financial profits, since that might entail what we regard as some unfavourable or less than preferred working conditions. Rather, while we may profit-maximise in certain activities, career choices generally reflect utility maximisation in desiring an overall package of 'goods and bads.' In some regards, the academic resembles the familiar image of the pre-modern artisan in terms of adjusting the actual hours of work, the nature of the work the intensity of the work, and the quality and quantity of output from work, all based on individual preferences. This is true, although as in the case of artisans, incomes may sometimes be low and jobs lost.

Clearly not all individuals have the same utility functions as do academics - most people pursue other occupations. And, of course, sometimes people make similar choices for rather different motives and concerns. Moreover, within academics, the choice among a broad range of possible disciplines still leaves ample room for differing decisions in finding the individual's desired mixture of subject matter and methods of analysis. Not all economic historians come with the same set of underlying concerns, and I can only describe features in my career choice. Some disciplines and questions were too complex and difficult, a few were not challenging enough, but that still leaves a diverse set of approaches and disciplines from which to choose.

As with most of my peer group in economic history in the United States, my graduate training was in economics. The basic definitions of the contents of economics, as also was the case for economic history, included two related but separable, issues. One was the study of the economy and the economic parts of life, the other was the use of the economist's tool-kit to study society, and to see how people behaved in situations where choices were made and constraints were dealt with. The importance of rational decision making from available alternatives, and the analysis of the implications of choices can be applied to a wide range of issues, from the rather narrow economic to the broadest of political, cultural, and racial issues, and training in basic economics provided a very useful way to try to understand individual and group behaviour.

This economist's approach, of course, need not lead to a simple answer to all questions that scholars might study. The complexity of people's psyches and also of events would seem to limit that possible achievement by one single approach, but that need not be a source of disappointment. Some scholars do believe that there can be one single answer to major questions, and often advocate the usefulness of specific types of approaches to reach that answer. Others, however, regard scholarship as more of a collective enterprise, with knowledge accumulating, and find the words of Adam Smith on the division of labour, applied to this different set of problems, quite sensible. Frankly, I find the Smithian view the more reasonable one, since it provides a more realistic approach to problems of data and interpretation. My feeling is that the actual day-to-day work of economic historians is to handle rather narrow, specific questions in working towards the broader view. By defining the precise nature of the question, and pointing to the answers desired, to help to determine what methods of data gathering and analysis are most necessary in each case. In short, much of what appears as debates on methodology, are less about methods than about what questions the particular scholar regards as interesting or important. It is the opportunity to ask and to answer a broad range of questions that has always made economic history seem such an interesting and enjoyable discipline to pursue.

Stanley Engerman (b. 14. 3. 1936) took his B.S. and M.B.A. from New York University. His Ph.D. is in economics from The Johns Hopkins University, 1962. He is currently Professor at Rochester and has published widely on US economic history, trade and slavery. He has been a pioneer in the use of both cliometrics and anthropometric history.

Economic and Social History: My Experience

Alan Everitt

The study of history seems to me like travel in time, a journey into the past. In this paper I shall mention a few of my own journeys, and the way they have led me into the study of local and provincial society in one of the world's oldest and most varied countries.

I do not remember a time when I was not interested in the past. I did not think of it at first as 'history' because it bore little relation to what we were taught at school. It was a human world, not an abstract one, that absorbed me. I wanted to know how people lived: to learn about their work, their family-life, their relationships, their manners and customs, and above all the houses they lived in. I longed to be an architect and bought every book on architecture I could afford, or work for, or beg for my birthday. When I left school and found that ambition impracticable, I began to see I was really more interested in buildings as historical evidence, as expressions of a society, than as symptoms of stylistic development.

These early interests went back no doubt to the way I was brought up and the place we lived in: an old market town of 10 or 12 thousand people in Kent, with buildings of every century from the thirteenth to the twentieth, and some fine country houses and farm buildings in the neighbourhood. My parents' own house was a good example of the Vernacular Revival movement of about 1900. It was full of books of a great variety, and that helped to awaken an interest in the 'realist' tradition in English literature. Though I did not read economic history as an undergraduate, I thus had a certain basis for the study of social history.

My first degree at St Andrews (1948-51) belonged to the rather rigid political and constitutional tradition of that time, but it had its value as an intellectual discipline. Firmly anchored in original texts, it forced the undergraduate mind to think closely about the meaning of words and phrases, their changing significance, and the development of institutions and offices of state. It gave one a sense of the long-term evolution of history, of Maitland's 'seamless web', and some sense too of the evolution of society behind it. Not a great deal, for it was difficult to incorporate in the old syllabus, but enough to link with my earlier interests. With my tutor's encouragement, I therefore began ferreting around in the university library for myself.

When we came to the Civil War period, it seemed as though a curtain was drawn aside upon society, and one was brought face to face for the first time with the real people of England. Naïve doubtless; but one book that made an impression on me then was W. Schenk's *Concern for Social Justice in the Puritan Revolution* (London, 1948). So much has been written since on Levellers, Diggers, Quakers, and Fifth Monarchy Men, that it now seems

70

unknown. Yet it is still worth reading for Schenk's insight into an unfamiliar world, and the human experience behind it.

When I began postgraduate work at the Institute of Historical Research in 1952, I had to move further in that direction. My subject was defined for me as 'Kent and its Gentry, 1640-60: a Political Study'. I had recently returned to the county after seven years elsewhere, in the army and at University, and several of us were then beginning to work on the shires. My supervisor was R.C. Latham, the editor of Pepys; but I also joined R.H. Tawney's seminar. The link with his work was obvious; we were all then talking about 'The Rise of the Gentry'.[1] Thanks to the liberal tradition of London, however, the special genius of the Institute under Goronwy Edwards, and the breadth of Tawney's own interests, neither he nor anyone else - Neale, Bindoff, Namier, Latham, Notestein, et al. - forced their views on us. I listened and learned, not least from a galaxy of able fellow-students, and revelled in that intellectual freedom. For the first two years I spent every evening until 9 p.m. at the Institute after my work at the Universities Association, and all my Saturdays in the Public Record Office or British Museum. There were no State Studentships; but in 1954 I won a Carnegie Scholarship and completed my work in two years full-time.

Mr Latham introduced me to the sources for tracing the Parliamentarian 'Committeemen' and Royalist 'Compounders'. He pointed out the *Catalogue of the Thomason Tracts*, the *Calendars of State Papers Domestic*, and a few other items; then, wisely, he left me to discover everything else for myself. Almost immediately a baffling problem came to light. When I put the lists of my Committeemen and Compounders together, I found that most of the former appeared also on the latter: at some stage, it seemed, the 'Parliamentarians' had become 'Royalists'. By reconstructing a detailed narrative of events in Kent, for which the evidence was enormous, I reached something of the answer. But I gradually realised I should also have to reconstruct the *society* in which those events took place if I was to understand their mercurial relationship with national developments.

For that purpose I made a systematic survey of all the gentry families in the county: their numbers, origins, and whereabouts; their standing, fortunes, and estates; their relationships, marriage-connections, and links of neighbourhood; their houses, family-life, friendships, and cultural interests. I was fortunate in the abundance of material I found on Kentish family history, and in the survival of so many manor houses. I was especially fortunate in the abundance of personal evidence I discovered in the form of private diaries, journals, account books, autobiographies, and family correspondence. The work of Peter Laslett on Sir Robert Filmer's *Patriarcha*, and on the cultural life of the gentry in 1640, shed a further shaft of light on the *mentalité* of the county.[2] I followed that up by tracing all my people in the catalogue of the British Library, and found another goldmine.

Quickly summarised, what came to light was an intensely personal dynastic society of about 800 families, for the most part quite minor, deeply rooted by ancestral ties, and closely inter-related; an evolutionary rather than revolutionary society, rising more by gradual accumulation of moderate wealth than by dramatic acquisition; deeply conservative in instinct, yet more preoccupied with the safety of the county, the stability of its government, the care of the family estates, and the welfare of kinsfolk and dependants than with outright 'Royalism'; concerned above all, I judged, with a circle of human and personal interests beyond the sphere of politics. In looking for an explanation of allegiance, in short, I had also found a *community* - a society with a life of its own. That discovery was to colour my subsequent work and thought on quite different aspects of provincial history.

In 1957 I was appointed Research Assistant to the *Agrarian History of England and Wales* for 1500-1640. I was already in touch with the English Local History Department at Leicester, which had published my first academic work, and where I was to spend the rest of my career. Working for Joan Thirsk on that great project, and then on my own behalf for chapters on 'The Marketing of Agricultural Produce' and 'Farm Labourers', marked a turning-point in my life.[3] It drew me further away from political history, though in 1960 my first book was published under the title of *Suffolk and the Great Rebellion, 1640-1660* (Ipswich).

When I began research on 'Marketing', friends said, 'You will never be able to do it; there are no sources for inland trade'. But although there are no systematic sources, such as port books, ample evidence of other kinds quickly came to light: in the State Papers, in Exchequer Special Commissions and Depositions, in probate inventories, account books, contemporary works, and so on. Important publications by Jack Fisher, N.S.B. Gras and others were available, notable theses by P.V. McGrath and Neville Williams, and much else.[4] But it was an unforgettable moment when I found, at a hint from Jack Fisher, a great mass of disputes about marketing in the Court of Requests. Eventually I went through about 800 cases in Requests, and then many more in Chancery Proceedings. They revealed the rapid expansion of 'private marketing' in the early-modern period, outside the legally-recognised 'open market', and the development of a widespread network of travelling factors, carriers, drovers, and other wayfaring traders. That led me to look into the history of inns, where so much of the new commercial activity took place.

The study of market towns was one natural consequence of working on the agrarian history. I started investigating their origins, buildings, and topography, as well as their economy. Over the years I built up a large slide-collection on the subject, in England and other European countries, and often lectured on it to student-groups and historical societies. On moving to Leicester in 1960 I was able to go further. At that time Leicester had the largest retail market in England, with 485 stalls in its vast medieval market place on three days a week. Though ramshackle to a degree, it was an amazing survival; some of the market folk had 'inherited' their stalls for two or three generations; to me it seemed like living history. Talking to the people, and working on the evolution and topography of the city's various markets and fair-sites, was a fascinating experience.[5] It provided an instructive 'model', moreover, when turning to other major trading-centres, such as Northampton.

From Leicester I also began work on Northampton. Though a smaller place, it was in several ways a remarkable microcosm of provincial society in the early-modern period. Its strategic situation made it a natural focus of the wayfaring community. Detailed investigation of its inns, particularly after the Great Fire of 1675, showed how they also developed as administrative, political, social, and cultural centres. Musical, intellectual, scientific, literary, dramatic, charitable, and leisure functions, as well as trade and transport, figured prominently among the activities they promoted; they were hives of unsuspected enterprise. During this same period Northampton burgeoned, moreover, as a notable centre of craft-training. Tracing the development of its numerous specialised skills, and comparing them with those of places like Exeter and Shrewsbury, seemed to light up some obscure corners in economic history. The infrastructure of skilled crafts, which underpinned so many aspects of our agrarian and industrial history, needs more thorough recognition.[6]

Developments of this kind were echoed in other provincial towns. But in the religious and humanitarian movements of the eighteenth century Northampton held an exceptional place. The origins of the missionary movement, the foundation of county infirmaries, the Sunday

School movement, the development of English hymnody, and the Evangelical Revival itself, may all be traced, wholly or in part, to this one town and county. Behind them all was the charismatic figure of Philip Doddridge (1702-51), the Independent minister of Castle Hill from 1729, and founder of the pioneering Northampton Academy. Tracing his impact upon society, through his travels, his academy, his diaries, his vast correspondence, and the thousands of subscribers to his publications, opened up an extraordinary network of family connections and personal friendships throughout Britain. Unlike Whitefield and the Wesleys, he founded no movement, and he was not a polemical figure. Yet although less well-known, his influence was in some ways more wide-ranging. It transcended denominational boundaries, reached out to all social classes, and rapidly spread to America, to other European countries, and ultimately to the Far East.[7]

After working on Northampton, I turned first to a study of rural dissent, and then to farming dynasties, country carriers, the evolution of settlement, and other subjects.[8] But in the space available, I must limit myself to my present work, on the extent and role of common land in English history. Until the nineteenth century 'manorial waste' was more extensive, in both Lowland and Highland counties, than is sometimes thought. It underlies many of our industrial districts, and many suburban areas, especially around London. In the 1690s at least eight million acres of common land survived, or one-quarter of the entire country, and in 1800 probably more than five million; the figure today is about one million. Though complete statistics can never be reconstructed, much may be discovered by working systematically from parish to parish and county to county. Utilising the evidence of place-names, topography, ancient jurisdictions, early maps, contemporary commentators, and many printed sources, I have now worked through about 2,000 parishes, in 20 or so counties, and many scattered places elsewhere.[9]

One notable conclusion to emerge is that piecemeal or 'concealed' enclosure of the waste (by private means) continued on a substantial scale throughout the parliamentary era. There were eight or nine ways in which that could occur, and the total acreage involved may ultimately have approached that enclosed under Act of Parliament. It was largely concentrated, however, in those regions that lay outside the 'Midland' or classic common-field zone, where parliamentary methods were dominant. It was particularly widespread in the kind of 'intermingled' or 'old woodland' countryside, characterised by scattered farms, isolated hamlets, and ancient lanes, which is so often found in counties like Kent, Sussex and Surrey, Essex and Hertfordshire, the Marcher counties, the Derbyshire-Nottinghamshire borders, and many parts of the North and the South-West.

Perhaps the main economic point to emphasise is the remarkable range of local occupations and industries the commons gave rise to, in addition to their use as rough pasture. For although they were usually unrewarding areas agriculturally, they were often rich in mineral resources, and in a great variety of trees, shrubs and wild plants. Industries based on extraction were especially likely to develop from obscure common-land beginnings: quarrying, brickmaking, potting, tilemaking, flint-mining and chalk-working, for example, as well as the familiar cases of coal, iron and lead. Resources of vegetation gave birth to scores of forgotten crafts, such as basket-making, broom-making, mat-weaving, rope-making, clog-making, hurdle-weaving and shovel-making. Such homely products may seem unworthy of notice, yet they often underpinned developments in industry, agriculture, transport and domestic life.

In providing a livelihood for the poor and dispossessed, common land also gave birth to many new hamlets - of potters, turners and charcoal-burners, for example - and new industrial

73

settlements like Lye Waste, Coalville and Woodville. The society of such places often contained a seasonal, migrant or fugitive element, and they were widely regarded as wild or lawless by more settled communities. Yet necessity was the mother of invention: and as the commons dwindled, it was in places like these that the spirit of ingenuity was most evident in exploiting the resources of the waste.

My travels have taken me to many types of countryside and community I never thought of when I set out 50 years ago. What has interested me in all of them is their 'native' or 'indigenous' life. No place of course, whether a county, a provincial capital, a market town, a village or a hamlet, can exist in isolation. All are linked by countless human ties of neighbourhood, dynastic network, dissenting connection, the web of wayfaring trade, the bush-telegraph of common-land society, and much else. Yet their place in the economy, their response to the world at large, is not merely automatic. They respond in their own way, for they all, like the community of Kent in the Great Rebellion, have a life of their own.[10]

Alan Everitt (b. 17. 8. 1926) was educated at the University of St Andrews and the Institute of Historical Research. He taught at Leicester University for most of his career, becoming Hatton Professor of English Local History there in 1984. He is a Fellow of the British Academy, and has been a member of the Economic History Society since 1960. He is currently researching the history of Common Land in England: its extent, usage, economy and society.

---

[1] Tawney, R.H., 'The rise of the gentry, 1558-1640', *Economic History Review*, XI (1941); Trevor-Roper, H.R., 'The Gentry, 1540-1640', *Economic History Review Supplement*, I, 1953.
[2] Laslett, T.P.R., ed., *Patriarcha and other political works of Sir Robert Filmer* (Oxford,1949); idem, 'The gentry of Kent in 1640', *Cambridge Historical Journal*, IX (1948).
[3] Thirsk, Joan, ed., The agrarian history of England and Wales, IV, *1500-1640* (Cambridge, 1967), Chapters VII and VIII.
[4] Fisher, F.J., 'The development of the London food market, 1540-1640', *Economic History Review*, V (1935); Gras, N.S.B., *The evolution of the English corn market...* (Cambridge, Mass., 1926); McGrath, P.V., 'The marketing of food, fodder, and livestock in the London area in the seventeenth century' (unpub. M.A, thesis, Univ. of London, 1948); Williams, N.J., 'The maritime trade of East Anglian ports, 1550-1590' (unpub. D.Phil. thesis, Univ. of Oxford, 1952).
[5] Everitt, A.M., 'Leicester and its markets: the seventeenth century' in A.E. Brown, ed., *The Growth of Leicester* (Leicester, 1970).
[6] Everitt, Alan, *Landscape and community in England* [collected essays] (London and Ronceverte, 1985), Chapters 2 and 8.
[7] Ibid., Chapter 9.
[8] Ibid., Chapters 3, 5, 11 and 12; Everitt, Alan, *Continuity and colonisation: the evolution of Kentish settlement* (Leicester, 1986).
[9] For a *résumé* of this work, see my chapter on 'Common Land' in Thirsk, Joan, ed., *The English Rural Landscape* (Oxford, 2000).
[10] Everitt, Alan, *The community of Kent and the Great Rebellion, 1640-60* (Leicester, 1966).

George Unwin (1870-1925),
Founder of the Manchester School of Economic History

D. A. Farnie

During his 15 years in Manchester Unwin radically changed the orientation of the new subject of Economic History. His death in 1925, at the age of 55, was lamented by the sober 'Honest John' Clapham as an 'infinite loss' to English Economic History.[1] Born in 1870 in Stockport, Unwin served for seven years as a clerk in a local hat-making firm. The next nine years he passed in study at the universities of Cardiff, Oxford, Berlin and London, graduating in 1897 with a First in Greats (Classics and Philosophy). Finally, he served for nine instructive years as a private secretary to the Right Honourable Leonard Courtney (1832-1918). By inclination and training Unwin was a philosopher whose interests lay in the fields of literature, philosophy and religion. He became a historian by vocation but he always regarded his work as a religious one. Throughout his life he embodied to the full the English tradition of Dissent, having passed under the successive influence of Baptists, Wesleyan Methodists, Unitarians, Congregationalists and Quakers.

In 1910 T. F. Tout (1855-1929), the founder of the Manchester School of history, made one of his most inspired appointments. He chose Unwin as the occupant of the first chair of Economic History to be created within the British Isles. In return Unwin raised the department of history to new eminence within the world of scholarship. Teaching within the department was in need of renewal. It had concentrated over much upon the royal court, the aristocracy and warfare. Thus it had proved 'frustrating and disappointing' in the years 1910-1913 to such youthful spirits as Ellen Wilkinson (1891-1947).[2] Unwin dedicated himself to changing the emphasis of instruction from politics to society and from the state to social ideas and social relationships. 'The essential element in my philosophy is my relegation of politics to an entirely subordinate plane of spiritual reality... I think the part played by state-power in history has been very largely evil.'[3] Unwin had early found inspiration in Adam Smith's abhorrence of 'that insidious and crafty animal, vulgarly called a statesman or politician'. 'Adam Smith was the first great economic historian, and ... to my mind he is still the greatest.' *The Wealth of Nations* 'was still perhaps the finest piece of Economic History ever written.'[4] One of the intellectual heirs of Smith and 'the greatest man I have known', Lord Courtney, exerted an immeasurable influence upon Unwin during the years 1899-1908. 'Lord Courtney represented, in its most clear-cut and uncompromising form, the Liberal Individualism of the mid-Victorian age, with its unquestioning faith in Free Trade, its dislike of all forms of state action, its disbelief in the British Empire, its whole-hearted pacifism. Compared with him Cobden, Bright or Morley were not infrequently backsliders, and Gladstone a mere trimmer.'[5]

Courtney's teaching was reinforced by that of William James, who supplied Unwin with one of his favourite quotations. 'I am against bigness and greatness in all their forms... I am against all big organisations as such, national ones first and foremost; against all big successes and big results.'[6]   Unwin contrasted with the coercive State the 'little platoons' revered by Burke and Bagehot.   Those private, voluntary and local associations had been formed for such purposes as common worship, mutual aid, education or recreation.   Such self-governing bodies served as the creative core-agencies of any society.   They became artificial families, recruited their members freely and enabled them to fulfil their highest aspirations.   Such communities of life, work and worship tended inevitably to absorb the whole personality of their members.[7]   In contrast more extended communities such as the nation-state could affect only a minor aspect of existence and could inspire only an attenuated loyalty.

Nationalist historians Unwin distrusted as intensely as national policies.   He could not abide 'drum and trumpet history' or 'the mythopoeic illusions of the patriotic imagination'.[8]   He regarded it as his mission to recall historians to a sense of their true vocation and expressed his conviction in a flow of searing aphorisms:

> 'The orthodox historians ignore all the most significant factors in human development'.
> 'History has become to a large extent the history of institutions'.
> 'Most histories hitherto written are pathological'.
> 'The beginning of wisdom is to distinguish between the State and Society'.
> 'History is a scrap-heap of discarded States'.
> 'Imperialism is immorality tinged with emotion'.
> 'The central feature of the English character, as seen by the intelligent foreigner, is hypocrisy'.[9]

Unwin would have been baffled by the very idea of a Welfare State and dismayed by textbooks portraying the advent of such a State as the culmination of British history. Community-building, on the other hand, he exalted as the most important aspect of history but also as the most difficult and the least studied aspect.   In the past history had been written from a national viewpoint and from national sources.   The records of voluntary associations had never been explored by historians.   Unwin recognised the differing value of public and private records.   He expressed a decided preference for modern economic records as being 'more many-sided and complete, more disinterested and reliable than the political records of the past'.[10]   He never believed that Economic History could be effectively studied on the basis of national and official sources.   He would have been bewildered by the readiness of later scholars to accept official statistics as an unimpugnable source of data.   Appropriately, one of his first published articles, in 1900, was devoted to the history of a seventeenth-century trade union.   His first monographs, published in 1904 and 1908, similarly comprised a comparative history of the gilds of Europe and Britain.   Paradoxically those studies focused upon London, the seat of the great Leviathan of the modern State.

Unwin came to exert an extraordinary influence upon both historians and economists.   The time, the place and the man came together in a unique conjuncture, so as to maximise his influence.   The cotton industry reached successive climacterics in 1913 and in 1920 but its history had remained unexamined.   That history was first revealed in detail through the records of four business firms, M'Connel & Kennedy of Ancoats, Samuel Oldknow of Stockport, the Gregs of Styal and Peter Stubs of Warrington, which Unwin uncovered between 1913 and 1923.   His own intellectual range was for ever expanding, as he added five modern foreign languages to his knowledge of Latin and Greek.   He always regarded history as a seamless web, forged in what Goethe had styled 'the roaring loom of time'.   His mind ranged freely through the fields of ancient, medieval and modern history and across the continents of Asia and Europe.   His omnivorous reading endowed him with a daunting knowledge of the sources for political history, which he turned to effective use in research. He captivated his listeners by the clarity of his thought and expression, by his passionate and transparent idealism and by 'the wealth of ideas and the stores of learning that he poured out.'[11] To his friends and colleagues 'he was not merely one teacher among others, but unique'.[12] In his closing years he was well on the way to becoming a legend.

Ernest Barker (1874-1960), his fellow-student at Oxford, 'was amazed by the power and the passion of his thought... He carried me further than I should otherwise have gone... I learned to follow his thought and to think more quickly myself.'[13] At Manchester he impressed Sydney Chapman (1871-1951) as 'a man outstanding both in personality and scholarship' and Frances Collier (1889-1962) as 'one of the most inspiring teachers our University has had.'[14] To Tawney he always remained 'the most original' of economic historians. 'One cannot hope to convey the impression of listening to the wisdom of experience rather than to the learning of the schools, which one felt in hearing him'.[15] For T. S. Ashton (1889-1968) 'my chief reason for wanting to go to Manchester was to be with Unwin': from him 'I gained more than in any other place or from any other man.'[16] For five years Ashton remained in daily contact with Unwin, transforming the quinquennium of 1921-1925 into the golden years of his existence. 'Ashton worshipped him as no other man in his whole life.' In 1957 Ashton described Unwin as 'scholar and saint,' an epithet applicable only to two other economic historians, Toynbee and Tawney. Perhaps the greatest of all of Unwin's achievements was to convert the hard-headed ex-miner George W. Daniels (1878-1937) from the study of Economics to that of Economic History. His passionate appeal to the power of ideas convinced Tout himself that his own approach to historical research had been misguided: towards the end of his life Tout confessed that if he had to begin his research anew then he would start with Aquinas rather than with the machinery of royal administration, whose history he had embodied in *Chapters in the Administrative History of Medieval England (1920-31).*

The Manchester school of Economic History reached the zenith of its fame during the years 1920-1924, when the city still regarded itself as 'the hub of the universe'. The school found its natural home within the Faculty of Commerce, which had been created in 1904. The teaching of Economic History in the university had in fact been pioneered by economists, by A. W. Flux (1867-1942) from 1893 and by S. J. Chapman from 1901 before H. O. Meredith (1878-1964) was appointed in 1905 to a lectureship in the Faculty of Arts.[17] In 1917 Unwin was elected Dean of the Faculty of Commerce. That appointment paid an unparalleled compliment to a professor in the Faculty of Arts: it contrasted sharply with the bitter experience of the 1930s, when inter-faculty rivalry denied chairs to two of the most eminent economic historians of the time, T.S. Ashton and his brother-in-law, Arthur Redford (1896-1961).[18] As Dean, Unwin rendered immense service to the faculty and gave a decided impetus to both teaching and research. G. W. Daniels published a pioneer study of Lancashire during the Industrial Revolution in *The Early English Cotton Industry* (1920). Unwin supervised two theses, one upon 'The Family Economy of the Working Classes in the Cotton Industry, 1784-1833' (1921) by Frances Collier and the other upon labour migration, 1800-1850 (1922) by Arthur Redford. He suggested in 1922 to G. H. Tupling (1883-1962) that he should study the Industrial Revolution in Haslingden. He inspired Mabel Phythian, who had graduated in 1919, to undertake research into the mechanics' institutes. In 1923 he introduced Julia Mann (1891-1985) from the London School of Economics to A. P. Wadsworth (1891-1956) of the *Manchester Guardian* and so paved the way for their joint authorship of a classic history of the early cotton industry. He also inspired the publication of three important monographs, his collaborative history of the industrial revolution at Stockport and Marple, *Samuel Oldknow and the Arkwrights*, (1924), T. S. Ashton's *Iron and Steel in the Industrial Revolution* (1924) and Conrad Gill's *The Rise of the Irish Linen Industry* (1925). The first of those books was Unwin's most important single work. It was devoted to 'the glorious epic of Stockport', whose history he found as interesting as that of the Holy Roman Empire.[19] It became the pioneer volume of a new Economic History Series published by the Manchester University Press, which Tout had founded in 1904. It established the pattern for a new type of Economic History, shifting the focus of interest from machinery to people and rewriting the history of the Industrial Revolution.

The position of Britain and Lancashire had been transformed by the Great War, with its 'carnage incomparable and human squalor' in the verdict of Wilfred Owen. The claims of the State to a universal competence had increased and its share of G.D.P. had trebled from 8% in 1890 to 26% in 1920. That increase validated the law enunciated in 1892 by Adolf Wagner (1835-1917) but only enhanced Unwin's loathing of the State. The story of his reaction, as a pacifist, to the war still remains to be told. He shared the view of William James that 'history is a bath of blood' and decided to study the influence of warfare upon the civilisations of Europe and America. In 1917 he compiled a draft syllabus for an introduction to general history which wholly excluded political history.[20] In 1918 he demolished the myth propagated by Cunningham of Edward III as 'a precocious Cobden' and the father of English industry.[21] In 1924 he was however deeply dismayed by the barrage of propaganda evoked by the British Empire Exhibition, which he dubbed 'Wembleyism.'

The lasting achievements of Unwin were two-fold.
1. He established the first academic school of Economic History in Britain, such as W. J. Ashley had failed to do in Birmingham. He enlarged the horizons of the subject and re-oriented it from the study of institutions to the study of growth and development within society.[22] He elevated Economic History into a higher criticism of political history.[23] He pioneered the study of urban, commercial and industrial history and first revealed the full complexity of the evolution of industrial organisation. Not only did he come to the very threshold of business history but he boldly crossed beyond it.
2. He established the first school of research into Economic History. He pioneered the study of the subject upon the basis of original records. He first undertook the collection of business archives in the Manchester region and inspired the Manchester Central Library to build up its own special collection of business histories.[24] His students benefited by access to that library which ranked as the best municipal library in the land outside London and had since 1878 been opened upon Sundays. Unwin profited by Tout's introduction in 1908 of a thesis in the third year of the undergraduate degree course. He sought to compensate for the isolation inseparable from individual research by encouraging team-work and by inspiring team-members with his own unfailing enthusiasm. He became keenly interested in the projected *Economic History Review*, the first issue of which appeared two years after his death and featured his own essay on the Merchant Adventurers.

In plans for his own research Unwin 'remained to the end an incorrigible Utopian', still building in 1924 'towering sky-scrapers of research, to be completed when he should obtain the necessary leisure'.[25] Thus he hoped to use his Creighton lectures of 1905 as the basis for a book on the origin and growth of the City of London. He undertook for the *Victoria County History* chapters on the social and constitutional history of London which were never published. His lectures on the Merchant Adventurers, delivered at Oxford in 1913, inspired a projected history of that association. He was indeed forced to abandon one of his most cherished projects, that for a history of commerce, as being too large to be capable of achievement.[26] He was however recruited by Professor Frederick Rees (1883-1967) to contribute a volume on the Economic History of Great Britain, 1558-1660, to a four-volume series to be published by Longman's.[27] Unwin also remained determined to complete a comparative study of medieval cities. In 1905 he had contemplated a history of industrial civilisation from the end of the Dark Ages and of the evolution throughout time of the English wage-earner. In the 1920s he seriously considered a whole series of volumes on the Industrial Revolution which would be truly comprehensive. Therein he wished not only to trace the origins of the English working class and of modern industrial democracy but also to portray the working life and ideals of the entrepreneurs of the period.

The early death of Unwin at the height of his powers was a major tragedy for the Manchester School. His brief but creative life was commemorated in a leading article by A. P. Wadsworth in *The Manchester Guardian*,[28] in the composition of superb memoirs by two of his close friends, Tawney and Daniels, and in the publication of his collected papers by the Royal Economic Society in 1927. Together with Lilian Knowles (1870-1926), he was however excluded from the pages of the *D.N.B.* by the editor, J. R. H. Weaver (1882-1965) who disliked the new breed of historians professing to find the quintessence of common humanity in the life of the common man. The work of Unwin was carried on by four of his intellectual heirs, Daniels, Ashton, Wadsworth and Redford. Daniels established the first British research school in the field of Economics. To that end he founded a new journal in 1930, the *Manchester School* and a faculty Research Section in 1931, in close co-operation with his old professor, S. J. Chapman, at the Board of Trade. He employed two highly competent research assistants, John Jewkes (1902-1988) and Harry Campion (1905-1996) and supervised the publication of a series of monographs on the industrial region of Lancashire. Thus the decline of the region's staple industry imparted an unprecedented stimulus to research by economists. More than any other scholar, Ashton popularised the study of Economic History. In 1939 he completed his monograph on Peter Stubs of Warrington and in 1959 he largely redrew the map of eighteenth-century British Economic History. To the encomiums composed by Tawney and Daniels he added three personal tributes to the teacher whom he revered.[29] Wadsworth venerated Unwin as much as did Ashton. From him he had learned to cultivate 'the long view and the synoptic outlook.' That perspective he embodied in a series of articles on regional history which remain uncollected. Wadsworth became a key figure in a second intellectual partnership, with R.S. Fitton (1925-1987), who was introduced to him by Ashton.[30] In the tradition of Unwin, Redford encouraged team-work in the research he undertook into the history of the trade and administration of Manchester. He inspired third-year undergraduates to study the Economic History of their own communities. The best of those theses was written by T. C. Barker and J. R. Harris, *A Merseyside Town in the Industrial Revolution: St. Helens, 1750-1900* (Manchester, 1954). The work of such scholars focused inevitably upon the Industrial Revolution, the region and the cotton industry, whose most significant product remained 'neither yarn nor cloth but the factory communities of "Cottonia"'[31] Their influence helped to widen the market for Economic History amongst the reading public for a full 40 years after the death of Unwin.

Douglas A. Farnie (b. 31. 3. 1926) was first introduced to the subject of Economic History in 1943 by R.M. Hedley and in 1950-51 by Arthur Redford, both of whom were students of Unwin. He taught at the University of Manchester for most of his career and currently holds a Professorial appointment at Manchester Metropolitan University, attached to the Centre for Business History. Since 1951 he has undertaken research into the history of the cotton industry.

---

[1] *Economic Journal*, 35, (1925) 157.

[2] Davies, Stella, 'The Young Ellen Wilkinson', Manchester Literary and Philosophical Society, *Memoirs and Proceedings*, 107 (1964-65), 36.

[3] Tawney, R. H.(ed.), *Studies in Economic History: The Collected Papers of George Unwin* (London, 1927), lxii.

[4] Ibid., 18, 72.

[5] Gooch, G.P., *Life of Lord Courtney* (London, 1920), 441, quoting Unwin's predecessor as secretary, Leo Amery (1873-1955).

[6] Tawney, 462.

[7] Unwin, G., *Samuel Oldknow and the Arkwrights. The Industrial Revolution at Stockport and Marple* (Manchester, 1924), 159.

[8] *Economic Journal*, 24, (1914), 277, G. Unwin in his review of J. A. Williamson, *Maritime Enterprise, 1485-1558* (1913).

[9] Tawney, lxvi, 5, 424, 445.

[10] Ibid., 16.

[11] *Manchester Guardian* 31 January 1925, 10iv, A. P. Wadsworth.

[12] Tawney, xliv, xlvi.

[13] E. H. Barker, *Age and Youth. Memories of Three Universities and Father of the man* (London, 1953), 294.

[14] *Manchester School*, 9 (1938), 68, 73.

[15] Tawney, lxvii.

[16] Ashton, T. S., 'Recollections of Four British Economic Historians', *Banca Nazionale del Lavoro Quarterly Review*, 158 (1986), 343, 346.

[17] Harte, N. B. (ed.), *The Study of Economic History. Collected Inaugural Lectures* (London, 1971), xxv, xxxv.

[18] Sayers, R. S., 'Thomas Southcliffe Ashton (1889-1968), *Proceedings of the British Academy*, 56, (1970), 270.

[19] Tawney, xii.

[20] Ibid., 43-45.

[21] Unwin, G. (ed.), *Finance and Trade under Edward III* (Manchester, 1918).

[22] Rees, J. F., 'Recent Trends in Economic History', *History*, N.S.34 (1949), 5-6 Chaloner, W. H., 'Working-Class History and Middle-Class Historians: The Webbs, the Hammonds and the Coles' in Farnie, D. A. and Henderson, W. O., (eds.), *Industry and Innovation. Selected Essays* (London, 1990), 202.

[23] Daniels, G. W., .*George Unwin: a Memorial Lecture* (Manchester, 1926), 31.

[24] Smith, Harold, 'Business Histories', *Manchester Review*, Spring 1954, 2.

[25] Tawney, xl-xli.

[26] Ibid, 133, 221.

[27] The third volume entitled *The Economic History of England 1760-1860* by Arthur Redford appeared in 1931 but the fourth volume covering the period 1860-1914 was never completed by H. L. Beales (1889-1988), who had graduated from Manchester in 1912.

[28] *Manchester Guardian*, 31 January 1925, 10iii-iv, 13iii.

[29] Ashton, T. S., 'Note on George Unwin' in G. Unwin, *Industrial Organisation in the Sixteenth and Seventeenth Centuries* (London, 1957, second edition, 6pp.). 'Unwin, George' in Sills, David L. (ed.), *International Encyclopaedia of the Social Sciences* (New York, 1968), 16, 199-200. See also end-note 16.

[30] Fitton, R.S. and Wadsworth, A.P. *The Strutts and the Arkwrights, 1758-1830. A Study of the Early Factory System* (Manchester, 1958).

[31] Farnie, D. A. *The English Cotton Industry and the World Market, 1815-1896* (Oxford, 1919), v.

Time on the Cross:
How and Why Not to Choose Between Economics and History

Marc Flandreau

I. Clio-Me-Tricks

I never intended to become an economic historian. I thought I had had enough in my early university years, with the mandatory courses in humanities dealing with the industrial revolution: where had It happened first? When did It begin? And had It really existed, after all? All the coal accounting, number guessing, vagueness, aggregating, etc., not to mention the description of innovations, was obviously the least exciting thing one could think of, and I felt about it very much the same enthusiasm one would feel for modern articles on the 'new economy', and how the internet is going to revolutionise economics and society at large.

On the other hand, there were two sister disciplines in which I found intrinsic beauty and appeal, which I decided to study separately. These were economics and history. The seduction of economics was its abstraction, its ability to operate a fairly sophisticated conceptual machine capable of moving at high speed and to land it, as a helicopter, in the tidy glades that can be found in even the most inaccessible jungles. The seduction of history came from qualities that are exactly opposite. The same jungles are explored on foot with a duty to collect every single exotic flower along the way, taking the petals, leaves and roots together, writing where they were picked in a booklet, and studying them back in the office both for themselves and in relation to each other. While in history elegance and scholarly achievement is often a thick book, in economics, it is a lean one. But how to choose between, say, Arrow's *Social choice and individual values* and Braudel's *Méditerranée*? I think that it is this continued refusal to choose that led me, in large part unwillingly (or at least unknowingly), to become an economic historian.

This however took time. The bridge between economics and history is by no means easy to erect, and in fact I did not feel any urge to build one. One legacy of the post-war triumph of technocratic-scientific administration in France has been the ascent of the engineer-economist: an improbable offspring of nineteenth century Comte style positivism and of the ideas that produced the Soviet system (except if you consider that positivism created the soviet system, which is possible). This type believes (a) that society, as any other physical body, is subject to the laws of nature and that (b) if only she or he were given decision making powers, she or he would improve society by making it conform to her or his idea of social good. Their scholarly ideal is a Minister of Figures, crunching numbers *sine ira et studio*, for the glory and advancement of Science and Mankind. The position of French historians in French society on the other hand had suffered some blows with the political default of the Third Republic. They had not been able to recapture their former role as a source of inspiration for pragmatic policy making. Their move to the far left after the Second World War had been one more dead end as the Fall of the Berlin Wall eventually showed, mimicking in a slower way what Berliners had done overnight, they could only offer to 'deconstruct'.

How to connect Malinvaud and Derrida? There was obviously no way, and obviously no interest in doing it. Moreover, economic history was by the 1990s in dreadful shape in France. One lacked a starting point. It is true that in economic history as in many other things, France had had its glorious time, long, long ago. One could still hear in some quarters the word '*Annales*' being whispered with due respect. But this respect was more akin to the one students of Ancient Greece experience when coming across a reference to the mysteries of Eleusis: nobody knew what was in there. Were the *Annales* dead and buried, or had they survived somewhere? The *Ecole des Hautes Etudes* had a claim on that and argued its case on *Jus Soli*. But in effect it had become, after Braudel's death, a place where heirs fought over inheritance. It still gobbled huge amounts of resources and lots of energy but did not produce much light.

To be entirely fair, there were, in French universities, a few exceptions to this doomed picture: they urged me to pursue my doctoral studies in a place where my uncomfortable balance, 'between two cultures', as Carlo Cipolla so nicely put it, might find some way to be resolved. To tell the entire truth I should add that these voices cautioned me against cliometrics. As I understand it now, the resistance was in part religious (isn't it a sacrilege to measure a Muse?), in part philosophical (can one really gauge events that have occurred using others that haven't?), and in part French (wasn't this discipline predominantly Anglo-Saxon?). But there was also a fascination: hadn't Ernest Labrousse himself developed, way before Cliometrics were even born, what can be called a fully fledged 'model' of the effects of wheat crises on agricultural economies? If practised with the required dose of Cartesian doubt, Cliometrics could after all have their virtue. Included in a broader framework of interpretation that would make sure that over-simplification would be resisted, counterfactuals were conceivable. And in the end, my attempts at arguing that the rise of the gold standard in the late nineteenth century was by no means preordained and that another course of events might have been possible, suggested that I had already crossed the Rubicon.

II. Changing Places

I first stopped over in London, still believing that I would turn, *nolens volens*, to macro-economics. In many senses this stay helped in a decisive fashion to make my way to economic history. Most modern French economists, for all their definitely Gallic taste for maths and economics-as-an-exact-science, are more or less living with a complex vis-à-vis their English speaking counterparts. Cases of cultural self-rejection are not uncommon and can reach the more neurotic point of an adverse relation to one's own language, which tends to be misused, often in seminars, sometimes even at home in the intimacy of family life. These phenomena are quite remarkable and probably not dicussed enough. In any case, for a student of economics, meeting the original proto-types that were so far only appraised through the mental reactions which they have induced on French scholars is a defining experience. It is a bit like a young adult who has only heard about his or her distant, impressive, grand parents through his or her parents and happens to meet them in person. The danger obviously is for the young to find a way to challenge his or her parents by seeking the praise of the grand parents. If such is the case one is bound to inherit the parents' neurosis. Alternatively, one may suddenly realise that the reasons for the parents' difficulty with dealing with their own parents belong to a time and history with which the young has nothing to do. In such a case, the experience may be quite liberating. This is how I decided that I would *NOT* become an economist, and how I landed in California, helped by a grant and an invitation from an American professor who was kind enough to offer to guide my next (or first) steps in economic history.

The early months, and in truth, the following ones too, were something not unlike the experience of the characters of the famous David Lodge novel. There was the sun and the weather of the Bay Area, the ambience of the campus, the extraordinary library facilities, and the rich supply of seminars, where everybody was open and relaxed, focused and concise, tolerant and attentive. In Euphoric State University, I gorged myself on reading, something which I had never been able to do on such a scale in the past, overexploited the possibilities of interlibrary borrowing, and discovered the charms of the 'government documents' library where all the official publications, statistics, etc. were so conveniently gathered. I also discovered that cliometrics was a subject that was respectable enough to be taught to (final year) undergrads. Economic history moreover featured as a full subject within the requirement of the PhD programs, and some students within the economics department would choose a historical topic for their dissertation.

III. Tricks or Treats?
At the same time, while the mass was still being said, and while there was a substantial supply of bishops and archbishops who knew their liturgy well, one had a sense that, as far as the original Clio program was considered (i.e. use ideas from neo-classical economics and apply them to revisit defining episodes of (American) economic history), the heroic times were over: a soon to be awarded Nobel prize (a distinction that honours the victors of old controversies whose whereabouts everybody has forgotten) would indeed be the R.I.P. of the First Clio Movement. It is not that there was no claim on direction. The Davidians announced that 'history mattered' and told stories about keyboards. It was not clear how useful such theories could be since the majority of economists anyway believed that history is 'bunk' (I had to look up the word in my dictionary). Historians, on the other hand did not need to be convinced: so why should they sound apologetic? The Northians on the other hand said they had discovered the role of institutions in economic development and wrote about British-style parliamentary systems and property rights. But any French high school student knows from the textbook that the problem with Russian rural development before World War One was that the Mir's communitarian structure did not provide people 'with the right incentives'. To a large extent, Clio seemed to owe much of its survival to the forces of inertia: there were syllabuses, journals, students and thus a natural tendency towards replication. After the original take-off of the Clio Revolution, growth was achieved through absorption of generations of technological progress. In the same fashion neo-classical economics had been applied in the past, and new waves of innovation, originating in economics, could be processed on historical matter. The new economics of information was (and still is) especially trendy. Bankers of the past became 'financial intermediaries' in charge of resolving 'informational asymmetries', and those who did not get access to loans were being 'credit rationed'. The mill could run at full speed, and the economic historians were precisely those intermediaries who derived a rent from knowing both the economists' tool (with a standard delay) and the historians' facts (with a standard error).

IV. Time on the cross

It is an important question to decide on intellectual grounds what economic history should be at the turn of the century. What was path-breaking 40 years ago cannot remain so forever, and there is no longer much novelty in the application of economics to history. The only possible renewal that would come from this continuing process would involve more narrowly defined historical issues: i.e. it might contribute, topic after topic, to change our insights and views about things past, with each new application of economic ideas. This natural trend would end up making economic history a junior planet in the economic galaxy. Located downstream in the intellectual process of investigation, economic history would derive its institutional status from providing illustrations to the glory and power of economics. The challenge would be for historians: a new swarm of techniques and findings would invade their fields every year. In this sense, the trend in economic history would be just that experienced by other social sciences - such as political science - which are being gradually transformed by the instillation of economics, to the point where they sometimes seem to lose their specificity.

Is another course of events, (desirable and even possible?), the current evolution of economic history may be an appropriate response from the point of view of institutional strategy: it may be better to be the poor cousin of economics than to experience a thorough and irresistible decline such as has occurred in France and in fact in many other European continental countries. At the same time, if economic history becomes a mere plaything for economists, it will certainly lose much of its appeal, and much of its usefulness. For again, it is the beautiful (or deadly) flowers that history throws up and that do not fit into the square explanations of economics which should provide the thrust and the energy for new research efforts. It is precisely because we deal with facts more than with stylised facts, with observations more than with introspections that we can advance the state of knowledge in social sciences. The first cliometric revolution did a wonderful job in proving that economics was an adequate tool to explore history. But isn't it time to show that these explorations have in turn something to tell us about economics? And wouldn't this be much more exciting than endlessly replaying the same old tune?

After years trying to strike a balance between economics and history - a balance that could in turn be called economic history - I have come to the conclusion that the essence of economic history is not about the appropriate proportion, the optimal dose which each part should have in the final product. It is rather in the very attempt at striking a balance, in the continuing sense of discomfort that one has as long as a clear and systematic explanation has not been found, and in the renewed sense of discomfort as soon as such an explanation - suddenly all too clear and systematic - has been found. This is probably why a perennial bridge has not been and shall never be built between the two cultures: because both banks of the river are moving or constantly changing, so that any bridge is bound to have its foundations weakened and be washed away at some point. And because economic history is about the effort at building the bridge, about crossing the river on the provisional construction, and about the view one gets from there - not about the bridge itself. I suppose that's how, unknowingly and unvoluntarily, by refusing to choose between economics and history, one may end up an economic historian.

Marc Flandreau (b. 1967) was educated at the Ecole Normal Supérieure, Paris, the University of Paris - Sorbonne (1986-1990), and his PhD was jointly awarded in 1993 by the Ecole des

Hautes Etudes en Sciences Sociales, Paris and the London School of Economics. He has been Fulbright Fellow at the University of California, Berkeley; Visiting Professor at Stanford University; Research Fellow at the Centre National de la Recherche Scientifique and is currently Professor of Economics at the University of Lille (since 2000). His research interests are money doctors; history, economics and politics of international financial expertise 1850-2000; the political economy of the Habsburg Empire; private responses to international financial instability pre-1914.

In at the Beginning of British Cliometrics

Roderick Floud

The excitement of discovery. That is what economic history has meant to me ever since, as a teenager, I received as a school prize *The Wool-Pack*, by Cynthia Harnett,[1] a children's novel about the medieval wool trade. Under its stimulus I chose to study economic history at 'A' level and my fascination with the subject has never left me. The excitement comes in several guises: the discovery of records which have never been used by an historian; teasing out causes of people's behaviour; statistical analysis which reveals patterns which no-one had hitherto discerned.

It was the discovery of a group of historical records which led me into an early involvement with what was then the new movement of quantitative history. I had chosen to write a doctoral thesis on the history of the machine tool industry in Britain before 1914. I wrote to all the surviving engineering firms which had been founded in that period to ask whether they had retained any records. Greenwood and Batley of Leeds replied that they had indeed kept a large volume of records but that I should visit them quickly, as they were about to throw the records away. A hurried trip to Leeds revealed that the firm, founded in 1856, had kept its accounts, describing the production of each order for machinery, in large ledgers; when each ledger was full, it was put in the basement where, with its fellows, it had remained ever since, accompanied only by thousands of machine drawings.

The necessity for what would now be called 'rescue archaeology' led me to return to Leeds with a van, load some hundreds of ledgers into it and return with them to fill my room in Nuffield College, Oxford. I was then faced with the question of what to do next. Each dusty ledger contained several hundred pages; on each, inscribed in clear copperplate, were descriptions of orders for machine tools, steam engines, guns and other engineering goods, with careful accounts of the amount of metal used in their manufacture and the work done on each order by five different groups of workers. The task of making sense of them seemed insurmountable.

It was a stroke of luck, which in my experience plays an extremely important role in historical research, that Professor Lance Davis was then a visiting fellow at Nuffield. He came from Purdue University, Indiana, which in the early 1960s had become the centre for a new kind of economic history which rapidly became known as econometric history or cliometrics. Its hallmark was the alliance between economic theory, shaping the questions to be asked about a problem or a set of data, and statistics, analysing the data so as to answer the questions. Its new tool was the computer.

When I showed Lance my records and expressed bewilderment as to what I should do with them, his immediate answer was 'use a computer.' This was a revolutionary suggestion for an historian or indeed, at the time for any British social scientist, let alone someone in the humanities. It was 1965, when electronic computing was still in its infancy and when its use was confined mainly to physicists and chemists; historians, if they counted at all, were still using mechanical calculators. At Nuffield, however, some economists and econometricians had begun to see the potential of this new tool and I was encouraged by my supervisors, H.J. Habakkuk and Max Hartwell, to join them.

The decision thrust me into a world which was new at the time but which has already wholly disappeared. In the 1960s, there were no package programs for word processing or statistical analysis; spreadsheets were not thought of and there were no data-base programs. There were no hard disks. Data was recorded by means of holes punched in cards or on reels of paper tape. Programs had to be written by the researcher in a programming language, normally either Fortran or Algol, which had only just superseded the use of even more basic instructions known as machine code; learning them was like studying a foreign language. Programs were needed for the simplest of tasks, such as calculating averages, and they had to be exactly right. A single mistake in writing them or in punching them onto card or tape would lead to the rejection of the program; then followed a laborious process of cutting up paper tape and sticking the correct version together with sellotape. The real penalty, however, was the loss of 24 hours or more – known as the 'turn-round time' - before the corrected program could be submitted once more to the computer. Then, since the machine read the cards or tape sequentially, a mistake in the next line of code could start the whole process again.

A major constraint at the time was that the processing of alphabetic data was in its infancy. Essentially, data such as the information about the customers for Greenwood and Batley's machine tools, or the place to which they were sent, had to be coded into predetermined categories, thus forcing the researcher to establish the outlines of analysis at a very early stage. It was difficult, if not impossible, to have second thoughts. This difficulty continued to haunt historians even when early programs for statistical analysis such as the Statistical Package for the Social Sciences (SPSS) first became available. SPSS would not, for example, sort data alphabetically, so that all alphabetic data had to be coded into numbers. In the late 1960s, I was still forced to write for myself an alphabetic sorting program – now available at the touch of a key in any word processor – to count and analyse the life-histories of engineering firms.

Computing was even physically difficult. It was necessary to carry heavy boxes of punched cards, or reels of paper tape, to and from the computer laboratory; disaster was to drop one's data, since cards could be damaged or tape turn into cats' cradles. The basic code for operating the computer was recorded on magnetic tape, then also in its infancy, but even here there were dangers. As a special privilege, I and other graduate students were allowed to operate the main Oxford university computer (the size of a large room but with less power than a modern PC) through the night, allowing us to escape from the tyranny of 'turn-round time.' One had to be especially careful to punch the buttons on the tape-decks in the right order and at the right time; if one got it wrong, 2400 ft of magnetic tape could unwind across the floor.

It is perhaps because of these experiences that I have never had much patience with philosophical discussions about quantitative history. To me, the computer is a tool, an inanimate and often irritating object which, with a great deal of difficulty, enables one to answer historical questions. It is the questions – whether British engineering was competitive with the United

States, whether the standard of living declined in the industrial revolution - not the technology, which are important and exciting. So too are the statistical and theoretical tools which aid analysis. Quantitative history in its early days was particularly reliant on one method, counterfactual analysis, and one statistical technique, regression analysis, both borrowed from econometrics.

Counterfactual analysis, at least so called, had its first impact with the work of Robert Fogel on the economics of the introduction of railways into the United States. It was received with suspicion if not outright hostility. When Fogel presented his findings to a meeting of the British Economic History Society in 1966, he was roundly attacked by Professors Jack Fisher and Arthur John from the London School of Economics, two of the leaders of the economic history profession. Fogel was, they argued, introducing imaginary or at least wholly hypothetical history when he sought to establish the impact of railways on America by building an imaginary network of canals and estimating how much it would have cost to transport goods along them.

Regression analysis, now a staple of quantitative history as well as of many other social sciences, was similarly received with suspicion. Its claim to be able to sort out and establish the quantitative impact of a number of different factors on an economic event was indeed a substantial challenge to older forms of economic history, which had either been entirely descriptive or had made untestable assertions about cause and effect. Regression analysis, and the testing of statistical significance which normally accompanies it, does indeed require the researcher to make a number of strong assumptions about the data which is being analysed. It is right to criticise studies in which those assumptions cannot legitimately be made. But much of the early suspicion of regression was not based on these arguments, but on a general distaste for statistical analysis and economic models which were seen as too simplistic to sum up the complex realities of economic history.

Early suspicions were, it is true to say, sometimes fuelled by the tendency of early econometric historians to display the zeal of the missionary. Not only did we sometimes claim more for our new methods than, with the advantage of hindsight, we would now judge appropriate, but we also sometimes sought – deliberately or inadvertently - to blind our opponents with science. Econometrics is, as has often been said, more an art than a science and it should not, in either case, be expressed obscurely or with jargon. In my first book, *An Introduction to Quantitative Methods for Historians*,[2] I therefore sought to demystify the statistical techniques which historians were beginning to use in the 1970s. Then, with Don (now Deirdre) McCloskey, I began in the late 1970s to edit *The Economic History of Britain since 1700*,[3] with the explicit aim of making accessible the results of the first generation of works in the econometric history of Britain.

Such work is sometimes derided as 'only writing textbooks.' This ignores both the fact that all teachers and researchers should have a mission to explain, but also the sheer intellectual challenge of explaining complex matters in simple language. Textbooks are, for this reason, actually more difficult to write than research monographs, even if they do not produce the thrill which can come from completing an analysis of a complicated data set or discovering new evidence. I gained satisfaction from both analysis and discovery from my research into the engineering industry. The former came, for example, from establishing the patterns of entry and exit of firms into and out of the industry. Of the latter, I remember in particular the satisfaction of locating a minute book of the directors of Greenwood and Batley. So confidential that it was kept separate from the other records, it recorded secret meetings at the Grand Hotel in Leeds with other engineering firms as part of a cartel to fix prices on government arms contracts.

My early initiation into quantitative and econometric history was turned in an entirely new direction, in the late 1970s, by an invitation from Robert Fogel and Stanley Engerman to join them in an analysis of changing patterns of mortality in North America since the eighteenth century. As they realised, if one was to explain mortality in the American colonies and the United States, one had to be able to assess the health of the migrants, principally from Britain, who travelled to and died in the new world. The novelty of their approach was to make use of a source of evidence which had been used before only once, by Emmanuel Le Roy Ladurie, in a study of French conscripts. This was records of human height, collected in their millions as part of the process of recruitment to the British, American and European armies.

Fogel and Engerman's insight, followed up by a number of other scholars, created a new sub-discipline of economic history, anthropometric history. It was soon apparent that the measurement of the average height of groups in the population could act as a proxy for what human biologists call the 'nutritional status' of the group; human physical growth reflects the net effect of nutritional inputs in the form of food, warmth and even love, as compared with claims on those inputs in the form of body maintenance, work and the defeat of disease. The biologist's concept of nutritional status thus bears a close, if still disputed, resemblance to the economist's and economic historian's concept of the standard of living.

The excitement of the early years of econometric history stemmed from new techniques and new technology. Anthropometric history provided new challenges. There was, first, the need to understand, so far as possible for a non-specialist, the concepts, methods and findings of human biology; this was greatly helped by the enthusiasm of some biologists, notably James Tanner, for the historical research which gave background and a new dimension to their own work in the modern world. A second challenge was that of the need to collect very large amounts of evidence, principally from military records, to provide sufficient sample sizes for statistical analysis. A third challenge, in this connection, was provided by the fact that most armies refused to recruit the shorter men who came forward, on the grounds that they would not be strong enough; this created a complex statistical problem of making inferences about the average height of a population from data where many observations were missing.

Luck once again played its part in the search for evidence. Professor Sarah Palmer happened to be showing a group of students around the archives of the National Maritime Museum in Greenwich. Pausing at random by a shelf, she took down from it a ledger recording the recruitment to the merchant and Royal navies of boys from the streets of London, charitable work by the Marine Society of London beginning in the middle of the eighteenth century. Noting that the ledger included information on the heights of recruits, she recalled my interest in height and told me of the discovery. There proved to be over 100,000 teenage recruits whose heights, addresses and parental occupations were recorded. This gave an unrivalled set of evidence on the heights and nutritional status of the London working class. Matched to the records of the Royal Military Academy at Sandhurst, the evidence provided an entirely new insight into the inequalities of nineteenth century society; all the Sandhurst recruits, the sons of the aristocracy and middle class, were taller at the ages of 14 to 17 than any of the boys from the London slums.

Evidence on population height, and sometimes weight and body mass, has now been collected for over 20 countries at different time periods and, for example in the work of Richard Steckel, is now being supplemented by analysis of skeletal remains for periods before the advent of written records. Anthropometric history has, like quantitative history, generated argument both among researchers in the field and between them and other economic historians who, at least initially, reacted with incredulity to the idea that heights could be of any use as an historical source. Particularly controversial was the claim, advanced for example in *Height, Health and History: nutritional status in the United Kingdom 1750-1980*,[4] which I wrote with Kenneth Wachter and Annabel Gregory, that the new material was relevant to the long-standing historical argument known as the 'standard of living debate.' Whatever the outcome of these controversies, it has been exciting to be part of them.

As this essay in intellectual autobiography has shown, I have been, and continue to be, fascinated by economic history. I do not wish to make any particular claims for it as providing particular insight into human history and behaviour. Other forms of history, and other social sciences, have at least equal claim to such status. I have found it, however, endlessly exciting and challenging; it combines the thrill of the chase – described so much more vividly than I can in A.S. Byatt's novel *Possession* [5]– with the intellectual challenges of economic theory and statistical analysis, the complexity of human biology and the puzzles which underlie the transformation of our world during and since the industrial revolution. I feel privileged to have been part of this endeavour.

Roderick Floud (b. 1. 4. 1942) was educated at Wadham College, Oxford, and Nuffield College, Oxford. He taught at University College London, the University of Cambridge, Birkbeck College, London and Stanford University California. His current position is Provost of London Guildhall University, President-elect of Universities UK. He is researching the anthropometric history of Britain since 1700.

---

[1] Harnett, C. *The Wool-Pack* (London, 1951).
[2] Floud, R. *An Introduction to Quantitative Methods for Historians* (London, 1973, 1979).
[3] Floud, R. and McCloskey, D. (eds) *The Economic History of Britain since 1700* (Cambridge: first edition in two volumes 1981, second edition in three volumes 1994).
[4] Floud, R., Wachter, K and Gregory, A. *Height, Health and History: Nutritional Status in the United Kingdom, 1750-1980* (Cambridge, 1990).
[5] Byatt, A.S. *Possession: a Romance* (London, 1990).

Challenges to the Economic System in the Twentieth Century

James Foreman-Peck

Economic history impinges on many fields- anthropology, archaeology and architecture, to consider only some early in the alphabet[1]. It is an integrative subject, grounded in the facts of social life, uncovering and accounting for fundamental social patterns, trends, cataclysms and discontinuities[2]. Such investigations and explanations can never be the province of a single discipline.

Far more important than defining the discipline in logically rigorous fashion is communicating the importance and the excitement of the activity. In keeping with the personal nature of the brief proposed by the editor, I will pursue the limited objective of discussing why some major twentieth century problems of economic history - challenges to the economic system- concerned me sufficiently to research them. These are:

- the conflict over private or public ownership of 'the means of production' -capitalism or socialism,
- criticisms of private management as a class,
- the charge that capitalism is ultimately unstable,
- the failure of the Russian transition to a market economy in the 1990s which raises questions about the under-pinnings of the market economy that are central to economic history.

Private v public ownership
At the beginning of the century, the ownership and control of national resources to ensure an efficient and fair economy was a question never far from the surface of public discussion in Europe[3]. Most economies gradually became 'mixed', a large block of state-owned sectors coexisted with private enterprise elsewhere.

Industrial acquisitions by the local or central British state in the century before the First World War had generally shown tendencies towards monopoly that undermined some of the advantages of private enterprise. Companies colluded to fix prices or tried merging to eliminate competition. Environmental and safety problems in industries such as water reinforced the case for tighter regulation. Influential pressure groups sometimes had their own reasons for wanting regulation 'internalised' by state ownership. Late nineteenth century municipalities saw utility companies as sources of revenue, for instance. Even that bastion of the British market economy, *The Economist*, concerned about the newspaper's telecommunications costs, complained of excessive profits of the Edwardian private National Telephone Company, and looked to lower prices in a state-owned network.

These acquisitions were consolidated and new industries such as coal and railways were added to the state portfolio by the Labour government elected in 1945. A statutory monopoly industry-wide corporation was the basic institutional form. At the end of the nationalisations of the 1940s, 40% of national capital expenditure was within the public sector[4] - an enormous volume of resources to misdirect if the allocation criteria were wrong.

Did these shifts enhance or reduce efficiency? Gas and electricity controlled cost comparisons showed little difference for private and public British firms in the early part of the twentieth century. Further removed from the taxpayers than municipal gas and electricity, unit costs of the nationalised telegraph rose with the expansion of the system. But whether this was solely because of state ownership must be questioned in the light of the poor productivity performance of the contemporary privately owned railway system. Institutionally most intriguing was the 'public interest corporation', the Central Electricity Board, empowered in 1926 to build a national transmission grid and rationalise electricity generation. The new regime reduced costs by one third, radically improving the utilisation of capital and boosting the average scale of operations. It did so by persuading private and municipal enterprises to accept central direction of the extent and timing of their electricity generation. This voluntarism saved on enforcement costs but perhaps one half of the industry cost reduction the CEB actually achieved by 1937 was apparently forgone[5]. In the British experience, there were some advantages from a shift from private ownership. The 'Morrisonian' corporations of the 1940s are far less amenable to efficiency comparisons because they were intended to cover entire industries. Precisely for this reason there must be some doubt about their performance. But soft budget constraints and ministerial interference with management point even more clearly in the same direction.

The unwinding of state ownership positions with the privatisations of the 1980s and 1990s stemmed from tighter financial control and ideological change- triggered by the inflation and political disorder of 1970s. Four factors generally boosted the performance of the now privatised industries

- simple management objectives,
- the separation of 'the natural monopoly' network structure from network services which could be competitive, if regulated correctly,
- novel forms of price controls, and
- the piecemeal approach which allowed successive privatisations to learn from preceding experiments, a considerable improvement on the creation of the monolithic nationalised industries of the later 1940s.

The moral of the story is that the long struggle over the ownership of the means of production was misconceived as far as efficiency is concerned; regulation, competition and management are far more important.

The Shortcomings of Management
Public ownership of businesses becomes more popular when private management is poor and private enterprise is insulated from competition by size, by exclusive contracts or by barriers to international trade. The international comparative literature does not rate British private business highly.[6] Some of this criticism has been misdirected- in particular the supposed unwillingness to create large multi-divisional firms.[7] But the downward slide in British productivity relative to most of the rest of the world over the twentieth century, to a position behind much of western Europe by the 1970s, suggests something more than the catching up of a former industrial leader.

Inevitably people make mistakes, not every businessman will be competent or lucky. But was, and is, the entire supply of British management talent nonetheless unusually low – sapped by a 'decline of the industrial spirit'[8] or other deficiencies? As well as being more competent, some individuals are more hardworking than others, some are more impatient, and some are more risk-averse. At the level of society these traits are supported or undermined by institutions such as particular religions, banks and other financial organisations, laws of bankruptcy and debt default, tax regimes and so on. One might distinguish a whole society that is in some way incompetent or lazy - has a high leisure preference say- from sections of it. The options are different if only a group from which managers and entrepreneurs are traditionally recruited exhibit such characteristics. In either case we can say these traits reflect a culture but this hardly constitutes an explanation; for that we must find the institutions that support the 'culture'.

One such approach is to consider the pecuniary reward of business relative to other walks of life. If it is low then the most ambitious may not be drawn to the activity. But the continuing entry of rich and successful businessmen into the British elite throughout the twentieth century is hardly consistent with the rewards being inadequate. Taking upward social mobility as a measure of success, then before state education became more widespread, business was by far the most effective means of advancement for the talented and energetic at the bottom of the social ladder-small as that chance was[9]. With the twentieth century extension of state education and state bureaucracy such mobility increased (but only a little by the 1970s).

The 'arms-length' style of traditional British management is a distinctive cultural feature; workers exclusively know about production while management merely regulates and provides incentives, devoting any efforts to finance, accounting and possibly sales.[10] This approach is likely to prevent management discovering their business' 'core competence'. Moreover, when decision-takers lack essential know-how for strategic repositioning, they will probably be inflexible in the face of technological or market change. The team piece rate system in Morris Motors in the 1960s was an extreme example of an uncomprehending 'arms-length' management style. The payment parameters were wrongly set, ensuring without further action the destruction of a large proportion of the industry. Then to avoid the approaching disaster, management shifted the wage system to the other extreme, time rates, and succeeded in bringing forward the collapse[11].

The share price of a badly run publicly quoted private company, in theory, should collapse, making profitable a hostile take-over bid by other management for the assets. Yet this did not happen; the capital market did not oust those responsible for poor performance. The explanation is the sheer size of the corporation into which the British motor industry had been merged and the consequent apparent commitment of the state to support it. The industrial policy lying behind this state-encouraged merger was therefore a culprit as well.

British management certainly could be catastrophic; selection and correction mechanisms were obviously defective in certain cases. Traditional institutions such as piece rate systems were poorly managed, as was state policy.

The Crisis of Capitalism
Incompetent business management combined with an inept governing elite is an indication that the market economy is not efficient and a recipe for its collapse. In the years between the world wars, central bankers were at the peak of their power. International institutions like those established at Bretton Woods in 1944 had yet to be created. Instead there was the supposedly

automatic gold standard, and the equally self-regulating 'most favoured nation' clause in international trade treaties.

The threat to the market economy of the world crisis of 1929 – and perhaps even the unemployment of the interwar years- was widely believed in the first generation after 1945 to have been averted by Keynesian economics. Then came Milton Friedman's counter-attack of monetarism- the US crisis stemmed from an institutional failure in the US[12]. Simulations show that the interwar US economy was indeed 'Keynesian'- it needed fiscal policy because of the extreme collapse of the monetary system, in part stemming from the US laissez-faire policy. In Europe, more prompt state action prevented such calamities and thus those economies, especially France, would have responded better to appropriate monetary policies. Britain had very little leeway with conventional policy instruments[13].

Britain's leaving the gold standard was bad for the rest of the world; the ensuing exchange depreciation exported unemployment and provoked retaliation, damaging the entire international economy[14]. The gold standard and (fairly) free trade could have been viable. It only required suitable fiscal and monetary policies. Maynard Keynes' tariff proposal was one way of raising the revenue for an expansionary fiscal policy. Had Britain temporarily adopted protection 18 months before abandoning the gold standard the debacle of September 1931 might have been avoided. Then the trade barriers would not have been raised in response to sterling depreciation and a bargaining tool would have been available to reduce other tariffs.

The gold standard was a means of promoting co-operation in keeping trade barriers down. With the benefit of historical hindsight, the policy problem that especially required co-operation (or leadership) was to avoid enlarging the policy instrument set to include devaluation, exchange controls and trade quotas. For Europe, but not for the much larger US, this might have been achieved by official international reserve lending sufficiently promptly and abundantly. But political constraints appeared to have ruled out this solution. A sufficiently powerful supra-national body may have been able to over-ride them. But the Bank for International Settlements, established only a year before the international crisis, was too late to defend the system against the Great Depression.

The Transition to the Market Economy

Market economies can be disastrously managed and lack appropriate institutions, as the 1930s shows. The transition of Russia from a communist war economy to a market system in the 1990s reveals related shortcomings. Economic history suggests some helpful analogies with British war economy transitions.[15]

When the U.S.S.R. disintegrated and Boris Yeltsin became undisputed leader of Russia, he asked Yegor Gaidar to design and manage a 'big bang' transition to a market economy. The reformers believed that the state was weak, intrusive and corrupt. They were determined quickly to minimise its interventions in the economy, relying primarily on markets, prices and decentralised decision-making. Since the crisis of August 1998, this Russian reform strategy over the preceding six years has generally been recognised as inadequate.

Even in a capitalist market economy not all information is conveyed by prices. The price system must be supplemented by implicit or explicit social contracts. Economies require an effective legal infrastructure and transactions inevitably are based on social trust and civil norms, as well as on market or plan signals. Well functioning economic systems possess intricate institutional fabrics and rely on social and organisational capital that takes time to produce. Effective governments are of crucial importance in ensuring the proper functioning of an economic system, although the scale of state intervention can vary substantially.

Although of course of far shorter duration, the British economies during both world wars were far closer in many respects to the Soviet command economy in relying on pervasive rationing, de facto nationalisation, and non-price control mechanisms, than is usually appreciated. During economic decontrol after world wars as well as transitions to market economies, institutional and cultural shifts matter greatly and depend on the historical legacy. For the Russian transition and for British decontrol the governments were confronted by similar challenges of shifting from a centrally controlled economic system, with negligible or attenuated private property rights, that was focussed on military production, to a market-oriented peacetime economy. But the transition policies adopted and the results obtained varied considerably. The rapid transitions in Britain after World War I and Russia in the 1990s were associated with numerous problems in reallocating resources and restructuring.

In contrast, the relatively successful transition of the British economy in the post-World War II period was based on continued government intervention and control. This case indicates that the state can provide useful interim guidance in the reallocation process of the initial phase of transition, which is dominated by 'noise' and disorganisation. State-directed conversion programmes were, on the whole, effective in directing resources to pay Britain's foreign debts, maintaining full employment, and providing a social support system that improved the well-being of the population. The implication is that a gradualist transition would have produced more sustainable institutional change, and superior economic performance in Russia as well, than did the actual programme of abrupt change.

Lessons

By helping us understand the past, economic history explains where we are today and allows us to predict where we will be tomorrow. The belief that transferring industrial ownership and control to the state would create a better world has been severely undermined by the twentieth century experience. Yet the desire for simple solutions – or 'big ideas'- remains strong. A more popular European present day recipe is 'Europe'. In both cases the empirical research of economic history suggests big ideas need testing and their implementation requires detailed understanding, if they are not to have the opposite effect to that intended[16].

Over the last hundred years, the rise of the corporate economy has created private sector bureaucracies almost matching the public sector in scale and other characteristics. Professional managers now pursue their careers with only distant accountability to board members and shareholders. The recruitment, training and rewards of the business elite in these organisations have profound implications for their competence, for the performance of the private sector as a whole, and thus for the national economy. It is to these variables we should look, rather than to 'culture', which is itself in part created by more objective institutions, such as payment systems.

Despite their enormous size in relation to many nation states, modern corporations are dependent upon a stable international economic framework, which in turn is supported by institutions and national policies. The consequences of the crumbling of this order in the 1930s are a sobering reminder of its importance. Whatever the shortcomings of the World Trade Organisation/GATT, the World Bank and the IMF, the lessons of the past suggest they could have performed much worse. The rapid economic growth and rising living standards of the last half century are a good advertisement for the regime now under attack by anti-globalisation protesters, compared with any previous period in history.

Fundamental to the whole world economy, emerging frequently in economic history over the millennia, is the proposition that the market depends on extra-market values. Impersonal honesty cannot be monitored and enforced across a whole society that does not share the value - the resource costs would be too great - yet markets cannot function without a minimum of it. Property rights must be defined and accepted if trade and production is to flourish[17]. Some institutions supporting these rights must be above the buying and selling of the market- without an effective police, defence and judiciary even existing supportive values can be eroded. It is likely that there are broader non-market requirements than these as well. The Russian transition to market economy of the 1990s demonstrates the importance of not taking institutions and values for granted. The more radical the proposed change, the greater the time that should be allowed to establish new conventions, for the market copes best with gradualism[18].

James Foreman-Peck (b. 19. 6. 1948) is Economic Adviser at H M Treasury[*] and Professor of Economics at Middlesex University Business School. Awarded a PhD by the London School of Economics, he was formerly Professor of Economic History at the University of Hull, and Fellow of St Antony's College Oxford. His *European Industrial Policy: The Twentieth Century Experience,* with Giovanni Federico, was published in 1999 by Oxford University Press.

[1] So I include Jared Diamond's fascinating *Guns, Germs and Steel* (Vintage 1998), in economic history for instance.
[2] Fernand Braudel's distinction (in *A History of Civilisations* Penguin Books 1995) between layers of history according to the pace of (structural) change appeals to me. Economic history is concerned with the more stable aspects of society- including the cultural features which often underpin differences between economies- not the rapid change of personalities and ephemeral events so often the concern of political history.
[3] Clause 4 of the Labour Party constitution is a case in point for Britain.
[4] Robert Millward and John Singleton. 'The ownership of British Industry in the postwar era; an explanation' in Robert Millward and John Singleton *eds The Political Economy of Nationalisation in Britain 1920-1950* (Cambridge University Press 1995) .
[5] James S Foreman-Peck and Chris Hammond 'Variable Costs and the Visible Hand: The Re-regulation of Electricity Supply 1932-37' *Economica,* 64 1997 15-30 ; James Foreman-Peck and Robert Millward, *Private and Public Ownership of British Industry in Britain 1820-1990* (Clarendon Press, 1994).
[6] Alfred D Chandler *Scale and Scope* Belknap Press 1990, is perhaps the most cited in this context.
[7] Leslie Hannah, 'Survival and Size Mobility among the World's Largest 100 Industrial Corporations, 1912-1995',*American Economic Review* 88(2), 1998.
[8] Judging by the impact of his book, Martin J Wiener, *English Culture and the Decline of the Industrial Spirit 1850-1980* Cambridge University Press 1981, counts as a 'cavalier' economic historians in the dichotomy of *1066 and All That-* he is wrong but romantic.
[9] James Foreman-Peck and Julia Smith 'Entrepreneurship and Social Transformation' *Middlesex University Business School Discussion Paper, Economics Series,* no 87, 2000; David J Jeremy *A Business History of Britain 1900-1990*s (Oxford University Press, 1998), Table 10.2; Leslie Hannah ' Cultural determinants of Economic Performance: An Experiment in Measuring Human capital Flows' in Graeme D Snooks ed *Historical Analysis in Economics,* (Routledge 1993).
[10] Howard Gospel, *Markets, Firms and the Management of Labour,* Cambridge University Press 1992
[11] Sue Bowden, James Foreman-Peck and Tom Richardson, 'The Post War Productivity Failure: Insights from Oxford (Cowley)' *Business History* 2001 (forthcoming).

[*] The views expressed in this article are those of the author and not necessarily those of H M Treasury.

[12] Milton Friedman and Anna Schwartz *A Monetary History Of the United States 1867-1960*, (Princeton University Press. 1963).

[13] James Foreman-Peck, Andrew Hughes Hallett and Yue Ma 'Optimum International Policies for the World Depression 1929-1933' *Economies et Sociétés*, Serie A F, 22: 4/5 (1996) 219-242 ; James Foreman-Peck et al 'The End of Free Trade; Protection and the Exchange Rate Regime', in A Marrison (ed) *Free Trade and Its Reception, 1815-1960*, (Routledge, 1998); James Foreman-Peck, et al 'A Monthly Econometric Model of the Transmission of the Great Depression between the Principal Industrial Economies' *Economic Modelling*. 17 (2000) 515-544.

[14] Both Barry *Eichengreen Golden Fetters; the Gold Standard and the Great Depression 1919-1939*, Oxford University Press 1992, and Peter Temin *Lessons from the Great Depression* (MIT Press, Boston, 1989), maintain that leaving the gold standard was desirable because it was deflationary.

[15] Christopher M Davis and James Foreman-Peck 'The Russian Transition Through the Historical Looking Glass: Gradual Versus Abrupt De-Control of Economic Systems' in P David, M Thomas and P Solar eds *Economic Challenges of the 21st Century in Historical Perspective* (Oxford University Press/ British Academy: forthcoming 2001).

[16] Alan S. Milward *The European Rescue of the Nation State* (Routledge 1992), for example proposes that the evidence of the early years of the European Community indicates a very different role from that perceived by many of its present-day proponents.

[17] Avner Greif 'The Fundamental Problem of Exchange' *European Review of Economic History* 4, 2000 251-284.

[18] This can even warrant an interventionist industrial policy that temporarily 'leans against the wind' of the market if necessary to maintain public confidence in the fairness of a market economy.

The Life of Society: The Public Role of the Social Historian[1]

Mark Freeman

In his inaugural lecture at the LSE in 1932 R. H. Tawney claimed that history 'is concerned with the study, not of a series of past events, but of the life of society, and with records of the past as a means to that end'. The historian's job, for Tawney, was 'to widen the range of observation from the experience of a single generation or society to that of mankind'.[2] This statement of the activities and aspirations of the economic and/or social historian suggests that the discipline can and should have a broader applicability to the world in which it operates; and this was certainly how Tawney and his contemporaries envisaged it. Tawney's work reached a relatively wide audience of educated general readers,[3] and he helped to inspire a generation of political activists and social reformers. Moreover, as Maxine Berg has pointed out, many women in the interwar period, Eileen Power for example, were attracted to economic history as 'a discipline to provide the ammunition of practical reform [at] a time ... when social policy was central ... to British intellectual life': social policy shaped the subject-matter and approaches of economic and social historians, who regularly discussed their work in the context of contemporary social issues.[4] Today the educated general readership for economic and social history, insofar as it existed, has largely vanished, and the links between the discipline and social policy are less evident than in Tawney's times. The historical profession as a whole is becoming more fragmented and more specialised, and as a consequence more inward-looking. As Martin Daunton, writing in 1985, argued, the institutional separation of economic history, although necessary for disciplinary self-protection earlier in the twentieth century, was by then counter-productive, making economic historians 'introverted, narrow, pursuing the increasingly marginal returns of a particular type of economic theory'.[5] Moreover, the problems associated with the institutional separation of economic and social history from 'straight' history are deepened by the questionable yoking together of economic and social history in the first place, despite their increasingly divergent subject-matter and methodologies.

Social history is in danger of suffering in a similar way. At one time it was hoped that wider interest in history would be kindled by an approach which sought to explain the experiences of the 'ordinary' people who had apparently lived, until then, below the historian's notice. These projects of integrating the forgotten masses into the historiographical mainstream encouraged academic involvement in amateur local social history projects, and in so doing promoted a collaborative approach through which communities were empowered and encouraged to investigate and explain their own histories. (The History Workshop movement is a good, if atypical, example.) Social history filled a significant gap in the historiographical canon. However, today it seems that many social historians have retreated into an academic shell, pursuing, to paraphrase Daunton, the marginal returns of social theory. As early as 1984, it was being argued in some quarters that new orthodoxies had come to attain the very monolithic status once supposedly held by the documentary-based empiricism that the 'new social history' sought to challenge.[6] This fear was rather exaggerated, but its airing emphasised some of the dangers we, as social historians, face. The subject is becoming less accessible: few people have a grasp of the terminology or theoretical underpinnings of the approaches used by many of the 'new cultural historians', just as few have the training required to understand the equally opaque articles that appear in many economic history journals. The penetration of economic and social theories into history is not new, of course, but it can be dangerous if it comes at the expense of engagement with the people who form the subject-matter of our history. I suspect that before 1963 posterity was not quite as condescending as we have been led to believe, but undoubtedly some of the romance has disappeared from the project of rescuing people from it.

I do not wish to invite caricature as a 'young fogey', unable to appreciate the importance of the theorising of certain aspects of social history: indeed, these developments should be viewed as a sign of disciplinary maturity. However, I would suggest that, by employing the past as a laboratory for the evaluation of social and economic theories, many historians come to conceptualise it on terms other than its own, and in a way alien both to those who experienced it and those who wish to read about it. The 'linguistic turn' has produced some interesting investigations of historical texts, but it is neither as new as has been suggested nor as helpful in understanding the fundamentals of the past and what mattered to those who lived in it. Patrick O'Brien briefly but memorably reminded us, at the Economic History Society's annual conference dinner in April 2000, that the new cultural historians too frequently overlook the fundamental aspects of the experience of those who live in the past. As Joan Thirsk, one of Tawney's students, argued in the Tawney lecture at the same conference, historians need to start 'listening to people' again. Thirsk used the phrase to describe her exploitation of descriptive seventeenth-century source material to illuminate our knowledge and understanding of agrarian practices in the past; however, she also indicated that 'listening to people' must involve a reappraisal of the historian's wider role in society. I would suggest that there are three key relationships that define this wider role. One is with general readers and those with a non-professional interest in history, who form a market in which the historian can and should operate; one with students in universities, whom the professional historian teaches; and thirdly and perhaps most importantly, a more public relationship with the society and the state from which historians take their licence to practice.

The 'general reader' has become rather redundant to the majority of professional historians; and yet history, even and perhaps especially in a rapidly changing world, exerts a powerful popular fascination. Pondering on his young son's question, 'Daddy, what's the use of history', Marc Bloch remarked that 'even if history were judged incapable of other uses, its entertainment value would remain in its favour ... it is incontestable that it appears entertaining to a large number of men'.[7] This 'entertainment value' is confirmed by the popularity of historical television documentaries, and by the success of books like Dava Sobel's *Longitude*. Yet social history, which should be inherently interesting to the majority of the population with whose experiences it is concerned, seems to reach only a fringe market. Those social histories, written by professionals, which have sold well, have been precisely those that have been the product of 'listening to people': Thompson's *Making of the English Working Class*, Ladurie's *Montaillou* and Ronald Blythe's *Akenfield* are examples. Others stem from the 'revival of narrative' in the late 1970s and early 1980s: the micro-narrative can create a seductive reconstruction of past events, and is also often able to tap into a local history market. Books which, through the geographical and chronological specificity of their subject-matter, lay themselves open to accusations of 'antiquarianism' are those which seem to attract popular interest. It is precisely the 'antiquarian' aspects of local research that are likely to interest the local historian, and thus inspire community-based social history projects: projects that examine the kind of subject-matter defended by the new social historians on the grounds of its potentially wider appeal than 'traditional' history. Through such collaborative local work, a community can conceptualise with greater interest and more understanding a past with which its people have an inherent affinity. This gives the 'entertainment value' of history a greater and more lasting worth.

Insofar as history is an academicised pursuit, which it is perhaps less so than many other disciplines, its students are also significant users, or consumers, of historians' output, broadly defined; and the implications of this go much deeper than simply the marketing of textbooks and the 'jazzing up' of lectures. Economic and social history is precariously positioned within the structure of most universities, but ultimately this might also prove an opportunity. It is viewed on the one hand as the historical wing of the social sciences – at Glasgow, where I am based as I write, the department is in the social science faculty – and, on the other, as a rather specialised version of 'straight' or 'arts' history. Whichever view is taken, the answer to many of our problems appears to lie in interdisciplinarity. As the quest for 'relevance' intensifies, among both funding bodies and students who increasingly view themselves as customers of a university education and are rightly concerned with the employment prospects afforded by their degrees, the broadness of the educational curriculum, long a feature of the Scottish university system, will need to be redefined. This can be a research-led redefinition: interdisciplinary research projects are multiplying and will continue to do so; and there seems no reason, beyond the inevitable problem of academic workloads, why this interdisciplinarity cannot be translated into undergraduate teaching. The traditional graduates whose degrees (in Scotland at any rate) have involved a small amount of a variety of subjects, especially in the early years of their courses, may be replaced by graduates who have undertaken more project work, probably with interdepartmental supervision. They will also be more IT-literate: the laboratory-classroom is a fertile, if at first daunting, learning environment, and it helps to equip students with skills that will serve both them and their CVs well. Taught effectively, computer-based historical work can be surprisingly motivational, as well as bringing primary sources, such as censuses, closer to students at an earlier stage in their university careers than might otherwise be the case. This in turn helps them to understand what history, of all kinds, is really about.

So much for the institutional survival of economic and social history, and, for that matter, history itself. As Tawney and his contemporaries believed, however, the discipline should not simply be a professional activity with no aims beyond its own continuance, and no duties except to interest the public, important and frequently neglected though this duty is. History should benefit from having become a profession rather than a pastime, and it should also confer reciprocal benefits on the society which allows it to be pursued as a profession. However, we cannot now expect economic and social historians to provide the 'ammunition' of social reform in the way the early pioneers conceived of their role: early twenty-first-century academic historians are usually, and rightly, expected to be more politically detached than their pre-war counterparts. We cannot recreate the Balliol of the 1880s or the LSE of the early twentieth century. In these institutions the experience of liberal education not only pushed graduates in the direction of social service and social reform, but also stimulated the academics, such as Tawney, into writing history, not with a directly reforming purpose, but to provide the background for a more general evaluation of the position at which society had arrived, from which might be deduced some of the possible outlines of its future progress. If we are to re-create this role for economic and social historians, the future for economic and social historical inquiry, as with teaching, must surely be more interdisciplinary. Paradoxically, this interdisciplinarity may help to save both economic history and social history from submersion under other disciplines within the university system. This is where the social-theory-driven rapproachement with other arts and, especially, social science departments might help us: our different disciplines can complement rather than interpenetrate each other if more interdisciplinary projects are undertaken.

I should declare my personal interest here. I am about to start work on a one-year interdisciplinary project at the University of York, evaluating the history of the Joseph Rowntree Charitable Trust, in which I, as a historian, will be working with colleagues in the politics and social policy departments: the sort of project to whose apparent relevance many funding bodies would be attracted. An even better example is the ESRC-funded 'Future of Work' project, based at the University of Essex, in which historians are providing the necessary contextual background to support researchers in other fields. I anticipate that in the future there will be many more such interdisciplinary projects, and this suggests a way in which the work of historical analysis can be allied to social reform and other more practical considerations. Such work will no doubt become more international as the world becomes more technologically, politically and linguistically united. This to me seems the best way of fulfilling the aims of the pioneers of our discipline, and, more importantly, of ensuring that academic economic and social history does not marginalise itself out of existence through the limitation of its scope and the over-theorisation of its various approaches to the past. If it is to be an academic pursuit, the broader relevance of what is done should be more explicit in the framing of our research. Interdisciplinarity should be evaluative: informed by theory but not theory-driven, constructive rather than de(con)structive. If this is the direction our discipline takes, economic and social historians may find themselves more frequently in the future, as Tawney and many of his contemporaries envisaged, working collaboratively with those whose interests lie more firmly in the present in order to help shape future social change.

Mark Freeman (b. 29. 8. 1974) read Modern History at Merton College, Oxford and gained his PhD on 'Social Investigation in Rural England 1870-1914' in 1999 from the Department of Economic and Social History, University of Glasgow. He was the Economic History Society's Tawney Fellow for 1999-2000 and is currently a Research Fellow in the History Department at the University of York.

---

[1] I would like to thank Hadrian Wise, Pete McKinney and Krista R. Maglen for their comments on earlier versions of this essay.

[2] Quoted in J. F. C. Harrison, *Early Victorian Britain 1832-1851* (London, 1979 [1st. ed. London, 1971]), p. 17.

[3] For example, *Religion and the Rise of Capitalism* (1926) quickly sold over 100,000 copies, and was translated into seven languages. (Ross Terrill, *R. H. Tawney and His Times: Socialism as Fellowship* (Cambridge, Massachussetts, 1973), pp. 59-60.)

[4] Maxine Berg, 'The First Women Economic Historians', *Economic History Review*, 2nd ser., XLV (1992), p. 319.

[5] *History Today*, Feb. 1985, p. 38.

[6] See Gertrude Himmelfarb, 'History with the Politics Left Out', in *The New History and the Old: Critical Essays and Reappraisals* (London and Cambridge, Massachussetts, 1987), pp. 13-32. (The article first appeared in 1984.)

[7] Marc Bloch, *The Historian's Craft* (Manchester, 1954), pp. 3, 7.

Through Which Looking Glass? Image, Reality and Historical Enquiry

W. R. Garside

Blame it on Hoover and Roosevelt. As an undergraduate student of economics in the early 'sixties, when access to university was pre-UCCA and by no means pre-ordained and when black-gowned Professors and Doctors were vested (at least in my mind) with a depth of understanding and scholarship that it was my weekly privilege to savour, the world began to take on a degree of precision, orderliness and certainty that had previously escaped me. Entrepreneurs (who were these people?) sought profit-maximising outcomes, states of equilibria existed and economic policymakers earnestly sought optimal bliss. Exposure to the principles of public finance, the theory of money and the niceties of perfect competition, oligopoly, duopoly and monopsony encouraged an unnerving feeling that the economic mess I had left behind in my native County Durham in 1962 was due in part to the inability or unwillingness of 'invisible' entrepreneurs to get their marginal and average cost curves in order or to understand the difference between arc elasticity and an automatic stabiliser.

Then came the great depression, at least in the form of a detailed examination on my part of American economic policymaking during the Hoover and Roosevelt administrations. The narrative was exciting enough and compared to my feeble efforts in a first year survey course to conjure up images of the South Sea Bubble or the repeal of the Corn Laws, one could enjoy moments of more relaxed intellectual endeavour unpicking FDR's homespun economic philosophy delivered during his infamous fireside chats. But it was the power of political expediency, the heady mix of certainty and uncertainty that 'informed' policy making and the contrast between the outcomes one might have expected from textbook graphics and what passed as strategic thinking that struck home.

This interest in the political economy of change would have been nurtured earlier had I undertaken a degree in economic history rather than economics. But it was the formal training in economics that drew me into economic history in more ways than one. Hailsham's cloth-capped visit to the north-east in the early 'sixties as an emissary of regional development (worryingly in retrospect without any firm departmental backing in Whitehall) nonetheless conjured up in my mind the prospect of my joining some economic task force dedicated to tackling (yet again) the already long-established North-South divide. It seemed the decent thing to do in recognition of the County Major University Scholarship which had released me from the terror of ending up with some unremitting and unrewarding job (discounting, of course, my subsequent post in academia). But a chance encounter with officials of the Durham Miners' Association saved Whitehall from that unsolicited application and the north-east from my economic meddling.

My study of the fortunes of the Durham miners and their industry during the turbulent years 1919-60 was driven in part by the rather vacuous accounts I had read earlier of Durham's determined stand during the 1926 general strike. It was conventionally represented as being characteristic of the fortitude and strength of community spirit within the county when in reality it had a great deal more to do with a complex relationship between wages and working hours that had been a source of local discontent since the late nineteenth century. Likewise there was at the time little information about the motives and actions of the regional coalowners or much discussion of the links between industrial decline, the market for coal, and the influence of geology except for the details buried in official and largely inaccessible sources. It was time to declare an interest.

On reflection my subsequent work bears out that early concern to view economic phenomena in as wide a context as possible. The absence of any systematic study of the sources and reliability of unemployment statistics from the mid-nineteenth century onwards, the relative neglect of employers' industrial relations strategies, and the manner in which the problem of interwar unemployment straddled the fields of contemporary finance, trade and economic ideology seemed to me to be worthy of greater attention. The latter subject also gave rise to Benjamin and Kochin's now celebrated exercise in economic modelling to demonstrate the extent to which a significant proportion of interwar unemployment was 'voluntary' in as much as the benefits system reduced the opportunity cost of idleness, inducing workers either to opt for leisure or at least to extend their search for a job. I welcomed the fall-out, not so much in terms of the contrary view to which I subscribed, but because of the way in which conventional understanding of the sources of persistent unemployment in the period had been challenged. There was a suspicion initially that the search for a more 'scientific' approach had been at the expense of careful investigation of the non-quantitative sources. Economists are apt to dress their formal modelling with as terse a summary of the historical context as they can conveniently find. It is often overlooked that in their effort to re-appraise Beveridge's contrast between pre-1914 and interwar unemployment, as part of their case, Benjamin and Kochin quoted the correct pages of the wrong book by Beveridge, arriving at precisely the opposite conclusion of Beveridge himself. But, that aside, it is part of the function of economic theory to help frame appropriate questions to ask of the past. It was gratifying to my mind that quantitatively-orientated economists had in the context of British interwar unemployment forced others to examine their assumptions of causality and to be aware of variables that might otherwise have been overlooked. More gratifying still was to find that to advance the argument further recourse had to be made to the musty administrative record.

I have never had any difficulty in accepting the benefits that can be derived from rigorous mathematical investigation of economic phenomena so long as its practitioners accept that the exactitude of their endeavours can only reveal part of the complexity of historical change. It is to the credit of those historians who brushed aside accusations of dullness and continued to worry over such issues of Britain's progress in education and training, industrial relations, the role of the state, and the power of prevailing orthodoxies, not only in Whitehall and the Treasury but also within firms. They brought to the forefront of current historical enquiry a range of influences upon economic growth and development that were previously and conveniently lumped together as 'exogenous'. It is no coincidence that the European countries which benefited most from post-war economic growth were those that established national institutions aimed at solving commitment and co-ordination problems without which neither wage moderation nor trade expansion could have taken place. Not all western European countries proved adept or willing to establish appropriate socio-economic institutions, the differing institutional responses going some way towards accounting for variations between countries in European growth performance. Britain conspicuously failed to develop the kind of domestic institutional arrangements that eventually emerged among her closest competitors. The country failed to address the distributional problem of who would bear the costs and who would reap the gains of structural change, failing to incorporate the legitimate concerns of employers about profits and the right to manage, and of the trade unions about redundancy and labour mobility. In consequence there was every likelihood that competing interests would continue to undermine a consensus to pursue growth.

What continues to interest me, therefore, is the range of influences upon economic change and development that might be less than fully appreciated if we focus only on key variables. The work of econometricians and others in providing a more robust and wide-ranging statistical underpinning to help us understand economic change over time must be welcomed. The greater part of the results, however, measure outcomes. It is as valuable an exercise to investigate, with as much rigour as the historical material allows, what combination of forces political, economic, attitudinal, or social and in what changing mix have played upon policy and performance in the past. In that way some sense can be gained of the complexity of historical change, however imperfect our conclusions or seemingly unscientific our approach. I remember as an undergraduate hearing of the conclusion of a detailed cost/benefit analysis, conducted according to the strictest economic criteria, concerning the relocation of a firm in either Leeds or Harrogate with the final judgement in favour of the former, only to learn that the latter had been chosen because the Managing Director's wife was more attracted by its leisure facilities and educational provision. Few now deny the importance of infrastructure but hearing the tale (apocryphal or not) only added to my sense of unease over historical determinism based only on what can be readily measured. Can we really understand the high growth years of Japan in the post-1945 period without accepting the critical role of consensus in politics and production? Will Britain's action and reaction within Europe stem only from a think-tank's assessment of relative economic gain or loss?

In many ways it should be easier and more gratifying today to teach recent economic history because students are bombarded whether they like it or not with media commentary on the importance of the exchange rate, on the significance of the service sector and on the impact of the public sector borrowing requirement, to take but a few examples. The fact that few of the horrors of economic mismanagement or the arguments over the priorities of public policy in the current climate are new to professional historians provides us with an opportunity to offer the wider perspective. In truth, however, most of us seem to be retreating more and more into specialised camps, writing for and to each other and often (with notable exceptions) in journals openly dedicated to a narrower and narrower audience.

Perhaps this does not matter as much as we might think it should. As economic historians join larger departments of 'old' History they might be persuaded to join the Vice Chancellors' chant that, after all, history is history however we cut it professionally. If colleagues are contributing RAE-worthy pieces on ecclesiastical history, gender history or economic history there is little reason for concern so long as the sum of the parts wins resources. Part of me accepts both the challenge and the opportunity facing 'academic artisans' working hard to mark their professional card with what our peers judge to be worthy or significant in a world where, we are also told, the monograph is dead and narrative is suspect. If my interest in economic history was to wane in such a climate, I suspect I would follow a vulgar instinct. The chance to write history backwards. To take a range of current preoccupations in the broad field of political economy and to trace the manner by which economic agents were often the victims of some ingrained prejudice, ignorance or obscurantism or when they believed themselves to be innovative, challenging and pro-active to find on reflection that they were the victims of what was only ever likely to be feasible or acceptable to vested interests, whatever theory or best practice suggested might be the outcome. Academics in post hope, of course, that there will be a continuous stream of undergraduates anxious to tread the evolutionary path of economic change, whatever the chosen time period or geographical scope. And yet there is an audience out there constantly told that when political posturing has all but ceased and when rhetoric is stilled 'it's the economy, stupid' that counts. This preoccupation with current economic affairs provides ample opportunity for gurus of various persuasions to provide 'the answer' to the uninitiated. Young and old alike are fed the same certainties about the sources of national competitiveness, comparative wealth, social and economic stability and welfare provision for all. We economic historians have heard and read it all before and sit open mouthed as a City stockbroker or financial analyst offers up a media soundbite of explanation that would be unworthy of a first year tutorial. But then, there is always that specialised article to write.

W. R. (Rick) **Garside** (b. 20. 11. 1944) was educated at the University of Leeds (BA, Ph.D). He is currently Professor of History at the University of Birmingham where his principle research interests are Government and the economy in the twentieth century, labour, industry and economic change, British and Japanese industrial policy since 1945. Publications include *British Unemployment 1919-1939. A study in Public Policy* (Cambridge University Press, 1990); *The Measurement of Unemployment, 1850-1979* (Blackwell, 1980); *Capitalism in Crisis.* (ed), Pinter 1993); *After the Slump. Industry and Politics in 1930s Britain and Germany* (ed.), (Lang 2000); *The Durham Miners, 1919-1960* (Allen and Unwin, 1970).

Is it Cold Out There? Economic History in a Business Climate

Edwin Green

Membership numbers in the Economic History Society have always been dominated by those who are *inside* the subject, teaching and researching in economic and social history in an academic environment. The great majority of the Society's members are past, present or future incumbents of history appointments in schools, colleges, universities and research institutes. As a contrast, this essay offers a view from the minority of the membership - those of us who are not economic historians in terms of academic appointments but who adhere to economic history in other types of career. It also offers the hope that economic and social history has an additional role and a future outside the teaching and research tradition.[1]

At first sight the business climate is not promising for economic history or for history in general. The imperatives of business apparently leave little room for the past. Those imperatives are shareholder value, profitability in the markets chosen by the business, high levels of service, and cost : income efficiency. This is a crude picture but it is still clear enough to suggest that history and economic history may not be a priority amongst the financial objectives of a going concern. Even when a company does recognise value in long-term care for its past, that company's attitude might change rapidly in the face of the sudden upheavals of business life. For the business horizon seems too short for history either in a generalised or a scholarly form. It is rare for the annual report of a company to look back or even give comparative figures for more than five years. More typically, today's business is assessed on each half year's results, or even the last quarter, rather than the familiar whole year.

In practice, the business climate for economic history is not nearly so grim. Company history and business archives, which are the two linked areas where I have worked for the last three decades, are examples of the hardiness of economic history outside the teaching and research traditions. In the UK, history and archives in a business setting have not only survived but have even thrived in the third quarter of the Society's life. This acclimatisation improves the opportunities not only for business historians but also for a wide range of historians, geographers, social scientists and other users of business archives.

By the early 1970s company histories by senior economic historians had become an accepted part of the public and internal presentation of major corporations. Examples included studies of Courtaulds by Donald Coleman, Royal Exchange Assurance by Barry Supple, and WD & HO Wills by Bernard Alford.[2] These projects helped to end the domination of what Forrest Capie has described as the 'great tome' tradition of business history ('books which, once you had put down, you could not pick up again').[3] Instead, the new approach provided organising ideas, full analysis, and a crusading zeal for the study of business history.

More recently this output has been both plentiful and robust. Work by the Business History Unit at the LSE and by other units has added variety and breadth to business history, while the flow of commissioned and freelance business histories has also been maintained. Over the last 20 years the number of entries for the Business Archives Council's Wadsworth Prize for Business History has averaged 10 each year. That same period has seen the completion of major commissioned histories such as the multi-volume histories of the British coal industry, BP, GKN and the Hongkong and Shanghai Banking Corporation.[4] Such projects were on an heroic scale, in which business gave its backing to the type of company history created by leading economic historians. That tradition continues to prosper in the shape of forthcoming histories of Unilever by Geoffrey Jones, British Railways (Terry Gourvish), and Wellcome (Roy Church). The durability of the company history tradition has also been maintained. Clive Trebilcock's second volume on the Phoenix Assurance survived not only the merger of the Phoenix with the Sun Alliance in 1984 but also the merger of the Sun Alliance with the Royal in 1996; it was published 15 years after the company's name had disappeared from the market - a tribute to the determination of the sponsors, the author and the publishers. Similarly the recent history of Standard Life by Michael Moss endured the stormy weather of the de-mutualisation debate in 1999 and 2000 and was published on time and in full at a time when many businesses might have turned their backs on history projects.[5]

Company history may be the most visible sign that economic history can grow in the business climate. Perhaps it is more important to economic and social historians, nonetheless, that the archives profession has made real gains in the modern business world. The number of formal company archives in the UK has increased from less than 10 in 1970 to 50 in 1985 and 87 by 1998. The financial sector is especially prominent, with 26 archive units in 1998, but the retail sector, the food and drink industries, the extractive industries, and the media are also well represented.[6] The population of business archivists (i.e. full-time professionals employed in the private sector) has increased in the same period from six in the late 1960s to over one hundred today. There are influential parallels in the USA. Ford (which should be the coldest climate of all if you listened to Henry Ford) has had a thriving business archive since 1951. The number of US companies making provision for their archives shot up from 44 in 1964 to 133 five years later and 200 by 1980. In the 1990s major US corporations such as American Express, Phillips Petroleum, Microsoft, Motorola and AIG added their weight by establishing their own corporate archives.[7]

Economic history has played its part in the modern development of business archives, certainly in the UK. In the late 1960s and early 1970s there was little formal training in business archives in comparison with the modules now available in the master's courses in archive administration. As a result early appointments in the business sector included economic historians or economists with archives experience as well as archivists moving from the public sector. In my own case economic history was the essential bridge into business archives. I was very fortunate that my mentors at Sussex, Malcolm Kitch and Michael Hawkins, strongly encouraged interest in original sources outside the well-trodden paths of the public records. My first research spells in the archives of a City livery company also pointed to the opportunities for history and archives in a business environment. Appointment as Hugh Cockerell's research assistant for the Insurance Records Survey at the City University in 1972 then led me into survey work, where economic history was already face-to-face with the business community.[8]

In the 1960s leading economic historians had argued the case for surveys of business archives and then carried them forward, notably Sydney Checkland, Peter Payne and Tony Slaven in the West of Scotland; Peter Mathias in the case of the shipping survey; and Leslie Pressnell in the first banking survey. Subsequently economic historians have continued to play a prominent part in the supervision of the many surveys carried out by the Business Archives Council and its sister Council in Scotland - as for example Peter Payne in the Company Archives Survey and Derek Oddy in the recent surveys of the pharmaceutical and veterinary medicine industries.[9]

By the early 1970s historians with a background or special interest in economic history were also being employed to carry out the practical discovery and listing work required in such surveys. That group included Pat Hudson, Charles Jones, Michael Moss and John Orbell and we all benefited from sharing information and ideas about the assessment and potential use of business collections. Some survey officers then moved to teaching and research in economic history. Others were appointed to business archives posts where (as a heresy to some in the archives world) we also became closely involved in history projects.

Surveys of business archives, with this strong influence from economic history, have generated double value for economic and social historians. Firstly they have encouraged businesses to ensure the future of their collections, either by establishing in-house archives or by depositing their archives in local record offices or other public archives. Hundreds of collections have been rescued in these ways in the last 30 years.[10] Secondly, and less obviously, the surveys have produced a generation of archivists who have been appointed as company archivists or as archivists in the public sector with special responsibility for business archives. Examples of former Business Archives Council staff in these roles include Alex Ritchie at the Historical Manuscripts Commission, Lesley Richmond at the University of Glasgow Business Records Centre, Alison Turton and Philip Winterbottom at the Royal Bank of Scotland, Serena Kelly at the Victoria and Albert Museum, and Melanie Aspey at the Rothschild Archive. In these and other cases, senior figures in business archives have worked in a tradition where the priorities and preoccupations of economic history have been well understood. This background can be highly relevant when the business archivist is placed in the role of unofficial supervisor to graduate and undergraduate researchers, particularly in the interpretation of the more difficult classes of business records or the business structures which lay behind those records.[11]

Hence the economic history and archives communities have continued to give mutual support in the business environment. Yet these favourable signs do not mean that the continuing stamina of company history and the development of business archives in the private sector are wholly or mainly for the greater good of social and economic history. I do not see senior businessmen hunched over the latest editions of the *Economic History Review* or *Business History* every three months. On the company history front, as Donald Coleman forcefully pointed out, business enthusiasm for history is only one possible element in the commissioning of a history. Other factors include the appetite for commemorating anniversaries; the public relations instinct to endow a company with the reputation and prestige of a major institution; and the related urge to imitate or compete with other business institutions.[12]

Similarly in business archives, the needs of the historian have been only one factor in the development of modern in-house collections. At HSBC Group Archives the number of enquiries from within the organisation outnumbers external enquiries (not just enquiries from historians) by over three to one. Many other company archives report a similar balance. This corporate use of archives includes management information about the organisation's history in particular markets, products or customer relationships; management information about business decisions or appointments; legal and statutory information for regulators, tax authorities, and special commissions and government enquiries; 'discovery' work, in which the company is required to answer claims or enquiries about the products or services which it has provided decades ago; media enquiries and marketing; and internal management education at different levels. An awareness of these other priorities is essential in the survival pack of any historian or archivist working in a business environment.

As to the future of history in the business climate, economic historians are likely to remain a small minority of users of business archives. In our own case at HSBC, at present historians provide less than 4% of the new enquiries which we receive each year and only 15% of all external enquiries. Both these percentages are on a declining trend over the last 20 years. That puts historians in the same statistical range as fine art specialists, family historians and direct media enquiries and is only just ahead of groups such as collectors and students of design and branding.[13] This pattern of demand has developed despite the accessibility of the Group's archives since the 1940s, the strong influence of economic historians and economists on the life of the collection, and a long list of publications based on the Group's records.

Many business archivists would prefer to see an increase in this level of use by economic and social historians. The records which have been saved and which are now open for research are matched to the preoccupations of the subject. Not least, economic and social historians are particularly well-equipped to harness and interpret these sources in comparison with other groups of external users. Unless the historian's voice is heard in this way, there is the persistent worry that his or her concerns will be forgotten or shouldered aside. Likewise the needs of the historian should surely be an important factor in decisions about the keeping of records. If the historian makes little use of those records, however, the preoccupations of other groups of users will continue to gain influence over the collecting policies of business archives in both the public and private sectors.

Mutual support between economic history and business archives is also needed in the training and recruitment of archivists. The four master's degree courses in archive administration in the UK are long-established and are in heavy demand. Many of the graduates from these courses are appointed, with great success, to posts with responsibility for business archives. Yet the number of graduates in economic and social history who apply and are then selected for these courses is tiny. At Liverpool, for example, in the five years from 1996-97 to 2000-1, only one graduate in economic and social history took the master's course alongside 37 history graduates (although some of these graduates may have studied options or modules in economic history).[14] This is a disappointing situation, in that archivists with a background or interest in economic history are ideally placed for posts in business archives. Their familiarity with the context and development of business and industry, together with their skills in quantitative methods, are valuable resources in dealing with the wide range of demands placed upon business archives. In this area the archives option should not be forgotten or ignored either by students or their supervisors. A larger showing in the archives profession by graduates in economic and social history would be a welcome boost for the future of business archives in the UK.

This essay does not claim that the business world offers an ideal climate for economic and social history. The subject does not offer business the direct, short-term answers which it often needs. In the related areas of company history and business archives, however, the climate is not so inhospitable as it might seem. Economic history has made gains in these areas in the last three decades, significantly improving the wider world's understanding of the history and importance of business. These gains in turn add to the opportunities for economic and social historians. Looking ahead, I do hope that members of the Society and their students can convert those opportunities into continuing activity in business history, into greater use of the rich resources of business archives, and even into careers in business archives.

Edwin Green (b. 16. 4. 1948) was educated at the University of Sussex. He is currently Group Archivist of HSBC Holdings plc, having originally joined the Group as Archivist of Midland Bank in 1974. He served as Deputy Chairman of the Business Archives Council from 1984 to 1995 and as Chairman from 1995 to 1999. His publications are mainly in the fields of banking history and business archives.

---

[1] I am very grateful to Lucy Newton and Sara Kinsey for their advice and comments on this essay.

[2] Coleman, D., *Courtaulds: An Economic and Social History*, 3 vols. (Oxford, 1969 and 1980); Supple, B.E., *The Royal Exchange Assurance. A History of British Insurance, 1720-1970* (Cambridge, 1970); Alford, B.W.E., *W.D.& H.O. Wills and the Development of the UK Tobacco Industry, 1786-1965* (London, 1973).

[3] Capie, F., 'The historiography of commercial banking', in Fase, M.M.G., Feldman, G.D. and Pohl, M (eds.), *How to Write the History of a Bank* (Aldershot, 1995), p.44.

[4] E.g. Church, R.A., *History of the British Coal Industry. Volume 2: 1830-1913. Victorian Pre-eminence* (Oxford, 1986); Ferrier, R.W., *The History of the British Petroleum Company. Volume 1: 1901-32* (Cambridge, 1982); Jones, E., *A History of GKN. Volume 1: Innovation and Enterprise, 1759-1918* (Basingstoke, 1987); King, F.H.H., *The History of The Hong Kong and Shanghai Banking Corporation*, 4 vols. (Cambridge, 1987-91). See also Mathias, P., 'The history of the firm: still an expanding business', in Fink, J., *Business Records and Business History* (Århus, 1998), pp. 47-61.

[5] Trebilcock, C., Phoenix Assurance and the Development of British Insurance, 2: The Era of the Insurance Giants, 1870-1984 (Cambridge, 1998); Moss, M.S., Standard Life. The Building of Europe's Largest Mutual Life Company, 1825-2000 (Edinburgh, 2000).

[6] I am indebted to John Orbell for this analysis, based on his notes for the Business Archives Council sessions at Liverpool University Centre for Archive Studies, 1998-99. See also Richmond, L., and Turton, A., *Directory of Corporate Archives* (London, 1997).

[7] Adkins, E.W., 'The development of business archives in the United States: an overview and a personal perspective', *American Archivist*, 60 (1997), pp. 8-33.

[8] Cockerell, H.A.L., and Green, E., *The British Insurance Business, 1547-1970. An Introduction and Guide to Historical Records in the United Kingdom* (London, 1976).

[9] Payne, P. (ed.), *Studies in Scottish Business History* (London, 1967); Mathias, P., and Pearsall, A.W.H., *Shipping: A Survey of Historical Records* (Newton Abbot, 1971); Pressnell, L.S., and Orbell, J., *A Guide to the Historical Records of British Banking* (Aldershot, 1985); Richmond, L., and Stockford, B., *Company Archives. The Survey of the Records of 100 of the First Registered Companies in England and Wales* (Aldershot, 1986).

[10] Green, E., 'Business archives in the United Kingdom', in Turton, A. (ed.), *Managing Business Archives* (London, 1991).

[11] Kinsey, S., and Newton, L., 'Bank archives and the user', in Pohl, M., *Bank Archives and the User* (Frankfurt, 1998), pp 28-38.

[12] Coleman, D., 'The uses and abuses of business history', *Business History*, XXIX (1987), pp.143-4.

[13] Other criteria such as the number of documents produced, or the time devoted to each user, give a higher score to the demand from historians but this demand still remains a small minority of usage.

[14] I am grateful to Caroline Williams, Director, Liverpool University Centre for Archive Studies, for this information.

Economic History: A Personal Journey

Knick Harley

Economic history is an examination of the dynamics of social change, particularly economic growth in both its successes and failures. It is also a journey of exploration. The intellectual excitement that comes when ideas and detailed archival evidence interact to produce unexpected discoveries is the great reward of scholarship. Economic history has been a journey that led me into unanticipated paths that appeared in the course of research. Because scholarship is a journey, everyone's mental map, although related through the scholarly community, contains unique perspectives.

We study history to understand human society. Traditionally history has focused on power, its distribution and transmittal but modern sensibilities direct attention away from this 'history as past politics' to the experiences of 'average persons'. In the modern era, economic growth and its variance has been the most pervasive force for change. So, to me, economic history is the study of economic growth. Interest in economic development and growth many years ago led me into formal training in economics and economics has provided both intellectually fascinating abstract logical thinking and a set of well-constructed tools for organising and understanding historical evidence. But modern economics' formal structure has often relegated serious attention to evidence about social behaviour to a secondary position. Within economics, economic history has proven an important exception in this regard (although some will accuse the 'new economic historians' of economics' preoccupation with theory at the expense of evidence). For me the excitement of discovering key evidence in archives has provided high rewards.

For my fellow students and I in Alex Gerschenkron's workshop in the Harvard economics department in the 1960s, economic history meant the study of 'modern economic growth' (the phrase is Simon Kuznets's – another teacher who influenced me greatly). We chose to study historical change with the tools of modern analytic economics, usually microeconomics that emphasised individual choice constrained by technology and market-determined prices. Because the growth economists showed that growth seemed to come mainly from technological change, many of us focused our research on this. Looking back, I see Albert Fishlow's work on railroads, Peter Temin's on American iron, Paul David's various projects, ostensibly on Chicago, Bob Zevin's on American cotton, Lars Sandberg on British cotton, Donald (now Deirdre) McCloskey on British iron and my work on shipping and shipbuilding all in that mould. Microeconomic training directed our attention to firms' profit-maximising choices, which we explored with detailed - often archival - historical evidence. We came to realise the complexity of technological change and that differences in factor costs and product detail led firms in different situations to different behaviour. At the same time, we found that even in industries that had often been criticised for inefficiency and technological conservatism managers' choices, conformed to profit maximisation within their market environments.

My thesis focused initially on the displacement of wooden sailing ships by metal steam ships in shipbuilding, and led naturally to the study of shipping. The technological change I was studying had driven freight rates down dramatically during the late nineteenth century fundamentally changing the nature of international trade. I was drawn to examine the impact of the near elimination of the barriers of distance on international trade and globalisation. The research led me to rethink Robert Fogel's famous analysis, which found a modest impact of American railroads and suggested a modest role for transportation in the history of the late nineteenth century. He showed that American railroads did not provide dramatically cheaper transportation than their water-based competitors, but since the same technology of iron and steam that lay behind the railroads had transformed water transportation his calculations underestimated the impact of the new technology. Furthermore, it became apparent to me that a focus on the United States overlooked much of the effect of transportation technology. Cheaper transportation in America mainly meant expansion of the frontier with little change in primary product prices; in Europe it meant cheaper primary products. Placing these developments into explicit modelling of global trade became my research agenda but I became somewhat diverted.

Economists' view of international trade involves general equilibrium analysis since trade theory emphasises the connection between imports and exports. By the 1980s advances in computer technology had made it possible to simulate realistic, if still highly simplified, general equilibrium models. The technique seemed the logical way to proceed with my research on market integration. The place to start, I felt, was John James's pioneering computational general equilibrium analysis of the American mid-nineteenth century tariff. James's analysis had concluded that the American tariff had allowed the American economy to increase the benefits it received from its near monopoly on raw cotton production but had little impact on the size of American manufacturing industries. As I became familiar with the details of James's model, I became convinced that the analysis was flawed by an oversimplified specification of the rest of the world. The model inadvertently conferred monopoly power in world food production as well as cotton production to America. Modifying the model to remove this feature fundamentally changed the results. The American tariff did not increase the benefits from America's cotton monopoly and American manufacturing industry seemed to depend on it heavily.

At about the same time, a nagging uneasiness I had long had teaching the British industrial revolution led me to examine the literature in detail. Deane and Cole's national income estimate formed the central focus of my vision but seemed difficult to reconcile with estimates of slow real wage growth. A worsened income distribution, of course, provided a possible reconciliation. Deane and Cole's estimates for the eighteenth century were indicative rather than definitive but Hoffmann's very differently based index of industrial production seemed to provide powerful independent support. My curiosity, however, led me to consider the possibility that the divergence between the wage data and the output estimates signalled a problem in the construction of the output estimates. Deane and Cole's procedure involved the somewhat improbable assumption that in many industries domestic sales grew at the same rate as British trade. As a matter of construction, Deane and Cole's acceleration of growth came from the late eighteenth century increase in trade. Hoffmann's index, for all the problems of data, seemed more satisfactory. Close inspection, however, showed that he had overweighted the growth of cotton textiles. When this was corrected, British output growth seemed to have been much slower and similar to the course of real wages. My conclusion, it turned out, reinforced independent work being done by Nick Crafts at about the same time. We have subsequently benefited from working together on these issues.

These two projects redirected my interests from the late nineteenth century international economy to the beginnings of industrialisation in Britain and America. I went back to the archives for detailed research into the cotton textile industries in both countries. My estimates of the impact of the American tariff were very sensitive to the likely effect of tariff reduction on the cotton textile industry. As a result, I felt compelled to examine price and cost data to establish the industry's vulnerability. My estimates of British industrial production growth depended to an important degree on the course of cotton textile prices between 1770 and 1841. In my initial work, I depended on unsatisfactory price information in secondary sources. Sharp criticism led me to look at primary material. The obvious archival material in Lancashire, to my astonishment, yielded a wealth of unexploited data. This has led me to extensive research on the British cotton industry during the industrial revolution - a topic on which I had long assumed there was little new to be said.

Perhaps because of the route I followed, I think of both British and American industrialisation firmly in their international context. I am convinced that international forces heavily influenced industrialisation in both Britain and American and that the special nature of both British and American industrialisation has made them unusual rather than general examples of modern economic growth. Consequently, I have come to believe that our careful study of the British and American experiences may have distorted our understanding of the beginnings of modern economic growth at least as much as it has illuminated it.

The simple picture of the history of modern economic growth discusses industrialisation and 'development' in which economic institutions change and evolve. This development process was often contrasted with 'mere growth' in which an economy expanded its traditional activities, usually resource-based agriculture and extraction. In much of the literature, particularly the literature in English, industrialisation is represented as a process that followed broadly similar lines in Britain and America. In both, technology first revolutionised textiles. The application of inanimate power to machinery in textile mills stimulated metallurgical and engineering industries. In due course, the railroads strengthened the demands for technically improved machinery and metals and industrialisation proceeded. This story, however, is somewhat suspect if, as I believe, international trade should be at the centre of the story. The Atlantic economy of the nineteenth century can be initially approached in terms of simple economist's models of international trade. An obvious paradigm sees the United States representing a resource abundant 'New World' and Britain representing a labour and capital abundant 'Old World'. During the century, declining transportation costs increased the opportunities for profitable trade and the integrated Atlantic economy emerged. Such a picture, of course, helps in understanding the main features of nineteenth century trade but it also raises a fundamental question. Trade theory indicates that two trading economies with significantly different resource endowments would experience divergence in economic structure. Yet the histories of Britain and America's industrialisation, and thus development, seemed strikingly similar.

In fact close investigation reveals that Britain and America's industrialisation were quite different. Britain was unique by being first. It was also unique because in cotton textiles and in metallurgy the technological breakthrough quite suddenly introduced a dramatic reduction in costs at a time when the Revolutionary and Napoleonic Wars prevented the spread of the new technology to other countries. As a result, British industrial growth rested primarily on technological leadership in a few important industries and not on factor supplies. The technological leadership was concentrated in textiles and metals. The ability of British firms in these industries to export and capture a large portion of world demand formed the basis of Britain's industrialisation. Industrialisation was enhanced by the structure of British agriculture, which released labour and eventually accepted food imports.

America's industrialisation was different. The industrial revolution created a surge in American exports, but the export was the cotton textile industry's raw material. Industrialisation came within a customs union that deflected the international specialisation which this demand for exports unleashed. Wartime isolation stimulated the initial American adoption of British textile innovations and then from 1816 the tariff provided vital protections for over a century. The key to American early manufacturing success lay in the fact that the United States was a large customs union with important agricultural regions that the tariff reserved to American manufacturing firms. Behind the tariff barrier, American conditions were unique. Manufacturing prices were largely disconnected from international prices. Labour scarcity and resource abundance - whose presence could have been expected to mitigate against industrialisation - caused American firms to follow different strategies of production and marketing than developed elsewhere. In due course in this environment, American firms developed mass production, modern corporations and world leadership.

All of this makes for interesting economic history and even interesting economics. But if we feel, as I think we should, that our main task is to understand the social processes that have generated modern economic growth, British and American examples show too many unique features to support much fruitful generalisation. Certainly careful investigation helps to identify special circumstances. Thus, I see the important generalisation from Crafts's and my research on the British industrial revolution to be that the industrial revolution was specific to a few industries, and less revolutionary and less important than it has generally been portrayed. The emergence of modern economic growth was a much more protracted process than usual stories suggest. Its roots lie not in the technology of Arkwright and Watt but in the social, and probably political, processes that worked over a longer period of time.

Where then do I envisage economic history and my research going? Certainly there are still many interesting photocopies and notes in my files that I extracted from archives over the years from which I was diverted. The search for the nature of modern economic growth remains the interesting issue. Britain and America's limitations as general example indicate an extension of research to other cases, particularly in continental Europe. As a 'New Economic Historian,' I see territory to be opened up with the aid of the maps and tools of economics and, undoubtedly due to my own history, that Alexander Gerschenkron's attempt to find a pattern in European diversity can still provide useful guidance. It is hardly surprising that various specifics in his outline have not stood up to detailed investigation. Nonetheless, I still find his idea that many of the structural and institutional differences among economies undergoing economic growth can be thought of as 'substitutes for missing prerequisites' fruitful. It seems to me that these substitutions can be understood with theoretical tools that modern economics has developed to think about problems of information, the relationship between principals and agents, and the nature of the firm. These tools provide ideas that can help us continue to develop better understanding of modern economic growth. With a focus on institutions and long-term processes, I find now that 'history as past politics' seems more central to my appreciation of economic history than it was when I saw myself as a young economist.

C. Knick Harley (b. 1943), received a BA in History and Economics from the College of Wooster in Wooster, Ohio and a Ph.D. in Economics from Harvard where he worked with Alexander Gerschenkron. He is currently a Professor of Economics at the University of Western Ontario. His research has concentrated on technological change, the Atlantic Economy and the industrial revolution (often in collaboration with N.F.R. Crafts).

My Economic History: From Revolutions to Routines

Mark Harrison

As a schoolboy I read Marx's *Communist Manifesto* of 1848. It stunned and excited me. I was captivated by the images of capitalism constantly revolutionising production and society, and the cheap prices of commodities battering down the Chinese walls of the barbarians. I didn't understand it at all; there was hardly anything in it to match my experience, apart from the stuff about the hypocrisy of the bourgeoisie on which I felt already pretty clued up. Parts of what Marx wrote seemed downright peculiar: marriage based on property? My parents' marriage was based on love! I asked my dad what he thought — was *any* of it true? He said he didn't know, which was honest and gave me permission to enquire further. I realised I *had* to know, and decided to study economics at university.

My first lectures in economic analysis were revelatory, and faintly disappointing. Aubrey Silberston told us about perfect competition and marginal cost pricing. A lad with a denim jacket, greasy hair, and a lower–class accent put his hand up and asked about exploitation. Silberston said he didn't think there was any. As that seemed to settle everything, I could not see what I was going to study over the next three years. My solution turned out to lie in economic history. We did Britain and France with Phyllis Deane and Brian Mitchell, Russia with Charles Feinstein, and India and Japan with W.J. MacPherson, and I still didn't understand, but I loved it.

Looking back I can see that my enthusiasms have changed. At that time I was gripped by the drama of revolutions: the industrial revolution, the French revolution, the revolution of 1848, the Russian revolution; smoking factories and locomotives, famines, and five–year plans. (Of the young, only the brain–dead were not in love with revolution: it was the late 1960s.) I believed in progress and the rationality of collective action. I also believed in quick results, and studied revolutions to see how they could be obtained. This was Cambridge after Keynes, so we learned hardly anything about the long run: all we *needed* to know was that the long run consists of a succession of short runs, in the course of which we will all one day be dead. I was instinctively antagonistic to writers like Alexander Gerschenkron who wrote persuasively about historical continuities in a long–run perspective. *Plus ça change, plus c'est le même chose*? I didn't believe it! I refused to read liberal critics of socialism like Peter Wiles. How dared they write so well?

The thread that bound us students into the Cambridge tradition was a belief that politics stood above economics. This belief was shared in various ways by Keynes and his successors; in

116

my time it made unlikely bedfellows out of Whitehall mandarins such as Nicholas Kaldor and Brian Reddaway, the tweedy Marxist Maurice Dobb, and Joan Robinson who hailed China's Cultural Revolution and wore clothing only from the Indian subcontinent. Keynes had thought the trick was to use correct ideas about economics to educate politicians, who would then do the obviously right thing. We saw politics as a means of making the world a better place, and government service as a higher calling.

Today we live in a more cynical world. The Soviet and Chinese experiments have failed. Inflation, the supply side, and the economics of the long run have taken their revenge. In America the use of governmental power to engineer a better society is abused as 'liberalism'. We understand that power corrupts, that politicians and public servants too are self–interested, that they will maximise utility, and that they will behave time–inconsistently if we let them and unless we punish them for it.

What is left of my early motivation, when I thought that the meaning of life lay in revolutions and that economic history could lay bare this meaning? Today I feel that the study of economic history is more thrilling than ever. One reason is philosophical. In a old pamphlet on a long–forgotten subject of immense obscurity my former comrade David Purdy wrote a sentence so wise that I committed it to memory from which I now paraphrase: 'instead of criticising history in the light of our ideals, the thing is criticise our ideals in the light of history'. In other words the verdict of history is not on Stalin or Hitler or Genghis Khan; it is on us, ourselves, and on our own preconceptions and illusions. As students of Soviet economic history we anxiously debated whether a decade of famines and purges had been an acceptable price to pay to overcome the centuries of backwardness and impoverishment. We were using our ideals to test history; we didn't see that history tests ideals, not the other way around. Like the historians that still get stressed over whether Stalin or Hitler was the bigger criminal, we were just arguing in the wrong court.

Besides, what if Stalinist terror had not accelerated but only complicated and held economic development back? As students we read Dobb's *Soviet Economic Development Since 1928*, then already in its *n*th edition; Dobb had been the first western scholar to treat the Soviet experience seriously in terms of academic economics. My contemporary Alison, daughter of the economic historian H.J. Habakkuk, argued that Dobb did not play fair: he ascribed Soviet economic difficulties before World War II to rearmament, without mentioning purges and repressions. At the time I passed this insight up, but later I understood that in a deep sense Alison was right. Whether or not Dobb's interpretation was correct, by being selective with the evidence he hadn't given history a fair chance to criticise his ideals. Since then I have seen my ideals tested, and maybe it was that they failed, or that their time had not yet come, but either way I want to know more!

Another reason that economic history has kept me in its thrall is practical: we know or can find out so much more about what happened in economic history than we did in 1970! We can look at the next 30 years after that: just think of everything that happened in them! There was an oil crisis and stagflation, European integration and monetary union, a world debt crisis, Thatcherism, China's Four Modernisations, an East Asian economic miracle (or was it?), and Gorbachev. Nelson Mandela walked to freedom, the Soviet Union collapsed, the cold war came to an end (or did it?), and the 'new economy' appeared (or did it?). It sounds naive, but when I started doing economic history I thought that history was all in the past; I didn't understand that it was still going on.

Naturally, because I am an economic historian of Russia, for me nothing in 'recent history' has compared with the end of the Soviet Union. And while the balance of happiness compared to pain that this event has brought to hundreds of millions of former Soviet citizens has so far been in doubt, it transformed my professional life without any equivocation. Suddenly I could do things that I'd never dreamed would be possible in my lifetime: travel back and forth with relative freedom, rent an apartment, buy a mate a drink in a bar, collaborate freely with Russian historians, sit in the archives, and read the once–secret documents that laid bare the inner working of the economic and statistical system. I felt like Schliemann discovering Troy. I shared the elation that German economic historians must have felt in 1945 when the archives of the Third Reich were thrown open. The best thing of all was that, if you were an economic historian, you didn't have to compete with the sensation–mongers for documents because they thought the stuff you wanted to see was *too boring*! All they wanted to know was whether Stalin murdered Kirov or whether Beriia was a paedophile. They couldn't care less about the allocation of budgetary resources or the monitoring of production and prices, although these things also profoundly shaped the lives of hundreds of millions of people. Finally, I witnessed at first hand the hyperinflationary disintegration of a major European economy, something that hadn't happened since the 1920s.

Today I am less interested than I used to be in revolutions themselves, and more interested in their preconditions and consequences, including what they change and what they leave the same. I am more willing to spot the continuities. I am more interested in analysing the long run, something for which a Cambridge education left me ill–equipped. I am more interested in economics, and in the scope and limits of its influence over politics. Getting to grips with the daily routine of the Soviet economic system seems more worth while than before, as well as far more feasible now that we have access to its copious paper traces in the Russian archives.

I have taken to heart Paul Gregory's distinction between historians and economic historians: he has argued that historians focus on events, anecdotes, and the aberrant behaviour of individuals, but *economic* historians have the task of trying to understand what was typical: long–run trends, routines, and averages. Typical of the Soviet system was the problems that officials faced when they tried to understand what people do when they work, and how hard they were working. One thing we can learn from the archives is just how important it was, and how difficult it was, for Soviet bureaucrats to solve this humdrum everyday problem. People may look busy, but what are they really up to? You can't tell by looking! Much of the mistrustfulness of the Soviet system stemmed from bureaucrats' realisation that people could seem to be working away to fulfil the plan, yet actually working to a different agenda, or not working at all. And how can you make them work harder? Planners were trying to reward producers for putting effort into plan tasks, and all the time producers were busy putting effort into trying to fool the planners. As for the secretiveness of the Soviet system, while some of it stemmed from real high–level national security considerations, we can see now that much of it was actually the result of low–level agents trying to defend the secret of what they were really doing when they wanted to appear to their superiors to be working to the plan.

I realise that I have written nothing about the things that divide economic historians in Britain today. Is economic history primarily about history or about economics — and, if economics, where does 'social' history fit in, if at all? Is economic history primarily analysis or narrative? Does it rest on fact or on rhetoric? I can contribute little to these issues except to say that I am proud to have trained as an economist and glad that the discipline of economics remains firmly stuck in nineteenth–century rationalism, safe from twentieth–century post–modernism. Above all what I do is fun and I don't think post–modernists get much fun. Wrapped up in their own discourse they don't get to do *real* things: design aircraft that fly, measure gravity, set Bank of England base rates, or understand time–inconsistent behaviour by central planners. The only thing that spoils the practice of economic history for me now is that, although the Soviet Union has gone, its habits are being continually recreated in British higher education by ever more burdensome regulation and inspection and proliferating performance indicators that are screwed ever tighter as people get better at fulfilling them and increased in number as people learn ways around them; in a Soviet context we called this mechanism the 'ratchet'.

At heart I am still a utopian. I look forward to a future society of material abundance in which the state has withered away, taking with it the HEFCE, the ESRC, the AHRB, the RAE and the QAA. Humanity's chief want will be to have fun, and we will all be able to do economic history to our hearts' content, for no reward but the sheer pleasure of it.

Mark Harrison (b. 6. 4. 1949). Undergraduate education and degrees: Clare College, Cambridge, 1967–70 (BA in Economics & Politics, 1970). Postgraduate education and degrees: St Antony's College, Oxford, 1970–73 (DPhil, 1974), Clare College, Cambridge, 1973–4. Employment: Department of Economics, University of Warwick where he is currently Professor of Economics. Co–editor (with John Barber) of *The Soviet defence–industry complex from Stalin to Khrushchev* (Macmillan, 2000), editor of *The economics of World War II: six great powers in international comparison* (Cambridge University Press, 1998), author of *Accounting for war: Soviet production, employment, and the defence burden, 1940–1945* (Cambridge University Press, 1996), co–editor (with R.W. Davies and S.G. Wheatcroft) of *The economic transformation of the Soviet Union, 1914–1945* (Cambridge University Press, 1994).

My Path to Economic History

Negley Harte

At my Lancashire grammar school in the late 1950s and early 1960s, O-level and A- level history was very political and constitutional, the sort of history laid out (as I came to know later - it was far from my understanding at the time) by Stubbs and by Pollard rather less than a century earlier. We did English seventeenth-century constitutional conflicts (Tanner and G.M. Trevelyan), we did British nineteenth-century political developments (Woodward, Ensor); Europe meant foreign policy and we did that (Grant and Temperley), and there was a special subject on the Italian Risorgimento (Trevelyan again). So far as I recall, we omitted the eighteenth century - no Namier, and certainly no T.S. Ashton.

This was the history that I did, so I must have to some extent found it interesting. But I was frustrated by it and I clearly remember trying to be interested in the history of the people, how actual individuals had experienced their lives and really coped with life and made their livings. There were two helpful strands in this pursuit. First, I read W.G. Hoskins. Two of his books were especially poured over: *The Making of the English Landscape* (1955) and *Local History in England* (1959). Why does the road turn here? Why is the church there in relation to the village? Why are the buildings of stone here and of brick there? Second, I discovered industrial archaeology just as it was emerging as a field of interest, or rather, I created it for myself just as it was being invented.

The mills of Lancashire were closing down throughout my childhood in the 1950s, many of them left empty and forlorn before the development of television assembly plants and the like, and long before the development of 'heritage sites'. I remember a man lovingly showing me the polished brasswork of the steam engine at one recently closed mill, saying sorrowfully that his father and his grandfather had been polishing it since 1870, and I recall wondering if continuing to polish the technology of the 1870s had anything to do with the decline in the 1950s. I now realise that this encapsulated an historical moment. I was present at another historic moment - the time when the Quaker Meeting in Rochdale voted to have the modest brass plaque saying 'John Bright worshipped here' removed from one of the benches where some Quakers had long thought it rankled as unQuakerly; Kenneth Moore, the calmly civilised Town Clerk of Rochdale, promptly pulled a screwdriver from the pocket of his tweed jacket and unscrewed it (a footnote to yet more G.M. Trevelyan). This must have been in 1962 or 1963, around the time I attended the first meeting of the Manchester Region Industrial Archaeology Society, of which I became one of the founder members.

I spent much time rummaging through all sorts of local history records in the splendid Central Library in Manchester and at the Public Libraries of Rochdale and of Bury. I tried to link maps showing farms and field patterns to urban building development, long before I knew that this was being pioneered by Jim Dyos elsewhere. I cycled round the south-west Pennines photographing weavers' windows, attempting to distinguish domestic loom premises from workshops, long before I knew of any other interest in the 'proto-factory', a useful but much later term. I became fascinated by ruined carding and scribbling mills on a few tributaries of the river Roch and their overgrown water-power systems. With a friend I embarked on a 'total history' of Ramsbottom and Peel and the Grants (the real 'Cheeryble Brothers' of Dickens), long before I had heard of *histoire totale*, much less of Stanley Chapman.

So in some key ways I had invented economic history for myself before I became conscious that others had in fact invented it before me. I applied in those pre-UCCA days to various universities to read history. My history master said prophetically, though I thought bizarrely at the time, that he saw me as 'a London man'. I applied to UCL, who turned me down, and to LSE, who accepted me, and then I noticed that LSE offered not only' history' but also 'economic history'.

When I went to the London School of Economics as a student, I discovered that there was an economic history beyond that I had developed for myself. My old economic history continued to show through. I tried to explain the interest of industrial archaeology to Donald Coleman, doubtless over-enthusing about my ruined carding mills on the Naden; 'I suppose its alright', said Donald suavely and devastatingly, 'if you can't think of a better reason for getting a girl up into the Pennines'. (I was only just discovering girls, and I found them much more threatening than industrial archaeology; it was many years before I realised that my interest in industrial archaeology was a sex substitute). My first-year moral tutor, as LSE then had for first-year students, was the distinguished Sovietologist Lenard Schapiro, and he was more tolerant when I explained my passion for local history; I remember his mild and bemused surprise when in my first term I asked him to sign my application for a reader's ticket at the Public Record Office.

But another vista was beginning to be opened up. 'What sort of agricultural system is revealed by the Gerefa?', asked Olive Coleman. 'Why is Postan always wrong about everything?', asked Tony Bridbury. 'It doesn't matter, does it, if the railway bends here or there - what matters is who financed it, and how...', said Malcolm Falkus. 'What impact might the spread of the wearing of artificial teeth have on entrepreneurial decline in late nineteenth-century Britain?', asked Theo Barker. Teachers asked questions. I had been used to teachers providing information. Some of their information had not excited me, so I had tracked down other information. But now a new world opened up. Facts were OK, but they needed to be shaped into answers.

I realised that there had to be questions before there could be answers. I realised that the concerns of many of the social sciences posed questions that historians could speculate about and formulate arguments towards answers. I went, of course, to Karl Popper's lectures, and also those of Lord Robbins, and Bob McKenzie's, and I discovered that there was a world of intellectual power to be set alongside surveying weavers' cottages in the Pennines. And above all there was Jack Fisher, the Professor of Economic History at the LSE, apparently astride all the social sciences, well-read and knowledgeable about pre-industrial England and virtually everything else. He was the first professor I ever met, and he was a transforming influence, wonderfully irreverent, fearless, witty and inspirational. I have tried to pay tribute to Jack's powerful influence in a few paragraphs in *London and the English Economy, 1500-1700*, edited by P.J. Corfield and N.B. Harte (Hambledon Press, 1990).

The transformation from my own economic history into the economic history tradition was not blinding or sudden. It was a gradual process. As it happened, at LSE in those mid-1960s years, there were some engagingly powerful students as well as some captivatingly powerful teachers. One wonderful summer - was it '64 or '65? - with David Ormrod and Jim Higgins, by happy chance fellow Lancastrians and the best fellow students one could possibly have, I cycled around various ruins in the area of Wigan and around Warrington and the length of the Sankey Canal, we went on a pilgrimage to Arkwright's mill at Cromford, and we drove off to Shropshire counting iron gravestones.

The visual and the intellectual gradually merged, much helped by Robin Craig - another fellow student of tremendous energy and influence, from whom I learnt the pleasures of seeking out and acquiring books. I already had a passion for antiquarian bookshops, but Robin fired me and made me read the books too. Jack Fisher loved acquiring books and he loved reading them and pointing out their inadequacies.

By 1969, when I was appointed to a Lectureship in Economic History at University College London, I felt a fully-fledged economic historian in various ways, conscious of the two different routes that had led me to the field, a subject that was self-consciously flourishing and booming and growing, as 'economic history' or 'economic and social history' evidently then was.

Lots of students wanted to do the Industrial Revolution in the 1970s and1980s, but then it fell off . . . Alan Bennett-esque-phrasing, but I remained committed to the economic history of what could be now a past heyday. London and Vienna and Venice and Berkeley, California, came to replace Rochdale and Bury in my life, and other important interests and concerns were developed. The roundabouts were not shown on the map, but the original path was well-trodden.

Negley Harte (b. 1943) was educated at LSE and has spent most of his career teaching at University College London with spells at Berkley. He is currently Senior Lecturer in Economic History at University College and Public Orator of the University of London. He has written histories of UCL, on the history of economic history and about various aspects of the production and consumption of textiles. He is now preparing *The Wig Interpretation of History*.

What Economic History Has Meant to Me

Max Hartwell

Economic history has given me a privileged life as an academic, has been the source of the intellectual problems that have dominated my thinking, and has given me a sense of purpose and a firm commitment to a life of scholarship based on critical inquiry. I describe my life as privileged with grateful conviction. Academic life is remarkably free, is well rewarded, is largely self-disciplined, and allows a degree of individual autonomy that is unique in the world of work. And, most important, I have had a working life in the company of clever young people who, generally, have been interesting to be with, and rewarding to teach. The abiding characteristics of the young, in my experience of half a century of close association, are energy and enthusiasm, curiosity and idealism, generosity and loyalty, a love of argument, a certainty of views bordering on arrogance and a proneness for fashion, whether in ideas or clothes. It would be invidious to mention individual students for their virtues or failings, so I mention only the first and the last students I supervised in Oxford as examples of the many students from whom I have learned so much: Patrick O'Brien, the first, and Anne Hardy, the last. Argument – debate in the form of a Socratic dialogue – is the essence of good teaching and controversy enlivens and clarifies thought and understanding. In my case, controversy was inevitable because my teaching life spanned a period when all academic gods were on the left whereas I had a pluralist view of society and institutions, seeing historical outcomes as the complex consequence of competing and co-operative forces. I was, and am, a radical liberal of the J.S. Mill and Adam Smith school: radical in the sense of believing that there are no given authorities and that authorities are only as good as their evidence and reasoning; and liberal in the sense that the individual, with varying degrees of autonomy, is the key actor in history, and that the good society, recognising individual differences, evolves institutions which reconcile those differences without serious conflict and which encourage individual enterprise and co-operative voluntary associations for a wide variety of purposes. I am sure that the constant company of the young sharpened my intellect, challenged my views, and made me firmly sympathise with them, even when they were demonstrably wrong, which they often were. And when they were wrong I felt that my task was to correct error, but not to indoctrinate. Indeed, the students with whom I had the least sympathy were those who accepted my views uncritically, although I always reminded them that the authority about whom they should be most critical was the one who teaches them!

Being an academic in any of the humanities or social sciences would surely have given me the sort of life I describe above. But being an economic historian had the particular advantage of making me aware of two historical phenomena which have dominated my intellectual endeavours, my teaching and my research. The first is what nineteenth-century social theorists called 'progress', but which I prefer to call very long term growth, the long haul from caves to skyscrapers. Why are we not still ape-like creatures, inhabiting caves? How can change and progress be explained? But equally important, how to explain dissimilarity, why some societies have not progressed, and why some societies grew more slowly than others, so that today different societies have different levels of progress? And why some societies have stagnated, declined, or disappeared? Interest in these questions was stimulated by my research on the histories of colonial Australia in the convict era, 1788 to 1850, and of industrial revolution England between 1750 and 1850. More interesting, and more important would have been to explain the progress of ancient Greece to produce that remarkable Greek civilisation of the fifth century BC, and the decline of ancient Rome, perhaps the greatest decline and fall of a civilisation in history, but I lacked the linguistic skills which would have allowed me to study ancient civilisations more seriously than I did for lectures on very long term growth.

I concluded on the basis of a study of economic change during the period 1750-1850, both in Australia and England, and of a wider reading about economic change over history, that growth of any duration cannot be explained by a simple formula, but only by a complex combination over time of changes in the classical factors of production - population, technology and capital (including human capital) - operating in a changing institutional context of the state and its agencies, and of law, custom and values. At any time entrepreneurs, seeing opportunities, initiate economic growth which is cumulative. But conditions varied from area to area, and over time, so that each growth path has been unique. For example there have been many industrial revolutions following 'the industrial revolution', and all of them different.

The second great problem that economic history gave me was how to explain historical controversy: why, on the basis of existing evidence, historians came to different explanations of what happened in the past. Two controversies stimulated my interest: whether Australia was a victim of imperialist exploitation; and whether the Marxist thesis of the immiseration of the working classes in a capitalist economy explained the standard of living of the English worker during the industrial revolution. It was obvious to me that the growth of Australia was a success story in a period of increasingly liberal policies in Britain, of increasing self-government in Australia, and of a mutually beneficial relationship between Britain and Australia involving migration, capital exports, and a growing demand for colonial exports to provide raw materials, especially wool, for the rapidly expanding industries of the industrial revolution, especially the woollen and worsted industries of Yorkshire. Workers, both in Australia and Britain, benefited, as the evidence clearly demonstrates. But historians disagreed on the consequences of the industrial revolution for the mass of the British population, and often disagreed disagreeably. Why?

I can best answer these questions by showing how my awareness of them developed, first at school, and then at teachers' college and university. I have always been suspicious of autobiographies in which the author has a life-enduring world view at a very early age, yet it is certain that in my case my growing up in a small and remote Australian village had an important impact on my view of the world and how it worked. The village was Red Range, near a small town, Glen Innes, about 450 miles from Sydney on the northern tablelands of New South Wales. The village, 13 miles from the town, was the centre of a small community of hard-working small farmers who were self-reliant, independent and resilient, and who prospered, or not, through their own efforts. They were good neighbours, and co-operated voluntarily to produce those goods which made a hard-working life more tolerable: sport (cricket and tennis), community singing and dancing, tea and supper parties (for gossip and camaraderie), picnics (especially for fruit-picking, particularly blackberries), bush walking and shooting (especially of that universal nuisance, the rabbit). There were three shops in the village, a butcher, a baker and a country store which sold necessities like tea, sugar and kerosene. There was no piped water, no gas or electricity, few cars and many horses. Mail came three times a week. There was a dirt-surfaced road to Glen Innes, and no bus services.

There was little awareness of the state and its agencies, except at election time, and the only continuous evidence of government was a small school (my father was the schoolteacher) and a post office with one employee – a postmistress – and the only phone in the village. With one or two teachers, the method of teaching was to teach one class, perhaps half a dozen students, verbally, while other classes worked on assignments with the help of wall charts.

One such chart, I believe, influenced me permanently. It was headed 'The Growth of an Empire Based on Political Freedom', the growth being charted by a series of dates and events, beginning with 'Magna Carta 1215' and ending with 'Australian Federation 1901'. Important also was a subject called 'Civics', which explained the responsibility of the citizen in a democracy, the Australian constitution, the parliamentary system, and the agencies of government which provided, for example, education and police. Once a week, the school was assembled in front of the Australian flag and we chanted: 'I honour my God, I serve my King, I salute my flag.'

The word 'empire' had particular meaning for us, although I never heard the word 'imperialism' until I went to university. We were proud to be part of world-wide empire 'on which the sun never sets', because to be a small colony in a large empire enhanced our importance and increased our self-respect. Also it gave opportunities to assert ourselves as a nation, whether it was playing against, or fighting beside, the British. And Britain gave us economic strength, being the provider of capital and immigrants, and the market for our products, especially wool. When I was told later that we were being exploited and that our identity was prejudiced by British economic and cultural imperialism, I was staggered by the implausibility of the claims! I grew up in the days of Donald Bradman's record-breaking batting and of Anzac Day celebrations on 25th April, the day in 1915 when Australians and New Zealanders landed at Gallipoli. Australians were at Gallipoli because they were British, and Australia still today can be understood only in terms of its Britishness. What is most significant about Australia is its democratic temper, its Westminster system of government, the common law, religious tolerance, education on the British model, a free press, British sports and, most important, the English language which has been modified to produce a vigorous and characteristic regional variant of 'the mother tongue'. We were at peace with the British background, and found the idea of being a victim of British imperialism implausible nonsense. The first book I wrote was an economic history of Van Diemen's Land (Tasmania) before 1850, whose rapid and successful development was the result of a mutually beneficial relationship with Britain.

Before going to Oxford I lectured on British economic history in the faculty of economics in Sydney University, and for the modern period relied heavily on Clapham and Ashton. I was most surprised, therefore, to find in England that Clapham was almost completely ignored, and that Ashton, though praised, was ignored when he generalised, in the last chapter of *The Industrial Revolution*, about the effect of industrialisation on living standards. I was not surprised, therefore, that the preferred interpretation of the social history of the industrial revolution came from Engels, Marx and the Hammonds. I now found myself disagreeing with both imperialism and immiseration, and asking why the most remarkable advances in technology, management and productivity could have reduced rather than increased living standards. The first article I published after arrival in England tried to explain the varying and contrasting interpretations of the industrial revolution, and I followed it with an article on the standard of living in England before 1840. I did not expect the extraordinarily hostile reaction to that article, nor the degree of passion it aroused. Why? Controversy, I knew, could stem from various sources, of which the following are the most important: the incompetence of some historians in a profession of varying talents; the discovery of new source material which negates existing interpretations; the failure to specify the questions being answered, so that historians talk at cross purposes; most important, the use of ideology and unchallenged authorities to prescribe solutions before research and inquiry.

Analysis of the controversy about the industrial revolution showed that the use of ideology and statistically biased sources were the main causes of disagreement. The ideologists were using history to make history and were determined to prove Marxist theories of historical change. They were more concerned with showing what should have happened than what did happen, and therefore felt that they had to denigrate those historians who disagreed with them. They were misled, perhaps, by the character of their main source, the British parliamentary papers which by their very nature were problem-oriented. Concern with the social problems that came with, or were accentuated by, industrialisation led to public inquiries which amassed a huge mass of material concerned with the ills of society, not its goods. In a process I call 'the public inquiry trap', parliament investigated, legislated and created bureaucracies of control, on the basis of inquiries which revealed real problems which, however, were not necessarily typical. The worst slums of London and Glasgow today do not accurately portray the condition of the working classes in modern Britain. Nor did they in the 1840s.

Controversy is surely good for history? Vigorous debate about 'contentious issues' stimulates research and the more careful scrutiny of evidence and conclusions. Much more is known about the industrial revolution as a result of the 'standard of living controversy'. The controversy, however, has meant much more to me than the need to refute error. It has inspired in me a recognition of the need for critical inquiry, a sense of responsibility about the writing of history, a passion for 'getting it right', a rejection of historical inevitability, a courage to criticise even the most admired and fashionable authorities, and a love of teaching and supervising research. The study of economic history has made me scrupulous about my own scholarship, and honestly objective in my use of evidence and in interpretation of that evidence. Objectivity comes down to a belief in the disinterested and critical examination of facts and problems; to a determination to understand and respect evidence from whatever source; to a belief that a proposition is either true or false, or that something is either the case or not the case; to a consideration of the grounds on which the validity of any generalisation depends; to a recognition that there is only one kind of truth and to a desire to seek that truth without rancour or prejudice; and to a belief in the art of civilised discourse rather than ill-tempered assertion.

Critical objectivity means, above all else, that the truth matters and that courage is necessary in the perpetual fight against prejudice and interest-based bias. Economic history has made me a serious historian, and one who believes that history matters, because it leads to a better understanding of the human condition in all its complexity. And in making me a better historian, I believe, it has also made me a better and wiser person. Many, I am sure, will disagree.

R. M. (Max) **Hartwell** (b. 11. 2. 1921) trained at the Universities of New England, Sydney and Oxford and subsequently taught at the Universities of Sydney, New South Wales, Oxford Virginia and Chicago. He has researched and written on the convict era in Australia, the industrial revolution in England and on the history of liberalism. He is currently Emeritus Fellow at Nuffield College, Oxford.

Agricultural History and Economic History

Michael Havinden

It is of course very flattering to be invited to contribute to this collection, but difficult to be certain what might be of interest. After having researched in agricultural history (British and Colonial) and taught economic and social history at the University of Exeter for 30 years, it seemed on reflection that a few thoughts on the importance of agricultural history and its relationship to the broader subject of economic and social history might be appropriate.

An inevitable, but still unfortunate, concomitant of modern scholarship is to direct every researcher into more and more narrow and specialised fields of study and to make the relationship of these specialised studies to the general historical picture increasingly difficult to achieve. Thus, agricultural history, already a sub-division of economic and social history, is broken down into many chronological and subject topics (agrarian structure, arable, pastoral, etc.) and has generated its own British Agricultural History Society and *Agricultural History Review*. These are admirable projects in their own right, but inevitably they tend to widen the division between agricultural and economic history and it requires constant effort to narrow the gap. The irony is that both subjects are scholarly abstractions; for despite the undoubted importance of economic activities throughout human history, there has always been more to life than earning a living and spending money. For scholarly purposes these divisions are no doubt essential, but we need always to be aware that in the last resort they are artificial constructs.

It is now perhaps time to consider the importance of agriculture in human history. It is not an accident that it is always referred to as the *primary* sector of any economy, for if the worst came to the worst we could give up our luxuries, dress in skins and live in caves, but we cannot give up eating and drinking (for most people at least three times a day). Hunting and gathering might sustain a tiny residual population, as it did for the first two million or so years of human history, but without agriculture, civilisation and current population levels would be impossible. All this is banally obvious, but in Britain, where the agricultural sector now employs only about 2 % of the working population, there is a tendency to downplay its significance, and even perhaps to regard it as a quaint hangover from the past-picturesque in its way, but not of any real significance in our high-tech society. But if we raise our eyes to a world level we see a very different picture, for worldwide, agriculture still remains by far the most important economic activity in the majority of countries, even if we cannot measure its total production in any completely accurate way, owing to the impossibility of measuring subsistence production, which is still so significant in Third World countries.

This leads me to a more personal reflection. I had the great privilege and pleasure of teaching economic history at the University of Sierra Leone in the late 1960s. This was literally a shattering experience which completely transformed my perception of economic and agricultural history, for instead of merely studying the pre-industrial economy, one actually lived in it and experienced it as if living in a time-warp. Exact comparisons with an earlier phase of European history are not really appropriate, but at that time Sierra Leone (then an orderly and peaceful country not yet torn apart by internal strife) had literally *no* industry of any sort, and hardly any services either. When my spectacles broke they had to be sent to London to be mended! This caused me two weeks of considerable inconvenience. The only two hotels in the country were in the capitol, Freetown, which did not exactly facilitate travelling. There was supposed to be a postal service and a telephone network, but they seldom worked. The roads were medieval, and the one railway which the former British colonial government had built, had been closed down (colonial rule had ended in 1963). In contrast to this archaic set-up there was an internal air service, and a large export of diamonds and iron ore to Europe and Japan. In that way the modern world had impinged on the country and partially shattered its 'medieval' image.

Nevertheless the great bulk of the population still lived by subsistence agriculture carried out in a timeless cycle of shifting cultivation, in which they circled their village each year, burning down a section of the surrounding forest to grow dry rice, vegetables and fruit. Much of the work was carried out communally, but each family harvested its own crops. In such a system there could be no question of individual private ownership of the land, but each village had its own land, and it was the chief's task to allocate a plot each year to each family according to its needs. Tropical fruits, peppers and spices were plentiful and the people seemed well nourished, though their diet was monotonous, and their simple huts almost devoid of furniture. The great majority of villages had no piped water, sanitation or electricity. They did however have a rich tradition of singing, dancing and music-making with home-made instruments, especially drums. To hear a village band in full swing was quite an experience. Hunting played a small part in their lives, and their small supplies of meat were mainly pork and chicken, since cattle and sheep could not survive in a tsetse-fly infested environment. They sometimes could buy dried fish brought by traders from the coast. Clothes were not really needed, but some people wove their own cloth from locally-grown cotton and made their own clothes. All this was so completely at variance with my previous European experience that it exercised a huge fascination and induced considerable thought about how economic development might take place, and a greatly renewed interest in how it actually had occurred in Europe. I believe every historian should undergo a similar experience if at all possible.

Perhaps at this stage, I might indulge myself briefly and say a few words about how I came to take up agricultural and economic history in the first place. After taking a history degree at Cambridge (about one-third of which was economic history) I spent seven years working on a small family farm and gaining some crucial agricultural experience; but it was a limited life, and an introduction to William Hoskins, the celebrated landscape and local historian, led to my decision to study for a B.Litt under his supervision at Oxford. The subject was the 'Rural Economy of Oxfordshire, 1580-1730' and it led to an intensive look at the Oxfordshire probate inventories, leading me to the conclusion that open-field agriculture had not been so backward as was then believed. Other scholars like Joan Thirsk, Eric Kerridge and Eric Jones were reaching the same conclusion, and it is gratifying that modern experts like Robert Allen, in his *Enclosure and the Yeoman* (Oxford, 1992) have reinforced this view based on a much wider study of the English midlands.

In 1960 I joined the research staff of the Museum of English Rural Life (now the Rural History Centre) at the University of Reading which led to my first book, *Estate Villages* (Reading, 1966) a study of the extensive Lockinge estate near Wantage. A Lectureship at the University of Exeter followed in 1965, and the Sierra Leone experience led to a broadening of my interests into British Colonial history, resulting in *Colonialism and Development.*

Britain and her Tropical Colonies, 1850-1960 (London 1993) with David Meredith, a former research student, now a Professor at the University of New South Wales in Sydney.

In conclusion there seems to be some evidence from the contraction in the number of University students taking the subject that Economic and Social History is declining. If so, this would be a tragedy, because in my view there is no subject equal to History- and its Economic and Social aspects in particular- in explaining how the modern world came to be as it is, and why different countries and societies are so varied in development and culture. It may be that schools are inadvertently to blame by beginning the subject with the Romans and proceeding to the Tudors and Stuarts and sometimes never reaching the modern world at all. This can make the subject seem irrelevant to modern life. I have often thought that perhaps history should be taught backwards, by beginning with a proper understanding of how modern economies and societies work and then moving backwards to show how they have evolved. We experimented with this at Exeter with some success.

Another possible reason for some students' lack of interest may arise from the increasing use of mathematics and statistics in economic history. The move towards more quantification is perfectly understandable and legitimate. The problem is that it is hard to make it appealing. Economic and Social History needs to be a lively, fascinating subject concerned with people and how they react to changing circumstances. History should never be relegated to a mere branch of mathematics if it is to captivate and enthral as it should.

Michael Havinden (b. London in 1928) was educated at Cambridge and Oxford Universities. He became Senior Lecturer in Economic and Social History and Dean of the Faculty of Social Studies at the University of Exeter. He was successively Secretary, Chairman and President of the British Agricultural History Society. He retired from Exeter in 1994 and is now a Senior Honorary Research Fellow at the Rural History Centre at the University of Reading.

The Value of a Grounding in Economic History

Richard L. Hills

The temptations as a boy to try and find out how things worked led me into taking to pieces clocks and other similar mechanisms. In those days, there were few electronic devices so it was often possible to make things run again by bending broken springs and similar dodges, to my great satisfaction. A couple of years' National Service in the Royal Artillery introduced me to new mechanical delights and motor vehicles. I am not certain whether I spent more time at Cambridge reading economic history under Peter Mathias or repairing a vintage car (which I still own and am still repairing).

It was while the National Health Service was trying to repair the damage done to a leg by a falling rock when I was instructing for the Outward Bound in the Lake District that the friends who were helping me restore the car took me to the Stretham Engine which they were also restoring. There I discovered a box full of records of the Waterbeach Level which this old steam engine had once drained. Some annual accounts (including the 'Special Drainage Account' of port and sherry), superintendents' and stokers' wages (one stoker became too large to fit through the manhole so he no longer had a little extra emolument for chipping scale off the inside of the boiler), purchase of coal, engine repairs, rainfall figures, hours run by the engine and other details were all there covering many years. These gave a glimpse of a microcosm of one small drainage area which had to be set against a more general background. So I launched into my first post-graduate research and book.

Why should the Great Level of the Fens have pioneered the use of the steam engine for land drainage when it might have been thought that other places, such as the Netherlands, the Norfolk Broads or the Somerset Levels, could have been earlier? This is where the economic background lying behind the various different industries which I have studied down the years has always been important for pointing to questions that ought to be asked, although, through lack of records, frequently I have not been able to find answers. Sadly, so often in my research, I have not been able to link technical developments with economic performance. Some reasons for the lead in drainage by steam engines in the Fens were lack of wind when compared with both the Netherlands and Norfolk where the life of windmills was prolonged, cheaper coal than the Netherlands due to taxation (or the removal of it in the case of the Fens in 1830), and less rainfall when compared with the Somerset Levels. But, ultimately, in the Fens it was a change in agricultural practices to a wheat growing country which made the extra capital expenses and running costs of steam engines a viable venture for the farmers. Here technological change was clearly supported by economic factors, although lack of figures, for say the incomes of individual farmers, made this difficult to prove.

My work on both the textile and paper industries has taken a different line because who am I to compete with such doyens as Chaloner or Musson in the textile world or Coleman on the paper scene. However, what I have written I hope may be of benefit to economic historians because I have studied the techniques which some of the famous inventors such as Hargreaves, Arkwright or Nicholas Louis Robert employed. An invention must be an advance on previous devices if it is to be adopted, and, implicit in that, must normally be economies in some form or another. I hope I have shown some of the limitations of the spinning jenny - a back-breaking machine to demonstrate with both hands doing different movements, as for winding on the spun yarn,... How nice to be able to sit back and watch Arkwrights' water-frame spin away on its own quite easily. But I still ponder how Arkwright was able to build a water-powered mill, fill it with all sorts of machines and yet sell cotton yarn more cheaply than that produced by women sitting at home with spinning wheels. I know from experience through spinning wool for my own pullovers just how slow is a hand wheel, but I have never seen production figures to compare with the early spinning machines (did someone mention quality ?).

Another machine about which there are still many misconceptions is the Jacquard pattern selection method for weaving. It is so often taken for granted that this presumed first computer-controlled device immediately caused a revolution in pattern weaving from the time it was patented in 1800 - far from it. The machine itself needed many mechanical improvements before it worked satisfactorily and easily, so it does not seem to have become popular until after 1830 in Britain. Another reason was the limitation in size of patterns which could be woven with it. But its great advantages were that the patterns controlled by the punched cards could be changed quickly and that it could be worked by only the weaver himself. Look at the superb patterned silk brocades and other cloth of the eighteenth century which were woven long before Jacquard. They needed a weaver as well as the drawboy who selected the pattern. The memory system on these looms was a series of loops of string with which the drawboy pulled out the appropriate warp threads through the harness, a time-consuming procedure but nothing compared with having to retie all the loops for a new pattern. Loops of string are not what is normally considered as an early computer memory. The economic advantages of the Jacquard are easy to see with hindsight but it took a long time before it could compete with the earlier system.

Yet it is in the fields of textiles and papermaking particularly that the old hand production methods have been a long time dying, in some ways defying economics. While in the 1830s an Andrew Ure could praise the regularity of cotton cloth woven on Roberts' power looms, the later arts and crafts movements have stressed the individuality of hand-made products. The snob appeal of the craft product makes no economic sense other than keeping alive what would otherwise be hopelessly uneconomic industries. A sheet of handmade paper has few advantages over that produced on a machine while its cost is many times greater. But at least its continued production does enable us to still see historic production methods and so have a better appreciation of why they have become uneconomic.

It is for these reasons that I tried so hard, when I was establishing the North Western Museum of Science and Industry in Manchester, to preserve the exhibits in working order and have them demonstrated regularly. Take John Kay's flying shuttle for example. It made one weaver redundant on broad cloth and increased productivity, hence the economic reasons for its introduction. But the flying shuttle could not have been dreamed up over night and must have taken a lot of experimentation before it worked properly. Kay may have been inspired by the way shuttles on contemporary ribbon looms were operated. Then he had to fit wheels which have to be angled to keep the shuttle running against the reed; the shuttle had to be shaped to fit against both vertical reed and horizontal race which were not at right-angles; the earlier loose pirn with the weft had to be changed for a fixed one wound differently and so on. So much of our understanding about this came through actually operating looms. Or take another example;

run one of the Otto-Langen atmospheric gas engines and it is easy to appreciate why it was a dead-end design and Otto only escaped from this impasse through the four-stroke engine. Sadly today in this museum, now at Liverpool Road in Manchester, fewer and fewer of these exhibits are being demonstrated so that fewer of our young people will be able to understand the origins of our present civilisation.

Another aspect of my work at the museum was the preservation of industrial archives. There was little interest and few attempts by other depositories to go to industries which were closing down in the sixties and seventies and preserve their records. What I could do at the museum with our minuscule staff and resources was little enough in view of the immense contributions made by industrialists in the Manchester region to technical development and the firms founded thereon. Often, while I was able to save something about the products, I was unable to preserve much about the financial performance. One partial exception was the famous railway locomotive building firm of Beyer, Peacock. This was partly achieved through the late Lord Bowden, then principal of U.M.I.S.T., on the understanding that the archives would be used for academic study and not profit. We had no museum, no money - I heard the Chief Accountant tell the Head Draughtsman, 'Well if we can't sell it, let Mr. Hills have it for the museum'. We had to move a ton and a half of glass plate negatives and I don't know how many tons of drawings and books of records (luckily the vintage car was running then). It is probably the most extensive archive of any private locomotive builder in Britain, but that meant that, when I was writing its history, I was unable to compare its economic performance with any of its competitors. But even here we come back to a problem of Economic History - how did this company with its reputation for producing some of the highest quality and costly locomotives, survive to be the last of the large private manufacturers, defying usual economic practices ?

Through having been the founding Curator of the North Western Museum of Science and Industry, I have been fortunate in being involved with so many different industries. I hope that what I have been able to write about some of them will explain to others, particularly economic historians, some of the stages in technological development on which they can build their own studies and interpretations on different aspects. Yet I still wish that I could have included in my work more economic aspects, which is especially so in the new biography that I am writing on James Watt, the improver of the steam engine. In all the mass of papers which make up the Muirhead, the Boulton & Watt and the James Watt Papers at Birmingham, there are few details about his personal finances. The canny Scot played his cards very close to his chest and told Boulton the truth, but not quite the whole truth, about debts incurred in Glasgow before they formed their steam engine partnership. Roebuck had taken over Watt's debts amounting to around £ 1,000 but £750 of that was to finance a merchanting venture for a shop and not the steam engine. Economic History can have its lighter side and put flesh onto the bare bones of technical history.

Richard L. Hills (b. 1. 9. 1936) was educated at Queens' College Cambridge, B.A. and M.A. Imperial College, London, D.I.C. University of Manchester Institute of Science and Industry, Ph.D. Now Honorary Reader in History of Science and Technology. North Western Museum of Science and Technology, founding Curator, 1968-1985. British Association of Paper Historians, founding Chairman, 1988.

Economic history – Part of My Life
My Life – Not Only Economic History

Riitta Hjerppe

When my economics teacher Professor Niitamo recruited me, a young student, as research assistant on his research project, I had no way of knowing that this would put me on the path leading to where I am today, giving direction to my entire career. Professor Niitamo, Director of the National Accounts in the Central Statistical Office of Finland, was also an exceptionally active teacher. He had gathered a lively group of young researchers and students around him to develop national accounting. Partly the same group also worked on the historical national accounts of Finland.

To be chosen as a research assistant was an unbelievable experience for a student. All around me people were discussing social sciences, real economic and social issues, national accounting and research. Instead of just reading about research work, I was doing it myself, experiencing the joys of searching and finding, getting insights. We were all highly enthusiastic and worked very hard, making friends with other like-minded young people. Later on, these friendships have proved to be of great value: many of my student friends have become holders of high offices in the civil service, university teachers, directors in various interest groups, etc.

Somewhat later, when the Department of Economic and Social History was established within the University of Helsinki, this Department offered working space for a young researcher, although ties to the Central Statistical Office were maintained. In the beginning it was a very small-scale operation: the entire research and teaching staff working in Economic and Social History consisted of one Professor, an Assistant and a few researchers. The historical national accounts of the Finnish economy, or Growth Studies – as we called it among ourselves – became a major part of the research carried out within the Department of Economic and Social History and the main research object for me. It functioned as a channel of scientific research training. It was one of the Department's links with the rest of the social science research field, especially with the Central Statistical Office, later on Statistics Finland, with economic research institutions, with the Economics Department and with the researchers working at the Bank of Finland, the Finnish central bank. A major role in these linkages was played by my husband, Dr. Reino Hjerppe, working as an economist at the Central Statistical Office and the Economics Department of the University. My economic and social history Professor, Sven-Erik Åström, also gave me his untiring encouragement, although he never worked in the historical national accounts field himself.

The Growth Studies constituted a huge project: a total of 15 works were published within it. From time to time, long, extensive research projects tend to land in financial difficulties threatening their continued existence and completion. This is what happened with the Growth Studies. At the final stages, the Bank of Finland was pressured, after a long break in the studies, to complete the project, initiated in 1959. The final report *Finnish Economy 1860-1985, Growth and Structural Change* was published in Finnish and English in the 1980s. Even though my contact with the daily running of the Bank of Finland remained a tenuous one, owing to the intensive research work, it gave me valuable acquaintances and friends.

The historical national accounts project was an international one as well. The Nobel Laureate Simon Kuznets had awakened enthusiasm for this theme in researchers in several countries; it was at Kuznets's behest that the Finnish study was launched. An almost accidental meeting in the mid-1970s between myself and Angus Maddison, an OECD researcher and later Professor in the University of Groningen, led to many interesting discussions, correspondence and invitations to international conferences for which I have been deeply grateful. It felt great to go, as a Finnish researcher, and present our first results and meet with other researchers 'speaking the same language'. They opened up the next 'new world'. Ties with other researchers, especially the Nordic ones, helped our work along.

Personally, the completion of the historical national accounts project gave me a new insight in long-range dynamic interaction between the progress of the economy and structural change. It opened new vistas into the workings of society and its change, although the time series as such do not directly reveal the reasons behind the change. This society, which I as a young student had started to study, opened up as a logical whole, a fascinating network of macro economic relationships, held together by the laws and regularities of the economy.

This understanding got its reward when I was invited to work as an economist at the Economics Department of the Ministry of Finance in the 1980s, at a point when my chances of a continued University career seemed to dry up. Forecasting economic trends and preparatory work in the economic policy field began with a surprising ease, as I could build on the groundwork of national accounting and against the perspective of the economic history trends. It was very concrete everyday use of my knowledge of economic history. At the same time, it was very interesting to learn to know an entirely different world, where the long-range approach of the research field was replaced by rather short-term assignments, but the constant curiosity of a researcher could still be applied. And what could be more interesting than standing close by when the means of bringing about recovery in the economy of a nation is discussed or choices are made resulting in a balance between various economic policy measures of the government.

The 1990s depression in Finland – even though an economic setback was expected in the late 1980s – came as a surprise to everybody in its depth. It caused serious depressions in the minds of the forecasting economists as well and reminded us that economics is not an exact science and that society occasionally acts in very unexpected ways. Information on economic history was again in high demand and I buried myself in the problems of the 1930s depression. Although Finnish society in the early 1990s was in many respects totally different from that of the 1930s, there were plenty of common features as well: the dangerously deep depression in the building sector and the slow recovery; the public sector troubles, with diminishing flows of revenue but no automatic reduction in outlays, where painful choices must be made; or regularities in foreign trade (during a depression, with low expectations, imports decline more than exports and for a longer period). While emerging from a deep depression, Finnish pre-depression trade deficits turned into rapid productivity growth, high competitiveness and exports surpluses, enabling the state to pay off the foreign debts.

The sudden opportunity systematically to follow daily economic progress also opened vistas that made it possible for me to link these two, today's economics and economic history, firmly with my later teaching and research, now that I am again working in the University. It is a rewarding experience to see that the Finnish public knows to turn to the economic history people, in search for background for today's events. Inquiries from government representatives, from the Bank of Finland and the media give me great pleasure, because they show that we have not laboured in vain.

While my Growth Studies had a macro-economic orientation, my doctoral thesis acquainted me with business history. It brought along other kinds of domestic and international contacts. This versatility has been of great use, for example when I have been introducing my doctoral students to the international economic history researcher community. Both lines of study have given rise to new study ideas and brought new researcher contacts. Economic history is an indispensable part of my life. On trips both in Finland and abroad, I keep instinctively commenting on the economic history factors in the cultural environment. On the other hand, economic history has helped me establish a network of interesting friends both at home and abroad which, I hope, will be of benefit to my students as well.

Riitta Hjerppe (b. 3. 10. 1944) has worked in various teaching jobs in the Universities of Helsinki and Jyväskylä, as researcher at the Academy of Finland and the Bank of Finland as well as at the Economics Department of the Ministry of Finance. She has published major studies of the Finnish economy and on Finland's economic growth.

75 Years of the Economic History Society: Some Reflections

Eric Hobsbawm

What can one who has been a member of the Economic History Society for about 55 of its 75 years, contribute to the celebration of its anniversary? Not as much as one might suppose, for memory is at best a notoriously defective historical source, and its density is inversely proportionate to its length. Moreover, in the course of time I have got rid of such few records as I kept of dealings with the Society and the *Review*, in which I took a life subscription for £9 when I joined the Society (by far the most successful investment in my lifetime). Nevertheless, survivors are sufficiently scarce for even their fragmentary impressions of the first post-war years of the Society to have some marginal interest.

In my undergraduate days (1936-39) Economic History in Cambridge meant M.M. Postan, who had come to the Cambridge chair from the London School of Economics. Looking somewhat like a red-haired Neanderthal survivor and speaking through a heavy Russian accent, he was nevertheless so brilliant and compelling a lecturer that he filled Mill Lane at nine o'clock in the morning, and attracted even Arthur M. Schlesinger Jr., then a visiting young Harvard man who made no bones about his 'lack of skill (and interest) in economic history'. For the bright radical (i.e. Marxist) history students of the time economic history was in any case the only branch of the subject then taught in Cambridge which was relevant to their interests, so we also sacrificed breakfast to attend his lectures, because, though deeply hostile to Communism, he was the only one of our teachers who knew about Marx, Weber and the great central Europeans and Russians of the late nineteenth century, and took their arguments seriously enough to expound and criticise. Every one of his lectures – intellectual-rhetorical dramas in which a historical thesis was first expounded, then utterly dismantled, and finally replaced by his own version – was a holiday from interwar Cambridge insularity. What other don would have told us to read the young *Annales*, arranged to invite Marc Bloch to lecture, and presented him to us (justifiably) as the greatest living medievalist? In short, it was natural that, among the available labels on the bottles of Cambridge history, I should choose 'economic history' and, on returning to Cambridge from the war, join the Economic History Society, and publish my first article in a professional journal in the *Economic History Review* (New series vol. I, 2-3, 1949).

Economic history in Britain in the later 1940s was still a small, almost family affair, presided over by the ancient, leonine figure of R.H. Tawney, ash on his trousers, making his way to and from his destinations slowly, with a small rucksack. He seemed older than he was, perhaps because of his injuries in World War I, perhaps because in 1950 seventy years was still the biblical expectation of life. Economic history, unlike economics, was not high on the academic totem-pole - before the war the British Academy had only elected Tawney and Postan's predecessor, (Sir) John Clapham - and it was slow to rise until after the mid-1960s. Of course, the expansion of economic and social history was only just beginning.

The global boom in higher education, which was to multiply the library subscriptions to the *Review* sixfold in 15 years, did not begin until the 1960s, although the Society grew comfortably in the 1950s and – thanks to the help of the Royal Economic Society – the size of the *Review* expanded substantially. The Economic History Society had an individual membership of the order of 7-800, mostly invisible. Presumably they included a fair proportion of the 300 or so who wrote or reviewed the first 10 volumes of the new *Review* (1948-58), but the number of those who actually taught economic history in universities and those who took an active interest in the Society was considerably smaller. Theo Barker records the attendance at the annual meetings, on which the *Review* relied for some of its heavy-weight articles, at about 40-60, which tallies with memory. 'The field' therefore consisted of people who knew each other personally, or who knew of each other through their teachers and supervisors, even of people who had been in the same few jobs then available, to an extent difficult to conceive of in the academic mass society of the twenty-first century. On looking through volumes I-X of the post-1948 *Review*, I observe that at the time of publication I personally knew a majority, sometimes up to four fifths, of the authors of the articles in *every* volume.

What unified this minority even more, was the domination of the subject by Cambridge and London (overwhelmingly the LSE). Manchester, home of the history as well as the reality of the Industrial Revolution was still present as a tradition – Redford and Julia Mann of Wadsworth and Mann were silently, and T.S. Ashton, much more vocally, on the Council - but it was now less influential. However, with Ashton's move to the chair at LSE in 1944, the North had been integrated into the powerful Cambridge-LSE network, which had been reinforced, during the war, by the evacuation of the LSE to Cambridge. Economic history as such was not prominent in Oxford, until the arrival – from Cambridge – of H.J. (Sir John) Habakkuk, although one brilliant and controversial young Oxonian, Lawrence Stone, who was later to leave Oxford for Princeton, was associated with the Society, joining its Council for a time in 1950. However, in the initial post-war years there was another London-Cambridge unofficial network with economic history interests that reached into Oxford also – that of the Communist students of the 1930s. Whatever the change in their views since then, they had known each other as friends since student days. In 1952 the Society's officers and Council contained several members of this group.

Inevitably, in the immediate post-war years the Society relied on economic historians already established before the war. Very few undergraduates of the 1930s had got to that point yet, so there was a distinct generation gap, before they began to play a major role. Hrothgar Habakkuk was probably the first of the 1930s student generation to make it into the Establishment – as Postan's assistant editor from 1946, on the Council from 1949, followed on the Council (shortly before his then much commented battle with H.R. Trevor-Roper) by Lawrence Stone. By 1952 the pre-war generation was clearly established: Kenneth Berrill (LSE/Cambridge) became Hon. Sec., Kenneth Connell (LSE), Rodney Hilton (Oxford) and myself (Cambridge) joined the Council, followed by Joan Thirsk and, a few years later, W. Ashworth, M.W. Beresford and Sydney Checkland. By the middle 1950s the first of the post-war graduate generation were already appearing on Council, that is to say the great crop of the late 1940s LSE economic historians – Walter Minchinton and A.H. John (1955-56) followed by Donald Coleman and Ralph Davies (1960-61). (One notes, in retrospect, the failure of the Society to pay sufficient attention to their contemporary Sidney Pollard, one of our most distinguished and original economic historians, and one persistently underrated in this country.) By the later 1950s an even younger generation (Peter Mathias, Barry Supple, Theo Barker) was knocking on the door. By the 1960s the pre-war generations had been reduced to an honorary masthead of the *Review* (now edited by the young) and (omitting the representatives of the Royal Economic Society) to four out of 23 members of Council.

London had been the base of the Society and the *Review* before the war. It was the war and the Postan connection that transferred it largely to Cambridge. (There is no sign that Postan's predecessor, the formidable (Sir) John Clapham, had taken much interest in it before or after his retirement.) The Society emerged from the war with two Cambridge dons as Secretary and Treasurer, who were soon replaced in both these functions by another Cambridge don. The *Review* retained exclusively Cambridge editors and assistant editors from the end of the war until into the 1960s.

This was by no means due to the administrative or editorial talents of Mounia Postan himself, on which even his friends preferred not to dwell. Nor did post-war Cambridge produce economic history graduates in unusually large numbers, or compete with the LSE as an employment agency for them, although all economics undergraduates were taught and examined in the subject in a version rather different from the one intended for the historians. Indeed the links between the historians' economic history and the prestigious Cambridge Economics faculty were surprisingly tenuous, except for Kenneth Berrill, with a foot in both camps, who played an important role in the Society. Even though Austin Robinson was one of the Royal Economic Society's representatives on the Council, the only Cambridge economists who reviewed more than once in the first 10 years, seem to have been Robin Matthews, the late Harry Johnson and (the later Sir) Charles Carter. In retrospect the gap between the debates on population history at our conference in 1949 and later developments in historical demography is perhaps equally surprising.

However, Postan's *Review* could benefit from two advantages. The first was the absence of a specific department of economic history in Cambridge, which, as Peter Mathias has observed, 'discouraged disciplinary frontiers'.[1] Young Cambridge historians of much wider interest gravitated into the economic history orbit: Gallagher and Robinson, Henry Pelling and Asa Briggs, who reviewed extensively in the early volumes. More specialised economic historians broadened out into what they had always wanted to be: general historians, for example H.G. Koenigsberger and, for that matter, Charles Wilson who would presumably have succeeded Postan, had he not chosen the Cambridge chair of Modern History first. Postan's own medievalism helped, since (especially in Maitland's university) even the most unreconstructed traditional scholars allowed that in the Middle Ages some notice had to be taken of social and economic matters.

The second asset was the editor's unique familiarity and contacts with the economic and social history scene on the European continent, including Eastern Europe. Who else would have introduced me in the late 1940s to Witold Kula, not yet the great figure in Polish history?[2] His contacts were particularly close with France, which was to make him (with Fernand Braudel) the co-architect of the new International Economic History Association, a body run for several decades as a virtual Franco-British condominium. His contacts with the *Annales* team, as we have seen, went back to the 1930s and it was that review's own in-house scholar, Paul Leuillot, who supplied the first regular surveys of French writings on social and economic history (vols. I, II, V of the new series).

However, the most eminent French historian to take part in the Society's conferences at this time was the great Ernest Labrousse, pillar of the Sorbonne, former Chef-de-Cabinet to Leon Blum, and Braudel's predecessor and later rival as the patron of the Paris historical world. I recall acting as translator for him at one of our conferences, and receiving in turn a firm warning never to have anything to do with *white* Bordeaux wine, which he considered unworthy of any self-respecting French drinker.

Except for the Low Countries, with which other Cambridge economic historians had excellent relations, most post-war contacts with other European countries came through

France, and particularly through the contacts made at the Paris (and indeed largely *Annales*-organised) 1950 IXth International Congress of Historical Sciences, the first after the war. As the co-rapporteur on the medieval part of a section obscurely entitled 'Anthropology and Demography' (with Jean Dhondt of Belgium, Carlo Cipolla of Italy and Philippe Wolff of France, both well-represented in the first post-war volumes of the *Review*) and as sole rapporteur on medieval economic history, Postan was evidently the only British historian involved in planning the main Congress programme. At least I cannot otherwise explain why I found myself nominated to preside over the 'contemporary' part of a rather vaguely conceived section on 'Social History' – the first time the subject appeared at these Congresses – introducing (to my surprise) the brilliant Polish specialist on feudal crises and the sixteenth to seventeenth centuries, Marian Malowist, whose writings appeared not long after in the *Review*. (Richard Pipes of Harvard once told me that he had been taught history by Malowist in a *gymnasium* of eastern Poland between the wars, but as the communist schoolmaster was put in jail during the long vacation, he could only return his vacation essay to him, when Malowist visited Harvard many years later: he had kept it.)

For obvious reasons, reinforced by the financial and technical limitations of the post-war years, the bulk of the UK's economic historians worked on their own islands. Yet insofar as they looked overseas, they remained remarkably eurocentric, or 'imperiocentric', including a heterodox interest in the history of the formal and informal British empires, inherited from the pre-war Marxist fashion. It was represented in the early volumes of the *Review* by such articles as those by H.S. Ferns and Gallagher/Robinson. However, what must still surprise the observer, is the relative lack of interest in the economic history of the USA before the 1960s. The stateside historians who interested us were those who worked in British or European history, or in general rather than specifically North American problems, and these were also the ones most likely to turn up an our doorsteps, like David Landes, Charles Kindleberger, Rondo Cameron or Walt Rostow. The Comments, Revisions and Essays in Bibliography and Criticism of the first 10 volumes include articles on the Mycenean Tablets and Economic History and the Ural Metal Industry, but none on the specific economic history of the USA. This is all the more surprising as the *Review* could – and did – mobilise people in Cambridge with considerable interest in and knowledge of the USA such as D.W. Brogan and Frank Thistlethwaite, and lists of books and articles on the economic history of the USA and Canada (compiled by business historians) appeared in several years of the 1950s.

The truth is, that, in spite of its giant economic – and now military and political – presence, intellectually the USA was not then a prominent part of the world of British economic historians. I can only note this, without being able to explain it. What changed this was not so much the competition of the American *Journal of Economic History* as the impact of the 'new economic history' or cliometrics in the 1960s. This was due, I think, to Bob Fogel's impressive combination of technical ingenuity and intellectual provocation, although the immediate pre-war and post-war generations of British economic historians only took a marginal interest in cliometrics. (Few of us paid much attention to Douglass North, the other future Nobel in Economic History.) The earlier American fashion for 'entrepreneurial history' made less of an impact, although it came up for (sometimes acerbic) discussion in our conferences – strongly supported at the time by a visiting David Landes, and the *Review* had sense enough to get A.D. Chandler Jr. to review for it in the 1950s, though the name as yet rang no bells.

In short, as I recall the first 15 years after the war, it strikes me that the Society evolved quite without knowing where it was going or wanted to go. Its relations to the rest of history were undefined, for while we knew we were not about cabinets, battles and treaties, we did not completely accept Trevelyan's definition that ours was 'history with the politics left out'. Our relations with the social sciences were imprecise, and by their standards many, perhaps most of us, would have counted as amateurs or autodidcats. Indeed, except for economics, the other social sciences were only slowly making their way into several universities, notably Oxbridge, sometimes against heavy resistance. People working in fields that had not yet developed their own institutions – social history, labour history and others – still sheltered under our umbrella. The Society did not even begin to survey its own field until the end of the 1960s, when the *Studies in Economic History* pamphlets edited by Flinn and the *Debates on Economic History* under Peter Mathias began to appear. Still, the post-1945 economic historians were convinced that the subject was advancing, even if one of our seniors, T.S. Ashton, joining hands with von Hayek, to whom nobody then listened, in *Capitalism and the Historians*, thought it was going the wrong way. At least, we all thought our arguments were important and, looking back, we had some lively ones. 'Quiet' is not the word to describe a decade of the *Review* that contained Hugh Trevor-Roper's frontal offensive against Lawrence Stone, the start of the Hobsbawm-Hartwell duel on the standard of living during the Industrial Revolution, the Wilson-Heckscher debate on mercantilism or, for that matter, Gallagher/Robinson on the imperialism of free trade. And, looking back on it, it is not easy to read into the *Review* of those days the tense ideological atmosphere in which we lived, wrote references and applied for jobs in the period between the Berlin airlift of 1948 and the victory of Fidel Castro in 1959.

Eric Hobsbawm (b. 9. 6. 1917) is Emeritus Professor of Economic and Social History at the University of London since 1982. He studied at the University of Cambridge and taught at Birkbeck College for most of his career becoming Professor there 1970-82. He holds honorary degrees at many major world universities and was, and is, a leading figure amongst British Marxist historians. His publications are legion and have been very influential in the formation of the discipline world-wide. His writings on politics and jazz are similarly held in high esteem. He 'continues to be interested in movements of social protest'.

---

[1] Memoir of C.H. Wilson in *Proceedings of the British Academy 105, 1999: Lectures and Memoirs*, p564.
[2] See for example Witold Kula (1962) *Economic Theory of the Feudal System* (Eng. Trans. London, 1976).

What Economic History Means to Me

Paul M. Hohenberg

How does one choose one's field of endeavour, and one's sub-field within it? Is it really chance, for example an encounter with a charismatic teacher, reinforced by strong path dependence? Or is it destiny, based on deep-seated, innate affinities and capacities?

My own training was in engineering, although I realised even before completing the course that my vocation lay elsewhere. The initial decision to study engineering had been made rather by default. My father felt that my temperament was unsuited for medicine and rather too well suited for law, which left only one legitimate profession, as it then seemed At any rate, I began the study of economics on my own after college, while holding an industrial research job, and wound up doing an MA in international studies by way of transition to the social sciences. Here I encountered economic history in the person of Charles P. Kindleberger, who would later supervise my doctoral thesis, and was hooked. That he happened to be studying France certainly had something to do with it, since I was a native and retained both francophony and -phily. The final sign came a year or so later, at MIT, when my interest in economic history survived unease at the overly teleological approach taken by Walt W. Rostow, this being the time of his too-famous *Stages of Economic Growth* [1].

At any rate, the die was cast, reinforced by the stimulating presence at MIT of M. M. Postan and the fine year I spent doing research in Europe, principally Paris. I could go on multiplying the names of scholars encountered, and places visited, from then onwards, but the point is quickly made. Economic history means keeping excellent company, as well as getting to know interesting places (often rather less superficially than most visitors can). While no generalisation can adequately describe all one's colleagues, most of them have turned out to suit my own intellectual style. They tend to show balance, of the single-minded or hedgehog economist with the dilettante – I use the word in its etymological sense of taking delight in – and fox-like historian. Yes, we can be pompous, dogmatic, overly critical, or lose our way among technical or factual minutiae. All in all, however, one is seldom bored with economic historians.

I have found other advantages to the field as well, in particular a use for my love of languages, books, and maps. On the other hand, being an economic historian has proved a mixed blessing in terms of a career. Not only has the field known ups and downs as regards fashion and therefore opportunity – in both history and economics – but the predisposition it encourages for work across and at the edges of disciplines can in itself be dangerous to one's professional health. At least in the United States, economics surely, and history probably as well, give great weight in matters of appointment, promotion, and tenure to the judgement of those who take it as their duty to guard the borders of the discipline. I finally found a home in a technological university where my research interests, while certainly tolerated, formed no part of my formal duties. This was not all bad, in the sense that I was forced to keep up my credentials as an economist and was also strongly motivated to participate in the collective life of the economic history profession, but it did not contribute to very rapid productivity.

Thus the community of economic historians has been important to my scholarly life, and I have been privileged to know many scholars from a variety of countries. These people have been more varied in their interests than would, I think, be typical of other small research communities. Economic history cuts across not only spatial units but also subjects and time periods, yet its active practitioners remain sufficiently few that a wide variety of specialists share conferences and journal pages. Most of us thus develop the habit of engaging without either excessive diffidence or presumption in discourse when the topic is relatively unfamiliar to some. The possible cost in superficiality seems bearable to me in view of the gain in flexibility, range, and courtesy. Particulars aside, one soon realises that many of the same issues crop up again and again in different contexts. And some of us, at least, are mindful of the need to limit the use of jargon, and so are able to clarify our thoughts along with our language.

The breadth of our profession and its practitioners is also manifest in their links to cognate disciplines, in my case population history, urban history, and the history of technology. All have standing as separate sub-disciplines, with the full apparatus of societies, journals, and meetings, but they are small enough to be, of necessity, open. Of particular importance in my own social practice has been the Social Science History Association. Long congenial to this generalist, it has undergone transformations that both attract and repel. On the one hand, historical demographers (and others) from outside North America have increasingly felt at home there, giving the meetings added interest. At the same time, and most surprisingly in view of the currents prevailing at the outset (1975), many fields of historical inquiry have been invested by post-modern and post-structuralist currents with their roots in the humanities. We have come far from the day when it seemed that social science - read quantification - would take over the humanities, and the turnabout is not one most economic historians find congenial. Whether the more recent European association is moving in the same direction is something I have yet to learn by direct experience.

Within the profession of economic history, one can distinguish those who build theoretically structured edifices and those who undermine or shake those constructs, those who advance theories or models and those who put them to the test. The distinction is akin to one made by Robert Solow between Big Think and Little Think types. Two things seem clear: that the two generally find one another uncongenial and even hard to respect, and that each in fact badly needs the other. Unlike the case of physical structures suggested by the metaphor I used above, the critics tend to exhibit more technical skill than do the system-builders. Deflating theories offers a wonderful opportunity to show off ingenuity in technique and/or diligence in going after primary data. We Big Think people, on the other hand – lest there be any doubt in which camp my tent has mainly been pitched – can usually just master the secondary literature, since we cover so much more ground. Ideally, of course, a scholar will cut her or his teeth on the grubby details – where no less a thinker than Goethe situated the Divinity – and only later, suitably armed with caution, venture into flights of theoretical fancy. Yet the realities of comparative advantage and natural temperament make us tend to specialise along this line of cleavage, no doubt to excess. My own approach has been to take from the theories of others what they have to give, without feeling the need to pass judgement on the whole, and with no compunction in turning their insights to whatever intellectual ends best suit my own project. Models, after all, are never true, at best only useful and stimulating.

Since my training is in economics, I barely qualify as an amateur historian. So it is best to leave to others extended reflections on the intellectual value of our field to that larger discipline. If history is indeed a seamless web, then economic history offers another cut through it, an alternative to the old focus on political and military highlights, yet something besides the currently fashionable emphasis on the victims of conflict. It is easy to forget that, in past times as today, most people have gone about their business most of the time neither triumphant nor desperate. What that business was and how it got done is all the more interesting as we too often take for granted our own, quite different, everyday experience of material life. Of course, as economic historians we synthesise, generalise, perhaps caricature. We throw around portmanteau terms such as medieval cities, European marriage patterns, mercantilist policies, proto-industrial modes of production, industrial revolutions, etc. Yet such constructs, fragile as they are, not only speak to real phenomena but are in fact unavoidable. Compared to other historians it is not so much that we are more given to generalising and theorising as simply that we are more explicit about it.

What then of economics, which reigns over the social sciences, though some would argue from a walled-up fortress? In my capacity as an economist who from time to time comments publicly on the issues of the day, I am frequently asked to forecast interest rates or share prices, etc. I then point out that, as an economic historian, I predict only the past. There is something to the point besides a prudent evasion of the question. Economics is about understanding as well as predicting (*pace* Milton Friedman), and economic history even more so. The counterfactual beloved of cliometricians is really nothing more than the plausible story one can tell of what should have happened but did not, for example (to take a case of very recent history indeed), an explosion of growth in post-communist Russia by analogy with post-1948 Germany.

Let me try to be a little more systematic about two contributions of economic history to economics. One is the treatment of time. Most economists deal with it reductively at best, or, fixated on equilibrium, ignore it altogether. Microeconomics texts' treatment of production merely distinguishes *the* short run and *the* long run, not even always recognising that decision making takes place on multiple levels with variable time scales. Others treat time as a pure discount meter, with the erosion of future value ticking away at the interest rate. Many focus only on the short run, bowing to bottom-line-obsessed investors and election-fixated politicians.[2]. The recent American debate on social security finance demonstrates how awkwardly economists respond when forced to contemplate the somewhat distant future. They persist in seeing the problem in fiscal terms, when its central feature is clearly the looming drop in the ratio of workers to total population. Even the study of economic development in the 'South', though it comprises far-reaching structural changes, often lacks a concrete sense of historical unfolding, of spurts, plateaus, declines, and stealthy development as alternative patterns to a lock-step advance. Here I must give the devil his due: for all its problems, Rostow's 'take-off' was at least grounded in (stylised) historical experience and therefore represented an advance on abstract models of accumulation and structural change. More generally, economic history, at least as I view it, points us toward underlying long-run factors to explain economic performance and change, as opposed to incidents of policy and personality or transient events (though these too have their historians).

If one can criticise the treatment of time in economics, things are much worse as regards space. It is not too much to say that geography has been the stepchild among social sciences, certainly in the United States, and economics stands convicted of severe neglect towards this poor relation despite some recent efforts to remedy matters. Even in the fields of urban and regional economics, space is most often reduced to cost of transport. When did you last see a proper map in an economics journal? Economic history offers the opportunity to take space seriously – as distance, landscape, topography, amenity, separation, and connection. Here my model must be Fernand Braudel – although the *Annales* School I once found so congenial has also veered away from its earlier central concerns.

The historical study of urban systems provides a good illustration of the importance of taking space seriously. My own work in this area (much of it together with Lynn Hollen Lees) departs from most other treatments in using a dual model, one that brings out both central place and network relations between cities, where others have worked with single urban hierarchies based largely on population size. The point here is not to justify this model, although it has found quite wide acceptance, but to recall its firm grounding in contrasting spatial patterns. Whereas central place models focus on interurban distances and geometric configurations of urban arrays, network relations are spatially flexible and follow lines of communication, notably waterways. I have argued that the contrast extends to many dimensions of urban life, from the links between population size and economic activity to politics and culture. But the starting point is clearly space considered as more than distance or cost alone.

What, then, of the future? How economic history will fare is no longer my direct concern from the point of view of a career. That was probably determined by my failure to join the cliometric bandwagon at the outset. Those who did so have been far more likely to gain acceptance from their fellow economists. Did the substantive achievements of the New Economic History fulfil the early claims and compensate for the weakening of ties to historians? I leave it to others to judge. Yet in the past decade or so, a number of these more forward-looking colleagues have clearly achieved for economic history a new place in the sun, from – to take only American examples – the Nobel Prizes awarded Robert Fogel and Douglass North to the prominence the media have given to work by economic historians on labour markets, technological change, property rights, and other 'hot' issues. To rub shoulders with such people and be at least marginally of their company has afforded me pleasure, profit, and pride.

Paul M. Hohenberg (b. Paris, 11. 9. 1933) was educated at the Universities of Cornell and Tufts, and at MIT. He is Professor Emeritus of Economics and Acting Department Chair at Rensselaer Polytechnic Institute in Troy, New York. He has written on European economic history including agriculture and urbanisation in the early-modern period and in the nineteenth century.

---

[1] Cambridge, 1960.
[2] My colleagues working in ecological economics do consider the long run, albeit in generally apocalyptic terms and with so little faith in markets that they risk losing touch with the rest of the discipline altogether.

On the Damascus Road
The First Steps in My Conversion to Economic and Social History

Colin Holmes

A collective biography of leading economic and social historians which throws light on the influences which brought them to the discipline and, simultaneously, assesses their work, is long overdue. However, that project is not on the agenda here. This essay is more restricted. It is personal. It sets out to trace the formative influences on my conversion to the discipline.

I went up to the University of Nottingham in 1957 to read History. I had studied the subject at 'A' level and also sat a Special Paper in the subject. My marks met all my hopes and satisfied my teachers' demanding expectations. The diet I had consumed in preparation for these examinations involved digesting a large slab of European political history from 1648 to the twentieth century, as well as a study of Britain between 1815 and 1914, which focused on high politics. Against that background, I looked forward to my University career. In particular, I relished the prospect of studying medieval history, a branch of the discipline I had thus far never tasted.

However, the transition to university proved difficult. The level of analysis required in the 'A' level and the Special Paper had hardly been exacting. In retrospect, it would seem that if one piled up the detail the marks followed almost automatically. It amounted largely to a Rankean exercise, a collection of facts in order to tell the past as it was. I soon discovered that at University rather more skills were required. The transition also proved stressful in another respect. I realised before long that I could muster little enthusiasm for certain periods of history. The politics of the Tudor years, for example, failed to grip my imagination and fire my interest. Moreover, the approach adopted towards medieval history turned out to be acutely disappointing. In one case the course assumed too much prior knowledge. In another the lecturer taught from yellowed notes, recycled over many years, and without any apparent interest in conveying the excitement of the remote past.

By the end of the second year I felt as if I had become trapped in an intellectual cul-de-sac, but, simultaneously, I glimpsed a possibility of an escape. Nottingham, at that stage, was one of a very small number of institutions which offered an honours degree in Economic and Social History. Robert Peers, who had taught economic history to students at University College, Nottingham, for many years, had exercised a major influence on this development in his role as Deputy Vice-Chancellor of the new University established in 1948. However, there was no Department. The unit appointed to teach the subject functioned as a sub-department of History under the leadership of J.D.Chambers, who was at that stage a Reader.

145

In my second year I attended Chambers's lectures and found them inspirational. He taught a course on Britain from the late eighteenth century onwards. He lectured on the Industrial Revolution and its economic and social consequences, concentrating on themes such as urban poverty, the standard of living, then a topic of intense and furious debate, as well as labour organisations. This course was supplemented for students by Peter Payne's lectures on the Economic and Social History of Europe and America. Payne, a graduate of Nottingham, had just returned from the United States to a temporary post in his own university.

When I told Chambers of my dissatisfaction with the endless history of popes and kings, he encouraged me to switch degrees. It was easier said than done. A.C.Wood, then Professor of Modern History dealt with my request to transfer. During the interview in the Trent Building in his spacious, book –lined room with its collection of Victoriana, I intimated at one stage that I wanted to become a university teacher. He dismissed the possibility. The nature of his intervention strengthened my resolve to transfer. Wood agreed eventually to my request. I never regretted the move. I relished the third year of my studies. My enthusiasm for academic work flowed back.

Compared with the loads imposed on today's students, I realise in retrospect how few courses we had to study. Robert Ashton taught Tudor and Stuart Economic History. The influence of Tawney ran thorough it like a thread and, for me, that dimension acted as a stimulus. The intellectual impact of Tawney's *Religion and the Rise of Capitalism,* which I read during my second year as an undergraduate, has remained with me. Chambers, for his contribution, took us on a deeper excursion into the history of the Industrial Revolution which introduced students to key documents of the period. He had a particular interest at this point in time in the memoir of Robert Blincoe and the events at Litton Mill.

In addition, we had to engage with a course on General Economic History. We studied intellectual developments of the day such as C.P.Snow's *The Two Cultures and the Scientific Revolution,* which had been delivered as the Rede Lecture in 1959. But much of the course focused on two themes. We discussed why industrialisation began in the Western World rather than among the Ancient Civilisations of, say, China or India. Rostow's recently published *The Stages of Economic Growth* and Wittfogel's *Oriental Despotism* were much thumbed in the course during the year. This theme of rich and poor nations has been the subject of recent high profile work by David Landes in his *The Wealth and Poverty of Nations* and also by Peter Jay in *The Road to Riches.* But we can be counted as pioneers in the study. Chambers's own interest in this theme can be detected in his Inaugural lecture delivered in 1960. He took for his subject, 'The Place of Economic History in Historical Studies'. The other major related emphasis on the course involved a consideration of Marxism and, in particular, the Marxist interpretation of history and its critics. Rumour had it that in his youth Chambers had almost been persuaded into Marxism by the arguments of Maurice Dobb whom he described to me on one occasion as 'the cleverest man of his generation'. However, Chambers retreated from the brink and spent a fair amount of his time and academic effort subsequently in attacking historical materialism. That intellectual stance can be read in his important article, 'Enclosure and Labour Supply', published by the *Economic History Review* in 1952-3, as well as in *The Vale of Trent 1670-1800* (1957). It appeared also in the position he adopted in seminars on the standard of living controversy. He stood four square in this debate behind the views of T.S.Ashton, with whom he enjoyed a personal as well as an intellectual relationship. The examination I sat on the General Economic History Paper in the summer of 1960 is still vivid in my thoughts. It amounted to one of the most difficult papers imaginable. How were third year students expected to cope with questions such as: 'Marxism was a characteristic product of mid-nineteenth bourgeois intellectualism. Discuss'?

The third year course required, finally, a dissertation. I chose to work on Chartism in Nottingham. This interest grew out of 'A' level studies. An extended piece of undergraduate work now afforded the prospect of interrogating original sources. I researched in the City's Public Library for much of the second year's summer vacation and proceeded to write a weighty dissertation. Shortly after it had been submitted, Chambers published an article in a Nottingham newspaper suggesting that Chartism in the City had died effectively in 1848. My assessment was that its life had been prolonged beyond that date. I have no idea of the mark I received for my work. What I do know, is that other historians have used the dissertation heavily and sometimes shamelessly. It remains a piece of work, now recollected in tranquillity, with which I remain reasonably contented.

Chambers became involved in a further decisive intervention in my career after I had sat Finals. He recommended me for the Revis Postgraduate Studentship, with the result that in the autumn in 1960 I commenced my graduate career under his supervision. My experiences with him in this connection proved to be mixed, for a variety of reasons. He insisted that I worked on the ' Life and Career of H. S. Tremenheere,' the first Inspector of Schools and Mines. 'If we (Nottingham) don't do it, then Beales at the LSE will put one of his students on to the topic'. In later years in the course of my supervision of research students I know how important it is for any postgraduate to be deeply involved in the choice of his or her subject. That option was closed off for me. The imposition of a topic counted as a bad start and my problem was compounded when Chambers, always delightfully eccentric and possessed of an impressive degree of forgetfulness, managed to lose the first chapter of my thesis. As a 'green' postgraduate student, I had not made another copy. Nevertheless, I persisted, even though it soon became apparent that insufficient materials existed for a doctorate.

Yet in more positive vein, Chambers made a further important intervention in my career. He saw his postgraduate students on Saturday mornings and in 1963, shortly before his retirement, he enquired, quite casually, whether I wanted to be considered for a University post. He had received two letters, one from Liverpool and the other from Sheffield, drawing his attention to vacancies. I responded positively and asked which of the posts he would recommend. His personal preference was for Sheffield. 'Sidney Pollard is a coming man – he's a Marxist, though', he replied. However, a problem arose at this point. Chambers's forgetfulness had triumphed once again. The closing date for the Sheffield post had passed. Chambers assured me that notwithstanding this difficulty he would write in on my behalf. How different from today's world . . . As a result, I travelled to Sheffield on a brilliant summer's day for an interview. I met Sidney Pollard, who's work I knew from my undergraduate reading, for the first time. I did not realise it then, but that meeting proved to be absolutely decisive for my future. In effect, Pollard made me into the historian I later became. But that, as they say, is another story. It is part of my later personal and career development.

I began by emphasising that there is scope for a collective biography of Economic and Social Historians. A study of the role of particular institutions in the history of the discipline is also needed. The careers of Power, Tawney, Ashton and Fisher, as well as Beales, were played out largely in the lecture rooms of the LSE. The Cambridge connection also needs to be considered. Cunningham and Clapham laboured as early pioneers and, closer to my own day, there was the redoubtable Postan, one émigré who has enlivened British intellectual life. Among provincial Universities, Birmingham provided a base for Ashley, early in the twentieth century and, later, for Court. In addition, the role of Manchester, the city which in many ways symbolised industrial capitalism is of central importance. Unwin and Redford worked early in the field and as undergraduates in the 1950s we were constantly encountering the works of Chaloner and Henderson. In tandem with these long-established institutions, the role of Nottingham would also call for attention.

When I went up to Nottingham in 1957 B.L. Hallward, the imposing Vice-Chancellor, addressed all the freshers. He began with the arresting remark: 'this is rather a good University and you are rather lucky to be here'. He had a vested professional interest in projecting this positive public image. Nevertheless, the young University contained what are now called Centres of Excellence and the Sub-Department of Economic and Social History certainly set a cracking pace. Among my contemporaries, either slightly ahead or later in the date of their admission, can be counted Roy Church, Stanley Chapman, Leslie Clarkson, Martin Daunton, H.E. Hallam, E.L. Jones, G.E. Mingay, Bryan Outhwaite, Peter Payne, Malcolm Thomis and Eric Richards. By any standard this list of research students is formidable.

I do not know why these scholars were attracted to Economic and Social History, but my involvement depended to a great extent upon personal influences and in particular the role of J.D.Chambers. Chambers's enthusiasm for his subject, his encouragement of students, his style of teaching, added to his informality, all appealed to me. In my case these qualities were supplemented by the fact that both of us had personal roots in Lawrence country. D.H.Lawrence was very much in vogue in Nottingham in the late 1950s and early 1960s, after a long period when his work had been sidelined in the University. Chambers was caught up in this activity. After all, he had appeared as a character in *Sons and Lovers,* as the child Hubert. But in addition to this personal influence, what the discipline of Economic and Social History offered, through Chambers particularly, also brought about my conversion. It was presented as relevant to the world I inhabited. This sense of relevance and significance had never been apparent from the lectures I received, say on the Crusades. Even the political history of the eighteenth century, which so fascinated Lewis Namier and which was well taught in Nottingham by Ron Fryer, was still presented as a slab of the remote past, frozen in space and time, when it could have been endowed with a different slant which drew out themes of general significance. Years later I noticed that an emphasis on understanding the present through a study of the past had been expressed by R.H.Tawney in his inaugural delivered in 1932 at the LSE I had not read this lecture by the time I had left Nottingham. I encountered it soon afterwards and it struck an immediate chord. In the course of his lecture Tawney remarked:

> I came to the study of economic history, not as one dedicated from childhood
> to the service of the altar, but for reasons so commonplace that I am ashamed to
> admit them. When I reached the years of discretion – which I take to mean the
> age at which a young man shows signs of getting over his education – I found
> the world surprising; I find it so still. I turned to history to interpret it. . .

I was searching unconsciously for that type of history. I found it. I could then begin to fashion my own work in the same mould.

Colin Holmes (b. 1938) retired from the University of Sheffield in 1998, where he held a personal chair. He still supervises research students at that University and is also a part-time Research Professor at the University of Sunderland. He has published widely, mostly on the subject of immigrants and minorities in British society.

Risk, Uncertainty and Profit: The Personal Challenge of Economic History

Julian Hoppit

My first sustained encounter with economic and social history was in the first week of my first term as a 19 year-old undergraduate in 1976. I was immediately smitten, if also infuriated. And that ambiguity is what economic history means to me.

Like many, at school the history I studied was primarily political, in which the emphasis was upon an appreciation of more or less detailed chronologies of events and the actions and motivations of a small number of purportedly key individuals. The focus was upon the particular and the short run. But in the autumn of 1976 economic history showed me a decisively different way of approaching the past: where the emphasis could be on the medium or long term; where the gaze could be upon the whole of society; where a simple, single chronology was often insufficient; and where the ideas and institutions which mattered were often inchoate and confused. In brief, it was the need to pursue complex analysis to undertake economic history which was so fascinating. However, the attractions of economic history were not merely methodological. It certainly helped, for example, that I was temperamentally, one might say politically or ideologically, sympathetic to placing a heavy emphasis upon material issues. I was fortunate too to have in Richard Overy an inspiring teacher. And my first efforts with economic history could hardly have addressed a larger question, the industrial revolution in Britain.

That fascination with economic history flourished as an undergraduate, not least in papers I took on the nature of European empires, on the history of Africa and on economic and quantitative methods for historians. But I retained that very first enthusiasm for studying the industrial revolution in Britain. Perhaps this was inertia, but I think it was because I sensed that much of the history of Britain between the Restoration and the early nineteenth century was then still *terra incognita*. So I chose to do doctoral research on bankruptcy in eighteenth-century England. If this was clearly a piece of economic history I very quickly discovered the importance of studying the legal and institutional arrangements within which bankruptcy took place. I was drawn here into not just the law, but politics and the culture of credit, all the while limiting the applicability of the neo-classical precepts so much of economic history begins with. That was a shift in perspective which, in retrospect, was decisive and ever since my approach to economic history has been less from the direction of studies of consumption, exchange and production than the mental frameworks and power relations within which economic issues at the time were framed.

Perhaps I should have seen that this shift would happen, as economic history was from the very first a problem for me. I struggled long and hard to write my first essay, but despite my best efforts the result was messy. I did not know it at the time but I was defeated by some of the tensions that are fundamental to economic history as an intellectual exercise. Firstly, that because the focus is often not upon discrete or clear events the subject matter is fundamentally determined by employing concepts and categories which are necessarily artificial and debatable. Secondly, I was struggling to marry quantitative and qualitative approaches to economic history. It was and is hard to say whether, for example, Deane and Cole had written more or less that same things about the fundamentals of the industrial revolution as Landes, having approached much the same subject from very different directions. Thirdly, if I was challenged by having to think about structural or impersonal forces as explanatory variables, then how were they produced by human action? Much of what I was reading about the industrial revolution was hardly about people at all. And, finally, there was quantification, at once powerful and liberating but also in places like quicksand.

My difficulties with economic history derived from a largely traditionally based scepticism of methodology and historiography informed by reading the reflections on history as a discipline by the likes of Bloch, Braudel, Butterfield, Carr and Elton. Such difficulties, however, are much more a sign of success than of failure of economic history, of its strength rather than its weakness. It is a discipline with a long tradition of vigorous jousting, witness the 'storm over the gentry' and the standard of living debate. However, for some years now the vitality of economic history as a sub-discipline has been in doubt, apparently powerfully evidenced by the demise of so many separate departments of economic and social history in British universities. It is within this environment that I have developed as an historian and as an economic historian. Unquestionably, there is a sense that economic history is not the powerhouse of historical enquiry it once was and so current debates often seem to take place elsewhere in the mansion of history. So, for example, the debates over and within post-modernism in the 1980s and 1990s seem to have touched economic history less markedly than other areas of history.

Many others have considered the 'decline' of economic history: of whether it is relative rather than absolute, whether caused by a developing wider suspicion of material issues, whether it has become too much of a social science, too categorically eschewing history's wider qualitative and narrative conventions, whether too preoccupied with modern history and of whether, as a mature area of intellectual enquiry, some 'stagnation' or diminishing marginal returns are not unavoidable. But such 'decline' is in some measure a matter of perspective, for cases could equally be made for the 'retreat' in recent times of political history and social history. What has been striking over the last thirty years or so is how increasingly we are coming to appreciate that history is indeed a discipline largely without borders and of how, in purely quantitative terms, more and more of it is being researched and written. History's vastness has become ever more apparent, such that once easily imagined ways of dividing it up have become less credible to all of its sub-disciplines. It is too easy to lament the trends and fads in this, but from this perspective economic history has less 'declined' than become part of a wider uncertainty, an uncertainty which I think should be embraced enthusiastically because without it we will not come to understand the past better.

The institutional advantages once enjoyed by economic history, in large part by virtue of the fact that it was among the first sub-disciplines successfully to erode the late-nineteenth century fortresses of political and constitutional histories, if personally valuable to many should not count for very much in pursuing the past. More important is economic history's continued intellectual relevance, and this seems to me still to be very considerable, providing 'economic' is broadly defined (a big 'if'). Most obviously, the histories of consumption, exchange and production, of the distribution of economic power if you like, are undeniably major areas to study. Economic history has at its core subject matter which can rarely be ignored by other historians. Secondly, more than most approaches to the past economic history is committed to the significance of the *longue durée*. Thirdly, as Clapham noted long ago, economic history is that part of history more conducive to quantitative approaches, the virtues of which are too often ignored – the explicitness, the attempt at conceptual clarity and the marrying of the general and the specific. By frequently painting with a broad brush it can show up just how much history now is unambitiously about the particular. Related to this, fourthly, economic history can provide powerful means of identifying change and continuity over time, of posing the general questions within much specific historical research can be located. So, for example, the relative growth and stagnation of the British and Dutch economies respectively in the eighteenth century provides a framework in which to consider a vast range of issues from culture, to politics, to resource endowments and more. Finally, what might be called the social inclusiveness of economic history is frequently (if silently) impressive. It is a sub-discipline capable of looking at the whole of society and its inter-relationships. To forget that, which has happened too often, is to forget a lot.

I have considered the value of economic history to me in intellectual terms, drawing out points from a comparison of my own development as a historian with those taking place within history more generally since I became a part of the academic business. This, naturally, leaves out much of the value of economic history as a scholarly community. I would not underestimate the impact of this on me, but I doubt that in social terms economic history is structurally distinctive here. The stories one might tell about its characters or moments are unlikely to be caused by its nature as a sub-discipline. So the lifeblood of economic history must rest upon the general relevance of its core and upon its intellectual vitality, flexibility and imagination. If that vitality has been doubted it is worth remembering just how many sub-disciplines it has helped to spawn, among them agricultural history, business history, demographic history, historical geography, the new institutional history, social history, transport history and urban history. If economic history defines itself generously and ambitiously – thematically, chronologically and methodologically – then such vitality can continue. But in a world of increasingly prescriptive research programmes, project-led endeavours and intrusive paymasters that is becoming harder and harder. The meaning of economic history should evolve overwhelmingly within the imagination of historians working in archives, libraries, studies and seminars, not in committees.

Julian Hoppit (b. 14. 8. 1957), was educated at Selwyn College, Cambridge. His PhD was supervised by Donald Coleman. He is currently Reader in History at University College, London. Among his published works are *Risk and failure in English business, 1700-1800* (Cambridge, 1987) and *A land of liberty? England 1689-1727* (Oxford, 2000). For 10 years he was heavily involved with the Royal Historical Society's British and Irish history bibliographies project.

Economic History, Political Economy and Society: Inseparable Interests?

Anthony Howe

Arriving at Oxford in 1969 well-schooled in the intricacies of medieval kingship, it was with some relief that I took up Cliff Davies's suggestion that I might like to tackle as tutorial topics issues such as the state of the peasantry in the thirteenth century or population change and economic growth in the fourteenth and fifteenth centuries. This not only led me into eye-opening new fields that I had scarcely considered part of the past – land-ownership, plague, trade – but also gave me a quite novel appreciation of the controversies which the past could provoke as I came to grips with the erudite works of Postan, Titow, and Bridbury[1]. In my second year I was keen to follow up this intellectual challenge and logically progressed to the further subject 'English Economic History 1500-1700', with Tawney and Power's *Tudor Economic Documents* (1924) as a set text. Attending Joan Thirsk's patient and intriguing expositions in her university classes - at a time when Oxford did not yet offer the study of Economic History after 1700 - I gained a sense of the importance of detail but also of how the accumulation of detail could revise commonly–held interpretations which commanded lazy assent by their outward plausibility. (Endearingly, even the sixteenth century tobacco close at Winchcombe, where I had grown up, rated a mention in an account of the Elizabethan economy). I also at this time absorbed the pages of Tawney's *The Agrarian Problem in the Sixteenth Century* (1912), confirming my sense that understanding the economic basis of society provided a field of interest as compelling as Tudor dynastic politics or the Reformation. Above all, however, it was around this time that I read Lawrence Stone's *The Crisis of the Aristocracy, 1558-1641* (Oxford, 1965). Stone's had been a name familiar to me since schooldays - in part the reason I had gone to Wadham, the college he had recently left. But *The Crisis* proved an inspiring intellectual catalyst, not so much for its thesis, but for the attempt to study all facets of the past – economics, politics, religion, education, mind and manners – to draw together all aspects of the structure and behaviour of a social group. By this time my own interests had been moving towards the late eighteenth and early nineteenth centuries, and it was on reading Stone that I first aspired to study what I vaguely perceived as a second crisis of the aristocracy initiated by the Wilkite movement of 1760s and taking full shape with the Industrial Revolution, a crisis which brought into play the then largely unstudied British middle class. Reading E. P. Thompson's, *The Making of the English Working Class* (1963) confirmed my sense that the 'class enemy' had been neglected.

My first opportunity to explore some of these issues and to touch on the study of modern economic and social history, came in my third year with perhaps the most influential of all Oxford special subjects in recent years, 'Social and Economic Policies during the Ministry of Peel, 1841-1846' under the guidance of the late Angus Macintyre. This proved of enormous importance – partly in drawing me to an enduring interest in economic policy-making but also in more clearly shaping in my mind the contours of the nineteenth-century middle class. In particular I now perceived as its leading members, the Lancashire mill-owning class, whose Anti-Corn Law League seemingly embodied an overt bourgeois challenge to the aristocracy. Despite of course readily conceding that the Repeal of the Corn Laws owed much to aristocratic self-interest and that, in political terms, the aristocracy remained dominant, it became apparent that the middle classes had been written out of English history to my mind to a quite inexplicable degree. I therefore now became attached to the idea of studying the cotton masters as a prototypical middle class group, modelling myself on Stone's 'histoire totale'. The real problem was how to go about such a study but here I found much of value in one of the few 'Annales' type attempts to extend their approach into the nineteenth century, Adeline Daumard's La Bourgeoisie Parisienne de 1815 à 1848 (Paris, 1963). Like Stone's Crisis, this based itself on a vast and disparate culling of archival sources and ranged from social stratification to the classically French participation à la vie collective. From both Stone and Daumard I conceived as the best possible way to study a relatively small social group to lie in collective biography – for while such a method ruled out studying the bourgeoisie as a whole, it did lend itself to treating sub-sections of it. Studying the industrial bourgeoisie was, in the 1970s, an idiosyncratic ambition in a university that still distrusted industry (were not the strike-ridden Morris Motors merely a source of disruption in a university town?) and in a faculty that believed the bourgeoisie mythical. But I won the support of my tutor, and soon to be a patient and long-standing supervisor Pat Thompson.

Ironically, having embarked, as I thought, to study the most influential group in modern British economic history, I soon found that this interest largely separated me from the discipline as it was then developing. That famous series of seminars at Oxford in the early seventies – Fogel, Engerman, North, Parker – served only to convince me that the emerging school of cliometric history held little in common with the concerns of the economic history of Tawney or Thirsk. However ingenious its techniques and strikingly revisionist its intellectual results – it did not promise to illuminate the areas of social behaviour of modern Britain in which I was interested. On the other hand, the prosopographical approach I had absorbed from Stone – if practised by few (and they mostly ancient historians) did seem to me to blend an element – amateur, no doubt - of quantification with the larger ambition to study a group in the round and to avoid casual impressionism.[2] This eventually, with the support of Max Hartwell as college supervisor at Nuffield, and Peter Mathias as temporary supervisor, encouraged me to adhere to my study as originally conceived (two theses, not one, as Peter Mathias warned) which was eventually published as The Cotton Masters, 1830-1860 in 1984.

Collective biography has remained relatively unfashionable but it still has much potential as a technique to study elite social groups, and to test common generalisations as to many facets of their behaviour and identity. This is easiest for the aristocracy but is also important for the continuing study of the British middle class, whose detailed study only began in the late 1960s and 1970s.[3] This necessarily involves the selection of subgroups amenable to study, as successfully done for bankers and regional elites by Cassis and Berghoff respectively.[4] For this reason it has been odd that until recently the vast amount of information collected in the Dictionary of Business Biography[5] has remained untapped. Only now have the articles of Tom Nicholas shown how prosopographical material can be used to test some hoary old questions as to the nature of British entrepreneurship and its alleged failure.[6] If the current post post-modern drift towards a largely uncritical cultural history is to be tempered by a quantitative approach, then collective biography is one potentially fruitful way forward. With the increasing availability of CD-Rom sources such as Who's Who 1897-1998, the Dictionary of National Biography and, in 2004, the New DNB the way is open to valuable studies of social elites and of occupational sub-groups, whether aristocratic wives, civil servants, generals, bishops, or businessmen. Economic historians concerned with people in the past need therefore not be confined to statistical people and should not shrug off the study of actual people. In particular, the history of the British middle class is still to be written.

154

The legacy of my own attempt to write one portion of that history was a determination not to become an 'economic historian' *pur sang* - but to resist sub-categorisation and to embrace as far as possible an approach to the past which based itself on underlying economic factors but did not omit power, society, ideas, foreign policy, and the administrative process. Finding myself in a department of International History at the LSE in the 1980s provided me with the opportunity to pursue this wider remit. It was a department which had in the past paid considerable attention to economic aspects of international history (as for example in some of the works of W. N. Medlicott[7]) and which had spawned at least one future professor of economic history (Alan Milward). Of course, in the days before departments, the first director of the School had himself lectured on themes such as the Economic Policies of the Great Powers in the nineteenth century.[8] In this institutional context, I took up the study of neglected issues in the history of international political economy, for example, a foray into the history of the bimetallic movement, a debate long forgotten by economic historians who thought in terms of the gold standard as if this had been eternal and uncontentious, simply a technical mechanism, rather than part of a hotly contested political and diplomatic process.

A second more important policy issue whose study had been also largely neglected, falling through the interstices between economic and political history was that of free trade. Of course there had been some attempts to study this from a cliometric perspective[9] but this also provided an example of where the quantitative approach had narrowed attention and diminished the significance of issues. The study of free trade was not simply that of the pursuit of the most growth-maximising economic policy but the interplay of ideas, interests, parliament, the people and morality. Oddly, historians hitherto had been greatly concerned with tariff reform, but free trade after the Repeal of the Corn Laws remained in the 1980s, as the unrepentant Cobdenite F. W. Hirst had called it in a different context, a 'cause without a history'.[10] I therefore attempted to write that history, seeking to explain the diverse ways in which free trade had become the dominant, integrating ideology in Victorian Britain, and explaining why Britain alone among the leading powers adhered to free trade after the 'Great Depression'.[11] Free trade broadly conceived embodied not only a fiscal and economic strategy with vital ramifications for the state but also a morality that helped bind together elite and popular cultures. The nature of the state and of political culture in turn provide crucial components of the explanation of economic policy, moving beyond the still all too common 'City' versus 'Industry' explanations. Such linkages between the state, culture and economy are now being profitably explored by younger scholars. Free trade in its crudest form had of course long been preconceived as the ideology of an ascendant bourgeoisie and in several shapes - whether evangelical, Ricardian or Cobdenite - it does provide an important aspect of the world-view of the middle class. But more importantly, as underlined in Richard Price's recent book,[12] free trade can now be seen as a vital and peculiar part of the way in which the political economy of modern Britain was constructed. Alongside themes such as empire and fiscal policy, it illustrates the impossibility of separating politics and economics. It suggests therefore that economic historians in the future should be readier to embrace the old sphere of 'political economy' if the subject is not to cut itself off from a new generation of historians. Through the study of political economy - by putting back in what the counterfactual historians have left out - economic history can fruitfully reconnect itself with many of the concerns of international relations as well as of social and political history.

Anthony Howe (b. 1950) was educated at Wadham College, Oxford, and Nuffield College, Oxford. He is currently Reader in International History at LSE. His interests include the formation of the Victorian middle class, industrial elites and the City of London 1815-1914,

Huskisson and the making of the nineteenth-century British state, and the international history of free trade from Adam Smith to globalisation.

---

[1] M. M. Postan, *Agrarian Life in the Middle Ages* (Cambridge Economic History of Europe, vol.1, 1966); J. Z Titow, *English Rural Society, 1200-1350* (1969); A. R. Bridbury, *Economic Growth: England in the later Middle Ages* (1962).

[2] See Stone, 'Prosopography', *Daedalus*, 100 (1971), 46-79.

[3] For example, R. J. Morris, whose path-breaking 1972 Oxford D. Phil. thesis partially surfaced beneath a Gramscian retread in *Class, sect and party: the making of the British middle class; Leeds, 1820-1850* (1990); V. A. C. Gatrell's influential thesis,' The Manchester Commercial Classes, c.1820-57' (Cambridge, 1972) has remained unpublished; R. H. Trainor, *Black Country Elites: The Exercise of Authority in an Industrialised Area 1830-1900* (Oxford: Oxford Historical Monographs, 1993).

[4] Y. Cassis, *Les Banquiers de la City à l'époque Edouardienne* (Geneva, 1984); translated as *City Bankers, 1890-1914* (Cambridge, 1994); H. Berghoff, *Englische Unternehmen, 1870-1914:eine Kollektivbiographie führender Wirtschaftsbürger in Birmingham, Bristol und Manchester* (Göttingen, 1991).

[5] Ed. D. J. Jeremy & C. Shaw, 5 vols. 1984-86.

[6] E.g. T. Nicholas, 'Businessmen and Landownership in the late nineteenth century', *Economic History Review*, vol.LII (1999), 27-44; id., 'Clogs to Clogs in Three Generations? Explaining Entrepreneurial Behaviour in Britain since 1850', *The Journal of Economic History* 59 (1999), 688-713; id., 'Wealth Making in Nineteenth- and Early Twentieth-Century Britain: Industry v. Commerce and Finance', *Business History* 41 (1999), 16-36.

[7] For example, W.N. Medlicott *The Economic Blockade* (2 vols, History of the Second World War, Civil ser. 1952) but also his *Contemporary England, 1914-1964* (1967).

[8] W. A .S. Hewins. See Hewins Papers, Sheffield University Library.

[9] Above all, D. McCloskey, ' Magnanimous Albion', reprinted in *Enterprise and Trade in Victorian Britain* (1981).

[10] F. W. Hirst, *From Adam Smith to Philip Snowden: A History of Free Trade in Great Britain* (1925).

[11] A. Howe, *Free Trade and Liberal England, 1846-1946* (Oxford: Clarendon Press 1997).

[12] R. Price, *British Society, 1680-1880* (Cambridge, 2000).

The Economic History of Life

Pat Hudson

I came to economic history in an effortless way: it was all around me as a child. Studying it has helped to make sense of my experiences of growing up in an industrial town on the fringes of Britain in the post war years. Afterwards, as I moved via London to West Yorkshire, Liverpool and South Wales my understanding of regional cultures and of their interactions with wider pulses of national and global commerce and power, has been formed by the sorts of questions which economic history provokes and by the observation and analysis which a social science training encourages. Economic history is thus an integral part of my life.

In Barrow-in-Furness in the 1950s ship yard cranes dominated the skyline and the buzzer marked out the working day. At its signal thousands of walking and cycling workmen rushed home across the bridge and past the town hall in the gathering dusk: a flow of humanity so strong that it could suck you in and drag you along. I watched the launch of some of the biggest P&O liners and the earliest submarines of the dreadnought class, sitting on my Dad's shoulders or waving bunting along with a school party. We had a great view from Walney island, close enough to hear the cheers of the workers in the Yard half a mile away, to see the clouds of dust raised by the snapping chains and to watch the backwash speed across the channel and splash against our feet.

My Dad worked as a self employed joiner. Before 1958 when he bought his first van (a Vanguard Standard pickup) he pushed all his tools and equipment in a hand cart. His workshop was next to my first school so sometimes I got a lift home in the cart along with the wood shavings and the hammers and nails. I can still smell those tools and hear the noise of the wheels turning.

First generation migrants from farming to the town, my parents took in lodgers, kept hens and rabbits and grew all our vegetables. The lodgers from the Yard were migrant workers who swelled the population of Barrow for the duration of building a particular ship. They were always from the other great ship building areas: they were Geordies, Scousers or from Belfast or Glasgow. Their accents were almost unintelligible. In different seasons we set long lines for flounders, went blackberrying and nutting, picked damsons and mushrooms. I knew the feel and the smells of the land and from my father I developed a keen knowledge of wildlife, especially birds. I was not a hot house plant.[1] I remember getting early recognition at junior school for writing a description of a disused canal: full of old prams and rubbish where narrow boats and horses had once been busy. Mallard, coot and minnows surviving amidst the rubbish. Nature reclaiming the landscape: economic history and natural history together.

Alongside the household chores and book keeping, Mum made all our clothes, - beautifully smocked and tailored - apart from socks, underwear and Dad's suit and trilby. She also worked at Listers factory, roving wool on the evening shift in the 1960s and 70s. Apart from mounds of rubble and concrete nothing remains of the building where she spent so much backbreaking time in the heat and noise. It's all quiet now: bracken and loostrife, clumps of birch trees, seagulls on the wet tarmac, a blackbird or two. A cycle of industry gone, along with the ship building, and so many lives and livelihoods.

We had holidays in Morecambe or Blackpool steaming along what must be one of the most beautiful rail routes in the world, skirting the coast and saltmarshes of Morcambe Bay with the Lakeland fells, enclosures and tenant farms in full view. We stayed as paying guests in boarding houses supplying our own food which the landlady cooked. We had to spend all day outdoors. Such places were full of Alan Bennett families on Wakes Week trips from the textile centres of Lancashire and Yorkshire. More occasionally, we went to London where we stayed with my disabled Great Aunt Maggie who had spent her working life in service there. She lived in a rented room, cooking on a primus. In 1953 we slept out on the pavement in the Mall to wave flags at the Coronation parade. Aunt Maggie was very ambitious for me. She took me to museums and bought me a trunk (when I was about eight) so that I would be able to come to University in London and become a teacher.

Fortified with free orange juice, antibiotics and polio vaccinations, provided with the opportunities of a grammar school education (now also for girls), my generation carried all the hopes for post war betterment. A burden of responsibility to fulfil the frustrated aspirations of our parents. But a small town grammar school with no social science, a childhood of flat caps, whippet racing, Royalism, deference, and bike rides with the Anglican Young Peoples' Association. None of this prepared me for the thrill of the metropolis, cinema and theatre, LSE sherry parties, esoteric debate, student revolt, feminism, atheism and my first encounters with economics and economic history. I stepped off the overnight bus at Victoria in October 1967, before the tube had started for the day. I remember nervously eating at a Lyons Corner House before arriving at cold, mice-infested digs, opposite St Olave's Irish Social Centre in Manor House. Every Saturday I empathised with the young Irish navvies who hung around the glare and noise of the dance hall adrift and lonely: the anomie of the migrant far from the culture of home.

I survived with the help of breathless and truly exciting lectures from a young man with a shock of hair, Dudley Baines; the laconic, gentlemanly wit and intelligence of Donald Coleman; kindly commitment from Arthur John and Jim Potter; and some doses of first principles of economics, as applied to the early modern economy, by Jack Fisher who taught in a room full of papers, overflowing ash trays and whisky bottles. Peter Earle, Eddie Hunt, Olive Coleman, and Charlotte Erickson also taught me: I was very lucky. The legacies of Tawney and Ashton, and the creative tensions which these provoked, were strong at the School. Alan Day and Alan Walters lectured me on supply and demand curves and a diminutive, worry-bead clutching Peter Bauer, operating well below his preferred depth, backed these up with some seemingly unrelated seminars idealising the free market. Impressed by my contributions (which tended to be less inhibited than those of my male peers but which were just common sense) he wrote a laudatory letter to my parents: 'intelligent without being a blue stocking'. Bernard (later Lord) Donahue, tutored me in politics with irony, sarcasm and *double entendre*. As a working class girl with a strong Cumbrian accent (which he and others mimicked to good effect), I never knew how seriously I was being taken but I slowly learned the rules of academic engagement in what was (even if you *were* a blue stocking - and certainly if you were not) a very gendered environment. The Tawney Society, then presided over by the exuberant and friendly (then post grad) Negley Harte, provided just the sort of alcoholic diversions that were required.

It was the days of student protest, angry young people, arrests on campus, obsession with revolutions, new sexual 'freedoms'. Not to be a Marxist was unthinkable and in any case it appealed to my already strong sense of the importance of the economic. Much time was spent talking politics, measuring life in coffee spoons. It took me four rather than three years to gain my degree but I had learned a lot besides economics and history.

After a year working for Unilever, I resumed an academic career by accepting a Pasold Research Fellowship at the University of York. The brief was to work with Eric Sigsworth in cataloguing textile business records which he had helped to salvage from the death throes of the Yorkshire trade. In early November 1971 on a wet and overcast day he introduced me to the industrial towns, villages and stone built hamlets of the West Riding, exploring derelict weavers' cottages above the tree line, visiting the sites of water powered mills, now hen houses or barns but often with their waterwheels still in tact and mill races and ponds clearly visible in the undergrowth. We ate sandwiches on a hill looking at the landscape: the road, rail and canal lines finding the easiest routes along the valley bottoms, chimneyed towns nestling in the wider floors and above these the hillside sites of earlier rural-industrial activity. I could have had no better nor more enthusiastic guide and I was hooked.

My subsequent research has focused upon industrialisation, particularly in Yorkshire, and upon industrialising communities, using regional, local and micro-historical approaches to address bigger questions.[2] I spent much time studying business records still in private hands or in the dusty basements of West Yorkshire museums. I met many very helpful (often eccentric) museum curators. In the days before orderly libraries and computer terminals, I recall with great fondness the cosiness of research with a coal fire blazing in the search room and the curator's dog asleep across my feet. My work has been much informed by economic analysis but, as Eric Hobsbawm nicely put it 'It is an obvious drawback of economics as a subject dealing with the real world that it selects out some and only some aspects of human behaviour as 'economic' and leaves the rest to someone else'.[3] As economics retreated further into formalism from the 1960s, economic history held out the possibility of comprehending economic activity which involved much more than constrained optimisation and supply and demand responses. Research, as well as experience of life, impressed upon me the inappropriateness of firm conceptual boundaries between 'economic' and 'non economic' activities and behaviour. In my research the fusion of economic, familial, social and cultural activities and networks has appeared central. As are the connections between the 'public' world of commerce and industry and the 'private' world of individuals and families, the importance in economic 'rationality' of group perceptions and subjectivities, and the role of tacit knowledge and unarticulated, often localised, understandings.[4] The embeddedness of economic activity within the social, cultural and personal fabric of everyday life means that the economic historian must ask additional questions and use other sorts of methods alongside those of the economist. This is what attracts me to economic history.

Despite its growing sophistication, with new institutional economics, new growth theory, bounded rationality, and new ideas about risk aversion, asymmetries and moral hazard, modern economics remains focused on the role of interests in explaining economic behaviour. Along with formalism this has contributed to the isolation of economics within the social sciences. It sets itself apart by being the only discipline defined by a methodology rather than by its subject matter. Rational choice theory has of course been very successful in spreading to areas of social and cultural analysis which were previously regarded as beyond its purview.[5] But this signals a growing rather than diminishing methodological polarity in social science because, unlike economists, most sociologists and anthropologists approach the same questions from a different starting point. Where economists start with interests and then take institutions and social behaviour into account, sociologists start with society, culture and institutions, explaining how economic behaviour (oriented towards interests or utilities) is 'embedded' within them. These approaches involve different methodologies which limit their potential for integration but economic history can be sited at their interface and this gives hope for the future.

That an understanding of the economic can best be approached by detailed ethnology and thick description which can then be brought to bear to illuminate and restructure models and ideas derived from social science (including economics) has been the lesson of my empirical work. The tension between a positivism based upon the science of large numbers (usually geared to policy making) and the value of detailed 'readings' and/or description in grasping underlying subjectivities, social interaction and structures 'in the process of structuring'[6], is one which inhabits all social analysis. It is this tension that keeps me excited about economic history.

The choice between history as poetry or history as science (history as a text to be read or as a model to be built and tested) is stark and overdrawn but is often posed in theoretical debate. In the sort of small-scale research which I am doing at present, both approaches are necessarily integrated and this promotes my engagement with broader theoretical issues. By approaching economics from the perspective of everyday life, micro-history and ethnology, I hope that my future work will make a contribution to rethinking the place of the economy in social analysis and also to debates about the methodology of the social sciences more generally. In this process, I like to think that, just as when I was a child, I am learning as much from observation as from abstractions.

Pat Hudson (b. 11. 12. 1948, in Barrow in Furness) gained her BSc. (Econ) from LSE and D. Phil from the University of York. She taught at the University of Leeds (1975-6) and at the University of Liverpool (1976-97) where she was promoted to a personal Chair in 1993. Since 1997 she has been Professor of History at Cardiff University. Her publications have focused upon industrialisation in Britain, the family economy, regional and local history. Her most recent book is *History by Numbers* (Arnold, London 2000) and her current research concerns the place of the economy in social science.

---

1. Lucien Febvre argued that historians of his time were hot house plants: most were raised too far away from the sights, sounds and smells of man's constant battle with the land and the elements for an empathetic understanding of pre-industrial history. Part of the Annales project, as he saw it, was to regain this contact by becoming more conscious of senses other than sight and sound: *The problem of unbelief in the sixteenth century: the religion of Rabelais* (1942, Eng. trans., Cambridge, Mass. 1983)

2.The approach used in my most recent research is that of micro-history allied to the 'thick description' first expounded by Clifford Geertz in *The Interpretation of cultures* (1973). The purpose of micro history is to say a great deal about the wider world and about wider structural forces but from a more concrete, less abstract, perspective, rooted in vernacular experience and expression. See H. Medick, 'Missionaries in a rowboat? Ethnological ways of knowing', *Comparative Studies in Society and History*, 1987 p.93. The relationship between micro history and theories of social systems is explored further in C. Ginzburg and C. Poni, 'La micro-histoire' *Le Debat*, 17, 1981, 133-3676-105. Although born partly as a reaction to positivism, micro history deliberately eschews the disabling relativism of post- structuralism favouring the use of traces, signs and details of evidence to grasp elements of an opaque reality. It also necessarily rejects traditional divisions of labour: for example, where the historian is assigned to gathering evidence and the economist encouraged to provide the theory. In this approach the two are inseparable.

3. E. J. Hobsbawm, *On history* (London, 1997) p. 109.

4.The sort of knowledge which Hayek argued was so fundamental that central planning could never work. F. A. von Hayek,

5. This started with work on the neoclassical economics of the family by Gary Becker but for recent examples see M. Tommasi and K. Lerulli, *The new economics of human behaviour* (1995) which uses the methods of modern economics to analyse sex, drugs, crime, marriage divorce, alcohol, religion, politics and crime.

6.A phrase most often associated with A. Giddens but found earlier in the writing of Geertz and recently taken up in important theoretical debate in sociology by Z. Bauman in particular: See his *Intimations of Postmodernity* (1992).

Economic History and Area Studies – the View from the Periphery

Janet Hunter

As an economic historian of Japan I have often felt myself located on the periphery of the economic history discipline in this country. The same, I suspect, has been true for many other economic historians working on the countries of Asia, Africa and Latin America. It is only relatively recently that many history and economic history departments have begun to extend their teaching beyond the primarily British (and to a lesser extent North American and European) focus which has long been the foundation of the discipline in the UK. This broadening out is, of course, welcome, but a glance at the content of papers at recent economic history conferences, particularly those by young researchers, suggests that the focus of economic history research in many British universities at the start of the twenty first century continues to be strongly 'British'. To call this an alarming insularity would be excessive, but I do think that, notwithstanding the excellence of much of this research, this situation should be food for thought.

It would, of course, be surprising if our comparative advantage did not lie in the vibrant study of British economic history. Research can build on the existing strong tradition of work in this area, as well as the accessibility of data sources. However, the extent of the continuing dominance of this emphasis is in some respects more puzzling. Firstly, such an intensive concentration on research on one's own country and region is not necessarily found elsewhere. In the case of Japan, certainly, more economic historians are studying their own economic development than that of any other economy, but this group does not constitute such an overwhelming majority as in the British case. Secondly, the increasingly multiracial nature of society not just in Britain, but in most of the countries from which students come to study in the UK, might have been expected to increase 'consumer'-led pressure for change, something to which many British universities have been inclined to respond with only too much alacrity. Witness the 20-plus posts in Chinese economics and management advertised last year under a major funding initiative. Economic historians have in general, perhaps, been slow to capitalise on their strengths in a university environment in which 'relevance' stands high on the agenda, 'globalisation' has been the buzz-word, and economics has been becoming increasingly theoretical and mathematical. Thirdly, the boom in the study of British economic history was at least in part a reflection and a consequence of Britain's status as the first nation state to industrialise, and its dominant position in the international economy. Given the tendency of academic research to mirror the fluctuations in economic fortunes, our discipline might have been expected to adjust itself accordingly.

That it has not done so is at least partly due to institutional constraints, notably the framework within which the social sciences, including history, have been taught and researched in the past. The study of non-European and non-North American societies has been primarily located in self-contained 'area studies' centres. Research students of economic history and the other social sciences working on non-Western areas have traditionally been taught in departments that brought together expertise on their chosen geographical area or country rather than their discipline. Most such students still work outside disciplinary departments. In the economic history recruitment market they can be quite correctly perceived, whatever their merits in their chosen area, as lacking in disciplinary depth, in the general economic history training that might equip them to teach the bread and butter courses already existing in the department to which they may be applying. The tendency is therefore for 'disciplinary' specialists to exclude those who share their interests, but who may be less well equipped to teach what has been considered the core of the discipline. At the same time area studies specialists have too often used their area studies expertise as a substitute for disciplinary excellence, resulting in the production of research that can be considered in disciplinary terms as second rate.

An associated factor is the extent to which a researcher possesses the theoretical knowledge or technical skills, particularly the quantitative skills, which have come to be so widely used in many areas of the discipline. Economic historians of non-European/non-North American areas are still more likely to be the product of an area studies environment, which may well not be able to provide them with such skills. The need to devote time to studying an Asian or African language, for example, can also detract from the time spent on acquiring other skills. It is thus the case even now that economic historians who work on Asia, Africa and Latin America are less likely to possess the sophisticated quantitative skills used by many of their counterparts working on Europe and North America. This is compounded by the fact that in the case of many developing economies, the non-availability of reliable statistical data on a scale that might permit quantitative manipulation even for the latter part of the twentieth century, let alone earlier, is likely to render such skills largely superfluous. Of course, economic history retains, and should retain, a diversity of approaches and methodologies, but this is one that is less likely to be accessible to many historians working outside the European or North American areas, and which is often a less appropriate tool for their research.

The pressures that universities have come under to sustain the research output of staff, and to ensure that graduate students complete their theses quickly have also played a part, by tending to promote research on more 'manageable' topics. While established researchers are likely to be better able to pursue their interests, we all know that staff at the start of their careers are under enormous pressure to publish, while graduate students have to be told that a Ph.D. is a hurdle rather than a major contribution, and discouraged from tackling anything too ambitious (and interesting). A clearly defined topic that relies on easily accessible data sources and is located in a well-established historiography has obvious advantages over one where the historiography is extremely limited, where the availability of data is uncertain, and where writing up is unlikely to be able to begin prior to the third year of research, following a second year of costly fieldwork outside the UK. Under the circumstances a British-European focus is entirely rational.

However, the present balance of study clearly has implications in terms of the interests of our student consumers, the pressure to take more overseas students, the closures and mergers of economic history departments that we have witnessed, and the shortfall in student applications. The experience at LSE, admittedly with a unusually international student body, is that cosmopolitan courses and research expertise have played an important role in helping to ensure our survival as an independent unit. Of course, institutions are different, and each must play to its own strengths, but there are good arguments to be made that these problems do not betoken a crisis in the discipline – economic history remains, after all, the very core of the historical experience – but may in part be associated with a failure sufficiently to extend the focus of the discipline beyond its traditional core. Particularly in a changing intellectual climate, in which academic contributions have challenged the belief that the economic history of Britain and the West is the essential starting point for our understanding of economic development more broadly, my own feeling is that if the UK is going to remain the centre of excellence in the discipline that it has been in the past, we cannot afford to be seen as anything less that international or transnational.

For me this is much more than just a marketing issue, though. Lying outside the 'mainstream' has been positively damaging when it comes to understanding and analysis of Japan's economic history. It has reinforced the notion of 'difference' which dominated Western perceptions of Japan's economic development for much of the twentieth century. As the first non-Western nation to industrialise, and that significantly in advance of its Asian neighbours, Japan always was going to be 'different'. Its pattern of development meant that it did not fit neatly into any category of industrial or developing economy, and yet its growth and industrialisation posed questions fundamental to our understanding of long term economic change. With few exceptions, though, analysis of Japan's historical experience was left to area studies specialists. In a climate of envy of Japan's success, and in the absence of rigorous application of the analytical tools and methodology of economic history, Japan became the 'honorary Westerner', whose achievement of that status remained something of a paradox. Explanations tended to revolve around a one-off combination of timing, hard work, good luck and a mysterious undefined ingredient often referred to as 'culture'. Lack of wider access to the substantial writings of Japanese economic historians helped to confirm this view.

We have, fortunately, moved on since the days when this catch-all 'uniqueness' explanation seemed to carry all before it. Application of economic theory to the Japanese case, the incorporation of Japan in comparative work, and the exhaustive study of some of the institutions of Japanese economic activity, have produced a much more nuanced view of what was really going on. The growth of other Asian economies has led to Japan's being increasingly analysed in its Asian context. As most specialists on Japan will confirm, the more one researches Japanese history, the greater the number of points of similarity and comparison one finds with other economies. Nevertheless, the view of Japan as 'different', as being more 'unique' than anywhere else, tends to live on, increasingly at odds with the reality we research. It is hard to conceive how such a seemingly innocuous concept has done so much damage both to academic analysis and international understanding.

Failure to examine the Japanese experience with sufficient rigour also skewed our research agenda. Most research on Japanese economic history over the last three decades has resulted directly from the stimulus of Japan's growing significance in the international economy from the 1970s. Understandably, many sought to learn lessons from Japan's 'success'. The growth in teaching modern Japanese economic history has likewise been a response to Japan's undisputed economic power, and recognition of this by the academic community and its student body. However, because Japan has tended to be treated *sui generis*, the questions and issues addressed have often not been 'universal' ones. In particular, Western economic historians of Japan were inclined only to ask why the Japanese economy had been so 'successful' and why it had grown. These are significant and valid questions in themselves, but ones driven by the crucially important task of having to interpret Japan for a Western audience. Many other issues that might show a negative side to that 'success' were neglected, with the result that scholarship was often too uncritical of the costs of Japanese growth, both those borne by the Japanese themselves, and those borne by other peoples. Japan's own historiography, strongly influenced by Marxism-Leninism, had long drawn attention to the structural features of Japanese economic development that pitted one class against another and exacted a heavy price, both in the early years of industrialisation, and during the postwar years of high economic growth, but the climate was such that these distributional issues were often overlooked in the search for the secrets of growth. Greater integration of research on Japan with the 'mainstream' of the discipline would, I think, have enabled us to achieve rather earlier the more balanced view of Japan's modern economic history that has begun to emerge over recent years.

How this institutional relationship works out in the future remains to be seen. Bridging the gap between the discipline, with its British/Western core, and the area studies 'periphery' has not proved easy for either side, and is likely to remain a problem. That there is a need and willingness for the discipline itself to evolve is apparent from the changing coverage of economic history teaching over recent years, but area studies will remain of major importance; no interests will be served if its members feel their research contribution will be undervalued. I hope that both sides will continue to be more inclusive and accommodating towards the other, in the interests of both academic excellence and practical survival. It is perhaps still legitimate to ask, however, why, when Japan has one of the richest and most powerful economies on earth, we still have so few scholars in the UK – in both history and area studies departments - who specialise on its economic development.

Janet Hunter (b. 18. 7. 1948). BA Hons University of Sheffield, D.Phil (Oxon). She has taught at the University of Sheffield and is currently Saji Senior Lecturer in Japanese Economic and Social History at the LSE. Her research interests are comparative economic development, economic and social history of modern Japan, development of the female labour market in prewar Japan and the history of Anglo-Japanese economic relations.

Economic History and the Big Picture

Harold James

Economic history (and academic history in general), where it has a bad reputation, owes that to a narrowness of focus. There have been a variety of neatly unpleasant literary parodies, which some practitioners will readily identify as negative caricatures of their own work: from Kingsley Amis's *Lucky Jim* working on fifteenth century shipbuilding back to Hendrik Ibsen's stultifying husband for *Hedda Gabler* ('Tesman is a specialist, my dear Judge. . . And specialists are not very amusing travelling companions - Not for long at any rate. . . Just you try it. Nothing but the history of civilisation, morning, noon and night. . . And then all this business about the domestic industries of Brabant during the Middle Ages. That's the most maddening part of all.').

These are unfair parodies, though: for the best part of economic history has always been the grand nature of its sweep. Our comparative advantage lies in large scale contrasts and comparisons. At its best, on the other hand, economic history, more than other types of history, has a capacity to illuminate really large issues that cut across centuries and continents. Why did particular forms of property relations develop in some societies, and not in others? How did some societies become more prosperous? How do prosperity and demographic behaviour interact? What sorts of institutional change are associated with increased prosperity? What sorts of geographical unit are most appropriate to the study of these changes? That one of only two Nobel prizes in economics, awarded to an economic historian, was given to Douglass North, seems an appropriate recognition that it is these big issues that matter.

Economic history also does best when it draws closely on the work of economists, not just by taking hand-me-down econometric models, and applying them relentlessly and promiscuously in a routinised way in order to put together assembly-line standardised articles, but by isolating issues that are soluble with the help of certain types of technique. It is striking that some of the most important and provocative studies of economic history of the last generation have been produced by economists who would not usually consider themselves to be economic historians: Amartya Sen's *Poverty and Famine*, Mancur Olson's *The Rise and Decline of Nations*, Partha Dasgupta's *Inquiry into Well Being and Destitution*, and Deepak Lal's *Unintended Consequences*.[1]

An accusation made against many types of historical writing is that they are distortingly presentist, 'whiggish' in Herbert Butterfield's terminology. They are said to take an agenda from current social or political or moral debates and impose that on an interpretation of the past, that consequently owed little to past realities but much to present dreams. It may be legitimate to worry that the current large questions are the result of particular modern concerns.

The converse of this problem of presentist orientation, however, is that history has a peculiar legitimacy when it tells us something unexpected about current problems. Economic history has something quite concrete to say - something which distinguishes it from some other types of historical writing which increasingly have taken pleasure in deconstructing, stressing the meaninglessness of modern meaning, and the amorphous and chance nature of thought. These may be interesting insights, but they can hardly be said to be helpful.

Periodically, the major emphases of economic history have shifted. For much of the early twentieth century, in an era of economic turbulence, it was concerned with immiseration, the condition of labour and the price of progress, in other words the 'standard of living debate'. For much of the second half of the century, it looked at development issues - what could be learnt from the European and North American story, and how those lessons might apply to contemporary 'under-developed' (later 'developing') economies. It was concerned with 'models of economic growth'. The opportunity of economic history at the turn of the millennium is that it offers an interpretation of a really quite challenging question. That is the issue of 'globalisation' - the creation of an integrated international economy, with a greatly increased level of interdependence of capital, goods and labour markets, and a rapid dissemination of technical and organisational change.

Often we believe that this process is irreversible, that it provides a one-way road to the future. But any kind of historical reflection leads to a more sober and pessimistic assessment. Globalisation is very old - one evidence is archaeological, the presence of imperial Roman coins in coastal areas in Sri Lanka and Vietnam. Henri Pirenne's famous thesis was about what might be termed 'proto-globalisation'. So the worry about globalisation is that it moves in pendulum swings between integration and disintegration. There have already been highly developed and highly integrated international communities that dissolved under the pressure of unexpected events. The momentum was lost, the pendulum changed direction, and went backwards. In Europe, for instance, the universal erasmian world of the Renaissance was destroyed by the Reformation and its Catholic counterpart and separatism, provincialism and parochialism. This break-up of globalism has its economic parallel in the succession of an age of transoceanic integration by an era, in most of continental Europe, in which resources were diverted into wars and an increasing opulence of the state.

There has now been a great deal of economic history literature, some of which has even seeped into more popular perception, of the late nineteenth century as a similar universal age to the Roman world or the Renaissance, in which integration and progress went hand in hand. At the beginning of his novel of the last turn of the century, *Der Stechlin*, the great German novelist Theodor Fontane described the remote Lake Stechlin: 'Everything is quiet here. And yet, from time to time, just this place comes alive. That is when out there in the world, in Iceland or Java, the earth trembles and roars, or when the ash from a Hawaiian volcano rains down on the Pacific. Then the water here stirs, and a fountain shoots up and falls again.' Fontane regarded the changes of his age with an elegiac, sometimes nostalgic pathos. Most of his contemporaries were much more optimistic, and looked 'ever onward and upward'. This is the world of globalisation and rapid technical change. We live in a world like Fontane's in which a financial earthquake in Indonesia shakes the City and Wall Street. But Fontane's dynamic and self-confident world was soon to break apart. The break-up destroyed the optimistic belief in co-operation across national boundaries, and indeed in human progress.

At the end of the last century, the world was highly integrated economically, through a mobility of capital, goods and people. Capital moved freely between states and continents. Trade was largely unhindered, even in apparently protectionist states such as the German Empire. Above all, people moved. They did not need passports. There were hardly any debates about citizenship. In a search for freedom, security, and prosperity (three values which incidentally are closely related to each other), the peoples of Europe and Asia left their homes and took an often uncomfortable journey by rail, across the oceans as well as in gigantic human treks in search of a new life and new fortunes. In the countries of immigration, the inflows brought substantial economic growth. At the same time, in the countries the migrants left behind, their departure resulted in large productivity gains as surplus (low productivity) populations were eliminated. Such flows eased the desperate poverty of for instance Ireland or Norway. The great streams of capital, trade and migration were linked to each other. Without the capital flows, it would have been impossible to construct the infrastructure - the railways, the cities - for the new migrants. The new developments created large markets for European engineering products as well as for consumer goods, textiles, clothing, musical instruments.

These inter-related flows helped to ensure a measure of global economic stability. Some forty years ago, the economist Brinley Thomas brilliantly demonstrated an inverse correlation between cycles in Britain and the United States: slacker demand in Britain helped to make the Atlantic passage more attractive. The new immigrants stimulated the American economy, and hence also British exports, and the British economy could revive. The mechanisms for these inter-connections of different markets have more recently been the subject of a large amount of work, some of it collaborative, by Jeffrey Williamson.[2]

This globalisation worked, however, only to the extent to which it was socially acceptable. In particular, it required compensation mechanisms that sheltered, at least to some extent, the victims of change, whether they were workers, or rich land-owners, or owners of capital. In the last third of the nineteenth century, as the previous age of globalisation came about, states began to apply protective measures: tariffs, welfare measures, interventions in the capital market. These were the price to be paid for integration. They also created an expectation of more similar measures in the future, and created in this way a mechanism in which anti-globalisation backlashes snowballed. The interventionist state derived a great deal of its legitimation from the process of globalisation, and became increasingly an impediment to integration. Mostly the logic of this process only came out after the shock of the First World War. It was in the Great Depression that those who opposed the freedom of migration, and of goods and capital transactions, saw the opportunity to move the pendulum back.

The question of globalisation thus raises the issue of institutional development. In the nineteenth century push to globalise there were nation states but the most important developments occurred across national boundaries. Regulation was left largely to a market which did not seem to require international organisation. It merely needed the rule of law in each country which participated in the global economy: it needed no or little international law. Managing international financial crises was left largely to private interests, such as the Rothschild family banks. On a national level this was also the case with J.P. Morgan being a de facto lender of last resort in the big financial crises at the turn of the century.[3] But the combination of a global economic world and national political units with weak powers of market regulation conjured up debates about how a more satisfactory interlocking of economics and politics might take place.

The nation-state appeared to be obsolescent, and instead prophets of the future saw huge empires, such as those of Britain, France, or Russia (even Germany and the United States went over late in the day to a fascination with blue water), or regional economic arrangements such as those envisaged by Friedrich Naumann for *Mitteleuropa*. Regarding crisis management, an increasing political pressure saw private sector solutions as open to abuse even when, as in the case of J.P. Morgan, the rescues were handled quite brilliantly - much better than by many twentieth century central banks. So there was a demand for national solutions (strengthened central banks) and even international organisations, such as the League of Nations, and later the World Bank and the International Monetary Fund.[4] Did these make the world more secure?

There is a current debate about globalisation and backlashes, in which many very prominent contemporary economists (Paul Krugman or Joseph Stiglitz) have intervened with only little consideration of the long-term historical picture of globalisation. They argue for increased international controls, and limitations on capital movements. Are we now living in an age in which the attempt is being made to use not a Great Depression, but the fear of one as a justification for moving back away from the world of the internationalised economy?

Economic historians should focus on the big picture issues. This is not to say that the study of 'smaller' topics can't be interesting and legitimate. A great deal of the most interesting recent work in economic history has been concerned with the application of micro-economics. But this work at its best actually gets at the same issues: how do institutional structures and economic results affect each other. In order to be convincing, such micro-studies need to be tied into those large debates and discussions: to show, for instance, how entrepreneurial action is not some constant that comes from a fundamental proclivity (Keynes's 'animal spirits'), but that a legal and institutional framework can determine if and how entrepreneurship is used. For much of the modern era, there have been two alternatives: economic innovation, or political rent-seeking. The options between these are the consequences of historical choices in institutional arrangement. Analysing those should be at the heart of our discipline.

Harold James (b. 19. 1. 1956) was educated at Cambridge University, was a Fellow of Peterhouse, and is now Professor of History at Princeton University. His books include *The German Slump: Politics and Economics 1924-1936* (Oxford, 1986), *International Monetary Cooperation Since Bretton Woods* (Oxford, 1996), *The End of Globalisation: Lessons from Previous Collapses and Crashes* (Harvard, 2001) and *The Deutsche Bank and the Nazi Economic War Against the Jews* (Cambridge, 2001).

---

[1] Sen, A., *Poverty and Famine: An Essay on Entitlement and Deprivation* (Oxford, 1981); Olson, M., *The Rise and Decline of Nations: Economic Growth, Stagflation and Social Rigidities* (New Haven, 1982); Dasgupta, P., *An Inquiry into Well Being and Destitution* (Oxford, 1993); Lal, D., *Unintended Consequences: The Impact of Factor Endowments, Culture, and Politics on Long-Run Economic Performance* (Cambridge Mass., 1998).

[2] Thomas, B., *Migration and Economic Growth* (Cambridge, 1954); Thomas, B., *Migration and Urban Development* (London, 1972); O'Rourke, K.H., and Williamson, J.G., *Globalisation and History: The Evolution of a Nineteenth Century Atlantic Economy* (Cambridge Mass., 1999).

[3] Ferguson, N., *The World's Banker: The History of the House of Rothschild* (London, 1998); Strouse, J., *Morgan: American Financier* (New York, 1999).

[4] James, H., *International Monetary Cooperation Since Bretton Woods* (Washington D.C. and New York, 1996); Pauly, L.W., *Who Elected the Bankers? Surveillance and Control in the World Economy* (Ithaca N.Y., 1997).

Economic History and Regional/Local History

Bernard Jennings

It is 50 years since I acquired a wife, a home and a research topic in one comprehensive action. The home was a wing of a country house in Swaledale. At the other end of the house I found the abandoned estate office of the major lead-mining royalty in Swaledale, containing 300 years of records in confused heaps – the raw material for a thesis on the lead mining industry of Swaledale.

I became particularly interested in the commercial organisation of the industry. In the eighteenth and nineteenth centuries most mines were let on 21 year leases. Left to themselves, the lessees might do little or no development work (driving levels, sinking main shafts) in the last few years of the lease, concentrating instead on cleaning out all the ore-bodies within sight and leaving the mine difficult to let. Consequently negotiations for a new lease usually centred on development work covenants rather than financial terms. In the middle of the nineteenth century a sensible solution emerged in Swaledale in the form of agreements that lessees would employ a certain number of men full-time on development projects, half of them working to the directions of the lessor's agent.

The supervisor of my thesis, Asa Briggs, raised my spirits when he told me that I had become an expert on the evolution of leasing systems in non-ferrous metal mines, as a result of which the academic world would beat a path to my door. Alas the path has remained completely untrodden for nearly half a century. My laments about this led on two or three occasions to well-meaning colleagues approaching me, their eyes shining with insincerity, to declare that they had always wanted to know about . . . But I was not deceived. I was not only the leading expert on the subject; I was the only person remotely interested in it. However, my work on the commercial organisation of the industry led Arthur Raistrick, who had an intimate knowledge of the technology of mining and smelting, to invite me to join him in writing *A History of Leading Mining in the Pennines*.

In the meantime the direction of my researches was being determined by the students in my WEA/extramural classes. Most of these were held in the Pennine dales, where the people tended to identify with the valley rather than the village. For example, when I began a class on the history of Nidderdale in Pately Bridge in 1958, the students came from all over the dale, and included farmers, farmer's wives, people involved in the local flax-spinning industry (including the foreman of a mill still using a water wheel), a council roadman, a reservoir keeper and even the owner of a limestone cave. They were interested in exploring broad economic and social themes rather than the history of particular villages.

When the class began there was no thought of going beyond a thorough study of the history of the dale for its own sake. As the students realised that the ground they were cultivating was both fertile and largely virgin, they began to say how interested the local community would be in their explorations. The end product was a 500-page book, *A History of Nidderdale* (1967). The book has gone through two subsequent editions incorporating further research (1983 and 1992), with a total print of 7,000. The profits of the first edition were used to start the thriving Nidderdale Museum, which has its own publication programme still keeping some of the 1958 students busy.[1]

Two classes in Harrogate wrote *A History of Harrogate and Knaresborough* (1970), which covered the extensive Honour of Knaresborough as well as the two towns.[2] R. Fieldhouse and B. Jennings, *A History of Richmond and Swaledale* (1978) was mainly the work of Roger Fieldhouse's classes in Richmond and Reeth. In 1974 I became Professor of Adult Education at Hull, where I used my Pennine experience to plan a part-time degree in Regional and Local History, but still kept in touch with my students in West Yorkshire. The Hebden Bridge WEA group wrote *Pennine Valley: A History of Upper Calderdale* (1992), and subsequently I worked with three other members of this team to produce *A History of Todmorden* (1996).[3] By no means all of my classes succumbed to 'the last infirmity of noble mind', but a kind of monitorial system developed, with experienced students acting as tutors of other classes. One such was Maurice Turner, who took early retirement as an industrial scientist, gained a doctorate in economic history, and has guided classes to publication, including *Kith and Kin: Nidderdale Families 1500-1750* (1995).[4]

Following the maxim that good style means 'courtesy to the reader', we have tried, without diluting the intellectual content, to present concepts and terms in a form accessible to 'the intelligent general reader'. Specialists can easily skim over explanations which they do not need. For the benefits of both kinds of reader we provide detailed references. The local market for these books is brisk. What use is made of them by specialists in economic history? The picture varied. The material on lead mining is readily harvested. The accounts of the flax-linen industry in *Nidderdale* and *Harrogate and Knaresborough* are recognised as making a useful addition to the limited literature on that industry.

There are, however, a few other topics which might be worth wider attention. One is mortality rates in the 'Great Pestilence' of 1349. From the court rolls and accounts of the Forest of Knaresborough it is possible to calculate, with only marginal uncertainties, the proportion of land vacated by death in the plague year, 46-49%. We are dealing not with some wild guess by local historians seeking ghoulish glory for their district, but with roll after roll listing the holdings of tenants who had 'closed their last day'. A different administrative system in upper Calderdale means that similar figures of 40% and 33% are understatements, by an uncertain margin. A third township in the same area was pronounced 'dead', and did not function administratively for over two years. Why bother about a few more Black Death figures? The above areas were rural, with much dispersed settlement, demonstrating that high mortality was not confined to tight concentrations of people.[5]

Extensive studies of probate inventories have provided a correction to Herbert Heaton's view, expressed in his masterly study of the Yorkshire woollen and worsted industries, that the two branches had contrasting structures c1700, woollens being dominated by small independent producers and worsted by large-scale capitalist employers. In fact the latter were just as important in woollens, and 'small independent clothiers' operated in worsted. Some households engaged in both branches, a sensible arrangement as the market for one kind of cloth might be brisk while the other was slack.[6]

A wider question relating to the textile, and other, industries is the origin and nature of the dual economy. Four decades ago Joan Thirsk's article on 'Industries in the Countryside' showed how the manorial custom of dividing copyhold properties between surviving sons stimulated industrial development in rural areas. In upper Swaledale (the manors of

Healaugh and Muker), the practice was not some ancient Viking Inheritance, but developed from letting off monastic granges and seigniorial vaccaries. These were large enough to provide adequate family farms during the early stages of subdivision on inheritance, and the practice evolved into a rigid manorial custom. Giving younger sons the chance to marry increased the population and accelerated fragmentation, some holdings being divided in the space of three generations into a number of parts ranging from 10 to 30. The alternative occupations here were hand knitting and lead mining. By 1800 most of the farmland was held in smallholdings by miners.[7]

The economic consequences of compulsory divisible inheritance are well known. There was, however, a system of discretionary divisible inheritance in some large lordships. In both the Forest of Knaresborough and Sowerbyshire (the upper Calderdale section of the Manor of Wakefield), the manorial rule of primogeniture could be circumvented by the practice of copyholders surrendering the title to parts of their land to their younger sons and receiving back a life interest. In the course of time this dual surrender in the manor court was replaced by the single surrender of a reversion. In Calderdale the system became so flexible that parents could transfer the title to parts of their land to their children with the right to reclaim it by a simple declaration. In both Swaledale and Calderdale freeholders often passed part of their land to younger sons, perhaps influenced by local copy practice.

In the Forest of Knaresborough and Calderdale the eldest son was not infrequently given a larger share of the land (not necessarily of the textile side) than the younger sons. The process of subdivision was not allowed to proceed to the extremes found in upper Swaledale. In the 'discretionary' areas subdivision and industrial growth were interactive processes, the possibilities of developing the textile side of the household economy, and to a lesser extent of intaking from the commons, encouraging copyholders and freeholders to pass land to more than one son.[8]

A general feature of the textile areas of west Yorkshire was the existence of extensive common lands on which it was difficult to prevent small-scale encroachments for building a cottage and enclosing a small plot of land. As every weaver needed five or six ancillary workers for such tasks as carding/combing/heckling and spinning, the cottage on the common was an essential adjunct to the dual-economy household. It would be interesting to test the hypothesis, for which there is some evidence, that where strict control of the commons prevented intaking and encroachment, the development of the textile industry was severely restricted.

The final example which I would offer is medieval farming and field systems in the Yorkshire uplands. Theses are sometimes described as predominantly pastoral areas in which common arable fields were unknown. In fact there were two quite distinct agrarian economies, especially before c1300. One consisted of monastic granges and seigniorial vaccaries, concentrating on large-scale cattle and sheep rearing. Fountains Abbey, for example, grew corn in the lowlands round the abbey and in the Vale of York; used Nidderdale for cattle rearing and the wintering of sheep; and in the summer grazed its sheep and young cattle on the high limestone pastures in Craven. The peasant in the parallel economy could not specialise in this way. Their 'cash crops' were normally livestock products, but for subsistence they relied on cereals, the great bulk in the form of oats, which could best withstand the cool and damp climate. Holdings consisting of intermixed selions subject to 'average' (the right to pasture stock after the harvest had been gathered) were found in the heart of the Pennines, although the cropping arrangements were different from the 'classic' lowland systems. When vaccaries and granges were split up and let off to tenants we find meadow and pasture being converted to arable, as shared fields.[9]

If the suggestion that scholars in the Deep South, i.e. the lands beyond Sheffield, should be more cautious in generalising about upland Yorkshire leads to accusations of Yorkshire chauvinism, I have the perfect defence. I come from Lancashire. If I am ever introduced, as a public speaker, by a Yorkshire chairman who offers a disparaging apology for my origins, I explain tactfully that I am eternally grateful to Yorkshire because I realised that there was no chance of someone with only moderate talents making a successful career in Lancashire. For some reason I never receive repeat invitations.

It would be unrealistic to ask writers on topics in English economic and social history to skim through all the more substantial regional and local histories in the country in search of relevant material. There are far too many such works. One answer to the problem might lie in a reconsideration of reviewing strategy, the regional and county journals looking at studies in the round, and the national journals, e.g. the *Economic History Review*, providing short reviews which concentrate on noting the additions to knowledge likely to be of interest to the readers of that journal.

There is room for improvement in the first category of journals. I would like review editors to urge reviewers to identify the main contributions to knowledge in a book, even if this means that they would no longer have room for such laments as being unable to find 'Quakers' in the index until they looked under 'religious life'. I am the last person to argue that regional and local studies should be regarded essentially as tributary streams to the great river of English economic and social history, but the use of short specific reviews would enable many more to be published. Such a review might say, 'This book makes a significant contribution to the discussion of the origins of the planned, nucleated village'; or even, 'This book satisfies the long-felt hunger of the academic world for knowledge of the evolution of leasing systems in non-ferrous metal mines'.

Bernard Jennings (b. 7. 4. 1928) was educated at London (BA) and Leeds (MA). His thesis was on 'The Lead Mining Industry of Swaledale'. He was WEA tutor from 1950-61, elected to North Riding County Council 1955, 1958, 1961. Department of Adult Education, University of Leeds 1961-1974, lecturer then senior lecturer in History. Liberal candidate in Huddersfield East, 1964 general election, won the bronze medal. Department of Adult Education, University of Hull, Professor of Adult Education 1974-1990, Professor of Regional and Local History 1990-93. National President of the WEA 1981-91. He is currently Emeritus Professor at the University of Hull and has two areas of research interest: the subject of Adult Education and regional economic and social history, especially in Yorkshire.

[1] B. Jennings (ed), *A History of Nidderdale* (Huddersfield 1967, 2nd and 3rd edns York 1983 and 1992).

[2] B. Jennings (ed), *A History of Harrogate and Knaresborough* (Huddersfield 1970).

[3] B. Jennings (ed), *Pennine Valley: A History of Upper Calderdale* (Otley 1992); M. and F. Heywood and B. Jennings, *A History of Todmorden* (Otley 1996).

[4] M. Turner (ed), *Kith and Kin: Nidderdale Families 1500-1750* (Summerbridge 1995).

[5] *A History of Nidderdale* (3rd edn), pp 483-5; *Pennine Valley: A History of Upper Calderdale*, pp35-8; J.F.D. Shrewsbury, *A History of the Bubonic Plague in the British Isles* (Cambridge 1970), pp54, 123.

[6] H. Heaton, *Yorkshire Woollen and Worsted Industries* (2nd edn Oxford 1965), pp264-71; *Pennine Valley: A History of Upper Calderdale*, pp 81-5; M. Dickenson, 'The West Riding Woollen and Worsted Industries 1689-1770' (unpub. Ph.D. thesis University of Nottingham 1974).

[7] Joan Thirsk, 'Industries in the Countryside', F.J. Fisher (ed), *Essays in the Economic and Social History of Tudor and Stuart England* (1961), pp70-88; A. Raistrick and B. Jennings, *A History of Lead Mining in the Pennines* (1965), pp312-3; R. Fieldhouse and B. Jennings, *A History of Richmond and Swaledale* (1978), pp135-9.

[8] B. Jennings, 'The study of local history in the Pennines, the comparative dimension', *Transactions of Halifax Antiquarian Society*, NS Vol. 3, 1995, pp 22-6; *A History of Nidderdale* (3rd edn), pp 56-7; Pennine Valley: A History of Upper Calderdale, pp 53, 78-82.

[9] B. Jennings, *Yorkshire Monasteries: Cloister, Land and People* (Otley, 1999), chapters 5-7; *A History of Todmorden*, pp25-30; *Pennine Valley: A History of Upper Calderdale*, pp28-32; *A History of Nidderdale* (3rd edn), pp 37-46, 94-105.

Migrations in Economic History

David J. Jeremy

This is an autobiographical piece. All my working life has been related to historical studies, either by teaching, research, or museum curating. However, in veering between institutions, historical sub-disciplines, time periods, and continents, my career has been untypical of British academics. Things began unexpectedly. Until I went to university (Keele) at the age of eighteen, I was not greatly interested in History and certainly not Economic History. My main passion was drawing and painting. My spare hours were spent cycling out into the Berkshire countryside in order to sketch a watermill here, a prehistoric fort there, a parish church somewhere else. My devout Nonconformist parents encouraged this tentatively. Around O Level time in 1955 they suggested that I think about becoming a draughtsman and try to get an apprenticeship at nearby Harwell, the 'Atomic Research Station'. To their surprise and mine I passed enough O Levels to enter the sixth form. This opened the possibility of getting a degree. Neither my parents nor my grandparents had schooling beyond the age of fourteen, so our family knew little about university except that a degree was a passport to a good job. I had better stay on in the sixth form and try to get onto a degree course: in Fine Art, I hoped.

A new headmaster, John L. Cain, arrived soon after I moved up to the sixth form at Wallingford Grammar School. Like the previous head, he was an Oxbridge man but was much younger, having served in the Second World War while his predecessor served in the First. In retrospect, John Cain's advice would prove crucial. Under Tom Beale's tuition, my artistic abilities and my hopes of doing a Fine Art degree flourished. At the end of the lower sixth year I passed A Level Art with distinction (and simultaneously scraped through A Level History). I imagined getting into a university Fine Art department would not be difficult. However, neither university to which I applied would give me a place. I was shocked and deeply disappointed. John Cain suggested that I try a general Arts course at what was then the University College of North Staffordshire. So I went to university on a State Scholarship in Art and History to take a degree that did not include the subject I liked best and in which I was most able.

My intellectual goals centred on getting a degree and becoming a schoolteacher. To keep my training down to four years, I took an Education Diploma alongside a degree in History and English. My results were mediocre: a 2.2 degree and an Education Diploma with commendation. Drawing and painting became hobbies, but were still useful in the classroom. Behind all this, four formative influences fed my appetite for historical research.

The first was family. My father was a GWR railway telegraph clerk, as was my mother before their marriage. He advanced his education through the GWR Social and Educational Union, the St John Ambulance Brigade, and the Wesleyan Chapel in Carmarthen. I suppose his taste for poetry and music gave my brother (who became a professional musician) and I our artistic preferences. Mother's horizons were more limited perhaps. She came from a family of smallholders in the Chiltern hills. Apparently her father was rather good at drawing. Dad was a Methodist lay preacher and Sunday School superintendent and, after 1945, a parish councillor.[1] Books and reading were therefore commonplace in our home. His long-widowed mother came to live with us during the war (along with another of her grandchildren), thereby cramming six people into our three-bedroomed council house in Didcot. Grandma's cousin was Professor Arthur Samuel Peake, the eminent Primitive Methodist Biblical scholar, and, though we had no contact with the Peakes, our family's respect for learning was high. This was augmented in the chapel where members included Harwell scientists and where, occasionally, we had distinguished visitors (Sir John Cockcroft was one). Above all and foundational for my brother and I were the sacrificial love of our parents and their constant encouragement to persevere with skills for which we showed some aptitude.

The second influence shaping my appetite for historical research was faith. Methodists believe in conversion: repentance and surrender to the rule of Christ. After a period of inward rebellion, at 14 I became a committed Christian, at a Billy Graham Crusade in 1954. While behavioural change came slowly, I did adopt certain attitudes and practices which have remained. One was the habit of seeking God's direction, believing that He had purposes for my life. This eased my switch away from Art: God had moved the points. Further, Christianity is an historical religion: history was one way to understand divine-human interactions. As well as that, if God wanted me to engage in historical research, the handicap of a weak undergraduate degree could be surmounted.

A third influence were my early History teachers: Mary Mollison (later Mrs Mary George) at school; Hugh R. Leech, a Balliol medievalist, at Keele. They taught me to write, to analyse and organise thoughts and data, to be questioning. Again, like my parents, they gave me encouragement. Miss Mollison encouraged me to take A Level, and then S Level, History. Hugh Leech persuaded me to work for a part-time master's degree (at Bristol) when I started as a school teacher in Swindon.

Last, there was the influence of my artistic inclinations. Traditional, representational art, 'my kind', has certain cognitive ingredients which can be transferred to historical research and writing. One is the quest for a new angle on the familiar. Another is the need simplify a welter of detail, yet select and retain significant minutiae. Another is the search for pattern, contrast, relationship, composition. And the practice of accuracy in representational art has obvious applications in historical investigation.

That I moved from part-time to full time historical research, and eventually shifted into areas of Economic History, was really due to my first wife as much as to my own inclinations. Theresa was a very determined person. While raising two daughters she gave me unstinting support in my studies. She loved cooking and entertaining, as visitors from the fraternity of historians discovered. She restrained, but did not entirely choke, my book-buying. She helped with masses of typing when I lacked that skill. Above all, perhaps because her faith was stronger than mine, she was the first to welcome new opportunities and to push my career forwards. Three big moves in particular turned me into an economic historian: to Hereford in 1963; to the USA in 1967; and back to the UK in 1973.

We started married life in Hereford where I had been appointed assistant lecturer in Herefordshire Technical College. Here I taught History, including A Level Economic History, O Level English, and recreational Art. That was pre-Mathias. Our A Level textbooks were 'Briggs and Jordan' and 'Pauline Gregg'. For the first time I studied Economic History! Simultaneously, my researches into the eighteenth century Wiltshire clothier Henry Wansey and his American journal of 1794 (a topic suggested and supervised by Peter D. Marshall at Bristol) were bringing me into contact with practising economic historians. Most generous in sharing information and correcting some of my early drafts was Miss Julia de Lacy Mann. Then living in Melksham, she was preparing her definitive volume on *The Cloth Industry in the West of England from 1640 to 1880* (1971). Chris Aspin, then writing on Hargreaves and the spinning jenny, kindly explained the workings of spinning machines (which then I had never seen in operation).

Editing a travel journal to eighteenth century USA from a base in Hereford meant forays to the British Museum Library and the Public Record Office in London, Rhodes House Library in Oxford, and the American Museum near Bath. These excursions had to be supplemented with a wide correspondence with librarians, archivists, and scholars in the USA. One correspondent, Julian P. Boyd, Professor of History at Princeton, commissioned me to do a small piece of research at the PRO and then in February 1967 invited me to spend a year as one of his research associates on his pioneering project, *The Papers of Thomas Jefferson* (at a salary of $8,000 a year).

At the age of 27, having gone from school to college to school, I felt that my lifetime experience was very narrow and blinkered. Here was a great chance to savour new horizons. But Theresa was pregnant with our second daughter, due that June. She had every reason to reject the possibility. Instead she was keener than I to see the USA. So we seized our second major 'life-enhancing opportunity'. We withdrew my state pension contributions to help pay our fares (totalling £206 14s 6d). On alien immigrant visas, with one daughter aged three years and another three months, we sailed to New York on the *Queen Mary* at the end of August 1967.

Beyond the flamingo pink skyscrapers, which greeted us in the morning light as we sailed up the Hudson, lay six years of wandering scholarship. From Julian Boyd I learned much about historical editing, not least, how meticulous and exhaustive editing could be. The year also enabled me to find an American publisher for my Wansey thesis.[2] As our time at Princeton came to an end, an acquaintance on Arthur Link's *Papers of Woodrow Wilson* project down the corridor, John Davidson, thoughtfully put me in contact with John Munroe, chair of the History Department at the University of Delaware. For a year I replaced John Beer (in Germany, following his history of science research) and taught 'European Civilisation'. For a new research topic I began to relate Wansey's view of 1790s USA to the wider question of technology transfer. Diffusion of technology, I think, I first encountered at Hagley (then the Eleutherian Mills Historical Library), the Du Pont-funded historical research centre with links to the University of Delaware. Here Eugene Ferguson, historian of technology, and George Rogers Taylor, economic historian, were teaching on a graduate programme and leading exciting seminars on early American history, some of which I attended. Meantime I applied to the Smithsonian Institution for a research fellowship and, through the good offices of Philip W. Bishop, English-born, LSE- and Yale-educated curator, I secured one for 1969-70 at the National Museum of American History (as it is now named). Thus began my quest to understand technology transfer. I also joined the Society for the History of Technology and encountered its inspirational prime mover, Mel Kranzberg.

Due to a stomach ulcer and operation, I did not think it wise to return to school teaching in England (our plan) so when Tom Leavitt and Jim Hippen from the Merrimack Valley Textile Museum[3] invited me to apply to succeed Jim as curator, I leapt at the chance. Over the next three years we enjoyed living in North Andover, Massachusetts. From the MVTM's and the Smithsonian's collections I learned almost all I know about textile technology. Simultaneously I made weekly visits to the Baker Library at Harvard, thirty miles away. Here I entered the scholarly world of early American business records, books, and historiography. Robert W. Lovett, archivist; Ken Carpenter, curator of the Kress Library; and Glenn Porter, editor of the *Business History Review* were frequently lunchtime companions on these visits. Al Chandler I met at Hagley and later when he visited the MVTM. Through Phil Bishop's introduction, the first academics I met when we moved to New England were Arthur H. Cole and Fritz Redlich, both venerable and alert.

We sailed back to England in 1973. I had no job in prospect. However, the move resolved the emotional and economic tensions we had long felt in straddling two countries and two cultures. I started again in schoolteaching, for a term as a supply teacher in Herefordshire and afterwards as head of the History Department at the Cecil Jones High School, Southend-on-Sea. Here I taught A Level Economic History, now equipped with Peter Mathias's *The First Industrial Nation*. During my time at Cecil Jones I completed a part-time PhD on the diffusion of textile technology between Britain and the USA in the early industrial period. This was supervised at the LSE by Charlotte Erickson whose unrivalled knowledge of nineteenth century transatlantic migration history guided me into the evidence of the US passenger lists and the movements of the mass of artisans. The thesis was published in 1981.[4]

An entirely new challenge came at the beginning of 1980 when I joined the Business History Unit at the LSE under the direction of Leslie Hannah. From American history and the history of technology, I now moved into business history. My assignment was to edit a biographical dictionary of business leaders in modern Britain (except Scotland, treated by Sydney Checkland and Anthony Slaven). The dictionary, containing 1,169 entries on 1,181 individuals, was completed by the editorial team, with the assistance of about 440 contributors, within budget and on time.[5] In reading all the entries one common thread attracted my attention: the frequency of church connections. A fresh research topic came into view: the interactions between entrepreneurs and religion. Supported by the Leverhulme Trust, I developed this into a systematic study.[6]

Eventually in 1987, impatient with the uncertainties of a research staff contract, I moved from the LSE to Manchester Polytechnic as a Senior Lecturer in Economic History. In the years that followed a small but strong Centre for Business History has developed in the Business School of what is now The Manchester Metropolitan University.[7] Our interests lie in the directions of company boardrooms, occupational health, the cotton industry, business ethics, and business networks. Much of this work has been funded by the ESRC, the Leverhulme Trust, and the Wellcome Trust.[8] A North West regional focus has been the common theme linking together these business history topics. We have also investigated comparisons with Japan's cotton region, Kansai, a project which has taken thirteen years to complete.[9]

So, what does Economic History mean to me? In essence it has meant the privilege of using my creative and social impulses in a working life. I have tried to understand the past on its own terms, seeking to explore the minds, personalities, and horizons of past societies, rather than building econometric models of hypothetical 'might have beens'. At the same time I have sought to illumine the past with the aid of modern theory and, conversely, to test that theory against the evidence of the past. As an historian of technology, I have been more interested in the interplay between people and technological environments than in a nuts-and-bolts approach to technical change.[10] As a business historian, I have been more fascinated by the personalities of entrepreneurs and managers than by economic theories or organisation charts.[11] I have regarded it as a duty to hold the mirror up to the past in the hope that the next generation may gain the perspectives and learn the lessons that will advance the social justice and material prosperity of their day.[12] At the personal level, Economic History has been a quest which involved not only myself but also my wife and family.[13] It took us across the Atlantic. It provided a career after returning to England. It has helped to tap those barely-understood springs of personality which in my case are summed by the dominant metaphors and experiences of the migrant, the pilgrim: inquisitive, restless, creative, moving onwards and, of course for a Christian, upwards.

David Jeremy (b. 17. 7. 1939) is Professor of Business History at Manchester Metropolitan University. He was educated at the University College of North Staffordshire, Bristol University and the London School of Economics. He has been Curator of the Merrimack Valley Textile Museum, USA (1970-73) and editor of the *Dictionary of Business Biography*, (1980-85). His publications include *Transatlantic Industrial Revolution* (1981) and he is currently researching culture and governance in British boardrooms in the twentieth century.

---

[1] Active in the local Labour Party, Jim Jeremy served as chairman of Didcot Parish Council in 1951.

[2] *Henry Wansey and His American Journal, 1794* (Philadelphia, 1970).

[3] Now located in Lowell and named the Museum of American Textile History.

[4] *Transatlantic Industrial Revolution: The Diffusion of Textile Technologies between Britain and America, 1790-1830s* (Cambridge MA; Oxford, 1981).

[5] *Dictionary of Business Biography* (6 vols, London, 1984-86).

[6] *Capitalists and Christians: Business Leaders and the Churches in Britain, 1900-1960* (Oxford, 1990).

[7] Current staff, besides myself: Dr Geoffrey Tweedale; Dr David Sunderland; Professor Douglas A. Farnie; and Dr Francis Goodall. Richard Warren is an adjunct member of the MMU CBH.

[8] ESRC grant R000-23-8347: for a study of 'Business leadership and industrial change in North-West England, 1750-1870', undertaken by Dr David Sunderland, 2000-2003. Leverhulme Trust Research Fellowship allowing me to take a sabbatical year to complete a book-length study of 'Boardroom culture and governance, 1900-1980s'. In addition Dr Tweedale has been supported by the Wellcome Trust in his studies of interactions between medical, occupational health and business interests.

[9] Douglas A Farnie et al (eds.), *Region and Strategy in Britain and Japan: Business in Lancashire and Kansai, 1890-1990* (London, 2000).

[10] See my *Artisans, Entrepreneurs and Machines: Essays on the Early Anglo-American Textile Industries, 1770-1840s* (Aldershot, 1998)

[11] See my *Capitalists and Christians*.

[12] This is one of the purposes of my textbook, *A Business History of Britain, 1900-1990* (Oxford, 1998). This didactic function also emerged in work on the records of the asbestos manufacturer, Turner & Newall. See David J. Jeremy, 'Corporate Responses to the Emergent Recognition of a Health Hazard in the UK Asbestos Industry: The Case of Turner & Newall, 1920-1960' *Business and Economic History* 24, no 1 (1995) and, more importantly, Geoffrey Tweedale, *Magic Mineral to Killer Dust: Turner & Newall and the Asbestos Hazard* (Oxford, 2000). But see also my MMU Business School Working Paper, *Business History for Business and Management Students: Why? What? How? A UK View with Some International Perspectives* (Manchester Metropolitan University, Research in Management and Business, Working Paper Series, 2000).

[13] Sadly, Theresa contracted cancer and died in 1991. Family, faith, and work were bulwarks in my grieving process. This past summer I have remarried and with Jean a new stage in the pilgrimage has begun.

Inspiring People - What Economic History Means to Me

Christine Johnstone

Trained as an economic historian, and then as a curator, I have worked for many years in museums run by local authorities. My current job title is 'Senior Keeper and Keeper of Social History' and my duties include developing strategy, managing staff, budgets and buildings, preparing funding bids, managing capital projects and (last but not least) organising the care and display of some 40,000 artefacts made since 1700.[1]

I do a little research, but mainly on potential funding, the demand for new displays, and the evaluation of visitor experience. I use secondary sources for information about the collections. About once every three years, I do 'original research' when I analyse census enumerators' reports on a street-by-street basis, for specific displays.

What then does economic history mean to me? I first came across economic history as an undergraduate at the University of York. Without ever studying social sciences at school, I had registered for social sciences, with the vague intention of studying sociology when I specialised in the second year. Three weeks into the first term, after only six lectures on the industrial revolution by the inspirational Christopher Storm-Clark, I was clear about my future. Sociology was out, I was going to be an economic historian. Why? Because economic history sought to explain how people lived in the past, and how events in the past had shaped everything I saw around me – industries, landscapes, wealth, poverty etc. It had a methodology that looked at evidence and reasons, and was not just based on hunches and opinion.

By my third undergraduate year, having been compelled to spend a good third of my final two years studying economics, I knew that I still wanted to study more economic history. There were two options – I could go and learn to teach it or I could do a doctorate. Teaching was not an attractive idea, and would involve learning about subjects other than economic history! So I aimed for a doctorate, and was fortunate enough to do so at a time when the government still provided adequate funding for such aspirations. Inspired by Eric Hobsbawm's work, I wanted to look at living standards during industrialisation. My professor wanted more research done on some particularly extensive textile wage records in West Yorkshire. So a D.Phil. on the standard of living of worsted workers in nineteenth century Keighley was born.

Towards the end of my three years of research, I had to ask myself what I wanted to do next. The answer was clear, I wanted to help other people find out about the history that had shaped their lives. But how? School teaching did not appeal, and in any case the curriculum left little time for nineteenth and twentieth century economic history. Academic teaching was out. Coming just after the great expansion of university provision, as I did, there were just not enough dead men's shoes to fill. In any case, the history I was interested in would, I thought, interest everyone, not just the minority who remain in education after the age of 16. Eventually I worked out that museums could be the answer, even though I had hardly ever visited any. For the next five years my goal was to work in museums, to 'bring history to the masses'. It is hard to think of a more difficult profession to enter, especially if you need paid employment, but eventually I became a curatorial trainee in the Modern Department of the Museum of London. With their support, I did the necessary post-graduate museums course, and attained my professional qualifications. Twenty years on, I'm still working in museums, still focused on the history of the last 200 years, and still using my knowledge and experience of economic history.

Museums are rather like ducklings on a lake. Spectators see a familiar, attractive and seemingly effortless sight. They cannot see the legs paddling frantically underneath, and they do not necessarily bring to mind what they know about floods, foxes and genetics. Similarly, museum users see displays, sometimes even reserve collections, often without realising how much work goes into producing and maintaining them. More significantly, museum users invariably underestimate how much the museum product is affected by the staff who work, or have worked there.

Everything that curators do affects the resources that museum visitors use, often in subtle and covert ways. To avoid abusing their power, curators have to be driven by a strong commitment to discipline and transparency and a strong belief in ethics. They must make a clear distinction between subjectivity and objectivity, particularly in relation to their own actions. For me, economic history is one of the touchstones which helps me to tell the difference between the two, and thus to do my work to the standard which I and my colleagues expect.

The term 'museum' covers a wide variety of institutions, organised in many different ways. Museums can focus on history, science or aesthetics; on tourists, local residents or researchers. They can collect artefacts, or specimens, or both; they can be funded nationally, locally, by universities, regiments or volunteers. They can be open one afternoon a week, or every day of the year. Even history museums can focus on a community, a building or an industry; on recent, earlier or ancient times. However, all museums have one thing in common. They agree what a museum is. Through the Museums Association, the profession has debated this issue at every opportunity, and has committed itself to the following definition: 'Museums enable people to explore collections for inspiration, learning and enjoyment. They are institutions that collect, safeguard and make accessible artefacts and specimens which they hold in trust for society'.[2]

All museums, whatever their specialism, balance contemporary public access with long term preservation of the collections they manage. An institution without users is not a museum, neither is an institution without collections. The core of a museum is the contact the public has with the collections, and museum staff work at this core, hopefully enabling the inspiration, learning and enjoyment that the definition focuses on. In a history museum, that inspiration, learning and enjoyment may come from aesthetic appreciation of the collections, or personal memories of individual artefacts, but usually it comes from the historical content.

In this context, museum staff, and in particular curators, have to guard against subjectivity. The existing collections are often biased. In 'social history' collections there is almost always an undue bias towards artefacts that are unique, long-lasting, or produced for the wealthy. Typically, from the nineteenth century, museums hold many samplers, flat irons and china tea sets. They do not hold much second-hand and re-used clothing or many beerhouse mugs and glasses. In the twentieth century, artefacts from both World Wars far outnumber those from student bedsits or interwar council houses. In many cases the chance to fill these gaps has long gone, as the artefacts themselves have failed to survive in private ownership. In these circumstances, museum staff have to ensure clear documentation of the existing collections, recording the fullest provenance and associations, simply to broaden the potential of the collection that is available to them.

Even with the collecting policies that all museums now have, current collecting can also be subject to curatorial bias. This is sometimes simply due to the lack of resources to do rigorous analytical collecting, but more often because curators follow their interest and expertise rather than use other people's knowledge. Biases like these have to be acknowledged, and remedied, or the museum may come to reflect the history of the curators it has employed, rather than the district or community it is supposed to focus on.

A less subtle expression of subjectivity is in the displays, both temporary and permanent. Museum staff generally choose the theme of the displays, decide which artefacts are both relevant and technically suitable for display, write the accompanying text, and select appropriate interpretation. Each of these actions is an opportunity to be subjective, to focus on one view of history which may only be personal to the curator, but which will be validated by its presence in a museum display.

The issue of perceived validation is important for history museums, particularly ones which focus on a geographical area rather than an industry or a building. Outside some of the major cities, the economic history of many of these areas has not yet been written. There may be a history of the town, full of names and dates, published in the 1880s; perhaps even well-researched articles on firms and individuals in local society magazines. There are often books compiled from recent oral history, and almost always volumes of historic photographs. National and sectoral research is available through *ReFRESH* (if a local institution subscribes to it) or through one of the numerous history programmes on television. But many enquirers and researchers will find no coherent published explanation of the development of the town or area they are interested in. The displays in the local history museum are often the only secondary source available to someone interested in local economic history, the only easily available context for the information they already have, and the only guide to potential primary sources.

In the district where I work there is a town called Castleford. After a brief, but important, flowering as a Roman fort and town, it became an important centre of coalmining, glass bottle manufacture, potteries and the chemical industry from the 1780s onwards. The people of Castleford value this 'heritage' and have just started a well-supported local campaign led by the Castleford Heritage Group. The aim of this group is to 'celebrate our past, Roman times, glass, coal, chemicals, our people, our future'.[3] This sounds very much like economic history to me, but the Castleford Heritage Group are not striving to write a book or publish an article, they want a museum.

Museum staff have to use the power that they are given in a very responsible manner. Curators, in particular, have a duty to respect the evidence they pick up and discard when they add to the collections and edit the displays. They must resist the temptation to present history as a united march to a pre-destined future. They should create displays which reflect both the diversity of views and experiences at any one time, and clearly distinguish between fact and opinion.

Recently, Wakefield Museum has installed completely new permanent exhibitions, including one on 'The Story of Wakefield'. This begins with hunter gatherers coming across the land bridge from what is now mainland Europe, and ends with a Teletubby and video footage of a

Saturday night in a Wakefield pub in 1998.[4] It is the only historical overview of the city's history in the public domain.

Obviously, the Story of Wakefield included a display on the 1984-5 miners' strike, as coal-mining was then one of Wakefield's major industries. In 1984-5, museum staff had appreciated the historical importance of the strike and had collected a wide range of ephemera, badges and photographs reflecting strongly-held opinions both for and against the strike. This collection had been added to more recently, especially after the preparations for the new display on this topic had been publicised locally.

As the curator, I had to ensure that we provided an accurate overview of events locally, not allowing hindsight, rivalries or my own views to bias the museum's statement of what happened. I included anti-strike material in the displays, but grouped together, not mixed with the pro-strike material. Where contemporary comments were available from the original donor or photographer, these were included, but provenanced and produced in a different type-face. The main text for this display was deliberately terse and factual:

> In 1984 the National Union of Mineworkers went on strike, without a full ballot. Margaret Thatcher's Conservative government vowed to break the strike, and thus the power of the N.U.M. After a long and bitter struggle, the government won. In 1985 the striking miners were forced back to work. Almost all of the pits in the Wakefield area closed down over the next ten years.

The secondary text made clear the provenance of the material on display, and the authorship of some of the individual captions: 'Across and around Wakefield, community groups organised support for the striking miners. Raffles, jumble sales and concerts were held, money collected and food parcels put together. Many of the objects here come from the Stanley Miners Support Group, others from Featherstone and Castleford. Richard Clarkson, a striking miner, took many of the photographs you can see. We have used his captions.'

My only editorial comment was in the sub-heading of the display: 'The Miners' Strike: Dissent and Control'. I had used the same sub-heading for a display covering the religious and political debates of the period 1810-50. In the six months since the new exhibition opened, everyone seems to have accepted the Miners' Strike display as a fair and unbiased historical record of the strike.

Economic history underpins all of the collection-based work I do as a 'Keeper of Social History'. It helps me focus on artefacts as products, to put them in the context of how they were made, who made them, what they were made for. More importantly, it supports the analysis of cause and effect that our users crave, and which is uniquely available at the museum.

So what does economic history mean to me? Certainly the shelves full of off-white journals in the spare bedroom, and the fond memories of happy days at York's concrete campus, but also a clear underpinning knowledge of why and how industrialisation changed people's lives. Post-graduate research gave me some useful skills in combining accuracy with an eye for detail, which have transferred very beneficially to my new role in preparing funding bids. Most importantly however, economic history inspires me, and others, to look for reasons, and to explore the past for our own, and others' enjoyment.

Christine Johnstone (b. 3. 12. 1950) studied economic history at the University of York, receiving her doctorate on nineteenth century living standards in 1979. Since 1980 she has worked as a curator in history museums in London, Hertfordshire and West Yorkshire, and is currently Senior Keeper and Keeper of Social History at Wakefield MDC Museums & Arts.

---

[1] Most small and medium sized museum services divide 'human history' collections into three groups, one by function and two by date. Artefacts which were made for aesthetic display by elites are almost always described as fine and decorative art, and curated separately. All other artefacts are usually divided into two groups, by date. The early group is usually called archaeology, the later group, social history. The dividing date is often 1700.

[2] Museums Association, 12 Clerkenwell Close, London EC1R OPA. Tel: 020 7608 2933. Fax: 020 7250 1929. Email: info@museumsassociation.org.uk Website: http://www.museumsassociation.org.uk

[3] Quoted from the cover of *Lagentium*, Bulletin No 1, September 2000. The Castleford Heritage Group, 8a Broomhill, Castleford, WF10 4QP.

[4] Alston, Judi, *Wakefield Nights*, (One to One Productions, 1998). Email: Info@one2one-films.demon.co.uk.

Economic Growth and the Wealth of Nations

William P. Kennedy

For me, economic history is an integral part of economics. As Robert Lucas has observed, once one reflects on the consequences of even small differences in economic growth rates sustained over time, it is hard to think about anything else.[1] It is therefore not surprising that economic growth, literally the wealth of nations, with all its implications for human welfare, should comprise a large, perhaps dominant, component of economics. However, the study of economic growth is inevitably largely historical. To be sure, as in all other areas of economics, evolving theory disciplines observation, interpretation, and research. Yet in understanding growth, economic theory primarily serves to screen out the implausible and identify the relatively small handful of factors capable of coherently explaining rising per capita incomes over time. The confirmation that technological progress is the ultimate engine of growth is certainly an important insight, but, in itself, is extremely limited. The important issues remain empirical and can only be clarified by historical research. Economic analysis cannot say (certainly not yet) what growth rates should be or even can be, let alone what they have actually been in the past. Indeed, here historical evidence is essential in defining precisely what needs to be explained and in this way informs economic theory even as theory shapes the understanding of history. When and where, for how long, and in what circumstances, has growth performance been impressively good (or bad)? Only against an empirical framework of historical observation can competing theories of growth be effectively tested and useful inferences drawn.

The 75th anniversary of the Economic History Society is a particularly useful point from which to survey those aspects of history's role in comprehending economic growth that most interest me. Consider the current economic and financial press, which, with academic journals not lagging far behind, is currently full of speculation about the implications of the 'revolution' in information technology (IT) for growth.[2] The 1987 observation of Robert Solow, - that 'You can see the computer age everywhere but in the productivity statistics' - has posed an enduring paradox that has prompted an increasingly intense interest in past industrial 'revolutions'. Above all, how does the IT 'revolution' compare with previous ones? Did steam engines, railways, electricity, and motor vehicles have a bigger, more immediate, impact on growth than computers are having now? Is it really true, as Paul David has suggested, that it took fully 40 years for the application of electricity palpably to affect aggregate measures of American productivity, and even longer in other advanced countries? Interesting as these debates are, more than abstract curiosity is at stake here. The 1990s saw an unusually sustained period of growth. Both the U.S. and the U.K. are currently enjoying record breaking expansions, at least in terms of longevity. However, this prolonged growth, especially since 1995 and especially in the U.S., has appeared to accelerate rather than follow precedent and fade as the expansion has matured. This growth in turn has, like the 1840s, the 1880s, and the 1920s before it, ignited what many believe to be 'irrational exuberance' in financial markets. The extent to which this undeniable exuberance is irrational (or otherwise) hinges crucially on how the possibilities of the current IT boom compare with previous episodes of pronounced technological advance. For better or worse, historical judgements on this matter, and on closely related issues such as the ability of regulatory and political regimes to accommodate technological advance, have become embedded in security prices. In response, the well-funded research departments of prestigious financial houses like Goldman, Sachs have discovered an interest in the market impact of the early phases of previous waves of innovation (in Goldman's case, the application of electricity). Historians are likely to find their gratification at such new-found interest in their craft tempered by their surprise at how long it has taken leading market participants to become explicit (and one hopes more discriminating) in their historical judgements. After all, historians have long debated the indirect and subtle ways in which technological advance plays out. When almost anything is possible, no disciplines offer infallible guidance to the future, but few are better than carefully examined historical experience in preparing economic decision-makers to anticipate the probable, while still keeping an open mind in complex, path-dependent environments.

But participants in financial markets have compelling reasons to appreciate historical experience well beyond simply gauging the locus and nature of the impact of technology, vital as that might be. By its very nature, economic growth, the product of a vast myriad of loosely co-ordinated decisions by countless thousands of agents, has never been a smooth process, but is punctuated repeatedly by turbulence of greater or lesser violence emanating from many different quarters in the real economy (wars, big and small; commercial rivalries among and between firms and states; the chance sequence of discovery of processes and resources; natural catastrophe – the list is long and can be altered to taste). Such inevitable turbulence in the real economy, for reasons still vigorously debated, is more often than not amplified in financial markets. Nor does the direction of influence flow only one way: turbulence stemming independently from financial markets has the capacity to add its own contribution to the intrinsic volatility of the real economy. In view of this, surely one of the most important products of historical research in recent decades has been the growing understanding of the role of monetary policy and regulation in anticipating and responding to financial turbulence. Technological change may be the ultimate river of growth, in the sense that in the absence of technological opportunity even the most flawless execution of monetary policy will not produce significant sustained growth, but equally, serious policy errors can deny the fruits of technological opportunity for decades, while causing great immediate misery. That surely is one of the more plausible accounts of American experience in the 1930s.

This perspective suggests that one of the most important audiences for economic historians consists of central bankers, whose lot is not an easy one. By its very nature, serious financial turbulence is hard to anticipate, for correct anticipation, as the efficient markets hypothesis persuasively posits, eliminates most, if not all, of the problem. As the Great Depression all too vividly demonstrated, turbulence in the form of wildly swinging and mostly falling prices has the capacity, if left unchecked, to curb and progressively disrupt all economic activity. Yet some of the bankruptcies and abnormal price declines that turbulence brings are essential parts of growth, as the consequences of flawed (or simply untimely) decisions are revalued in a Schumpeterian process of 'creative destruction'. Hence central banks cannot intervene too quickly and too supportively as lender of last resort. Indeed too great eagerness to cushion agents from the consequences of their own decisions may create moral hazard, making turbulence both more likely and more destructive. Yet to let 'liquidation' of past mistakes (or presumed mistakes – what insights do central bankers possess to discern better than the market the value of assets?) rage on too long and can all too easily cause real damage to the underlying economy through systemic impairment. Similarly, an exaggerated fear of latent inflation and other manifestations of 'irrational exuberance' may needlessly restrict growth and employment. The stakes are huge and the margin for error either way small. Economics has come to offer central bankers and financial regulators a vast array of aids in framing and executing policy, including elaborate structural and forecasting models buttressed by extensive databases. Policy-makers can also draw on wide-ranging research produced by their own staffs, considering in detail various factors – such as the impact on consumption of rapidly rising (or falling) house and share prices – that have yet to be satisfactorily incorporated into operational models. Yet when the largely unexpected crunch comes, policy makers, and central bankers in particular, have little but historical wisdom, however acquired, to guide them. As turbulence unfolds, models become temporarily useless and on-going research untimely, they must act, for better or for worse, within a mater of days, if not hours, upon their 'gut instincts'. While their own post mortems can perhaps sharpen their models and operating procedures (and possibly their historical understanding as well) in preparation for future bouts, only the depth of historical understanding they take into a crisis will help in the heat of the crucial moments. Reliable historical understanding must be built on a detailed knowledge of how a wide range of previous crises – occurring at different times, in different places and in different contexts, in sufficient number to instil an instinct for fundamental processes – arose and were resolved (or not).

Early fascination with economic growth led me to economics. The fascination did not arise from the clarity of Lucas-like deduction, but from a more primitive adolescent interest in military history, a central lesson of which was that brute economic capacity was often a deciding factor in armed conflict – that the big, well-armed, technologically advanced battalions usually won. Such early, dim awareness of the importance of economic growth was reinforced by being asked to read, for my freshman week at Rice University, Walt Rostow's *Stages of Economic Growth.* That was followed a year later by my first formal introduction to economics. The key textbook was Paul Samuelson's *Economics* and reflected his long-standing interest in the role of financial systems within economies, as well as his obvious interest in growth and the policy mechanisms that might foster it. Already primed by an interest in economic growth, stemming from historical interests, Samuelson's *Economics* was a powerful revelation that induced me to study economics as my major subject, with a minor in history, my first formal European history course also having a big impact. Although the 1960s were a time of relatively buoyant growth in the U.S., there was nevertheless (in retrospect, quite rightly) widespread unease at relative growth performance. Western Europe and above all Japan were growing much faster and also making significant technological advances of their own, suggesting that their performance was no fluke, while the Soviet Union showed a disconcerting ability to generate militarily important technologies, which might also translate into enhanced economic growth at some point. These considerations led to a closer examination of British economic growth in the nineteenth century, for there seemed intriguing similarities with American experience a century later. Both had once enjoyed a commanding economic lead based on earlier, clearly superior performance, but both in their periods of ascendancy had gradually come to experience slower growth than that of important comparators. For neither in their respective periods of ascendancy could the most obvious explanations of economic difficulties – military disaster or ill-judged state intervention – be held responsible. More worryingly, for both there were signs of competitive failure (or at least important weaknesses), but without ostensible cause, for both were outwardly market-oriented economies, with open, sophisticated financial markets, surely able to benefit fully from the presumed virtues of competitive enterprise (insofar as an undergraduate could discern them).

Arriving at Northwestern University with ideas of a Ph.D. topic in economics ill-defined beyond some aspect of growth, Jonathan Hughes encouraged me to pursue more seriously my early musings on the British experience. Course work, not least Stanley Reiter's careful exposition of Debreu's *Theory of Value*, drilled home the strategic importance of investment, the only lever that might consistently affect growth, while more reading revealed the imposing extent of Britain's foreign investment. Then, in my final year at Northwestern, at Jon Hughes' urging, I read early conference copies of Michael Edelstein's research on risk-adjusted Victorian investment returns. Edelstein's work seemed to me then, and still does, to have asked with great accuracy the right questions and to have set about answering them in the right way (indeed Edelstein introduced me to the then newly emerging field of portfolio theory, an area that my graduate courses had neglected, although the standard regimen of econometrics meant I had little excuse to remain ignorant.) The answers he offered, however, were more problematical. How could it be that the outcome of rational investment decisions emerged so underweight in the great growth opportunities of the time? Theory identified technology as the key to growth, but Victorian experience, played out in the most sophisticated and informed financial markets the world had ever known, seemed to say investment in technology didn't pay. Resolving that paradox became the task of my thesis and has remained my main preoccupation ever since. Jon Hughes always said that a good thesis topic should last a lifetime (and maybe more).

And so it has proved with me. I feel I was fortunate that, just as my funded time at Northwestern was drawing to a close, the offer of a post in the Economics Department at the University of Essex appeared. Essex in 1971 wasn't a lot closer than Northwestern to the Victorian era that had come to exert such a fascination for me, but it was a little closer nonetheless, and the offer, for two years in the first instance, was too good to resist. The two years just flew by, and at their end my wife and I were not ready to return to the U.S. Contrary to the plan, there was too much in Britain and the rest of Europe still left unseen and undone, not to mention a thesis still uncompleted. Fortunately, I was able to extend my contract at Essex, so we stayed. Although economic history was never at the very centre of the work of the Economics Department at Essex, it was appreciated and I found it a stimulating place to work. Appreciated but not central had also been the position of economic history at Northwestern, so the cultural shock of moving between the two departments was small. But as at Northwestern, many people at Essex had strong interests in historical issues and were more than willing to read papers and listen to seminars. Moreover, the Department was committed to having at least one economic historian on the staff at all times, and two when circumstances permitted, which it did from time to time – both Leslie Hannah and Tim Hatton were colleagues at Essex (but not at the same time).

I would like to end by saying that for me the interest in the manifold aspects of economic growth has never waned. Indeed as I learn more, the interest deepens. There has been more than enough in the subject to have provided me with intellectual stimulation throughout my working life (and perhaps beyond). A close friend once said that the key to a good life was to get paid for what you wanted to do anyway. While it may not have been gold-plated, economic history has done that for me. I can't complain. I hope others will find it so too.

William P. (Bill) **Kennedy** (b. May 1944) gained his BSc from Rice University, Houston, Texas, and Ph.D. from Northwestern University, Evanston, Illinois. He taught at the University of Essex (1971-79) and currently teaches at the LSE . His research field is the finance of innovation in advanced industrial economies, particularly in the late nineteenth century.

---

1. Robert Lucas, 'The Mechanics of Economic Development', *Journal of Monetary Economics*, 22 (1988), p.5.

[2] See for example the panel 'Productivity Growth: Current Recovery and Longer-Term Trends', in *American Economic Review: Papers and Proceedings*, 89 (May, 1999), pp.109-128; Dale W. Jorgenson and Kevin J. Stiroh, 'Raising the Speed Limit: U.S. Economic Growth in the Information Age', *Brookings Papers on Economic Activity*, 2000:1, 125-235; Pam Woodall, 'Untangling E-conomics: A Survey of the New Economy', *The Economist*, 23 September 2000.

Looking to the Future

Eric Kerridge

To an historian like me, economic history is an avenue leading ultimately to history in the whole. Economic history has little in common with theoretical economics as nowadays usually understood. Nearly all the economic history essential to an economic historian is either common knowledge and expounded in pithy sayings and proverbs or is to be found in the works of the medieval Scholastics. Reading fashionable economic theories will only addle a man's brains and tempt him into the sin of reading history backwards, when his true mission is to work forwards in time and discover and explain what happened. Fortunately for me, as a student of what, disregarding conventional periodisation, may be called early modern England, Englishmen were then even less given to economic theory than now. The very word 'economy' meant no more than the business of a family or household. Thus the king had his economy and so did the ploughman and the fisherman. The Crown's policies for the exercise of its absolute prerogative in such matters as war and peace, dues on foreign trade, and law - enforcement, were designed for the defence of the realm, the keeping of the seas and public order. The Crown in Parliament concerned itself also with commonwealth matters like curbing usury and rural depopulation, relieving the impotent poor and disciplining able-bodied idlers. But neither the king nor anyone else had a national economic policy.

Any one man usually had several activities and several different sides to his character. In one or more ways he had to gain an income on which to live and from which to spend. He had also a family life and a religious one. As a sidesman or churchwarden or overseer of the poor or in some higher office, he had an administrative side; as a juror in his guild, manor or superior court, and perhaps as a litigant, a legal one. And these and other activities drew him into some form of calculation and accounting. Then he had also some social life in the course of his work and his leisure hours. His biographer would natural first abstract each of these aspects, subject it to close scrutiny, and then proceed to bring all the abstractions together to form a rounded picture of the man as a unique individual.

History, being the study of great numbers of men, is usually and best studied in an analogous way. Economic history is an abstraction from general or whole history, and agricultural, industrial and commercial history, and so on, are abstractions from economic history. The sole purpose and justification for such primary and secondary abstractions is that they concentrate the mind on a particular aspect of general history in order to unravel its mysteries. The secondary abstraction should throw light on the primary one and that in turn on the whole. The other primary abstractions include political, constitutional, religious, legal, medical, naval, military and educational history and so on, and each has its secondary abstractions. The crucial thing for the student of a secondary abstraction is to bear in mind the primary one, and of a primary one, the whole from which it was drawn.

The historian's greatest joy comes from venturing into unknown territory, treading where no man has trod before, and discovering what no one previously knew of. The joy of discovery has no equal in this world. The historian's second greatest joy is in his later re-assessment and reformation first of the matter of the secondary, then of the primary abstraction, and then of the whole from which both were derived. As he writes an account of what he has found, he will find delight in penning the first draft, pleasure in processing the second, decreasing satisfaction from the third onwards, and after a dozen years or so of making amendments, mere weariness, so that he has to force himself to finish off by dreaming of pleasures awaiting in pastures green and new.

In all this work the historian inevitably makes contact with, and learns from, his fellows labouring in other abstractions. Thus one working in the history of agriculture or landownership has to come to terms with those engaged in legal and industrial history, the political specialist with the ecclesiastical, and so on. One cannot fathom the depth of Charles I's deeds without acquainting oneself with economic history and the abstractions from it. Nor can one understand early modern England without consulting the Holy Bible, for this laid down the rules and laws Englishmen lived by. Christian religion was an essential part of their lives and was reflected in everything they did. The merchant who spent most of his time trading, the landowner who rode and managed his estate, the lawyer who haunted the courts and helped to decide what was and was not a lawful transaction, might on occasion be called upon to sit in a Parliament. Almost without exception, Englishmen were Christians and all had an impact on local and national government, and how they spent their working days and Sundays told in what ways they influenced the realm as a whole. Political and constitutional historians miss much when they fail to read and learn from the work of economic historians. We historians are all working side by side and cannot ignore each other. We all have to learn from each other in the reformation of history as a whole. The penultimate task facing all historians is precisely this reconstitution, this reformation of general history. The final one is its presentation in a lifelike form, satisfying to scholars and understandable by the writers and readers of textbooks and popular works.

These awesome tasks are difficult and endless, but we should not shirk them. Indeed, historians of all kinds have already taken steps in this direction. We see political historians reaching down to probe local politics county by county or town by town, and this is all to the good. But the political and constitutional historians who preside over historical studies in England take few pains to read economic history; they usually content themselves with cursory glances at the more readily available works and with making some casual remarks about agricultural, industrial and commercial events. This leads them into ridiculous blunders about such things as the relation between rises in prices and in population, when there is no means of knowing which came first and when common sense suggests that increases in population, if not from increased longevity, are likely to stem largely from the birth of children, and that though this will cause their parents' spending patterns to alter, as in buying napkins instead of neckties, this cannot affect prices in general and can do no more than make the prices of napkins and neckties higher and lower than otherwise they would have been. Other historians blandly assert that the so-called `price revolution' was caused by the influx of precious metals, all without pausing to wonder how and why they flowed in and why part of this influx was coined and part not. (Postan once asked some exponents of this myth why all the silver was not made into chamber-pots.) Such wild excursions into economic history make one shudder.

But political historians carry only part of the blame, for economic history has carelessly allowed itself to be infected with intellectual diseases. First, economists have penetrated history and brought with them their unhistorical cast of mind. This is true even of the best of the Austrian school. Ludwig von Mises and Friedrich von Hayek, for example, have much to say that is highly instructive to an historian, but their forays into history are intended to enhance their economics rather than to further historical studies. Schumpeter was in many ways an exception, but then he was cast out by the true Austrians and condemned to internal exile. And at the other end of the scale, a thoroughly bad economist like Keynes long succeeded in dazzling and deceiving undergraduates and graduates alike.

Secondly, statisticians have infiltrated. All that can be said against statistics in general has long ago been said; statisticians mind little what they count as long as they count it. The chief interest in statistical studies lies, indeed, in the curiosity they arouse about the data from which they have been compiled. But cliometrics is a special case. It is unhistorical; designedly or not, it disrupts historical studies. It gives rise to historical absurdities, such as the assertion that the standard of living amongst the lower ranks of sixteenth and seventeenth-century English society was deeply worsened. This is done by comparing the assessed rates of daily pay for day-labourers with market prices in large towns, and all without a hint of enquiry as to how many days the men worked and how much they produced for themselves, or the slightest acknowledgement that it was the food and drink their masters provided either free or at well below even local market rates that was a large part of their wage. To take another example, when a cliometrician proves to his own satisfaction that the diffusion of technical improvements in one age was bigger and therefore more important than those in another, he never stops to consider how important the improvements were to people in one and the other age; it is simply that, reading history backwards, they seem more important to him personally. And all cliometrical studies are replete with misplaced concreteness, as when the price of wool is traced (whereas nobody bought wool as such, but only some particular variety of it) and with fearsome technical terms and undefined algebraic formulae that blind the unsuspecting reader with science.

Thirdly, there is the invasion of economic history by contrafactual history, which is against not only facts but also elementary common sense. Nobody in his right mind would try to work out what course history would have taken if pigs could have flown. But a pair of scholars prove to their own satisfaction that if railways had never been heard of, traffic in the United States would have moved just as well on the rivers and canals. In truth, historians have more than enough to do to find out what happened, never mind what did not.

Fourthly, with resurgent Marxism, in North America especially, economic history is no longer any more immune than other historical abstractions from crude, utterly false and subversive generalisations in terms of 'class struggle'. Fifthly, in the field of early modern English history, all these intrusions come together with a variety of socialist beliefs to torment some mystical ogre called 'capitalism' and accuse it of having robbed and impoverished the mass of the population, a proposition diametrically contrary to all known facts. It is hardly surprising, then, that the mere sight of these blemishes in economic-history publications puts historians studying other abstractions off economic history altogether. Professor Hexter, for example, when confronted with an exercise in cliometrics, condemned it as inappropriate to his period and shied away from economic history.

By default, then, the burden of unifying historical abstractions falls mainly on economic historians; they are best equipped for the task and are being prodded into it by sociologists who have taken to reading history and might almost be said to have created sociological history. Their works often provoke thought and provide valuable insights, but sociologists will never be historians.

One way and another, the process of unification and reformation has started. We see a growth in local and family histories and biographies that combine findings emanating from several different historical abstractions and so achieve unification on a small scale. Then we have books that concentrate of one sphere of activity and unify the abstractions within it, for instance, G.D.Ramsay's two volumes on *The End of the Antwerp Market*, and others devoted to short but crucial periods, notably Professor Brenner's *Merchants and Revolution* and Professor Aftalion's *French Revolution*. No doubt other examples will spring to the reader's mind. These seem to me the best ways forward for economic history and history in general. First should come works of limited scope and later, works covering wider field and longer periods.

Finally, even re-integrated and reformed history should not be regarded as an end in itself. History is not something to be studied merely for its own sake. It enables us to travel from the present day and acclimatise ourselves in a former and strange period, but we are still left with a large part of our being in the present, and the greatest and highest objective of the historian should rightly be to use his knowledge of the strange past he has discovered to contrast it with the present-day world in order to advance our understanding of it. For instance, the works of Professors Challis, Aftalion and others on the past debasements of coinages and currencies should enable us to understand the far longer-lasting debasements of our own day and to point to their causes and consequences. As semi-outsiders we are better equipped than most to see the good and the bad in current events and to find and explain their significance.

Autobiographical excursus

Born in a suburb of Ipswich in 1919, I was educated at St John's Church of England School and at Ipswich School. In 1938 I went to read medieval and modern history at University College, London, and graduated in 1947. From 1940 to the end of 1945 I served in the Royal Artillery and was almost constantly on the move from one rural location to another in all quarters of the United Kingdom and in France, Belgium, Holland and Germany. Ever since the age of 18 I had wanted to devote myself to early modern English history and in Sir John Neale I found the perfect mentor. In 1947 I embarked on research in agrarian history and have since moved in natural progression from that. Thanks to charitable endowments, I had six years of full-time research. After a year or two foot-loose, I became a lecturer in the economics department in Bangor. There my hours of lecturing and tutoring rarely exceeded three a week for two terms, but for many years I also lectured once a week on English agricultural history in the agricultural department. In addition I was called upon from time to time to lecture on the economic history of various countries in a number of periods. Latterly, I lectured for a few years on English financial history. Towards the end of my stay in Bangor I was given a personal chair. It was for family reasons that I retired early in 1983, but by then the academic climate had so worsened that I was glad to escape, and former colleagues, finding themselves chained by higher authorities, have since grown to envy me my freedom.

Eric Kerridge (b.1919) is Professor Emeritus, University College of North Wales where he taught from 1960 to 1983. He is currently working on three projects: Christian teachings on usury and interest to1854; The debasement of money, AD.1000-2000 and The foundations of the English nation, c.1300-c.1800

What Does Economic History Mean to Me?

Charles P. Kindleberger

M.M. Postan has twice characterised economic history in ways that appeal to me, in one case saying that it is for economists in their dotage, in another that it was produced, like the mule, by cross-breeding between economics and history, though he felt under no compulsion to indicate which of the parents was asinine nor to judge whether the outcome was sterile.[1] I am not disposed to disagree with the first of these put-downs, but would argue that economic history is more fertile than Cartesian economic theory, which often derives its conclusions from its assumptions rather than from facts. My escape from international economics started with a paper in 1951 noting that the responses of European countries to the fall in the price of grain in Europe after 1875 varied more widely than economic theory would have predicted – tariffs or no tariffs,[2] supported three decades later by Stephen Magee's finding that tariff pressures in the United States were pushed by industries, combining land, labour and capital, not by the scarce factor as the Stolper-Samuelson theory would explain.[3] Somewhat later I produced a paper on the bankruptcy of international economics, despite a fairly successful textbook on the subject. I cannot find it on my shelves, nor remember what it said.[4]

Having insulted economic theory, I proceeded to do likewise to economic history spurred on by an editor who wanted to end *Economic Growth in France and Britain* with a bang. Reacting to the series of mono-causal explanations for growth in one or the other country - coal, exports, technology, *mentalités*, etc. I produced:

> Economic history, like all history is absorbing. Beguiling, great fun. But, for scientific purposes, can it be taken seriously?[5]

I have since recanted in full and in print. After quoting the passage came:

> This gave offence, and offence was taken. General equilibrium remains difficult to the point of being impossible, both in theory and in historical problems such as growth. But I now take economic history seriously indeed, and urge a similar born-again attitude on my fellow current and prospective economists. [6]

Economic Growth in France and Britain made a point that is still germane in most history, that mono-causality is an illusion. Most of social sciences involves many necessary conditions but few sufficient ones. Albert Hirschman has a paper 'Against Parsimony' that belongs in every economist or economic historian toolkit.[7] It is true that there are models or economic laws with strong historical support that lend themselves to many problems. In *Economic Laws and Economic History*, I lectured on four 'laws' that have a stood up well, but perhaps only in certain circumstances: Engel's law, the iron law of wages (a.k.a. the Arthur Lewis (Marxian) model of growth with unlimited supplies of labour), Gresham's law, and the law of one price that might be ascribed to Adam Smith.[8] Each requires other circumstances. In the Lewis model, an elastic supply of labour holds down wages and holds up profits, but for growth the profits have to be invested productively. H.J. Habakkuk, writing on technology in Britain and the United States in the nineteenth century, produced an analogue to the Lewis model, in effect growth with unlimited supplies of land (in the United States), which required for growth that labour was highly mobile.[9] Today's analogue might be unlimited supplies of (venture) capital.

I have often quoted Joseph Schumpeter and Joan Robinson that economics and economic history require toolboxes with many tools.[10] The analyst is required to choose carefully which tool fits a particular problem, whether one of understanding a complex situation (or to satisfy curiosity), or of policy. I especially am unhappy with Jan Tinbergen's five-step routine which he holds is the only valid approach to economic analysis:

1. List the variables involved in the problem (this is as far, he asserts, as literary economists get);
2. Formulate the relationships assumed to exist among the variables;
3. Collect empirical data;
4. Test the assumed relationships until statistically reliable results are obtained;
5. Use the model with the estimated parameters to obtain optimal policy. [11]

This strikes me as entirely too mechanical, with the technique liable to go awry at any one (or more) of the steps. Important factors may be overlooked, change with time, or be unmeasurable. Strong priors may corrupt in one or more ways, overlooking negative evidence, discarding results that fail to confirm the starting hypothesis. Specialisation in the choice of problems or the use of tools may well produce increasing returns, but also run the risk of solidifying opinions held at the start.

If there were only one technique for solving problems in economics or economic history, we would not be left with so many debatable issues: the standard of living in Britain after the industrial revolution and the Napoleonic wars until 1850; the great depression of the 1880s, the causes of the world depression of the 1930s. At the moment I am engaged in a debate whether financial bubbles have existed, or whether financial markets are always efficient, though they sometimes have trouble adjusting to policy-switching by governments.[12] This debate is related to a wider one about the relative efficiency of markets and governments, in which some claim that government bureaucrats are generally self-serving, more interested in their own positions than in the public good. This last strikes me as a political position rather than one about which generalisations do well. The United States made many mistakes after World War I over the League of Nations, reparations, war debts, foreign aid, but learned from them, I would think, as evidenced by the Atlantic Charter, Lend Lease, the British Loan, Marshall Plan, and other steps in world aid.

Economic history, in my judgement, has two major tasks, to understand the complexity of social interaction, satisfying scientific curiosity, and to test with historical data, to the extent possible, the various measures undertaken or proposed to solve economic problems as they arise. In many questions there will be no easy answer, or perhaps many possible answers among which choice depends on non-economic factors of politics, culture, the difficulty of effecting change in institutions or attitudes. As an example, there is the clash between economic and social optimal size: for economics it may be the world, as Robert Mundell said of currency areas;[13] in social terms the optimum is likely to be much smaller, a unit in which the individual feels that he or she counts. Circumstances may determine the outcome. Subsidiarity, or pushing decision-making down to the smallest unit may be desirable in quiet times, for political participation, but must be focused in a central unit in times of crisis. The difficulty, a serious one, is how to move from one pattern to another when circumstances change.[14]

Neither economics in rigorous formulation nor economic history can solve all or even most problems in society. They help, however, especially in combined form, in which economics is infused with lessons from the past. *Economic History and the Modern Economist*, edited by the late William Parker, and with contributions from Kenneth Arrow and Robert Solow, finds it distressing that more and more graduate training in economics is dispensing with its needed ingredient, history.[15]

Charles P. Kindleberger (b. 12.10. 1910) was educated at the University of Pennsylvania and Columbia University. In the late 1930s/early 1940s he was researcher for the Federal Reserve System and Joint Economic Committee of the United States in Canada. After distinguished wartime service he became advisor on the European Recovery Programme 1947-48. He has taught at many colleges and universities around the world, and was Professor of Economics from 1951, then Ford International Professor of Economics Emeritus from 1976, at the Massachusetts Institute of Technology. He has published extensively on international finance and the international economic order.

---

[1] Kindleberger, C.P., *Historical Economics: Art or Science?* , New York:1990, p. 353, quoting M.M. Postan without citation, and pp. 12-13, citing S. Pollard, 'Economic History - A Science of Society?' in N.B. Harte, ed., *The Study of Economic History*, London:1964, p. 291.
[2] Kindleberger, C.P., 'Group Behaviour and International Trade', *Journal of Political Economy*, 59 (1951), reprinted in ibid., *Comparative Political Economy: A Retrospective*, Cambridge, Mass:2000, pp. 51-72.
[3] Magee, S., 'Three Simple Tests of the Stolper-Samuelson Theorem,' in Peter Oppenheimer, ed., *Issues in International Economics*, London: 1980.
[4] Kindleberger, C.P., 'Assets and Liabilities of International Economics: The Postwar Bankruptcy of Theory and Policy,' Monte dei Paschi di Siena, *Economics Notes*, 2 (1982).
[5] Kindleberger, C.P., *Economic Growth in France and Britain, 1851-1950*, Cambridge, Mass.: 1984, p. 332.
[6] Kindleberger, C.P., 'A Further Comment,' in W.N. Parker, ed., *Economic History and The Modern Economist*, Oxford: 1986, p. 90.
[7] Hirschman, A.O., 'Against Parsimony: Three Easy Ways of Complicating Some Categories of Economic Discourse,' *American Economic Review*, 74 (2), May 1984.
[8] Kindleberger, C.P., *Economic Laws and Economic History* (Raffaele Mattioli lectures), Cambridge: 1989.
[9] Habakkuk, H.J., *American and British Technology in the Nineteenth Century*, Cambridge: 1962.
[10] See e.g. Kindleberger, *Essays in History: Financial, Economic, Personal*, Ann Arbor, Michigan: 1999, p. 5.
[11] Tinbergen, J., 'Optimal Development Policies: Lessons from Experience,' *World Economy*, 7 (1), 1984.
[12] See Peter M. Garber, *Famous First Bubbles: The Fundamentals of Early Manias*, Cambridge, Mass.: 2000, which takes exception to my view that manias were the result of excessive speculation (*Manias, Panics and Crashes: A History of Financial Crises*, 3rd ed., New York:1996. Policy Switching is discussed in Robert P. Flood and Peter Garber, *Speculative Bubbles, Speculative Attacks and Policy Switching*, Cambridge, Mass.: 1994, Part III.
[13] Mundell, R .A., 'A Theory of Optimal Currency Areas,' *American Economic Review* 51 (4) (1961).
[14] Kindleberger, *Centralisation versus Pluralism: A Historical Examination of Political- Economic Struggles and Swings within Some Leading Nations*, Copenhagen: 1996.
[15] cf supra, note 6.

Why Economic History?

S.A. King

In the second year of my undergraduate degree at the University of Kent, I came across Gordon Mingay for the first time. His opening gambit in one of his courses was a story about J.D.Chambers. It went like this. There was a fresh faced 17 year old who wanted to come to university to do economic history. He was invited to an interview with J.D.Chambers and duly turned up on the day. The secretary showed the fresh faced youth in and Chambers immediately started asking him questions. The secretary closed the door and waited for the interview to finish. Half an hour passed, then 45 minutes, then an hour and then an hour and a half. Getting worried, the secretary knocked on the door and went in. The young man was sitting stone still and Chambers was snoring away in front of him. Chambers had been asleep for the last hour or more but the young man had been too afraid to either wake him up or leave.

My first impression of economic historians, then, was that they were, literally, a funny bunch. More importantly, my first impression of economic history (albeit disguised as rural history) was one of a fun course delivered in an easy and jovial style. I learnt more in one course than some of my undergraduates learn in three years, and it is no accident that four undergraduates who were sitting in that room when Mingay told his stories are now academics in British or European Universities. These stories remain firmly implanted in my memory, as does the discovery of numerous stylistic and substantive approaches to economic history amongst the generations of historians before the 1980s. Economic history was a vehicle for learning the skills of the historian, an end in itself and a bridge around the sub-disciplines into which 'history' was fragmenting in the 1980s. I was eager to learn and read everything on the reading lists given to me by Alan Armstrong, Sean Glynn, John Lovell and Roger Scola.

How times have changed. Across Europe economic history is under pressure, fewer and fewer people want to do it at undergraduate level, professorial positions are being abolished and while some of my students still retain a sense of wonder and an eagerness to learn, not one of them feels comfortable with reading much of what appears in *Economic History Review*. Quite a few scholars feel the same way and have remodelled themselves into something else in some other branch of history. More widely, a disturbing number of talented people are giving up on the discipline of history altogether and going to do MBAs, sell books, travel or whatever. Sit back and think of the names that have disappeared and those who are about to go. Surprising, isn't it?

So what went wrong with economic history in particular? I was still an undergraduate when the first econometricians really started to make an impact in print, and I remember a conversation with one well known historian which ended with the memorable line 'all this econometrics spells the end for economic history'. I don't pretend to understand econometrics but this analysis was wide of the mark. Something did go wrong though. It might have been the students. I have noticed since about 1991 an astounding lack of numeracy on the part of undergraduates; 'I can't do numbers' has become a familiar refrain outside the last bastions of

British economic history at places like the LSE. The problem is that when you put a sources and methods course in front of them, most of these students *can* do numbers, some of them better than me. An alternative is to blame politicians. On the whole not a very bright lot, they have been all too eager to dismantle history teaching of all sorts in British schools, with the Industrial Revolution a notable casualty amongst five-eleven year olds for instance. On the other hand, interest in local history and genealogy gets stronger by the year. Just look at the magazines in the stands of a decent newsagents. Even young people are to be found 'doing history' through genealogy at the back of most local record offices.

No, the question of what happened is more complicated than these simple explanations allow. I was forced to confront the issue in 1997 when I taught for the first time on an Aims and Methods' course which asked first year undergraduates 'what is history and why do we do it'. The first topic on the lecture and seminar list? 'What is economic history and how does it differ from social, cultural or gender history ?'. To be honest, I did not have the foggiest, and nor did my students. At the end of the first session I walked behind some students going for a beer. As well as the usual tirade of abuse against the course, the lecturers, fellow students, each other etc. there was an analytical gem. Buggins turned to his friend and announced 'this b****y course is too hard - too many books to read, too many opinions and all these stupid little groups of historians'. Buggins failed his first year which saved me having to teach him in year two, but he did have a point which is relevant to my argument. You see, it dawns on me that at the very time a bunch of not very clever politicians were redrawing the boundaries of history teaching in schools, economic history ceased to be the bridge between disciplines, the path to making sense of a variety of sub-disciplines that stand relatively isolated, and ceased to be fun. Economic History became simply an end in itself. You can look back at the pages of numerous journals to see it happening. The back catalogues of our major publishers tell the same story. And in becoming an end in itself, the art (and it is an art) of teaching economic history began to pass away. How many people now engage their students with the sorts of stories with which I was regaled at Kent? Not many. Yet as cultural historians have shown us, stories of all sorts can capture the imagination.

So I had a problem. How to convince people like Buggins that an Aims and Methods course might be interesting and useful, and, more importantly, how to convince people like Buggins to take my (essentially economic history) courses in years two and three. Not an easy task. The starting point was to tear up the existing reading list and start again, getting students to read the sort of economic history offered by Mathias, Checkland and Hobsbawm. Facts, figures, analysis and an intuitively easy style. This was what I grew up on, and it still fires the imagination. The next task was to show the students how economic history was pushed onto a branch line in historical debates from the 1970s onwards. Not difficult, as I have suggested. The third task though was to get them enthusiastic about the subject. To do this I took familiar themes (demography, courtship, poverty and welfare and rural society) and reviewed the most recent debates to suggest to them how the basic principles of economic history (quantification, systematic analysis and linkage of significant datasets, a concern with the quality and representativeness of evidence and an awareness of the limitations of historical generalisation) could have a fundamental impact even on substantive areas that students (and many historians) might assign to the broad categories 'social', 'cultural' or 'gender' history. I suggested to them that economic history could be a vehicle for learning the skills of the historian and that economic history was the essential navigation tool around an increasingly fractured history discipline. Recent books have helped me a lot. Diana O'Hara's perceptive analysis of fifteenth and sixteenth century courtship processes takes what students assume to be a cultural phenomenon but places the negotiation (and quantification) of property settlements at the heart of the decision of when and who to marry.[1] Pat Thane's excellent discussion of old age in history melds administrative history, social, cultural and gender history with the sort of traditional economic history that I cut my teeth on.[2] And Alan Kidd's analysis of nineteenth century poverty and welfare structures has an economic history agenda at its very heart.[3] Add to volumes of this sort a field trip to Otmoor (currently being restored by the RSPB to its pre-enclosure state) and we have an interesting recipe for engaging students with the issue of what and why economic history. This little recipe must work. My third year special subject on poverty and welfare has graphs, numbers and econometrics and yet it recruited 90 students last time it ran.

Above all, though, my first year course has lots of stories about the characters of economic history. My favourite goes like this. There was this young PhD student who was invited to give a paper on his research at an Oxford college. The talk went well, and was followed by 30 minutes of questions. Towards the end of the session, the professor who chaired the session called out the name of an eminent but recently unpublished historian who was going to ask the final question. The PhD student looked startled and failed to answer the question. Over sherry afterwards, the student approached the eminent historian and apologised for his surprise and incoherence. He added, 'but I really thought that you were dead'. The eminent historian looked at him over his sherry glass and said 'economic historians never die, they just constantly re-invent themselves'. And re-invent ourselves we must if we are to stem the potentially terminal decline in our discipline. The vast ranks of local historians, genealogists, Open College and access students and undergraduates out there wait to be tapped again by economic historians who do not regard economic history as an end in itself but as a way of teaching the skills of the historian and a means if unifying fragmented historical disciplines.

Steven A. King (24. 11. 1966) took his PhD at the University of Liverpool after studying at the University of Kent. He was lecturer at the University of Central Lancashire and is presently the Director of the Humanities Research Centre at Oxford Brookes University. In 1998 he was visiting Professor at the University of Trier. He has published widely on aspects of historical demography seventeenth to nineteenth century, the regional dynamics of proto-industrialisation, poverty and welfare, and medical history.

---

[1] O'Hara, D., *Courtship and constraint: Rethinking the making of marriage in Tudor England*, (Manchester, 2000).

[2] Thane, P., *Old age in English history: past experiences, present issues* (Oxford, 2000).

[3] Kidd, A., *State, Society and the poor in nineteenth century England* (Basingstoke, 1999).

Thoughts and Worries about Economic History

David Landes

Economic History has changed, for better and worse. To be sure, no scholarly discipline should stand still. But some of the changes are worrisome.

When I began as a graduate student in history, almost 60 years ago, I chose to do economic history because it seemed to me that this was the most important, the most informative aspect of history. The dullards could do political or diplomatic history – battles, elections, anecdotes. Smart people would want to know about the material aspects of human development: getting and spending; wealth and power; why some are rich and some poor. I was not a Marxist; service in the army had cured me of any illusions about the virtues of command from above. But I was a believer in the pre-eminence of things.

So I took courses in history, economics, and economic history, the last of which, at Harvard, was taught by Abbot Payson Usher in the economics department. And thanks to a newly inaugurated programme and centre for research in entrepreneurial history (Arthur H. Cole director) I lived and worked with a range of social scientists, among them Talcott Parsons, economist by training, sociologist by practice, who introduced me to Max Weber and other authorities on the human and cultural aspects of economic behaviour. This informal education was reinforced by years spent as junior fellow of the Society of Fellows: financial support, no degree obligations, freedom, freedom! Plus weekly dinners with some of the brightest people around. The biggest visitors to Cambridge came to these Monday evening gatherings and chatted with the eager fellows afterward. Sometimes one learned invaluable things about new directions of research; sometimes one listened to trivia. Isaiah Berlin came, gathered a throng of worshipful listeners, regaled them with tales of cheeses and good dining on the byroads of France. I gave up on that one. Berlin more than made it up to me later on.

It was as a junior fellow that I began work on my dissertation (one could obtain a doctorate at the end of one's term). My thought was to do something on French entrepreneurship, which in those early days I thought of as a contradiction in terms. I took a year to travel about France to look for documentation. Not easy, because French firms saw curious strangers as possible agents of the fisc; and since they were all looking for ways to fool the fisc, they could hardly afford to have nosy outsiders poking about. Here I was helped by my foreign status. As an American, I was unlikely to be looking for breaches of French tax law.

So I found a few firms ready to be helpful. The biggest proved to be the records of one of the great merchant banking houses, De Neuflize, Schlumberger et Cie of Paris, offices right across from the Bourse. When I look back now on this stroke of luck, I realise that part of my good fortune was due to indifference: the people then running the bank had no direct personal identification with their predecessors. In any event, they agreed to let me look around; nay more, to let me take home and work on the dossiers that interested me. Unheard of.

More luck. (The more I think of it, the most important asset in successful research is luck.) I was bringing a stack of papers back to the bank officer assigned to help me. We met every two weeks in the vaults of the Bank of France. It was one of the dossiers I hadn't even looked at. It was labelled 'Ottoman Affairs'. What interest did I have in Ottoman affairs? But at the last minute I felt guilty. Did I have to return the papers without even looking at them. So I opened the folder and found the most extraordinary correspondence between the bank in Paris and a correspondent in Alexandria, Egypt – detailed, personal, intimate, candid, immensely revealing. And there was my dissertation, later published as *Bankers and Pashas*.

Meanwhile economic history was changing around me. These were the birth years of the so-called new economic history – history by and for economists, full of numbers and calculations, guided by economic theory macro and micro. Inevitably, the matter of economic history changed with the technique: analyses of economic growth, estimates of the so-called residual, and productivity, and other subjects that make for important but less than exciting reading. Except for a handful of stars who bridged the old and new worlds, most of the new work consisted of exercises in quantitative zeal and ingenuity.

The effect on the discipline may well be imagined. Where once membership at the meetings and contributions to programmes divided more or less equally between economists and historians, the historians now tended to withdraw, along with their students: people who once would have trained in economic history now chose social or anthropological subjects. In the United States things reached the point where economist-historians attended general historical meetings and, guided by topics offered, tried to recruit participants for forthcoming economic history meetings. A noble effort but it is hard to participate, even by invitation, if one does not understand the techniques and vocabulary of the other side. Like having a 30 course Japanese meal: best not to ask what one is eating.

Inevitably, this rift translated into major revisions. Where once students of North Atlantic history explained the revolt of the American colonies against Britain in terms of resentment – of the taxes, levies, and restrictions of the mother country – now statistical measures proved that these burdens were relatively light, almost trivial. Not enough to justify or account for a revolution. Or were they? Numbers, it would appear, are not the same to one person as to another, nor the same in one context as another.

In the same way, one of the great themes of economic history, the Industrial Revolution, became a battleground. Where an earlier generation of scholars had inherited and accepted this terminology, which went back to the mid-nineteenth century, and had buttressed the thesis by simple time series of outputs over time, the 'new economic historians' chose to show their quantitative potency by the construction of aggregate models, masterpieces of ingenious extrapolation, interpolation, and imaginative invention. The effect, inevitably, was to round off the corners and tame the breaks and leaps. Finished was the idea of rupture, or revolution, of a new direction; rather, now we had a gradual rise going back hundreds of years.

Ingenious calculation, but bad history. Fortunately, some of the 'new economic historians' are still wedded to the principle that history should make sense as history. Thus the new book by Chris Freeman and Francisco Louçã, *As Time Goes By: From the Industrial Revolutions to the Information Revolution* (Oxford, 2000). And some of the old-timers are still writing, viz my own 'Fable of the Dead Horse; or, the Industrial Revolution Revisited', in Joel Mokyr, ed., *The British Industrial Revolution: An Economic Perspective* (Westview, 1993), and François Crouzet's *History of the European Economy, 1000-2000* (University of Virginia, 2000). There lies hope.

In the meantime, the cliometricians must take care. They feel superior to historians, but where do they stand within economics? Many applied economists feel that they are better equipped to analyse numerical data than their economic historian colleagues. And the state authorities and university hierarchies are showing their sense of the contribution, realised and potential, of economic history by liquidating the autonomous departments. Chairs go to economics or history, but no longer to economic history as such. I am told that the largest department of economic history is no longer to be found in Britain, once the home of the subject, but rather in Uppsala. Good for Sweden, but not for Britain. And not a good omen for the subject and its future.

David S. Landes (b. 29. 4. 1924) was educated at City College, New York, and Harvard University. He is currently Coolidge Professor of History and Professor of Economics, Emeritus at Harvard University. He has written widely on industrialisation, technological change and clocks, including the prize-winning *The Wealth and Poverty of Nations. Why some are so rich and some so poor* (New York, 1998).

On Economic History

A.J.H.Latham

The book which drew me to work on economic history was J.U.Nef, *The rise of the British coal industry*.[1] It was not recommended to me by a teacher, but a fellow student when I was writing an essay on the Tudor economy as an undergraduate at the University of Birmingham. It opened up a new world of the pre-industrial economy, and its concept of an Elizabethan industrial revolution fascinated me. Its documentation of the Lancashire coal industry, centred on my home town of Wigan, frankly amazed me! That Nef was an American, not English, was also staggering. Who would have thought an American would dedicate so much time to such an unfashionable and obscure topic?

Because of this book I chose to write a dissertation on 'Economic Growth in the Parish of Wigan 1540-1640' as part of the requirements for my BA in Medieval and Modern History. This was supervised by R.H. Hilton, with whom I was delighted to work. This gave me my first taste of working on primary sources, at the Lancashire Record Office in Preston. But in working on agricultural aspects of growth in this period I came across another major work which had a profound influence, R.N. Salaman, *The History and Social Influence of the Potato*.[2] Again I was impressed by the extensive and detailed documentary research which had gone into this, especially with reference to the establishment of the potato as a key crop in Lancashire in the seventeenth century, where it was well suited to the cold wet climate, and where wheat would not grow. The coming of the potato raised incomes and demand for industrial products, and was a vital link in the move to industrialisation. Wigan had Europe's first potato market, in the 1680s! In both these books what was apparent was the way in which ordinary people went about the business of securing their existence, operating of their own free will within a market environment, and making key innovations, enhancing the prosperity of all.

Later I came to work for my Ph.D. at the Centre of West African Studies, Birmingham, with A.G. Hopkins. I think I was his first research student! It was the time of de-colonisation, and there were great hopes for the future. I chose to work on Old Calabar, a major port of the West African slave trade, in what is now Nigeria. Although I never put it that way at the time, my research was really concerned with the question of economic rationality. Were Africans motivated by markets and prices as we are? Or were they motivated by other considerations? In particular, how did they respond to the end of the external slave trade, and their loss of earnings from this source? Did they seek other external sources of income, or did they turn inwards to some communal idyll? It soon became obvious that Africans were economically rational as we are. Faced with the end of the slave trade, they soon found another source of income. Palm oil and kernels were exported to be made into soap and margarine. Far from turning to some communal utopia, they continued themselves to be major slave holders until the British colonial authorities abolished slavery and the internal slave trade in the early years of the twentieth century. They had money and markets, and invested heavily in capital goods like canoes.

Having worked on Africa, my interests turned to Asia. In many respects less work had been done by the late 1970s on Asia than on Africa, even though Asia was so much more important in economic terms. Ever since reading Salaman I had been interested in agriculture, and my interests focused on the international rice trade, and its influence in the dynamics of Asian economic life. While researching in Singapore, I came across another major work which influenced me, K.G. Tregonning, *Home port Singapore: a history of the Straits Steamship Company Ltd, 1890-1965.*[3] Written as a company history, and using what fragments of evidence could be put together after the devastation of the Pacific War, Tregonning had written a most evocative piece, a pleasure to read. It portrayed the mesh of inter-island trade within the Malayan archipelago, and South-East Asia in general. Again, the trading network of local produce resulting from man's innate motivation to produce and exchange was made plain. As a result, and working in collaboration with Larry Neal (University of Illinois, Champaign-Urbana) we were able to produce a series of rice prices right across Asia, showing an intra-Asian market in rice. But rice prices were linked with wheat prices in India, which grew and exported both grains. From the quantities of both grains traded internationally, and the interaction of their trade flows, it was possible to show that by the late nineteenth century one world market for basic food grains had emerged, in which rice and wheat operated together. Asia was fully integrated into the world economy. A world glut in both grains in 1928 was to lead to the depression.

So where does this place me? Why am I interested in economic history and indeed, what use is economic history if any? Crucially it seems to me that the study of economic history helps us understand man's economic motivation. The need to produce and trade to achieve greater personal wealth and prosperity seems a fundamental drive, in all periods of history. Africans and Asians are driven by these forces just as we are. In trying to create development strategies for countries at any stage of economic development, these fundamental principles must be recognised. If people cannot keep for themselves the product of their own labour, they will simply cease to work. Economic history does not itself butter many parsnips, but it does explain the forces which ensure there are parsnips to be buttered, and how much butter there will be!

A.J.H. (John) **Latham** (b. Wigan, 30. 3. 1940) was educated at Ashton-in-Makerfield Grammar School, Merton College, Oxford, and the University of Birmingham. He took his Ph.D. at the Centre of West African Studies. Since 1967 he has been Lecturer and Senior Lecturer in International Economic History at the University of Wales, Swansea. He has also been Visiting Professor of Economics at the University of Illinois, Champaign-Urbana. He is currently working on a history of the international rice trade: (A.J.H. Latham, *Rice: The Primary Commodity* (London, 1998); A.J.H. Latham and Heita Kawakatsu (eds), *Asia Pacific Dynamism 1550-2000* (London, 2000).

---

[1] Nef, J.U., *The rise of the British coal industry* (London: George Routledge & Sons, 1932).
[2] Salaman, R.N., *The history and social influence of the potato* (Cambridge: Cambridge University Press, 1949).
[3] Tregonning, K.G., *Home port Singapore: a history of the Straits Steamship Company Ltd, 1890-1963* (Singapore: Oxford University Press, 1967).

The Child is Mother to the Woman

Anne Laurence

It was not until I read Maxine Berg's study of Eileen Power that I realised how much I had been influenced by Power's work. The inscription in my copy of *More Boys and Girls of History* records that my parents presented it to me on my ninth birthday, certainly a gift prompted by my earlier enthusiasm for *Boys and Girls of History*.[1] Both books consist of accounts of children, of both sexes, in various historical settings, enlivened by detailed descriptions of clothing, accessories, food and household utensils. The first contains more material on the middle ages, but both volumes reflect Eileen Power's own interests in apprentices, in nuns and in the wool trade, and also in dress: she is described as elegantly dressed and fashion-conscious, making trips to Paris to buy clothes.[2] Power was concerned not only with popularising history, but also with the history of women, making a 'conscious attempt to connect the history of women to broader social history'.[3] Her influence extended to G.M. Trevelyan who dedicated his outstandingly successful *English Social History* to her.[4]

Economic history entered my formal education relatively late. Its significance was first borne in on me in the early 1970s, during the research for my D.Phil thesis on chaplains in the English civil war; my interest was further aroused in the 1980s, when I started work on a text-book on women in early modern England.[5] Economic history had not featured prominently on the syllabus of the History Department at the University of York, where I did my first degree in the 1960s (presumably because economic history was being taught in the Department of Economics). We were introduced to Annales school historians, but there was little formal teaching of economic history, and political theory was taught in preference to economic theory.

In Oxford, where I was a graduate student in the 1970s, economic history prospered under the protection of Peter Mathias. What I knew of it, from working on college accounts for the History of Oxford University as research assistant to Trevor Aston and to J.P. Cooper, seemed very austere by comparison with the work on the revolutionary movements of the civil war to which I was attracted and which, inspired by the writings of Christopher Hill, Keith Thomas and others, seemed to contain messages for the children of 1968. To my uninitiated eye, Joan Thirsk and her students seemed to be concentrating on developing local studies. The contents of the *Economic History Review* for 1972, the year I began work on a D.Phil, reveal historians' pre-occupation with production and capital formation: with land use, with the traditional industries of cloth and coal, and with trade and slavery. Although the cost of living appears, there is nothing about consumption and little about economic transactions as anything other than balance-sheet items.

Working through the accounts of the Parliamentary army to discover the identity of its chaplains, it became clear that the finances of the army were a key to its role in society. Provisioning, quartering, arming, feeding and clothing the soldiers, transporting materials and troops, and providing and paying for nursing and ancillary services to both field armies and garrisons, made considerable demands on the economy, creating manufacturing and investment opportunities for clothiers, carriers, cheesemakers, and armourers. Quartering and nursing brought country people into contact with central government through their claims for payment for providing food and services. There was (and still is) a thesis to be written on how the economics of the army affected its relations with civilian society.

Much work has been done, chiefly by Ian Gentles, on how the armies were funded. However, discussion of the arrears of pay due to soldiers has taken place primarily in the context of how far arrears were the grievance which finally led to the Vote of No Addresses with the king, rather than in the context of a larger concern with the economic infrastructure of the army.[6] The history of the armies as a purchasers and consumers, as yet unwritten, may be the key to knowing more about its place in society, which the existing histories of battles and campaigns on the one hand, and politics and religion on the other cannot reveal. The idea of material objects telling a story of the relations between the army and the civilian population in the 1640s is an inspiring one.

It was Joan Thirsk's work and, in particular her 1975 Ford Lectures, which awakened me to the idea that economic history could be the history of how people came to have things, and their relationship with the manufacture, purchase and use of goods.[7] This informed the way in which I approached the history of early modern women. Their participation in the market, both as producers and as consumers, placed them in the centre of economic life rather than at its margins. Research by Lorna Weatherill, Beverly Lemire and others on the trade in and use of particular objects and on women's increasingly prominent role in consumption, and on less visible forms of trade, affords a way to approach otherwise intangible and unrecorded aspects of the lives of women.[8]

Such work perhaps owes more to anthropology than to classical economic theory, as we may see from the influence of Mary Douglas and Baron Isherwood's book, *The World of Goods*, first published in 1979 and re-issued in 1996.[9] It has brought to historians a greater concern with the material world, not just in the recording of material objects, but also in the ways in which the material world survives and is preserved. Roberta Gilchrist's work on nunneries exemplifies this approach.[10] We see also a greater interest by historians in such subjects as painting, in, for example, Simon Schama's approach to the societies he has studied; this has been matched by art historians' concerns.[11] It is a pity that attempts to popularise the use made by historians of the material world have been poorly served by recent television presentations of the past.[12]

Women's involvement in the market is not merely confined to those who have substantial disposable incomes. Pam Sharpe has shown how poor women were also a part of the market, they were not the movers and shakers of economic life, but created the substance of its millions of small transactions.[13] Women and credit, women in business, and women and paid work have provided important subjects for investigation in recent years, by established scholars and research students alike.[14] This kind of economic history is plainly the social end of a spectrum of economic history at whose other end lies econometric history: much of it is empirical and it draws more heavily on such disciplines as anthropology and sociology than upon classical economics. It is concerned with consumer behaviour and the actions of individuals rather than with the history of the movement of the market.

The histories of the behaviour of individuals as economic beings had earlier roots among women economic historians. Eileen Power was interested in the contribution of anthropology and sociology to economic history. Elizabeth Levett, an early member of the Economic History Society, wrote a history of consumers in 1929.[15] Yet consumption as a significant subject for historians' interest had to wait until the 1980s with such works as Lorna Weatherill's on the pottery trade.[16] By the nineties, larger studies had started to appear, differentiating between various kinds of consumption and examining the activities associated with it.[17]

The development of a history of consumption casts an interesting light on the observations codified by Joan Thirsk as 'Thirsk's Law':

> whenever new openings have appeared in the English scene, whether in crafts or in trade, and, in the modern world, in new academic endeavours, or in the setting up of new organisations in the cultural field, women have usually been prominent alongside the men, sometimes even outnumbering them.... But that situation has lasted only until the venture has been satisfactorily and firmly established.... when... [it] fall[s] under the control of men.[18]

It is noteworthy how many of the historians writing the history of consumption are women. Joan Thirsk herself has argued that women writing social and economic history are concerned with all aspects of people's lives, rather than simply with their public activity, which has stimulated interest in women as economic beings.[19]

If recent publications reflect contemporary concerns with consumer demand, how does the *Economic History Review* compare? By comparison with 1972, its contents betray a concentration on work, on migration and on the cost of living, though textile industries and agriculture continue to feature; population history seems to be assuming the role formerly occupied by the economic origins of the industrial revolution. Is this where the reaction against Marxist and Marxisant history is really taking place? Has population history replaced the history of class as the explanatory framework for social change?

It is clear that economic history does not have to be the history of market movements, exchange rates, banking and financial institutions, on the one hand, or of labour relations, transport, industrial processes and the debate about industrialisation on the other. It can be the history of consumption, of work and of the participation in the market of people with the most modest means. Are the women historians who are leading the way in this history also leading a retreat from class?

Anne Laurence (b. 1949) studied history and politics at the University of York, graduating in 1971, and moving to Oxford for her D.Phil. Since 1976 she has worked at the Open University where she is Senior Lecturer in History. She has published on the English Civil War, Anglo-Irish relations in the seventeenth century, and women in early modern England. She is currently working on a comparative study of women in England, Scotland, Ireland and Wales. Also in progress is a larger study of women, patronage, consumption and building in the seventeenth century.

[1] Berg, Maxine, *A Woman in History: Eileeen Power 1889-1940* (Cambridge, 1996), pp.230-1; Power, Eileen and Rhoda, *Boys and Girls of History* (Cambridge, 1926, reprinted 1953); eadem, *More Boys and Girls of History* (Cambridge, 1928, reprinted 1953). These books were adapted from a collaboration between the two sisters on a series of school history talks for BBC radio in the 1920s.

[2] Berg, Maxine, *A Woman in History: Eileen Power 1889-1940* (Cambridge, 1996), p.154.

[3] ibid, p.130.

[4] Trevelyan, G.M., *English Social History* (London, 1944).

[5] Laurence, Anne, *Parliamentary Army Chaplains 1642-51*, Royal Historical Society Studies in History, 1990; op. cit., *Women in England 1500-1760: A Social History* (London, 1994).

[6] For example, Gentles, Ian, 'The sales of crown lands during the English revolution', *Economic History Review*, 2nd ser., XXVI (1973); idem, 'The arrears of pay of the Parliamentary Army at the end of the first civil war', *Bulletin of the Institute of Historical Research*, XLVIII (1975); idem. 'Arrears of pay and ideology in the army revolt of 1647', in Bond, Brian and Ian Roy (eds), *War and Society* (London, 1976) vol.1.

[7] Published as Thirsk, Joan, *Economic Policy and Projects: The Development of a Consumer Society in Early Modern England* (Oxford, 1978).

[8] Weatherill, Lorna, 'A possession of one's own: women and consumer behaviour in England 1660-1740', *Journal of British Studies*, XXV (1986); idem, *Consumer Behaviour and Material Culture in Britain 1660-1760*, (London, 1988); Lemire, Beverly, 'Developing consumerism and the ready-made trade in Britain 1750-1800', *Textile History*, XV (1984); idem, 'Consumerism in pre-industrial and early industrial England: the trade in second-hand clothes', *Journal of British Studies*, XXVII (1988); idem, 'The theft of clothes and popular consumerism in early modern England', *Journal of Social History*, (1990); idem, *Dress, Culture and Commerce: the English Clothing Trade before the Factory 1660-1800* (Basingstoke, 1997; Shammas, Carol, *The Pre-industrial Consumer in England and America*, (Oxford, 1990); Spufford, Margaret, *The Great Reclothing of Rural England* (London, 1984); Ginsburg, Madeleine, 'The tailoring and dressmaking trades 1700-1850', *Costume*, VI (1972); idem, 'Rags to riches: the second-hand clothes trade 1700-1978', *Costume* XL (1980).

[9] Douglas, Mary, and Baron Isherwood, *The World of Goods: Towards an Anthropology of Consumption* (London, 1979, reissued with a new introduction 1996).

[10] Gilchrist, Roberta, *Gender and Material Culture: the Archaeology of Religious Women* (London, 1994).

[11] Schama, Simon, *The Embarrassment of Riches: An Interpretation of Dutch Culture in the Golden Age* (London, 1987); idem, *Rembrandt's Eyes* (London, 1999); Baxandall, Michael, *Patterns of Inattention: On the Historical Explanation of Pictures* (New Haven, 1985); Freedberg, David, *The Power of Images: Studies in the History and Theory of Response* (Chicago, 1989).

[12] The Open University has for 30 years been trying to develop a genre of 'academic' broadcasting, presenting serious scholarly debate. Recent attempts on mainstream television to present historical subjects have been of mixed success, as, for example, the BBC series on the Renaissance presented by Andrew Graham Dixon and the BBC series on the history of Britain presented by Simon Schama. The Channel 4 series, 'The Day the World Took Off', was a valiant attempt to present economic history with stimulating discussion, and pictures that did not match the quality of the debate.

[13] Sharpe, Pamela, *Adapting to Capitalism: Working Women in the English Economy 1700-1850* (London, 1996).

[14] Beverly Lemire and Barbara Todd are both, for example, working on women and credit. See the theses of Lane, Penny, 'Women and proto-industrialisation in the 18th-century East Midlands' (unpub. Ph.D. thesis, Warwick University, 1998); Wiskin, Christine, 'Women, finance and credit in England c.1780-1826' (unpub. Ph.D. thesis, Warwick University, 2000).

[15] Levett, Elizabeth, *The Consumer in History* (London, 1929).

[16] Weatherill, Lorna, *Consumer Behaviour and Material Culture in Britain 1660-1760* (London, 1988).

[17] Brewer, John and Roy Porter (eds), *Consumption and the World of Goods* (London, 1993); Berg, Maxine and Helen Clifford (eds), *Consumers and Luxury : Consumer Culture in Europe 1650-1850* (Manchester, 1999); Rappaport, Erika, *Shopping for Pleasure : Women in the Making of London's West End* (Princeton, 2000).
[18] Thirsk, Joan, 'The History Women', in Mary O'Dowd and Sabina Wichert (eds), *Chattel, Servant or Citizen: Women's Status in Church, State, and Society*, Irish Historical Studies XIX (Belfast, 1995), pp.1-2.
[19] ibid. p.7.

People in Time, Space and Place: A Historical Geographer's Debt to Economic History

Richard Lawton

Although I have been a member of the Economic History Society for nearly 50 years, I cannot regard myself as an economic historian. My work is in the field of historical and population geography, with particular research interests in population change and mobility, urban development and rural decline in Great Britain from the mid-eighteenth to the late-twentieth century. Since 1949, when I began my academic career, I have seen these develop from multi-disciplinary studies (mostly within traditional disciplines of economic history, geography, social history etc) of social, economic and cultural life in a rapidly changing environment and society to much more closely related interdisciplinary studies. Inasmuch as I have participated in the field of economic history it has been through working alongside economic and social historians (for example in the Centre for European Population Studies at the University of Liverpool), attending interdisciplinary conferences, such as those of the Urban History Society, and, above all, in benefiting from the progressive unravelling of the changing dimensions and structure of the British economy, both quantitatively and over time, by economic historians. One of the most important influences on my work, which has been primarily orientated towards the spatial dimensions of change, has been the publications of the Society, in particular its journal, the *Economic History Review*. My battered and much-thumbed set – always read on a par with the major geographical research and teaching journals, not least the excellent reviews section – is still often consulted and the new issues probably read more thoroughly than my geographical journals, the *Journal of Historical Geography* excepted. A geographer with little formal training in economic history – though with an intuitive historical approach – economic historians and economic history have influenced my work in three main ways: first, their complementarity; secondly, in aiding understanding of the complex relationships of time, space and place in processes of economic and social change; thirdly, their methodologies, and analytical tools.

As an undergraduate at Liverpool between 1946 and 1948 I soon became aware of the importance of economic historians in studies of the historical and economic geography of the British Isles. Clapham's magisterial sturdy of modern Britain (1926-1932) was a key text for both Clifford Darby's Historical Geography of England and Wilfred Smith's Economic Geography of the British Isles courses which formed the backbone of the Part One Geography Honours year. Darby was fond of quoting R.H. Tawney's advice to fellow-historians to put on stouter boots and get into the field to support documentary evidence (advice that Maurice Beresford (1954) was to put to such notable effect in his study of lost villages), though it was said that falling into a swollen Pennine stream on a field excursion marked a switch to the dictum that historical geographers should become more immersed in the archives! Wilfred Smith, who succeeded Darby in the John Rankin Chair of Geography at Liverpool, drew extensively on the work of economists and economic historians in his locational analysis of Britain's changing economic geography (Smith, 1949). Much of my subsequent work has been placed within chronological and conceptual frameworks that owe much to techniques of econometric analysis and related models of economic growth developed by economists and economic historians, a theme to which I will return: they are matters on which economic historians had a considerable effect on the thinking of historical geographers of my generation.

A major concern has been the idea of the industrial revolution as articulated by Arnold Toynbee in his classic Oxford lectures of 1884. However flawed, this has been modified and refined by successive generations of economic historians, most recently by Pat Hudson (1992). Both econometricians and quantitative historical geographers have contributed to the refining of measures of production in the various sectors of the national economy and studies of shifts in the regional location and structure of economic activity, along with a widening concern for their roots in demographic and social change. The outcome has been to provide a much wider-ranging view of both the causes and mechanisms of what is now regarded as a series of transitions from a preindustrial to an industrial economy and society – or, to use E.A. Wrigley's (1988) phrase, from an organic economy to a mineral-based energy economy – over a lengthy period from the sixteenth to the early-twentieth century, affecting different sectors of the economy to differing degrees at different times.

Despite substantial advances in the understanding of processes and consequences of change for the nation, their regional origins and impacts have been relatively neglected, not least by historical geographers. Those of my own generation were, perhaps, over-concerned with technology and its influence on the character and location of farming systems and individual groups of manufacturers. In the chapter on 'The Industrial Revolution' for the essays presented to the Twentieth International Geographical Congress in London (Watson, 1964) I focused on the geographical consequences for the British Isles and the peoples of 'a long series of economic and technological changes'. A subsequent, and much fuller, study (Lawton and Pooley, 1992) – though set within a wider framework of 'economic and social development, . . . demographic change, . . . evolution of landscapes and the emergence of new regional structures' – is essentially systematic in its approach. Similarly, the essays in Dodgshon and Butlin's (1990) study of England and Wales are viewed in terms of changes in population, agriculture, industrialisation, urban systems, urban social geography, landscape and overseas expansion rather than of regions. Yet economic historians have made important contributions to regional studies – Dodd on North Wales, John on South Wales, Chambers on the Vale of Trent and Allen and Court on the West Midlands amongst others – and some still regard 'A regional perspective [as] important in examining the causes and dynamics of change' (Hudson, op. cit., p101; and 1989). Where economic historians and geographers have independently approached the impact of change on a regional economy and society, as in the studies of West Yorkshire by Hudson (1986) and Gregory (1982), it is clear that the contrasts in approach both benefit and owe much to the two disciplines. One of the most successful overviews of the regional impact of change in the industrial revolution is, appropriately, the atlas to which both geographers and economic historians contributed (Langton and Morris, 1986).

The concept of the trade cycle has long been regarded as crucial to an understanding of both short- and long-term fluctuations in economic activity in general and of regional responses to their impact on different sectors of the economy. One of the most persuasive developments of this idea, not least for geographers, is Rostow's concept of stages of economic growth (1960). Its phases of pre-conditioning, take-off, drive to maturity and mass consumption, coupled with the Kondratieff long waves (as elaborated by Schumpeter, 1939), seem to many geographers to offer a more coherent chronological framework for studies of sectoral and regional change that that of the 'period picture' focused on arbitrary dates or large data-sets linked by studies of change between these periods (e.g. Darby, 1973). For me, an economic framework provides a persuasive setting for a study of transformations in Britain between the mid-eighteenth and the mid-twentieth centuries over three broad phases: from the 1740s to the 1830s; the 1830s to the 1890s; and the 1890s to the 1940s (Lawton and Pooley, op. cit.). the validity of such cycles is crucially dependent on reliable statistical time series (from often imperfect data). Historical geographers have been grateful, therefore, for the broad statistical framework set out by Mitchell and Deane (1962) and the ongoing revision and reinterpretation of statistical series through more sophisticated econometric methods by Crafts (1985) and others, to which they themselves contributed substantially as the 'new' quantitative geography revolutionised spatial analysis of historic data from the late 1960s.

But there is more to modernisation than economic and technological innovation: the role of people, individually (as inventors and entrepreneurs) and collectively (as both workforce and market for increased outputs from the land, industry and commerce) was crucial for sustained growth. Whilst the study of individuals in business and industry has continued to yield a rich harvest for economic and business historians (e.g. Coleman (1969) on Cortaulds; Mathias (1959) on brewing) there have been significant advances in the study of the role of the workers, epitomised in the classic studies of Thompson (1963) and Hobsbawm (1964). These, together with vigorous debates such as that on the standard of living in the industrial revolution, have drawn population and society to centre stage.

Despite notable advances in aggregate population studies of England by the interdisciplinary centre at Cambridge (CAMPOP) (Wrigley and Schofield, 1981; Wrigley et al., 1997), much remains to be done at the regional and local scale. My first encounter with such studies was with both census tabulations and, especially, the rich material of the mid nineteenth-century census enumerators' books (Lawton, 1954). Proto-industrial societies provide ample evidence for the ongoing debate over early industrialisation. One central theme – which has influenced regional studies by both historians and geographers – is the extent to which handicraft industry encouraged earlier, marriage and, through larger families, accelerated population growth, further stimulating agricultural output and, in advance of large-scale factory production, the demand for consumer goods. A second aspect is the importance for shifting labour markets of greater labour mobility and the more substantial role of migration in local and regional population trends. Both have important implications for studies of demographic change.

It is no coincidence that the downturn in mortality from the 1740s and the late eighteenth-century surge in birthrates in Britain, is associated with economic growth and accelerated population increase. The relationship between a changing economy and vital rates continued through the eighteenth and nineteenth and twentieth centuries. Along with social changes it is an important factor in fertility control. And, despite the adverse effect on mortality or urban overcrowding and associated problems of control of epidemic disease, the gradual improvement in life expectation accompanying rising living standards continued (Woods and Shelton, 1997). In both systematic and regional studies of this demographic transition, the work of economic historians and historical geographers fruitfully overlaps.

However, the role of migration in population change is often neglected by demographers, though it is crucial for the understanding of local and regional population trends and the operation of the labour market. Economic historians have contributed notably to the latter and, from the classic study of the early nineteenth century by Redford (1926), have provided both the context for studies of the operation of the labour market (Hunt, 1981) and for the analysis of difficult data on the regional and national impact of migration (Baines, 1985). Recently geographers have, through studies of lifetime patterns of individual mobility, greatly illuminated the general picture of labour migration. My own involvement with such studies comes from family background which led to studies (based on census birthplace data) of patterns of movement and their impacts on population growth and structure in the West Midlands (Lawton, 1958). In seeking understanding of the causes and processes of migration the scale of analysis has shifted from regional to national contexts and to local and micro-level studies of individual and family decision-making (Lawton, 1987).

Studies of Victorian Liverpool (Lawton, 1979) provide a further focus on change in nineteenth-century society shared by other historical geographers (Dennis, 1984) and interdisciplinary studies of urban history (Dyos and Wolff, 1973). Many of our models of urban development were derived from the Chicago School of sociologists, emphasising behavioural approaches – social and humanist, rather than economic – to the study of population, and qualitative rather than quantitative methods of analysis. For context I now tend to consult the *Cambridge Social History of Britain* (Thompson, 1990) rather than the economic counterpart (Floud and McCloskey, 1981, 1994). Yet my debt to economic history is considerable as ongoing work on rural areas of West and North Yorkshire in the nineteenth century, which emphasises occupational rather than social structure, shows.

Richard (Dick) **Lawton** (b. 9. 3. 1925) was educated at the University of Liverpool where he taught for most of his career, becoming Professor of Geography. He was an active leader in the Institute of British Geographers for many years and is an Honorary Fellow of the Royal Geographical Society. He is currently Emeritus Professor, University of Liverpool and his research interests are urban, social and population development in Britain c.1750-1950 and rural change in nineteenth century Yorkshire.

Works cited
Baines, D., *Migration in a Mature Economy* (Cambridge, 1985).
Beresford, M., *The Lost Villages of England* (London, 1954).
Clapham, J.H., *An Economic History of Modern Britain* (3 vols., Cambridge, 1926-32).
Coleman D.C., *Courtaulds: an economic and social history* (2 vols., Oxford, 1973).
Crafts, N.F.R., *British Economic Growth during the Industrial Revolution* (Oxford, 1985).
Darby, H.C. (ed), *A New Historical Geography of England* (Cambridge, 1973).
Dennis, R., *English Industrial Cities of the Nineteenth Century* (Cambridge, 1984).
Dodgshon, R.A. & Butlin, R.A. (eds), *An Historical Geography of England and Wales* (2nd edition, London, 1990).
Dyos, H.J., and Wolff, M., *The Victorian City. Images and Realities* (2 vols., London, 1973).
Floud R., & McCloskey, D.J. (eds), *The Economic History of Modern Britain* (2 vols. Cambridge, 1981, and 3 vols. 1994).
Gregory, D., *Regional Transformation and Industrial Revolution: A Geography of the Yorkshire Woollen Industry (*London, 1982).
Hobsbawm, E.J, *Labouring Men* (London, 1964).
Hudson, P., *The Genesis of Industrial Capital: A Study of the West Riding Textile Industry c.1750-1850* (Cambridge, 1986).
Hudson, P., *Regions and Industries: A Perspective on the Industrial Revolution in Britain* (Cambridge, 1989).
Hudson, P., *The Industrial Revolution* (London, 1992).
Hunt, E.H., *British Labour History, 1815-1914* (London, 1981).
Langton, J. & Morris, R.J., *Atlas of Industrialising Britain 1780-1914* (London, 1986).
Lawton, R., 'The Economic Geography of Craven in the early Nineteenth Century', *Transactions of the Institute of British Geographers*, no. 20 (1954), pp 93-111.
Lawton, R., 'Population movements in the West Midlands, 1841-1861', *Geography*, 46 (1958), p 164-77.
Lawton, R., 'Mobility in nineteenth-century British cities', *Geographical Journal*, 145 (1979), pp206- 24.
Lawton, R., 'Peopling the Past', *Transactions of the Institute of British Geographers*, new ser., 12 (1987), p 159-83.
Lawton, R., & Pooley, C.G., *Britain 1740-1960. An Historical Geography* (London, 1992).
Mathias, P., *The Brewing Industry in England 1700-1830* (Cambridge, 1959).
Mitchell, B.R., & Deane, P., *Abstract of British Historical Statistics* (Cambridge, 1962).
Redford, A., *Labour Migration in England, 1800-1850* (Manchester, 1926).
Rostow, *Stages of Economic Growth* (Cambridge, 1960).
Schumpeter, J.A., *Business Cycles* (2 vols. New York, 1939)

Smith, W., *An Economic Geography of Great Britain* (London, 1949).

Thompson, E.P., *The Making of the English Working Class* (London, 1963).

Thompson, F.M.L., *The Cambridge Social History of Britain 1750-1950* (3 vols. Cambridge 1990).

Watson, J.W. (ed), *The British Isles: A Systematic Geography* (Edinburgh, 1964).

Woods, R. & Shelton, N., *An Atlas of Victorian Mortality* (Liverpool, 1997).

Wrigley, E.A., *Continuity, Chance and Change. The Character of the Industrial Revolution in England* (Cambridge, 1988).

Wrigley, E.A., & Scholfield, R.S., *The Population History of England 1541-1871: A Reconstruction* (London 1981).

Wrigley, E.A., Davies, R.S., Oeppen, J.E., & Schofield, R.S., *English Population History from Family Reconstitution 1580-1837* (Cambridge, 1997).

What Economic History Means to Me

Clive Lee

I first encountered Economic History as a first year student of history. Like many of my fellow students I found this compulsory course to be rather difficult, a fear compounded by our college supervisor, the redoubtable Mr Hyde, a tall thin man with an acerbic wit and a voluminous knowledge. He once engaged me in a detailed debate on back-to-back housing and the iniquities of northern slums before declaring that he had never been further north than Cambridge. The idiosyncrasies of our supervisor, and the vagaries of the Cambridge tripos meant that our study of English Economic History encompassed only the period from 1500-1800. (I later completed my mastery of the discipline by taking a special subject on the British economy covering the period 1900-1932.) However, it was during this first and compulsory year of study that I found my enthusiasm for Economic History. The question that caught my imagination will be most familiar to all students of the 1960s vintage, namely whether population increase in the eighteenth century was the result of rising birth rates or falling death rates. I have made absolutely no contribution whatsoever in the subsequent four decades to this important debate. But it stimulated an interest which has evolved and changed but never waned, and one that has given shape to my career, provided me with many colleagues who have become close friends and, more than anything, has provided me with a vehicle to explore with great self-indulgence those historical and economic issues which hold enduring fascination for me. It has not been a smooth progression, but there is very little that I regret.

After graduation, I drifted into research as a means of delaying a decision on a career and consequently turned down a number of promising opportunities, decisions I now regard with hindsight as evidence of manifest insanity. The decision to undertake research was probably correct, but I made my first major mistake in taking advice. My inclination was to continue to develop my interest in the interwar period that had been kindled by my final year special subject, and to explore the depression in the context of one of the regions of high unemployment. In retrospect, I think this would have been both a good choice and a suitable selection for me. But I took advice, well meant and from a senior member of the profession, so that I fell among business historians and, more particularly into the McConnel & Kennedy 'archive' at the University of Manchester. The location of the so-called archive was a very dirty cellar underneath the library of the Department of Economics in Dover Street. I was not the first, nor indeed the last person to consult these documents. But I can probably claim the distinction of being the only individual to steal the entire set, by the briefcase, to transport them to the hall of residence where they could be inspected under superior conditions, such as daylight. I returned all the records to the archive. They were, after all, both dirty and boring. While I found the subject moderately interesting, I realised that, for me, the attractions of business history, and archives, were limited.

The next critical event probably needs careful explanation given current academic market conditions. I was headhunted for a lectureship and, as the only available candidate, was duly offered the post. In the mid 1960s, at the beginning of the decade of expansion, there were more jobs than potential incumbents. So I looked for Aberdeen on the map and attended an interview that comprised a general discussion with future colleagues over coffee in a hall of residence cafeteria. Despite this easy introduction to the world of academia, I felt ill prepared and soon became even more sharply aware of my limitations. My appointment was within the Department of Economics where I made up a quartet of economic historians. I knew very little economics, and the discomfort of the environment was soon increased by rumours of strange new developments called counterfactuals initiated, it seemed, by a somewhat sinister figure called Fogel. My economist colleagues predicted that we would all be swept away by this revolutionary advance. In fact, I rather enjoyed life amongst the economists and discovered a taste for manipulating statistics and exploring the quantitative dimensions of the subject. I also returned to my first enthusiasm, regional development, and began writing.

Within three years a fundamental change really did occur. It was decided that the next vacancy in Economic History would be to a professorial appointment and that, when that a post had been filled, a separate department would be established. This met with the strong approval of all my colleagues, and probably with that of the economists, but I was less than keen. By this time my interest in both economics and statistics made me reluctant to leave. I even considered retraining as an economist but decided to hang onto the job I already had. So, in 1969, I joined the new Department of Economic History under the leadership of Peter Payne. The five original members eventually grew to nine in the boom of the early 1970s, to be whittled away to six by the time the Department was closed two decades later.

The Department of Economic History had a fairly peaceful existence for most of its two decades. We put on a full honours degree programme that attracted a steady but modest number of students. Those students seemed to be very satisfied with the programme, and the smallness of the classes and the department engendered a friendly and informal atmosphere. It was also an environment in which experiment was possible. This allowed me to explore my enthusiasm for quantification, and my growing belief that it was an integral and essential component of the discipline. Thus we became one of the first departments to include teaching in what was known, then as now, as 'new' Economic History. Our students did not seem unduly troubled by these unusual impositions. In sum, the Department of Economic History had a very honourable record. It maintained good personal relations between its staff (for most of the time), and with its students. It developed an interesting, varied and stimulating programme of courses, and its members produced a sound body of published research.

In view of this epitaph, one might wonder why the Department was closed. Indeed it was one of the first such departments to be merged into some larger unit. The problem lay in the performance of the University in the early research reviews that resulted in financial losses throughout the 1980s as a result of poor ratings for expensive faculties such as medicine and science. As a long established university, seeking to provide a full range of academic provision, Aberdeen had a large number of small departments. The obvious route for economy was to merge or close some. The policy was executed with the kind of expedient ineptitude that seems to characterise academia. A voluntary severance scheme ensured that the losses fell randomly and without regard to academic merit. In such a context, we were highly vulnerable and, at one point, were informed that the Department would close. We spent a few days contemplating unemployment and our lack of transferable skills. Then an advisory group, seeking to rationalise the provision of teaching in Economic History, suggested that we merge with the Department of Economic History at Glasgow, a prospect distinctly more frightening than a few years on the dole. There followed a summer of surreal opportunity. A scheme was developed whereby universities could transfer staff and acquire

215

'subsidised academics'. So we adjusted swiftly from contemplating unemployment to considering the overtures of virtually all the universities that had ever heard of Economic History. For a few weeks we were like football stars, considering alternative contracts and pondering various regius chairs. Reality, of course, eventually intruded and we were informed that the University had decided to retain three and transfer three of its stock of economic historians. We never found out why the decision was taken or who identified those to go or stay. The original plan was that we should return to the Department of Economics from which we had emerged two decades previously. But local politics intruded and the decision was changed so that four of us were absorbed by the Department of History, and the other two accepted transfers to other universities. I managed to secure an appointment with a foot in both economics and history and remained in that unstable equilibrium for three years.

Our experiences in the enlarged Department of History were predictably uncomfortable. Historians, the most traditional of scholastic sects, seemed unwilling to entertain or support specialist interests like economic or social history. Further our new colleagues had a long tradition of factional dispute and chaotic organisation, both of which were unattractive novelties to us. My experience in the Department of Economics could not have been more different. I felt welcomed and valued, and took the opportunity when it arose to become a full time member. This gave me a new lease of academic life, and my time in the Department of Economics has been the happiest of my career. A variety of factors contributed to this. Firstly, I was greatly attracted to the discipline both as an interest in itself and as an essential body of knowledge for an economic historian. I am convinced that the improvement in my understanding of economics during the past ten years has greatly improved the quality of my understanding of Economic History. Beyond that it was nice to belong to a medium sized department which was both ambitious and focused on improvement, and which was under no threat of closure. A couple of years ago I attended an Economic History conference and overheard an animated debate about departmental merger. It was just the kind of discussion that had taken so much of my time years earlier. But what shocked me was the fact that I simply had not thought about these issues for several years.

One of the major surprises I found when I joined the Department of Economics was the fact that my new colleagues were not hostile to historical economics, the new label I acquired to distinguish me from my erstwhile colleagues. For some years I did teach one course of Economic History, on the world economy in the twentieth century, and this did attract a respectable number of economics students. However, it clashed with teaching in some other courses in economics, so that the treatment of third world economies duplicated teaching in development economics, and the exposition of financial regimes replicated teaching in international money. So the course was abandoned, a decision I eventually took as head of department. The teaching of Economic History survives within a number of courses, although it tends to be labelled as applied economics. So there are problems involved in keeping Economic History alive within an economics department, although I could have kept my course alive by abandoning the post 1945 period to concentrate on a 'purely' historical context.

Economic History has been squeezed in the past two decades by the abandonment of independent departments and absorption into larger units, usually departments of history. My colleagues who joined the Department of History in Aberdeen found an increasingly unsympathetic environment, their degree programme was scaled down and the introductory first and second year courses, vital for progression, were abandoned. The belated appointment of a new professor of Economic History, Professor Leboutte, might halt that decline. When I retire I expect to be replaced but, almost certainly, by a mainstream economist. In institutional terms, I suspect this depressing tale is very common and does not bode well for the future of economic or social history as the basis for a degree programme.

But the organisational problems encountered by the discipline have not prevented the growth of its literature that has expanded in both quantity and quality in the last four decades. The vibrancy of the discipline reflected in books and journals thus stands in marked contrast to its treatment in many universities and its diminished role within many degree programmes. My progression through the disciplines has been mirrored by my equally self- indulgent writings. From my initial interest in regional problems stemmed two prevailing interests in quantification and in the macroeconomic aspects of growth. More recently, I have been drawn to the problems of the Scottish economy, partly because they are intrinsically interesting, and partly as an obligation to the country in which I shall spend my entire academic career. This has also brought me full circle, as one of the editors of a new history of Aberdeen, commissioned by the City Council during a period when the lord provost was a teacher of history. One of the little known benefits of being an editor is writing those chapters for which suitable contributors cannot be found. In this case, I became the author of chapters on, respectively, 'local government' and 'health and welfare'. Thus I returned to the to the discipline of general history.[1]

Despite having become an administrator, a writer of reports and memoranda, which is the province of the head of department in the present day academic system, I am still fully committed to writing and to exploiting my varied accumulations of skills and knowledge. Indeed my principal research projects at present bring together the traditions of social science and history. The new Economic History of Scotland, which I am writing in collaboration with scholars from several of the Scottish universities will draw extensively on these varied traditions.

During the past four decades Economic History has grown substantially as an academic discipline, with a great increase in its literature and the number of those contributing to it. It has also experienced substantial contraction in its institutional manifestation, a prime victim of university economies and a hybrid nature. Its essential problem has been its uneasy position between history and the social sciences and, it has tended to fall between them. Most of the amalgamations saw absorption into departments of history, often with the consent and collusion of the staff concerned. This is very understandable but, in my view, a profoundly unfortunate trend. My belief is that the future of economic and social history lies firmly within the social sciences where they are recognised and respected. Further, the great improvement in the quality of the literature in recent decades is a function of the increased influence of the social sciences, in analytical thinking, formal theorisation and the rigorous testing of hypotheses. So I believe that Economic History will survive and flourish as an integral element in the pantheon of social sciences. And I still hope to add to its literature, perhaps even to write my definitive study of British demography.

Clive Lee (b. 1942). Graduate of Fitzwilliam College, Cambridge (MA and Mlitt). Previous editor of Scottish Economic and Social History and previous convenor of Council of Economic and Social History Society of Scotland. Currently Professor of Historical Economics and Head of Department of Economics, University of Aberdeen. Recent publications include *Scotland and the United Kingdom: The*

Economy and the Union in the Twentieth Century (1995), and *Aberdeen 1800-2000: A New History* (2000), edited with W. H. Fraser.

---

[1] Fraser, W. H. and Lee, C. H. (eds), *Aberdeen 1800-2000: A New History*, (Edinburgh 2000).

Economic History as the Integrating Core
of Social Science

Christopher Lloyd

Economic History as a semi-separate area of enquiry with particular topics, problems, and methods is in institutional decline in Anglophone countries. Economic History is being absorbed into economics and history and other disciplines but this decline and absorption does not mean that the intellectual foundations as a distinct discipline are no longer valid. Nevertheless, those foundations are in need of new examination and defence. Many of the old methodological questions that underlay to varying degrees the work of Smith, Roscher, Marx, Cunningham, Weber, and other founders, concerning such issues as the relationships of economic to social and cultural and ideological aspects of the social totality, static to dynamic aspects of economy and society, theoretical to empirical aspects of enquiry, the historical and descriptive to the abstract and universal in conceptualisation, and the behavioural to the institutional aspects of socio-economic life, are still of vital concern to economic historians and should be to all social scientists. Indeed, economic historians along with scholars in closely related and overlapping fields such as social history, historical sociology, historical political economy, and historical geography, have traditionally been and continue to be concerned with these issues to a degree that is unknown in other branches of social science. The concern with the history, particularly the long-run history, and the *historicity*, of the patterns and structures of society unites these fields and raises these knotty methodological issues. Thus the intellectual separateness of economic history as a discipline may well be in doubt for reasons other than the imperialism of orthodox economics.

Economic behaviour and processes occur at the interface of human society and external nature through the production process. Therefore social and natural science meet at the economic interface of human society and nature. It is the realm of the economic that links humanity to nature through technology and production and in fact makes humans as humans. In other words, in a fundamental sense, a sense that only became apparent to thinkers in the seventeenth century in Europe but which has become all-pervasive in our time with the emergence of industrial economies, modern human kind is truly *homo economicus*. But in a longer-term sense, humanity became *homo economicus* through the process of its socio-economic co-evolution with nature. Accordingly, the biosphere has steadily become, over the past 10 or 15,000 years and rapidly recently, an economically-moulded sociosphere. This realisation of the fundamental role of economic activity has influenced the development of the social sciences in positive and negative senses. Positively, it has led to a great concentration of effort by economists upon delineating, analysing, theorising, and scientising the study of the economic domain in attempted imitation of positivistic natural science and for some economists, from that viewpoint, seeing neo-classical economics as the key to *all* human social understanding.[1] Negatively, at least in recent times, it has led to a denigration by many such 'scientific economists' of what was taken to be non-economic thought and a consequent neglect or sometimes subsumption of all the connections that economic processes have with non-economic processes in society. In these ways, orthodox economics has tried to realise its own self-image as the only legitimate and well-founded positive social science. Some economic historians have been seduced, unfortunately, by the supposed power of orthodox economic theory to the extent of becoming applied economists rather than historians. Applied economics has a quite different objective (the verification of theory) from history, which is concerned with the empirical explanation of the actual complexity of the world.[2] But whether this narrow economics is so viewed or not, there are more significant features of what we can loosely call the 'broad field' of economics beyond orthodoxy that are of crucial significance for economic historians today who wish to retain the methodological balance or tension between the various aspects of subject matter and method that the founders used so creatively for explanation building, and which bear upon how we now find ourselves institutionally and intellectually.

Thus this essay[3] outlines three general contentions, which together constitute the meaning that economic history has for me as a practitioner: (a) the intellectual framework of economic history should be a broad and *integrated* historical, institutional, sociological, and ecological approach to the economy; (b) economic history can therefore be the foundation or core of socio-historical science; and (c) this broad historical discipline can serve as the necessary interface between the macrohistorical sciences of society and nature. I think it's important that economic history does become more influential for the sake of the continuing validity and influence of social science generally and more particularly for the discipline of economics. Economic history founded upon these principles can become, I believe, the saviour not only of economics but the means to provide historical and theoretical foundations for all the social sciences.[4]

My proposed intellectual framework for economic history can be summarised by a series of connected propositions. First, if the economy is conceptualised as the dialectical process of the constantly evolving human appropriation and transformation of nature through technology and the constantly evolving technological conditioning of society's institutional organisation of production and social relations, the fundamental problematic for economics is not a behavioural issue. Rather, in order to be able to explain this constantly changing collective process of social and natural interaction, there must be a focus on the socio-institutional-agential interconnections for social relations and human interaction are always institutionalised in one form or another. In other words, economic and all other social activity in all times and places has to be understood and examined as *institutionally* organised, bound, and directed. And among the manifold institutions of society at any one time and place the institutions that are focused primarily upon material production, distribution, and exchange are of fundamental importance. Therefore the study of the economy is indeed a fundamental social enquiry but such a study is not mainly a behavioural enquiry, as it is in orthodox economics today, but an institutional, social, and historical enquiry.

Second, we have to re-emphasise the place of historicity in the social sciences. Economic historians are well equipped to do so providing they hold onto the view of the study of economic history as being concerned with institutional-structural *change*. The institutional structures of societies have to be examined for their dynamic, ever changing and evolving character under the determination of historically-specific endogenous and exogenous forces. The historicity of society cannot be ignored for a moment. By historicity is meant not just change but also chance, contingency, rupture, continuity and discontinuity, and long-run evolution. A historical process is one characterised by both stability and novelty. Economic history as a branch of social science has, ever since the Enlightenment, always tried to bring together economic and historical perspectives.

Third, it is important to view the history of the economic-structural foundations of society as an evolutionary rather than a teleological process. By this is meant the idea that structures exhibit a dynamic that has no subject or goal. There is no external causality nor directional force at work nor unfolding of an essence. Progress is a culturally-specific and unscientific term. The historical natural sciences of cosmology, solar systematics, and geology have long since abandoned teleology and progress. Biology is still engaged in a struggle with teleological views of primitive creationist and sophisticated progressivist kinds. The social sciences are still bedevilled by anti-scientific teleological thought, which is a mark of their immaturity. Scientific evolutionism of the neo-Darwinian kind developed by natural historians, a powerfully persuasive and supported theory, seems to me the only serious basis for theorising the long-run history of economic and social structures.[5]

Fourth, the long-run historical evolution of economies, which should be viewed as a socio-natural process occurring at the interface of natural and social is but one such process that takes place in the world and universe all of which can and should be understood using a similar scientific realist methodology and the evolutionary concept of punctuated equilibrium. Punctuated equilibrium refers to the paleontologically observed and theorised pattern in the history of genera whereby species exhibit long periods of stable equilibrium in their morphology interspersed with short periods of rapid change in which numbers of species either become extinct or branch to form new species. In other words, the history of the process of speciation (i.e. the evolution of life) is not one of gradual transformation of species or of steady accumulation of new species and/or extinction of species, but exhibits a record of very differential rates of speciation. The main explanation for this is that environmental change, to which species and genera have to adapt, also exhibits a punctuated equilibrium, that is, periods of stability interspersed with short periods of rapid change. The geological record strongly supports this idea. There is much controversy among biological evolutionists about punctuated equilibrium versus gradualism.[6] I am much more persuaded by the former view because of its inductive-empirical foundation within natural historical observation. Punctuated equilibrium can also now increasingly be seen as the process at work in the solar system, the earth's geological history, and in the long-run socio-biological and socio-economic history of humanity. Adopting a punctuated equilibrium approach thus implies adopting a neo-catastrophist view of historicity rather than a gradualist view. Just as there is mounting evidence supporting catastrophism in the historical natural sciences so there is in the long-run social sciences.[7] Neo-catastrophism is closely related to, perhaps is an essential component of, the new complexity/chaos theory. That is, large-scale, complex, evolved historical systems such as the solar system, earth tectonics, the macroecosystem of the biosphere, world economy, and world geopolitical system, are increasingly being understood as characterised by a dynamic interplay between structural inertia, chaotic equilibrium, mutations or innovative novelties, and large shocks causing major shifts or transformations between relatively stable eras.

Fifth, a theoretical-comparative approach must be adopted which continually sifts theoretical and empirical levels of enquiry through the sieve of comparison of both data and concepts. Only by thorough comparison of all or strategically chosen empirical cases can any part of the world be known and only through a comparative examination of the conceptual apparatus through which the world is examined and understood can conceptual advance be attained and so explanatory power improved.

Sixth, economic history in the sense of being at bottom the study of very long-run socio-economic change is, as pointed out above, but one of several such sciences – of the cosmos, the solar system, the physical earth, life, as well as of social organisation/ production – all of which have striven during the nineteenth and twentieth centuries to develop general theories to try to unify explanation in their own broad field. The gropings of economic historians towards such general theories have so far not met with success.[8] Many theorists and philosophers have rejected the possibility of such a level of general theory but without it there can be no science. On the other hand, it's doubtful that a very general level of unified theory can encompass all long-run structural processes of the planet or solar system.[9] Given the foregoing propositions, an appropriate general theory should probably take the form of a structural-chaotic evolutionism combined with catastrophism, which finds the fundamental locomotives of history in a combination of innovation in response to environmental and social change, occasional structurally-induced chaotic disequilibrium, and endogenous catastrophies or sudden shocks emanating from the natural environment and social pressures.

Seventh, economic history is already widely understood by many of its practitioners and others outside the discipline as an essential aspect of several existing synthetic approaches in the social sciences. These include historical political economy, historical sociology, historical geography, historical geopolitics, some branches of archaeology and anthropology, and, indeed, most general approaches to comparative historical social science. Integration of these new approaches around certain broad problematics, such as the long-run history of socio-environmental systems and globalisation studies, is now occurring.

I come back to the issue of economic history forming a core for all social science. The idea of a core implies the idea of an essential or central part on which other parts depend in some way. I think the foregoing outlines an argument for seeing the study of the long-run history of economies, conceived essentially as institutionalised social structures of material production, as foundational for all social enquiry. But the existence of a foundation or a core does not mean there has to be ontological or epistemological reduction in order to make explanation. This implies a view of the totality of society as a complex, interconnected structure that depends upon but is not reducible to the economic sub-system. Thus the study of social complexity cannot be reduced to a study of the economy alone. The question then becomes one of the historical (i.e. actual and evolving) interconnections between material production, socio-economic and political institutions, the physical environment, culture, ideology, and so on. Exploring all these interconnections is essential if economic history, in the wider sense I've been trying to sketch, is to play the important role I believe it should. Environmental, social, political, and cultural histories all interpenetrate with economic history. Thus economic history should not only be *open* to other branches of the social sciences but should *integrate* with them. *Intellectual broadening* seems necessary not just to save the economic history discipline in a time of institutional shrinkage but, as I have argued, to make it the essential core of social science, as its early progenitors and defenders (including Smith, Marx, and Weber) believed it should be. Furthermore, as a methodological core it would provide the site for theorising the evolving long-run interconnections between material production, social relations, institutional arrangements, culture, and ideas. Homo economicus would then be homo universalis!

Christopher Lloyd (b. 18. 12. 1950) was educated at Universities of New England, Sussex, and Oxford. His interests are in historical methodology and theory, Australian economic history, environmental history, institutional change, and industrial relations. He is currently Professor at the School of Economics, University of New England, Armidale, President of the Economic History Society of Australia and New Zealand and an executive committee member of the International Economic History Association.

[1] A recent example is Olson and Kähkönen (2000).

[2] The relationship of applied economics to economic history has been discussed in Lloyd (1994). See also Kindleberger. The approach of the historical economists privileges deductive theory over inductive empirical inference and has the effect of subordinating history to uncritically adopted neo-classical behavioural theory.

[3] Some of this essay draws on sections of Lloyd (1997b).

[4] Graeme Snooks has been making a similar argument in recent work but from a somewhat different perspective. See Snooks (1993, 1996).

[5] The best known proponent of the natural history approach to evolutionism is the palaeontologist Stephen Gould. See especially Gould (1992). See also Lloyd (2000).

[6] See Gould (1997).

[7] On catastrophism see Schubert (1992), Keys (2000).

[8] There have been general theories of economic history proposed ever since Adam Smith's pioneering work in the 1750s. Forms of evolutionism were developed in the late nineteenth century and have recently returned to favour. Neo-classicism has developed a rational choice theory based on behavioural psychological assumptions and recently sociobiology, social psychology, and ecology have influenced thinking. Insofar as they contain teleological notions they are vitiated.

[9] See the attempt to outline such a theory in Spier (1996) and the critique in Lloyd (1997a).

Works cited

Gould, S.J. (1992), 'Punctuated Equilibrium in Fact and Theory', in A Somit and S.A Peterson (eds), *The Dynamics of Evolution* (Ithaca).

Gould, S.J. (1997), 'The Darwinian Fundamentalists', *New York Review of Books*, June 1997, 34-37.

Keys, D (2000), *Catastrophe: An Investigation into the Origins of the Modern World* (London).

Kindleberger, C.P. (1990), *Historical Economics: Art or Science?* (Berkeley).

Lloyd, C. (1993), *The Structures of History*, (Oxford).

Lloyd, C. (1994), 'Historical Economics or the History of Institutional Structuring? From Theory to Historical Complexity' (unpublished lecture, Braudel Center, SUNY Binghampton), School of Economics, University of New England.

Lloyd, C. (1997a), 'Can there be a Unified Theory of Cosmic-Ecological World History? A Critique of Fred Spier's Construction of Big History', *Focaal: Tijdschrift voor Antropologie*, 29, 1997: 171-180.

Lloyd, C (1997b), 'Can Economic History be the Core of Social Science? Why the Discipline Must Open and Integrate to Ensure the Survival of Long-Run Economic Analysis', *Australian Economic History Review*, Vol 37, No 3.

Olson, M. and Kähkönen, S. (2000) 'Introduction: The Broader View', in *A Not-so-Dismal Science: A Broader View of Economies and Societies* (Oxford).

Schubert, G (1992), 'Catastrophe Theory, Evolutionary Extinction, and Revolutionary Politics', in A Somit and S.A Peterson (eds), *The Dynamics of Evolution* (Ithaca).

Snooks, G (1993), *Economics Without Time: A Science Blind to the Forces of Historical Change* (London).

Snooks, G (1996), *The Dynamic Society: Exploring the Sources of Global Change* (London).

Spier, F (1996), *The Structure of Big History: From the Big Bang Until Today* (Amsterdam).

From the Mediterranean: about Scylla and Charybdis

Paolo Malanima

Italian economists do not believe that Economic History is such a basic pillar in the study of economics. Italian economic historians, on the other hand, despite their efforts, are not able to convince their colleagues that history is that essential for the economist. They can certainly talk as they might remembering Schumpeter's and Keynes's ideas about the importance of a historical formation for the economist. The impression is that their appeals remain totally unheeded. An economic historian, the wife of a well known economist, recently told some friends of her husband's opinion, a poor opinion, of her usefulness; not as a wife, but as a university teacher of Economic History in a Department of Economics. The struggle within the Departments to gain new positions is making Economic History weaker and weaker and on the defensive. Some counter examples - very few - are insufficient to support an alternative view.

We have to draw a distinction, in any case, within the field of Economic History. There is an increasing number of economic historians - let's call them 'historical economists'- who cannot be easily distinguished from the economists, except the most theoretical ones. In the near future the distinction will become harder. The language they are using, the topics they are studying, the themes they are teaching in their university classes, are not easily distinguishable from those of economists. Let's take a congress on unemployment, or on transaction costs, or on regional economies, or on institutions... Here the only visible difference between economists and historical economists is that, while the former usually address their attention to the last decade, the latter have a somewhat broader view and can go as far as the last half century. As for the rest there is hardly any difference: the same models, the same econometric tests, the same multiple regressions, the same interests in economic theories...

In university courses the attention of these economic historians is almost totally concentrated on the last hundred and fifty years, sometimes the last two hundred; no longer. As far as I know, from conversations with these colleagues, courses are more or less organised the same way. There are one or two initial lectures on the pre-industrial world: once upon a time economic growth did not exist; the world was dominated by Malthusian traps; capital formation was very modest or non-existent; techniques were stagnant; people were not interested in innovations... In the first two hours of these courses, millennia of economic growth, decline, changes, become something indistinct and indistinguishable, dominated only by backwardness and poverty. Then the Big Bang of industrialisation and development and modernisation took place.

The cluster of modern historical economists is rapidly increasing. Farther and farther away are the times when, to win a national competition for an Italian university, you had to have published at least some article on Medieval book-keeping, on a Renaissance Florentine woollen shop, or on an ignored early capitalist merchant. The balance is rapidly changing in favour of modern history. The growing squad of these historical economists will sooner or later be welcomed in the army of economists. It is only a question of time. Towards them the behaviour of economists is increasingly tolerant.

In addition to this, there is in Italy another squad of economic historians. A distinction from the others we spoke of may be made on the basis of their prevailing interests in Medieval and Early Modern Economic History. They could be defined as narrative economic historians or, perhaps better, using Vilfredo Pareto's words, 'literary economists' – *les économistes littéraires* he spoke of in his *Cours*. Their aim is – as they believe and sometimes say – to reconstruct what really happened in past centuries in the field of economic activity: a very simple - even if old and once authoritative - kind of epistemology. They do not believe that a deep knowledge of economics is either useful or necessary for a historian. As to statistics, their opinion is that in pre-industrial economies, given the scanty presence of numerical sources, statistics is a useless encumbrance. Their economic and statistical common sense is enough. Nothing to add. When you speak to them they have always just made some decisive discovery, in an archive, of an important file of documents... absolutely interesting, to publish in a 'Bulletin' of their local historical society.

It is apparent to everyone that economic history is becoming more difficult day by day and that if, let's say, 20 years ago everybody, even if not particularly cultivated, could read everything about economic history, nowadays it is no longer so. Sometimes even a professional economic historian may find it hard to read an article on a theme just a little removed from his research field, so quickly is formalisation advancing and so widely is the use of statistical, economic and even mathematical procedures taking place within the discipline. Let's take as an example the proceedings of a Historical Demography Congress held some 20 years ago and compare them to those of a conference held today, to appreciate the big changes which have occurred. Historical demography is kind of a younger sister of economic history but if the case of demography does not seem appropriate, let's take, then, a Congress of Economic and Social History. Pages, in the conference proceedings are different too, just at first glance: from the grey ones in earlier times, made up of lines, only lines, one next to the other, to pages full of graphs, diagrams, formulae today. Literary economic historians I spoke of, are conscious that economic history is no longer as it was thirty years ago, and know the many changes undergone. They think, however, that all this is an unnecessary complication and that what matters is historical sensibility: historians trying to become acquainted with the new languages of statistics, economics, econometrics, are just wasting their time. Historians do not need particular training in those formal disciplines. What 'Annales' historians wrote 40 and even more years ago on the meeting of history with other cultural worlds - geography, sociology, anthropology, ethnography – is more than enough.

We could believe that this may be only a small group destined to succumb within a few years in front of the rising wave of those historical economists we saw before, interested in the history of the last few days with the use of economic and statistic technicalities. This is, after all, the way economic history is going; not only in Italy and not only since yesterday. But it is not so! Even if the two squads we are speaking of are more or less equally numerous - some dozen people each - their weight in the academy is not the same; not at all. The second squad - that of the 'économistes littéraires'- is far more powerful. They are able to control the metabolism of the University system, and are reproducing themselves day by day in an uncontrolled way. One might think that, going against the main stream this faction is predestined to be overcome, but this is wrong; or may be wrong for a long time.

Only a few academics exist in between: between, that is, the two groups we spoke of. They risk being crushed. The few units share the conviction that Economic History is too broad a subject to be flattened on contemporaneity alone, and that there is much to learn from a larger view of the past. In this they share the literary economic historians' opinions, which usually, as we have seen, have research interests a little further back in time. On the other hand, however, they believe that it would be a serious impoverishment for the discipline to adopt a superficial use of those tools economists are utilising to do research on contemporary economies. They share then, from this viewpoint, the modern historical economists' convictions on the relevance of more formal procedures in the study of economic history. The lack or scarcity of quantitative data on the more distant economic past does not mean that statistics is superfluous. Sometimes it is more useful when quantitative data are scarce than when they are plentiful. The study of pre-modern economies may deepen our knowledge of how the economy works in different civilisations: that is the main contribution of history to the study of economy. The knowledge of contemporary economies is important, but not sufficient. The risk of concentrating attention only on the contemporary world is that of imagining that the economy was and always will be working just as it is working now, in our civilisation. Widening our perspective the variables in play appear to be many more than we can imagine when we are using the logic of *ceteris paribus* so dear to the economists. In applied economics - which is Economic History - *ceteris paribus* procedure does not exist at all: everything acts on everything in the complexity of the real world. To do research on these far-off worlds the historian needs, in any case, a non-superficial knowledge of economics; and a training in statistics may prove more useful than palaeography was to past medieval historians. To adapt and change, when necessary, economic tools for application to remote civilisations, so different from ours, one first has to know well how those tools are working.

As far as we can see, these few Italian academics seem to be finding an increasing number of colleagues abroad. There are, however, - at least looking from the Mediterranean - a Scylla and a Charybdis of which to be careful. The first danger to avoid is that of acting like the 'économistes littéraires' we spoke of before. Their work consists, more or less, of inferior versions of what Italian economic historians of past generations - from Gino Luzzatto to Roberto S. Lopez - already did very well, but we do not seem able to continue to do well various decades later. The other danger, a really serious one according to what we see everyday on the pages of specialist journals, is the increasing use of formal languages - which may be a good thing - combined with a superficial experience of research in the archives and on documents - which is certainly a bad thing. Once - and perhaps still nowadays - an anthropologist lacking a long field practice in some African or Australian settlement of a primitive society, in touch everyday with the local population he had to study, was seen as an example of superficiality and dilettantism not to be followed. A serious professional needed a long training in contact with the concrete problems of those concrete peoples he had to study. Work in the archives, in touch with documents, is for the historian (economic historian included) what field work is for the anthropologist. We need the contact with the concrete ground of our research. The use of data, usually quantitative data, without a minimum knowledge of the ways they have been collected and worked out, and their processing, even by means of the most sophisticated techniques, cannot suffice. To define and redefine our problems, field work is as unavoidable for historians as it is for anthropologists. Carlo M. Cipolla once wrote that to be an economic historian without this kind of experience is like a surgeon who has learnt surgery from textbooks, and only on textbooks, without any practice. Would you consent to be operated on by such a surgeon? In history, fortunately, possible consequences of this kind of dilettantism are not as serious as in surgery. Too often today, however, there are examples of medieval economic historians who have never seen a medieval document, who do research on materials they do not know at all, assembled as they are by others with their own criteria. They use prices and price indices, but do not know what their reliability may be because they have never tried to get prices in the archives from documents. They use data on population, but do not know how these data were collected and the many problems involved even in the simple and apparently mechanical collection. They use series of wages, but, lacking research experience, do not know what a wage really was in pre-industrial economies and in civilisations different from ours... Today, also, as a consequence of the computerisation of our work, it is no longer so hard or tiring to become all of a sudden an amateur econometrist. All of us know people who, without knowing what they were really looking for, have once found, nearly by chance, by pressing a simple key on their computer, a series of lines full of mathematical functions they later began to decipher and more or less understand. The work of an economic historian cannot consist only of this. As Cipolla wrote some years ago, economic history is the daughter of two cultures – history and economics. An economic historian cannot embrace the first by losing contact with the second, but he cannot get rid of the first as a useless dead weight.

Paolo Malanima (b. 1950) was educated at the University of Pisa and the Scuola Normale Superiore in Pisa. He is currently Professor of Economic History and of Economics in the University (Magna Graecia) in Catanzaro - which is not far from Scylla and Charybdis. His research interest is preindustrial economic history and particularly in Italy.

What Economic History Means to Me: A Retrospect

J. D. Marshall

The economic history of one's youth is hardly that of one's supposedly more mature years. It is well known that the earlier stages are built upon all kinds of emotional identifications, which have deeper foundations than many are willing to admit. More than this: it is not always helpful to assume that the very latest version, one's own *dernier cri*, is necessarily the most complete utterance of wisdom. A private recital of one's follies, sometimes made selectively public for the benefit of really promising students, is no bad thing.

But one must also be willing to admit that follies are necessary to the creative historian; they spring from the inductive leaps that are part of his *modus operandi*, and demonstrate not only that he is bold to the edge of vulnerability, but also that he has, at some point, been a reasonably complete human being. Many economic (and social) historians of considerable talent are lacking in human roundedness, and this is what ultimately limits them as historians. It is not that their statistics and methodologies are without ingenuity, nor even that they have failed to shed light in dark places; it is that they do not quite rise to the peculiarities of behaviour of which humanity is capable. Their insights do not fully match the challenge.

This is to pass judgement on some economic historians; the reader will doubtless find that the cap fits extensively. But what about the 'Me' of the title, who is engaging in some sharp rifle fire from a position of security? It is well to remember that some of us are closely linked historically to the earliest stages of the subject, and that correspondingly we face huge disadvantages as well as advantages. We were trained to have moral attitudes, as Tawney and the Hammonds were. Not only did Tawney pass judgements on the 'prescriptive wickedness of the rich'; he benignly invited his students to 'conquer the devil in detail' when launching themselves on an essay. If you are going to make a case, do it properly.

I am writing of days of innocence, Wordsworth's 'very heaven'. Philip Larkin, a suitably cynical spokesman for the generation which ruled 50 or so years later, wrote what was originally meant to be an epitaph for the unknowing lambs of 1914 – 'Never such innocence again'. But, had he been interested in the disciplines of the subject in 1954 or 1964, he could have said the same thing. Innocence had been on the ebb since the years of demobilisation. The wartime cohorts had marched back and made their mark, and in its way the Attlee government had listened, and the Health Service lasted through the century - but without much idealism.

I come into this story, not in the years of Attlee, but in reality earlier. The 1920s and 1930s were not, as is sometimes believed, years of misplaced idealism; they consisted partly of a massive Slough of Despond, a marsh of hopelessness which left its contamination in much of the industrialised world. But a large part of that world was intensely respectable and self-centred. It was also full of the spirit of Joynson-Hicks, and was disposed to enjoy an improving quality of life behind its privet hedges, in the 1930s especially. This was not the result of political endeavour, but of economic circumstances. Labour was under a cloud during most of the inter-war years, and idealists tended to join the C.P or the I.L.P. The international scene was one of defeats for the left. Yet, economic and social history (nobody knew what the 'social' really stood for) were developing in a debate which consisted largely of certitudes, moral or other. The present, even then, was shifting and uncertain, and was dominated by the imminence of war. My youthful generation was looking for moral certainties, and it tended to take truths for granted, like the wickedness of the rich. Entrepreneurial historians will be shocked at this; but they should be locked in a room with some of our local coal owners of that age, and even they would have to make some mental adjustments. We needed history that would reflect such truths, and would also polish them brightly. Economic history by Tawney, Cole or the Hammonds had this moral probity. The Webbs went further, and deployed a massive apparatus of scholarship, as in the *History of English Local Government*. But they were also reaching out into the attainable, and were not just filling space. On the right, Clapham was moved by the same need to establish certainties, and by a spirit of positivism that led to the consolidation of somewhat different truths.

Clapham's writing is also suffused by a love of country; he is almost poetic when writing about 'The Face of the Country', and one can set some of his paragraphs in such a way as to assert the presence of poetry. C.R. Fay is vigorously sentimental about the personalities of Georgian England, and in the hands of such a writer economic history could be declamatory. But facts, too, had their own special validity, and every one of these writers instinctively sought the clinching facts when reaching into the previous century. When I fell under their influence, sometime in the late 1930s and early 1940s (and that meant that one was wearing uniform for part of the time), this search for the validating and dominating facts was a central feature of the historical scene. Nobody reading the writings and conventional wisdom of Lilian Knowles could doubt this; but, in a very different setting, the work of Ephraim Lipson, planted in a rich garden of original sources, still has interesting facts to offer (the author may have been shoddily treated during his own lifetime, but his work can still be used by the wise).

Such authors, then, helped in the formation of economic history as we now have it. I was able to bring my own special experience to it; brought up in one of the regions most affected by the supposed industrial revolution in cotton-spinning, and most clearly influenced by the world of coal-mining, canals and railways, I was never short of an image, a structure or a sound that appeared to fit into the logic of industrialism. This world of mine had its own poetry, just as it had violence and brutalities, and I was prevented equally from indulging in sentimentalities (I had seen people dying from dirt and neglect), and from exaggerating the ills that already existed or had certainly existed. My first residence as a young married student was a framework knitters' cottage with four tiny rooms, built, according to the deeds, in the 1840s, and if its inhabitants had not know starvation at some point, then they had an excellent setting for the experience. I quickly learned that buildings like this could provide evidence. However, such subtleties seem to have escaped some of my earliest teachers, who were too given to following fashion and to setting tedious essays on Hammondism and anti-Hammondism, or worse, on 'pessimism' or 'optimism' in interpreting the industrial revolution. These debates, one had to concede, laid bare some interesting antitheses, but there was a whole world out there to interpret.

That world was also one of poetry, harsh, grim or utterly memorable. The otherwise sour and soggy towpaths along the canals were, as J.D. Chambers once reminded me, the key to a minuscule scene which was unique in our country. Meanwhile, I was studying, in a vague and romantic way, mill buildings when still in my early teens. I should have been frightened by the term industrial archaeology, but the names of Strutt and Arkwright resounded in my memory, and the title *Sir Richard Arkwright* had an unforgettable grandeur, there on his mill at Matlock Bath. My perceptions of this great ghost had not then been linked to the overbearing fat man thrusting his finger at James Watt and telling him how to improve the steam engine. (A true story – look in Watt's letters.)

Economic history came along to organise these scattered impressions. Just after the war, I was able to commit myself to it as Special Subject in the London Economics degree, and Chambers (whom I remembered as an adult education tutor from pre-war days) became my mentor. He, too, was a local lad, and we spoke more or less the same language, until I stuck to Marx and Tawney and he moved to the more fashionable right. Never mind; we both believed in counting populations and continued to consult each other until his death in the early 1970s. One form of quite vivid regional history resulted, a negation of the story that ideologies are sterile.

And what was happening to economic history in those years just after the war? It was becoming a little like a small-scale Heritage Industry, very popular as a teaching subject until the sheer, overpowering dullness of a younger generation of specialists, interested in their own self-promotion, threatened to engulf the subject completely. Meanwhile, economic history, like many another area of academic interest, was breaking to pieces beneath their feet; no sooner had it begun to spawn new specialisms then it found itself unable to synthesise the fragments. I found that one could deal with the wreckage reasonably well, and make it hang together in the workings of regional projects; but that was after I had turned down at least one straight teaching post in economic history, generously offered by the late Sidney Pollard. Synthesis was not popular at this time, unless one wished to write a textbook, and it was far more advantageous to pursue a new or newish specialism.

In these years (the 1950s and the 1960s), a number of major specialisms were already appearing, like urban history and historical demography. But they had no apparent relevance to the central concerns of economic history; the accumulation of wealth and the growth of national economic power, the break-up of feudalism and the manorial system, the gilds, channels of national and international trade, the increasing role of the state, technological change and its consequences, the agrarian 'revolution', the Navigation System (note the capitals), the factory system, and so forth. The first form of specialisation to have any effect was 'agricultural' or agrarian history, which itself sprang partly from the bucolic interests of local specialists like Finberg and Hoskins. Transport historians had organised themselves a few years earlier; both areas of interest seemed to attract the learned collector. Business and labour history set up mutually unsympathetic political enclaves at the end of the 1950s, and thereafter, to the severe loss of urban or regional history, did not speak to each other.

It is very much to be doubted that the examples of 'breakaways' so far given added greatly to the scope and stimulus of the main or parent subject. They provided detail, most certainly, often of a dull and antiquarian kind, and sometimes (but too rarely) they brought human interest. More often they simply added to the length of student reading lists.

The great success of the specialisation movement was undoubtedly that of local historical demography, led by the so-called Cambridge Group from the mid-1960s; they got local historians throughout England aggregating parish registers (often already printed), and added an entire dimension to the study of local history and demography. Probably economic history gained very little from this impressive operation, although the Cambridge pioneers had intended that it should benefit the former appreciably. Perhaps the lack of effective application of economic history at the local level, even in the midst of a major development of urban history, was responsible for this sad state of affairs.

It was plain that in a more general sense, the study of economic history did in fact gain from these outgrowths and embellishments, and hundreds of dissertations and theses remain to demonstrate the truth of this assertion. But, as has been pointed out, there was an increasingly prevalent fragmentation of subject-matter in all historical studies, as their subject-topics became more numerous. The specialisation movement was in a sense a safeguard against such pressures; meanwhile, as far as mainstream economic history was concerned, the basic subject-matter remained more or less in place for several decades. One can check this for British history by comparing Southgate's original chapter-headings of 1934, 32 in all, with the fare offered in degree schemes 20 or even 30 years later. Much depended on the scheme offered, and the requirements of the qualification sought, not to mention the originality and eminence of the main teachers. An economic history sub-department might have genuine freedom of operation, but would be less likely to have the latter in an economics department. Economic history could be recited, as Southgate's famous primer demonstrated, and it could be reproduced with embellishments – which sophisticated teachers could further embroider, or could torpedo at will. I was saved from this kind of reproduction by the need to humanise history, which was in itself a creative force. Telling young miners the story of their jobs could actually bring a period of almost respectful silence. (A painstakingly vivid presentation received the accolade; 'Good programme, Sir!'.) Records suggest that historical geographers were the people who promoted urban history and gave it a formally solid foundation; local historians struggled desperately with it, boasting for long the sole inimitable example of Hoskins on Exeter. As departments and therefore research became regionalised, economic historians attempted to interpret towns and cities, the major push forward coming in the 1960s from Dyos and his colleagues. Urban history could in any case swallow whole any kind of conventional economic history. Later, a truly massive fragmentation took place, as is pointed out in my book *The Tyranny of the Discrete*.

Two other major historiographical events followed, both in the 1970s. Humanisation found its most extreme expression in the foundation of the Oral History Society (1971). Economic history had to face a direct threat to itself when the familiar 'and social' could not be automatically added to its title, when the Social History Society was formed in 1975. The writer was involved in almost all the post-1960 specialisations so far listed, except the last, and can therefore give useful testimony to the motives that lay behind their formation. The cardinal motive was boredom with existing sources or approaches to a given set of problems. But, that apart, there was a powerful urge to seek and find real vertebrate material for one's subject; this certainly applied to historical demography, as it did to labour and urban history – although the latter was, and remains, something of a mess. Regional history, the arch-synthesiser, was not taken very seriously when these specialisms were taking shape.

Social history, which drew a salutary and extensive migration of bored economic history teachers into the social fold, was in no danger of encompassing the extinction of the economic variety. The latter has lost its charm and novelty, but it is a good and tidy teaching subject with a real educational function. To be sure, most teachers of economic history will recoil in horror at the thought that their work might have an educational function – a point wittily made by Charles Wilson at an annual Economic History Society conference a generation ago ('in Professor Ashton's mouth, the word education took the shape of an obscenity'). But economic history has run through a long course of development, passing through several phases; early or primitive construction, respectability, relative richness of historiography, Cold War political fixation, first phase centrifugal shedding (thinning out of subject matter as specialisations take effect), the need to be unusually intellectually tough (for survival purposes?), and, at the recent stages, reliance on sheer ingenuity and cost-cutting to keep up student numbers.

The writer, like many other colleagues, chose to ride away (1966) on what was then seen as a specialism, but what is now the most integrating and holistic of all – it can even bridge the gap between historians and geographers, and, working away quietly, it has never tried disreputable empire-building tactics. I am writing these comments in a centre for regional studies, of which there are more than a dozen in peaceful corners of Britain. Its time will come, as regional development is taken more seriously.

As for economic history, its real significance has been as a propagator of seeds and a producer of specialisms, some of the latter enriching and some of them sterile. It has contributed greatly to the study and formation of agrarian, urban, transport, business, labour, demographic, social and (to be fair) regional history. Not an insignificant record.

John Marshall (b. Ilkeston, Derbyshire, 1919) studied economic history under J.D. Chambers at Nottingham and wrote a thesis on the history of Barrow in Furness while teaching Coal Board apprentices. Its success, when published as *Furness in the Industrial Revolution,* enabled him to obtain employment at Bolton College, which trained teachers for technical colleges. And when the new University of Lancaster was founded, he was appointed to teach regional history. At Lancaster his imaginative and challenging teaching and research flourished, he founded the Centre for North West Regional Studies, and developed his muse for poetry. Retiring through ill-health in 1980, he remains an active writer and researcher. His most recent book is *The Tyranny of theDiscrete, a critique of the methodology of local history* (1995).

Still Living with the Neighbours

Peter Mathias

I was born and bred up as an economic historian in the Cambridge history school after 1948 – not amongst the Whigs of Trinity, the mystical Christian right of Peterhouse or the leftish (if not formally Marxist) groups in Kings or Trinity, but in Jesus College, a rural fastness of traditional Anglicanism, where Charles Wilson became my main mentor. The Jesus historians had little truck with Fabian-inspired economic history, then the most prominent current in the tide of the subject in Britain. Nor was Charles Wilson much enamoured of the impact of formal economics or sociology; he remained a shrewd, perceptive empiricist who always saw individual human endeavour as a driving force in history, whether in political or economic affairs, and considered political forces as strong in their effects as economic.

I did enter a different intellectual world through M.M. Postan, who had brought deep knowledge of continental scholarships (Weber, Dopsch, Durkheim, the Marxists. . .) to the history faculty, while being as much at home with the Cambridge economists. Postan's weekly seminar at Peterhouse was the liveliest forum for the subject in Cambridge at that time. Then T.S. Ashton's seminar at LSE, together with Charles Wilson as supervisor in Cambridge, set my initial course in research. An invasion of a quite new (to me) methodology reached Cambridge with Walt Rostow's lectures on the *British Economy of the Nineteenth Century* in 1949, followed a few years later (in the Economics Faculty) with his series on *The Stages of Economic Growth*. But the main influence, still transatlantic, came during a year at Harvard and MIT in 1952-3. I was there to take graduate courses in economics but, as it proved, also to participate in the programme of the Research Centre in Entrepreneurial History, then in full swing spreading the heritage of Schumpeter. He had departed to the great macro-economy in the sky several years before but at the Centre it still seemed that he might reappear at any moment. An active academic year in the United States exposed to a wide range of intellectual styles (as well as the wider experience of living in America) was perhaps the most influential single year of my life as an economic historian – as it doubtless has been for many others in my position.

At all events that experience left stronger influences behind than more numerous but briefer excursions to the *Sixième Section* of the *Ecole des Hautes Etudes* in Paris, where Fernand Braudel then held court, during the gestation of the International Economic History Association in the later 1950s. Braudel and Postan formed the diarchy behind the new Association, negotiating like two mutually suspicious heads of state who both needed a treaty. I suppose that this was the globalisation of economic history. The gene pool of British economic history, it seemed to me, was then mainly enriched by North American penetration, while historical demography and social history responded more to France and *Annales*.

My own views about economic history can best be derived by drawing conclusions from what I have written. An inaugural lecture enforces a brief interval of self-awareness and *Living with the Neighbours* did that for me as long ago as 1970 in Oxford. I still believe that the lot of economic history is to go on living with other social sciences conceptually, although they are more numerous and pressing now than they were, while both its principal progenitors, history and economics, have also changed, if not beyond recognition.

For a while when, econometric history – disguised behind that brilliant label 'the new economic history' (where new equals good and old equals bad) – was seen as the new dawn, I feared that economic history was painting itself into a corner, being defined against itself ever more narrowly. Only quantifiable economic variables could be covered by the equations: everything else was non-analysable. This was bad enough conceptually but, more practically, access was only possible for those with the necessary expertise in econometrics, which put most students in history departments beyond the pale. A great diaspora to social and cultural history took hold. The long-standing radical tradition in British historiography, centred in economic history from the first generation of academic economic historians, departed to live with the neighbours in social history. Driven out by quantification, protesting that the new economic history offered quantified expressions of bourgeois ideology, they marched off the battle-field under a banner that proclaimed 'thou shalt not judge by real-wage indices alone'. Qualitative data, or at least data which could not be construed in the same economic matrices which dominated the assumptions of neo-classical theory, was legitimised again in a different mode.

Other trends, more conceptually congenial to good old economic history, as it has seemed to me, then came on the scene with further advances in economic theory. The full implications of one such, indeed, had lain largely hidden since the 1950s. All the exercises in 'accounting for growth' had revealed a large, if unidentified, residual when growth over time was measured in relation to quantified inputs of capital, labour and resources at constant levels of productivity over the period in question. This, by definition, lay outside the terms of the equations – literally a residual – part of the higher mysteries of growth. Technological change and 'improvements in human capital' were assumed to be the main components of the residual but, equally, institutional change, improvements in organisation and other changes in the context of the economy were also potentially relevant. Even entrepreneurship, which could be rejected by definition under neo-classical assumptions of perfect competition, could be an activating force for improving the performance of other variables.

And then came Douglass North and others with the new 'institutional economics' which opened doors wide enough for all of us to re-enter the temple. The momentum for economic change (or the sources of inertia holding back the process) were to be found deeply entrenched in the fundamental institutions of society, the state, together with the political process and the legal system, which embodied in large measure underlying social and cultural determinants. The 'incentive structure' within which an economy operated was identified as being all-important, and this depended on the development of private property rights, economic and tax policies, finding the appropriate balance between freedom of action and the regulatory framework which conditions the operation of all markets. 'Agency relations', the fostering of personal trust and confidence which underlies commercial dealings and contractual relations, formed another dimension of the reality of how an economy actually worked. All these issues recognised that economic action and institutions were socio-cultural constructs embedded in a wider society and its values.

The balance between incentive and inertia could be analysed conceptually, if not always measured, through the means of 'transaction costs' which set the terms for the interplay of these relationships governing change. But 'transaction costs' could arise from a multitude of things – climate and resources, transport, the political and legal system, the efficiency of communications and information flows in a market economy, the business system, the level of risk (itself arising from many aspects of this context) and other issues.

All this came as no surprise to economic historians accustomed to investigate aspects of the empirical context through primary sources and contemporary commentaries. They did not need a sophisticated conceptual apparatus to tell them how complex matters were in practice. But it has broken through constraints in formal economic theorising and dramatically widened the agenda for analysing economic growth, which had been operational in the other social sciences for a long time. The range of relationships which the new conceptual apparatus in economic theory brings to the analysis of economic change includes many non-economic variables, as described, and, although many of these may invite quantification on their own terms, they cannot be captured within a single general model, being too numerous and heterogeneous, although organically part of the process of change. This has opened up the discipline conceptually again, as the methodology of cliometrics had narrowed it, providing a basis for reconciliation, if not a symbiosis, between the older and newer traditions of the historiography and bringing the conceptual and the empirical into relationship in new ways. I see that as a great gain. But will the students ever come back?

Peter Mathias (b. 1928) was educated at Jesus College, Cambridge, and Harvard University. He taught at Queen's College, Cambridge before becoming Chichele Professor of Economic History and Fellow of All Souls, Oxford (1968-87). He was Master of Downing College, Cambridge 1987-95. He was awarded a CBE in 1984. His research interests are primarily eighteenth and nineteenth century economic and business history.

Economic History: A Doomed Love Affair!

Ranald C. Michie

I did not know that I was in love with Economic History until I went to University. The explanation for that was simple – I had never met it before. As a child I had a passion for History, devouring books on such topics as Napoleon and the Vikings. As a teenager I switched to current affairs, using my pocket money to buy the *Manchester Guardian* rather than comics. That fostered an interest in both economics and business as providing an explanation for what was taking place in Britain and in the world in the early 1960s

Consequently when I went to Aberdeen University in 1967 I decided to study History and Economics along with Mathematics – the school I attended (Elgin Academy) was very science orientated and virtually everyone did Mathematics. However my first year was a great disappointment. I found the history rather boring. It covered modern European History and was much the same as I had done at school. In economics I really enjoyed the applied aspects, dealing with Britain's current economic performance and the policies being followed. In contrast I found economic theory too divorced from reality and unable to explain the complexities of everyday economic life. Though I could handle the mathematics I did not enjoy it and realised that was not where my talents lay. Having passed all of the exams – what was I then to do as a degree?

Friends in the first year had mentioned Economic History to me as a course they had taken and enjoyed and so I went along to the department to ask about the subject and see whether I was eligible. On enquiry it appeared that Economic History combined all the things I had been interested in so I signed up to do both the first and second year courses in the coming October. That left me to choose between History and Economics. In the end I picked History which, in retrospect was a mistake!

There existed a joint honours programme between History and Economic History, whereas none was available with economics. This was despite the fact that the Economic History Department had just been carved out of the long established department of Political Economy where Maxwell Gaskin was Professor. Peter Payne had arrived from Glasgow as the newly appointed Professor of Economic History and he ran the first-year course on British Economic History from its medieval origins to the twentieth century, with a strong focus on the industrial revolution. This was exciting stuff with Rostow's *Stages of Economic Growth* and Deane's *First Industrial Revolution* as central texts and I absorbed it all like a true devotee. The second year module in Economic History was taught by Bob Tyson, and covered the economic development of the United States. This was immensely enjoyable and Bob was an excellent lecturer. I lapped it all up, spending most of my time in the University library reading anything I could find on these subjects. In contrast the history course was immensely dull, being a general history of modern Britain. Compared to the analytical drive to be found in Economic History courses, in general British History appeared to be all

236

narrative and no explanation. At the end of my second year I came first in both Economic History examinations and won the first and second year prizes. My love for Economic history had been reciprocated – the subject loved me back!!

As no single honours Economic History degree existed at Aberdeen at the time, I had to continue with general History combining it with further Economic History modules, such as the British Economy since 1914 (Clive Lee), Comparative Imperialism (Malcolm Gray) and comparative economic development – India, China and Japan (Richard Perren). I enjoyed all these and found them immensely interesting. This led me to browse the library shelves for books and articles omitted from the bibliography. Above all I found the special subject on the British Economy 1870-1914 the most interesting, as taught by Payne and Tyson. I found myself at the very cutting edge of the subject as it was being taught in the 1960s. The question of Britain's economic decline was central to the course, especially the debate on entrepreneurship. This was explored from the angles of iron and steel, with Peter Payne, and cotton textiles with Bob Tyson. It was all very exciting with the work of Donald McCloskey coming to challenge that of Aldcroft and Richardson. In contrast the only History course I actually approached with enthusiasm was that on tropical Africa, taught by Hargreaves and Bridges. The whole debate on Imperialism was a live issue at the time with the appearance of Robinson and Gallagher's book *Africa and the Victorians*.

As it was, I graduated in 1971 with a First Class Honours degree in History/Economic History. From that it was an easy and natural step to stay on and study for a Ph.D. with an SSRC grant. In retrospect that was another mistake as I had already been in Aberdeen for 4 years and a change of scene would have helped my perspective. The topic I began, supervised by Peter Payne, was on capital formation in north-east Scotland during the nineteenth century. This reflected current thinking on the subject, with capital formation being seen as the key explanation of economic growth rather than a consequence of it. As the records of the Aberdeen Stock Exchange had recently been deposited in the University Library that appeared to be a convenient starting point – of course it was not! The Aberdeen Stock Exchange dealt in a small number of locally promoted companies which revealed much about financial market activity and nothing about the process of capital formation. After a year pursuing this subject I realised that the research I was doing was contributing nothing towards the Ph.D. I was meant to be writing. I was also becoming stale and Economic History was losing its appeal. It was at that stage I took one of those decisions that was to change my academic life completely. Realising that the records of the other Scottish stock exchanges had also become available I decided that, using my Aberdeen material as a basis, I would study the development of the securities market in Scotland during the nineteenth century. Peter Payne agreed to this and so I spent time in Edinburgh, Glasgow, Dundee and Greenock reading what I could find on the subject. This renewed my love with Economic History which again proved fruitful as, in 1974, I obtained a lectureship in Economic History at Durham University. This was much to my surprise as I had not yet finished writing up my thesis.

When I arrived in Durham in October 1974 the Department of Economic History had just been set up and my designated task was to teach International Economic History. What the content was to be was up to me. All I had to do was deliver 42 lectures and handle all of the tutorials. The Professor of Economic History was Frank Spooner, a rather remote and autocratic figure whose experience and reputation lay in Europe – a friend of Braudel – and in the United States – a friend of Gerschenkron. All the other staff were lecturers. Duncan Bythell (Handloom weavers) handled the first year course – Industrial Britain: origins and development (1750-1914), Richard Britnell (Medievalist) taught nineteenth century European industrialisation and Martin Daunton (Urban History) provided the twentieth century British Economic History. Mike Turner (Agricultural History) was Frank Spooner's Research Assistant. All of us, apart from Frank Spooner, did tutorials on the large first year module which was taken by all the students studying Economics, Politics and Sociology, plus the small number of Economic Historians (around 120 in all). Frank's sole contribution to teaching was a course on Early Modern Europe.

In my second year I was asked to offer a course on the Economic History of the United States – another 42 lectures – while in my third year I put on a special subject on Investment and Imperialism (20 seminars). We certainly did a lot of teaching in those days and there was no system of re-distributing teaching loads. Junior lecturers were easily exploited. Nevertheless, I enjoyed it and Martin Daunton and myself were both young lecturers pleased to have posts. With all this teaching and preparation my Ph.D. was getting no nearer to completion. However inspired by Martin's productivity – he had published his BA dissertation in the *Welsh History Review* and was well on his way to converting his Ph.D. on Cardiff into a book – I decided I would just have to sit down and complete my Ph.D. By then my reading had given me a much broader perspective on what I was doing. I had become impressed by the work of Rondo Cameron and his associates and I saw an opportunity for myself to follow in his footsteps but focusing on securities markets, which were largely ignored in the literature at that time. Thus, beginning after the end of the finals in June and not stopping until October, I wrote non-stop, completely revising what I had already written and adding chapter after chapter. By the end of that summer I had a draft of the whole thesis, which I then revised the following summer and added a few general chapters. One covered the securities market and investment and the other the relationship between London and the Scottish Stock Exchanges. The thesis now extended to two volumes - luckily for me there was no word limit at that time. Eventually after some delay, as Peter Payne wanted Sir Alexander Cairncross as the external examiner, I was awarded my Ph.D. The viva that I had was another turning point because the searching questions that Sir Alexander asked prompted me to rethink my views on the role played by the securities market. The result was not only to re-write my Ph.D. as a book, but also to begin work on a number of general articles. It was at this stage that I decided to focus on London. I put on a special subject on the City of London and started work on the London Stock Exchange records in the Guildhall Library. My love affair was deepening and the subject was still growing. Though Martin Daunton and Mike Turner had left Durham (UCL and Hull respectively) others had come, namely Penny Summerfield (Social History – soon left for Lancaster) and then Roger Middleton (British Economic history), Philip Winston (History of European economic integration) , Martin Jones (Twentieth century economic history) and Dick Lomas (Medieval Economic history). The result was that we had an extensive degree programme covering Economic History from Medieval to Modern, as well as Britain, Europe and the United States, and themes such as capital, labour, enterprise, technology and the international economy. Apart from Frank Spooner all of us now contributed lectures and tutorials to the first year course, offered a second year option, provided a specialised third year subject and supervised dissertations. It was a happy close-knit department where the staff and students knew each other well. All of us were research active and we had set up a series of visiting speakers and developed an active staff seminar programme. Applications were strong - 90 for 12 places – and we did a phenomenal amount of service teaching for the rest of the University. We were also contemplating further expansion in such directions as the Economic History of the Middle East as that area was a Durham strength, and were planning an additional first year course – The Economic History of the British Empire. Personally, my own research was blossoming after a spell in the United States in 1982. I was now working on my second book – a comparison of the London and New York stock exchanges 1850-1914.

Then, in the mid 1980s disaster struck. Frank Spooner decided to take early retirement, Duncan Bythell took a college post and went half-time, Roger Middleton was given two years leave of absence to accompany his wife abroad, Martin Jones joined the Bank of England and Philip Winston went off to the City. The University was facing one of its bouts of financial stringency and so it was clear to us that **no** replacements were available. As there was no way that those of us who remained could cope with the demands of one single and two joint honours programmes, and provide service teaching, we had to seek a merger with another department. Economics was the obvious answer as we shared a building with them and had a long, well-established relationship. Denis O'Brien, one of the Professors of Economics, was on our board of studies, and we expected a sympathetic hearing as his speciality was the History of Economic Thought. That was not to be. The Economics department regarded Economic History as marginal and were much keener to build up accountancy in its place. In no uncertain terms they let it be known that as we were not a "buzz" subject we could "buzz" off. Luckily for us Paul Harvey, the professor of Medieval History, who was also on our board of studies, was very sympathetic to our position, being an economic historian himself. Thus, in 1985 the Economic History department was absorbed into the History department and the staff physically moved into their building, leaving Economics to occupy the space we vacated. The love affair was turning sour.

The one consolation of the merger was that the University gave us a three year temporary lectureship to facilitate the running down of all the Economic History degrees. Peter Wardley (British Economic History) was appointed (now West of England). The History department also made available courses to Economic Historians or permitted them to transfer to single honours History. Though Roger Middleton did return form abroad he never settled into History in Durham and moved to Bristol, where there was still an Economic History Department at that time. Eventually Dick Lomas and Duncan Bythell took early retirement while Richard Britnell flourished as a born again Medievalist. After several failed attempts I managed to create for myself a small niche within the History degree programme by focussing on British economic history and the City of London. As a degree programme Economic History at the University of Durham had ceased to exist by the late 1980s, surviving only as a marginal component of the single and joint honours degree programme, and almost totally ignored by the Economists who had once provided most of our students. All that remained of the connection with Economics was a joint-honours programme with History but as the economists insisted on candidates for this degree having A-level mathematics, it did not flourish. (It is now in the process of being withdrawn) The subject I had studied, had a degree in and loved, now no longer existed in Durham in any distinct form. As what had happened in Durham had not yet taken place elsewhere, our plight was ignored by fellow economic historians where Departments and strong groupings still existed. At Economic History conferences I found myself isolated and ceased to attend. The love affair was over. All that remained was my own research and that grew from strength to strength as I established myself as a leading authority in financial history, focussing on the history of stock exchanges and the City of London. This gained me a group of international colleagues which compensated for the lack of a community of Economic Historians in Durham or elsewhere in the UK. I found myself better received at conferences abroad than in Britain. Nevertheless the love affair was now over to be replaced with a series of transitory friendships. In retrospect all that was inevitable though it came to me earlier than most of my colleagues in Economic History in Britain. Economic History's mistake was to cut itself off from the objectives which had given it life. Detached from Economics it was no longer able to serve that subject as it changed in focus and complexity. Detached from history it became too technical, so making it difficult for general Historians and students to access the subject. This left Economic History with no natural constituency, so making it vulnerable in an age of university austerity. However, I am sure I was not alone in not only not recognising these fundamentals but also ignoring the signs and warnings that were evident throughout the 1970s and 1980s. I well recollect Jack Fisher prophesying the demise of Economic History at a conference dinner and few of us believing him.

So what did Economic History mean to me. In the end it meant a subject I enjoyed and discovered I was good at. It also meant entry to an international field of scholars who shared my absorbing interest in the specialised area of financial history. For that I have no regrets. However, it also meant being marginalised within both History and Economics, with no access to the mainstream of either subject. That I do regret because I firmly believe that Economic History has much to contribute to both subjects. Without a knowledge and a real understanding of the long-term past Economics becomes an arid and rather empirical subject that has little to contribute to an understanding of the everyday concerns of ordinary people or even provide the ability to predict the future in the face of discontinuities and uncertainties of a non-economic nature. Similarly, it seems inexplicable to me that History concerns itself with such subjects as politics and culture while ignoring the economic fundamentals that have made possible all that modern societies have enjoyed and fought over. Economic Historians must be forever ready to both dispel an economist's simplistic views of the past and persuade historians that they must give greater prominence to the substance of the past rather than its froth. Economic History remains a subject worth fighting for even if all the current battles appear lost. However, it is now two subjects being split between economists and historians, leaving the likes of me stranded in a no-man's land in the middle rather than having a foot in both camps. It is like still being married with all the disadvantages and none of the advantages!!

Ranald C. Mitchie (b. 12. 5. 1949) was educated at Aberdeen University. He has held visiting research fellowships in the United States and Canada, and is currently Professor of History at Durham University. His research has concentrated on modern financial history and related areas. He has written extensively on the history of stock exchanges and on the City of London. His most recent publication is *The London Stock Exchange: A History* (1999).

From Economics to History

Robert Millward

I started academic life as an economist in the heady days of the 1960s when there was great optimism about the scope for social engineering. Teams of economists were pouring into Whitehall - not just the Treasury but also the spending Ministries: transport, fuel, power, agriculture, later on health and education. I have an intrinsic interest in economic organisation and was caught up in the great debate about how the modern public sector should be run. Cost benefit analyses of water resource schemes, new road programmes, railway investments were being undertaken in both the developed world and in the less developed countries in Asia and Africa and generated a large literature in academic journals. The French, overshadowed in many areas of economics, lead the way in the analysis of the links between economic and engineering issues in electricity supply, in the debate on the pricing rules for public sector industries and in the introduction by Éléctricité de France of the famous time - of day Tarif Vert. I had a spell in the early 1970s working as an economic adviser for the East African Community (a common market body like the European Union) based in Arusha, Tanzania, where we were heavily involved in drawing up 5 year development plans and training African economists.

I mention these matters only to indicate that for many academics the trade of the economist was, intellectually and financially, a very attractive profession. Yet in the 1970s I gradually shifted my interest to economic history for the simple reason that I found it more interesting. My main interests have proved to be in the long term features of economic organisation, though that was not so obvious at the time. Economics, including its Keynesian variant, appeared to be most useful in the diagnosis of short term changes in the economy. The optimism about social engineering in the Third World and in the public sector in Western Europe started to decline as policy prescriptions were ignored or proved inappropriate. Much of the neo-classical diagnosis and policy prescriptions are concerned with promoting the use of markets and price systems and useful as these may be (and the message was certainly swallowed whole by governments throughout the world in the 1980s and 1990s) they do not capture many of the dimensions of the long term historical experience of economy and society outside frontier America. In any case it had become clear to me, and to many others, that the objects of policy decisions - British railways, the banks, farming communities in Africa, the Ministry of Fuel and Power - had a life of their own which needed to be understood and explained. For some academics the path lay in formal models of behaviour of, for example, public sector institutions, and this was the starting point for public choice theory. I was more interested in studying the long term features of institutional change and was not too worried about whether the answers could be formalised into elegant mathematical theorems.

One of the ways of studying long term features of economic organisation is to focus on the property rights which characterise different institutions and to try to explain them. Why were the peasant land holdings in medieval open fields arranged in the form of scattered strips? Why was the classic proto-industrial firm in textiles organised in a putting out system? What is a firm - as Ronald Coase asked in the 1930s? Why did some towns in nineteenth century Britain municipalise their water and electricity supplies whilst other towns left operations to private companies? Why did British manufacturers in the twentieth century delegate more power to shop floor employees and maintain craft production methods longer than their American counterparts? Several brief allusions to historical issues in the work of the economists I was reading in the 1970s (Armen Alchian, Harold Demsetz, Oliver Williamson), started an interest in the shift to the factory system in eighteenth century Britain. The predecessors of the textile factories were putting-out systems where merchants based in towns like Leeds and Nottingham arranged for raw material, wool, cotton, flax, to be spun into yarn in rural cottages, passed on to weavers sometimes in different cottages, and finally transported to bleachers and dyers. This was a curious form of economic organisation since the domestic workers were geographically spread, were not supervised and yet the merchant retained ownership in the processed material throughout. This was the start of my interest in economic history and several colleagues at Salford - Greg Anderson, Barbara Ingham, Colin Simmons - directed my attention to the huge literature on the shift to factory systems. My answer to the putting out puzzle was published in *Explorations in Economic History* 1981. These initial forays into the literature on the putting-out and factory systems had been stimulated by another factor. Anyone working and living in the Manchester region has the history of the cotton industry all around them. The cottage industries of the Pennines, the Trough of Bowland and the Rossendale valley (where my grandparents lived) had a clear place in that historiography. Precisely what role did they play in the success of Lancashire cotton? We now have fairly good answers to these questions from the mushrooming literature on proto-industrialisation which, given my own early interest in putting-out, formed the basis of the lectures which I offered in Manchester in the 1990s in a course on Economic Organisation in Theory and History which also included a large chunk on the economic history of serfdom.

The interest in serfdom was a big leap but had developed from my exposure to pre-industrial history. By the early 1980s I had taken the bait. Douglass North's *The Rise of the Western World* was an obvious next step as also Maurice Dobb's *Studies in the Development of Capitalism* (with its wonderful first chapter on the usage of the term 'capitalism') which led to the whole debate on the transition out of feudalism, thence to Michael Postan, Robert Brenner, Immanuel Wallerstein quite apart from neo-classical economic historians like Deidre McCloskey writing about the scattered medieval strips. I developed a particular interest in Eastern European serfdom, in part I suspect because many of my generation were conscious of the economic backwardness of that area in the early twentieth century and the way it had formed the battleground for capitalism, fascism and communism for much of the century. I do not read Polish or Russian and could not therefore unearth new sources or data but was able to bring to this subject my own interests in economic theory and property rights and was greatly stimulated in this by the work of Stefano Fenoaltea, a really outstanding economic historian. In addition there is a literature by Eastern European scholars (especially the Polish historians like Witold Kula, Jerzy Topolski, Leonard Zytkowicz) which has been translated into English or French so that, in conjunction with the large number of American studies of Russian history, I was able to put together a very detailed picture of Eastern European agriculture. I was particularly interested in why the condition of enserfment was invariably associated with labour services rather than forced rents in money or kind and sought an answer in the role of supervision (*Journal of Economic History* 1982).

At the same time in the 1980s I was following another intellectual thread from early days in academic life. Only one month before I was due to take up my first academic post, aged 22, I was told by Charles Carter to put on a full 40 lecture course on Public Enterprise Economics, about which I then knew nothing but which led thereafter to a permanent interest in the growth of the public sector in Britain. Now one of the great virtues of history as a discipline is the way it readily demonstrates the fragility of ideas and policies. I currently teach a course on the British Economy since 1945 and an important theme is the way the fashion for macroeconomic demand management in the 1950s gave way in the 1960s to national economic planning (a phrase which, after 1967, never passed the lips of a British politician), to the support for leading firms ('champions') and Italian-style holding companies in the 1970s, to monetarism and free markets in the 1980s and 1990s. I have been particularly struck by the way one form of economic organisation, the nationalised industry, had become discredited, in the writings of economists, by the late 1970s and this led to a search for the causes of this apparently misconceived institution in the early decades of the twentieth century and indeed to the long term origins of public ownership, including nineteenth century municipalisation. (It turned out that many of the economic reasons for privatisation in the 1980s were similar to the reasons advanced for nationalisation in the 1930s and 1940s). Were the Victorians as successful in building up the country's infrastructure of water pipes, railway lines and sewer systems as we have sometimes been led to believe? The rapid growth of cities in nineteenth century Britain and the attendant problems of crime, poverty and squalor are known as much from the English novel as from the works of historians though books like Anthony Wohl's *Endangered Lives* have been equally evocative. Was the huge blight which accompanied industrialisation avoidable? Did we have the scientific insight to solve the problems? Was it, perhaps, instead, deficient administration and a resistant ideology? The scope for more historical research in this important period is still large. The modern development of computers has allowed new large data sets to be developed and I have found this particularly fruitful in my research on the growth of sanitation systems and its links with urbanisation, public health programmes and mortality in the nineteenth century.

My interest in economic history has therefore distinctly different roots from those of my colleagues who from the beginning were history scholars. Historians are not readily drawn into current policy matters - their cynical reaction, into which I have been successfully indoctrinated, is to ask what particular fad, ideology, career move is motivating the policy adviser. Perhaps the influence of historians can be at most indirect. Why, for example, has it proved so difficult for capitalism to flourish in Poland, Hungary, Russia and certain other parts of Eastern Europe? The first seeds of capitalism, planted in the nineteenth century, were overthrown in the communist revolutions in the first half of the twentieth century. Now communism has been overthrown and teams of advisers from Western Europe and America are trying to promote the spread of free markets. The agenda of many Westerners initially was for a very rapid transformation but the process has been painfully slow. There have been catastrophic declines in national output and life expectancy and robber capitalism is a phrase increasingly used for what is emerging in Russia. The economists from the West and from Eastern Europe are well aware of the importance of certain institutions for the successful development of capitalism - good capital markets, clear enforceable legal codes to underpin private property, strong infrastructure of communications. Historians on the other hand know also that these countries still had, as late as 1914, nobility-dominated governments, a large agricultural sector interlaced with vestiges of feudal relationships, strong village communes, repressive policing systems and a very small indigenous capitalist class whilst the non-indigenous class emigrated or was wiped out in the twentieth century. Perhaps we should keep reminding people of this.

Robert (Bob) **Millward** (b. 11. 12. 1939) was educated at Hull (B.SC. Econ) and Manchester (Ph.D). He has been Professor of Economic History in the Manchester History Department since 1989, having previously been Professor of Economics at the University of Salford. Recent research with Frances Bell on public health and mortality in Victorian Britain has been published in *Continuity and Change* July 1998 and in *European Review of Economic History*, December 1998. Other research areas are East European serfdom, the putting-out system, nationalisation and the history and economics of public utilities. Recent books include *The Political Economy of Nationalisation 1920-50*, Cambridge 1995 (with J.Singleton).

What Economic History Means to Me: An Italian Perspective

Giorgio Mori

November 2000 marks exactly 30 years since Peter Mathias, then Fellow in economic history at All Souls College in Oxford, chose a title for his Inaugural Lecture that was both a popular expression and extremely appropriate to the subject - 'Living with the Neighbours'. In his lecture, he outlined the topical moment the discipline was passing through, experiencing both the discovery of new facts and new approaches. He did this with great shrewdness and calm and without concealing his own opinion on the subject. This period had begun - and it is an unnecessary reminder in a forum such as this - with the progressive affirmation in the United States of a research mindset that was openly and aggressively hostile to the traditional intellectual horizon and its standard work method. This new mindset was named 'new economic history' by its promoters and, after various modifications, in the end took on the name of 'historical economics.' It was the first, and the nearest of the disturbing 'neighbours' of which Mathias spoke. However, it was no longer the only one. Aside from 'entrepreneurial history', a second neighbour, new social history, moved in. It had a long and notable tradition in England and was in a phase of obvious redefinition. This redefinition was being guided by sociological theorizing which was more lively, yet still of great depth. This included, among others, Smelser's study and the little known work of Chayanov published in the 1920s, but only recently translated into English. These neighbours, as well as the new ideas and methods put forward by historical demography, were able further to shake up the operative certainties of a 'young' discipline like economic history. The cool reception which Mendels's article on proto-industrialization received, just two years after Mathias's Lecture, provided undeniable proof of this, as if there had been any need for it.

I will return later to the evolution over the years, of the picture painted in Mathias's Lecture but I think it essential to start with a brief examination of the condition of economic historiography in Italy at the close of the 1950s, the time when I had just begun my research activities and upon which I will dwell precisely for that reason. In Italy, as in many other countries, the first reports of the work of the scholars on 'new economic history', arrived rather late, more or less towards the end of the 1960s. The same can also be said, with some modest differences of timing, of information on new social history and on historic demography. Until then, the discipline (which Croce's restrictive judgment as to its servile nature had influenced much more than was apparent at the time) had witnessed undisputed and energetic protagonists, people of great and well-deserved fame whose interests focused essentially on the medieval and modern eras: Luzzatto, Einaudi (to whom we owe an excellent book on the Italian economy and society during the war of 1915-1918, as well as the founding in 1936 of the *Rivista di storia economica*), Sapori, Dal Pane, Barbagallo (who published *Le origini della grande industria contemporanea* in 1930), Borlandi, Melis, and the very young Carlo Cipolla. The century following Italy's unification was *terra incognita* or at least almost so, despite Corbino's Herculean work (in 1951, he sent the last of five volumes of *Annali dell'economia italiana*, to be printed - a resource which has been invaluable and has been used by many), and the arrival of two books on the history of Italian industry by Tremelloni and by Fossati, which added to the work done by R. Morandi on that subject and which were published in 1931.

These are all works which, in addition to others of lesser note, spurred both novices and well-established experts to face many questions regarding the history of the national economy from 1861 on (and during the half century prior to that time). However, much less attention was devoted to the questions raised regarding the twenty-year period of fascism.

I found myself living through the final phase of the first, fiery disputes of that period set in motion by Rosario Romeo in 1958, before reaching the point of no return described by Mathias. In one of his works, Romeo addressed the period from 1861 to 1887. He was able to take advantage of two new works on economic development published by Nurkse and Lewis and of the pioneering, even if not always reliable, *Indagine* of national income from Italian unification to 1956. This survey was the Italian contribution to the ambitious project of the Social Science Research Council of New York, promoted by Kuznets. Romeo's thesis was simple and unambiguous- by heavily taxing agriculture, the state had collected a volume of capital that was sufficient to set up and articulate an endowment of fixed social capital, including the railroads. This was a painful option for the ruling class made up of large property owners, but even more so for the poor peasants, but it seems to have stimulated the system along the road to industrial development, thanks to, among other factors, the extremely low wage levels and the protectionist tariff of 1887. The discussion that immediately followed publication of this article involved a large number of Italian historians and economists and even Gerschenkron took part (he had in 1955 compiled his well known 'Index of Italian Industrial Output: 1881-1913'). Despite the fact that many participants retreated to their rigidly fortified positions, the discussion was anything but sterile. In fact, in addition to other factors, it was also because of this discussion that I decided to consider industrial history as the field in which I wanted to specialize. On the one hand, the generalisation and fragmentation, which are often inevitable, with the slow pace of research, had not escaped me. On the other hand, a crucial and manifest gap existed; the almost total omission of any reference to the impact on the Italian economy, either pre-unification or post-unification, of the budding and spreading of industrialization in north west Europe and the consequent reactions of the ruling classes. I thought of Habakkuk's much earlier lecture, in which he distinguished between the 'imitative' types of reactions and the 'non-imitative' types, the latter of which the ruling classes opted for at the time of unification, and perhaps in part, prior to unification (as Richard Cobden, the great industrialist-politician-intellectual had hoped for). It was precisely for this reason that I chose a university course in 1960, entitled 'The Industrial Revolution and Italy', a theme that I would come back to many times.

My training in the subject started with a monograph on local history and I was influenced from the beginning by the books of Dobb and of Hobsbawm, but much more so by my studies of *Quaderni del Carcere* by Gramsci, and of *Das Kapital*, as was natural for me, since the first complete translation into Italian was completed in 1955. In the latter in addition to the notes on the national economy, I lingered over Marx's reflections on Ricardo's concept of a 'distinct market' and on the implicit potential logically to deduce, distinct from value theory. The connections to Marx's work were clear, as well as the grip of the 'law of large numbers' as an analytical tool (in the presence of state intervention in the economy and of the opposition of the popular masses abandoning passivity, a process that was already in motion in the mid-1800s and not only in the British isles).

I think it necessary to add that my career and study seemed more inviting after reading other works of those years. The most noticeable of these were *Industry and Trade, General Theory* and *Business Cycles* and especially the writings of Gerschenkron and Rostow, as well as Landes' powerful essay in the *Cambridge Economic History of Europe*, vol. 6. But, Schumpeter's work was undoubtedly the most important, because of the considerable attention that his distinguished, unprejudiced and original portrait of Marx published in 1942 received. My interest was aroused most by the final lines of the third part, which I must cite in full (asking pardon for its length, when presented in a context such as this). The great Austrian economist wrote that, for economists, 'the facts entered theory, if at all, merely in the role of illustration, or possibly of verification of results. They mixed with it only mechanically. Now Marx's mixture is a chemical one; that is to say, he introduced them into the very argument that produces the results. He was the first economist of top rank to see and to teach systematically how economic theory may be turned into historical analysis and how the historical narrative may be turned into *histoire raisonnée*. The analogous problem with respect to statistics, he did not attempt to solve. But in a sense it is implied in the other.'

I clearly remember that despite their peremptory tones, I did not feel any particular sensations of unease or of rejection concerning the proposal enunciated by the voices of Mathias's neighbours that seemed to me to be louder and more insistent. While I was very interested in the works of social history, because of its novelty for me, the complex and formally rigorous project of the historical economists did not seem new to me because of the readings I mentioned above. Apart from the extensive practice of treating original and already known quantitative data and interpolating it with continually evolving statistical techniques (and I must acknowledge that it is no small thing), its more original and somewhat more promising side left me with many questions which seemed neither unreasonable nor rhetorical and to which I could not find satisfying answers. Why did they speak of neo-classical 'theory' and not of theories? Why were only the results of econometric applications on historical series (constructed on a theoretical model that was tried but also simplified by definition, and how much?: clearly a precarious situation) considered to be 'scientific' and therefore trustworthy as a thorough interpretation of the historical phenomenon examined? And why should such appreciation be denied *a priori* to so-called 'traditional' or 'literary' (in the worst sense of those two adjectives) economic historiography? At its highest points, it had reached a degree of understanding that was not inferior to that reached by the theoretical and technical tools that were gaining increasing control. Besides, how could it be denied that one of the 'discoveries', deriving from the two paradigms (historical economics and social history), was the irrelevance of the concept of the industrial revolution (or its dilution over a long period of time), confirming views attributed to Clapham and then to Beales? We have witnessed repeated and vehement disputes over the last few years among historical economists exactly on this question, which has in turn created greater confusion among less prepared readers. As I remarked in the 'Introduction' to the first Italian translation of Mantoux's magnum opus (1971), - why was state intervention in the economy, especially in the United States and Great Britain (until 1846) so ignored by economists and social historians? These interventions had more direct and indirect effects than interference of groups and social classes on the states themselves. In 1971, Supple, in a work on the subject, which does not seem to have been adequately appreciated, suggested 'this is not to say that the state... reflects the exact distribution of effective power within a society... But it is to say that a government draws its aims as well as its legitimacy from existing elements in a particular society.' Why, in paying honor to the neoclassic model, was technical progress considered some type of accident, a 'residue', while there were scholars, like Abramovitz, who considered it 'the measure of our ignorance'? And finally, why did the new social history have to exclude the substance, if not the form, of the more or less radical modifications that appeared in a given economic system, concentrating its meticulous and clear analysis on the subjects active within it - groups, communities, families, classes (and on their cultures)?

In light of these rhetorical questions, of the reasoning presented here and of the many years I have been studying this area, I will now try to express my point of view on the present condition of economic historiography. It is necessary to be brief but I hope not to be disorderly or simplistic. The task is not easy because of the extraordinary expansion of the literature over the last few decades - a reality which has now become uncontrollable, but was acknowledged in 1977 by

Barraclough in his magnificent and courageous world overview of historic studies. I will continue to confine myself to the specific geo-cultural area of Western Europe and the USA.

Important points

a) Ignoring, if possible, the academic difficulties the discipline is facing, I think its state of health is better than good and I would say the most vital symptoms are the average quality of the studies, (much higher that a few decades ago) and the practice of dealing with controversy in a way that no longer falls into bitterness.

b) We must notice a boundless tendency, to methodological contamination, which should be accompanied by a rejection of all 'opportunism' and the hurry to arrive quickly at an ideal interpretation. Not the least problem with economic history is which word will be adjective and which one noun, this sets the basic concept of this branch of study - it is either 'Historical economics' or 'Economic History'.

c) A prudent but committed inspection of the extended historic series of great aggregates constructed masterfully by Kuznets, Denison, Maddison and others is urgent. (Such studies widely influence the organization and carrying out of all types of research). Neither can we ignore the connection of those series to the preceding phases of the economic system's dynamic.

d) We must consider Solow's exhortation of 16 years ago to be irreproachable and inalienable. 'That kind of model is directly applicable in organizing a historical narrative, the more so to the extent that the economist is conscious of the fact *that different social contexts may call for different background assumptions and therefore for different models...* If the proper choice of a model depends on the institutional context - and it should - then economic history performs the nice function of widening the range of observations available to the theorist. Economic theory can only gain from being taught something about the range of possibilities in human societies.'

e) Time is also ripe critically to assimilate the lines of research stimulated by 'endogenous growth theory' above all regarding the role assigned to human capital, that has put the neoclassical model under attack and which has had a salutary effect on the studies of 'historical economists' upon which the model is based.

f) It goes without saying that we economic historians - whose often-justified distrust of any form of modelling is far from being dissolved - should in any case, both incorporate and develop theoretical elements borrowed from other disciplines, and better earlier than later and to a greater extent than we currently do. We can start trying this with economics both in the formulation of our questions and in the development of our critical narrative. This means therefore, that we need direct and updated knowledge of economics, with the aim of arriving sooner or later at an independent place for our discipline.

Giorgio Mori (b. 1927) was Professor of Economic History at the University of Modena (from 1968) and the University of Florence from 1974. He has been President of the Scientific Committee of the International Institute of Economic History 1987-93. He has written books on the industrialisation of Italy and also researched the 'economic miracle' of Italy in the post-war years.

Meandering in Klondike Spaces Between Histories of Art and Histories of Material Progress

Patrick K. O'Brien

A volume of commemorative essays invites autobiography, recollections of a misspent youth (or career?), visits to the tombs of illustrious predecessors, and nostalgia for the subject's golden age, concluding with an elaboration of methodological prescriptions for a better future. I decided to resist these appealing temptations. Instead, perhaps because my memories of economic histories and economic historians go back a fairly long way, I am moved to say something about the cyclical nature of the lectures, seminars and publications that have filled my academic life for these past 50 years.

To impose coherence, structure and chronology on the volume of erudite words I have read and the cacophony of enlightening voices I have heard is rather difficult. I can recall cemeteries of dead friends, universities of colleagues and students and whole libraries of books, articles and working papers representing the evolution of the subject during and before my own half century in the field. Alas, no scholar has written a history of economic history on an international or (I believe) on a national basis. There seems to be nothing on the shelves like those multi-volume magisterial histories of physics, chemistry and astronomy that help natural scientists to comprehend from where their disciplines originated, how they developed, and to point up horizons towards which they are travelling.

In the absence of reliable histories and since many vacations are spent looking at paintings, the notion that comparisons with European art might provide some cautionary reflections and illuminating analogies for economic history has matured into an attractive way around the problem of writing something brief and possibly interesting for this anniversary volume.

Of course economic historians work with words and print and not with paint and canvas. Nevertheless, what the sources and recorded histories of western art provides us with is a way of perceiving and encapsulating past, present and future flows of knowledge for our own circumscribed, recondite but equally important discourse about the human condition. Art does just that with enviable ease simply because you can see the original sources displayed before you in marvellous colours on the walls and ceilings of galleries, palaces, villas, cathedrals and churches. Once in Rome, Paris, London, Vienna, Berlin, New York, Washington or in any of the innumerable smaller but delightful cities of our continent, we have merely to 'gaze' for a couple of hours in order to reflect on the heritage and future of this visually accessible mode of humanistic discourse.

Thus, at a superficial level the totality and chronology of the history of art is much easier to 'grasp' and 'to order' than the range and evolution of printed and documented material that constitutes the record of our economic past. Nevertheless both domains can be compared. To start with, the organisation of production for the two 'industries' is similar. Paintings have been constructed in thousands of workshops. Scales of production are small. Craftsmen jealously guard their personal autonomies. Each site includes masters, journeymen and apprentices, loosely co-ordinated or networked into guilds that regulate their terms and conditions for employment. At some sites training and so called best practice became rigidly prescribed. The methods, styles, subjects and obsessions of 'masters' leave indelible impressions on the work of the young. At best apprentices produced arresting variations on established and fashionable themes. At worst they became imitators, clones and clients of oppressively hierarchical systems of patronage. Many masters of the past are revered; some are loved and quite a few inspire dislike for their ungenerous dispositions towards journeymen and apprentices alike. It seems to be the case that (apart from Rubens) virtually no great artist taught pupils to become as enduringly innovative in their own right.

Moving this protracted (but hopefully heuristic analogy) on from a focus on producers and the organisation of work to consider the diversity and flow of output through time, other parallels come to mind. For example, is it not clear that chronologies for the history of art and for the mere two or three centuries of scholarship and craftsmanship devoted to the construction of histories of material life could be divided into cycles of innovation, consolidation, stagnation and revival?

Furthermore, when they appeared, innovations in the techniques, colour, styles and subject matter involved in the making of paintings also diffused from site to site. Some places (e.g. Sienna) resisted change. Others (Venice) adapted slowly and in their own way to new ideas. Other Burgundian towns insisted that their own Northern Renaissance took precedence and remained superior to anything going on in Italy. Perhaps too many sites and artists became merely slavish in their emulation of once fashionable and all too brashly advertised 'scientific' prescriptions from Florence.

At all times what they perceived to be original ways of differentiating their products from the 'obsolete' work of their elders has exercised a powerful hold on the rhetoric and behaviour of the ambitious young. Nevertheless throughout the centuries perhaps a majority of artists have continued to paint familiar subjects in established ways. Innovation and fashion have rarely swept the board because before that happened something emerged to transform the 'modern' into yet another stultifying tradition.

For every demarcated period a vast quantity of art appeared. Most is of professional quality, but 'on display' much of it emerges as more of the same or it can be represented as variations on fashionable themes and techniques. Yet when art historians look back over the very long chronology and diverse range of paintings that has somehow survived since Byzantium, they find that they can only grasp the sources and tradition that they study by imposing vocabularies, taxonomies, order and coherent narratives upon their unusually accessible and easily communicated body of historical evidence.

Compared to histories of science our colleagues in art history are disinclined to write of 'development' or of 'progress', let alone of standing on the 'shoulders of giants'. Historians of Western art prefer to separate their diverse bodies of evidence into cycles or tendencies in the history of painting; each explicable or assessable for a particular stage of evolution but in the fullness of time moving on to a different style, to new emphases in terms of subject matter and to the adoption of current innovations in technique. Clearly art history recognises change, but accords no status to leaps into improvement or falls into decline. It merely records and explains a passing from one phase to the next.

In contrast, in recent years, too many European and North American scholars have published eloquent laments on lost golden ages and the decline of economic history. That is why I labour the point about art because I wish to recommend that we consider the history of our tribe in the same way. After all our subject is at least three centuries old. Try to visualise its products (books and articles) on display or as a comprehensive exhibition of achievements from say Adam Smith to Fernand Braudel and Bob Fogel. Could we not agree that analogies with other genres of historical scholarship might be fruitful to contemplate?

For example we might consider tracing 'classical' histories of 'material life' all the way back to Herodotus and on through a series of ad hoc observations in Roman and Christian ethnography and geography to the Enlightenment which is where Donald Coleman's investigation into 'History and the Economic Past' begins. By that time, and after several centuries of regular commercial contact (initially within Europe), but from 1492 onwards with the peoples of Africa, Asia and the Americas enough hard information had accumulated for intellectuals to publish something valid about the economies and economic histories of Europe and Asia, Christendom and Islam, Europe and Africa, Europeans and Amerindians as well as more cogent analyses concerned with the environmental, demographic, political, legal and cultural conditions that produced variations in incomes, wealth and power across their own familiar continent of Europe.

However limited the reflections of Bousset, Montesquieu, Voltaire, Hume, Turgot, Smith, Robertson, Ferguson, Millar and the Gottingen school may now seem to modern economic historians, they can be repositioned in histories of economic thought as the origins of serious enquiry into the wealth and poverty of nations. Voltaire, for example, wanted to know 'how men lived in the interior of their families.' Hume conducted 'a general survey of the age as regards manners, finances, arms, commerce, arts and sciences'. At the end of his universal history (written in 1751) Turgot analysed what he regarded as the highest stage of economic development - urban, commercial society. We all know that Adam Smith reflected deeply on the differences between competitive and regulated systems of production as well as on variations in the levels of real wages in Europe, China and India.

Perceptions and embryo research into economic change that appeared during the Enlightenment eventually matured into the modern academic subject of economic history. But as Postan amusingly insisted, our discipline (like that useful animal, the mule) emerged as the offspring of two ill-matched parents: economics and history. Alas, the former soon neglected its responsibilities. After a brief interregnum when Adam Smith's 'great enquiry' into the Wealth of Nations, was at least pursued intermittently by a line of classical economists (including Malthus, James Mill, Senior, Wakefield and McCulloch), John Stuart Mill observed (as long ago as 1862) that 'it is only in the backward countries of the world that increased production is still an important subject. In most advanced countries what is economically needed is better distribution'. Mill's observation reflects the early hegemony of a mainstream and persistent trajectory within economic thought which followed Ricardo and aspired to be 'scientific'. By the time of Alfred Marshall, economics had become almost a-historical and preoccupied with individual choice, distribution and allocative efficiency. As Walt Rostow recently concluded 'growth theory had moved to the periphery', which left economic history to mature within the household of a single rather indifferent parent, but secure in the knowledge that it was actively engaged in the study of something of paramount and universal significance for mankind. After all, for most of recorded history the majority of the world's population has been preoccupied with obtaining the food, shelter, clothing and other manufactured artefacts that people everywhere require to sustain either a basic, a comfortable and only latterly an agreeable standard of living. That universal preoccupation is what we study; that is why we see most other (albeit methodologically sophisticated, imaginative and interesting) forms of historical investigations as subsidiary and subordinate.

Between its emergence as a project of the Enlightenment and its 'Renaissance' during the

1960s, economic history survived, coped and eventually matured into an academic discipline without a great deal by way of intellectual support from economics. Yet in no way was our absent parent rejected by previous generations of scholars. Economic historians writing during that 'Classical Era' did not find the insights derivable from abstract theorising about consumer preference, the rational behaviour of firms under idealised market forms, the properties of general equilibrium or conditions for steady state growth, particularly useful, let alone empirically verifiable for their own concerns. Most read some economics, imported its more arresting vocabularies and kept their minds open towards relevant theories and prospects for measurement. Meanwhile, the majority researched and wrote within the inductive tradition of the historical school of political economy. Their canonical 'grandmasters' included: Schmoller, Sombart, Bucher and Weber from Germany; Bloch, Labrouse, Levasseur from France' Pirenne from Belgium; Vives from Spain; Cunningham, Ashley, Tawney, Postan, Clapham and Ashton from Britain and Day, Gras, Usher and Innis from North America. They favoured case studies bounded by and specified for every conceivable level of disaggregation. Furthermore, and as historians, they displayed no hesitation in crossing the frontiers of territories demarcated as 'domains' by social scientists. They insisted on incorporating politics, law, institutions, religion and culture into their explanations for the behaviour of firms, farms, industries, social groups and they utilised all areas and types of historical knowledge that could conceivably help to explain the economic success and retardation of nations.

Just a superficial reading of the canon could persuade that the vocabularies and taxonomies of neo-institutional economies, the exhortations of new institutional economic history, notions of path dependency, the significance of human capital formation, the constricting or promotional roles of culture, religion and ideology are all there in the canonical writings of the German historical school and its European tributaries - awaiting rediscovery once the barbarism of the modern German state faded into historical memory and when cliometric history had run its momentary but brilliant course.

When cliometrics emerged in the early 1960s it represented the reappearance of our absent parent and a reassertion of the Ricardian tradition. Economic history was to be refashioned and reconfigured as applied economics. Without economics the subject was considered to be untenable. 'Florentines' (from across the Atlantic) led the tribe through a Renaissance and instructed us in the hallmarks of best scientific practice that included: the careful specification (or more often the import) of a model from economic theory, the search for and proper calibration of data and finally, how to deploy statistical and econometric techniques designed to test the model against historical evidence in order to offer qualified conclusions, based upon transparent sets of assumptions.

There can be no doubt that the Renaissance of the 1960s engendered intellectual excitement, enjoyed a period of fame and imposed rigour and standards of proof on historians who try to explain long term economic growth. As the paradigm and its prescriptions shifted from location to location, lessons were absorbed, modified and transformed into different styles of scholarship. Within a decade the limitations of counterfactual history, the constricting dependence on ceteris paribus assumptions and reliance upon models drawn overwhelmingly from neo-classical economics had been exposed. Former converts to cliometrics began to evince their dissatisfaction with methods that they predicted would perhaps produce little more than quantitatively insecure elaborations on the 'proximate determinants' of economic growth. With little more than a fraction of their predecessors' erudition and avoiding anything more than tangential engagements with history, by the early 1970s evangelicals from even further to the west advocated a reallocation of attention to the 'deeper structural determinants' of economic growth - such as institutions, legal systems, states, ideology, social behaviour and culture. In effect, Savonarola and the friars preached a return to basics, but in evocative metaphors congenial to their peers and colleagues in neo-institutional economics. Their sermons made virtually no reference to libraries of relevant research built up by generations of European historical scholarship from Schmoller and Pirenne to Weber and Braudel. But then and from its inception, this movement fashioned itself , not as a Restoration (which it clearly was and remains), but rather as a Revolution. Revolutionaries in search of niches for differentiated products rarely consider the antecedents or precedents for their entirely traditional agendas. Nor, alas, have they found enough time to fill the empty boxes of their conceptual vocabularies and taxonomic distinctions with empirical detail and properly validated historical examples.

Meanwhile the cliometric Renaissance ran into diminishing (not negative) returns. Work currently emerging from what used to be innovationary sites of production can be represented as 'Mannerist' - namely as examples of increasingly complex elaborations of models and techniques that 'demonstrate' that for long periods of history, markets worked. Although the insistence on methodology and quantification has carried economic history forward to levels of analytical sophistication not expected from most other areas of history (especially its fashionable postmodern varieties), there are self-evidently whole ranges of significant problems for the study of long run growth which cannot be resolved through trade with even the most modern and realistic of economic theories and the most useable and secure of econometric techniques. Yet there are scholars who continue to find 'chain saws' of yesterday's theory attractive for clearing their way through the trees and woods of history, and others who tempt us to avoid the tedium and risks of historical research by transforming their suggestions into novel vocabularies imported from the social sciences.

Given that the Berlin Wall came down in 1989, could we not agree that there are and have been several varieties of capitalism and for many activities markets usually work. We might then concentrate (for this our Baroque era of economic history) on the meta question of how and why markets for commodities, factors of production and especially for knowledge and new technologies emerged and operated more efficiently on some continents and in some states, regions, cities and cultures long before others?

Was it not the case that after the Renaissance had reintegrated classical learning into European consciousness, artists, scientists and intellectuals of the Baroque Era re-addressed universal questions and grand themes left over from the turmoil of Reformation and produced art, architecture, science and humanistic scholarship on the very grandest of scales. In this cosmopolitan century of globalisation is it not time for economic historians to re-engage with the big questions that preoccupied their masters - Schmoller, Sombart and Weber, Pirenne, Bloch, Braudel, Usher and Gras? Our parents (economics and history) can certainly help, but currently they seem a little too confused about their own identities to offer strong intellectual guidance, let alone paradigms for research programmes. There is a Klondike space between them waiting to be occupied and exploited.

Patrick K. O'Brien (b. 12. 8. 1932). Undergraduate degree at LSE. Postgraduate degree at Nuffield, then Lecturer and Reader in Economic History with reference to the Middle East. University Lecturer and Reader in Economic History (Europe) and Fellow of St Anthony's College, Oxford then Director of the Institute of Historical Research and Professor of Economic History at the University of London. He is currently Centennial Professor at LSE. His research interests have been the modern economic history of the Middle East, the early modern and modern history of Britain, France, Italy and Holland, and he has worked on most themes and areas within the field. He is currently interested in global history, and is writing a book on Historians of Material Progress (sic) from Herodotus to Pomeranz.

A Dialogue with the Past

Avner Offer

Adam Smith was surrounded by material scarcity. It is understandable that he regarded tangible goods as the hallmark of value. Only labour that fixed itself in some durable or vendible commodity could set in motion the benign cycle of growth. Services added no value, and were merely 'unproductive labour'. Of public servants, entertainers, menial servants, churchmen, physicians, men of letters of all kinds; players, buffoons, musicians, opera singers, etc., Smith wrote, 'like the declamation of the actor, the harangue of the orator, or the tune of the musician, the work of all of them perishes in the very instant of its production.'[1] Our discipline largely persists in this tough-minded bias, that production is paramount, and economic growth the final measure and justification of social activity.

When goods are scarce, increasing their supply is a high priority. But one of the basic tenets of economic theory is that the marginal utility of output diminishes as consumption increases. The subjective value of an increment of goods declines as more of them are acquired. That is not to say that goods inside the margin become less valuable. It is the incremental dose which is valued less. This qualification is important. Back in the past, when many basic needs remained to be met, material output and productivity deserved to occupy a much more central place. Increasing material abundance remains a high priority in societies still striving for affluence, and wherever deprivation persists in affluent societies.

There is empirical support for diminishing returns. It is normally assumed that marginal utility is positive, but that it falls as consumption increases. The elasticity of the marginal utility of consumption measures the percentage rate at which the marginal utility falls for every percentage increase in consumption. There are several approaches to this calculation, and current estimates place the figure at a range of -0.8 to -1.5 for the UK.[2] Other methods indicate a somewhat wider range over several different countries (c. -0.4 to -2.8).[3] A curvilinear, strongly declining marginal utility of consumption is also suggested by plotting a cross-section of welfare indicators in many countries against income per head,[4] and the same result is indicated in some simple time-series models.[5] Under affluence, it requires a great deal of additional income to increase welfare by very little. These estimates are simplifications: actual rates differ, from country to country, among individuals, cohorts, and classes, over the life cycle, and over historical time. But the pattern is clear: in affluent societies, for every increment of economic output, the marginal increment of utility is progressively smaller.

Britain is about 12 times wealthier than 200 years ago. And yet the focus of our discipline continues as if all that counted was to increase output. In a world of plenty, it is still preoccupied with scarcity, with productivity, and with production. But the utility of material goods diminishes much faster even than that of consumption as a whole. This is shown by the shift in output composition, from material production to services, in the course of economic growth. Services account for most of the output of every advanced economy, but their value defies precise measurement. Large premiums are paid for intangibles like brand recognition and corporate goodwill. It is increasingly understood that one of the main goods consists of human interaction, in the supply of status, attention, and regard, both in the market place and in the household.[6] Government output, between a third and one-half of GDP in most countries, is composed almost entirely of services, mainly health, education, and security. This disjunction between what matters to society, and what matters to scholars, may be one reason why economic history has lost some of the compelling relevance it used to have in the post-war period, when the world was emerging from the deprivations of depression and rationing.

Economic and social history might be considered (much like economics) as the study (over time) of choice under constraint. It needs to account, over long stretches of time, for the basket of consumption, a changing mix of rewards, tangibles and intangibles, leisure and work, domestic toil and wage labour. More pressing than the production function for goods, is to understand the production function which converts them into satisfaction, welfare, utility, well-being. To understand the spectrum of commodities, more attention is required to the spectrum of desire, and to the psychic impact of goods and services. It may be necessary to deviate from the orthodox view of rational choice (though not from experimental approaches to rationality). How is choice actually driven? How much is known about human nature in general as distinct from its manifestations in place, time, and culture, its range of wants and needs, and how it frames, experiences and reflects on choice? Imperfect information and limited mental capacity are points of departure. Choice is sometimes far-sighted, sometimes myopic, sometimes rewarding, occasionally disastrous. It may well be, as Stigler and Becker insist, that there is a limited repertoire of wants, reflected in stable preferences.[7] These may be modulated by systematic patterns of perception, experience, habituation, recollection, and regret.[8] The kaleidoscope of cultures, like the abundance of goods, ever-changing and unfolding in pursuit of betterment and in response to habituation, might merely be an elaborate means to satisfy a restricted array of wants. These might include food, shelter, love, education, dignity, freedom, self-expression. Psychologists, anthropologists and behavioural economists are trying to establish what this array might be. Economic and social history can bring a wealth of evidence to bear. It also provides a reality check on theory.

But the motives and actions of individuals do not simply scale up. Society is more than the aggregate of its components. The logic of collective action captures some of this difficulty: self-interest can be self-defeating. Social dilemmas arise when the incentives faced by individuals undermine their interests as members of a community. But rather than dwell on why collective action is so hard, we might study how it is achieved. History abounds with solutions to social dilemmas. This is one of the frontiers of social investigation: how are 'tragedies of the commons' averted – and if not, why not? The New Institutional Economics provides some leverage for these investigations, principal-agent theory in particular. Conflict, conformity, and agency are staples of social life, and historians have a methodological freedom of inquiry, which no other social science quite enjoys.

Apart from the confounding influence of post-modernism, there is a strong movement of convergence in the social sciences; sociologists, political scientists, economists, psychologists, increasingly share a common language, based on approaching social behaviour from the point of view of the individual. The encompassing subject matter and method of our discipline place it at the point where the others converge. Such a shift into the study of mental and social life does not mean 'going soft' – it is where the problems are leading. It holds out

255

the hope of moving away from a provincial periphery, to the very centre of social inquiry.

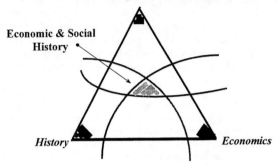

Behavioural Sciences:
Politics, Sociology, Psychology, Anthropology

Economic & Social History

History

Economics

Going beyond the Ashtonian preoccupation with business firms and their institutional context, beyond neo-classical or endogenous growth models, requires an awareness of other explanatory perspectives. In particular, a stronger focus on the individual as the motivator of outcomes, as both an economic and a psychological actor, as a consumer as well as entrepreneur, as a dissonant bundle of emotion and reason. More data and sources are always welcome, but it is understanding we are short of: more sharply defined questions, framed less in terms of our traditional debates, and more as contributions to larger issues of the social sciences.

Another expression of the shift from material output to services and intangibles may well be the appeal to students and scholars, so puzzling to many of us, of linguistic and cultural approaches to the past, and of the apparent unreason of some post-modern theory. How far to go down that road is an interesting question. At some point it appears to cross over the boundary from investigation to recreation. The traditional role of social inquiry, like science as a whole, has been to establish reliable knowledge about the world, or at the very least, to counter error. In linguistic and cultural inquiry, meaning is fluid and infinitely variable; in some post-modern approaches, the very notion of truth is denied. As the physicist Wolfgang Pauli remarked, 'some theories are not even wrong!'.

But History is not merely about explanation. In a short story a character complains, '… in what lousy book is it written that everything can be explained? My theory is, *nothing can be explained*.'[9] History is valued also for the pleasures it provides (akin to those of fiction), of identification, empathy, arousal, terror and suspense. It is approached as a repository of uncommon experiences and events, which is nevertheless accessible to the 'common sense', allowing the facts 'to speak for themselves'. It is archival and documentary investigation that generates most of the enduring issues. It would be unwise to discard the 'story' in history.

And yet, it seems to me that economic and social history is not primarily about the great dramas of history, but about the small ones that give rise to the conflicts of ordinary life. It seeks to frame those experiences in conceptual terms, to show that there is more to them than meets the eye, to explain them in terms of the timeless regularities of incentive, motivation, choice, social action and outcome. It has a commitment to explicit explanation, and some understanding of what this requires in terms of framing hypotheses and arguments, and of what counts as evidence.

F. W. Maitland wrote in 1898, 'Such is the unity of all history that any one who endeavours to tell a piece of it must feel that his first sentence tears a seamless web.'[10] The claim that in history everything connects with everything else, is sometimes taken to justify a chronological narrative approach, and to be incompatible with the problem based, method-driven investigation advocated here. But what kind of web is it that encompasses every scrap of archival information, while excluding the scientific understanding of motive and action that can make sense of it? In any case, the ideal of a positive, single history in which everything knowable is written down, has long been defeated by the impossible logistics of historical research. The stock of secondary literature and of primary sources is so vast, that any attempt at encompassing them must be selective and incomplete. Instead of a 'seamless web', history may be seen as a deep resource, which anyone can quarry for her dialogue with the past. But not only a personal one. Societies also want to pose their questions to the past, and they reward the historians who can do it for them.

But if explanations are timeless, the problems are not. We shall remain a progressive discipline if we accept that cherished preoccupations can become obsolete. As economies and societies evolve, economic and social history needs to follow, in order to remain as dynamic and flexible as its subject.

Avner Offer (b. 15. 5. 1944) was educated in Israel gaining a BA in History and Geography from the Hebrew University of Jerusalem. He was a graduate student at Oxford, and taught at the University of York before becoming a Reader in Recent Social and Economic History and Fellow at Nuffield College Oxford. He is currently Chichele Professor of Economic History at Oxford. Research interests include affluence and well being in the USA and Britain since the 1950s, international political economy c. 1870-1920, urban and rural land tenure, law and society.

---

[1] Smith, Adam, *An Inquiry into the Nature and Causes of the Wealth of Nations* (1776; Glasgow edn., Oxford 1979), vol. 1, Bk II, ch. 3, p. 331.
[2] Pearce, David and Ulph, David, 'A Social Discount Rate for the United Kingdom', *Centre for Social Research on the Global Environment Working Paper* GEC 95-01 (University of East Anglia, Norwich, 1994), pp. 10-17.
[3] Price, Colin, *Time, Discounting and Value* (Oxford, 1993), pp. 231-3.
[4] Offer, Avner, 'Economic Welfare Measurements and Human Well-Being', in David, Paul, Solar, Peter and Thomas, Mark (eds.), *The Economic Future in Historical Perspective* (forthcoming, London, 2001).
[5] Pearce and Ulph, op. cit., pp. 10-19; Offer, op. cit, using data in Crafts, Nicholas 'The Human Development Index and Changes in Standards of Living: Some Historical Comparisons', *European Review of Economic History* 1, no. 3 (1997).
[6] Avner Offer, 'Between the Gift and the Market: The Economy of Regard', *Economic History Review*, 50, 3 (Aug. 1997).
[7] Stigler, George J. and Becker, Gary S., 'De Gustibus Non Est Disputandum'. *American Economic Review* 67, no. 2 (1977), pp. 76-7.
[8] See Kagel, John H. and Roth, Alvin (eds.), *The Handbook of Experimental Economics* (Princeton, 1995).
[9] Singer, Isaac Bashevis, 'Gifts', in *The Death of Methuselah and Other Stories* (Harmondsworth, 1990), p. 163.
[10] Maitland, Frederic William 'A Prologue to a History of English Law', *Law Quarterly Review*, 14 (1898), p. 13.

What Economic History Means

Helen Paul

Economic history is a subject that many economics students do not realise they are studying. Its influence upon modern economic theory and practice can be found in all fields of economics. However, it seems to peek out from behind the formal models and vast array of current data, rather than being openly discussed. I did not study it as a separate discipline until I became a postgraduate. However, it has helped my understanding of the world and my enjoyment of my studies. Even if I have to abandon it professionally to earn a crust, I hope to set down here what it means to me. Despite the challenges the discipline faces, economic history still acts to warn the complacent.

Modernity versus History

A quotation of which economists seem inordinately fond is Keynes' dictum about policy-makers being reliant upon some long defunct economist.[1] Perhaps writers of dry economics tracts are fond of imagining the day when they too will be defunct and their doctrines will start to be put into practice. However, they might be concerned to learn that the influence they may exert will be shared with a whole army of ghosts – namely all those decision-makers high and low who ignored their advice when alive.

Current decisions are often taken within a framework that has been inherited from others. Such a framework concerns our ideas of how the world functions and what our objectives should be. Examples could include the belief in the existence of a class system, or the importance of equality. Morgan termed these constructions 'psychic prisons'.[2] This might seem a term of abuse, as we require some way of making sense of our complex world. Whilst simplifying the world for us, such frameworks also act as a limiting mechanism which may be very difficult to overcome. It is for this reason that Morgan terms them 'prisons'. They interact with the workings of the economy, as they are what policy-makers use to interpret economic behaviour and to decide upon their objectives. Evidence will come to light to overthrow the old certainties – as in all disciplines. People may choose the devil they know, their cosy 'prison', rather than face new ideas. This may be the case even against reasoned argument, as people invest so much effort in constructing and maintaining these frameworks. Whilst economic history constructs its own frameworks, it also acts to periodically attack those which have become obsolete. It can be revolutionary, as it strikes at two separate disciplines.[3]

Kill the messenger

Modern economies must have put roots down which are likely to affect their future growth. This might seem to guarantee economic history's place as a key to understanding the world.

However, it seems a point of honour that everything about the economy should be shiny and new. People seem genuinely afraid to confront early mistakes. The problems of the past are said to have disappeared with the *bad old days* – for example, the dark satanic mills. Miraculously, whatever it was which promoted past successes in the *good old days* has a strange staying power, and is bound to work its charms in the future. In this category we might find anything that the British press believes is the envy of the world.[4] Even if all the current generation has in common with past decision-makers is a shared nationality, it is noticeable how strongly many people identify with their predecessors. Reflected glory must have blinding properties as it is certainly not illuminating.

Choose your poison
Those who do not fall into the trap of over-confidence have built another one for themselves. They believe that past 'mistakes' continue to hurt them today. (In the case of a lack of investment in human capital in the UK this is probably true, but often old grievances have lost their practical effects.[5]) To take the doctrine too far is to restrict action or to invite over-confidence. A good warning could be taken from a card prominently displayed in my supervisor's office. It reads, 'People in olden times were stupid!' Economic history tells us what people in olden times actually did, and more importantly, why. It also reminds us that they had to cope with the leavings of their own ancestors and so should we.

Why not ask the experts?
Surely someone else's essay will contain the warning that he who does not remember history is doomed to repeat his mistakes.[6] Knowledge of history is one of those markers by which the well-rounded person identifies him/herself as being different to the pleb on the Clapham omnibus.[7] Unfortunately, this 'knowledge' is most often used as a tool to impress or to win an argument. The repeatable mistake will be looming, but history is not used to foresee it. As far as economies are concerned this mistake can devastate the lives of millions of people.[8]

Economic history suffers from being a strange hybrid of two competing disciplines. History is seen as wordy and economics as being concerned with money – not so much chalk and cheese as corduroy and chrome. Many people on that Clapham omnibus do not know that both subjects are in fact branches of social science. (Judging by the behaviour of many economics graduates, perhaps this is a misnomer and economics has a cold heart after all.[9]) Economic history manages to combine all the menace of the dismal science with the historian's gift for telling people what they do not want to hear. Perhaps it is not surprising that the financial rewards for Cassandras are less than those granted to the true believers in Mammon.[10]

It is strange therefore that the dismal scientists themselves are such a cheery bunch.[11] As an Economics Professor once said to me, in economic history there are lots of women and not much backstabbing.[12] He also told me not to go into academia, as the pay was bad. Perhaps the economic historians stick with it for the privilege of being right or perhaps because it is more rewarding for them than following a crock of gold. As an undergraduate, I studied management and economics at Oxford with proto-management consultants. The course emphasised that we would find many optimistic texts heralding the new dawn across several generations.[13] It was also interesting to see how much of the propaganda we were fed by the media and society was bunk. There was always a lot of pressure at that time to 'put the Great back into Great Britain'.[14] The remedy proposed was always a quick fix. Economic history showed me how countries had reached their current situation and where they were likely to go next. At the time, this was a revelation. Economies were no longer pushed forward by some special (and perhaps faintly diabolical) 'national culture', but by such down-to-earth factors as well-educated workforces and a lack of red tape.

Future Histories[15]

Economic historians manage to massacre a few sacred cows and that can be no bad thing. However, the low profile of economic history and the dwindling ranks of practitioners mean that future students may miss its benefits entirely. If this can happen within an economics department, it can only be imagined how little many policy-makers, pundits and voters truly understand the lessons of the past. What is even more frightening is the suspicion that they are aware economic historians can put them right on a few things, but they make the 'informed' choice not to know.

Helen Paul (b. 20. 11. 1975) is studying for a PhD at St Andrew's University where she has completed a Masters degree in Management, Economics and Politics. She previously studied Economics and Management at St. Anne's College, Oxford.

---

[1] Keynes, J. M. quoted in Roll, E., *A History of Economic Thought*, Faber and Faber, (London and Boston, 1992) p.5.

[2] Morgan, G., *Images of Organisation,* Sage (London, 1986), chap. 7, pp. 199-232.

[3] A classic example would be Fogel and Engerman's research on the productivity of the American slave system in the Antebellum South. They showed that slaves as a group were not lazy or ineffectual. This prompted a re-examination of current race issues and highlighted discrimination suffered by the freed slaves and their descendants. Fogel, R. W. and Engerman, S. L. *Time on the Cross: The Economics of American Negro Slavery,* W. W. Norton and Co. (NY/ London, 1989).

[4] To be fair, this is something which newspaper editors are familiar with worldwide.

[5] Crafts, N. F. R., *British Economic Growth during the Industrial Revolution,* Clarendon Press (Oxford, 1985), 159.

[6] No doubt those bright sparks will have correctly attributed the quotation as well.

[7] 'That most limited of specialists, the "well-rounded man"'. Fitzgerald, F. Scott, *The Great Gatsby*, The Bodley Head (London, 1958) vol. 1, p. 22.

[8] Note the repeated attempts to assist LDCs, especially in Africa, without reforming the political system.

[9] See any newspaper article concerning the dearth of economics lecturers as graduates head for the City. For an academic viewpoint see Machin, S. and Oswald, A., 'UK Economics and the Future Supply of Academic Economists', *Economic Journal*, 110 (June) 2000, 334-349.

[10] The *Economist* has been waging a pitched battle with those who argue that the current expansion in the United States is self-sustaining due to something being radically different about the 'wired economy'. See for example, *Economist,* April 15, 2000, p. 15.

[11] I take no responsibility for Eeyores whom I have not met.

[12] Perhaps these factors are related to one another and not to the subject.

[13] The course was designed to make us consider why certain theories appeared at certain times, and not simply look at the latest blueprint. It was perhaps an example of economic history by the back door.

[14] I apologise for yet another unattributed quotation. Suffice to say it has been uttered by more than one politician, and one of them is likely to have been Margaret Thatcher.

[15] I hope that this does not turn out to be an oxymoron for the subject.

Works cited

Crafts, N. F. R., *British Economic Growth during the Industrial Revolution,* Clarendon Press (Oxford, 1985).

Fitzgerald, F. Scott, *The Great Gatsby*, The Bodley Head (London, 1958) vol. 1.

Fogel, R. W. and Engerman, S. L. *Time on the Cross: The Economics of American Negro Slavery,* W. W. Norton and Co. (NY/ London, 1989).

Machin, S. and Oswald, A., 'UK Economics and the Future Supply of Academic Economists', *Economic Journal*, 110 (June) 2000, 334-349.

Morgan, G., *Images of Organisation,* Sage (London, 1986).

Roll, E., *A History of Economic Thought*, Faber and Faber, (London and Boston, 1992).
Economist, April 15, 2000.

Theory, Imagination, Eclectic History

Robin Pearson

I have only once taken part in an archaeological excavation. Over the Easter of 1977, I spent several weeks digging in the ruins of a Byzantine villa, situated on a dusty hill-top perched on the Israeli side of the Israel-Lebanon border, north of the town of Nahariya. It seemed an isolated and peaceful place, with views looking down over the coastal plain and the Mediterranean sea. This was a time of relative calm in the area. Within the year, Nahariya had been shelled by the P.L.O. and Israel had invaded southern Lebanon. The excavation team was an odd but jolly bunch of theology and archaeology students from Edinburgh, together with a few Israelis, and a couple of burly Catalan priests, who would hoot with laughter at their own (to the rest of us, incomprehensible) jokes, like a pair of bearded Friar Tucks. On our lunch-breaks we played football with the lads from the local Jewish settlement, and at Passover the children brought us small bags of crushed matzoth and sugar. Our evenings were spent strolling in Nahariya, or arguing over the archaeological foundations of the Old Testament, debates to which I could hardly contribute, but which fascinated me nevertheless.

The work was hot and slow. The villa had been burnt down in the sixth century and the scorch line of the fire was still visible in the remains. The walls had collapsed inwards, destroying many artefacts, but also burying others in a protective layer, which it was our task to dig through. Fragments of a mosaic floor in the entrance hall, a few amphorae, some utensils and tools were the principal finds. My initial enthusiasm with a pick-axe resulted in a few broken shards, and I was banished to the kitchen area, to sieve through the left-overs of countless Byzantine meals. However, this too was interesting – the seafood and fruit diet of the villa's residents was clearly to be seen in the gastronomic detritus they had left behind.

That experience lived for me because it worked upon both my imagination and my intellectual curiosity at the same time. While it is true that I knew almost nothing about the social and economic history of the late Roman empire, and only a little more about Byzantine architecture, I imagined the pleasure of living in that place for the villa's wealthy inhabitants and the disaster which struck down their house. For me, a few artefacts, a historic site, the shadows of the past – but not the artificial constructions, however worthy, of a modern 'street life' museum or a colonial Williamsburg - can draw a visceral response: wonder at the scale of Roman Ephesus, or at the fragility of La Isabela, the first European settlement in the Americas; gloom at the ghostly redoubts of Yorktown battlefield, or at the clan burial mounds on Culloden Moor; aversion at the disturbing grimness of Buchenwald or the slave cages on Macarthy island. I have always had a soft spot for Collingwood's story of his 'childish passion' for the battle of Trafalgar, as he tried to understand what the different combatants had wanted to do.

'History did not mean knowing what events followed what. It meant getting inside other people's heads, looking at their situation through their eyes, and thinking for yourself whether the way in which they tackled it was the right way'. [1]

I have no doubt that imagination and its lesser cousin, empathy – the latter enshrined in the English school history curriculum during the 1980s – have a part to play in writing economic and social history. What I am uncertain about is the prominence of their role. Like most academic historians, I read 'popular history' with varying degrees of impatience and irritation, and like to think that I can spot a 'romantic' view of history from some distance and be able to cross the street in time. I admonish my students for narratives devoid of analysis, and urge them to preface their essays with questions, and to place their questions within a hypothesis. An emotive response to a subject simply appears out of joint, even contradictory to the favoured 'scientific' method of theoretical postulation, hypothesis formulation, data collection, and inductive reasoning. In most of my publications I have solemnly relied upon the latter, which most regard as the methodological feature which marks economic and social history as a social science. This, however, is too comfortable. To be sure, history writing is hard labour, no stream of consciousness. It is the work of builders getting dirty rather than architects with their pristine thought-plans. There is a tension between construction, perspiration and inspiration, but the scales are heavily loaded on one side only. Nevertheless, inspiration, sensibility and imagination must have a place, not least because they can underscore the value which most economic and social historians instinctively place on the extraordinariness of ordinary lives.

We are all historical materialists. What an outrageous assertion in this postmodern era. Yet we have to be to write economic and social history. We know that to think, to talk, to write, to paint, we must first possess consciousness. To be conscious we must first exist. To exist we must eat, and this requires work, even in the most primitive form of scavenging for food. Labour then is a prerequisite of consciousness. Consciousness, closely followed by language, then help shape labour, in crafting tools and baking bread, and in turn lead to human systems and relations of production, distribution, exchange and consumption, societies, cultures, political and religious identities. Economic and social history is the history of these systems, relations and identities, of the processes and structures of resource allocation in the past, about how and why people lived the way they did, and what they believed in. Thus, while bearing in mind the proclivities of those who ruled and commanded, the policy- and strategy-makers of the past, economic and social historians spend much of their energies uncovering the expectations and choices which confronted the more anonymous individuals who cultivated, manufactured, sold, bartered, stole and begged. Brecht's questions are never far away when approaching the economic and social past. 'Every page a victory. Who cooked the feast for the victor? Every ten years a great man. Who paid the bill?' [2]

A concern with the material circumstances of everyday life – with the price of wheat, the stature of children, the experience of mothers under the poor law, the fiscal constraints on a business – is not a licence for vulgar economic reductionism, a *reductio ad absurdum*. To 'be' a historian requires finding one's way into the minds, the attitudes and *mores* of those in the past, to infer these elemental forces from the evidence of their behaviour or the legacy of their rhetoric, not to deduce behaviour from production relations or gender or class position. However, even the best attempts at imaginative 'readings' of historical texts - such as Douglas Galbi's recent essay on factory girls[3] – do not analyse language without also exploring the social and economic context in which their subjects find themselves. Of course one drags one's own intellectual baggage into the inquiry. Imagination cannot save us from this. As Kant insisted, 'percepts without concepts are blind', and concepts are not universal, but vary by time, place, culture and individual inclination. Of course we impose our own 'projects' on what we write. The sources require a voice, they 'do not speak for themselves'. But we should not need post-modernism to tell us about the invisible hand of the author or remind us of the need constantly to examine and re-examine paradigms, ideologies, 'readings' and 'projects' – to ask just whose voice is being heard, whose concept is being applied and why?

Indeed, in the grand push to eliminate all deterministic meta-narratives, some directions in social history have come to resemble the final motion in the centrifugal pull of history writing towards the history of ideas.[4] Their purpose is to abandon all vestigal notions of socio-economic causality in order to assert the subjectivism of reality and the complete autonomy of language, politics and culture. Social history thus becomes not an effort to determine cause and effect, but about analysing 'the social display of subjectivity'. Attempts to step back from this black hole have already begun. According to Cabrera, for instance, language gives reference and meaning to reality, but it cannot exist without it, and is in turn modified by it. Thus Cabrera's rescue plan for social history is predicated upon the existence of entities outside of language, waiting to be articulated.[5] This appears to satisfy the demand for the primacy of discourse as the place where meaning is constituted, without severing history from the material world and 'scientific' methodology. However, it remains to be seen whether this circle can really be squared.

Unlike cultural or social history, economic history generally has not undergone the process of twisting itself around the linguistic turn. This is surprising, for it can be easily claimed that economic concepts and quantitative data are also sites where meanings are constituted, as, for example, in the use of political arithmetic in eighteenth-century Britain, or in the role played by accounting in the shaping of labour discipline and notions of productivity during the industrial revolution.[6] Economic history would undoubtedly profit from a dose of epistemology, and from some of the deconstruction of meanings to which the categories of social history have already been subjected.

It is urged upon us that all history is the history of thought captured in the language of the past, and articulated in the language of the present. Whether or not we accept all or any of this, it is true that imagination itself is an historical construct – at one time mystical and spiritual, at another mechanical and neurological.[7] Thus the application of imagination, allied to the 'scientific' method, remains inadequate as an approach to history writing. For economic and social history to develop further, to add new dimensions, its authors must articulate a consciousness - critics would say become more conscious - of their own inputs. These should be drawn from as wide a range of influences as possible. It has been often pointed out that economic history was born of mixed parentage. However, economics and history apart, its kith and kin in the social sciences - sociology, anthropology, demography, geography, 'political science' - have also had an influence on its upbringing. Economic and social historians should not just be comprised of historians who know a little economics, or economists, who know some history. To write the history of society and the economy – of people and their interactions, of resource allocation and the elements determining the growth and changes in production, distribution and consumption – one needs to write a porous history, where influences flood in from all directions, where nothing is venerated, and where nothing is taken as an absolute.[8] History is not about a given past of 'events', but about a series of processes and relationships through time and space, a continuum with shocks and giant technological and attitudinal leaps. As Faulkner put it, 'the past is never dead. It's not even past'.[9] History is also about the present and the future, a continually remade venture which is always employing new materials and methods, and redeploying some old ones.

Economic and social history should thus strive to be an eclectic, piratical form of history, where theory is sometimes a starting point, but more often a toolkit ready to be plundered. Quantitative and qualitative data are the materials to be worked with these tools, and history writing becomes a process of imaginative excavation, reconstruction and simulation. I would certainly not claim to have succeeded in this in my own work, although on occasion I have tried to prospect across disciplinary boundaries for ideas and methods. Unsurprisingly, one of the advantages enjoyed by historians of insurance is the relative abundance of data available to those willing to dig deep enough in the archives. A modest dabbling in cliometrics has helped move me a little closer to finding answers to some of the questions which I am interested in, for example, on the nature of the relationship between economic development and the growth of financial services, although the task of data collection and comparative analysis has only just begun.[10] This particular approach has had less relevance to my other areas of current interest. A paper on business networking has been informed by insights from institutional economics on the relationship between changes in information costs and the institutional structure of an economy, by Granovetter's work on the social embeddedness of economic relations, by Offer's idea of 'regard' as a transaction benefit, and by Fukuyama's thoughts on high trust and low trust cultures.[11] Ongoing work on perceptions of risk and moral hazard in Georgian England has been enriched by the new literature on fear and popular responses to natural disasters, as well as by writers such as Daston on the history of probability theory, and by Beck's notion of risk as a product of the struggle between 'scientific and 'social' forms of rationality.[12] An analysis of shareholder-boardroom relations in nineteenth-century insurance companies has been influenced by Habermas's discussion of the public sphere, and inspired by the parallels recently drawn by Alborn between political and corporate change in Victorian England. [13]

As the institutional face of economic and social history in Britain drifts inexorably towards 'mainstream' history, and as the latter imbibes still more intoxicating influences from social and cultural history, we may see a large part of the 'new history' recasting itself as a behavioural science in a social science mould. Attitudes, perceptions, emotions, social psychology, contested notions about community, ethnicity, nation, empire, credit, trust, risk, leisure, poverty, wealth, sexuality, gender, morality, are already becoming the stuff of a grander history project. To retain its distinctiveness – and all the recent journal evidence suggests that the quality of economic and social history research remains high and for that reason alone worth preserving [14] – it must hold onto its economic inheritance, and continue to engage with developments in econometrics, microeconomics, industrial economics and so on. However economic and social history cannot be sustained by the economic or historical method alone. Human lives are multi-dimensional and behavioural motives are usually highly complex and non-reducible. Economic and social history should embrace its multi-disciplinarity and multi-dimensionality as a renaissance strength, and not regard these as signs of an identity crisis in a managerialist age of labelling. It should continue to move towards a truly eclectic form of history and continue to inspire the imagination.

Robin Pearson (b. 18. 12. 1955) was educated at the Universities of Edinburgh and Leeds. He was visiting Professor at Philipps-Universität Marburg, Germany in 1998, and is currently Senior Lecturer in Economic and Social History at the University of Hull. His research interests are modern European economic and social History, business history, insurance history and urban history.

---

[1] R.G.Collingwood, *An Autobiography* (Oxford, 1978), p. 58
[2] 'Questions from a worker who reads', in B.Brecht, *Poems*, eds. J.Willett and R.Manheim (1976), p. 252.
[3] Galbi, D.A., 'Through eyes in the storm: aspects of the personal history of women workers in the industrial revolution', *Social History*, 21 (1996), pp. 142-59.
[4] Jones, G.S., 'The determinist fix: some obstacles to the further development of the linguistic approach to history in the 1990s', *History Workshop Journal*, 42 (1996), pp. 19-35.
[5] Cabrera, M.A., 'Linguistic approach or return to subjectivism? In search of an alternative to social history', *Social History*, 24 (1999), pp. 74-89. For a different approach to the same problem, see Steinberg, M.W.,

'Culturally speaking: finding a commons between post-structuralism and the Thompsonian perspective', *Social History*, 21 (1996), pp. 193-214.

[6] Hoppit, J., 'Political arithmetic in eighteenth-century England', *Economic History Review*, 2nd ser., XLIX (1996), pp. 516-40;

[7] Rousseau, G.S., 'Science and the discovery of the imagination in enlightened England', *Eighteenth-Century Studies*, 3 (1969), pp. 108-35.

[8] Wright, P., *On living in an old country* (1985), p. 255.

[9] Faulkner, W., *Requiem for a nun* (1953), p.85.

[10] Pearson, R., 'Growth, crisis and change in the insurance industry: an historical retrospect'. This paper is forthcoming in a collection of essays shortly to be published by the Association of British Insurers. See also *idem.*, "Ein Wachstumsrätsel: Feuerversicherung und die wirtschaftliche Entwicklung Großbritanniens 1700-1850", *Zeitschrift für Unternehmensgeschichte*, 44 (1999), pp. 218-34.

[11] Pearson, R. and Richardson, D., 'Business networking in the industrial revolution' (unpublished paper); Casson, M., 'Institutional economics and business history: a way forward?', *Business History*, 39 (1997), pp.129-50; Granovetter, M., 'Economic action and social structure: the problem of embeddedness', *American Journal of Sociology*, 91 (1985), pp. 481-510; Offer, A., 'Between the gift and the market: the economy of regard', *Economic History Review*, 2nd ser., L (1997), pp. 450-76. Fukuyama, F., *Trust: the social virtues and the creation of prosperity* (Harmondsworth, 1995).

[12] Pearson, R. 'The cost of (dis)trust: moral hazard and the assessment of insurance risk in eighteenth- and early nineteenth century England', (unpublished paper); Naphy, W.G. and Roberts, P. ed., *Fear in early modern society* (Manchester, 1997); Johns, A., ed., *Dreadful visitations: confronting natural catastrophe in the age of enlightenment* (1999); Daston, L., 'The domestication of risk: mathematical probability and insurance 1650-1830', in L.Krüger, L.J.Daston and M.Heidelberger eds., *The probabilistic revolution* vol.1 (Cambridge, Mass., 1987), pp. 237-60; U.Beck, *Risikogesellschaft: Auf dem Weg in eine andere Moderne* (Frankfurt, 1986).

[13] Pearson, R. 'Shareholder democracies? Insurance companies as business republics in early nineteenth-century England' (unpublished paper); Alborn, T.L., *Conceiving companies* (1998).

[14] Pearson, R., 'Review of periodical literature, 1999', *Economic History Review*, LIII (Feb.2001), forthcoming.

266

Working with Economics and History

G. C. Peden

I find it easiest to explain what economic history means to me if I adopt an autobiographical approach, for thereby I can not only explain my perspective on our discipline, but also acknowledge some intellectual debts. I first encountered economic history when I matriculated at the University of Dundee in 1968. The head of the Department of Modern History, Donald Macdonald was a social and economic historian whose publications included *Scotland's Shifting Population* (1937) and *The State and the Trade Unions* (1960). He insisted that all students of history should also study economics for at least one year. It was a wise prescription, and it was reinforced by the fact that an element of economic history was integrated into most general history courses. In 1972 I went to Oxford to do research on the topic of 'The Influence of the Treasury on British Rearmament in the 1930s'. The fact that my supervisor, Norman Gibbs, was the Chichele Professor of War History, and not an economic historian, did not matter, for I had been sufficiently well trained at Dundee to understand the economic arguments that I encountered in Treasury papers (including arguments by Keynes, whom I took to be the best source of economic wisdom), and some of my closest friends at Brasenose College were students of economics who were only too happy to discuss their subject over cups of coffee and recommend books and articles for me to read. I returned in 1975 to Dundee, where I enjoyed a salary as a tutorial assistant, unlike grossly exploited, hourly paid TAs today, and, when the lecturer who had been due to take a course on twentieth-century British economic history took ill, Donald Macdonald gave me the chance to take over the lectures. At Dundee I also enjoyed the friendship of a lecturer in economics, Alastair Lonie, and through him I was invited to give a seminar paper on Keynes and the Treasury to members of the Department of Economics. After the paper the Professor of Economics, Kit Blake, who, unbeknown to me, was a director of Scottish Academic Press, asked if he could read my thesis, and the upshot was an offer of a contract.

The thesis was revised during the year 1976-77, which I spent at Leeds as a temporary lecturer, teaching mainly on courses on international history. Had the post been made permanent, I might have focused my research interests on economic aspects of international relations. However, Leeds was in no hurry to make up its collective mind and I was glad to move to Bristol in 1977 to the security of a permanent lectureship in economic and social history. William Ashworth, the head of the then independent Department of Economic and Social History there, asked me what particular contribution I could bring to a course on the Economic and Social Policy of the State in Britain since 1890. I said that I thought that a Treasury perspective would be different from what the students would encounter in their reading. Given that the course had been devised by Martin Jacques, who was leaving the department to become editor of *Marxism Today*, I am pretty sure that a Treasury perspective represented a change in the way the course was taught, but I learned a lot from reading the works that he had listed in the course handout. Ashworth was kindness itself. He took the trouble to read the proofs of my forthcoming book, now entitled *British Rearmament and the Treasury, 1932-1939*, and, as the author of *Contracts and Finance* in the official history of the Second World War, he was well qualified to criticise it. As it happened, he endorsed my arguments, but with typical economy of language he summed up the book in a single sentence: 'What you seem to be saying is that the Treasury ensured that there would be an orderly flow of contracts'.

I lectured on economic and social policy, and used the experience to write *British Economic and Social Policy: Lloyd George to Margaret Thatcher* (1985) and *Keynes, the Treasury and British Economic Policy* (1988), and developed a special subject on British Economic and Social History, 1931-1945. However, the range of my understanding of economic history was greatly extended by teaching with colleagues on a course on Industrialisation and the International Economy (for which my 'bible' was Ashworth's *Short History of the International Economy since 1850*) and, in particular, a final-year course on Comparative Economic History, which had been devised by Ashworth and Bernard Alford. Doing the reading necessary to teach Comparative Economic History was the best training I had in economic history: Alec Cairncross's *Factors in Economic Development*, Simon Kuznets on economic growth, Ashworth on typologies, Alford on entrepreneurship and management structure, Rondo Cameron on banking, Harry Braverman's *Labour and Monopoly Capital* and Alfred Maizels's *Industrial Growth and World Trade*, to name but a few. I learned to probe the weak points in the arguments of W. W. Rostow, *The Economics of Take-off into Sustained Growth* and Robert Fogel's *Railroads and American Economic Growth*, and all the time one had the stimulus of bright students who had been thoroughly trained in economics.

There were also contacts with economic historians at other universities. I read through and puzzled over Keynes's *General Theory of Employment, Interest and Money* in the summer of 1978, and the stimulus of giving a seminar paper to Professor Leslie Pressnell's Monetary History Group at LSE led to the publication of an article on 'Keynes, the Treasury and Unemployment in the Later 1930s' in *Oxford Economic Papers* two years later. About this time I struck up a friendship with a postgraduate at Cambridge, Roger Middleton, and learned a lot from discussing with him the research that was to lead to his thesis on 'Fiscal policy and Economic Management in the 1930s' (published in revised form in 1985 as *Towards the Managed Economy: Keynes the Treasury and the Fiscal policy Debate of the 1930s*). Keynes was the focus of a lot of economic history then, and Susan Howson was kind enough to comment on my unpublished work, including the draft of *British Economic and Social History*, even though I had ventured to make marginal criticisms in print of her *Domestic Monetary Management in Britain, 1919-38* (1975). The dilapidated state of my copy of her book is evidence of how much I have relied on it over the years.

I have never been able to escape from research on the Treasury for long. I was encouraged by Sir Alec Cairncross (who had examined my thesis) and Barry Supple (who had heard me give a paper on 'Economic Aspects of British Perceptions of Power on the Eve of the Cold War) to apply in 1986 for a British Academy Research Readership to work on what, eventually, appeared in 2000 as *The Treasury and British Public Policy, 1906-1959*. Over the years I accumulated many intellectual debts. There were my postgraduates: in particular, Russell Jones (M.Sc. thesis on 'The Wages Problem in Employment Policy, 1936-48'); Andrew McDonald (Ph.D. on 'The Formulation of British Public Expenditure Policy, 1919-1925'); and Neil Rollings (Ph.D. on 'The Control of Inflation in the Managed Economy: Britain 1945-1953'). A number of economists, economic historians and other historians commented on drafts of the book, and, as regards the economic aspects, I am particularly grateful to Sir

Alec Cairncross, Peter Clarke, Martin Daunton, Roger Middleton, and Tom Wilson, but mention should also be made of Gill Bennett and Kathleen Burk (for international relations) and Jose Harris and Pat Thane (for social policy). The book was intended for readers from more than one academic discipline, and I was pleased that the first review to appear was by an economist, Sir Alan Budd, in the politics section of the *Times Literary Supplement* (2 June 2000). When our president, Patrick O'Brien, urged members of the society at the annual conference in Bristol in April 2000 to 'go out and colonise' other disciplines, I felt that I was heading in the right direction.

However, colonisation is not an easy process. In order to engage in debate with cognate disciplines we have to find time in which to keep up with developments in these disciplines. Nick Crafts gave a talk to the Standing Conference of Representatives of Departments of Economic and Social History in October 1999 on the theme of 'living with big neighbours', in which he pointed out that the new economic history of the last three decades relies on a type of economics that is no longer shared by economists (Economic History Society, *Newsletter*, May 2000). Another problem is that, in many universities, departments of economics are not particularly big neighbours; it seems that in recent years there has been a shift in students' preferences away from economics towards business studies. I write from the perspective of someone who has been head of the Department of History at Stirling for most of the time since 1990. The department is in the Faculty of Arts and most of our students do not go near the Department of Economics; consequently economic history has to be taught on the assumption that they have no previous training in or understanding of economics, which is something of a pedagogical challenge. Conversations with colleagues at other universities suggest that our situation is not unique.

My experience since 1968 is that economics is the closest social science to economic history, but in my research on public policy I have benefited from the fact that I had also studied politics over two years as an undergraduate, and in teaching social history I have encountered useful works by sociologists. Ideally all historians, not just economic historians, would have an understanding of all three of these social sciences, including their quantitative forms. We should, of course, also be able to read several foreign languages. Indeed the ideal economic historian would never be employed as such, if he or she were economically rational, since anyone with all these attributes would earn much more in some other field. In the absence of the ideal individual, we must play to our strengths, while trying to keep up with as much of the literature as we can. The wider the perspective that we can bring to our own research the better. I certainly feel that I improved my understanding of the British economy by reading about other economies. Likewise, a broad reading of social history is required for an understanding of the development of the welfare state or, indeed the social consequences of, and impediments to, economic change.

There are always new fields to explore. In my case, returning to my native Scotland has made me aware of how little I know about its economic history, and, in agreeing to edit with Clive Lee a volume of essays on 'The Evolution of the Scottish Economy, 1700-2000', I have committed myself to learning a lot from him and our fellow contributors. However, I have not abandoned Keynes or the Treasury. I have undertaken to edit for the British Academy's Records of Social and Economic History a volume of Treasury papers, provisionally entitled: 'Keynes and His Critics: Treasury Responses to the Keynesian Revolution, 1925-46'. As a longer term project, I am gathering ideas and material for a monograph on the influence of the Treasury on British defence policy in the 1950s and 1960s, which would be an opportunity to integrate economic and other forms of history.

I have already had the opportunity for such integration in my teaching at Stirling. When I arrived in 1990 I was able to team up with Robert McKean, a general historian, to revive a final-year course on Britain and Europe since 1918 that had originally been set up by, among others, Roy Campbell and Maurice Kirby. Among the students who have taken the revived form of the course was Martin Schaad, a German who chose to take his first degree at Stirling and who went on to Oxford to do a D.Phil thesis which, in revised form, has been published as *Bullying Bonn: Anglo-German Diplomacy on European Integration, 1955-61* (Macmillan, 2000). When Martin wrote to let me know about the publication he commented that he had not only profited from the integrated approach to economic, political and international history taken by the course, but he had also been influenced by it in his choice of thesis. Teaching on integrated history courses can thus be very rewarding.

George C. Peden (b. 16. 2. 1943) was educated at the Universities of Dundee and Oxford He taught at the University of Bristol, 1977-90 where he became Reader in Economic History. Since 1990 he has been Professor of History at the University of Stirling. His research interests and their development are described in the essay.

What Social History Means To Me

Harold Perkin

I became a social historian because I was born into it. My extended family covered almost the whole gamut of class, from the poorest working potters through skilled paintresses and managers to the owners of 13 factories which they expanded into one of the largest combines in the Potteries. My father was a building foreman, who ran a small house-building firm on behalf of the owners. He had come down in the world: his father had been a prosperous insurance agent who earned five times a labourer's wage in 1903 when my father was born. Father's younger sister, an early liberated woman, rose from typist in the family firm to become one of the top managers below the directors. My cousin Bruce was a Christopher Robin whose pretty-boy cast-offs his mother sent us - which I and my four siblings made fun of in our dressing-up games.

I might just as easily have become an economic historian, since we lived in a small terraced house between a 'pot bank' and a marl pit, where they dug the clay for the saggars in which the biscuitware was baked – I used to pass a saggar-maker's bottom knocker at work in a basement as I walked to school - and I was acutely aware of the three-day week which my aunts and uncles worked during the depression. My father, on the other hand, benefited from the housing boom between the wars, and so was never unemployed. In fact, he moonlighted at building repairs to earn his pocket money - he gave my mother all his wages for housekeeping - and to pay for our clothes and occasional treats and holidays. The Grand Union Canal ran through the nearby park, and there was an engineering works at the end of the street where you could glimpse huge machines being made for export.

But I was more interested in people than in things: I found them endlessly fascinating. I went to Methodist chapel on Sundays and to Church at school on Monday mornings, while the childless aunt and uncle whose Sunday lunch I always shared were Catholics, so I had an early introduction to comparative religion. Principally, however, I was interested in inequality. I could not understand why some of my relations were rich and others, who seemed to me just as intelligent, moral and amusing, were poor. Luck was a partial explanation, education another, and undoubtedly life style: my father didn't drink, while other fathers in the street, well-paid miners and steel workers, did to the detriment of their families. But there was obviously more to it than that. My mother was a widow's child and poorer than most, but she was determined that her five children should be the equal of our rich cousin, and so I became aware of social mobility and its opportunities.

Education was an obvious ladder. I was lucky to be born under a Labour city council, who pioneered nursery education and generous scholarships to the grammar school. I had an early start, at the age of three, and never looked back. Having a quick mind and a good memory, I enjoyed exams and earned prizes every year of my school life. At a grammar school that had never sent a boy to university for years I had the good fortune to find a history teacher, with us for only three years, who knew how to apply and prepare for Oxbridge scholarships one of which I won, in 1945 just in time to escape the war. We discussed, in Oxford-type tutorials, questions of prime importance to real people's experience, notably the industrialism we could see all around us, and why it began in Britain first. At Cambridge, where I was one of the 10% straight from school, along with veteran scholars and exhibitioners from the war years, I was taught by such eminent dons as Michael Postan, Denis Brogan, Charles Wilson, and Michael Oakeshott, and learned how to disagree with them.

Most of the courses were strictly political or, even narrower, constitutional history. There were 'starred' economic questions, one only required, on the political papers. The only social questions I remember were on the poor law. People, other than politicians, philosophers and entrepreneurs, scarcely existed. My parting of the ways between economic and social came when I had to choose a special subject for my final year. I stood outside H. J. Habakkuk's room wondering why I had been recommended his Economic Growth, 1870-1930 and suddenly decided it was not for me. I rushed away and registered for R. J. White's Age of Castlereagh, 1810-1820. It was the best decision I ever made. It was a study in class conflict, in riots and mass demonstrations of the age of the Luddites, parliamentary reform, and classical economists at the end of the Napoleonic wars. It had the feel of people power upwelling from below, over political control, income distribution, bread riots, machine breaking, and all the issues that impacted on people's lives. That course has influenced all my work ever since. It determined me to spend my life pursuing the development of modern society, which I saw as stemming, not only in Britain but throughout the advanced world, from the Industrial Revolution.

After National Service as an education officer in the RAF, I applied to my old college, in view of my starred first, to pursue graduate research. They answered that 'your ability though considerable does not seem to us to lie in the direction of academic research'. They had good reason. I had spent some of my time - most, it seemed to them – in non-academic pursuits: rowing (which would have been acceptable enough), helping to edit *Varsity*, dancing in Handel's Solomon, and playing the leading lady in the Footlights. They softened the blow by saying that later I would come to see this as 'a happy chance'. So it turned out. I was saved from the dreary experience of working for a Ph.D. on a narrow subject - business history was then the flavour of the month at my college - and liberated to pursue my main interest, the Industrial Revolution as a social revolution which created modern class society.

I found a job, with the help of my WEA and RAF experience, as an extra-mural tutor in an adult college of Manchester University. Then came a lucky break: the Clapham Subcommittee of the University Grants Committee had recommended an expansion of the social sciences in British universities. Arthur Redford, professor of economic history, applied for three posts, in history of social thought, European economic history and, as a pennyweight, an assistant lectureship in social history. I applied for the last and, to my surprise, was appointed. I thus became the first person in the country appointed specifically to teach social history. I was asked to teach two courses of English social history, 1500-1850, and 1850-1950. This was in 1951, so I was obligated to teach contemporary history - exactly what I wished to do, to explore the origins of modern society.

Apart from Trevelyan's *English Social History* there were no suitable textbooks, so I was forced to use original texts, from William Harrison's *Description of England* (1577) to Patrick Colquhoun's *Treatise on Indigence* (1806), and from Chiozza Money's *Riches and Poverty* (1905) to David Glass's *Social Mobility in Britain* (1954). Redford, who thought that 'social history was economic history with the hard parts left out', asked me to produce a seminar paper on 'What is social history?' I argued that, since everything happened in society, it was nothing less than the history of society. He also suggested I study the domestic organisation of great country houses, and I duly visited and researched the archives of Chatsworth, Knowsley, Keele, and other great estates. I was rapidly diverted, however, into the role of property in British life and politics, and produced a long essay on 'Land Reform and Class Conflict in Victorian Britain', a study of the failed movement by Cobden, Bright and others to reform the land laws that kept the great landlords' estates together and underpinned their political and economic power.

One opportunity to test my holistic approach came when Tony Birch and his social science colleagues got a research grant to survey Glossop, one of the few really new towns of the Industrial Revolution, and asked me to write the historical introduction. I found it an extraordinary place, with more millionaires, in cotton, printworks, and paper-making, than any other, and a paternalism in schooling and religion that echoed the 'moral economy' of pre-industrial England. It illustrated how class and hierarchy could co-exist in the same community.

A by-product of my evening class work, an essay on working-class literacy and the origins of the popular press in *History Today*, led to another opportunity. Routledge and Kegan Paul asked me to write a book and, more importantly, to edit a series of volumes on social history. This resulted in contacts with most of the younger people working in the subject, and to a series of monographs, more than 40 in all, on many topics in English and foreign social history.

All this was grist to my mill of explaining the origins and rise of modern society, which I continued to pursue through all the creative opportunities of an academic life. I was diverted into a variety of mini-careers. One was, through an attempt to reform the authoritarianism of Manchester University and election to its Council, a career in the AUT, which took me to the Executive, the Chair of the Development Committee and the Presidency during the Robbins expansion, and negotiation with both Labour and Tory Governments of the new salary negotiating machinery and of the new USS pension scheme. It became my social laboratory, dealing with government and the then hot issue of higher education policy. Meanwhile, I wrote *Key Profession: The History of the AUT*, which argued that the university, the creator of human capital, was the axial institution of modern society. I also became involved in Granada Television, doing evening news spots on current affairs, culminating in my own two series of programmes on the Ages of the Railway and the Automobile - which I presented as the impact of communications on the development of English society, culminating in two more books.

Finally, I migrated from Manchester to the New University of Lancaster, where I became the first Professor of Social History, so-named, in Britain. There, in the midst of establishing a university of a new, more flexible kind, and founding the Social History Society of the UK, I managed at last to complete my major work, *The Origins of Modern English Society, 1780-1880*. The Industrial Revolution, I argued, was a social revolution with social causes, a social process, and profound social effects. The main effect was the creation, out of the old paternalistic society, of a new class society. The new entrepreneurial ideal based on capital and competition challenged the old aristocratic ideal of passive property and the 'Old Corruption' of patronage, but was itself challenged by the working-class ideal of the labour theory of value and the alternative of co-operation.

My most novel discovery was the 'forgotten middle class', the professional or non-business class, which played a much larger role in society than its numbers. As the intellectual class it provided the other three with the language of class and influenced the social and economic policies of government. Its ideal of trained expertise and selection by merit challenged the other three classes, denying the privileges of the aristocracy, modifying the competition of the business men, and seducing the working class from violence into peaceful bargaining. The rise of a more complex urban, educated, technological, and administered society gave the professionals more work to do and more opportunities to influence the future.

The next step was to complete the story of the evolution of English society down to the present, which resulted in *The Rise of Professional Society: England since 1880*. Here the argument shifted to the post-industrial revolution, the swing from agriculture and industry to services, and thus to the central role of human capital and professional expertise. The organising theme was the rivalry between the two halves of the professional class, the public sector professionals in government, health, education, and so on, and the private sector professionals, the increasingly powerful managers of the big corporations. This led to the most contentious issues in modern politics, the struggle for taxation and income between welfare and private enterprise and the use of society's resources for public services or for consumerism and private profit. It involved the conflict between communitarian democracy and the free market ideology which lay behind Thatcherism. Whether public or private, however, post-industrialism was to be a version of professional society.

This became obvious in the graduate courses I came to teach at Lancaster and then at Northwestern University in greater Chicago, one of the top ten universities in the United States. In these I traced the rise of modern society in the leading industrial and post-industrial societies across the world: Britain, France, Germany, the two Germanies, America, Soviet Russia, and Japan. The second of these led to *The Third Revolution: Professional Elites in the Modern World*. There I argued that industrialism and post-industrialism were modes of enterprise which mutated as they moved from one society to the next, according to the structure, mores and values of each. The six or seven societies lay on a great arch, stretching from the most free-market oriented to the most central command economies, from the United States through the European social market economies and the government-steered Japanese model to the unified controlling elites of the Soviet system. Professional societies were as flexible and variable as the industrial societies from which they evolved.

The advanced countries led me on, quite naturally, to my current (post-retirement) interest in global history, stimulated by membership of Patrick O'Brien's seminar at the Institute of Historical Research. Here I have pursued what I take to be the central issue in the organisation of historical societies, the extraction of surplus by the ruling elites from the subject population. All societies need to extract resources from the producers, for law and order, defence, welfare, and other common services. This is justifiable as long as it is fair. But elites are always tempted to extract too much, to turn extraction into exploitation, and exploitation into predation. This results in malaise, crime, protest, rebellion, refusal to defend the frontiers, and finally into revolution or defeat in war. Unfortunately, as the Reformation, the French and Russian Revolutions, and the collapse of the Soviet Union all bear witness, elites are loath to give up their lovely cake and eat it, and so sooner or later all empires and superstates decline and give way to new. If social and economic history means anything, it is that elites, and human beings generally, are extremely slow to learn from it.

Harold Perkin (b. 11. 11. 1926) was educated at Jesus College, Cambridge (BA, 1948; MA, 1952) and was RAF Education Officer, 1948-50. He was Lecturer at Manchester University, 1950-65, Senior Lecturer at Lancaster University 1965-67 and Professor of Social History (the first in Britain) 1967-84. He became Professor of History and Higher Education Northwestern University and is currently Emeritus Professor , Northwestern and Lancaster Universities and Honorary Professor at Cardiff University. He is author of 10 books and over 60 articles on English social education and global history and his current interests are chiefly globalisation and contemporary society.

A Personal View

Richard Perren

I began my career in economic history in the early 1960s as an undergraduate in David Chambers' Department at Nottingham. Under his leadership this was a lively place, not least because of his personal enthusiasm. It was formerly a sub-department of the History Department but David had found this unsatisfactory as he wanted to develop an honours degree in economic history and the historians had opposed this. He and his colleagues always argued that the two subjects were entirely different. History relied on a number of general approaches – at the time it was, I suppose, a vaguely liberal one that guided its judgements of the past – but economic history was always based on a definite system of theoretical analysis which was economic theory. As a result economic history was analytical, looking – not always successfully as it has turned out – for the causative factors and driving forces in the topic investigated. He stressed that the subject asked questions and looked for answers, rather than just being content to provide an exhaustive narrative. The other important feature he stressed was that it was a quantitative subject and the success of any research depended on the careful extraction of relevant data from the historical sources. But the use to which any data was put and the sort of questions that are asked needed to be clearly framed and informed by economic theory; without this it was just history with numbers. In contrast, history was non-quantitative and depended on accurate description and informed opinion, rather than any attempt at objective analysis. However, we all bring a set of opinions based on present day values to the study of the past and so I had some reservations about David Chambers's verdict on the two disciplines. But over the years I have come across more examples that support his view than refute it.

During my final year I was rather at a loss about what to do next and David Chambers suggested I might think about research. He said that the family papers of the Dukes of Sutherland in the Staffordshire Record Office were a rich archive of material. He even suggested the topic of railway and canal rivalry in the West Midlands, as the family had invested in both. This seemed a convenient way of avoiding an entry into the world of commerce and its problems. I had always found the eighteenth, nineteenth and twentieth centuries more interesting than either medieval or early modern and this encouraged me to go to Stafford and see what might be done.

On my first visit to that rather unexciting town and its Record Office I met Richard McKinley then the assistant county archivist - later to establish a formidable reputation on the history of English surnames. In a text book display of the guidance a really good archivist can provide, he conducted me around the Leveson Gower archives, which he explained was the family name of the Dukes of Sutherland. He also explained that they came to pronounce their name 'Looson Gore' when they had accumulated sufficient wealth to purchase a position in the higher echelons of society. He gave a graphic demonstration of why there was not enough material for a PhD on my suggested topic by pointing out the mere ten feet of shelf space devoted to the railway and canal material. By doing the same with the sixty feet on late nineteenth century agricultural depression he showed there was enough to sustain one on that. This quantitative demonstration, backed up by a couple of days consulting a judicious sample of items drawn from the shelves, largely at Richard McKinley's suggestion, was compelling enough. I felt that this was a suitable topic, being one of some importance and with an established body of literature, which I could investigate at a regional level by using primary sources. So in the eighteen months after graduating I lived in Stafford sifting through the primary materials, then six months back at my parents' home in west London doing secondary reading in the British Museum and working on the local Parish Agricultural Returns at the Public Record Office in Chancery Lane. This was followed by a third year back at Nottingham writing up the final version of *The Effects of Agricultural Depression on the English Estates of the Dukes of Sutherland 1870-1900*.

The department's research culture was a strong one as David Chambers had built up around him a large number of full-time and part-time research students, the latter mostly local grammar schoolmasters. About three times a term he would arrange a Saturday morning seminar with the department at which one of the group would give a presentation based on their research so far, generally at about a third of the way through our subject. These meetings were supported by the presence of economic historians from other universities, some of whom were former students in the department, reinforcing the message economic history was a growing and developing subject. Discussions and comments were always searchingly rigorous but quite fair, and it was always stressed that the primary purpose was to offer any advice and suggest any correction before an individual reached the point where it was impossible to change, and suggestions made at these meetings were always constructive. When it came to my turn there seemed to be approval of the way I was going about my task, which was a relief as I could see no other way of conducting the investigation.

In addition, supervisors were seen each term and provided with written reports and sections of chapters. At that time research students were treated in a far less formal way than with the system of almost monthly meetings, reports and written recommendations that is favoured today. There was certainly never any question of spending the whole of the first six months attending research training courses and reading the background literature. Although the present method is meant to prevent those occurrences where a new researcher starts off inadequately prepared and pursues the wrong avenue of investigation, I am not convinced these reasons were ever an important cause of failure to complete. Modern research training does provide a useful filter for research students as it gives individuals a chance to reflect and decide if they really want to commit the next three years to a single project with an uncertain outcome. But in my experience the main reason for lack of completion, both before and since its introduction, is that most often personal decisions intervene. On many occasions individuals give up when they see the costs in terms of time and effort outweighs any benefits. The most obvious example would be where an individual has struggled on and made financial sacrifices for two, or perhaps even three, years and then is offered employment outside the academic job market and told it does not matter if they have a higher degree.

That being the case, it was perhaps as well that I had never looked for a job until completion was imminent. When I finished after two years and eleven months in the summer of 1967 I joined four others already teaching economic history in the Department of Economics at the University of Aberdeen. Since then I have taught various courses in eighteenth to twentieth century British - that is Anglo-centric - economic history, and nineteenth and twentieth century Japanese economic history. My research interests have never been confined to one area. The business aspects of British agricultural history have always held more interest than its plough and cow features. No doubt this is a legacy from initially having to regard the Leveson Gowers' late nineteenth century estates as primarily a business enterprise, albeit not a particularly profitable one, rather than a series of social buttresses and mutual obligations for all involved therein. In addition, I have always been a townsman who dislikes getting mud on his shoes and, apart from walks on warm sunny days, prefer to keep the countryside at a respectable distance. In rural matters urban influences have often been unwelcome and frequently deleterious. But one great advantage of limiting the involvement with agrarian history is it has left time to write about other sectors that are not part of what is always the declining sector of economic importance in any growing economy. This perspective has allowed forays into food history, the nineteenth and twentieth century business history of North-east Scotland and, more recently, its urban history.

In the last flush of post-Robbins university expansion, shortly after I began at Aberdeen, it was decided in 1968 to appoint a chair of Economic History which was filled by Peter Payne the Colquhoun lecturer in business history at the University of Glasgow. After some debate about whether we should continue to stay where we were, the decision was taken to set up a new department. I had no particularly strong feelings either way, but most of my colleagues believed independence was the road to expansion, and they were probably right, as the economists, although friendly, regarded economic history as a separate subject that was not essential for them. Over the next twenty years we underwent the various phases of modest expansion, stagnation, decline, partial dispersal, and eventually an uncongenial and entirely unproductive amalgamation into a history department. This fate has been common to the majority of free standing economic history departments. During that time a number of features have emerged regarding both the research in and teaching of the subject which I feel may help to account for its ultimate decline.

One problem has been that it inhabits an uncertain middle ground between two larger disciplines. The inability of the subject to evolve an entirely separate body of theory is not surprising, nor indeed would it be appropriate. But the necessary reliance on a system taken from a larger discipline inevitably introduces an element of dependence. The tendency to see economic history as a 'help subject' has added to its difficulty in remaining entirely free standing at a time when teaching and research resources have been concentrated into larger units. But concentration, to acquire the benefits of providing the 'critical mass' of workers in a particular topic necessary to provide mutual support, has never fitted in well with the way in which economic history departments have been run, or their work managed. Traditionally, the approach has involved a small or medium scale department, most of whose members worked on their own areas of research. This has never ruled out collaborative work between people in different departments, but for all of those projects in which I have worked the immediate unifying influence has been the volume's editor. The other has been a strong level of general agreement among all parties about what a joint project requires, but this has hardly amounted to strong direction from the centre and reflects a long and rather gentlemanly tradition where the close details of approach are left to the individual.

This is not surprising, as there have been comparatively few areas where the really large-scale research project has been appropriate. It has been possible for historical demography, where large samples of data have had to be coded and checked, but this has applied in few other areas. The work of the Cambridge Population Group and, on a lesser scale, the Edinburgh project for the population histories of England and Scotland, are somewhat unusual in that they both employed large numbers. But although demographic growth was an important part of general economic growth, the industrial revolution in both countries has been the subject of individual researchers. Most economic history research has been carried out by lone academics because their subject offers far less scope for the joint project than either economics or sociology. Historical data is, for the most part, patchy and unsystematic and often never collected for the purpose for which it is now needed. This alone rules out the need for some of the large scale research surveys that can be undertaken by the branches of social science which focus on the present rather than the past. It has also helped to confirm the subject as one best studied in those small departments that have been so vulnerable in the cost-cutting climate since the 1980s.

Economic history's necessary reliance on quantitative data and some quantitative methods has probably deterred some students and obscured the fact that many important changes in people's lives are difficult to measure in any direct manner. The whole process of economic change in eighteenth and nineteenth century Britain involved a variety of contrasting developments which can only be fully appreciated by description, both contemporary and later, as well as measurement. This can hardly be otherwise, given the range of historical experience involved in those changes that may have transformed the lives of some but left those of others practically unaffected. These changes were not simply a case of the division between rural and urban dwellers as the lives of some farm workers were transformed just as much as those of town dwellers.

The eclectic approach that the subject demands, with a blending of qualitative and quantitative data and methods is probably one of its most exciting and rewarding aspects, and yet the one most often dismissed as a narrow concentration on the purely mechanistic aspects of historical change. In fact a perusal of the main journals in Britain and Europe and the United States reveals a broad range of approaches. There is certainly no evidence that those in which the data gathered is tested by a more or less formal model have ever dominated the subject, in spite of some of the gloomy predictions in the 1960s and 1970s. There has also been little to justify any assertion that cliometric techniques are now out of fashion, as they never dominated the subject in the first place. What they did was to introduce new ways of considering old topics and serve as a timely reminder that no academic discipline can remain rooted in the traditions of the 1950s.

However, their use did widen the gulf within the subject between those who prefer to keep any methodological framework in the background and others who move more towards the use of economic history as test bed for their economic models. Such diversity of approach has been both healthy and vigorous but can also be mistaken as a symptom of uncertainty and disunity. One of the consequences is that there has been little agreement about what exactly constitutes a basic training for a first degree in the subject. Unlike economics, beginners are not given an initial thorough grounding in basic microeconomic and macroeconomic theory. In economic history a foundation course can be either an outline of global economic development or that of almost any particular continent, country and region over virtually any time period. Possibly the only strong point of agreement is that the nature of modern economic growth, or the reasons for its absence, should be discussed. The 'broad church' approach to the subject in its initial stages is one of its healthiest aspects as a discipline, yet it may also be a decided liability as a recruiting agent.

Richard Perren (b.16. 8. 1943) was educated at the University of Nottingham (BA and PhD). He has taught at the University of Aberdeen since 1967 and is currently Senior Lecturer in Economic History in the Department of History. His main interests are business history and agricultural history since 1750. He was Secretary of the British Agricultural History Society from 1990 to 1996 and a contributor to the Cambridge *Agrarian History of England and Wales, volumes VI and VII* and *Aberdeen Since 1800: A New History*. He is Reviews editor for *Scottish Economic and Social History*.

The Force of Tradition

Karl Gunnar Persson

I started to study and teach economic history at about the same time. It was not because of unusual personal gifts but because in the latter half of the 1960s students flocked to economic history classrooms in numbers seen neither before nor after at Swedish universities. So the demand for teaching assistants was outrunning orderly supply. Heads of departments should have been happy if it had not been for the fact that the economic history sought after was not what was taught or could possibly be taught with some respect for academic standards. Students those days had high expectations of economic history - not as a subject preoccupied with boring things like index problems, national accounts, price analysis etc. - but as the key to all history *and* to society *and* to ideas *and* to culture. That causal links from economy to society and culture were strong, uni-directional, irreversible were beyond dispute.

This appetite for big, no, BIG, and difficult questions and inevitably woolly answers was not exactly met by Douglass C. North's *Growth and Welfare in the American past* which introduced new economic history and was made compulsory reading, despite classroom protests, at Lund University. However the virus of *new economic history* was there even if it turned out to have a long incubation period. How was it that this generation of economic historians which was drawn to economic history for other reasons than the real attraction or hidden charm of economic history generated so much good, sometimes even excellent economic history later on in their careers? The answer, I believe, is the force of tradition.

When I drifted into the study of social (im)mobility I was driven by social critique - a motivation for scientific inquiry as good as any - but I found myself very soon to pursue rather conventional socio-metric studies in the tradition of sociologist Raymond Boudon. I am afraid neither society nor social mobility changed much because of my published research.[1]

Others took up research where their supervisors had left off and produced good monographs on sectors, industries and firms. The Lund department had a wide variety of research programmes running including price history, historical national accounts reconstruction, historical demography and the history of ideas. However, I took the step over the Sound and started to work at an the University of Copenhagen Economics department. A life-long apprenticeship in economics started.

Looking back at the seventies and early eighties I can think of just a handful of contributions which actually meant a great leap forward from the radical critical thinking that emerged from the sixties. The verbally advanced but low-substance French 'structuralist' debate was rather sterile. However, John Roemer rescued the concept of exploitation from the outdated 'labour theory of value' and re-invented it in the concepts of mainstream economics.[2] G. A. Cohen made a consistent theory of historical materialism by showing that the only way to interpret it was as a functional explanation.[3] Re-casting the theory in a familiar and standardised mould and using the analytical rigour of modern 'Anglo-Saxon' philosophy made it much better. The force of tradition strikes again.

But at that stage, the early 1980s, the economic determinism of historical materialism was losing its attraction to historically minded researchers despite the fact that the Cohen version was academically impeccable and coherent. It was no longer politically correct in an era of 'cultural studies' which reversed the causal order of things social and economic. I was, however, attracted by the similarities between G. A. Cohen's 'historical materialism cum functional explanation', that is 'institutions thrive because they promote efficiency' and Douglass C. North's neo-institutionalism, the main difference being that Cohen was more careful to point out how vulnerable functional explanations are to misuse. Quite a few economic historians and economists still take the view, let us call it 'vulgar functionalism', that if an institution is stable it is efficient. An often desperate search for efficiency characteristics in all sorts of institutions became the order of the day: open field agriculture as a risk pooling device when natural accidents are local, share-cropping contracts as an efficient means of sharing risk etc. While I think it is a promising first strategy to look for efficiency characteristics in stable institutions, the literature on path dependence has made us sceptical, and rightly so too of stability of an institution as proof of its efficiency. But I insist, it is a reasonable first strategy. Who would deny, for example, that banks emerge because they are efficient in solving some of the asymmetries of information between lenders and borrowers by specialising in the costly collection of information on borrowers and by building up a reputation which makes risk-averse lenders trust them. Or that money is an efficient means to jump from bilateral barter to extended trade.

Although I was first thrilled by the relationship between neo-institutionalism and historical materialism I came soon to see the weakness of both . With friend and colleague Francesco Galassi I quarrelled about the inefficiency (my view not his) of the manorial organisation in medieval agriculture.[4] If institutions rely *not* on unrestricted and costless renegotiation of contracts but on one party having not only a monopoly of a crucial resource , say land, and on top of that a monopoly of coercive power, the institutional set up could be anything but efficient, yet, the manorial or 'feudal' institution would remain stable.

The next problem was this. If we, with the neo-institutionalists, argue that private property rights and incentives for purposeful search for new technologies, that is patent rights, are conducive to economic growth (or if we follow Karl Marx arguing that capitalist institutions are key) - what generates growth in their absence, say in the medieval and early modern phase?

Do we believe that there was not much growth to talk about? Well some do. The hubris that was typically a mark of the sixties optimism was helpful in redirecting my search into the causes of preindustrial growth An entire tradition of Malthusian thinking had to be reinvented on the way. I first looked into the theoretical structure of the Malthusian creed as echoed in the writing of Postan and Habakkuk. My colleague Peter Skott then at University College in London helped me a lot. We embarked upon what I now believe must be the natural way of historians and economists to collaborate, that is combining historical research with state of the art economics. We investigated a growth model with some traditional Malthusian attributes, such as fixed land,

and hence diminishing returns in agriculture, and population growth as a positive function of income per head. But we allowed for technological change, which Malthus sometimes did but mostly did not. An important result surfaces showing that in this bastard 'malthusian' model the higher the rate of technological change the higher the constant rate of positive population growth and the higher the constant above subsistence per capita income. The standard 'malthusian' result of population stagnation with subsistence wages was just the very special case of a zero rate of technological change. For an economist this might be the end of the project. But for me as an economic historian it was just the beginning. Was there positive technological progress despite the absence of growth-promoting institutions? Yes, there was I argued because there is learning by doing and Smithian specialisation effects. And what were the precise effects on income? This was the *new economic history* or *cliometric* question. How do you measure productivity or income change when you lack output or income data?

Sir Tony Wrigley suggested a simple device looking at changes in the relative size of occupational groups only.[5] His was a special case with the marginal propensity to consume food at zero, no trade and no income difference between rural and urban occupations. I used a more realistic (Engel-type) consumption function with marginal propensities of around 0.5, introduced foreign trade and admitted for urban/rural income differences. Changes in occupational shares, in particular the relative increase in the urban professions revealed productivity increase in the agrarian sector provided you controlled for trade and income distribution. The actual accounting formula I developed was derived from a conventional national income identity but I did not need income or output data. Needless to say I could not tell you anything about income or productivity *levels* but could say something about changes in income over time and income gaps between regions and countries.[6]

Others have since developed that approach further but the major empirical finding applicable for medieval economies remains.[7] There were great income and productivity differences between regions which could not be explained by resource abundance or scarcity. Rich regions were typically densely populated, they had little but efficiently used land per capita, and had fairly well developed markets for goods and in some cases also for capital. So the direction of the research for explaining differences in performance must be institutional. If you want to understand why some regions lagged behind look for market imperfections or worse lack of proper markets: look for poor institutional set-up.

Working with economists is rewarding because - unlike history - economics is a discipline rich in *new* hypotheses based on first principles rather than *ad hoc* conceptualisation. And besides you come close to their neighbours: the econometricians. I did my basic econometrics in 1968 when the obsession econometricians had for *'stationarity'* almost sounded counter-revolutionary. In the 1990s when I embarked on a study of market integration I found that the newest developments in time series analysis of - what a co-incidence - *non-stationary* time series was particularly well suited for that purpose. Can two price series each of which is a random walk of, say, wheat at two markets, be related so that a constant price ratio is secured? If so they are *co-integrated* as it is called in the technical jargon? At first sight it appears unlikely that two random walk series are co-integrated. However trade and arbitrage if efficient are the economic mechanisms securing market integration and by consequence co-integration. The new co-integration techniques and the related equilibrium error correction models gave a much richer analysis of the nature of market integration and its evolution over time.[8] However, my route to these techniques came by way of my excellent colleagues in the field and from my desire to solve a BIG historical problem: why were pre-industrial markets regulated and why did that regulation give way to free markets in a long process of institutional change lasting a hundred years from the mid eighteenth century to the mid nineteenth century. The simple answer was that market integration improved market performance and made regulation obsolete. The long answer takes a monograph.[9]

Karl Gunnar Persson (b. 9. 3. 1943 in the textile centre of Sweden, Borås). He was educated at Lund University and has been teaching at the University of Copenhagen , where he is now a professor, since 1975. He was founding president of the European Historical Economics Society and a co-editor of *European Review of Economic History*, 1996-2000. He is currently working on the relationship between information transmission and the efficiency of markets in history

---

[1]. A series of papers were published of which I select one which catches the spirit fairly well: 'Pure mobility and pure exchange mobility' in *Quality&Quantity*, 11, 1977,pp.73-82.

[2] J. Roemer developed these ideas rigorously in *A General Theory of Exploitation and Class*, Cambridge, Mass., 1982.

[3] See G. A. Cohen, *Karl Marx's Theory of History, A Defence*, Oxford: Oxford University, 1978.

[4] This debate was started by my 'Was Feudalism Inevitable?' in Scandinavian Economic History Review, 1, 1991, pp68-76 and was followed up in 2, 1992.

[5] E.A.Wrigley's paper was published as 'A simple model of London's importance in changing English society and economy 1650-1750' in *Past and Present*, pp. 44-70, 1967. I remember I presented my own -may I say more general version without sounding too cocky- at a seminar at a LSE in the mid-eighties but at the time of writing the paper I was not aware of Sir Tony's paper. That is until shortly before my presentation. However, since Tony was at LSE at that time he most certainly would show up at the meeting- and he did. I managed to include his paper in the reference list the last minute.

[6] See my *Pre-industrial economic growth*, Oxford:Basil Blackwell, 1988 and Labour productivity in medieval agriculture: Tuscany and the 'Low countries' in B. M. S. Campbell and M. Overton (eds) *Land, labour and livestock, Historical studies in European agricultural productivity*, Manchester: Manchester University Press, 1991, and 'Was there a productivity gap between fourteenth-century Italy and England?' in *Economic History Review*, Vol. XLVI (1993), pp105-14.

[7].See the recent paper by Robert C. Allen, Economic structure and agricultural productivity in Europe, 1300-1800, in *European Review of Economic History*, 4:1, pp.1-26.

[8] Error correction models can estimate the speed at which an equilibrium of price relatives between two markets is restored after a shock in one of the markets. By introducing transport costs between markets you can actually test for the transport cost adjusted 'law of one price'. See M. Ejrnæs and K. G. Persson, 'Market Integration and Transport Costs in France 1825-1903: A Threshold Error Correction Approach to the Law of One Price' *Explorations in Economic History*, 37 (2000), pp.149-173.

[9] *Grain markets in Europe,1500-1900. Integration and Deregulation*, Cambridge: Cambridge University Press, 1999.

How Economic and Social History Strikes Me

Brian Phillips

Instinct highlights one route to economic and social history for me, followed by more general judgement on the subject. How I became entangled in this amazing sub-culture leads to my conclusions.

I

Left of my window at home is a green circled by bungalows; models in construction and siting to suit their elderly occupants. Six months after planning, the first two couples were greeted by Reginald Bevins, Parliamentary Private Secretary to the Housing Minister.[1]

To my right, our turning joins the distributor road using the valley floor. Obvious traces of the winterbourne finally disappeared into a pipe when the playing field was built on in recent years, but noxious flooding has reminded neighbours of it. Local authorities and the water company shuffled responsibilities. Such drainage concerns and disputes also arose in the change from landed to housing estate, with such a full and frank exchange of views that the correspondence (which I listed archivally) will remain closed for 66 more years.[2] The town centre became celebrated as an early victim of floods in autumn 2000.

Residents of the next road report Roman pottery, alas off the record. Half a mile away was a corn-drying kiln of the first century AD: rare evidence of agriculture in the Weald during that period, when the region was probably an Imperial estate reserved for iron production. Earlier settlement is indicated by Mesolithic flints in the adjoining valley and measurable alteration to the natural vegetation pattern by then in the Sussex Ouse basin generally.[3]

Turning left, the estate roads join a former A-class road, busier than when one employee of the *Maiden's Head* inn calmly trundled a wheelbarrow containing the colleague he had murdered, late at night, to be dumped and soon found in heathy scrub. Soon afterwards, in 1974, here was the last authenticated sighting of Lord Lucan, a quarter of a century ago, after the murder of his nanny and attempted murder of his wife. Were this the inner city, it would be an infamous spot.

To the west, across a Roman road and head of a river navigation project at Shortbridge, the thoroughfare reaches Piltdown. Here, Charles Dawson (the strongest suspect) supplied in 1912 the ready intellectual market awaiting the 'missing link' in human evolution. Dawson was a local solicitor and administrator and amateur archaeologist and historian. Perhaps his amalgam of medieval skull and monkey teeth was intended to make his scholarly reputation, or merely aimed to deflate pompous professionals, which his sudden death four years later prevented from revealing: an early challenge to traces of the past from a post-modernist? A demolished ceiling in the Public Hall brought down documents of Dawson's civic activities, another surprise left for succeeding generations.[4]

My immediate surroundings, ignoring the town centre, thus provide leads to prehistoric and Roman activity, the process of post-war housing development, near-contemporary violent crime in contrasting tiers of society, the Edwardian urban elite and a hoax in scholarship.

The town grew rapidly after the railway arrived in the mid-nineteenth century. But it was already a hub of turnpiked roads and an urban and administrative centre for the surrounding farming villages. Those parishes were larger while more thinly settled; indeed it was a small but fairly sovereign chapelry close to the parish church.

A thirteenth century custumal shows a range of occupations, a brace of revolutionary fulling mills, shops, and even burgesses (though borough status never rated celebration). It served the large manor of South Malling, a ninth-century royal grant to the Archbishops of Canterbury (more speculatively a Celtic entity).[5]

This look at the town as a whole and one key primary source has touched further significant themes. More emerge at some specific locations within and around it, which I summon when leading historically-oriented walks. The parish poorhouse and the site of the Union workhouse recall the different phases of poor relief administration. The pair of cemetery chapels resulted from a four-year argument between Nonconformists who wanted the economy of one alone and Anglicans who insisted on segregated worship. Stretches of never-used railway embankment colonised by trees commemorate the investment slump of 1866. People who turn up for these events seeking a stroll with a little distinctiveness appreciate an introduction to these important issues while happening upon the associated spot.

Ramblings, in more than one sense perhaps, shape my feelings of economic and social history.

II

A first reaction may well be that this is actually local rather than economic and social history. A superficial defence is that I did not emphasise that my focus was Uckfield, or that it is particularly special in history, or inflict on the reader obsessive topographical detail to link what I said. Failure to provide a map, a somewhat random order of material, presented in awesome, breathless fashion with an assumption that everyone will be fascinated by the content would betray features of the worst sort of local history.

In practice, much economic and social history is local in scope while wider in significance, if only to keep research manageable. The distinction is surely in emphasis. The typical local historian starts with that particular place, while the 'Leicester school' would study the fate of a community over a major period of time. Economic and social historians will select a place to be important or typical, and/or richly documented for the argument.

Thus, to me, avid consumer but marginal producer, much of the subject intends and succeeds in conveying a sense of place. The diversity of experience is recognised. Scholarship accumulates more cases for generalities, but also more apparent differences. Proto-industrialisation, for instance, may eventually be explained by a novel unified theory, jettisoned as unwieldly redundant scaffolding, or otherwise developed. But its pursuit since Franklin Mendels' first model has been highly productive of perspectives and linkages.

History of the economic and social kind especially balances the unique and general, the ephemeral, regular, discordant or enduring, over various time-spans - because it can frequently measure these, quantitatively or qualitatively. To investigate virtually any part of past human experience, it has expanded the range of sources worthy of exploitation. In tandem, familiar material has new uses, to construct surrogate measures and otherwise extract additional information from documents commonly compiled for administration.

My undergraduate research initiation was the fashionable parish register demography: adapting entries to count births, marriages and deaths. Court examinations and depositions were scanned for migration data, the circumstances of offences and disputes and the background rhythms of life scarcely recorded elsewhere. Routine fare now, these stratagems still deserve our celebration.

Of course, political and administrative studies do not take their sources at face value but search for truer hidden meanings, if in a more restricted sense. On the other hand, contemporary social sciences have common interests with us, but can usually find or create direct evidence. Economic and social history must often be ingenious in method simply to start.

Economic and social history thus does the extraordinary for the sake of the ordinary. E. P. Thompson most famously expressed the mission 'to rescue...from the enormous condescension of posterity'.[6] But this campaign to enlarge history was won some time ago. Traditional concerns such as politics are now often informed by economic and social perspectives. These now even appear in the Historical Journal. Elsewhere too the influence has spread so that the editor of a local history periodical, after a conventional career in history teaching, wrote recently: 'in much of my own reading and researches I am seeking to understand the four As: attitudes and assumptions, aspirations and achievements'.[7]

In contrast I recollect 20 years ago a Past and Present conference where a questioner belittled the study of ideas at a popular level and a Historical Association gathering where another dismissed Le Roy Ladurie's *Montaillou* as 'News of the World history'.

Economic and social history is beset by institutional menaces, most apparent to those in place. Dissent also surfaces; Urban History Group conferences have included those keen to leave 'before the men in grey suits arrive' or 'unable to understand what they are saying' at the Economic History Society afterwards. Post-modernists have succeeded only in tougher scrutiny of evidence and methods, rather than discrediting the whole endeavour: our valuable court jesters? Greater reliable computing power will process more data more thoroughly and crossing traditional periods will assemble new concepts: ways I see the subject developing in the future.

III

My introduction to economic and social history was in infants' classes. I knew history would come later. By chance in a more advanced year's room, I inspected a book which fascinated and enthused me: R. J. Unstead's *Looking At History*. In each section, a page or two covered monarchs and major events, but its emphasis as the introduction said, was 'the everyday life of the ordinary people'.[8] I secured my own copy before long, still here, minus spine, if not now my staple reading.

Despite using Unstead, I do not recall much economic and social content to history in our junior school, and there was even less as we progressed through the ages. The next seminal influence was a Christmas present at age 11; I suspect my parents' choice was on the casual, desperate basis that 'he likes history'. So I encountered W. G. Hoskins' *Fieldwork In Local History*. It was a struggle, though I suppose the landscape descriptions were easier than discussions of documents and the societies revealed. In parallel as I read, Hoskins' first few pages showed him puzzling as schoolchild over the meaning of his Devon landscape, plus wrestling at 15 with Maitland's *Domesday Book And Beyond*. The absence of such topics from my prescribed education doubtless enhanced their appeal.

I think we devoted just half-an-hour to the economy of Tudor and Stuart England during two years of A-Level study. The grammar school I joined was now comprehensive, so practices such as reserving the economic and social history option for the streams deemed less academic persisted. Lewes Priory's philosophy of history had wider educational significance, for in the 1990s one of my teachers and his department head, in dispute with the authorities over choice of examination board, founded the History Curriculum Association, which brands economic and social history as dumbing-down.

After leaving school, while applying for a traditional history degree course, I commuted with long journeys to fill. My intake ranged widely, but certainly included the iconoclasm of A. R. Bridbury. A cloud formed on the horizon of my formal education meanwhile.

Undergraduate study at Kent entailed a multi-disciplinary first year, so that as a humanities student the unappealing prospect of philosophy and (even worse) English literature loomed. Fortunately, the 'Alternative Part I' permitted me to choose economic and social history, economics and politics courses from the social sciences faculty instead. In this escape route was 'The transition to industrial society in Britain'.

Under this heady influence I changed my degree registration to history and economic and social history. This led to a body of knowledge and an eccentric culture and camaraderie. There was a challenge in a lecture by Professor Gordon Mingay. He mentioned that everybody read the Hammonds on enclosure, while Gonner was ignored, an author guaranteed to induce sleep. Absorbed until about three a.m. in *Common Land And Enclosure*, I was different. Another marker was a dream sequence about buying the *Economic History Review* at a W. H. Smith railway bookstall from a certain Council member; that still awaits explanation.

IV

I have approached this question from micro, macro and narrative- chronological levels. From the fringes, my outlook must be what the subject has done to me, rather than the any impact I have had on the discipline. To me it rings as homely, or at least connecting with the homely, while profound too. It is at once local and global, beyond the topographical sense, so I have felt attached and comforted even through adverse circumstances. But my packaged version is deplorably anglocentric or even a tiny pays imaginaire and reified to boot.

Beyond self-indulgence, I see a recreational appeal to a history-conscious public, attracted to places of interest and reading broadly within economic and social history. Here is a pool from which to find future students and supporters, with carefully constructed bridges between syllabuses and sybaritism. Those repelled at school by dates and the politics of then and now can still respond to our perspectives on the past.

Journals usually occupy my bus and rail journeys, but it was the collection *Progress And Problems In Medieval England* which sparked a reaction once. A previously-rowdy youth on alighting noticed I had reached Jenny Kermode's essay on the trade of Chester and mentioned he preferred the Dark Ages to that later period. Friends we have not yet met may lurk anywhere.

Brian Phillips (b. 6. 2. 1956) undertook postgraduate research on migration in the early modern world at the University of Kent at Canterbury. He also researched the landscape of Sheffield Park for the National Trust. Subsequently he has worked for the Public Record Office and the East Sussex Record Office. He has published articles in local history periodicals.

[1] *Sussex Express and County Herald* (Uckfield & Crowborough edition), 2 Jan., 3, 10 July 1953, p.1.

[2] East Sussex Record Office (hereafter ESRO), Streatfeild archive, ACC6497/137.

[3] Tebbutt, C.F., 'A first century corn drying kiln at Uckfield', *Sussex N. & Q.*, 17 (1968), pp.25-26; Cleere, H. and Crossley, D.,*The Iron Industry Of The Weald* (2nd edn., Cardiff, 1995), pp.66-69; Scaife, R.G. and Burrin, P.J., 'Floodplain development in and the vegetational history of the Sussex High Weald and some archaeological implications', *Sussex Archaeol. Coll.*, 121 (1983); Hemingway, M., 'Further explorations at the Rocks early Mesolithic site, Uckfield, East Sussex', *Sussex Archaeol. Soc. Newsl.* 30 (August 1981), p.243.

[4] ESRO ACC6614.

[5] Redwood, B. C. Wilson, A. E., eds., *Custumals of the Sussex manors of the Archbishop of Canterbury* (Sussex Rec. Soc.,LVII, 1958), pp. 74-83; Jones, G. R. L., 'Multiple estates and early settlement', in P. H. Sawyer, ed., *Medieval settlement: continuity and change* (1976).

[6] E. P Thompson, *The Making Of The English Working Class* (Harmondsworth, 1968), p. 13.

[7] S. Wright, 'Editorial', *Hindsight*, 6 (2000), p. 3.

[8] R. J. Unstead, *Looking At History: Britain From Cavemen To The Present Day* (2nd edn., 1963), p. v.

What Economic History Means to Me

N.J.G. Pounds

I have always admired – and envied - those scholars who have been able to adopt a single, narrow field of study, and have been able to make themselves complete masters of it. I once had a friend whose interests were limited to the spurs worn by armoured knights in the Middle Ages. I have watched him make a rubbing just of the spurs represented in a late medieval monumental brass; no attempt to copy the rest, to understand the style of armour, the heraldry and the social and economic relevance of it all; only a dedication to the form of the spur through time. My career has been the reverse. I have wandered from one subject to another, one area of research to another radically different in content and techniques, just as the bee 'flits from flower to flower'. I do not always know what prompted the change. It could have been a chance conversation, a visit to an historical site, even a period spent lecturing to the troops stationed in Germany during the dark winter of 1945-46. And all my working life I have been looking for a thread, a highest common denominator, which might serve to link these disparate topics together and to give my work a unity comparable with the simplicity shown by my friend and his spurs.

I first came to economic history in 1931, when I sat at the feet of Sir John Clapham as he traced the economic history of this country from the Middle Ages until late in the eighteenth century, when time ran out and the Tripos loomed. His was a very broad and traditional treatment,[1] but I felt little inclination to follow his example. At the same time I listened to G.G. Coulton's lectures on the Middle Ages, and, in the company of a small group of like-minded students, accompanied him on my bicycle to visit parish churches in South Cambridgeshire. There we would discuss the social significance of graffiti cut into the stonework.[2] This must have been one of the earliest attempts by a professional academic historian to link field-work with classroom lecturing.

These were the foci from which my interest expanded. A year in the Geography Department of Cambridge University further broadened my historical perspective. Geology and Geomorphology threw light on the building methods and materials seen in those Cambridgeshire Churches, and at the same time the recognition of stone from Barnock, Purbeck or Portland raised the purely economic questions of transport methods and costs as well as those of personal preference and choice.

Circumstances allowed me to make a more intensive study of the economic development of Cornwall, and, at the same time, a close association with Charles Singer, then engaged in planning his monumental *History of Technology*[3], took me into the field of invention and technological development. A visit to Germany during that cruel winter following the war included a spell amid the ruined factories of Krupp and Thyssen and introduced a new facet into my growing ragbag of intellectual interests. Cornish mining, Singer's technology and the German experience led on almost inevitably to the history of metal-working, the rise of the modern iron and steel industry, and the book on the Ruhr.[4]

Migration to the United States led on to the task of developing a multi-discipline institute for the study of Eastern Europe in a major American university.[5] The interests generated by the Ruhr, Eastern Europe and technological development then spilled over into a study of the 'Eastern Ruhr', the industrial region of Gorny Slask[6] or Upper Silesia. In the 1970s physical circumstances compelled a further change in my interests. Library and desk work had necessarily to replace field-work. Tawney's dictum about the economic historian's need for strong boots had not lost its force, but there comes a time when, with the best will in the world, the legs cease to be able to wear them. The result was twofold, in the first place a return to those antiquarian interests which had been stimulated by Coulton, and, secondly, a suggestion dropped into my ear by those who examined me on my PhD thesis on the 'Historical Geography of Cornwall' in 1944: an historical geography of Europe, period by period, along the lines which H.C. Darby was already tracing at Cambridge. These two germs have continued to grow, perhaps to cross-fertilise, certainly to crystallise in several books. But all the time I have been troubled by the thought that these writings have been too diffuse; that they do not belong to a specific field of knowledge or a discipline. On the other hand I have been comforted by the thought that the cross-fertilisation of two or more fields can sometimes yield results; that important advances have often been achieved at the margins between traditional disciplines. There must have been many who felt torn between the attractions of a narrow, discrete field, if not quite as narrow as that of medieval spurs, and those of distant intellectual horizons, which beckoned one to venture more widely. I rationalised this as a conflict between the intensive and the extensive, between 'more and more about less and less' and its converse. And there can be few scholars who have not faced this quandary.

But this is a false dichotomy, if only because the study of the most trivial subject, if pursued, must lead into other fields. The prototype of the spur was almost certainly made of steel. Where had it been fabricated? What was the source of the iron? How had it been smelted and carburised? In the opposite direction one might ask how had it been used; had it been worn in battle, in tournament, or just for bravado; or, indeed, was it no more than an artistic convention, gratuitously accorded to its wearer who may never have possessed a suit of armour? And what does this tell us of the social and economic standing of its wearer?

No field of study, however trivial and apparently autonomous, can ever stand alone. It is not, to borrow the words of John Donne, 'an island, entire of itself', but 'a piece of the Continent, a part of the main' body of knowledge. There is a chain of causation linking facts, events and ideas, and there is no limit, except that which for convenience we set for ourselves, to their pursuit. I cannot conceive of knowledge as compartmentalised, divided into little hexagons set side by side as in Figure 1:

Figure 1

289

One thing which I learned from nearly 30 years in an American university is that academic departments are merely an administrative convenience; a means of organising courses and syllabuses and of recruiting students and teaching staff. The walls which separate them are subject to a kind of academic osmosis, encouraged and facilitated by the ease with which American students can hop from department to department in their choice of lecture courses and subsidiary fields of study. Indeed, I have made this transition myself, moving from History to Geography and back again. In doing so I have asked myself: is there any fundamental difference between the content and method of the two fields? And I have been obliged to answer: 'Not much'. I could discover in my lecture notes only a difference of emphasis. As an economic historian I would have more to say on currency and money matters, investment and capital accumulation. When wearing my geographer's hat, I would have emphasised the role of environmental factors and the usefulness of cartographic analyses. But basically I would have been covering the same body of material in similar, if not quite the same ways. Others, on both sides of the intellectual divide, would discover more profound differences than I have been able to do. The geographer would probably claim that his or her unique contribution to the debate would be the emphasis on the role of the environment, amounting in some instances to a kind of determinism, and, secondly, a reliance on distribution patterns as represented on the map.

Take, for example, a study which has long exercised my diminishing capacities: the relations between the elaboration of parish church architecture and the local resource base in both materials and agricultural production and expendable capital. This amounts to the equation of two distribution patterns which can best be represented and analysed cartographically. This in turn necessitates the selection of representative features of the buildings, and sometimes even of surrogates for them, and their evaluation . In many instances this can be done only in the field. The question is an historical one, but its sources and analytical methods are basically geographical. How often do we find historians using a kind of 'verbal' cartography? Why not the more precise and more objective map itself? How often do articles in our own *Review*, notably one in the most recent issue, call out for cartographic illustration. Of course, cartography of publishable quality is expensive, but a more important reason for its neglect is surely that historians have not, in general, learned to think cartographically. Maps of, for example, geology, soils and aspects of medieval churches, might offer insights that mere description cannot.

Another discipline which, in my own thinking, overlaps both Economic History and Historical Geography is Archaeology. It is essentially geographical in its use of maps, since the distribution of objects is an essential factor in their interpretation and understanding. Cultures are essentially distributions or spatial aggregations of specific objects. To return briefly to the analogy of the medieval church building, the mapping of its most significant features: mouldings, tracery, ground plans is primarily an archaeological pursuit, but it feeds directly into both Historical Geography and Economic History.

To resume briefly my historian's hat, I would plead for an even broader interpretation of Economic History. I view it, not as a field, cut off from others by firm demarcation lines, but as a point on which other, sometimes remote disciplines make their impact and on which the historians should be able to call for source material and the techniques with which to use it. Figure 2 is a model which elucidates at least a personal view of Economic History.

Figure 2

The inclusion of psychology may require justification. Much of my writing in recent years has concerned the history of population and of popular culture which manifests itself in buildings, style, decoration and folk practices of all kinds. These must be entered into the equation if only because they cost money and use up resources. In any consideration of these activities *homo economicus* must be dismissed out of hand. People have always spent heavily on *un* economic activities. Why were vast sums spent, often by communities which, by all the criteria now available, could not afford them? Religious belief, the lack of other means of investing temporary surpluses. Local pride, and the desire to out do the comparable efforts of neighbours all played a part. So must also the psychological need for action and variety. The American sociologist, C.C. Homans, wrote of 'superfluous behaviour'; he could as readily have written 'decoration' as demonstrated by the mindless graffiti of today. He was, no doubt, thinking of 'a boundless world of humorous forms and manifestations opposed [to] the official and serious tone' of ordinary life.[7] It was a world of masks, costuming, charivari, parades and rituals. These served to loosen the rigours of a more structured society. They were a safety valve, and thus a precaution against more violent and destructive action.[8] They became a regularly occurring and necessary part of life. Without in any way condoning the activities of the 'fans' who make the tumult of football even more violent and irrational than it is, their activities were such that Rabelais and Bakhtin would have understood. Superfluous to the business of life it may be, but without 'superfluous behaviour' that business might proceed even less smoothly. It therefore becomes, marginally at least, an economic activity.[9] It is part of that web of knowledge which I and countless others have attempted to explore under the all-embracing umbrella of Economic History.

And so the answer to the question posed at the beginning of this essay is that a unique and autonomous field of investigation is a figment of the imagination, and its realisation possible only at the most naïve and superficial level. I see in the variety of the subjects which I have chosen to investigate over a very long period of time a convergence on something which for lack of any better title, I call the people of the past in 'the ordinary business of life', a phrase devised almost a century ago by Alfred Marshall. I have viewed them as producers and their standards of living as a measure of their success. Such studies spread ever outwards like ripples, endlessly drawing in other fields of study. There is however, a limit. Three score years and ten are not enough, and one who has exceeded the allotted span by almost another score can only see, stretching before him, other fields which he will never tread.

N.J.G. Pounds (b.February 1912) was educated at King Edward's School, Bath and Fitzwilliam College, Cambridge (MA); London School of Economics (Ph.D). Tutor, Fitzwilliam College, Cambridge, 1944-50. Indiana University: Associate Professor to Distinguished Professor Emeritus of History and Geography, 1950 to 1977. Visiting Professor at University of Wisconsin; University of Kansas, University of Idaho. Honorary Fellow, Fitzwilliam College, Cambridge; President, Royal Archaeological Institute, 1986-89; President, Cambridge Antiquarian Society, 1994-96. Has written about 20 books and 50 papers.

---

[1] J.H. Clapham, *A Concise History of Britain form the Earliest Times to 1750*, Cambridge, 1949.

[2] He had already published the results of his own field-work: G.G. Coulton, 'Medieval Graffiti, especially in the Eastern Counties', *Proceedings of the Cambridge Antiquarian Society*, LXVII, 1915, pp. 53-62.

[3] Charles Singer, *A History of Technology*, 5 vols., Oxford, 1954-58.

[4] N.J.G. Pounds, *The Rurh*, London and Bloomington IN, 1952.

[5] *The Institute of East European Studies*, Indiana University, Bloomington IN.

[6] N.J.G. Pounds, *The Upper Silesian Industrial Region*, Indiana University, Slavic and East European Series, XI, 1958.

[7] Mikhail Bakhtin, *Rabelais and His World*, trans. H. Iswolsky, Cambridge MS, 1968, p.4.

[8] Natalie Zemon Davies, 'The Reasons of Misrule', *Society and Culture in Early Modern France*, London, 1975, pp. 97-123.

[9] Keith Thomas, 'Work and Leisure in Pre-Industrial Society', *Past & Present*, No. 29, 1964, pp. 50-62.

What Economic History Means – Then and Now

Roger L. Ransom

In the fall of 1965 I attended the meetings of the Economic History Association for the first time. It was the 25th anniversary of the association's founding and I can still recall the excitement I felt as I listened to the commemorative address by Herbert Heaton.[1] I was only two years out of graduate school, and I found Heaton's account of the efforts to establish the association in 1940 and the subsequent evolution of the EHA and its journal to be inspiring. 'It may be,' Heaton concluded,

> that the golden jubilee banquet speaker will talk about old truths and new errors of 1965-1990. For his evidence he will be able to draw on the next 25 volumes of the *Journal [of Economic History]*. And if those volumes show as great an advance in knowledge, visions, and understanding as can be traced in the first 25 our shades will rest content.[2]

Twenty five years later I had the honour of introducing that speaker to the jubilee banquet of the Economic History Association in Montreal. As I listened to Richard Sutch praise the accomplishment of the founders and affirm that there had indeed been profound advances in knowledge, I could not help thinking how much my own conception of what economic history 'meant' had changed over the intervening 25 years.[3]

In 1965 what was then called the 'New Economic History' was only beginning to flex its muscle. I was one of a cadre of young Turks who had studied economic history in graduate programs housed in economics departments and went forth to spread the gospel of a new methodology. For me, the 'new' economic history meant an emphasis on quantitative analysis and the application of economic theory to 'explain' a host of problems in economic history. As is so often the case with intellectual revolutionaries, we attacked the established 'truths' of the time. By the end of the 1960s the new economic historians had proposed a whole series of 'reinterpretations' of problems in American history:[4]

- The Navigation Acts were not a burden on Britain's 13 American colonies.

- Slavery in the antebellum South was profitable to southern slaveholders.

- The cotton economy of the antebellum South was a leading sector promoting the economic growth of the United States before 1860.

- The American Civil War was not a 'Second American Revolution that paved the way for industrial growth. The United States had already 'taken off' into industrial growth in the two decades prior to the Civil War.

- Railroads were not 'indispensable to the economic growth of the United States in the nineteenth century.

- Farmers' complaints of a deteriorating economic position in the late nineteenth century were not based upon real economic hardships.

- The New Deal did *not* get the United States out of the Great Depression.

The theoretical arguments behind these assertions were supported by the collection and refinement of quantitative data on an unprecedented scale. By the mid-1970s the 'new' economic historians had assembled an impressive collection of macro economic data that documented the course of American growth. In 1975 the Census Bureau published *The Historical Statistics of the United States;*[5] a statistical compendium that would become the indispensable companion of every quantitative economic historian in the United States.

All of this did not happen without a certain degree of tension among the fraternity of economic historians. Scholars such as Fritz Redlich pointed out that proponents of this new approach were 'standing on the shoulders of traditional economic history'.[6] While Redlich felt that 'older exponents' of the new approach understood this he complained that

> a still younger group now coming out of their seminars with the arrogance which is the privilege of youth seem to believe that their approach will take the place of the original one, that they will rout economic history as practised by the old fogies. They will in time mature and learn, or so it can be hoped.[7]

Redlich's hope would be only partly realised. Maturity would make the young Turks less arrogant, but their view of economic history would remain rooted in *economics* since they had learned the meaning of economic history in departments of economics, not departments of history. And as they pursued their academic careers, it would be their economist colleagues who would judge the value of their research. As 'economists' who wanted to specialise in economic history they had to convince their colleagues that the discipline of economic history really was important. This proved to be a formidable and enduring challenge[8]

Still, as a group, the new economic historians managed to prosper in the world of economists. By the 1990s, the new methodology had a new name – *cliometrics* – and it was no longer 'new'. Indeed, it had become the dominant methodology in the Economic History Association. As Richard Sutch put it in his presidential address at the golden jubilee:

> The first battle had been with the traditional economic historians; the objective had been to defeat them. The second conflict was with the economic theorists. The objective was to seduce them: first, to attract their attention; second, to help them see the contribution that historical methods and information could make; and finally, to fill their request for stories and historical data that address the concerns of theorists.[9]

Sutch judged that cliometrics had succeeded on both counts. However, in the course of winning these battles, the meaning of economic history had become blurred. The effort to 'sell' economic history to economists pulled the cliometricians away from the discipline of history towards a greater emphasis on economic theory in defining the 'problems' of economic history. Sutch called for the profession to tackle a third task: 'We must now make economic history relevant and required for the writing of good history. We should seek to integrate economic history back into the discipline of history: make economic history part of the core and make cliometrics part of the historiography.'[10]

This would prove to be no mean feat. Two decades earlier Lance Davis, who was himself one of the early cliometric pioneers, had observed that '[Cliometrics] will never be literature.'[11] Davis' remark points to a fundamental difference in the way cliometricians and traditional economic and social historians present their research. Historians write *books* that explore several facets of some historical situation; cliometricians write *articles* that focus on a carefully defined problem of economic history.[12] It is not coincidental, I think, that one of the few areas where the work of cliometricians quickly became part of the historians' historiography was their treatment of slavery and the American South. The research of scholars such as Stanley Engerman and Robert Fogel, Richard Sutch and myself, Claudia Goldin, Robert Higgs, and Gavin Wright appeared in books that reached audiences far beyond the readers of academic journals specialising in economic history.[13] It is not unfair to say that this work substantially revised the way historians viewed slavery and the South both before and after the Civil War. By the 1990s the cliometric interpretation was discussed in history textbooks as part of the historiography of the American South. While it would be premature to say that Sutch's challenge to integrate cliometrics and history has been fulfilled, at the end of the 1990s there is promise of a growing dialog between those who approach economic history with a background in economics and those whose training has been in the discipline of history.[14]

I developed a strong personal interest in this dialogue between historians and cliometricians. In September 1984 my appointment in the economics department at the University of California at Riverside was officially transferred across campus to the history department.[15] In a sense, my switch from economics to history reflected how the meaning of economic history to me was changing over the years. I began my career as a fervent disciple of the 'new' economic history, asserting that history was the blending of economic theory, statistical analysis, and history. My work on the American South with Richard Sutch convinced me that the process of historical change confounded the assumptions and at times defied the logic of economic models. By the time I joined the history department, my youthful confidence that historical models based on economic theory would provide the key insights into the process of economic and social change had been badly shaken. Teaching in my new academic department would further erode my confidence in the power of economic models to explain historical processes of change – particularly when those changes involve some dramatic discontinuity such as a major war.

The American Civil War provides an excellent example of how historical analysis can become warped if one focuses solely on economic growth. One of the earliest targets of the 'new' economic history was to debunk the accepted wisdom that the Civil War introduced major structural changes in the American economy that accelerated economic growth in the United States. Quantitative evidence clearly showed otherwise; in a purely economic sense, the war was an unfortunate interruption to the continuation of antebellum economic growth. So much for the Hacker-Beard thesis.[16] But does it make sense to claim that the outcome of the war had no significant implications for the economic future of the United States simply on the basis of measuring economic output? Suppose we ask the counterfactual question: 'what if the war turned out differently?' Would emancipation have still taken place? Would the dissolution of the United States have changed the patterns of economic development in North America? Answers to these counterfactual questions hardly suggest that the world would have remained unchanged in the face of a Southern victory.[17] By narrowing their focus to a question of economic growth, critics of Hacker-Beard threw out the baby with the bathwater. The irony of all this is that it was the new economic historians who made counterfactual history a cornerstone of their methodology forty years ago – and they were roundly criticised for it.[18] Since then cliometricians have narrowed the focus of their analytical models and the counterfactual approach has often become little more than sensitivity analysis within the confines of an economic model. In limiting the scope of their analysis, cliometricians have tended to overlook the larger issues that a counterfactual approach to a problem, such as the economic effects of war, might offer. Economists, as Robert Solow once observed, are 'determined little thinkers'.[19] Being an economic historian, it seems to me, means being a 'big thinker'.

My story has come a long way from my youthful reaction to Herbert Heaton's 1965 address celebrating the 25th anniversary of the Economic History Association. After three and a half decades – with roughly half of that time spent in an economics department and half in a history department – what does economic history mean to me today? What was once a simple task no longer seems so simple. The one constant in all this is that every society must somehow solve the 'economic problem': what to produce; how to produce it; and how to distribute the output to society members. It seems to me that the task of the economic historian is to take the historical record and make sense out of society's efforts to meet the challenges of that problem over time. If we can make sense out of the past, we will be in a better position to make sense of the present and, perhaps, be in a better position to deal with the future

Roger Ransom (b. 5. 9. 1938 in Berkely) has been Professor of History and Economics at the University of California, Riverside since 1984. He was educated at Reed College Portland and the University of Washington . His publications include (with William Breit*)* The Academic Scribblers: American economists in collision (1971, 1982, 1998), the award winning *One kind of freedom: the economic consequences of emancipation* (with Richard Sutch) (1977, 2000) *and Conflict and compromise: the political economy of slavery, emancipation and the American Civil War* (1989).

---

[1] Herbert Heaton, 'Twenty-Five Years of the Economic History Association: A Reflective Evaluation,' *Journal of Economic History* 25, (1965).

[2] *Ibid.* p.479.

[3] Richard Sutch, 'All Things Reconsidered: The Life Cycle Perspective and the Third Task of Economic History,' *Journal of Economic History* 51, (1991).

[4] A good summary of the reinterpretations by 'New' economic historians in the mid-1960s can be found in Douglass C. North, *Growth and Welfare in the American Past: A New Economic History* (Englewood Cliffs: 1966). Somewhat more technical assessment of the reinterpretation, is in Susan Previant Lee and Peter Passell, *A New View of American Economic History* (New York: 1979). My own reinterpretation of American economic history be found in Roger L. Ransom, *Coping with Capitalism: The Economic Transformation of the United States, 1776-1980* (Englewood Cliffs: 1981).

[5] Bureau of the Census United States, *Historical Statistics of the United States, Colonial Times to 1970*, Two Volumes vols. (1975).

[6] Fritz Redlich, '"New" and Traditional Approaches to Economic History and Their Interdependence,' *Journal of Economic History* 25, (1965), p. 494.

[7] *Ibid.* p. 494.

[8] An excellent example of the effort by economic historians to convince economists that economic history was 'relevant' for economics is the article by Donald N. McCloskey, 'Does the Past Have a Useful Economics?,' *Journal of Economic Literature*, (1976) .

[9] Sutch, *op.cit.* pp. 271-288, p. 276.

[10] *Ibid.*, p. 277.

[11] Lance Davis, '"and It Will Never Be Literature": The New Economic History: A Critique,' *Explorations in Economic History* 6, (1968).

[12] I realise this is a sweeping generalisation that cannot easily be verified. It is based on my personal observation that in order to obtain tenure within a history department, most major research universities in the United States would demand that scholar have published at least one book with a reputable press. Moreover, to advance beyond the level of associate professor a second book is typically necessary. I do not see a similar emphasis on book-length manuscripts on the part of tenure reviews in economics departments.

[13] See Robert W. Fogel and Stanley L. Engerman, *Time on the Cross: The Economics of American Negro Slavery*, Two vols. (New York: 1974); Claudia Dale Goldin, *Urban Slavery in the American South, 1820-1860: A Quantitative History* (Chicago: 1976); Robert W. Fogel, *Without Consent or Contract: The Rise and Fall of American Slavery* (New York: 1989); Roger L. Ransom and Richard Sutch, *One Kind of Freedom: The Economic Consequences of Emancipation* (New York: 1977); Roger L. Ransom, *Conflict and Compromise: The Political Economy of Slavery, Emancipation, and the American Civil War* (new York: 1989); Robert Higgs, *Competition and Coercion: Blacks in the American Economy, 1865-1914* (New York: 1977); Gavin Wright, *The Political Economy of the Cotton South: Households, Markets, and Wealth in the Nineteenth Century* (New York: 1978) and *Idem, Old South, New South: Revolutions in the Southern Economy since the Civil War* (New York: 1986).

[14] My own research interests causes me to focus on the literature of the American South as the primary example where cliometric research findings were quickly incorporated into the historical literature. This is, of course, not the only area where the two methodologies joined forces, however I believe it is the most spectacular case of a cliometric interpretation dramatically altering the conventional historical wisdom.

[15] The decision to change disciplinary affiliations highlighted some of the difficulties in being a specialist in two fields. For a discussion of the change, see Kerry Odell, 'An Interview with Roger Ransom,' *The Newsletter of the Cliometrics Society*, Summer 2000, and Ransom, *Conflict and Compromise: The Political Economy of Slavery, Emancipation, and the American Civil War* .

[16] The Beards and later Louis Hacker argued that the Civil War was a 'second American Revolution' necessary to permit the industrial expansion of the last third of the nineteenth century. See Charles Beard and Mary Beard, *The Rise of American Civilisation*, vol. 2 Volumes (New York: 1927) and Louis Hacker, *The Triumph of American Capitalism: The Development of Forces in American History to the End of the Nineteenth Century* (New York: 1940). This thesis was the accepted historical wisdom of the impact of the Civil War until it came under attack from quantitative historians in the 1960s. The best summary of the criticisms of the Hacker-Beard thesis is Stanley L. Engerman, 'The Economic Impact of the Civil War,' *Explorations in Entrepreneurial History* 2nd Series 3, (1966).

[17] For an analysis of the implications of a Southern victory in the Civil war, see Roger L. Ransom, 'Fact and Counterfact: The 'Second American Revolution' Revisited,' *Civil War History* 45, (1999).

[18] In the debates over methodology in the 1960s the use of counterfactual analysis was perhaps the most controversial aspect of the 'new' economic history. In 1962 Robert Fogel added fuel to the flames when he claimed that if there been no railroads in the United States in 1890 the effect on GNP would have been negligible. Fogel, 'A Quantitative Approach to the Study of Railroads in American Economic Growth: A Report of Some Preliminary Findings.' *Journal of Economic History* 22, (1962). Critics leapt on the implausibility of Fogel's assumptions to discredit the analysis, claiming it was not 'history'. Fogel stuck to his point; insisting that *every* historical question carried with it an implicit counterfactual situation that should be addressed. See *idem, Railroads and Economic Growth: Essays in Econometric History* (Baltimore: 1964). I strongly support Fogel on this point; see Ransom 'Fact and Counterfact…'.

[19] Robert Solow, 'Son of Affluence',' *Public Interest*, (1967). The reference was in regard to the sweeping generalisations of John Kenneth Galbraith, who Solow characterised as a 'big thinker.' Solow illustrated his point with an analogy to the household where the wife makes all the unimportant decisions such as what job they should take, where they should live, and how to bring up the children, while the husband makes the important decisions on what to do about the Middle East, the United States policy on China, and the like.

What Economic and Social History Means to Me

Alastair J. Reid

My first memory of consciously thinking about a historical problem was when I was revising enlightened despotism for A-level and began to ask myself why these monarchs had adopted their new policies. The answer I came up with was that, since their reforms created more jobs for government officials, perhaps those people who expected to benefit from employment had been exerting pressure for change. I may already have read about this somewhere, but I was aware of asking a question about a broad process and coming up with some kind of insight by way of an answer, rather than just memorising endless detailed information about events. This was a very exciting experience, and of course it also provided a basis for the selection of information and made it easier to remember details because they now had some meaning. I had always been interested in my history lessons at school and enthusiastic about reading widely at home, but now I had a sense of what of it might be all about. This was then almost immediately confirmed by coming across Christopher Hill's textbook on seventeenth-century British history (*The Century of Revolution, 1603-1714*, 1961), which gave only brief narratives of events for each period and followed them with substantial analyses of economic, constitutional and intellectual history: for me this was both highly unusual and exactly what I wanted to be reading at the time.

When I went on to study as an undergraduate at Cambridge University, I was very fortunate to find my way into Gonville and Caius College without really being aware of the special nature of the history school which was flourishing there in the early 1970s. Not only was it highly organised, with specialist supervisors able to provide up-to-date reading lists and draw on their own research experience for each subject, it was also strongly weighted towards economic and social history. As a result, my first two terms there were spent studying eighteenth- and nineteenth-century British history with Neil McKendrick and Vic Gatrell, focusing on the main economic themes in the Industrial Revolution and then on the corresponding social background to popular politics. I am very grateful to them for the care with which they supported my studies, encouraging me to follow my own interests but also challenging me to bring the results up to a proper professional standard. Though my ideas may have moved on from what we discussed then, the general approach they helped to shape has remained the basis of the way I still think today.

This was also an exciting time to be encountering university history more generally, for it seemed to be expanding rapidly in all directions, especially in terms of the range of issues which it was legitimate to study and the innovative methods which were being adopted to approach them. Broadly speaking, post-war structuralism was at its peak and, whatever one's own temperamental or political preferences, it was hard to avoid the influences of the British Marxist historians and the French Annales school. The sheer scale of major works by such figures as Edward Thompson (*The Making of the English Working Class*, 1963, pp. 848) and Fernand Braudel (*The Mediterranean and the Mediterranean World in the Age of*

Philip II, English translation 1972-73, pp. 1375) was just as exciting and impressive as the actual arguments and evidence they put forward. So, as often as not, it was less a matter of following their analyses of specific topics than of being inspired by their iconic status to try to do history in a particular way: focusing on the economic basis of social life, and complementing it with a reconstruction of the distinctive 'culture' or '*mentalite*' of each social group.

This was also a time when 'revolution' was in the air, fuelled mainly by news of dynamic democratic movements overseas: the student revolt of May '68 in Paris, the counter-cultural experiments in North America, the collapse of dictatorships in southern Europe and the brief period of progressive regimes in Latin America. Our nearest British equivalent was a peaking wave of trade-union assertiveness: the unofficial strikes in the car industry, the work-in at Upper Clyde Shipbuilders and above all the miners' strikes in the coal industry, which brought about power cuts, the three-day week and the fall of a Conservative government. Many of us who were eager to apply new methods to the understanding of our own situation were then naturally drawn into studying aspects of the history of industrial relations which, despite important contributions by the older generation of Marxist historians, had the added advantage of being largely uncharted territory as far as the twentieth century was concerned. There was a sense in which Marxism then contributed to its own demise. For, having heavily underlined the importance of the general structuralist focus on the economic basis of events, it encouraged us to start out on sustained inquiries into such issues as the impact of machinery on manual tasks and the systems of authority within companies. And this eventually had a profoundly deconstructive effect on widely-held assumptions about general trends towards deskilling and increasing managerial power which had been the basis of much of the appeal of the Marxist approach to history and politics.

Having become more involved in aspects of the history of industrial organisation than we might initially have intended, most of my peer group moved gradually into a new kind of business history, mirroring the shift of power away from the unions and towards the employers under the Thatcher regime. But I continued to focus more on the experiences and attitudes of trade unionists, which I am increasingly inclined to put down to the influence of my early years in Scotland. For Scottish society in general seems to have been suffused with a more democratic ethos, embodied above all in the traditions of the Presbyterian church which took a particularly intransigent form in the West of Scotland south of Glasgow where I grew up. There, every village had a memorial to the 'martyrs' of the century-long campaign by the Covenanters for the right of local congregations to appoint their own ministers, a right which continues to be exercised down to the present day by the elders in each parish, including my own father. A healthy disrespect for established authorities of whatever political colour, a curiosity about what keeps institutions running behind their public faces, a deep respect for the contributions of ordinary people and a strong commitment to local democracy: it has proved impossible for me to shake off these regional values. Thus they continue to inform my study of the past, which from this point of view could be seen as a kind of secularised Protestantism.

By now it should have become clear that what economic and social history means to me is not so much the study of certain specialised aspects of history, though that is indeed also involved, but rather an aspiration to develop a certain approach to the study of the past as a whole. And that implies both an interest in all aspects of history and the pursuit of insights into how societies are made up and held together as whole ways of organising people's lives. At first this was influenced by an 'economic' approach, in which history was seen as being structured like a layered cake: once you had studied the level of material interests, such as who got jobs out of enlightened despotism, you felt you were on your way to grasping the underlying causal dynamics. Gradually, it came to be more influenced by a 'social' approach, in which history was seen as being more like the orbiting particles of sub-atomic physics: you could describe a series of interactions but you could never be quite sure that you had broken them down into their fundamental components, after all, why had the European middle classes wanted government jobs in the first place? But whatever the approach, the central concern remained to understand what keeps whole economies and societies going and, however alluring the manoeuvres of high politics and the products of high culture may be from time to time, to uncover the mass of ordinary life which sustains them.

Thus a working agenda would include: employment relations throughout the economy, including both company organisation and industrial relations; law and policing as they affect not only criminal behaviour but also attitudes towards the functioning of institutions in general; religious belief, as an important phenomenon in itself and also for its impact on wider social and political values; the family as a fundamental site of biological reproduction and primary socialisation; education and training as reflections of social values and vital systems for inculcating them in the next generation. And alongside the inquiry into social organisations would be a concern to develop certain skills: to grasp the outer shape and inner workings of distinctive historiographical schools; to assess critically the reliability of different kinds of source material and the more or less subtle implications of depending on them; to deploy a range of explanatory concepts in a flexible way, along with an appreciation of their limits; to enter into and understand the ways of thinking and feeling of the people being studied.

Over time my reading has deepened and my perspective has broadened, so that I now see our current academic discipline as the tip of a much bigger iceberg. Thus the agenda I have been outlining might indeed be characterised as a form of 'historical materialism' without being confined within recent arguments over Marxism. For, as Karl Marx himself acknowledged, all the elements of his approach had been fully developed before he steered them towards a particular set of conclusions. The emphasis on the material basis of social relations had been a primary characteristic of the eighteenth-century Enlightenment attack on established religion, especially in France and Scotland where influential figures such as Montesquieu and Adam Smith began to bring together the fundamental elements of systematic thinking in what we now call sociology and economics. More or less simultaneously, the emphasis on contextually-specific world-views had been a primary characteristic of the Romantic defence of inner subjective life against the onslaught of this materialist generalisation, especially in Germany where influential figures such as Friedrich Schleiermacher and Leopold von Ranke began to lay the foundations for the professional study of the distinctiveness of cultural products and the uniqueness of historical processes. If in the longer term these two originally competing tendencies have come to seem more complementary, that is partly because they already drew on shared resources, above all on the inheritance of ancient Greece and Rome, which still formed so much of the core of the educational curriculum of the time. This is perhaps most evident in the general reflections of David Hume and Wilhelm Dilthey, deeply rooted in what would once have been seen as competing traditions of British and Continental philosophy, but reaching remarkably similar conclusions about the limits of causal explanation in the human sciences, and the importance of combining pluralism over attitudes and values with a grasp of the common underlying features of human psychology. And in both cases their thinking drew quite self-consciously on traditions stretching back to the various schools of Hellenistic philosophy, especially the Sceptics and the Stoics.

From time to time we may change the focus of our studies and re-evaluate our approaches to them, a process which may well feel confusing and even painful, as well as being distorted by sudden swings in fashion. But an intellectual activity which has such deep historical roots, and has for so long played such an important role in the self-consciousness of literate

Europeans, is not likely to come to an end or to change out of all recognition in the foreseeable future.

Alastair J. Reid (b. 12. 9. 1953). Educated at Gonville and Caius College, Cambridge. Fellow and Lecturer in History at Girton College, Cambridge. His publications include *Social Classes and Social Relations in Britain, 1850-1914* (New Studies in Economic and Social History, Cambridge University Press, 1995). He was an editor of the video series *Interviews with Historians* (Institute of Historical Research) which includes a number of distinguished economic and social historians.

The Australian Option

Eric Richards

Frank Thistlethwaite famously remarked that skill is like 'a radioactive tracer in the blood stream' of mass migration. Skill, of course, has been a passport for much academic emigration for two generations, not least among economic historians trained in Britain in the 1960s. There was a distinct exodus to Australia of which I was a part, leaving for Adelaide as a graduate in 1962. Some of that fortunate generation is now gracefully subsiding into retirement. But the Economic History profession, especially in Australia, is now much less comfortably placed.

Any skills I carried to Australia were mainly acquired at Nottingham in the days of J.D. Chambers, Bob Coats and Robert Ashton. Nottingham was already a sort of labour exchange for recruitment to Commonwealth universities. But 'the meaning of Economic History' had reached me before I faced the professionals at Nottingham. I was an adolescent economic determinist at school in Shropshire, already seduced by Marx, Tawney and the *New Statesman*. I seemed to know that economic forces ruled the world, that politics and society were governed by structures beneath. Exposure at school to conservative historians like Elton and Pollard simply confirmed the notion of 'vested interests' as the driving motive in the grand dramas of English History, usually reducible to economic advantage. Adam Smith made the interplay of economic interests logical, perhaps beneficial to the world at large. So to understand and influence the world, Economic History was clearly the most important field to explore. It was somehow also combined with the problems of class discord, and re-balancing the scales of society.

Being at University, in 1959, on a scholarship, was a way to indulge this passion. Born at the right time, our lucky generation reaped some of the most tangible rewards of British Socialism and Keynesian growth. (For me it was the first time anyone of my family had been anywhere near a university). Moreover Economic History was an inspiring arena in which were tackled the great questions of society and economy in real world contexts. It was essentially an earthy struggle with the practical and concrete issues of the way the world was made. This, to me, was the true fascination of Economic History, and the centre of its meaning to my mind. It was an outlook powerfully reinforced by the almost bucolic empiricism of David Chambers. When he asked what actually happened to the rural population during industrialisation, it was not an intellectual puzzle but an actual search for the people of that time. Though the approach at Nottingham did not exclude all theory and conceptualisation, one felt that the answers were to be found in the documents, in the parish registers, in the handloom cottages and the sweatshops, in the estate ledgers and in the fields, and much less likely in the formulae of the theorists.

The intellectual demands on Economic History in the 1960s inevitably burst these banks and became more testing and exciting. The agenda was big enough to engage any mind: the springs of economic advancement, the rise of capitalism, the distribution of the spoils of progress, the war against poverty and exploitation - these were, of course, meat and drink to Economic Historians. In 1960-1 the issues were sharpened by the exciting engagements of opposites - Hobsbawm versus Hartwell, Chambers *et al* versus E.P.Thompson, Marx (and legions of others) versus Rostow.

Economic history was to my mind a series of grand questions to which it was possible to imagine, even as an undergraduate, making small but useful inroads, explaining how the world worked. This engagement came with a creed: at Nottingham it entailed an immersion in the archives. The Honours thesis gave rapid access to research, and could yield something original, even publishable (as Gordon Mingay had demonstrated). Chambers had set utterly crucial questions: notably the twin problems of explaining the chronology and mechanics of industrialisation, and the demographic framework of that process. At Nottingham one was always aware that the ghost of the East Midlands prophet, D.H Lawrence, hung over these matters. He, of courses, had denounced industrialism with an eloquence which was matched by the opposite vision passionately enunciated by his childhood friend, Chambers himself.

The consequences of industrialisation were the central concern of Economic History (even though they later seemed to slip off the agenda). When I joined the profession the study of industrialisation was never an abstract puzzle. Industrialisation was the vital discontinuity in the lives of most families in modern western societies - the great majority, in actual historical memory, have indeed been detached from the land and become urbanised. This universal experience came to my own family late in the piece. In 1940 only 5% of the British workforce was left in agriculture. Out of generations of small farmers and agricultural labourers in North Wales, my own father and mother had taken the path from the cottage and village to the local town (Wrexham) as part of this great historical disjunction and transition. I was conscious of being virtually the last to depart the land at the end of one of the critical processes in Economic History.

The long secular boom and the expansion of the universities gave the graduates of the early 1960s employment opportunities which must look extraordinary to the present generation. The road to Australia was easier still: in 1962, half way through a Ph.D., I simply applied to Australian universities and was immediately offered several positions. As a '£10 Pom' I became a Tutor in Economics at the University of Adelaide. Accounting for emigration, like intellectual influences, is notoriously hostage to rationalisation, but it seemed uncomplicated at the time.

The Australian option required adjustment: Economic History in Australia was housed mainly in Economics Faculties and was heavily influenced by N.G. Butlin and his school at A.N.U. Butlin exerted an almost imperial control over the subject and he had fixed a rigorously quantitative framework on the study of Economic History. He established the critical dimensions of Australian economic development and set the agenda for the measurement of the identifiable variables in the past economy. To a newcomer it was both impressive and bracing. The approach was severely conceptual and required not only measurement but theorising and model-building. It was highly abstracted Economic History, devoid of recognisably human forms. This was a shock and did not blend well with the British tradition of that day. It was, nevertheless, intellectually invigorating, and gave a much sharper edge to my own work which, via the study of an aristocratic estate, had come to deal with the canal/railway transition during industrialisation and, less predictably, the history of the Scottish Highlands. Surprisingly, it was possible to conduct this sort of research from Adelaide, which, together with its other attractions, made the Australian option highly acceptable.

But the lure of the new British universities was powerful. An opportunity arose in 1967 to work with George Rudé in the first days of Stirling University in Scotland. This was my return migration which helped to consolidate the lines of my research in Economic History for the next two decades. I worked on the transformation of the Highlands (which increasingly I came to see as a particularly painful variant of the agrarian transition) and on the social consequences of industrialisation in different regional settings. Exposure to Rudé's ideas also set me off in the direction of social protest during rural turmoil, that is into riotology. These new preoccupations seemed to me large and central questions which gave further meaning to Economic History, liberally defined.

Second migrations are commonly better informed and more rational. I returned to the new Flinders University in Adelaide in 1971, to a free-standing Department of Economic History with Seymour Broadbridge, exchanging the drizzle of Stirling for the dazzle of Adelaide. Broadbridge soon departed for England and I diverted to History proper, though I carried most of my old intellectual baggage with me. I devoted myself to Social History which now seemed more exciting and also dissolved my tension with the Australian brand of Economic History which had become increasingly arid and inward. In our place an extraordinarily strong Economic History Department was built at Flinders, with W.A. Sinclair, Ralph Shlomowitz, G.D. Snooks and Wray Vamplew. This was a 'dream team' of Economic Historians, with R.J. Holton in the same School, in disguise as a sociologist. It is a glum commentary on the shifts that have overtaken Economic History here (and elsewhere, of course) that the Flinders Department has since disintegrated and no longer exists. After about 1985 not even the very best combination of economic historians was able to sustain the Discipline. In its wake even Economics has declined, to become a mere servant of the once despised Commerce and Management sector of an increasingly vocational University.

None of this melancholy story diminishes the meaning of Economic History: the great questions remain and are mostly far from resolved. One of the attractions of working in Australia was that of exploring the genesis of entirely new economies constructed in a virtual wilderness (ignoring the Aboriginal question for the moment). In the Australian context it is possible to witness the creation, evolution, and mutations of economic behaviour and structures from almost Robinson Crusoe-like conditions. For me this has long been a beguiling juxtaposition with my continuing study of the convulsive changes experienced by the old economy of the Scottish Highlands at about the same time. Writing about old and infant economies in parallel always brings into sharp focus the problem of the price of economic progress which, in my view, tends to be underplayed in present-day Economic History. Other currents were at work too. Thus the stimulus of Feminism caused me to speculate about the role of women during industrialisation. And I have been much engaged in the ironies of displaced Scottish Highlanders recruited as the direct agents in the destruction of Aboriginal societies in colonial Australia.

By this circuit I returned almost to my original inspiration, to Tawney and to the springs of economic change. I have been exploring the mentality of entrepreneurship by way of that neglected *genre*, the economic biography. Specifically I have been dealing with an extreme case, namely that of Patrick Sellar - a man charged with massive evictions in the Highlands in the 1810s, the vehicle of sudden and explosive economic transformation on the recalcitrant fringe. This happens to be a remarkably well-documented case, with access straight into the mind of the developers. In this instance the main attraction is that of observing men of intellect and sophisticated education (indeed from the very centre of the Edinburgh Enlightenment) grappling with the social consequences of their economic engineering. This is ultimately about the balance sheet of economic change, which I have always regarded as the paramount responsibility of Economic History. It inescapably leads to some kind of evaluation of the agonies that 'progress' commonly demands of the social fabric, as well as its uneven effects for the different sectors of society in the throes of economic change. It is about the distribution of the necessary costs of industrialisation.

These 'meanings of Economic History' for me are linked. I see a continuum of questions which derive from rural transformation. The disengagement of the people from the land has always entailed their displacement to other places, other economies, other forms of human existence. How this necessary part of industrialisation has been managed and realised - and how it has been vilified and demonised - are grand themes in our agenda. The process of modernisation is almost universally accompanied and characterised by bitter social turmoil, often captured in song and tradition. The juggernaut of rural transformation is generally greeted with revulsion, often with active opposition, which delays though rarely prevents the outcome. My own work at present is given special meaning by the underlying and still mysterious connections between rural displacement, the demographic upsurge of the late eighteenth century, and the phenomenon of mass migration, especially in its international dimensions. Having collected hundreds of individual accounts of emigrants from the British Isles, the trick is now to relate them to the wider structures of change so well sketched by Thistlethwaite and his successors. Beyond this I find inspiration in a growing conviction that the emigration of the nineteenth century might be regarded as one of 'the great proletarian achievements' in British history, invisible though much of it has been.

Back in the 1960s there were debates about 'The Tasks of Economic History'. We might coolly ask whether we now know more than that generation. In the fields in which I have worked great strides have undoubtedly been made, and great intellectual advances consolidated. Economic History has become more rigorous, more precise, more knowledgeable, and better framed than it was thirty years ago. And so it should be with the intellectual investment that has been made in that time. But I am not so sure that the progress is cumulative. Sometimes it seems that fewer people than ever are actually listening to economic historians. (In South Australia, for instance, the state has recently passed through a decade of exceedingly painful banking crises, yet this is a society which knows virtually nothing of its banking history). Currently almost all Economic History Departments in Australia have ceased to trade under their own flag. Economics and Commerce are now taught without context, perspective or knowledge of past experience; History is increasingly taught without its foundations. This is a strange and disappointing outcome. And, consequently, the 'Australian option' barely exists in the new century.

The idea that there are no great challenges and causes left would be preposterous. Most of our explanations of economic change are inadequate. Our understanding, for instance, of the role of women in the economy; of the roots of population change; of how and why certain economies after decades of stagnation, quite suddenly begin to grow rapidly; of the ultimate causes of the great diasporas - to mention a few matters - are still far from resolved. It is surely time for revival.

Eric Richards (b. Holt, Denbighshire, 3. 8. 1940) was educated at Notttingham University where he obtained a Ph. D. He was employed in Economics at the University of Adelaide in 1962, in History at the University of Stirling in 1966 and in Economic History at Flinders University in Adelaide in 1971. Some of his sabbaticals have been spent at Glasgow, Warwick, Birkbeck and Florence and he has strong connections with the RSSS at the ANU. He has been Professor of History at Flinders since 1975. His books include: *The Leviathan of Wealth. The Sutherland fortune in the Industrial Revolution* (1973); *A History of the Highland Clearances: Vols. 1 and 2* (1982 and 1985); *Patrick Sellar and the Highland Clearances: Homicide, Evictions and the Price of Progress* (1999) and *The Highland Clearances. People, Landlords and Rural Turmoil.* (2000).

The Long Period is with us Every Day of Our Lives

W. W. Rostow

Keynes commended to economists the dictum: 'In the long run we are all dead.'. His most famous work, *The General Theory*, was framed by short period assumptions. I have held to the view that the long run is with us every day of our lives. That goes for both history and the active world of policy. It should be added immediately that Keynes practised his craft mainly in inter-war Europe where unemployment rarely fell below 10% and reached, say, 25% or more in the Great Depression of the 1930s. It was natural for him to concentrate on the urgent problem of putting idle people to work. That required that he focus on the short-run demand factors in play, although he was thoroughly capable of speculating a hundred years ahead.[1] In our time, however, I am inclined to hold that my dictum better fits the case than Keynes's *bon mot* of the inter-war years.[2]

My commitment to the Marshallian long period means a commitment to take account of the short-run supply as well as the short-run demand factors in the life of economies, above all changes in population and the work-forces as well as technological change which lies at the heart of economic growth. But it means also taking account of non-economic factors as they affect the economy, as they often do; e.g., wars, the play of politics, non-economic factors which often can weaken or strengthen the will of peoples to absorb new technology. Thus my work at Yale and Oxford, requiring year-by-year, cycle-by-cycle analysis of the British economy, set me on this course both as an academic economist and as a public servant.

My direct answer to the question: What Economic History Means to Me is, therefore, quite simple: economic history has taught me that the long and short periods were, in modern economies and societies, always intertwined, and they are separated at great analytic cost. On the other hand, the introduction of long period factors requires increased complexity that must be faced in academic life and the making of policy. Mathematics is a first approximation and, sometimes a poor approximation of reality. As J. S. Mill wrote on the first pages of all six editions of his Principles: 'Except on matters of mere detail, there are perhaps no practical questions, even those which approach nearest to the character of purely economical questions, which admit of being decided on economical premises alone'.[3] Now that proposition was and is no news to economic historians. We make our living after all, mainly by studying long period factors: birth and death rates, technological breakthroughs and trends, institutional changes, development patterns through time, price trends and their causes, etc.

Malthus spoke for all of us when he and Ricardo probed vigorously but with great mutual respect, at their abiding difference.[4]

> 'The first business of philosophy [science]', said Malthus, 'is to account for things as they are . . . Where unforeseen causes may possibly be in operation, and the causes that are foreseen are liable to great variations in their strength and efficacy, an accurate yet comprehensive attention to facts is necessary . . .'

And down to about 1870 historians have had little to complain of so far as the classics in economics are concerned. The ties of David Hume and Adam Smith to history were direct and unembarrassed. And, with the partial exception of Ricardo – he was, after all, a pragmatic member of Parliament – the classics were in the spacious tradition of political economy, not in the tradition of the economics that succeeded it.

The change happened around 1870. Mainstream or orthodox economics ceased to trouble itself about economic growth and to focus on the precise distribution of income and the determination of price and output in an equilibrium, competitive market system. Essentially these systems were static; equilibrium was set in a short period framework, and it was therefore reversible.

This revolution did not capture all major economists of this period. The best of them – Alfred Marshall – not only contributed to so-called 'marginal' or 'utility' analysis but he dramatised that the ceaseless working of increasing returns rendered the favourite tool of the revolution – differential calculus – incomplete or non-operational. Therefore, Marshall concluded, economics should be a biological rather than a Newtonian science.

While mainstream economics went its merry way and dominated the university departments which began to appear in this era (1870-1914), economics not only narrowed, and became more elegant and precise, but it fragmented into new disciplines: demography; the history of science and technology including Schumpeter's innovations; welfare economics, which led to the first national income estimates; business cycle analysis; institutional analysis; and, of course, economic history. Economics has never recovered from this diaspora, even if the latter-day practitioners were located down the hall or on the next floor. Each speciality had its journal, its annual gathering, its more or less mannerly inner debates. The only thing lacking was that they paid little attention to one another. There was little authentic dialogue between them.

Since I shall shortly make the case for reversing 1870, let me give you one example of what happens when a serious question is addressed only in short period terms. Economists focused in the Great Depression and then after the Second World War on a thoroughly legitimate question: was capitalism inherently unstable and, therefore, was radical government intervention required to achieve and to maintain full employment? Or was it inherently stable? There were three answers.

First, there were the pessimists who dominated the conventional expectations of the future immediately before and after World War II. They more or less accepted what was known as the Harrod-Domar model which refined that analysis in Keynes's *General Theory*. Essentially they argued that the capitalist system was on a knife's edge. It would not generate sufficient investment to achieve and sustain full employment and would have to be supplemented on the side of effective demand by governmental action to avoid falling off the knife's edge.

Then came the post-war period which saw full employment and prosperity in the 1950s and 1960s in the industrial world. Round about the mid-1950s, the economists caught up with reality by producing models that automatically self-adjusted to maintain full employment and steady growth. There was the Cambridge Mass. Version which alleged that stability was achieved if one assumed the capital-labour ratio was variable: the substitution of labour for capital in depression, capital for labour in prosperity. Robert Solow, the father of this change of assumptions, concluded triumphantly:[5]

> [W]hen production takes place under the usual neo-classical conditions of variable proportions and constant returns to scale, no simple opposition between natural and warranted rates of growth is possible. There may not be – in fact in the case of the Cobb-Douglas function there never can be – any knife edge. The system can adjust to any given rate of growth of the labour force, and eventually approach a state of steady proportional expansion.

This doctrine was answered from Cambridge, England, by Nicholas Kaldor *et al*. Kaldor evoked a different change in the Harrod-Domar assumptions: a change in the proportion of income saved and spent in the course of the business cycle.[6]

> . . . a rise in investment, and thus in total demand, will raise prices and profit margins, and thus reduce real consumption, whilst a fall in investment, and thus in total demand, causes a fall in prices (relatively to the wage level) and thereby generates a compensating rise in real consumption. Assuming flexible prices (or rather flexible profit margins) the system is thus stable at full employment.

Then came the sudden rise of wheat and, especially, of oil prices, in 1972-1973. There was immediately a rapid subsidence of the debate about stable growth[7] and a highly volatile world economy operated awkwardly for a decade or more.

I have gone through this story because all three models were, by assumption, set up in short period terms. In the two decades of relatively stable growth and full employment there was, in fact, both a continent to repair and an enormous flow into the world economy of inventive innovation and technology hitherto not applied. Moreover the industrial countries enjoyed a passage of favourable terms of trade (after 1951), to say nothing of the baby boom which lasted until about 1960 in Europe and North America. All these and other long term factors were ignored. A homeric generation of growth was debated by the reigning economists in short period terms.

I have recalled this highly stylised history of our profession as a prelude to the second half of my paper which is about population in the twenty-first century, an urgent long-term problem of mortal significance. There are, in fact, an ample number of problems for the century ahead: social equity, privacy, the suppression of violence, the very fast technological revolution in the computer and the mapping of the genome – both driven as never before by rapid advances in basic science. But there is something special about what is going on in population. Not since the mid-eighteenth century has the human race faced, declining or, at best, stagnant populations. We stand right now between an almost universal decline of fertility and a foreseeable decline in populations. The gap is not long by a historian's standards. In fact, the decline in population has begun or will shortly begin in the former Soviet Union and Japan. Fertility is rapidly on the way down in more than 60 countries.

Here are a few statistics which show what is happening on a global basis. As background, a gross fertility rate of 2.1 (children per family) defines the replacement rate. Above that number a population rises in time; below, it falls. There is a general tendency of fertility (and, later, population) rates to correlate inversely with urbanisation, income per capita, education, and the proportion of the population using modern methods of birth control (see Table 1). These four determinants are obviously, to an important degree, related to one another.

Table 1
Total Fertility Rates

	1970	1992	2000 (estimated)
Low Income Economies	6.0	3.4	3.1
Lower Middle Income Economies	4.5	3.1	2.9
Upper Middle Income Economies	4.8	2.9	2.5
High Income Economies	2.4	1.7	1.4
World	-	-	2.9

Source: Reprinted by permission from *World Development Report, 1989* (New York: Oxford University Press, 1989), p. 216, Table 27.

There are a number of transitional countries, including some with large populations, whose fertility rates are rapidly decreasing; and a few already have fertility rates below 2.1 as shown in Table 2.

Table 2
Fertility Rates, Sample Transitional Countries

	1970	1980	1992	1999
Thailand	5.5	3.8	2.2	1.7
Turkey	4.9	4.3	3.4	3.0
Brazil	4.9	3.9	2.8	2.3
Mexico	6.3	4.3	3.2	2.8
S. Korea	4.3	2.6	1.8	1.7
Indonesia	5.9	4.3	2.9	2.7
India	5.8	5.0	3.7	3.3
China	5.8	2.5	2.0	1.8

Sources: The figures for 1970 and 1992 are from *The World Bank: The Development Report, 1998-1999*, Table 26. Those for 1980 and 1999 are from *The World Bank, Entering the 21ˢᵗ Century, World Development Report, 1999-2000*, Table 7, pp. 242-243.

Since the late eighteenth century, both birth rates and death rates have been falling; but the fall in death rates out-paced the fall in birth rates until the Great Depression of the 1930s. After the Second World War, however, world population rose sharply, due to the spread of the new antibiotics and the control of malaria. Birth rates have subsequently declined and converged with death rates almost irrespective of stage of growth (see Table 3).

Table 3
Death Rates, (excluding India and China), 1970 and 1992 (per thousand)

Countries by Income	1970	1992
Low Income	19	12
Lower Middle Income	12	9
Upper Middle Income	10	7
High Income	10	9

Source: Reprinted by permission from *World Bank Development Report 1989* (New York: Oxford University Press), 1989, p. 216, Table 27.

While the length of life in most countries has crept up, the circulatory diseases and cancer have thus far set a kind of limit to the fall of death rates. Africa south of the Sahara is a regional exception to the pattern with a fertility rate of 5.6, not far below the maximum.

Against this background, the overall long run estimates of peak global future population have systematically been falling. The medium figure now centres at about nine billion. At the edge of politics the future of welfare is being discussed or even acted upon, as the number of people in the working force declines relative to those retired. In the United States the age of retirement, for example, has been quietly raised by two years (from 65 to 67) and the question has been raised of putting a part of pension funds into private markets.

Meanwhile, Chinese leaders are publicly sharing the enormous calculated rise in the retired population: from roughly 10% of the total population in 1997 to 21% by the year 2030. We are talking about creating a safety net in 2030 for 339 million people.[8] But, none of the measures taken around the world thus far, including fiscal subsidies to having extra children, have stemmed the decline in fertility. The demographic forces now underway promise in time to engulf a good part of the world unless the population question moves away from the periphery to the centre of global politics; unless a positive vision of the future is agreed among the political leaders and peoples of the affected countries; and unless a policy capable of reversing the trend already so strongly underway, is mounted and sustained on a proper scale.

The vision is to attain (or in many countries to re-attain) a fertility level that will guarantee the replacement level of population (2.1). This should be backed by R & D and innovation which will in the short run, raise the productivity level per worker in the time of attenuation of the workforce; and for the long pull to reconcile a static population with a steady improvement in the quality of life and the standard of living.

The policy that is needed to implement this vision has three components.
1. *A time-buying programme* that will expand the workforce and its productivity during the period of decline of fertility and of rebuilding the workforce. The main components of this policy are: A) a rise in the retirement age. Those above 65 who are able should be induced to stay in the workforce. B) An increase in immigration can play an important role but has limits. A rise in income per capita plus a relative increase of the elderly population in the country now exporting labour will reduce candidates for immigration. Politically significant resistance in the host country to 'excessive' immigration is already evident in a number of European countries. C) Increased training for the workforce of those now on welfare or in low-level jobs. This is not now merely a matter of morality or of social welfare budgets, but an essential element in maximising the size of the workforce. D) Increased labour-saving innovation, for example robots, will raise productivity and, in effect, expand the workforce.

2. *A consensus achieved by men and women* which will permit an expansion of the fertility rate to 2.1 for countries below that level; and, for those now above that level but falling, to achieve a levelling off at 2.1. This will require a kind of *de facto* treaty in which the women continue to expand their role in the workforce while families are provided with well-run nurseries (close to the place of work); pregnancy leave, for men as well as women, and men sharing more than they do now the tasks of the family and household. This non-economic and non-technical part of the task is the most difficult; but it runs with the grain of a world-wide trend.

3. *Acceptance, as a long- term goal, of a constant population with continued R & D and innovation.* This would not only permit a regular growth in income per head but an increase in the quality of society. This will require private and public investment and/or an increase in private consumption to fill the gaps of perhaps 50% in investment previously related to an increase in population – an unfamiliar problem, but one capable of solution. Incidentally, J. S. Mill suggested this formula a century and a half ago.

In short, we can no longer take population increase for granted. The human race must assume responsibility for its destiny.

Returning to the central theme of this paper, I believe that it is time to reverse in spirit the revolution of 1870 and the diaspora which followed; to talk to one another at least; to work together if possible. The prospect for the twenty-first century is for dramatic, and hopefully related, changes in two major long period factors: technology and population. There is not much use in elaborating the technological possibilities if we do not solve the population problem. Ideally, the two revolutions should support one another. More broadly, it is now time for us to bring what we have learned in our several disciplines, in our time of separation, to bear on these grand long-term factors on which our destiny depends.

Walt Whitman Rostow (b. New York City, 17. 10. 1916) was educated at Yale University and was Rhodes Scholar at Oxford University. He served in the Office of Strategic Services and as a major in US army during the war. Taught at the Universities of Oxford, Cambridge and MIT, returning to government service as Deputy Special Assistant for National Security Affairs and in the Policy Planning Council, and as Special Assistant to the President during the Kennedy administration. He then taught at the University of Texas. Has written seminal works on economic growth and fluctuations.

---

[1] J. M. Keynes, 'Economic Possibilities for our Grandchildren' in *Essays in Persuasion* (London: Macmillan, 1931).

[2] W. W. Rostow, *Concept and Controversy: Sixty Years of Taking Ideas to Market*, mss., Chapter 13, p. 1.

[3] W. W. Rostow, *Theorists of Economic Growth from David Hume to the Present* (New York: Oxford University Press, 1990), p. 94.

[4] W. W. Rostow, *Theorists*, p. 53.

[5] W. W. Rostow, *Theorists*, p. 335.

[6] W. W. Rostow, *Theorists*, p. 336.

[7] W. W. Rostow, *Theorists*, p. 333.

[8] W. W. Rostow, *The Great Population Spike and After* (New York: Oxford University Press, 1998), p. 203.

Economic (*and Social?*) History

Edward Royle

In their quest for intellectual respectability, academics with special but marginal interests are driven to create new disciplines to define their territories and claim equal treatment with more established subjects. So, in the last third of the nineteenth century, when university curricula were still dominated by mathematics and the classics, the social sciences and history staked their claim to be subjects for the modern world. The new social sciences in England received an important addition to their credibility in 1900 with the admission of the London School of Economics and Political Science to the University of London,[1] while, in the older universities of Cambridge and Oxford, history became the most popular humanities subject.[2]

An important development at the older universities was the emergence from within Economics (or Political Economy) and History of a hybrid, Economic History, the identity of which in Britain was shaped by the lectures and publications of those who pioneered the subject before the First World War. In Cambridge, William Cunningham taught 'Political Economy and Economic History' for the new History tripos and produced a text book, *The Growth of English Industry and Commerce,* first published in 1882.[3] Here, and in the lectures of Arnold Toynbee at Oxford, economic history was, rightly or wrongly, identified with the history of economic development in the first industrial nation of the western world, setting out to explain the economic greatness of Britain at that moment when the Great Depression was calling it into question.

In staking a claim for their subject, teachers of Economic History needed an equivalent to that cornerstone of constitutional history, William Stubbs's *Select Charters* (1870). They found it in *English Economic History. Select Documents*, compiled by A. E. Bland, P. A. Brown and R. H. Tawney, to serve the needs of their adult education students in the Workers' Educational Association. Their selection illustrates the problem of definition implicit in the emergence of 'economic history' as a separate subject for study. As they put it, 'we are not so incautious as to be tempted into a discussion of what exactly Economic History means'. Indeed, they admitted to having neglected some topics which might be thought central, such as taxation and foreign trade, whilst paying 'excessive attention' to, among other things, social conditions. In an effort to counter the 'natural bias' of economic historians towards 'those aspects of economic development which come under the eyes of the State' they had included illustrations of 'the humbler but often more significant movements which spring from below'.[4]

So from the start Economic History had a crisis of identity which readily assumed a political dimension. As the story of economic development, it could easily slip into what Herbert Butterfield was to condemn as 'Whig' history.[5] Parallel to the celebration of English constitutional liberty could easily come the celebration of English capitalism. Who could deny the wonders of economic progress? Bland, Brown and Tawney hinted at an answer - those concerned with 'history from below'. Cunningham had shown an awareness - and some unease - at the implications of industrialisation in considering human welfare during the age of *laissez faire*; this was taken further and with more overt sympathy by Lawrence and Barbara Hammond in their studies of the labouring classes.[6] But was this Economic History, or was yet another sub-discipline of history emerging - Social History?

Though what is now called Social History had roots in the new Economic History of the pre-Great War generation, other traces can be found in legal history which led not so much to a history *from* below as a history *of* below as recorded in English law. The greatest of these works was F. W. Maitland's *Domesday Book and Beyond*, first published in 1897, which touched on issues of contemporary interest - land law and taxation. The origins and nature of feudalism in England were of significance to a generation concerned about the aristocracy's monopoly of the land and the distribution of hereditary wealth. It was within this radical context that the pioneering book on living standards was written in 1884, J. E. Thorold Rogers, *Six Centuries of Work and Wages*. Rogers was both an Oxford political economist and a politically active Radical.

From these roots, in law, politics and economics, Economic History grew. Perhaps the most influential individual bringing these strands together was J. H. Clapham, who between 1908 and 1935 used his lectures to undergraduates at Cambridge to take them through the economic development of Britain 'from prehistoric times to our own'. If anything has defined the subject, both in its day and since, it was this lecture series, immortalised after his death in a published version up to 1750, arranged by John Saltmarsh whose own lectures at Cambridge continued the Clapham tradition into the 1960s.[7]

In his sequel to 'Clapham's *Concise*', W. H. B. Court of Birmingham showed himself aware of the moral as well as intellectual difficulties of interpreting an age with different values and expectations from one's own.[8] He was referring to the controversy over the standard of living in the early Industrial Revolution which dominated historiography from the 1920s to the 1960s and which still fuels articles in economic history journals. Though the fissure lines are neither straight nor neat between the two schools of thought, the 'optimists' in this famous controversy tended to emphasise economic data and argue from the point of view of the national economy, whereas the 'pessimists' looked at history from below, stressing the human experiences of those who were the 'victims' of economic change. This division broadly coincided with the ideological division between the 'right' who saw in the advance of capitalism and *laissez-faire* economics a generally benign and improving influence and those on the 'left' who thought the contrary. Though to orthodox Marxists capitalism was a necessary evil, to others on the left it was a wrong turning, made to appear necessary only with hindsight. The phrase 'industrial revolution' had, after all, been adopted by Friedrich Engels in 1845, borrowing the language of politics to describe the social impact of the economic changes of his day.[9] When Arnold Toynbee introduced the phrase to academic scholarship in his Oxford lectures over thirty years later, like Cunningham at Cambridge he still included some matter on social conditions but devoted more of his time to economics, establishing what became the standard interpretation of the industrial revolution located firmly on the economic side of history.[10]

With careful argument and much evidence to support their case, the 'establishment' in Economic History teaching, from Clapham to T. S. Ashton, supported the optimistic view of the industrial revolution while the liberal and Marxist left, from the Hammonds to E. J.

Hobsbawm, led the pessimists. A critical turning point came in the 1960s when Marxism, social history and history from below converged in a powerful and radical alternative to the accepted ideas of Economic History. Its flagship was E. P. Thompson's *Making of the English Working Class* (1963). Thompson was in no doubt as to the identity of 'the enemy'. With incisive, barbed and memorable wit he characterised the standard of living debate: 'The 'average' working man['s] . . . share in the 'benefits of economic progress' consisted of more potatoes, a few articles of cotton clothing for his family, soap and candles, some tea and sugar, and a great many articles in the *Economic History Review*'.[11] Thompson's book was, in the words of the *Guardian* headline over Peter Laslett's review of *The Making*, 'Unfair to Capitalism'.[12]

The emergence of Social History, like a cuckoo hatched in the nest of Economic History, caused a double crisis of identity. Economic historians had come to assume that their subject was a coherent 'discipline'. Its purpose was to study past economies and economic development, not in a disembodied way, but within the context of past societies. Social history was therefore an integral part of their subject. Now social historians were asserting their independence, demanding the same space and recognition that economic historians had earlier carved out for themselves. At the same time, economic historians, wishing to strengthen their credentials as historians of the economy, were turning to the more theoretical and mathematical aspects of their subject and away from both the immeasurable depths of human experience and the taint of amateurism carried over from the Tawney WEA tradition (within which Thompson also operated). To validate their independence, social historians responded in kind, with the application of social theory and social science methods to their study of history.

The forces building these disciplinary boundaries within history are understandable: identity is important in the market place; books need to be advertised in publishers' catalogues and placed on certain shelves in libraries according to known and accepted if not always acceptable criteria. As the subject matter being studied becomes more specialised, demanding particular expertise, so too do the journals, monographs and courses. The explosion in academic life since the 1960s has produced fragmentation, yet another step in that long process from general to particular knowledge whereby as we know more, we know it about less. But against the centrifugal forces of modern academic existence are contrary pressures. As resources become increasingly scarce no subject wishes to yield territory to another. Economics and Economic History departments have not been keen to recognise the independence of their social historians if that means transfer of resource. Neither the Economic History Society nor the *Economic History Review* have felt that their restrictive titles should preclude them from continuing to represent social history as a legitimate interest. Economic History retains its claim to Social History but at a cost to the latter. In ESRC-funded training for social historians, a knowledge of economics is given priority over other social science skills. The assumption remains that Social History is a part of Economic History, which itself is closely allied to Economics. In that classic compromise worked out between the British Academy and the ESRC, Social History was defined by its methodology not its subject matter. This may be a sensible expedient, but that methodology should no longer be assumed to relate principally to Economics: many modern social historians would see a closer ally in the other social sciences; in particular, Sociology.

Apart from bureaucratic structures, scare resources have also countered the Balkanisation of the past. Economic and Social History alike have seen their academic identities threatened, either by absorption into Economics departments greedy for student numbers in a growing A-level subject; or into History departments; or into colossal schools of The Past in which

Classics (largely reduced to Ancient History), Archaeology, History and Economic History have merged. For those who have carefully cultivated their distinctive identities, fostering the 'hard' edges of their disciplines, and whose livelihoods depend on such distinctiveness, this attack on their independence is a serious threat to their aspiration to be a science amid the softer and more numerous ranks of mere historians.

Yet there is also a gain in this. There is a danger that, in dividing the past into different disciplines for political, financial and academic convenience, we forget that the past itself is not so divided. Academic divisions can limit understanding. In their early defence of teaching English economic history, Bland, Brown and Tawney asserted, 'That Economic History cannot be studied apart from Constitutional and Political History is a commonplace to which we subscribe'.[13] Though as an apologetic this was certainly diplomatic, it was nevertheless true. Rather more aggressively defending Social History in the early 1940s, G. M. Trevelyan wrote, 'Without social history, economic history is barren and political history is unintelligible'.[14] Emphasis may determine subject matter and a variety of methodological tools might be used, but for a rounded understanding of human experience in the past, all approaches - economic, social and political - are needed simultaneously by the student and researcher alike. Marc Bloch's *Feudal Society*, completed in 1940, remains a challenge and reproach to the fragmented nature of our modern subject.

This essay, like all history, is personal and the telling of a history reflects the historian. Much has been omitted which should have been included and in abridgement lie the dangers of superficiality and bias. This has been an essay born of the experience of Cambridge in the early 1960s. Even so there has been no mention of the inspirational lecturing of M. M. Postan, a giant in reputation if not in stature, or other significant figures in the making of Economic History. Instead there has been the recollection of a social historian struggling to be born in a world torn between entrenched traditions of Constitutional and Economic History, with the latter giving only grudging recognition to a misunderstood fragment of what passed for Social History. And there is the further recollection of a bewhiskered John Saltmarsh intoning the 'Economic History of England', concisely, to a still-crowded lecture hall three mornings a week, including that memorable lecture when, almost shyly, at the mention of E. M. Carus-Wilson he produced from beneath the lectern a model of a thirteenth-century fulling mill, flicked the water wheel round, and let the hammer rise and fall.[15] Within months, Thompson had produced his passionate account of the Luddites. The world for me could never be the same again.

Edward Royle (b. Huddersfield, 29. 3. 1944 in the former workhouse within yards of where the Luddites murdered William Horsfall in 1812). He was a student at Christ's College, Cambridge, but his research on Jacob Holyoake and the Secularist Movement was supervised by George Kitson Clark of Trinity. After four years as a Fellow of Selwyn College he moved to the University of York in 1972, where he is now a Professor of History. He has published widely on the social history of Britain since the mid-eighteenth century, with particular interests in freethought, religious organisations and beliefs, radical politics and many aspects of local and regional history.

---

[1] McGregor, O. R., 'The Social Sciences' in Thompson, F. M. L., (ed.), *The University of London and the World of Learning, 1836-1986* (London, 1990), pp. 209-24.
[2] Roderick, G. W. and Stephens, M. D., *Education and Industry in the Nineteenth Century: The English Disease?* (London, 1978), pp. 92-6.

[3] Kitson Clark, G. S. R., 'A Hundred Years of the Teaching of History at Cambridge, 1873-1973', *Historical Journal* 16 (1973), p. 537; Kenyon, J. P., *The History Men*,2nd edition (London, 1993), pp. 246-52.

[4] Bland, A. E., Brown, P. A. and Tawney, R. H. (eds), *English Economic History. Select Documents* (London, 1930), pp. v, vii.

[5] Butterfield, H., *The Whig Interpretation of History* (London, 1931).

[6] Hammond J. L. and B., *The Village Labourer, 1760-1832* (London, 1911); *The Town Labourer, 1760-1832* (London, 1917); *The Skilled Labourer, 1760-1832* (London, 1919).

[7] Clapham, J. H., *A Concise Economic History of Britain from the earliest times to 1750* (Cambridge, 1949, reprinted 1957), pp. v-vi.

[8] Court, W. H. B., *A Concise Economic History of Britain from 1750 to Recent Times* (Cambridge, 1954, reprinted 1958), pp. v-vi.

[9] Engels, F., *Die Lage der arbeitenden Klasse in England* (Leipzig, 1845). Engels used both *die industrielle Revolution* and *die industrielle Umwälzung*.

[10] Toynbee, A., *Lectures on the Industrial Revolution in England* (London, 1884).

[11] Thompson, E. P., *The Making of the English Working Class* (London, 1963), p. 318.

[12] *Guardian*, 22 Nov. 1963.

[13] Bland, Brown and Tawney, *Select Documents*, p. v.

[14] Trevelyan, G. M: *English Social History,* 2nd edition (London, 1946), p. vii.

[15] See Clapham, *Concise Economic History* (1957 reprint), pp. 154-5.

What Economic History Means to Me

William D. Rubinstein

Economic history is often seen to polarise around two methodologies, econometric economic history, dominant in the United States, and economic history with a social historical or sociological emphasis, as has been dominant in Britain, especially prior to the 1970s. In many respects they have little in common. The extreme practitioners of one kind, as a rule, are not truly at home with the alternative view of economic history. Indeed, economic historians on the sociological side of the divide are not technically qualified to work with econometric formulae and frames of reference. There may be evident differences in the temperaments of the two poles, with econometric history more hard-nosed and 'masculine' compared with sociologically-oriented economic history.

My own work in this field has largely been an attempt to describe the evolution of Britain's elite structure since the mid-eighteenth century, based especially in a comprehensive analysis of wealth-holding from the probate and income tax records. The aim of my work has thus always been very definitely on the sociological side of the divide, in the tradition of, among others, Harold Perkin, but employing very considerable, far-reaching, and painstaking quantitative evidence from which to infer conclusions about the composition and evolution of Britain's elites. I am personally not at all at home with econometric approaches to economic history, and have never attempted to employ them in my work. On the other hand, I admire the penchant of econometric history to address the big questions, in contrast to socially-oriented economic history which often studies the small-scale. The conclusions which are drawn from the evidence on either side is often subjective, but non-quantitative economic history runs the risk of virtual pure subjectivity, as, for instance, with the 'standard of living' debate of a generation ago, which largely reflected the ideological presuppositions of its participants.

During the past 20 or 25 years, economic history as a discipline has certainly declined as a single, unified field of study. American-style econometric history has become more solidified and confident as has, on the other extreme, social history of a type which, in the Social History Society of the U.K., is probably too self-indulgent and lacking in methodological rigour. Also, many sub-disciplines and interest groups have, in essence, hived off from the centre – urban history, labour history, feminist history, and so on – leaving a greatly attentuated core discipline, which I take to be the type of historical issues discussed and debated at the Economic History Society conference and in the *Economic History Review*. In one sense this is a great pity, and this sense of pessimism has been enhanced for me by the trivial nature of much of the material which the editors of the *Review* have chosen to publish.

Economic history, at least until one reaches some of the more extreme areas on the social historical wing of the divide, is *a priori* the field of history most immune from the undermining of historiography *per se* advanced by the 'post-modernists'. Economic history relies wholly, or almost wholly, on both the objective meaningfulness and the objective accuracy of economic and other quantitative data from the past, which, for most economic historians, enjoys an epistemological priority over subjective evidence or the 'narratives' of individual persons. This is, in my view, all to the good. The curious popularity of 'post modernism' seems to me to be almost wholly deplorable, although there may be some merit in emphasising the highly ambiguous nature of individual identities and beliefs. It carries with it its own none too well-concealed set of ideological presuppositions, being very largely a replacement for now-discredited Marxism, with a similar *a priori* unproven central tacit assumption that there is always an 'establishment' which is reactionary and repressive. Paradoxically, although post-modernism claims to prioritise the individual beliefs of 'ordinary' people, the notion of history of the person in the street is invariably that of 'kings, dates and battles', history of a kind which most academic historians would view as beneath contempt. The fate of the Princes in the Tower, or whether the *Titanic* was deliberately sunk by a conspiracy of its owners, is, to most 'ordinary' people, much more the very substance of history than anything we study.

The viewpoint about British history with which I have been generally associated – the 'gentlemanly capitalism' school, although my interpretation derives from very different evidence than does that of Cain and Hopkins – has happily become more popular and mainstream over the past thirty years. The crucial importance of the City of London in Britain's economic development, virtually ignored or unknown thirty years ago, has since become if not exactly a commonplace, at least widely acknowledged. There is less sheer prejudice against studying the rich than I encountered 25 or 30 years ago, either from old-fashioned right-wingers aghast at intrusive foreign vulgarity, or from left-wingers who objected to 'hero-worshipping' the exploiters of the poor. Today, the various Rich Lists have become an accepted part of social information. This change is not wholly for the better. Few people, I think, would prefer to live in a society which, like the United States, has money as its only social value or test of worth. Britain has, however, gone very far down the American road, and shows no signs of turning back. This was, I think, almost wholly unpredictable 25 years ago. Who now recalls the enormous growth in Marxist studies and Marxist-derived academic publications of the 1970s and early 1980s? Today these seem quaint, their artifacts sitting on university library shelves as unread as so many volumes of Thomistic philosophy. This change has not necessarily been wholly desirable. Whatever else might be said about it, Marxism provided both intellectual rigour and a sweeping view of history which was, for so many intellectuals, both convincing and moving. The 'end of ideology', so widely hailed in the 1950s, has in fact become a reality today, for better or worse. The old ideologies disagreed on 10,000 things, but they had in common a core belief in history and an intellectual enterprise combining rigour with imagination to sustain it. However destructive the old ideologies might have been in practice, their passing – we are all vague liberals now – is something of a tragedy. We may be the last survivors of a vanished age.

William D. Rubinstein (b. 1946) was educated at Swarthmore College and Johns Hopkins University, and has held chairs at Deakin University in Victoria, Australia and (since 1995) at the University of Wales, Aberystwyth. He is the author of *Men of Property: The Very Rich in Britain since the Industrial Revolution* (1981) and *Capitalism, Culture and Decline in Britain 1750-1990* (1993), among other works.

Understanding Ourselves in Time and in Comparative Perspective

Osamu Saito

Economic history is the study of the economic past by a present-day historian. This, on the face of it, seems to be taken to imply that, just as in political history and other branches of traditional historical inquiry, its concerns are all about change. But economic history means, to me at least, a history in which both questions of 'what changed' and 'what remained unchanged' should be addressed.

Changes in prices, trade, consumption, production and population are topics the economic historians are usually concerned with. All these changes, according to the Braudelian tradition of the tripartite scheme of historical time, belong to the medium *durée* (unlike political and diplomatic historians, we do not necessarily need to arouse a sense of the days or months passing). Some economic historians are more interested in longer-run changes, especially transition paths to modernity. They often postulate that on each side of the transition period there is something synchronic. But the chief concern of the economic historians of that kind is not to discover something constant over time, but to delineate broad contrasts and changes that are supposed to have taken place in the period of transformation. However, are we right in assuming that we can ignore things remaining unchanged even for the pre-modern/modern transition period?

Take, for example, Peter Laslett's *The world we have lost.*[1] Originally the book was the author's attempt to elucidate the 'structure of English society as it was before the Industrial Revolution, and to make some comparison with its structure in the twentieth century', in the hope that the contrast established as such would help the readers understand themselves in time.[2] However, despite this aim, which is manifested in its title *The world we have lost*, it is not necessarily a book about changes English people experienced over the past centuries. It is also about what remained unchanged in English history. Based on research done at the Cambridge Group, the book rejects the view that today's nuclear families evolved from the regime of large and complex families in the past. The age at marriage was relatively high in the English past, reflecting that the formation of a new household was tied with marriage, one of the key demographic variables. The demographic profiles sketched in the book are now fully supported by the monumental work by Tony Wrigley and his associates. With the empirical evidence established, we can now distinguish real changes that took place during the three-century period, from what kept functioning throughout this time of transformation.

Another case in point is the work by Tom Smith, who has written widely on the economic and social history of both traditional and modern Japan. His fine articles on various topics, ranging from demography to time discipline (assembled later in a book of essays entitled *Native sources of Japanese industrialisation*), are attempts to find 'native sources' of the success Japan achieved after the encounter with the West.[3] However, what he discovered as undercurrents in the course of the country's remarkable transformation was the persistent operation of factors that made 'modern Japanese society similar to but profoundly different from Western counterparts'.[4] In other words, he too has found what remained unchanged in Japanese history, and it was his argument that much of the country's modern transformation was made possible by elements that had been operating there for a very long time.

My own research on a more specific topic, work patterns, also lends support to such interpretations. My interest was in the work patterns of men and women in the household context and how those patterns changed over time in relation to economic and population changes. What I had in mind initially was some theoretical expectations of a 'backward bending supply curve' of labour giving way to the normal, familiar one illustrated in the textbook of economics. The 'backward bending' type was thought to be able to describe nicely the ways in which people of the pre-industrial age behaved, a set of behavioural traits distinctly different from labour supply patterns common to us all living in modern times.[5] The research plan was to work on two structurally different societies, England and Japan, in the hope that two different sets of characteristics would be found in two different types of pre-industrial society, and that we would to able to trace two separate paths to the modern regime, i.e. a process of convergence. The more I knew of the cases I chose, however, the more sceptical I became of the assumption lying behind this view, a way of thinking that assumes a sharp divide between industrial and pre-industrial, modern and pre-modern. The evidence I could assemble suggested strongly that English labouring families and Japanese peasant cultivators in the past, on the one hand, and present-day office workers in any developed country, on the other, all operate on the same principles, i.e. necessity and opportunity.

Think of a 10-year-old boy who had to work in a nearby colliery because of high prices of bread bringing the real value of his father's weekly earnings down below the level of the Speenhamland table of 'what should be the weekly income of the industrious poor'; and a Tokugawa farm girl who was sent into filthy, urban service because her peasant father could not pay the rents because of successive harvest failures; and also a teenager in any country of today's developed world, who is forced to give up going to college and to take a low-paid job instead after a substantial cut in family benefits was announced. They are all driven by 'necessity'. In contrast, 'opportunity' works in a different direction. A woman of dexterity lured by rising wages, be this in an English lace-making area or in a Japanese silk-reeling district, was probably not so much motivated by necessity, but was trying not to miss an opportunity to improve her material wellbeing, just as is the case with a present-day qualified woman applicant for an administrative post. The actual change in the aggregate supply of labour, which we can observe in a particular country of a particular time period, is an outcome of whether necessity outweighed opportunity, or the other way round. This is a sort of micro-economic truism.

Although this is almost self-evident, it helps us understand, not just why it is difficult to get rid of, for example, women's and children's low-paid employment even in an industrialising, expanding economy such as England in the late eighteenth and early nineteenth centuries. We can also understand why growth of Japanese agriculture and its commercialisation kept the peasantry on the land despite the country's successful industrialisation in the nineteenth century. In the former case, the necessity factor operated in the direction we would normally expect: in lower sections of the society, any decline in household income meant an increase in the necessity of family members to go out to work in order to supplement the household earnings. Put differently, it implies that married women's and children's participation in the labour force would decline as the economy grew – unless income inequality widened.[6] In the

321

latter case, on the other hand, the same necessity factor functioned in the *opposite* direction – the expansion of sericulture and other forms of market-oriented farm activities, plus a gradual output growth in rice farming in nineteenth-century rural Japan, reduced the necessity for the peasant farm households to force their family members to take up low-paid industrial employment. Indeed, it is established, though for a later period, that the effects of both farming and sericulture were negatively related to the hours actually worked by farm family members in *non-farm* employment. When agricultural growth began to taper off, or when the overseas silk market collapsed, however, the shift of workforce from the agricultural to the industrial sector would speed up and, hence, the rural-urban wage differentials would widen. Indeed, these are what actually happened in the Japanese economy of the interwar period.[7]

Such English-Japanese differences are half structural and half cultural. Structural, because the Japanese peasant, however poor he may have appeared, was self-employed and, unlike his English counterpart, had family labour and other means of production at his command. Cultural, because the Japanese peasant family was governed by the rules of a vertically constructed stem family household system (not of a nuclear type, nor of a multiple type), which had significant implications on labour supply behaviour and the age and gender divisions of labour as well as on marriage and fertility profiles, making those attributes look very different from the English.[8] In short, both *necessity and opportunity* are at work in both pre-modern and modern times, as well as in both England and Japan.

Clearly, we must not draw a hasty conclusion from seemingly contrasting statements about past and present situations. It is widely agreed that seventeenth- and eighteenth-century English authors witnessed that the labouring poor exhibited a tendency to be idle when real wages were higher[9] whereas modern economists, be they classical or neo-classical, see that workers ready to offer more labour for higher wages, conforming to the general law, that the higher the price the greater the supply. Does this difference in observation reflect an actual change in people's behaviour? Is a view of modern scholars always more realistic than that of their ancestors? According to evidence we now have, it is likely that the ways in which labour supply was determined remained largely the same from the eighteenth to the nineteenth century. I have argued elsewhere that for the working poor in the English industrial revolution, the *aggregate* schedule of labour supply, if constructed, may have been 'negatively sloped'.[10] In other words, the shape of the supply schedule turned out to be the same as in the days of 'backward sloping'. The only difference is that the seventeenth- and eighteenth-century economists were concerned with periods of higher wages, i.e. a move to the right on the slope of the supply curve whereas, in the days of industrialisation, more problematic was a move to the left on the same slope, by which lower wages resulted in an excess supply of labour.

A similar point may be made in relation to assumptions about peasant behaviour. The peasant has often been depicted as an agent having little to do with the modern *homo economicus*. As the above account of the Japanese peasantry indicates, however, it is not unlikely that there is some rationality in the peasants' economic behaviour. A majority of them are undoubtedly risk averters, operating on the 'safety-first principle'. Their profit motive may not particularly activate them, but it does not necessarily mean that they cannot weigh costs and benefits of their own action. As far as the allocation of time within the household is concerned, between leisure and income-earning activity, between domestic and productive tasks, and between farm and non-farm activities, they cannot be irrational. Indeed, what Tom Smith's work, as well as my own, has suggested is that the Japanese tenant cultivator was the 'rational peasant' in the sense that the eighteenth-century English labourer was.[11]

Undoubtedly there were genuine changes taking place in modern economic and population history. Various factors contributed to expand opportunities and remove some of the necessity factors (while necessity was still operating nonetheless), all of which are associated with industrialisation, rising living standards and the growth of the collectivity. But the timing of change seems to have been different from what the conventional chronology indicates. The real break with the past came much later in both countries, since traditional elements tended to continue to function during the first phases of modern economic growth. Some of those traditional forces were carry-overs from the past. However, some others were not just carry-overs bound to disappear as time went on. The point Peter Laslett made in his book is that, without knowledge about the past familial regimes, it is difficult to decide how to make welfare provisions for lonely elderly and other socially disadvantaged people in industrial society. As for Japan, it was Tom Smith's contention that her industrial success was made possible by the traditional elements, such as those associated with the ways in which the peasant family economy was run. How industrial activity was accommodated into household activities, how the structure and composition of the family workforce was maintained, and how time discipline was developed within the household economy – these were resources fully mobilised in the process of industrialisation.

Technological progress, state growth and global contacts are the forces to bring change into our material life, while the combination of micro-economic truisms and familial systems plays the *basso continuo* in history. Economic and population history appeal to me because they attempt to advance a balanced view of what changed and what did not change in the past in comparative perspective: this is nothing but 'understanding ourselves in time'.

Osamu Saito (b. 1. 4. 1946) was educated at Keio, Tokyo, where he subsequently received a D.Econ. Having lectured in economic history at Keio, he became a research professor at the Institute of Economic Research, Hitotsubashi University, a post he still holds. He is currently Director of the Institute and has held visiting positions at the University of Sheffield and the Cambridge Group for the History of Population and Social Structure. He has written on protoindustrialsation and various topics in historical demography, but his unabated research interest is in work patterns of men and women and their household behaviour in the past.

---

[1] Laslett, P., *The world we have lost: further explored*, 3rd edn (London, 1983). Its final chapter is entitled 'Understanding ourselves in time'.
[2] Ibid. p.xv.
[3] Smith, T.C., *Native sources of Japanese industrialisation, 1750-1920* (Berkeley, 1988). See also *Nakahara: population and family farming in a Japanese village, 1717-1830* (Stanford, 1977).
[4] Smith, *Native sources*, p.1.
[5] A concise account of this supposed transition is found in P. Deane, *The first industrial revolution*, 2nd edn (Cambridge, 1979), pp.149-150.
[6] Saito, O., 'Labour supply behaviour of the poor in the English industrial revolution', *Journal of European Economic History*, 10 (1981). See also 'Occupational structure, wages, and age patterns of female labour force participation in England and Wales in the nineteenth century', *Keio Economic Studies*, XVI (1979), and 'Who worked when? Lifetime profiles of labour-force participation in Cardington and Corfe Castle in the late eighteenth and mid nineteenth centuries', *Local Population Studies*, 22 (1979), reprinted in D. Mills and K. Schürer, eds., *Local communities in the Victorian census enumerators' books* (Oxford, 1996).
[7] Saito, O., 'The rural economy: commercial agriculture, by-employment and wage work', in M. Jansen and G. Rozman, eds., *Japan in transition: from Tokugawa to Meiji* (Princeton, 1986).
[8] On women and children, see O. Saito, 'Gender, workload and agricultural progress: Japan's historical experience in perspective', in R. Leboutte, ed., *Proto-industrialisation: recent research and new perspectives* (Geneva, 1996) and 'Children's work, industrialism and the family economy in Japan, 1872-1926', in H. Cunningham and P.P. Viazzo, eds., *Child labour in historical perspective, 1800-1985: case studies from Europe, Japan and Columbia* (Florence, 1996).
[9] Such views are documented in E.S. Furniss' classic, *The position of the labourer in a system of nationalism: a*

study in the labour theories of the later English mercantilists (Boston, 1920; reprint edn New York, 1957), especially ch.iv.

[10] Saito, 'Labour supply behaviour', p.648.

[11] For the debate on 'rationality' and the 'safety-first principle' in peasants' behaviour, see J.C. Scott, *The moral economy of the peasant: rebellion and subsistence in southeast Asia* (New Haven, 1976), and S.L. Popkin, *The rational peasant: the political economy of rural society in Vietnam* (Berkeley, 1979).

Memories and Reflections

Michael Sanderson

I came late to economic history. My sixth form course in the 1950s consisted almost entirely of history as politics and high diplomacy with ancient textbooks by Sir John Marriot. The subtext was how efficient governments suppressed dissent at home and acted in a suitably proud manner to foreign nations abroad. But economic considerations scarcely entered the picture. I suppose that we were following some old A level syllabus. Also my history master had suspicions about the intellectual respectability of economics (which in my school was linked with geography) and of industry generally – compounded by a false career start in a Birmingham bolt factory. He was a recent graduate of Trinity College Cambridge and led me to believe that economic history was not fashionable at Cambridge. This was dangerous advice since when I repeated it in my Cambridge entrance interview, the interviewer was a young (and to me unknown) Peter Mathias, He expressed concern that I had been given this impression which he assured me was false. nevertheless he let me in.

Perhaps, as if to offset my naïve misconception, I put special effort into my first undergraduate economic history essay. As I earnestly droned through all the duties of the reeve and hayward on a mediaeval manor, Peter sank deeper in his tutorial chair and concluded with kindly encouragement that 'that was very – thorough'. But I did very little economic history as an undergraduate, devoting much of the third year to French intellectual history. I still enjoy teaching French history to third years. When it came to choosing a Ph.D. subject my original intention was something on the political thought of state education but was advised that a topic dealing with realities based on unpublished documentation was preferable. Work on education in Lancashire during the industrial revolution entailed grinding through county, urban, national and ecclesiastical archives. The Lancashire County Record Office was then one table and a chair; the Chester Diocesan Archives were in the old gaol. It proved a good self education in research and brought me more into the area of economic and social history. Peter Mathias (who was not my supervisor) also helped by pointing me towards contemporary writing on the economics of education since economists were then becoming interested in the relevance of education for industrialisation. In my final year of research I began thinking about jobs and my then research interest related more closely to economic history than to other traditional categories. Accordingly I began a re-education, attending the courses of David Joslin on the British economy 1900-1930, Neil McKendrick on the Industrial Revolution and R.C.O. Mathews's first year economics lectures. I was fortunate enough to gain an assistantship at the University of Strathclyde which was then starting its economic history department with a very good team – Edgar Lythe, John Ward and Richard Wilson. Thence I went to UEA with Roy

Campbell. Economic History departments were proliferating in universities in the 1960s and as my reading deepened I became increasingly committed to the subject.

I had met Roy Campbell a little earlier when I attended my first Economic History Society Conference in Edinburgh in, I think, 1963. He was leading a coach tour on a wet, misty day, at one point trying to point out to us the 'Coldstone Slapps' a gap in the hills through which cattle used to be driven from the Falkirk tryst. As we peered through the gloom at we knew not what, Max Hartwell could not resist making exhuberant humour of the situation – 'What, What? Coldstone Slapps! Where is it, What is it? I cannot see it'. The serious courtesy of Roy Campbell and the schoolboyish ribbing of Max Hartwell was an interesting contrast of two differently attractive personalities. I was not to know it but in the near future both were to be important to me; Max Hartwell who examined and passed my Ph.D. and Roy as my excellent and much respected Professor at UEA. I am grateful to them both.

When UEA began, economic history was part of a School of Social (later Social and Economic) Studies, linked with economics, sociology and philosophy – but not politics. This reflected the attitudes of the first Vice Chancellor, the American historian Frank Thistlethwaite, whose own degree studies had been an eclectic mix of history, economics and English. He wanted forms of history combined with other disciplines rather than as an independent department. However this became less satisfactory over the years. As the economists, for their own professional reasons, became more mathematical they seemed to have little interest in the real world and even less in the past. As financial constraints bit in the 1970s and 1980s economists appeared more as predatory competitors for resources than likeminded collaborators. Moreover 'pure' English and European historians elsewhere in the University were increasingly adopting economic and social approaches in their own work. These included some major figures – Patricia (later Baroness) Hollis, Paul Kennedy (later at Yale), Richard Evans (later at Cambridge) and Geoffrey Searle – to whom we felt greater intellectual affinity than to our over-theorising sociologists and mathematical economists. Accordingly all the historians in the University joined in creating first a separate history degree in 1981 and then under the leadership of the economic historian Professor Roy Church, a School of History in 1994. This has worked well, gaining a five rating in the last RAE.

The former department of economic history has merged into the new arrangement as is probably a common experience in many British universities at this time. It leaves the problem of whether to retain a specific economic history degree. I incline against this on two main grounds. Firstly I think that history is still valuable as a first degree when it presents the student with a wide range of the concerns that make up human life – economics certainly, but also culture, politics, international relations, religion and so forth, and above all the interrelations between them. But this is linked with another matter which can compound too much specialism at the undergraduate level. There is an increasing concern with postgraduate degrees. BA dissertations and Special Subjects track on to MAs, MPhils and Ph.Ds with the demands of the postgraduate degrees casting their influence backwards creating a deepening but narrowing experience.   One understands the drives – the TQA requires structured 'progression', the RAE a 'research culture', the grant giving bodies evidence of research potential in undergraduates and, above all, the universities need the postgraduate fees. But a first degree already specialised to one aspect of history risks being pressurised even more so by these demands. It is as if we are too concerned to produce research students and future professional historians – any good department advertising a post will get over 100 applicants as it is. A broader degree is more appropriate for the mass of students – who are not going to be historians but move into other spheres of life.

The discipline also faces a dilemma about how mathematical it should be. The tradition of prose argument, informed by economics, of, say, Ashton, Mathias, Pollard, Daunton etc, is joined by the more econometric one of O'Brien and Crafts whose insights into French and British economic growth are comprehensible even to those who do not follow the detail of the methodology. Yet it is strange that Jeffrey Williamson's famous 1984 essay on growth in the Napoleonic Wars is regularly cited in reading lists and footnotes though there cannot be more than a handful of historians in Britain who really understand every line of the mathematical working. It raises issues. As economics becomes more like physics (and Alfred Marshall was a physicist) and economic history moves more to economics than towards history so it risks losing some if its constituency. The steadily falling membership of the Society since 1974 and the closure and merger of many departments of the subject may reflect this. Amid its concern for increasing professionalism the subject must not lose its wider following. The success of television in covering subjects like the history of women, old age, the War and the recent series 'The Day the World Took Off' suggest that it is there. When I edited the Society's NESH series 1992-1998 I tried to develop some of these social themes – childhood, sport, education, towns, science, war – and when possible to show how the past illuminated the present. Also if the subject demands increasing quantification skills then students possessing them, and a sense of economic rationality, will rightly prefer to deploy such skills in the engineering, management consultancy and accountancy professions rather than in pursuing academic problems of the past. Dedication may soon appear to be wilful eccentricity.

However the diminishing membership of the Society quite underrates the transforming influence of the subject on other forms of history. I have seen this in some areas where I have had a research interest. Theatre history used to be the preserve of students of English Literature and largely an account of plays. In recent years there has been increasing involvement of economic and social historians in entertainment generally with first rate books on film music, broadcasting, feminism in theatre and film. Likewise, educational history used to be confined to teacher training colleges as an account of great reformers and legislation. As I had to review recent literature on education and economic decline in a booklet for the Society it became clear how many publications had come not from traditional educationalists but from leading economic historians (e.g. Derek Aldcroft, Roderick Floud, Sidney Pollard, Stephen Nicholas, Eric Evans, Mary Rose etc) better known for other things. As the subject has declined in training colleges so it has been absorbed into the broader sphere of economic history and been enriched thereby. The same is true for medical history, of which UEA is a major Wellcome centre, sport, military history and I am sure many others. It can no longer be possible to study that kind of narrow political narrative history that was my A level pabulum. This is a measure of the transforming change brought about by economic history.

My latest work has been a substantial history of my own university. It has entailed getting to know something of a wide range of interdisciplinary matters from Sir Denys Lasdun's architectural building techniques in the 1960s to Lazard's investments policies in the 1970s, from trends in Sir Robert Sainsbury's art collecting taste in the 1930s to the John Innes Institute biochemistry of genetically modified foods in the 1990s. Lots of archival documents and lots of interviews. It is the kind of history that I like and I only wish that I were better at it.

Michael Sanderson (b. 1939) was educated at Queens' College, Cambridge, MA, Ph.D. He is Reader in History at University of East Anglia, Norwich. Council Member of the Economic History Society 1993-1999. Editor of the Society's Studies in Economic and Social History 1991-1998. He recently completed the official history of the University of East Anglia 1900-2000, and has special interests in educational and entertainment history.

Economic History: A Reminiscence

John Saville

I attended a well-organised grammar school and was able to take Economic History as one of four subjects for the London Intermediate Examination; the equivalent of today's A levels. In my first year at LSE (1934-1935) academic members of the department of Economic History included Eileen Power, R.H. Tawney, M.M. Postan, H.L. Beales with Jack Fisher as the assistant lecturer The B.Sc. (Econ) degree, which most students took, included three compulsory papers - two in economics and the third in economic history-with three papers in a special subject, including economic history, two optional papers from quite a wide choice within the social and political sciences, and a compulsory essay for all. The compulsory paper in economic history covered industrial development on a world scale so that everyone would know something of the emergence of the United States and Germany as world powers by 1914 or of the Wall St. crash of the autumn of 1929. I sometimes wonder how many economic specialists these days know anything about the crisis of 1929.

The war years, as for most of my contemporaries, took me away from academic life, and after six years in the Army (I was in the Artillery) and one year or so in Whitehall in a research job, I was appointed as lecturer in economic history at the University College of Hull. My predecessor, for two years, had been O.R. Macgregor. By the autumn of 1947, the date of my appointment, the teaching at LSE, as reflected in their examination papers, had been much influenced by the publication of Rostow's book on the British economy in the nineteenth century, and for several years I followed Rostow in my own teaching. I began to have some criticisms of Rostow's approach and I put my doubts in an article in one of the early issues of the newly founded *Past and Present*. At a conference soon after its publication I was asked by a distinguished historian why I had used such an out of the way journal (or words to that effect), the implication being that its founders and editors were not quite 'kosher' in the intellectual atmosphere of the day. It was, it must be recalled, the days of the cold war, and while the academic situation in the UK never approached the hysteria that was generated in the United States, the general atmosphere was a good deal colder than is often appreciated. Christopher Hill made several unsuccessful applications for professorial chairs. and he once told me that in 1957, after he had left the Communist Party, he was asked by one member of the committee he was going to meet, if he could give an assurance that he would not write for the *Daily Worker*.

There were certain advantages in this. There were a number of University Colleges in the years between the wars .They managed their own affairs with one major exception. The syllabuses and the examinations their students sat were the University of London's External Degree, and examination papers were marked by London's examiners. First year students normally had an examination at the end of the year as, of course, they did at the end of their third year. What this meant for the University College lecturers was that during the summer term of each year there was very little teaching except to the second year. So from the beginning of the Easter vacation and the start of a new session in late September economic historians, as in other subjects, were largely free to read and research. There was almost no bureaucratic interference and life was very pleasant and hopefully productive. When the University Colleges became full Universities - most by the middle 1950s - the syllabus for economists often included economic history. At Hull, for example, we took over the B Sc. (Econ) from the London syllabus almost unchanged, and as student numbers began to increase, as they did from the middle fifties, so the demand for economic history also grew.

There were other reasons why the subject of economic history was to become increasingly attractive in academic circles, among both undergraduates and postgraduates as well as their tutors. The subject had the great advantage of a succession of outstanding scholars in the field, beginning with Cunningham, the Hammonds and Lipson, and above all John Clapham whose three massive and wonderfully erudite volumes provided the basis for teaching for several decades. The subject was to attract an increasing number of excellent postgraduate research students, numbers of academic staff continued to increase through the sixties and seventies, and the volume of financial grants greatly widened with economic history supported by the research monies then more easily available.

If we look back over the century the intellectual consequences of two world wars were of central importance in the growing sophistication of economics and economic history. One should, perhaps, distinguish quite sharply between theoretical economics - but not the Keynesian kind - and applied economics. What was crucial was the emphasis upon statistical data for the latter, and this certainly involved an increasing interest in the past history of individual economies. In 1960, my department was still teaching a general economic history paper for all B. Sc (Econ) students. As I have already indicated this followed the pattern of the teaching at London which concentrated mostly upon the development of industrialisation in the United Kingdom. At this date I still had only one other colleague in history although our numbers were to increase to seven by the end of the coming decade. But in 1960 I decided it would be interesting to compare Britain with another industrialising country and I chose Japan on the grounds that its history and modern development was so different from European experience. For this first year, therefore, it was possible to assess with more understanding the nature of the industrialising processes against quite different social and political structures, and one always hoped that the comparison of differences was analytically helpful in the further two years of study before Finals.

Full employment and state interventionism greatly encouraged the study of the social sciences in general, and alongside the growing interest in the economic development of individual societies went an equal concern with their social histories and evolving social structures. The third quarter of the century was to witness changes in political and social ideas - intellectual and political ructions might perhaps be more appropriate terms for some aspects of the changes. This is not the place to offer an analysis of the intellectual and social movements of a complex period except perhaps to note the headings of any serious evaluation. These would include the aftermath of the 1956 speech by Khrushchev which had such a devastating impact upon much of the communist world; the political influence of the New Left; the mass campaign against nuclear weapons ; the founding of the Society for the Study of Labour History in 1960; the notable emergence of a militant feminist movement in the United States and then in western Europe; the vigorous movement against the war in Vietnam on both sides of the Atlantic. This is not an exhaustive list and the items noted are certainly not of equal significance. It omits, for example, the intellectual influence in Britain of the

Communist Historians' group or the impact of the establishment of a number of greenfield Universities, beginning with Sussex, and their vigorous debates concerning the ways of teaching traditional subjects as well as new ideas about the combination of subjects. The publication of Edward Thompson's *The Making of the English Working Class* in 1963 was an important influence upon the development of social history in general. The year most remembered is of course 1968, when student sit-ins affected many universities and generated different kinds of politics and movements (most of which did not survive as organisations).

The Social Sciences Research Council, established in the mid-1960s, began to make available research scholarships and the Economic History Committee was able to offer two places a year to most institutions. These grants were only available to research students in economic or social history, and it became a practice that the Committee began to receive subject titles in which the word 'social' had been inserted from straight history departments whose outside funding was less generous. I was a member of the Economic History Committee for most of the seventies and its chairman during the years 1977-9.My term of office fortunately came to an end a few months after the election of the first Thatcher government when research grants began to be cut back almost immediately. My successor as chairman complained to me half way through his term of office of the 'can of worms' he had been left with.

During the 1970s the Economic History Committee decided to visit university departments and assess how they 'adjusted' their research students. It was a series of illuminating experiences. Our first meeting was with the whole department and it was dominated by the senior academic members. We therefore decided to interview separately on future occasions beginning with the head of the department and any other professors, then the academic staff and finally all the research students. Our most dramatic occasion was a visit to a well respected, university, with four professors in the social sciences and a good research reputation. We interviewed the professors first and received very positive replies. Then we spoke to the lecturing staff with only half of those present who could have been with us, and whose responses were not wholly satisfactory. Finally we spent an hour and a half with the research students This could only be described as calamitous, with a well-argued stream of complaints. Our next committee meeting in London confirmed what we had provisionally agreed, namely to withdraw the annual allocation of research places. The decision naturally brought about major protests which in the end were settled in the not unknown manner of academic compromise.

Part of my academic life in the 1960s, and also thereafter, was the encouragement of the reprint of important periodicals and books now difficult to consult. Augustus M. Kelley, had begun publishing his *Economic Classics* in the late nineteen fifties. I was introduced to Kelley by Ralph Miliband, and we became friends. I persuaded Kelley that he could move into the field of economic and social history and I offered in most cases to write a longish introduction or to find someone to undertake the job. So in the sixties I spent a fair proportion of my research time on searching out suitable volumes for reprints. I was firmly against the trivial two page Introduction and in the beginning had to argue with Gus Kelley that a serious, probing Introduction was the only way that we were going to achieve the proper levels of scholarship in social history. I wrote Introductions to reprints of Harney's *Red Republican* and *The Friend of the People,* W.E. Adams's *Memoirs of a Social Atom,* Gammage's *History of the Chartist Movement* (with an introduction of 25,000 words - this was the 1894 edition) and half a dozen other titles. I had also, early in the sixties, started on the *Dictionary of Labour Biography,* but I was much troubled by the arguments I had within myself as to the structure and its contents, and the first volume did not appear until 1972.

I retired from the University of Hull in 1982. Although my research interests were mainly in social history I always taught the compulsory courses in economic history for both the first and third year students. My retirement was a year earlier than my contract allowed, but there was a 20% reduction in the University's income, and a large number of the academic staff were encouraged to take redundancy. I still accepted the occasional research student for supervision, and I still kept my room until recently because of the *Dictionary* (volume 10 was published early in 2000). My old department and the University were very helpful and I had all the facilities required. What I did become aware of was the declining importance of economic history in most universities, with many economic history departments being absorbed once again in the departments of economics. But we all know the changing emphases within the general subject of history in this past couple of decades, and these are matters for serious debate, at economic history conferences, and indeed throughout the land.

John Saville (b. 2. 4. 1916) was educated at LSE and taght at the University of Hull for most of his career. His many publications and his resaerch interests focus upon labour history, Chartism, and British economy, society and politics, especially in the nineteenth century. He is a leading figure among British Marxist historians.

A Global Sense of Community: Economic History and Personal Experience

Pam Sharpe

In 1997, on the day following the examiner's dinner at Bristol University, I boarded a plane to Tanzania with 68 kilos of luggage. We were heading for the mission hospital at Rubya. This was a day's drive to the south of Kampala on increasingly poor roads, and situated to the south of Lake Victoria, within near reach of the border with Rwanda. My husband, a geotechnical engineer, had been asked to prepare an assessment of a failed aid project: a dam for a hydroelectric scheme that had never been built. He was to look into the possibilities for bringing electricity to a large settlement and hospital. We were not the only people in the airport queue who were laden with luggage, but probably the only ones whose excess consisted of a large number of books and photocopies of seventeenth- and eighteenth-century documents, as well as sundry computer equipment because, although I was fascinated to be spending the next three months in a remote part of Africa, I assumed that I needed to carry enough academic work to fully occupy my time.

In case the point of this story is not obvious, suffice it to say that some of the academic texts I carried remained unread throughout our stay in Rubya but that this particular period in Africa showed me what economic history means to me. My husband is South African and we had already travelled and holidayed in southern Africa on several occasions. But such fleeting engagements cannot compare with deep immersion in the workings of a local community. In this case our own living conditions, with an intermittent water supply and periodic electricity from a dodgy generator, gave an insight well beyond that of how it might have been to live in an early modern village.

Fairly rapidly, it became apparent that the construction of the failed dam was not entirely, or even mostly, an engineering problem. Sorting through the hospital archives we started to piece together a story of political and ecclesiastical corruption with mismanagement of past charity funds. This was a classic disaster of early 1980s aid: the hydroelectric scheme was designed for massive population expansion and was too big for local needs. It was managed from overseas with insufficient local input or accountability. The gap between the desires of the community and the flush of funding from willing church congregations in Europe appeared glaring. On our first day in Rubya, we took shelter from a torrential rainstorm in the hospital engine room and viewed an On/Off switch for electricity from the hydro, which was never to be turned 'on'. An eleven kilometre power transmission line had been erected by the hospital maintenance staff and could be tracked across the countryside ending in a sorry pile of rocks at the dam site. Rusting penstock pipes and ageing earth-moving equipment were scattered around the area.

A handful of European expatriates, ranging from Dutch doctors with practical know-how, through to the Catholic priest who lived in the area and specialised in solar power ('Solar

Father' as he became known) had put in their twopenneth to try to bring power to Rubya. But a holistic view was required. What were the real needs of the community and how could electricity best be supplied?

This area of Tanzania is densely settled and the small farms, (many run by women while men work as migrant labour elsewhere), yield cash crops of coffee and bananas. Population pressure meant the bride price has risen in recent years and marriage age is later than it used to be. When we were there, the swollen population was further increased by the presence of Rwandan refugees. Boys could receive a good education in the mission school and some progressed to university. Opportunities were less good for boys from poor families such as the teenagers who spent the day carrying nile perch from Lake Victoria, up the escarpment to the village making fish available in the marketplace late in the day. When we left Rubya, we took an orphaned boy to Kampala to be trained in carpentry, finding him clothes and shoes in the local town on the way. Girls, by contrast, had an opportunity for vocational training in the village but almost no academic outlet. As a result of land pressure, new areas are being cleared within a day's drive of Rubya. We visited the clinic in one such village at the margin of cultivation and advised on the design of a water supply there.

Partly due to the basic need for clean water the entire region is impoverished by chronic illness. AIDS and malaria are enormous problems. This area has one of the highest incidences of AIDS in Africa. We saw villages of deserted houses decimated by the disease. The local village was a scene of destitution with many houses serving as brothels. Yet the influence of Catholicism was such that condoms could not be distributed and to be known to be suffering from AIDS was a terrifying stigma. We were in Rubya in malaria season and often witnessed sick people being delivered to the hospital carried aloft on a chair, serving as a makeshift wheelchair. Sick children were three or four to a bed in the overcrowded hospital. Many of our trips out of the village were to procure quinine, which was in short supply. The ululations of mothers from the hospital every morning, made it possible to count the number of children who had died in the night.

Some external attempts to help appeared to be misguided, however. What was apparent from the vantage point of the village was the distorting influence that aid agencies were having on the district. The refugee camps in Rwanda were draining medical personnel from the struggling hospitals of the region, paying doctors and nurses three or four times the local salary. Médicins Sans Frontiéres, the premier international medical agency, flew in all their supplies from Europe thus providing no gain to the local economy. Some of the supplies, such as packs of sanitary towels, were a novel, and potentially environmentally-damaging, addition to the lives of local women. Many aid workers are, of course, recruited because of their specific skills rather than their cultural sensitivity or local awareness.

Other images are difficult to forget because of the incongruous interface with the developed world. The focus of the week was Rubya's Sunday market. Here piles of (donated) second-hand western clothing were sold by middlemen. Winter coats might be left aside, but women who had never worn underwear were buying bras while men purchased second-hand baseball caps. At the same time, rural tailors were finding they had much less to do: they no longer fashioned traditional clothes to sew but merely made alterations to Western cast-offs. More apparent still was the fact that the only vehicles we saw were shiny white Aid agency four-wheel drives. And one day we unpacked a box containing the latest portable computer, directed from an aid agency and not too useful when the only supply of electricity was a faulty, inadequate hospital generator.

Or was it? By the end of our stay all options for electricity had been investigated, and negotiations to bring the national grid to Rubya had begun. A year after our stay, we were amazed to receive an email from Rubya hospital. Rubya had no communication with the outside world when we were there. Like a throwback to the medieval world, letters would arrive at the hospital from the bishop by a courier in a land cruiser. Now Rubya skipped many stages in the evolution of communication and hit the 'e' revolution.

Finding solutions to practical problems in Rubya required a community effort, an integrated approach and a hefty dose of cultural awareness that should be a part of the methodological training of all historians. An apparently technical dilemma actually needed consideration from the standpoint of the local economy and society. For example, the erection of the power line had caused a spate of land speculation along its route because a rumour had circulated that neighbouring houses would be provided with (or could help themselves to) free electricity. What would be the impact of alternative sources of power? I was ancillary to the project but felt that my training in demographic, social and economic history could provide a useful insight into contemporary human interaction and the interrelated issues at the heart of the problems confronting this particular community. As an economic historian, I am forced to assess how wealth is created and why there is a concurrent increase in poverty. My detailed study of early modern Colyton in Devon might seem a world apart from Rubya, but both reinforce the fact that it is not possible to divorce political, economic, social and other factors in the dissection of a local community.

In my academic work, I have usually concentrated on the effects of economic differentiation on marginal groups: women, the poor, or migrants. The trend of economic history in recent years has been a greater emphasis on quantitative methods and my experience of the utility of history in this particular context suggests the clear need to preserve the human element. My own interdisciplinary interests, in this case anthropological, also helped my assessment. Indeed, it seems to me that economic historians can play a very effective part in interdisciplinary teams and there is now an increased willingness by scientists (at least here in Australia) to carry out collaborative projects with social scientists. Abandoning old disciplinary barriers is something that most economic historians have had to contend with in recent years but it may be no bad thing in the long run. Economic historians lean more naturally towards joint projects than traditional historians, and one of the major beneficial elements that social and economic history might bring to history departments is a greater sense of community, however scarce this may seem to be in these days of funding pressure and intense competition.

Since arriving in Western Australia, I have become embroiled in a very effective community action campaign about heritage in the beach suburb where I live. This area was the first coastal resort of Western Australia but in recent months, as a result of soaring land prices, many of the characteristic early wooden cottages have been, quite literally cut in half and towed away. What has emerged in a protest involving the State Premier, the Minister of Heritage and Planning, and much television and newspaper coverage, is the not very profound fact that a sense of place matters to people. These ordinary homes are infused with the cultural heritage of the area, and with the sort of rich, associative memories that are revealed in oral history projects. Again, the focus on one cottage, revealed the many stakeholders in the heritage of a particular place and the impossibility of isolating a certain set of influences in the situation.

A sense of community is central to my own *modus operandi*. Influenced by W.G. Hoskins, the first significant economic history work I did was the local history of the mining community in which I grew up. Situated on the Derbyshire/ Nottinghamshire border, this was a deeply industrial area and our village was a very close-knit community. The identity of the parish, shaped by coalmining culture, was created in the late nineteenth century with the advent of deep mines. In this golden era, my great-grandparents migrated to the coalfields. In

1887 and ahead of his time for new unionism, my great-grandfather, an impoverished Somerset agricultural labourer struck for a pay rise from nine shillings to eleven shillings with two fellow workers and was denounced from the pulpit for forming a union. The local schoolmaster told him the new Midland Railway was advertising for men and he went north, became a pointsman, then a guard on goods trains. For him, the building of the railway quite literally offered an escape route to a different life. He renounced the church forever. My grandfather was not christened and he and his brothers could not go to the local school because it was a church school. Also drawn by coal, another great-grandfather left a wandering life of entangled personal attachment in Ireland, another gave up the life of a horseman in Yorkshire, and yet another was a struggling stockinger who could no longer maintain his craft and became a recruiting agent for the local 'works'. Only a decade after his migration the Somerset labourer, seeking another type of escape, this time from the coalfield, caught malaria in South Africa in the Boer War, and never recovered. My great-grandmother, uprooted from her childhood home to live in a colliery house, reputedly died of grief when her second youngest son, who had falsified his age, fell on the Somme. My own starting point for economic history came through these family stories of struggled livelihoods, crushed and recreated in an industrial heartland.

Without the disciplinary springboard of economic history there would be no micro-history of the sort fostered by what we might call the 'Cambridge School' of early modern social and economic history. Economic history was also the basis for the parish-centred studies of local demography that have developed over the last forty years. Yet this is a local history very different from the nostalgic hankering after a lost rural world. What economic history means to me, in these global times, is the ability to write the small stories of ordinary people and their habitations onto a larger canvas, to analyse the different elements that come together to form a local community in a holistic way, and perhaps now and again, to offer an insight into contemporary life situations and social problems.

Pam Sharpe (b. 28. 3. 1962) has been Queen Elizabeth II Research Fellow in the Department of History at the University of Western Australia in Perth since 2000. She was formerly Lecturer in Social and Economic History at University of Bristol 1993-1999. She gained her doctorate at the Cambridge Group for the History of Population and Social Structure. She was Secretary, then Chair of the Women's Committee of the Economic History Society 1994-99 and was on Council 1995-2001. Her publications include *Adapting to Capitalism: Working Women in the English Economy 1700-1850* (1996, paperback 2000); *Chronicling Poverty: the Voices and Strategies of the English Poor 1640-1840* (co-edited with Tim Hitchcock and Peter King, 1997) and a student reader *Women's Work: the English Experience 1650-1914* (1998).

A Marriage of Convenience? A View of Economic History and its Partners

Deborah Simonton

When asked to write on the question, 'What is Economic History?', I asked myself, 'Am I an economic historian?' I had never labelled myself as such, and yet I was aware that a form of economic history clearly permeated my thinking and writing. So the question, 'What is economic history and what does it mean to me?' was fundamental to my self-perception as a historian.

As a young student, my first encounters with economic history were in studying the economies of nations and of economic trends in the past. It was sometimes also the history of industries and places, a study of economic growth, change or decline. But it did not appear to relate to individuals or groups of individuals. Some of the methods and approaches of economic history, particularly the quantitative, tend to embed this notion of macro-history, a history distanced from real people and the actors of the past. These methods seemed to suggest an implacable series of forces at work. But as I found my feet as a historian, I began to recognise the potential narrowness of this view. I began to recognise the wisdom of William Ashley's view that economic history is, on the contrary, quite broad encompassing 'the history of actual human practice with respect to the material basis of life'.[1] Jordanova has captured the sense of this, writing that 'economic history concerns itself with production on the one hand and consumption on the other'.[2]

My interest was in what people of the past were doing, why they acted as they did and what factors impinged on their decision making. I was looking for a broader notion, one which allowed a study of 'society', which asked questions other than economic ones. This latter felt more like what I perceived as social history. To quote Jordanova again, 'If social history is an approach, then it can be connected with the conviction that the lives of ordinary people, not just elites, should be studied; that weight should be given to lived experience; that complex relationships between people, no matter what kind, should be explored; that whatever phenomena societies throw up should be investigated historically'.[3] Clearly, the boundaries I had set up between these two approaches were uncomfortable, and I could not ask nor answer the questions about the past that I considered important by employing the labels and concepts in this way. Indeed, for me history and the practise of history cannot be compartmentalised, and should not be. Thus social and economic history are inextricably linked in the way I work and think.

An important feature of economic history and its development over the last quarter of a century is the way that it has developed a more explicit role in writing the past of people and groups. In some senses it has managed a marriage with social history to enable historians to write more nuanced historical accounts of cultures, societies and people. It is notable that Chartier, in defining cultural history, lumps social and economic history together, sometimes as socio-economic history.[4]   Similarly Lynn Hunt treats them together, citing the emphasis on both by the *Annales* school. Even E.H. Carr refers to them in the same breath: 'Since the preoccupation with economic and social ends represents a broader and more advanced stage in human development than the preoccupation with political and constitutional ends, so the economic and social interpretation of history may be said to represent a more advanced stage in history than the exclusively political interpretation'.[5] This suggests that historians, myself included, have some difficulty in separating the two. Yet, this is not to argue that economic and social history are the same thing, nor that they necessarily exploit the same materials or approaches. Clearly not all economic history is also social, nor is all social history economic. But at the interface of the two, there is important work going on. The recent surge of interest in luxury and consumption is one such area which has thrown up some of the best historical research and elucidation of the past.

Economic history and social history are not only intrinsically linked, but they both have become increasingly eclectic, absorbing new ideas and approaches, exploiting other disciplines and unearthing new sources and new ways to read sources. The methods of social science, including methods of statistical analysis, data collection and reconstitution have added to both social and economic history, by finding new ways to shed light on the structures and trends of the past. And yet, in their most austere form, they have led to criticisms, not the least of 'unintelligibility'. Such cliometric economic history in its severest and unreformed version is reminiscent of debates about 'new trends in history' in the late sixties and seventies, which Lawrence Stone encapsulated by saying 'It is appalling if two men studying the same phenomenon just walk past each other and have nothing to say to each other'.[6] There is, however, a danger in defining economic history, or indeed social history, in terms of large data runs. Such a view tends to diminish the variety and vigour of the fields and undermines their focus. Thus, obviously, economic history itself has a history, and the way it is written and the way historians have used it in collaboration with other models and approaches is movable.

In much of my research and writing I want to know how women created an identity within a culture and community, how they fit in the economy and society, how much agency and independence they had. In studying eighteenth-century education, apprenticeship and work, I have used a variety of sources and materials, and worked to begin to form a holistic account of girls and women in society as a whole and women in specific urban and rural communities in particular. I have used quantitative approaches to answer some of the questions, such as the extent to which the provision of educational opportunities in a community could enable girls in that community to go to school; or to evaluate the comparative experience of girls and boys as apprentices. Yet these approaches only told a part of the story. Other factors gave sense to the quantitative material and analyses. It was in trying to understand the economic, social and cultural constructions which surrounded women, that the fuller picture emerges. While this research focused on women and gender, it was situated largely in a social and economic context which gives the whole study shape. In particular I became interested in the relationship between education, work and status. Thus the economic factors and context within which women operated were fundamental. So was the meaning those contexts had for the women themselves, and for their relative position in society.

The relationship between woman and her labour is mediated by a number of issues. Some, such as the nature of work available, its urban or rural character and the work process, affect men as well. In addition, key issues for women concern family and female life cycle. But work is mediated by ideology and by concepts of gender, status and power. These are less about the work itself than about relationships and the psycho-social needs which work fills above and beyond its economic rôle. While women's work is delineated by factors such as economy, class and demography, society's notions about woman's place and its beliefs about gender roles are significant determinants. Similarly definitions of work reflect society's perception of the values placed on different forms of labouring activity. The most obvious of these is whether or not unpaid work in support of the home is construed as work. These factors, outside of purely economic considerations, influenced women of all classes, though with varied effects determined partly by class and partly by culture. Society's understanding of women's activities is usually situated within male definitions of work, while important ideas about women's work were derived from their positions within the household. Even if women's work was crucial, the gender roles of society were often about other things altogether, such as status, masculinity, power, and control. The question of skill is particularly significant since women were excluded from many established routes to male-defined expertise, which were closely associated with status, prestige and political rights.

From my point of view, the strength of economic history is how it enables the understanding of a set of factors which shape the way people of the past operated. It does not have an exclusivity which suggests that people only operated in the face of instrumental concerns,[7] but it helps us to shape a more accurate picture which reflects economically, socially and culturally constructed paradigms. People's decision-making process comprised complex considerations that included emotional and moral values as well as economic considerations. For example, to argue that women working on their own in urban Europe in the eighteenth century sought independence, or that they were forced into it only through instrumental concerns, is oversimplification.

Chartier wrote that, 'Unlike economic or social historians, who reconstitute what was, the historian of mentalities or ideas seeks not the real but the ways in which people considered and transposed reality'.[8] In posing a contrast between what he sees as two different approaches, he sets up a false dichotomy, and I believe, misreads what social and economic historians have to offer. I have trouble suggesting that my researches have turned up 'the real' in women's lives; I tend to believe that I am able to offer an approximation of what women experienced. In doing so, I employ the methods and approaches of both an economic and a social analysis situated in the cultural context.

Deborah Simonton (b. 2. 11. 1948) is a graduate of Arizona Statue University and the University of Essex. She is the author of *A History of European Women's Work, 1700 to the present* (Routledge, 1998) and co-author of *Gendering Scottish History: An International Perspective*, (Cruithne Press, 1999) and *Women and Higher Education, Past, Present and Future,* (Aberdeen University Press, 1996). Her research interests are in women, work and education primarily in the eighteenth century.

---

[1]Ashley, W., 'The Place of Economic History in University Studies,' *Economic History Review,* 1, (1927), p. 1
[2]Jordanova, Ludmilla, *History in Practice,* (London, 2000), p. 51
[3]Ibid., p. 38.
[4]See for example, Chartier, Roger, *Cultural History, between practices and representations,* (Cambridge, 1988), pp. 2-3.
[5]Carr, E. H. *What is History?* pp. 164-65. See also, Lynn Hunt, ed., *The New Cultural History,* (Berkeley, 1989), pp. 3-4.
[6]New Trends in History', *Daedalus,* (Fall, 1969), p. 894. See also Gertrude Himmelfarb, 'Social History and the Moral Imagination,' in *Art, Politics and Will -- Essays in Honour of Lionel Trilling,* edited by Quentin Anderson, (New York, 1977), pp. 28-58, reprinted in R.S. Neale, ed., *History and Class, Essential Readings in Theory and Interpretation,* (Oxford, 1983), pp. 248-70.
[7]See, for example, the argument about family strategies and child labour in Cunningham, Hugh, *Children and Childhood in Western Society since 1500* (London, 1995), pp. 87-89.
[8]Chartier, *Cultural History,* p. 43.

The Interpretation of 'Industrial Revolution' in the Second Age of Malthus

Victor Skipp

In his 1926 volume *Population problems in the age of Malthus*, G. Talbot Griffith insisted that, 'under the existing conditions' of Malthus's lifetime, 'the truth of the main [Mathusian] proposition was so clear and strictly relevant that it was hopeless to argue against the author, much as one might rail against him . . .' As of the 1920s, Griffith commented, 'With all the fertile waste and semi-cultivated land there is in the world, it must obviously be a long time before there is any need for the world to find itself in the position England was in when Malthus began to write'.[1] Yet, with global population doubling between 1930 and 1980 – like England's did between 1790 and 1840 – and very probably with global population doubling again between 1980 and 2030, if Griffith had been alive today he would presumably have announced the second 'age of Malthus'.

Those believing that Malthus made 'one of the most egregious mistakes in the history of economic thought'[2] would be dumbfounded at such a backward looking suggestion. Potentially, however, the idea is also forward-looking. Because the really distinctive thing about the age in which Malthus lived, and over which he cast such a spell, was that it was *both* a period of dire demographic pressure, and therefore widespread penury, and of massively countervailing technological and economic advance. And the same surely applies today, even if Malthus is ignored.

Malthus himself was aware of the technological and economic advance. In 1803, when the gargantuan second edition of his *Essay on Population* was published, he noted that 'We [the British] have now stepped out of the agricultural system, into a state in which the commercial system ['of manufacturers and traders'] clearly predominates'.[3] More substantively, after charting the enigmatic waverings of the first industrialising nation's 'development' for a further 30 years, shortly before his death in 1834, Malthus is recorded as saying that he 'thought well, on the whole, of our manufacturing prospects', which 'depended in the main on circumstances, not subject to fluctuations, such as our abundance of fuel or mechanical ingenuity, our great capital, our rapid and cheap communications, the efficiency of our labour'.[4]

Not that this meant – in such an intrinsically dichotomous period of metamorphosis – that the younger Malthus had been *wrong*. As a fellow economist, Deacon Hume, was still problematising the situation in 1835, 'If the increase of population should not comprise a body of new manufacturers . . . the country would become little else but one great poor-house'.[5] Arguably, even this late, Hume was being more than a little sanguine. For, to the present author's own knowledge, at least one part of Britain (which may not have differed conspicuously in this regard from many others) – despite boasting an 'increase of population' that (partly!) comprised 'a body of new manufacturers' – had nevertheless been, since the early 1790s, and was to remain until the late 1840s, 'little else but one great poor-house'. It may likewise be the case in virtually every part of the contemporary world which has had an 'increase of population' that (*partly!*) comprised 'a body of new manufacturers' over the past 50 or 60 years. After all 47.8% of the 1995 global population of 5.43 billion live on an annual average *per capita* income of $1,600, or $4.38 per day; and a further 36.8% on an average of $400 per annum, or $1.10 per day.[6] And year after year, unreckoned numbers die of starvation. Thus, far from Malthus being condemned in perpetuity for his 'egregious mistake', he ought rather perhaps to be lauded – and indeed, a great deal more closely scrutinised – for his exemplary ability to at least keep within his intellectual purview the whole of early nineteenth-century Britain's developmental situation as it actually (and changingly) was.

Why is it necessary to revive, and indeed replicate, Griffith's long forgotten 'age of Malthus'? Because hopefully, this concept may help give shape, as well as bite, to the essay's principal position. Namely that – both 'then' and 'now' – the reason we find massive technological and economic advance chronologically coinciding with dire demographic pressure and widespread penury, is simply that there is a high degree of *causal interconnectedness* between them. So high that – at least from one point of view – it represents the actual dynamics of what is conceived here as the 'industrial revolutionary' process.

It was many-faceted research into the history of Birmingham and its rural hinterland that enabled this complicated interconnectedness to be teased out.[7] Throughout most of the period 1790-1850 – or (as again, conceived here) 'the [high] industrial revolution' – many of the region's inhabitants lived virtually on the margin of subsistence. At first – aside from Birmingham's export difficulties during the Napoleonic wars, which must have been considerably offset by bumper military purchases – the most obvious problems were 'Malthusian'. Rapid national and local population growth brought a succession of critical food shortages; a persistently high cost of subsistence (never mind living); and therefore inadequate demand for industrial products. With population growing at a faster rate than jobs, there was also escalating unemployment; an oversupply-dictated downward pressure on real wage levels; and, in such harsh circumstances, the inevitable (and indeed salvatory) use of desperately vulnerable people as cheap labour. From 1822, cheaper food lowered the cost of living. Unfortunately, by then, with 'what is blasphemously called the 'surplus population''!![8] still increasing, another 'non-Malthusian' (or 'industrial-revolutionary') problem was augmenting the nation's woes. Steam-powered mechanisation meant systematic labour *saving*; a preference for low-paid female and child labour, and therefore widespread adult male redundancies; the killing off of uncompetitive domestic employment; the manufacture of goods wildly in excess of demand, and therefore shut-downs, lay-offs, prolonged industrial depressions. So, whatever its advantages, the substitution of machines for skilled human labour greatly intensified the once merely '*Malthusian*' unemployment/low-wage syndrome.

Reportedly from 1791 onwards, 'Birmingham suffered from . . . stagnation of trade, and the very high prices of provisions'.[9] Famine conditions prevailed in 1794-6 and 1799-1801, with way above average burials and below average marriages and baptisms. The combined industrial stagnation and food scarcity of 1808-13 was similarly marked by troughs in nuptiality and fertility and by unprecedentedly high mortality throughout 1810. At last, the end-of-war years brought the 1814-15 economic (and demographic) boom. But, with cut-throat competition for home and overseas markets, and with industrial depression, plus the grinding impoverishment of the post-war agricultural depression sapping demand, there followed six more unprofitable and dispiriting years. Eventually, cheaper corn, plus the dazzling boom of 1824-5, *promised* progress. Yet, with the tide of mechanisation now in full flow, and still all too few people having much to spend (and help make work), 13 of the next 22 years fell (nationally; and locally) into 'three intervals of prolonged unemployment' namely 1826-32, 1837-42, and 1846-48.[10]

'We only ask to have it placed within our power to earn honest bread by honest labour . . .', ran a petition which ' the artisans of Birmingham' submitted to parliament in April 1817. 'But some cause which we cannot understand has deprived industry of its reward, and has left us without employment and without bread, and almost without hope'.[11] To all intents and purposes, these distraught and bewildered men might have been speaking, not merely for themselves in a particular *annus horribilis*, but for two full generations of Birmingham artisans – to say nothing of those similarly afflicted elsewhere. Yet, the 'cause' which they could not 'understand', has never come anywhere near to being understood since. And never will be unless and until it is realised that its 'hidden key' lies in the intricate and reciprocal – indeed key-like – *interrelationship* between the '*Malthusian*' and '*industrial-revolutionary*' forces at work.

And correspondingly, by implication, and even in terms of an ever mounting body of contemporary evidence, the same intricate and reciprocal interrelationship could well prove as applicable to the demographic predicament *cum* golden economic opportunity which the now six billion strong human race (as a whole) finds itself facing today: in this, the second 'age of Malthus'. Or what, in its complete opposite or (to borrow from quantum theory) 'complementarity' or 'alternative' manifestation, is 'the global industrial revolution' or 'the second industrial revolution'.[12]

Returning to Birmingham's almost Third-World like experience, despite its post-1790 economic and demographic difficulties, according to the early decennial censuses, numbers went up from 73,670 to 85,755 between 1801 and 1811, and had risen to 106,722 by 1821. This implies a 45% increase for the first two decades of the nineteenth century – and possibly an overall 55-60% increase since 1790. Even after 'about 12,000' of 'the town's sons' had 'volunteered for war service between 1797 and 1805', and 'one would have expected, that, when such a number of labourers were taken away , there would have been a want of hands' in fact, 'The reverse was the case: there were still too many hands for the manufacturers here'.[13]

William Hutton, Birmingham's first historian, had recently boasted that 'Wherever the view of profit opens, the eyes of a Birmingham man are open to see it'.[14] The prospect of exploiting the 'too many hands' as a source of cheap labour – and by this the other questionable means producing cut-price goods that more people could afford – opened such a 'view of profit'. As early as 1800, a Birmingham pamphlet lamented the 'springing up among us of a spurious kind of mongrel race who can be called neither *merchant* or *manufacturer*, but are a common enemy of both'. Such 'men of all work' are further pilloried as 'dealers chiefly in discretionary orders, usually given from plundered patters'. And they 'understand precisely the beat of every man's pulse and how to make use of him'.[15] All of which sounds incredibly like the sudden and, so far as 'the old order' was concerned, patently unwelcome arrival of unfettered business competition. Or of a not merely 'free', but perhaps distinctively 'industrial-revolutionary' (and/or 'Malthusian') '*free-for-all*' market.

Matthew Boulton had been archetypcally churning out precision manufactured copper coins from his steam-driven Soho Mint since 1788. Nevertheless, it seems to have been only *after* the arguably *pivotal* advent of this free-for-all market that steam-powered technology was widely adopted in Birmingham. When this happened, it brought the automation of – and the ability to apply cheap unskilled labour to – countless local production processes, thereby enabling the long established businesses to regain the competitive edge from their upstart rivals. Unfortunately it also involved dismissing many highly paid traditional craftsmen who had until then produced predominantly hand-fabricated wares for the 'gentlemen' of what, by the 1860s, was being looked back upon as an 'Augustan age'.[16] Such craftsmen, once the deadly mix of mechanisation with child and female labour forced them into redundancy, would have little option but to join the 'mongrel race': either as endemically insecure 'small-masters', or as *their* inadequately remunerated workers.

A mere 13 rotary steam engines are listed as being installed in Birmingham during the 24 years 1783-1807. This implies that, thus far, for some reason (complacency? – aversion to risk-taking? – lack of technological wherewithal or know-how? – not being pushed?) most 'Augustan' businessmen had held back from a technologically comprehensive – but also, alas, socially disruptive – restructuring. At the earliest, that nettle was only grasped in the prolonged food scarcity and industrial stagnation of 1808-13, during which a total of 20 rotary engines were installed – closely followed by an annual record of eight more in the downturn of 1816.[17]

Particularly when one bears in mind that steam engines were often used locally by more than one business, this might well be regarded as the 'take-off' of automative and/or mass-production manufacturing in Birmingham. Yet, instead of that epoch-making breakthrough being unambiguously self-generating, as is often tacitly assumed, it appears rather (or also) to have been market (or *crisis*) driven; or, in straightforwardly 'Malthusian' terms, cheap labour, or *demographically*, driven.

Nor is it impossible to detect similar signs of intercausality in what William Greider visualises as today's now *single* 'one-world' economy. The microchip apparently had its 'origins' in 1958-9. But in the early 1970s – long before that technology revolutionised manufacturing – 17 US semiconductor companies decided 'in rapid succession' to move 'chip production to Kuala Lumpur and Penang': the idea being to find 'a new locale for low-wage final assembly'. Countless other businessmen in countless other industries soon followed, until the practice of taking advantage 'of the gross surpluses of human labour that exist around the world' became 'the most powerful and convenient incentive for global commerce'.[18] Or, again in 'Malthusian' terms, an overwhelmingly potent *demographically*-rooted (as opposed to merely *economically*, or *technologically* rooted) element in the emergence (or re-emergence) of a *de facto* nineteenth-century-style 'free' – and 'free-for-all' – market.

Even after the establishment of the new market and new technology, the causal interconnectedness of 'Malthusian' and 'industrial-revolutionary factors remains observable. As for instance, in relation to the dreaded 'crises' which are so disruptive (and promotive) of early capitalistic advance. For, in an ultimate sense, it is surely the *coincidence* of demographic rampancy with technological rampancy, of overpopulation with overproduction (or the coincidence of too many destitute people with – for them – too many impossibly unaffordable manufactured goods), which leads in turn to the seemingly inescapable emergence of widespread and chronic overcapacity, with its associated tendency towards 'superabundance' or 'gluts' of manufactured goods (and eventually *redemptive* price-lowering!). In the wretched industrial stagnation of 1840-43, Thomas Carlyle expostulated: 'Over-production, runs it not so? "Ye miscellaneous, ignoble manufacturing individuals, ye have produced too much! . . . Millions of shirts, and empty pairs of breeches, hang there in judgement against you . . . And now there is glut, and your operatives cannot be fed!"'[19] 'Crudely stated', echoed Greider – just as the 1997-8 'Asian crisis' was making the penalties of today's overcapacity plain for all to see – 'the technology competition leads companies to invest in more output of goods than the global marketplace of consumers can possible absorb . . . The resulting surpluses are often lamented by business leaders but are generally regarded as a revolutionary condition beyond anyone's control . . . Of all the imperative driving the behaviour of global enterprises, this constitutes a central cause of their anxiety'. For it 'represents a fundamental disorder', and 'the threats that accumulating overcapacity will lead to some sort of decisive breakdown'.[20]

It was about the time the Economic History Society was founded (and Griffith was wrestling with his *Population Problems . . .*) that. 'following on from the work of Planck and Einstein', physicists began thinking of 'light as possessing both the qualities of waves and particles'.[21] Three quarters of a century later, in the midst of what we are here suggesting might usefully be thought of as *both* 'the second age of Malthus', *and* 'the (current) second industrial revolution', could it perhaps be time for *economic historians* to consider the 'quantum leap?

Victor Skipp (b. 25. 8. 1925) was educated at Emmanuel College Cambridge He was Head of History at Sheldon Heath Comprehensive School, Birmingham, 1955-59; Principal Lecturer in History and Head of Environmental Studies, Bordesley College of Education, Birmingham, 1963-78. He led the 'Discovering' series of Birmingham University Extramural local history research courses, 1956-90 and published *Crisis and Development: An Ecological Case Study of the Forest of Arden 1570-1674* (Cambridge, 1978). Thereafter (aided by John Townley, and many others) he has extended the same 'ecological' approach to the rise of modern Birmingham.

---

[1] Griffith, G. Talbot, *Population Problems in the Age of Malthus* (Cambridge, 1926), pp. 91-2.
[2] Mokyr, J., 'The Industrial Revolution and the New Economic History', in Mokyr, J. (ed), *The Economics of the Industrial Revolution* (London, 1985), p.20.
[3] James, P., *Population Malthus: His Life and Times* (London, 1979), p250.
[4] Winch, D., *Riches and Poverty: An Intellectual History of Political Economy in Britain, 1750 – 1834* (Cambridge, 1996), p.370.
[5] Hilton, Boyd, *Corn, Cash, Commerce: The Economic Policies of the Tory Governments 1815-1830* (Oxford, 1977), p.305.
[6] *Times Literary Supplement*, 19 March 1996, p.4.
[7] For a fuller arguing of this whole case, see the author's hopefully forthcoming *Industrial Revolution: Then and Now* (seeking a publisher).
[8] Attwood, T., *The Distressed State of the Country: The Speech of Thomas Attwood, Esq. . . .at the town's meeting in Birmingham on 8th May 1829* (Birmingham,1829), p.11.
[9] Guest, J. (ed and continuator), *The History of Birmingham by W. Hutton, F.A.S. with considerable additions* (sixth edn) (Birmingham, 1834), p81.
[10] Gayer, A.D., Rostow, W.W., Schwartz, A.J., *The Growth and Fluctuations of the British Economy 1790-1950* (Oxford, 1953), pp 636-7.
[11] Dent, R.K., *The Making of Birmingham* (Birmingham, 1894), p.350.
[12] Greider, W., *One World, Ready or Not: The Manic Logic of Global Capitalism* (Harmondsworth, 1997), p.11; Honeyman, K., (book review) *Economic History Review*, 2nd ser., L (1997), p.845.
[13] Pratt, S.J., *Harvest Home: Consisting of Supplementary Gleanings . . .* (London, 1805), II, p.376.
[14] Guest, *History of Birmingham*, p.132.
[15] Woodward, C.J., 'Birmingham trades and industries during the last century', *Transactions of the Birmingham Archaeological Society*, XXX (1904), pp. 36-46.
[16] Timmins, S. (ed), *Birmingham and the Hardware District*, (London, 1866), p.433.
[17] 'Table of steam engines in the borough of Birmingham in 1835', *Report of the Birmingham Philosophical Institute*, 1836 (Birmingham, 1936); 'Steam Engines in the borough of Birmingham up to December 1838', *Journal of the Statistical Society of London*, 1840 (London, 1840).
[18] Greider, *One World*, pp. 27, 88, 59.
[19] Carlyle, T., *Past and Present* (London, 1843), p.230.
[20] Greider, One World, pp. 103-4.
[21] Bullock, A., and Trombley, S. (eds), *The New Fontana Dictionary of Modern Thought* (third edn, London, 1999), p.717.

Economic History and Human Welfare

Richard H. Steckel

My thoughts on the general question of 'What economic history means to me' are put forward in the form of an observation and some advice. The observation, based on many years of attending conferences, untold informal conversations, and extensive reading of books, book reviews and journal articles is this: Economic historians are united by their interest in describing and explaining the economic past, but divided by their ideas on interesting and worthy research topics. If this seems like a contradiction, I'll explain.

If a common interest in understanding the past can be taken for granted, how can this shared curiosity be shadowed by alternative conceptions of valuable research agendas? My most vivid, early experience with the ideas that divide us occurred when I was a young assistant professor attending the Economic History Association meetings at Toronto in 1978. At the banquet, Douglass North was introducing the new president, Robert Fogel. North and Fogel are old friends and the introduction was warm and upbeat, but along the way he became evaluative, chastising Fogel for absorbing so much of the profession's time and energy in studying slavery, especially when he thought there were far more important topics to be considered. To be sure, the remark was made partly in jest, and at a time when the debate over *Time on the Cross* was in full swing. Yet, the comment drew hardy but serious laughter and the point was intentional.

Since that banquet, I have heard or read innumerable remarks in the same vein. Although most were far less dramatic, I have observed that economic historians (and other academics, too) readily supply their opinions or judgements on what makes an interesting research topic. Passions on this subject are easily aroused, and not just over drinks or in similar informal settings. Debate is intense and serious during the hiring season, when candidates rise or fall in the eyes of hiring-committee members based on the specific topics in their research programs. I am not arguing that technique and data sources are irrelevant, but if some modest qualifications in these areas are met, often the specific topic of study confers the upper hand in decision-making.

Why can't economic historians agree, or at least be more agreeable, on what constitutes interesting research? Can anything be done about it? While I have not given careful scientific study to the first question, I am willing to venture this hypothesis: individual scholars are attracted to specific subfields of research for reasons that are substantially idiosyncratic. In principle, detailed research agendas could be formulated by carefully ranking the returns to alternative investments by studying a wide variety of research problems, assessing their potential for contributions to valuable knowledge, and making decisions accordingly--much as an investor in stocks or bonds would decide how to manage a portfolio. No doubt expected returns (including monetary ones) play some role for most people, especially for those on or near the margin of various related career choices. I suspect, however, that graduate students and other young researchers who are forming careers know that they lack the breadth and judgement required for success with these methods.

Far more influential in directing the process for specific individuals, I think, are accidental circumstances and emotions. A person may study globalisation, banking, the integration of labour markets, schooling, health, or innumerable other subjects largely because the topic was presented in an enthusiastic and interesting way during a course the person happened to take. Or because it happened that financial aid was available in their graduate program for studying the topic, or because they discovered that relevant data were readily available, by chance a friend was also interested in the subject, or a persuasive professor insisted the topic was interesting. The list of specific reasons may be almost endless. I suspect that a survey of economic historians would reveal a long and varied list of specific explanations leading to the choices of research topics early in their careers.

Whatever the explanations, once choices are made, any investment of time and research energy tends to reinforce beliefs about what is interesting. Additional reading or study revels new research problems, dialogue with other scholars working in the area often extends the excitement, and soon the individual researcher acquires an identity leading to requests for book reviews in the area, to referee papers, and to give papers at conferences, which creates professional inertia that is often difficult to change even if research tastes change later in life. Changes in research agendas do occur, but they are frequently to neighbouring areas. Thus, I am arguing that persistence occurs for many reasons, which reinforce initial choices made heavily by chance. Hence, as scholars we often cannot justify our choices of research topics because frequently they were not made in ways that are defensible, i.e. by carefully weighing numerous alternative research projects based on pure intellectual merit. Emotional appeal, random events and forces leading to persistence guide much of the process.

If it is inevitable that random forces play an important role in shaping research interests, perhaps the best we can do as a profession is to seek common standards for evaluating research output. More often, we should ask of our work McCloskey's grand question, 'So what?' I am proposing, however, more than just enthusiasm for the question. The next logical step is to formulate methods for comparing the value or importance of disparate research findings. In my view, the most relevant criterion would be the work's contribution to understanding the evolution of human welfare. In a very broad sense, we study little else. Even advances in technique, a research area that appears to have a life of its own, are ultimately useful insofar as they have practical applications for studying welfare.

Human welfare is a complex subject, and most economic historians would agree that it has several dimensions, including material living standards, health, and a psychological component that embraces freedom, among other things. While we may never agree on its precise meaning, our research can do much more in striving to define it and in explaining how our research findings may relate to it. Too often our work stops short of this last effort. Studies of labour or capital integration, for example, usually end without attempting to estimate their contribution to economic growth. Similarly, many studies of public health practices may fail to approximate their importance to longevity. Too often the psychological dimension of human welfare is ignored altogether.

To the extent that research in economic history is published in short articles, it may be unrealistic to expect each paper to link results to human welfare (or one of its commonly accepted proxies such as income or longevity). This is all the more true if linkage would be a major project in itself. At least more could be done in the small space of most articles to set forth a research agenda that would help connect results to living standards or to the quality of life. Moreover, books are not so constrained by space, and reviews of the literature could certainly do more to associate the findings of a body of work with the evolution of human welfare, thereby creating common ground that would help guide the profession's allocation of research resources.

Richard Steckel (b. 28. 6. 1944). AB, Oberlin College 1966; MA University of Oklahoma, 1970; MA University of Chicago, 1973; Ph.D., University of Chicago, 1977. Except for sabbaticals (both at Harvard – 1985-86 and 1993-94) he has spent his career at Ohio State University in Columbus where he became Professor in 1989. Two years ago he was elected Vice-President of the Economic History Association. He has held an appointment in anthropology (courtesy) since 1995.

What Economic History Means to Me

Barry Supple

The roots and course of any academic commitment are extraordinarily difficult to disentangle. The influence of personality (one's own as well as others'), personal history and experience, ideological concerns, intellectual provocation and excitement, accidental events - all intermingle beyond the point of feasible ordering into some hierarchy of explanation. Perhaps, like the putative Industrial Revolution, the development of an academic, and especially an economic historian, is beyond systematic comprehension.

Superficially, my own career as an economic historian was fashioned by a limited number of people and a logic of cause and effect that a later age might have labelled 'path dependence.' And that story should be mentioned first. At the outset, I was influenced by a combination of aversion and attraction. After my first few weeks as a callow undergraduate at the London School of Economics, I decided that what seemed from an impetuous perspective to be the aridity of an economics specialism (or at least of the preparatory tooling-up for such a specialism) was not for me. On the other hand, along with a relaxed group of *epigone*, the exotic reassurances of sixteenth- and seventeenth-century social and economic development, as mediated through the attractive cynicism and scathing wit of F.J. (Jack) Fisher, provided a self-contained intellectual, and even social, world of it own. There was something intangibly comforting about studying a period and a society which, although so much unlike the present, seemed comprehensible and logical. Thus the illusions of youth and the charms of a role model worked their magic.

After LSE, needing financial support, I was fortunate enough to secure a research studentship at Cambridge. There, I encountered a different and more oblique sophistication, in the form of my supervisor, C. H. (Charles) Wilson. In the context of a **very** unstructured graduate programme, he conducted me, with benign neglect albeit rapidly, through the process of a PhD on early seventeenth-century trade fluctuations and economic policy. Much of what I have written about since then seems to echo this first perspective, although with the rationalisation of hindsight we can all detect long-running themes and continuities in our lives. Thus, in the following decades, as I went to teach in the United States (where I learned a vast amount from Alex Gerschenkron's remarkable analytic insight into the relationship between social institutions, levels of development and the role of the State) and then Canada, before returning to England for successive posts at Sussex, Oxford and Cambridge, my preoccupation with the interaction between economic dislocation, economic thought and public policy does indeed now seem to have been rooted in my initial study of commercial crisis and change. This variegated theme seemingly logically reappeared in my excursions into the history of economic growth, the economic role of the early-modern State, nineteenth-century thrift legislation, the comparative history of the State's relationship with economic change, the British coal industry before nationalisation, the nature of Britain's economic 'decline', and the moral aspects of structural change and macro- and micro-economic policy in twentieth- century Britain.

Of course, few themes are without a counterpoint, and while I was toying with these insistent topics, I was also developing a parallel interest in business history. That interest was initially stimulated by the obligations of my first teaching appointment (at the Harvard Business School), which itself resulted from the intermediation of my Cambridge supervisor, Charles Wilson, whose history of Unilever established the *genre* of company history in this country. When I returned to the United Kingdom, I retained a vestigial interest in the subject. This interest was fanned into profitable flame by a commission to write the history of the Royal Exchange Assurance, and was then sustained with somewhat more professional assertion than substantive achievement. On the other hand, in later years my work on the pre-nationalisation coal industry was closely concerned with business structures and problems, and I happily agreed to act in an advisory capacity to a number of business histories since then - including, in poetic fulfilment of my postgraduate association with Charles Wilson, current work as consulting editor for the fourth volume of the History of Unilever.

But told in this way, the story of this biographical progression is superficial, and the 'reasons' for it banal. The really interesting questions relate to the deeper origins of such concerns and the implications for my own view of economic history.

Here, of course, it is difficult - probably impossible - to escape rationalisation. But after almost 50 years it seems reasonable to argue that my reiterated return to the themes of political economy has reflected a concern with both the practicality of economic issues and basic political questions which transcended (or perhaps shied away from) the drama of day-to-day party politics. At the same time, to someone as ill equipped as I to deploy the methodology of advanced economic theory, it was logical to approach the field historically and in the round. How economic change occurred and affected people, how they perceived their economic problems, how these perceptions and the pressures resulting from a diversity of perceptions related to what was attempted by way of amelioration, and what the effect of consequent policies was on the situation which had given rise to the thinking in the first place - all these perspectives could and perhaps had to be dealt with in broad, even rough, terms.

Taking this point even further, it might well be argued that the nature of my interest in economic history was itself profoundly shaped by the issues that surrounded me and my contemporaries. As I wrote in the Introduction to *The Experience of Economic Growth* (1963):

> It has been said that each new generation rewrites its own history. And this is as true of economic as of other varieties of history. One striking feature of the progress of economic history (as of theoretical economics) over the last few generations is the extent to which each generation has tended to be preoccupied with specific topics, and the extent to which such topics, although considered in their historical context, have been derived from contemporary problems.

Whether this is a truism or only a first and rather crude approximation to an understanding of the roots of history, the content still strikes me as important and usefully provocative. As scholars, we are what we experience. Of course, our experiences and the way we process them vary enormously between individuals and groups. But they also change over time. I was a child of wartime and a youth of post-war Britain. And I now feel that my interest in economic history was in large part an outgrowth of the resulting reactions to circumstances: a confused sense of the personal importance of economic performance, the problems now defined as structural (changes in people's livelihoods and welfare), the ways in which different communities enjoyed or felt deprived of its fruits, the rationalisations and systematisations which pass for economic and political thought, the reactions of those in power to the pressures and potentials, and the impact of what they did.

For a few years after the War my father ran a small and unsuccessful tailoring workshop. Sometime in the late 1940s or early 1950s I read an article in the *Economist* which, almost in an aside, referred to the need to raise interest rates in order (I paraphrase) to squeeze some of the fat out of the economy - and abruptly realised that my father's income and my welfare were part of the 'fat' to be eliminated. It was a salutary realisation, even though I was (just) sufficiently 'mature' to catch the glimmer of a point to which I returned at more length 50 years later - namely, that the fact that the costs and benefits of macroeconomic policy are unevenly distributed is an argument not for eschewing the pursuit of such policy but for paying a good deal of attention to the equity with which its effects are experienced.

What, then, are the implications of all this for economic history? To return to my own biographical and personal terms of reference, they are perhaps that whatever else it aims to achieve (and no one could deny the multifarious nature of the task) the subject must be concerned with the lives of people, the patterns into which those lives fall, and the outlooks and relationships which characterise both the people and the patterns. When I was an undergraduate, R. H. Tawney, although retired, gave a series of remarkable lectures at LSE. Like so many of my generation, I was deeply influenced by his writings and his comforting mixture of morality and irony. As a graduate student I went to see him for advice, and was warmly received in an atmosphere marked by gentle courtesy and herbal tobacco smoke. But I soon deduced that my choice of an ostensibly attractive research topic was not in itself sufficient to make a mark. Attractive topics, like book proposals, are easy to specify and therefore innumerable and frequently unrealistic. What are needed to make a mark are insight, originality and achievement. In a curious way, therefore, I was a little chastened by the great man's relaxed off-handed reaction. Nevertheless, my apparent rebuff did not undermine my admiration. For me, Tawney remains a pillar of economic history, and its human face.

Yet no building is adequately sustained by one pillar. And from this viewpoint I sense that the full realisation of the human values of the subject needs other characteristics. It needs, for example, the sharp and unexpected insights and even the hardness of mind that I found in Jack Fisher (of whom it was said by a friend that, on seeing a clergyman burning at a mid-sixteenth-century stake, whereas Tawney might suffer in sympathy, Fisher would pass by, pausing only to take his pipe out of his mouth and express his mild and powerless, if genuine, regrets). I should also wish to recruit the devotion to impersonal analysis and the recognition of economic realities that Charles Wilson exemplified in such a demanding, humane and affable way. And I should like to be able to make good use of the intellectual breadth, the social and institutional insights, and the cross-cultural vision that Alex Gerschenkron brought to the study of economic development.

All this is phrased in terms of specific personalities and experience. But it is not my intention to hold up particular role models to the constituency in general. Rather, I cite this team as representative of what is needed if economic history is to fulfil what I hope is an important function: linking the world of economic change with the lives of the people who inhabit it; linking the way people think with the way they act; linking theory and policy, economics and politics; linking realism with morality.

Throughout the world the twentieth century witnessed violent swings in political economy as huge changes in economic performance interacted with equally huge shifts in expectations. The resulting confrontations between the State and the Market, between regulations and competition, between collectivity and individualism, are major topics in their own right. But they, and the resulting trends in welfare provision and public and private enterprise, also provide a powerful context for the work of economic historians, who can bring to bear analyses which range far beyond the temporal limits of the last 60 or 100 years. At its most promising, economic history is positioned at the intersection not only of disciplines but of some of the central preoccupations and moral needs of human society. Of course, very few of its practitioners can hope to contribute any large insights into these matters. But if we do not try, we have sinned by neglecting to make the best use of our potential.

Barry Supple (b. 27.10.1930) has been Director of the Leverhulme Trust since 1993. He trained at the London School of Economics and at Cambridge University. In the period 1965-78 he was Professor of Economic and Social History at the University of Sussex, acting also as Pro-Vice Chancellor there. He was Professor of Economic History at Cambridge, 1981-93 and has spent periods at Harvard University as visiting Professor. His reaserch interests and many publications have covered early modern trade, the insurance and coalmining industries, business history and economic thought.

Reminiscences of Britain and Financial Revolutions

Richard Sylla

In 1975, I had earned my first sabbatical year, and Patrick O'Brien was kind enough to invite me to spend the academic year 1975-1976 at St. Antony's, Oxford. At the time, the two of us were struggling young scholars trying to get our work done as well as leading somewhat normal family lives and making ends meet. Now, a quarter century later, Patrick is the president of the Economic History Society, and I am the president of the Economic History Association, its US-based counterpart. On behalf of all E.H.A. members, I want to congratulate the Economic History Society on reaching its 75th anniversary, and to salute Patrick for his stellar leadership of it. It has been my good fortune to be a member of both groups for three decades, an arrangement I heartily recommend to all in the economic history business.

Before getting down to business, I cannot suppress a desire to reflect on what a few acquaintances in Britain were doing a quarter century ago. Patrick, of course, was an Oxford don, not yet a professor in London and potentate of economic history. Avner Offer was just beginning to hone his ideas as a St. Antony's research student, but one already could detect their uniqueness. Charles Goodhart was at the Bank awaiting instructions from the government on how much money to print, not in his later position of telling the Bank from his chair at LSE how much it ought to print. Paul David had not yet left Silicon Valley to improve his perspectives on technological change from the sanctuary of All Souls, where one supposes that working typewriters were still available for hypothesis testing. Niall Ferguson was a wee lad in Scotland; dandled on his grandfather's knee, he began to wonder with each bounce if every big fact implied a counterfactual question, and who really were the villains of the Great War. Compared to these nomads, Phil Cottrell has been a pillar of stability; he was teaching economic history in Leicester in 1976, and he still is.

I came to Britain in 1975 with the general goal of studying the development of the British banking system, with a particular interest in tracing influences of British banking institutions and practices on US banking development. What I knew at the time, from my American perspective, was that the British North American colonies before 1776 had had no modern-type banks. British merchants and financial institutions did most of the financing of colonial trade with the rest of the world. The absence of banks, however, led the Americans into a major financial innovation. To economise on specie, which was precious foreign exchange, the colonists introduced fiat paper money. Initially issued by Massachusetts in 1690, the innovation spread to all of the 13 colonies by the late colonial era. Fiat money became an important medium of exchange in the domestic colonial economies. During the American Revolution, fiat money was issued to excess and became discredited. The US Constitution of 1787 took away the right of states to issue it. From the 1780s forward, the US introduced banks, and with the rapid expansion of the US banking system after 1790, bank money became an increasing proportion of the US money stock. Colonial America, having gone off on a tangent from the main direction of European financial development, returned to that direction as an independent United States.

It was in the period from the 1780s to the 1830s, then, that I expected I might find influences of British banking and financial practices on US developments. There were some. The leading US financial thinker and doer, Alexander Hamilton, was familiar with British and other European financial history and practices. As the first Secretary of the Treasury starting in 1789, Hamilton introduced British-style public finance, a national bank on the model of the Bank of England, and a US dollar anchored, like the pound sterling, in a monetary base of specie, into which bank money was convertible.

In banking, however, I quickly learned that differences between Britain and the United States were more striking than any similarities. Apart from the corporate Bank of England, which was rather like the Bank of the United States (although it would not have the latter's branches until later), British banks consisted of London private bankers, small country banks in England, and, in Scotland, a small number of banks on the Bank of England model and a larger number of banking companies with branches. Almost all of the British banks were partnerships with unlimited liability. In the United States, on the other hand, almost all the banks were corporations with limited liability chartered by state governments. The numbers of these banks increased with rapidity. There were 4 in 1790, about 30 in 1800, 100 by 1810, more than 300 by 1820, and nearly 600 by 1835. The American state banks raised their capitals by issuing tradable shares to investors. It was not unusual for the state governments that granted corporate charters to the banks to hold some shares in them. These governments also received up-front payments for granting bank charters, on-going tax and other revenues from the banks, and in the charters they often directed the banks to perform public services and make public investments. In Britain two centuries ago, there was nothing like these close and cosy relationships between banks and governments.

Looking back, the most interesting discovery I made during that British sabbatical year was an anonymously authored 1828 pamphlet in the celebrated collection of the Goldsmiths Library, *Report and Observations on the Banks, and other Incorporated Institutions, in the State of New York*. Somehow I determined (and would later discover that others already knew) that it was the work of one James Buchanan, who at the time was the British consul in New York City. In the report, the consul expressed amazement at all the banking, insurance, and Lombard saving associations that were being chartered by the New York State government, a development that had no counterpart in Britain or Europe. Some of his amazement was negative. Often the paid-up capital of the banks and other financial corporations was far less than the capital authorised in the charters, and often the enterprises over-issued their own liabilities and failed. The US financial system, it seemed, was awash with fictitious capital. Buchanan further noted the considerable corruption that seemed to be inherent in the politics of chartering corporations.

But consul Buchanan's amazement was also positive. By issuing so many corporate charters the state legislature, he noted, had 'sought to draw forth the energies of the people', and on the whole the experiment was a great success, unleashing a productive capability that 'in the history of nations affords no parallel'.[1] To drive his message home to his intended readers back in Britain, Buchanan contrasted the results of New York's experiments with conditions in 'our own territories' to the north. The contrast was 'a reproach to British rule' because 'crossing the St. Lawrence from any part of the state of New-York into Canada', a traveller immediately had 'an opportunity of comparing the enterprise, energy, and industry of one country, with the lassitude, torpidity, and indolence which prevail in the other'.[2]

Having gone to Britain in 1975 to study similarities in British and US financial development and British influences on the early United States, I returned in 1976 with a much greater impression of the differences that arose between the two countries' experiences in the early decades of US history. I explored these differences directly in a paper on the significance of corporate banking.[3] In the 1830s, there was a debate of sorts between the American economist H.C. Carey and the British banker J.W. Gilbart on the relative virtues and vices of corporate limited-liability banking versus partnership and joint-stock unlimited-liability banking. Carey said that the corporate form was the better system, and Gilbart the opposite. Data on banking failures I gathered from both sides of the Atlantic appeared to support the American, Carey. So did subsequent history, as the British eventually allowed banks to adopt the corporate form, and nearly all banks now are corporations. The explanation is that the corporate form, while seeming to limit the assets standing behind a bank's liabilities compared to an unlimited bank, actually increases them because it attracts more investor interest and leads to more highly capitalised banks.

Another co-authored paper explored the implications of the close relationships that developed between US banks and the state governments that chartered them.[4] One implication was good. Since the states had a strong fiscal interest in chartering banks, they chartered lots of them, encouraging the spirit of enterprise early identified by British consul Buchanan. The United States by the early twentieth century became uniquely a nation with tens of thousands of independent banks, many with single offices, while most countries including Britain consolidated their banking into a smaller number of institutions with extensive branch systems. On the other hand, the close identification of American banking with state governments and state boundaries prevented a rationalisation of the system right down to our own time.

Another benefit of that British sabbatical a quarter century ago was that I became familiar with the concept of a 'financial revolution'. Britain's occurred in the late seventeenth and early eighteenth centuries, well before American independence. Further investigations convinced me that Britain had adopted much of its financial revolution from the Dutch Republic, which had its own financial revolution a century before. Somewhat to my surprise, I also learned that Lt. Col. Alexander Hamilton of the Continental Army during the American Revolution, at age 23 in 1780, was quite familiar with the British and Dutch financial revolutions, and also with the promise and pitfalls of John Law's system in France. Hamilton had determined that the main reason the Revolution against British rule dragged on so long was that America's public finances were chaotic, not because of military disadvantages. He used the lulls in eighteenth-century warfare to bone up on financial history and to sketch out a future US financial system based on best practices elsewhere. After leading a bayonet charge at Yorktown, the success of which led him to predict Cornwallis's surrender and ultimate American success, he further studied finance and engaged in reforming the US governmental system.

In 1789, as Treasury Secretary, Hamilton at last had the opportunity to put his learning into practice. In just a few years, he implemented a US financial revolution that had taken decades to happen in the Dutch Republic and Britain. In honour of Hamilton's political party, I call it 'the Federalist financial revolution.'[5] Directly, it involved restructuring US Revolutionary War debts, stabilising public finances, founding the Bank of the United States, and introducing the hard-money US dollar. That took two years, 1790-1791. Indirectly, as all of the new US debt

354

securities (with interest and principal payable for the first time in hard money) and the shares of the Bank of the United States were issued, trading markets for these securities quickly arose in Boston, New York, Philadelphia, and other cities. And as the Bank of the United States began to open branches in a number of cities, the states began to charter more banks (and other corporations) of their own lest they cede the turf of banking to the federal government. The bankrupt country of the 1780s suddenly had an articulated, modern financial system, and was off and running. By 1803, when Thomas Jefferson successfully used his arch opponent Hamilton's financial system to double the size of the United States, half of all US securities, public and private, were in foreign hands, representing the early stages of one of history's greatest international capital flows.

When British consul Buchanan looked in on the US financial revolution in the 1820s, it was going full tilt. State and corporate securities were crossing the Atlantic, with the proceeds used to finance canals, railroads, and other enterprises in America. By that time, by my rough calculations, the United States, even though its population was smaller, had more than twice the capital invested in banking than did England and Wales, and the capital of American corporations already roughly equalled the par value of all the equities listed on the London Stock Exchange, or at least those listed in *Course of the Exchange*, the newspaper that reported the London list.[6]

The US financial revolution preceded and assisted the developments that are usually cited as explaining US economic modernisation, namely the industrial and transportation revolutions and the opening up of the vast territories of the west. It is worth noting that the Dutch and the British financial revolutions also came early, before the economies in which they were embedded became world leaders. The same could be said of Japan in a later era. When it was a relatively poor and isolated country in the late nineteenth century, Japan too had a financial revolution, and then went on to become the prime example of a non-Western country fully to modernise its economy.[7]

I think it is suggestive that what many would consider to be the four leading economies of the past four centuries all had financial revolutions early in their histories, before they became leading economies. To me it suggests that we need to re-examine whether the Anglo-centric view of economic history, namely that the industrial revolution that began in eighteenth-century Britain has been the key to economic modernisation throughout the world ever since, is indeed correct. Maybe the industrial revolution depended to an extent, perhaps a large extent, on a prior financial revolution. A critic of such a heretical view might say, 'But look at the poor Dutch. They didn't have an industrial revolution and were left behind'. My response would be that in modern history the Dutch do not ever seem to have been poor. Most comparative statistics show the Dutch having higher average incomes and output per person most of the time than the British, before *and after* the industrial revolution. An industrial revolution is a means, not an end in itself.

That is what I began to learn in 1975 on my sabbatical pilgrimage to the home of the industrial revolution. It was a formative experience for which I shall always remain grateful.

Richard Sylla (b. 16. 1. 1940) is Henry Kaufman Professor of the History of Financial Institutions and Markets, and Professor of Economics, Stern School of Business, New York

University, and Research Associate, National Bureau of Economic Research. In 2000-2001, he is president of the Economic History Association. His research and many publications have concentrated upon the history of finance.

[1] Anonymous (James Buchanan, British Consul in New York), *Report and Observations on the Banks, and other Incorporated Institutions, in the State of New York* (New York, 1828), pp. 10-22.

[2] ibid.

[3] Sylla, R., 'Early American Banking: The Significance of the Corporate Form', *Business and Economic History*, 2nd ser., 14 (1985), pp. 105-123.

[4] Sylla, R., J.B. Legler, and J.J. Wallis, 'Banks and State Public Finance in the New Republic, 1790-1860', *Journal of Economic History*, 47 (June 1987), pp. 391-403.

[5] See Sylla, R., 'U.S. Securities Markets and the Banking System, 1790-1840', *Federal Reserve Bank of St. Louis Review*, 80, no. 3 (May-June 1998), pp. 83-98.

[6] See Rousseau, P.L., and Sylla, R., 'Emerging Financial Markets and Early U.S. Growth', National Bureau of Economic Research *Working Paper 7448*, (December 1999).

[7] See Sylla, R., 'Emerging Markets in History: the United States, Japan, and Argentina', in R. Sato, et al., eds., *Global Competition and Integration* (Boston: Kluwer Academic Publishers, 1999), pp. 427-446/

The Meaning of Economic History: An Interdisciplinary Perspective

Rick Szostack

Research on the nature of disciplines and subdisciplines (e.g., Salter and Hearn, 1996) has found that these can generally be identified at any point in time by five evolving characteristics: a certain subject matter, a preference for certain theories, an emphasis on certain methods, a 'worldview', and a set of 'rules of the game' including guidelines for publication and career progress. It is widely, though not universally, recognised that such a disciplinary structure imposes arbitrary limits on academic understanding: certain theories, methods, and perspectives are brought to bear on some questions but excluded from others. Yet while this observation may seem obvious at the global level, it is too easily obscured at the level of the subdiscipline.

Flexibility can only be assured if subdisciplines are defined in terms of only one of these five characteristics. We must, then, choose which of these defines economic history (and how), and then ensure that we are not unnecessarily restrictive with respect to the other four characteristics. There is an increasing tendency to identify disciplines with methods, and disciplinary specialisation by method *instead of* (not in addition to) subject. This may be advantageous if it is harder to master method than subject. Traditionally, though, disciplines have been defined by subject matter, and I suspect that the vast majority of economic historians, faced with the choice, would prefer to define our field in terms of subject than method. I remain convinced that it is much harder to understand the course of history than the intricacies of any method.

What is the subject of economic history? The easiest answer would be that we study any economic phenomenon as this occurred or evolved in history. Beyond begging the question of how to define the set of 'economic phenomena' (and note that the postwar economics profession has until recently devoted scant attention to institutions or technology, two phenomena which deservedly occupy much of our time and effort), such a definition seems entirely too broad to provide useful guidance to either practitioners or those in related fields (both on what we do, and why they should care). I believe that economic history is and should be (and was, much more clearly, in its early days) focused on the study of the causes and consequences of economic growth throughout human history (note that economic history is thus often performed by development economists and some economists in other fields). To be sure, as in any science, some of our research is only loosely related to this grand theme. But I think it important nevertheless for us to appreciate the grand goal of our collective enterprise, both to guide the decisions of researchers and referees, and to enhance our ability to defend our place to other economists and historians. It is a travesty that 'economic growth' is identified by economist colleagues and students as the subject of a series of simplistic models taught as an afterthought in macroeconomic coursework (especially since the growth process generates fluctuations in economic activity much more so than the reverse). It is our exploration of the dynamic interactions among technology, institutions, demography, and a host of other phenomena which has and will be the primary source of academic understanding of economic growth processes.

We might define ourselves instead in terms of the application of economic theory to historical events or processes, but such a definition would simultaneously constrain our subject matter and theory. It would also encourage both economists and historians to question our value added. And the simple fact is that most economic theory deals with efficiency rather than growth. While the two goals are not unrelated, they are far from identical. Moreover, most existing theory is essentially static (though this is slowly changing), while growth is an inherently dynamic process. And the limited body of formal 'growth theory' which exists casts an almost imperceptible light on real world growth experiences. It is often a good strategy first to see how much of a particular event or process can be comprehended within existing theory. But economic historians must stand ready to add to our body of theory. And we do this primarily by seeking out 'regularities' among relevant phenomena: what effect do particular types of institution have, and how are the institutions themselves and their effects shaped by yet other phenomena?; what range of factors encourage technological innovation, and how does this in turn affect growth and fluctuations? The uniqueness of institutions and innovations, as well as the complex web of interactions between these and other phenomena, require a complex theoretical structure with room for hundreds of different causal links, and in which discussion of each causal link is littered with caveats. I firmly believe that this body of theory can only be built up by detailed and comparative analysis of diverse historical experiences. And only if we recognise this as our purpose.

Rule (1997) argues convincingly that a/the major problem in social science is a focus on testing theory as opposed to explanation. This has two costs: research becomes useless as theories go out of vogue, and we ignore observations which have no implications for our theory (e.g. the highly unusual timepath of technological innovation during the interwar period has no place in macroeconomic models). An explanation-driven approach requires that we be open both to a variety of theories and observations, and particularly to the development of new theories to cope with new observations. Reder (1998) notes that economists cannot generally test theories very well, and they thus emphasise theory over empirics. We as economic historians must strive to avoid this sin, for if we cannot shed light on actual historical growth processes we can say little (that is reliable) about why and how growth occurs.

Common sense dictates that, *for any scientific field*, evidence that comes from more than one of the ten or so methods employed by scientists is to be preferred to exclusive reliance on one method. The study of economic growth is no exception. Few would query the value of mathematical models and statistical tests; yet the uniqueness of particular institutions and innovations guarantees that detailed case studies will always have a place in our efforts to achieve reliable generalisations. Moreover, as we have long since recognised with respect to the Industrial Revolution, important technological and institutional changes can occur which do not show up in the aggregate statistics; we must be able to see the trees as well as the forest.

Most economic historians in the English-speaking world work in Economics departments, where methodological flexibility is still an alien concept. We must stand ready to make a collective case that it is essential to at least our subdiscipline. If we do so, we will take an important step toward identifying the unique mission of economic history (as pretending to be just like other economists has not done). And we will simultaneously make our field more attractive to those in History departments.

Some would argue that a better path to impressing economist colleagues is to show them that the past provides useful tests of economic theory and method. To be sure, the reliance of the wider economics profession on a few decades of data severely limits the range of observation over which theory and method are developed and tested. And I would emphasise that applying existing theory and method to past events and processes is an important part of the economic history mission of identifying how, when, and why various phenomena influence the process of economic growth. But we would go sadly wrong if we were to see this as our goal rather than a means to a greater goal. And experience again suggests that such a narrow view hardly impresses our economist colleagues of our worth.

Others would see our role as proselytising for economic theory and method among historians. I doubt that such a mission would excite either discipline. While we can usefully encourage a more explicitly analytical (but not necessarily formal) approach among the broader community of historians, we are much more likely to impress them of our worth, and encourage more of them to join our ranks, if we stress the importance of economic processes in history, and recognise explicitly that there is room for more than one method in the field.

Interdisciplinarians debate what is meant by a disciplinary 'worldview'. I suspect that it strongly influences, and is influenced by, a discipline's theoretical and methodological preferences. Thus flexibility within economic history in those realms will both encourage and depend upon flexibility in the worldview of economic historians. While I can not attempt a complete inventory of what this might mean, I would highlight two important aspects. One is humility. We have taken as our focus perhaps the most complex set of questions in all of human science. Economic growth is influenced by, and in turn influences, a host of phenomena, many of which are difficult to quantify or even precisely define. While we should celebrate both individually and collectively every advance we make in our understanding, we should not fool ourselves into thinking that we know more than we do. We should be clear about what is left out of our models. When we use static theory to define a supposed 'upper bound' on the effect a particular phenomenon has/had, we should remain open to the possibility of heretofore unimagined dynamic effects. When neoclassical theory *seems* to explain half of an event or process, we should be as conscious of that which is left to be explained. We should not pretend to an unattainable precision, and accept that sometimes qualitative analyses, and huge margins of error, are the best that we can do. We should, in particular, not abuse the rules of statistical analysis by ignoring - or not admitting - the huge margins of error in many of our estimates. Nor should we hide behind tests of statistical significance; we must worry about the historical explanatory power of an argument (as McCloskey has long advised). And we should not be so confident of our pet theories that we ignore the theories and evidence contributed by others (a corollary: we should read widely lest we ignore through ignorance). In addition to humility, we need to admit to, and then consciously act to limit, our inevitable subconscious biases: we should not assume that either governments or markets are always better, that progress or regress or circularity is the inherent nature of human history, or that some received theory must be right. We should be honest with ourselves as with others.

What then should be our 'rules of the game'? We should judge research by the simple and single criteria of whether it adds to our understanding of economic growth; to do otherwise would place an unnecessary constraint on our pursuit of understanding of growth processes. We would thus seek to balance precise answers to 'small' questions with fuzzier answers to big questions. We would not expect any answer to be perfect, and would thus be wary rather than impressed by claims that all loose ends have been tied up. Philosophers of science recognise that 'proof' and even 'falsification' are impossible; we can and must embrace this conclusion, while appreciating that we are still capable of judging good evidence (of various sorts) which adds to (or reduces) our collective confidence in a line of argument. We should look for what is good in a piece, rather than damning it for the slightest of flaws: this latter practice can only encourage a focus on trivialities and the pretence of an unattainable precision.

A mind is a terrible thing to waste. If promising young faculty feel compelled to pursue a narrow form of inquiry in order to get published, they will contribute less while young to our collective understanding than if encouraged to pursue their curiosity. Moreover, they may lose sight of our collective purpose long before they achieve the sort of job security which allows them to do the type of research which they think best. We have a collective duty as referees and editors to ensure that our rules of the game create incentives appropriate to our mission.

And we must remember the complexity of growth processes. As noted above, case studies which seem at first glance distantly related to the big questions of our field may nevertheless provide an important empirical base for larger speculations. Methods, too, may be developed by one scholar and usefully applied by another (a more explicit recognition of the potential for specialisation here could halt the regrettable practice of publishing works that get the history wrong but introduce a new method). Nevertheless we should never forget that our purpose is the elucidation of history; we will fail if we view method as a goal rather than as a means. A recent survey of the most influential works in sociology found that these were generally more famous for introducing a new theory or method than for explicating any sociological process (Clawson, 1998); Reder (1998) argues that fame in Economics comes from mathematical theory or econometrics. We must strive to keep the focus of our field on historical events and processes. Theories are fine, and even essential - I've developed a couple myself - but are to be appreciated not for their beauty, and not for the generation of new research projects, but for how much light they shed on (one or more) growth processes. We must always stand ready to make our theories both uglier and better by adding caveats.

What does economic history mean to me? It is a field devoted to perhaps the most important set of questions in all of human science, concerning why growth occurs more rapidly at some times and places than others. As such, it is an intellectually stimulating endeavour, yet not without inherent frustrations. It is a field that demands humility, openmindedness, cooperation, and awe. Its practitioners must cope with a wide range of causal links, theories and methods. They must be willing to leap across disciplinary boundaries in pursuit of understanding. As with all sciences, they must appreciate both that which we understand and that which we do not. Part dream and part reality, my economic history is very much a work in progress, sometimes glorious in its discoveries, often overzealous in closing off fruitful lines of inquiry. Like any noble quest, it has its choices, its challenges, and its glimpses of truth. If true to itself it will survive and prosper. If we mistake our purpose, though, we will fail in our quest. And the quest is too worthy for that.[1]

Rick Szostak (b. 27. 10. 1959) is Professor of Economics at the University of Alberta. He is the author of six books, *The Role of Transportation in the Industrial Revolution* (1991), *Technological Innovation and the Great Depression* (1995), *Technology and American Society: A History* (with Gary Cross; 1995), *Econ-Art: Divorcing Art From Science in Modern Economics* (1999), *A Schema For Unifying Human Science: Interdisciplinary Perspectives on Culture* (forthcoming), and *Unifying Human Ethics* (under review), as well as several articles spanning the fields of economic history, history of technology, economic methodology, and interdisciplinary theory and practice.

---

[1] The author thanks Herb Emery for helpful comments.

Works cited
Clawson, Dan, ed. (1998) *Required Reading: Sociology's Most Influential Books.* Amherst: University of Massachusetts Press.
Reder, Melvin (1998) *The Culture of Economics.* Chicago: University of Chicago Press.
Rule, James B. (1997) *Theory and Progress in Social Science.* Cambridge UK: Cambridge University Press.
Salter, Liora, and Alison Hearn, eds. (1996) *Outside the Lines: Issues and Problems in Interdisciplinary Research.* Montreal: McGill-Queen's University Press.

What Economic History Means to Me

Yoshiteru Takei

My undergraduate supervisor once said that scholars' academic fields tend to be decided almost by accident. In my case, however, I chose economic history with definite intention. Whether one's field is chosen with intention or not depends much upon the characteristics of the times. When I began to research Japanese economic history, immediately after World War II, the confusion that ranged in Japan was so acute that those brought up after the War may find it hard to imagine. Most Japanese felt not only physically destroyed but also mentally desolated. Some people believed that a socialist revolution would take place in Japan in the near future. Others, who had believed so comprehensively in the Tenno (Emperor) regime, were mentally devastated by its defeat and tried to express their prostrate minds through ideas such as existentialism. Not happy with either of these approaches, I tried to find a way of forecasting the future of Japan through reconsidering Japanese economic history since the Meiji Restoration.

Unfortunately, there were no reliable books on Japanese history at that time. Almost all history books published before the end of the War were written under the influence of the Kokoku-shikan, that is, the historical view that the Emperor would eternally rule Japan. The only books permitted to take a more critical stance were those pertaining to Japanese capitalism. These books were written by economic historians belonging to the Koza-ha or Rona-ha schools.

Let me explain the difference between the Koza-ha and Rona-ha schools of thought. The Koza-ha were a group of historians who regarded the Meiji Restoration not as a revolution but as a reform. Therefore they insisted that Japan should be regarded as a semi-feudal or immature capitalist country. The Rona-ha, on the other hand, regarded the Meiji Restoration as a revolution that had cleaned up all the relics of Japan's feudal past. Hence according to Rono-ha theory, post-Restoration Japanese society was one of mature capitalism.

Needless to say both these approaches were grounded in Marxism. The semi-feudal atmosphere, which had derived from the landlord-tenant relationship, remained in urban as well as rural districts. In addition, militarism was growing more fanatical day by day. Hence historical materialism should have been a powerful and effective way of analysing Japanese capitalism. Although the work of these scholars had been repressed and their books prohibited, these restrictions were lifted immediately after the War and their books were reprinted and popularised among young scholars and students. They became, as it were, the starting point of the 'scientific study' of Japanese economic history in the 'newly re-born Japan'.

As I read these works, one after another, I noticed that the economic historians of both schools regarded the whole process of the growth of capitalism in England as a model of modernisation, as Marx himself had done. Whenever they remarked on the 'distortion of

Japanese capitalism', they appeared to compare it to the 'normalcy' of English capitalism which had built up in their minds through Marx's works. Furthermore, the distortion, according to their theory, was caused by the tension between the relics of a feudal society (or feudal uklad, so to speak), and an immature capitalist one. The more feudal relics that remained, the more difficult the transition to a mature capitalist society would be.

I therefore concluded that it was necessary for me to research into the economic history of England before researching that of Japan. At that time, I intended to return to Japanese economic history before long. However, I became so deeply involved in economic history of England, that 45 years later it is still part of my research. I began, at first, to research the medieval period, in particular, the medieval borough. There were two reasons that made me decide on this as my first subject. Firstly, there was a tendency amongst Japanese economic historians, whose specialist field was basically the transition from feudal to capitalist society, to look back at medieval economic history simply in terms of a source for those aspects that appeared to originate from the medieval age. I, on the contrary, wanted to research into the break up of the English feudal society from inside the feudal system itself.

Secondly, I was, in those days, particularly interested in medieval boroughs because they had appeared as the antithesis of the agricultural society on which the feudal system was founded. I believed that if I researched into those aspects of boroughs that made them distinct (such as burgage tenure, *firma burgi* and free election into the mayoralty, none of which had developed in Japanese medieval cities or towns), I might be able to find clues as to the reason why English society shifted so 'typically' from feudalism to capitalism. The growth of medieval boroughs into modern industrial societies was frustrated by the oligarchic rule of the privileged merchants, who organised the livery companies, and further thwarted by the Test and Corporation Acts. However, in the same way as guild registration, while acting as a barrier to profit-seeking capitalism, had inevitably led to the development of a rational account system (Max Weber), I believed that some of the characteristics of medieval boroughs had extended and spread beyond the borough and laid the foundations of a democratic social system.

This brings us to the pre-modern or semi-feudal subordination of the tenant to landlord which basically distorted Japanese capitalism. In England, the subordination of villein to landlord had begun to break up in the early thirteenth century. The spread of commutation accelerated the independence of villeins and as a result, the number of self-sustaining peasants rose considerably as early as the sixteenth century. By the middle of the eighteenth century, however, as a result of the stratification of property, this group had separated into prosperous landowners and farmers on the one hand and poor peasants on the other. When I look at the violent means of enclosure taken by the former at the expense of the latter, I feel the landlord versus villein system was not completely over.

In Japan, in contrast, the self-sustaining peasant in the strict sense of the term, did not come into existence until the end of World War II. Their existence came about as a result of the Land Reform that took place under the US Occupation. Although since then the traditional landlord versus tenant system has almost disappeared from rural districts, the semi-feudal social consciousness which had derived from it was retained in almost every inch of Japan. Such a social consciousness, to my mind, is based on a sort of sense of hereditary *status*, which could not be distinguished with ease. The bureaucratic hierarchy of Japan, for example, can be said to have been strengthened by this social consciousness. The functional *posts* in a government or firm, therefore, were associated with a feudal or hereditary *status* not only within but also outside of the office. That this social consciousness is based on a kind of hereditary *status* can also be seen in industrial relations.

Although lifetime employment is labelled a peculiarity of Japanese firms, I see it also in the English firm. M. Dupree, R. Fitzgerald, P. Joyce, and R. Whipp point to a considerable number of cases of lifetime employment, sometimes extending across generations. Industrial relations in these firms have been, as a result, as paternalistic as most Japanese firms before the 1990s. However, on closer examination, I could not help noticing a difference between these two sorts of paternalism. In England paternalism was not as powerful as the contract between employer and employee, except in the case of the factory village where the firm was also the landlord of the employee lodgings. In Japan, in contrast, employees could be forced to work over and above the contract, particularly in hard times. Often this was done solely to the benefit of the employer. It must be said that the balance of power between employers and employees was not bilateral but one-sided. So I cannot help but recognise that relics of the subordination of tenant to landlords exist still in industrial relations.

In conclusion, what does economic history mean to me? To me it is a mirror in which we see a reflection of the virtues and vices of the social system of Japan.

Yoshiteru Takei (b. 1929) was educated at the University of Nagoya where he gained his doctorate in economics. He is currently Professor Emeritus Shizuoka University and Visiting Professor Shizuoka Sangyo University. His research interests are; industrial paternalism in England c.1870-1945 and personnel management in the cotton industry in the first half of the twentieth century.

What Economic History Means to Me

Eric Taplin

Economic History has not only been of absorbing interest but has provided me with a fulfilling career in teaching and research extending over 40 years. Yet I came to the subject by a somewhat unusual route and this brief autobiographical sketch may be of interest to readers.

I left school at the age of 16 during the Second World War and it was only in 1947 when I had been demobbed that I had to consider a career. As my education had not been interrupted by the war I was ineligible for a grant, which prevented me form going to university even though the University of Manchester had offered me a place. I chose to become a teacher and, after training, taught in a primary school. Encouraged by my headmaster and the low pay of classroom teachers at that time I studied for a degree by correspondence course. Those were the days before the Open University and it was not uncommon for mature students to study for an external degree of the University of London by that method. Metropolitan College provided me with booklets and reading lists and essays were submitted to anonymous tutors. So during the day I was teaching lively young children and each evening was given over to studying. It was a lonely furrow to plough with no face-to-face contact with either tutors or other students and the material I received from the College often left much to be desired. However I graduated with a B.Sc. (Economics) in 1957 having specialised in Modern Economic History. By then I was so absorbed in the subject that I was determined to learn more in less frenetic circumstance and to teach the subject. I became briefly a part-time evening teacher at the then Regent Street Polytechnic in London (now Westminster University) where Philip Bagwell was senior tutor in Economic History. I owe him a great debt in that his encouragement, wisdom and enthusiasm for the subject were of immense stimulus to this fledgling historian and led to an enduring friendship.

I moved into further education and spent three unsatisfactory years at Llandaff Technical College in Cardiff. I had been led to believe that the work would be teaching Economics and Economic History at GCE Advanced Level but this never materialised. So I was teaching a number of subjects at GCE O Level and Liberal Studies to vocational students. Teaching Liberal Studies to gas fitters is an experience never to be forgotten – the scars remain to this day! Moreover the teaching hours were excessive. In one year I had no less than 27 hours a week of class contact. In 1960, however, I managed to escape by securing a post at the Liverpool College of Commerce. There at least I was able to develop Economic History as a special subject for the External B.Sc. (Econ) of London University. I recall how helpful Walter Stern of the LSE was in giving me advice. But I was involved in teaching on a number of other courses and subjects (including for one year the Economics of Packaging which up until then I had assumed was a matter of brown paper and string). Teaching twenty hours a week again prevented any research being undertaken.

It was not until the formation of the Liverpool Polytechnic, which absorbed the college, that teaching hours were reduced. With the development of our own honours degree, validated by the Council for National Academic Awards, research was not only expected by staff but also demanded. Thus during the 1970s I was at last liberated to specialise in the teaching of Economic and Social History and to undertake research although when I became Head of Department in 1972, administrative duties took up a disproportionate amount of time.

My research interests increasingly drew me towards labour history. My higher degree examined the origins of New Unionism and since then I have concentrated on the development of the Liverpool labour movement and, in particular, the organisation of dock workers and their social conditions. I have always been moved by the contribution that 'the common people' have made to the development of the British economy. In most cases their sweat and toil is the basis for the functioning of the economy. In spite of the efforts of such scholars as G.D.H. Cole and Raymond Postgate it was not until after the Second World War (and especially since the formation of the Society for the Study of Labour History in 1960) that serious efforts have been made to examine their contribution, their struggles and their aspirations. It is not an easy task. Few working people kept diaries or wrote their autobiographies; they were too concerned with the daily struggle to make ends meet. Nevertheless labour historians have thrown much light on hitherto dark corners through a judicious mix of economic and social research. It has given me considerable satisfaction to have made a minor contribution in this respect.

The fascination of Economic and Social History derives from the analysis of such a wide spectrum of human activity. I recall the words of Sir John Clapham written many years ago but which are still relevant:

> Of all varieties of history the economic is the most fundamental . . . Economic activity, with its tools, fields, trade, inventions and investment, is the basis of a man's house . . . The economic basement may be dull, but it need not be . . . As most men and most ages have had little leisure, it is a comfort for the economic historian to remember that the sun seldom failed to get into this basement of his.[1]

As a student in the 1950s Clapham's encyclopaedic three volume *Economic History of Modern Britain* was an indispensable reference work. Other scholars such as R.H. Tawney, T.S. Ashton, Asa Briggs, G.D.H. Cole and D.C. Coleman among others through their books and articles deepened my knowledge and sharpened my intellect. As my research interest in labour history developed so the work of Eric Hobsbawm, Edward Thompson, John Saville and Hugh Clegg raised important issues of debate that could be fruitfully applied to my own work.

From 1960 until recently I attended the annual conference of the Society. At the outset I recall that Philip Bagwell and myself were the only two non-university participants. This gradually changed as polytechnics were formed. Nevertheless with the wisdom of hindsight it could have served the subject well had a more positive effort been made in the early 1960s to encourage participation by schoolteachers and college lecturers. This might have prevented the vicissitudes the subject has suffered from over the last few years. Nevertheless attendance at conference allowed me to widen my contacts and exchange views. I remember, in particular, the incomparable talks by Jack Fisher and the near-incomprehensible comments of Michael Postan!

After some 40 years as a student and teacher of Economic and Social History my interest in the subject remains undimmed. It has been a rare privilege to have had a career of such intellectual interest. It has permitted me to meet and learn from colleagues of high quality. My 75th anniversary predates the society's by one year. I was born in the year of the return to the gold standard; the society was formed in the year of the General Strike. When I retired from the Liverpool Polytechnic (now Liverpool John Moores University) and was invited to become a Fellow of the University of Liverpool I had little idea that as the venerable old 'fellow' in the School of History I would still be making a minor teaching and supervisory contribution 16 years later.

Eric Taplin (b. 22. 2. 1925) was Head of Department of Social Studies, Liverpool Polytechnic (now Liverpool John Moores University), 1972-84. He was founder member and Chair of the North West Labour History Group and is currently Fellow of the University of Liverpool in the School of History (since 1984). His research interests are British labour history, the labour history of Merseyside and the history or dock workers and their unions.

---

[1] Introduction to J. H. Clapham, A Concise Economic History of Britain from the Earliest Times to 1750 (Cambridge, 1949).

From the Danube to the Cam

Alice Teichova

I was born in Vienna in 1920 and came to England after the *Anschluss* on the day of the signing of the Munich Agreement in September 1938. After some vicissitudes I succeeded in obtaining a scholarship at Leeds University where I studied economics from 1942 to 1945. My interest in, love for and commitment to economic history was inspired by H.D. Dickinson. His lectures and seminars on economic theory, history of economic thought and economic history of Britain were convincingly presented, thought provoking and questioning traditional interpretations. Looking back I realise that, in particular, Dickinson's expertise and enthusiasm for socialist economics as well as for studies in capital, investment and finance[1] must later have influenced the direction of my research in economic history.

Dickinson thought that I should pursue economic theory and its application to contemporary economic and political problems as the end to the war seemed to be in sight during 1944-5 and as planning for the post-war economy became more urgent. Therefore he tried to discourage my aspirations to work for a PhD in economic history and encouraged me to turn my attention to one of the urgent contemporary socio-economic problems.

Life, however, did not allow me to realise any of these ideas after the end of the war. My husband, Mikuláš Teich, returned to his country Czechoslovakia, and I was to follow him with my firstborn child, Peter. In the meantime I had to earn a living by teaching at a Modern Secondary School in Nottingham. This, I thought, was my chance to imbibe my pupils with knowledge about economic history. How mistaken I was! The headmistress admonished me that I need not teach the girls anything in particular but I had to keep them busy! Nevertheless I smuggled into the lessons of hygiene and civics spelling competitions as their English was appalling. The nearest I came to economics was by talking to them about shopping and prices of consumer goods.

I was able to join Mikuláš only in Spring 1949. By then Eva had been born and I moved to Prague with two children. Above all, I had to learn Czech. By 1950 I was able to start an academic career at Charles University, at first teaching history of Western Europe to students of English Language and Literature in English until my Czech was proficient enough for the main history courses. Again economic history seemed to pass me by because it did not appear in the lecture list of Charles University. Students could not be examined in this subject unless they chose to study at the Prague High School of Economics. I held my lectures at first on medieval history which gave me the chance to teach medieval legislation about dues and duties of peasants rather than about kings and lords.[2] Later I lectured on the modern history of Western Europe against the background of economic development. During the later 1950s I was able to enthuse a few students to form a research group on the history of large enterprise, concentration and cartel formation in the first half of the twentieth century. Although there was no obvious academic advantage to be gained in the form of exam results students found the search for literature and archival sources exciting. Thus in 1958-1959 the first three prizes of a nationwide competition of students' essays in history were won by members of my economic history group.[3] Still, economic history remained outside the recognised subjects offered by Charles University. Indeed, my habilitation thesis for the *docentura* (Readership) on 'Foreign investment in interwar Czechoslovakia', which I defended in 1964, was recognised as pertaining broadly to Czechoslovak history and not narrowly to economic history.

In the meantime Professor Arnošt Klíma[4] had attended the first International Economic History Congress in Stockholm and had organised a small circle of historians to form the Czechoslovak Economic History Society which I joined as a foundation member. The Czechoslovak group became associated with the International Economic History Association and I was able to attend my first international congress in Munich in 1965. Arnošt Klíma had been elected as member of the International Committee and was preparing the participation of Czechoslovak economic historians at the International Congress at Bloomington in the fateful year of 1968. Both of us, Mikuláš and I, were invited to give papers. My paper - revising traditional views on the distribution of foreign investment in interwar Czechoslovakia - was scheduled for Peter Mathias's Session. On 19 August 1968, one day before the troops of the Warsaw Pact countries invaded Czechoslovakia, I handed in my manuscript on 'International investment in Czechoslovakia 1918-1938' to the Publishing House of the Czechoslovak Academy of Sciences.[5] We were to leave Prague for Bloomington via Paris the day after the invasion had taken place. In an adventurous and dramatic manner we managed to leave the country by train since all airports were occupied and, eventually, landed in Cincinnati and got to Bloomington in time for the Congress. In a highly emotional atmosphere my paper on Czechoslovakia was seen as a protest against the rape of a small country in which the reform movement to build 'socialism with a human face' had made immense progress.

As planned, we spent the year 1968-1969 at the American universities of Yale, Harvard and Wisconsin and decided not to return to Czechoslovakia. We returned to England where we had been during the war and where we joined our children. Mikuláš was invited to a Visiting Scholarship at King's College Cambridge and I was elected to a Bye-Fellowship at Girton College Cambridge where, at last, I could pursue teaching and research in economic history. During this time I was invited to give a paper at the Economic History Department of the London School of Economics and Political Science where I met Donald Coleman. He asked me what my paper was to be about. When I answered that it was to deal with British investment in Czechoslovakia before 1938 he remarked that 'this will be a short paper because there wasn't any'. I was, however, able to convince the audience, including Donald Coleman, that Britain held the greatest percentage of foreign direct investment in the pre-war Czechoslovak economy.

In re-establishing an academic career I was greatly supported by Peter Mathias in Oxford and Michael Postan in Cambridge. Their opinions about the future direction of my teaching and research differed greatly. Michael Postan advised me that, as no-one was interested in Central and Eastern European economic history in Cambridge, I must needs change to British economic history. I did begin teaching British economic history at Girton College, but having reached the age of 48 I was reluctant to change direction and offered a trial lecture at Cambridge University on 'Economic growth and stagnation in Eastern Europe'. 20 students came and stayed the course. Very soon - from 1971 - I could develop the field of European economic history, including prominently Central and Eastern Europe, in both teaching and research at the University of East Anglia in Norwich.

As it happened, my experiences in the USA where cliometrics was hotly discussed, and in Britain, where the debates on imperialism, on the Rostowian stages of economic growth and his 'anti-communist manifesto', as well as Gerschenkron's ideas on relative economic backwardness filled the pages of economic journals, showed that the theory and methodology of economic history was posing questions which were very pertinent for Central and Eastern Europe. It was argued that for the economic development of former colonies the Eastern European historical experience could supply the model for industrial development in economically backward areas. Even though the Eastern European example has neither produced guide lines nor solutions for developing countries, discussions of the 1960s and 1970s did, for a time, bring together economists and historians.

In this atmosphere of searching for explanations for economic development or the lack of it Peter Mathias put me in touch with Michael Kaser of St. Antony's College Oxford with whom we started an international research project on the economic history of Eastern Europe.[6] The three volumes on *The Economic History of Eastern Europe* (from 1918 to 1975) document, on the one hand, the West-East gradient of economic development, on the other, they disprove the generally held view of Eastern Europe - especially during the Cold War - as an undifferentiated socio-economic formation and show the diversity of economic growth or stagnation from West to East (from Czechoslovakia to Bulgaria) and from North to South (from Poland to Yugoslavia).

Since the 1970s I have attempted to examine the history of multinational enterprise, trade, finance and banking in Central and Southeast Europe within the framework of international economic and political development. As a rule, I have been working with teams of economic historians from European countries.[7] Most fortunate and productive became my academic contacts with Austrian economic and social historians which began with an invitation to Vienna from Herbert Matis in 1976 and branched out into several guest-professorships as well as long-term international research projects on interwar Central and Southeast European economic history supported in the 1990s by the Austrian Federal Ministry of Science and Research.

The events of 1989 led to the enrichment of the Central-European research teams since contacts with Czech and Slovak colleagues could be re-established. The starting point were letters from the Historical Institute of the Czechoslovak Academy of Sciences in Prague for Mikuláš and from the Paedagogical Faculty of Charles University for me which we received a month after the events in Czechoslovakia described as the 'Velvet Revolution'. In them an apology was offered for the wrongs that had affected our professional and personal lives and we were invited to come to Prague to discuss these matters, including possibilities of future co-operation. After 22 years of absence we travelled to Prague at the end of January 1990. Since then old contacts with Czech and Slovak colleagues have been renewed and new ones established and work along these line continues.[8]

My itinerary from the Danube, via the Vltava to the Cam has thus been accompanied by economic history.

Alice Teichova (b. Vienna, 19. 9. 1920) is Emeritus Professor of Economic History, University of East Anglia, Honorary Fellow, Girton College, Cambridge and Senior Research Associate at LSE. Her research is the comparative economic history of European countries in the twentieth century with special emphasis on central Europe and the economic policy of National Socialist Germany in occupied Europe.

[1] By 1942 when I entered Leeds University he had published the following books: H.D. Dickinson, G.D.H. Cole, *et al.* (eds.), *Studies in capital and investment* (London, 1935) and H.D. Dickinson, *Economics of Socialism* (Oxford, 1939).

[2] For this course I translated Anglo-Saxon documents which were later published: Alice Teichová, *Prameny ze st_edov_kých d_jin západní Evropy* (Sources of medieval history of Western Europe) (Prague 1961). I had started organising a team of Czech authors with whom I prepared a textbook for students on medieval history. During the 'Prague Spring' it was published in two volumes *D_jiny st_edov_ku* (History of the Medieval Age), (Prague, 1968). Because of my editor- and authorship, it - together with all my other publications - was put on the index of prohibited books. However, as I was told in 1990, students used xerox copies of it as textbook for all the intervening years.

[3] These were published in *Sborník školy pedagogické* (Collected Studies of the University of Education),Historie II (Prague,1959).

[4] Arnošt Klíma refused to recognise the invasion of the Warsaw Pact Troops as 'aid to Czechoslovakia' and thus was officially ostracised. Although unable to travel abroad he was for the next 12 years continually re-elected to the Committee of the International Economic History Association. Also his articles were published in the West. He died after a long illness in 2000.

[5] After further research during my Fellowship at Girton College Cambridge the book was published by Cambridge University Press: *An economic background to Munich International business and Czechoslovakia* in 1974. It was to appear in Czech only after the fall of the communist regime: *Mezinárodní kapitál a _eskoslovensko v letech 1918-1938* (International capital and Czechoslovakia in the years 1918-1938) (Prague, 1994).

[6] This was supported by the Social and Economic Research Council. The result was a three-volume publication: *The Economic History of Eastern Europe* edited by M.C. Kaser and E.R. Radice (Oxford 1985-89). My part in it was 'Industry', Chapter Five, Vol. I (Oxford, 1985), pp.222-322.

[7] Among the publications resulting from research projects supported by the British Economic and Social Research Council (ESRC) were, for instance: Alice Teichova and Philip L. Cottrell (eds.), *International Business and Central Europe 1919-1939* (Leicester -New York, 1983); the same, Philip L. Cottrell and Håkan Lindgren (eds.), *European Industry and Banking 1920-1939. Review of Bank-Industry Relations* (Leicester - London - New York, 1992) and the same, Terry Gourvish and Agnes Pogány (eds.), *Universal Banking in the Twentieth Century, Finance, Industry and the State in North and Central Europe* (Aldershot, 1994). The following two volumes contain results of research supported by the ESRC which were presented at the International Economic History Congress in Bern 1985: Alice Teichova, Maurice Lévy-Leboyer and Helga Nussbaum (eds.), *Multinational enterprise in historical perspective* (Cambridge, 1986) and *Historical studies in international corporate business* (Cambridge, 1989).

[8] From this research resulted publications, such as e.g.: Alice Teichova and Herbert Matis (eds.) *Österreich und die Tschechoslowakei 1918-1938 Die wirtschaftliche Neuordnung in Zentraleuropa in der Zwischenkriegszeit* (Vienna-Cologne-Weimar, 1996) and the same, Alois Mosser and Jaroslav Pátek (eds.), *Der Markt im Europa der Zwischenkriegszeit - The Market in Interwar Central Europe* (Karolinum Prague, 1997).

371

My View of Economic History

Joan Thirsk

For me, history is about people, and economic history is about breathing human beings, getting a living in a constantly changing world. I do not separate economic and social history into two compartments. By concentrating solely on economic factors when explaining the course of economic events. I believe I am grasping only half the story, and sometimes seriously misrepresenting, indeed distorting reality.

So, in order to get at the welter of motives, consequences, and explanations that lie behind economic actions, I have to get inside the minds of our forebears, and try to encompass all aspects of their lives. I hope thereby to get a better understanding of their way of life, their priorities, and the logic of their actions. People's past purposes and choices sprang from just as complex a set of circumstances and considerations as that surrounding us. But they were rooted in a wholly different world of assumptions from our own. I know that I can be beguiled by simple explanations, visible at the surface of things, when the full truth lies deeper, hidden under a multitude of layers. So I am always digging deeper, and I find it well worth all the patience and effort of getting there; it is extremely satisfying as well as sobering.

Of course, at the end I aspire to trace out some larger pattern in the course of events that fits into the story of national developments. Alternatively, I recognise that my results may upturn some long established beliefs about economic development, and then I shall have to defend an argument that will take a long time before it is fully evaluated. Along this line of thought, one of my growing interests in economic history in recent years has been to see changes in the basic assumptions of historians themselves. We are taught to accept certain narratives and explanations of events, and it is not easy to alter that mindset. I have taken a special interest in tracing out the way in which agricultural history has been mapped out for, and by, us in the last seventy or so years. To get a different perspective from our own, I go back to read narratives written a hundred years ago, now virtually ignored. In fact, the 1880s and 1890s bear so many resemblances to our agricultural circumstances today, that books from that time are some of my most enlightening reading. I have learned, moreover, that the wheel turns and turns again, and our viewpoints are always being revised. That adds a further relish to my studies, for I watch for the wheel to turn again!

Among other lessons in the course of my 50 years of studying economic history I have learnt to respect our forebears deeply for their shrewd perceptions, resourcefulness and ingenuity. We are tempted sometimes to think ourselves far more intelligent than those who have gone before; I do not hold that view. We certainly have a greater command over our natural resources, and we are often far better informed in all sorts of ways, but we are not always wiser or more farsighted than they in reaching our final judgements.

All this means that I analyse economic developments in a mood of some humility, doing my best to see them from every angle, and knowing that the most convincing explanations will be far from simple. Sometimes writers from the past bring me up abruptly by their accounts of events that they themselves experienced; they alight on causes and consequences which I would never have arrived at for myself. I realise that we often lack any perception of the practicalities that counted for much or most in their final score. So I habitually search in quite obscure places for enlightenment. The explanations of contemporaries, dwelling in the farthest corners of the kingdom, are just as important to me as the judgements of those more sophisticated characters walking the streets of Westminster. And I often get my best insights from individual people whom I can locate in a particular place at a particular date; better still if I can give individuals a name and set them in a family circle. Like a squirrel I collect many fragments far and wide, and I am grateful to be a local, as well as an economic, historian, for then a combination of local details with the national generalisation brings the scene to life in a remarkably vivid way, and in my final analysis I feel more than usually confident in attributing motives and offering explanations.

A reassuring experience that opened up for me deeper levels of understanding happened recently when Michael Zell cited a document written by Walter Morrell, an early seventeenth-century projector, explaining exactly how he first realised the urgent need to find ways of employing the poor.[1] I knew the place, the date, and the circumstances in which that flash of understanding struck our projector. He lived for a year in Enfield in 1603, he said; he was fleeing plague in London, and happened to have inherited a house there (though, in fact, the plague followed him). It was only when he saw the multitudes of poor scraping a living from the free resources on Enfield Chase that he fully realised the scale of the problem. David Pam, a devoted local historian of Enfield and Edmonton, has told us so much in recent years about that piece of country, on the high road out of London, that we can see it all![2] Morrell's encounter with innumerable poor on Enfield Chase nurtured ideas that grew into a grandiose scheme for creating a new textile industry in Hertfordshire and then in many other counties as well; the documents show how Morrell's plans grew ever larger and bolder. I fancied that he must surely have had a charismatic presence and style of speech to convince so many politicians. It gave me one small but jewel-like illustration of projects and projectors, enough to fill and explain a much larger canvas depicting the mood and aspirations of many others in the early seventeenth-century.

Yet another recent example of detail shedding a flood of brilliant light on a larger scene, has come from Margaret Spufford's delving into the life of Gregory King.[3] His is a household name among economic historians because of his estimates of national population and the proportion of different classes in the kingdom in 1688. Now Margaret has found him as a young man working in Eceleshall, Staffordshire, as steward, auditor, and secretary to Lady Jane Gerard at Bromley Hall. She tells us so much about the parish in his day that we can see him riding round its village and several hamlets, observing the plight of its landless poor, and almost certainly paying out wages to some of its casually-hired labourers. Gregory King's national population figures lie coldly on the printed page, and leave us wondering how he put them together.[4] It is true that we have long had his working notebooks, but the figures take on a deeper meaning for me now that I know something of his work and his movements in his twenties and thirties.

The aim of historians in the end is to see larger patterns of development, and put our much studied people and events into a wider context. My viewpoint makes it clear that I have to work from the bottom up. I never start with theoretical models, though I do, of course, ponder mixtures of possibilities, and I read the opinions of others. But I start with a mind that is virtually a clean sheet, building up many scattered fragments of evidence until a larger structure that I do not attempt to predict begins to take shape.

I realise that I started in this vein when looking at one single episode, the confiscation of Royalist lands, in the period of the Interregnum, way back in 1950. I was asking who were the new owners of this forfeited land and what they did with it. I came face to face with many different kinds of property, sitting in highly varied economic and social locations in south-eastern England - some in the forest country of Buckinghamshire, some in manorialised countryside where the gentry reigned supreme, some in the crowded streets of London. Purchasers dealt in different, and sometimes quite eccentric, ways with their property, and one or two alerted me to ideals as well as economic considerations governing their behaviour. So I never assume that self-interest determines all. I moved after that into another small, but very different world when I studied farmers in the fenland of Lincolnshire in the sixteenth century. That taught me at once the vital importance of making comparisons. One can never see the full significance of one set of circumstances until one has looked at others, however superficially similar. I knew already what the textbooks had told me about English farming as a whole, but here in the fenland I encountered a routine and an economy that was entirely different. The contrasts were so striking as to leave me permanently with a sceptical attitude to all generalisations. I went on to measure these Lincolnshire fenland lives in the sixteenth and seventeenth centuries against farmers' lives in other fenlands, as in Somerset, and to uncover yet more widely differing routines in forest country, on moorlands, and in the flat vale country of central England. That comparison of regional differences led on and on, and I recognised in myself a natural disposition to watch for differences, rather than uniformities. I relish and rejoice in diversity: *'Vive la différence'* is my motto; indeed, it constitutes a veritable principle of life.

I have said that I look askance at most generalisations as misleadingly simple, but I *do* move towards one generalisation that has implications extending far beyond the realms of economic history. I suspect that women on the whole rejoice in differences, while men prefer to identify (and sometimes impose) the uniformities. I find examples to support that bold generalisation all over the place. So I watch, from a rather special viewpoint, present developments both in the writing of economic history and in the development of the economy, as England, Wales and Scotland begin to move along separate paths, and prompt varied responses to what I see nowadays as a revitalised interest and appreciation for diversity.

Joan Thirsk (b. 19. 6. 1922) started as a student of Modern Languages (German, French, Spanish) at Westfield College, London University, but after one year and war service, changed to History. Her research for her Ph.D. at Westfield was supervised by Professor R.H. Tawney (1947-50). She was Senior Research Fellow in English Agrarian History at the Department of English Local History at the University of Leicester, 1951-65, and was Reader in Economic History at the Oxford University and Professorial Fellow of St Hilda's College, 1965-83. Her research interests are English agricultural history, principally though not exclusively, in the sixteenth and seventeenth centuries; rural histories; women historians in the nineteenth century; the history of food, 1500-1750.

---

[1] M.Zell, "'Setting the poor on work": Walter Morrell and the New Draperies project, c. 1603-1631', forthcoming.

[2] D.Pam, *'The Rude Multitude (Enfield and the Civil War)*, Edmonton Hundred Historical Society, Occasional Paper, NS., 33, 1977'; idem, *The Story of Enfield Chase*, Enfield, 1984; idem, *A Parish near London. A History of Enfield, vol. 1. Before 1837*, Enfield, 1990, esp. pp. 93-4.

[3] Margaret Spufford, 'Eccleshall, Staffordshire: a bishop's estate of dairymen, dairy wives, and the poor', in Joan Thirsk, ed., *The English Rural Landscape*, Oxford, 2000, pp. 303-6; Margaret Spufford and James Went, *Poverty Portrayed: Gregory King and the Parish of Eccleshall, Staffordshire Studies*, 7, Centre for Local History, Keele University, 1995.

[4] For the cold figures on the printed page (though they show that King did debate many uncertainties), see *Seventeenth-Century Economic Documents*, ed. Joan Thirsk and J.P.Cooper, Oxford, 1972, pp. 765-98. Notice on p. 775 King's prediction that in the year 2300 the population of England would have doubled to 11 million!

On Becoming an Economic Historian

F.M.L. Thompson

At the age of 75 it is rather easy to say that economic history - or some might say social history - has meant a career, bread-and-butter, and a pension, and goes on providing a source of fascination and occupation which makes retirement a continuation of life before sixty five under another name. No one in their right mind could say, in the year 2000, that it makes sense to become a professional economic historian for the sake of the money, or for that matter for the prospect that any academic career - possibly except for those of university economists and lawyers, and a sprinkling of physical scientists and stars of Eng. lit., who can use their university posts as the springboard for outside earnings - will provide a reliable basic life support system for such other-worldly characters as choose to devote their lives to indulging in the non-profit making pursuit of knowledge and understanding. Things may have been different half a century ago when I embarked on a career in economic history, in the sense that it was at that time a reasonable assumption that university teachers, with a starting salary of £500 a year, could look forward to a job for life - subject to good behaviour and an apparently self-monitored measure of good performance (in practice this was peer-group monitored, in an informal way) - remunerated if not generously then at least within shouting distance of other professions, in the law, medicine, civil service, engineering, surveying, architecture, school teaching, and even such a dull and highly-paid profession as accountancy. That, however, was taken for granted, and career choice was certainly not preceded by any enquiry into the relative rewards and prospects of the different possibilities open to an ex-service History graduate in 1949; there was no conscious material or financial motive for choosing economic history.

Donald Coleman (1920-95), later to become senior Editor of the *Economic History Review* to my junior, and Professor of Economic History at Cambridge (1971-82), five years older than myself, recalled that when he took a first in the London B.Sc. (Econ.) in 1949 'no course of action other than to go on to do research seemed remotely worthwhile'. That sums up the atmosphere and the expectations of the time: as an undergraduate one was fired up by the subject being studied, and so impressed by the example - and, I suppose, the intellectual and social status - of the especially inspiring and exciting tutors, lecturers, and authors one encountered, that the highest ambition was to follow in their footsteps should the chance occur. In Coleman's case the path to follow was indicated by his specialisation in the economic history option in his first degree, and by the advice of Jack Fisher to choose the economy of Kent under the later Stuarts as his research topic on the grounds that the sources were near at hand - in Chancery Lane and Maidstone - and that Kentish beer was good. I stumbled into economic history rather more accidentally, and with no alcoholic stimulus. The Oxford History degree which I took contained no economics - though I had read some Adam Smith, John Stuart Mill, and Alfred Marshall, and had certainly heard of Keynes, multipliers, and accelerators, probably without understanding them - no separately identifiable economic history, and my Special subject had been the French Revolution. Admittedly the French Revolution was undergoing searching economic explanations, which seemed quite convincing at the time, and one was more involved with taxes, bread prices, assignats, and sansculottes than with constitutions and rights of man, although the economic interpretation of events sat rather uncomfortably alongside power-based and military theories. At any rate, description, preferably of the lower orders, followed by analysis was good, simple narrative was bad: in terms of English History (which was thought of as indistinguishable from British History) G.M. Trevelyan was out, G.D.H. Cole was in. Moreover, the teachers who influenced me most strongly had no connection with the French Revolution. I was willing to get up early to be in time to hear A.J.P. Taylor lecture at 9 a.m. in Magdalen on subjects that were later to form part of the *Struggle for Mastery in Europe*, but had no wish to become involved with his kind of cock-up versions of diplomatic history and enough self-knowledge to realise that I could never emulate his cult of the paradox; though I think I learnt from AJP that history is fun because of the chance of uncovering the absurd, the incongruous, the bizarre, the inconsequential, or the hypocritical in human affairs. The greater influences were closer to home, in my college, The Queen's; John Prestwich, almost straight from Bletchley, a medievalist with a razor sharp mind and a world view dominated by finance and taxation and sustained by his monopoly on Hubert Walter, Richard I's justiciar and King John's chancellor; his Welsh wife Menna, in the full flood of expounding the faction theory of history based on her study of Cranfield and Jacobean politics, full of bribery, corruption, business deals, and monopoly profits; and Edmund Dell, later Labour's best Chancellor of the Exchequer who never was and in the late 1940s a marxist historian of the English Civil War, associated with Christopher Hill in supporting 'the good old cause'. Not believing that after four years in the gunners with a spot of liberating Sumatra and keeping the peace in East Bengal I could actually get a first in History, I made no plans for what to do after finals apart from visiting my Dutch girlfriend. When the possibility of staying in Oxford and doing my own historical research for a D.Phil. dawned on me in June 1949 I therefore had to decide in a hurry on a topic in order to have something to say when applying for a postgraduate award: medieval history seemed to present the most challenges and opportunities for detective work, but as my Latin was barely rudimentary it was ruled out. In any case since none of my tutors exactly fell over themselves to suggest research topics in their own fields the message seemed to be that I had better look at other centuries than theirs: the eighteenth century was out, having been temporarily reduced to a yawn by Namier, so it had to be the nineteenth century, which in Oxford the young Asa Briggs was beginning to make exciting. I chanced to have read quite recently Hrothgar Habakkuk's famous article on English Landownership, 1680-1740, and so almost on the spur of the moment announced that I wished to look at English landownership in the nineteenth century, initially giving the topic a distinctly political-cum-marxist definition by making the main objective an explanation of why the middle class gained power in 1832 while the landowning class remained the wealthiest until the 1880s. This hastily constructed research proposal did the trick; it gained me a Harmsworth Senior scholarship at Merton, and Asa Briggs as a supervisor - to be succeeded in 1950 by Habakkuk himself when he moved from Cambridge to Oxford. Thus I slid sideways into economic history.

At this point I had but the haziest idea of what that was, and with hindsight it could seem that neither had my first supervisor, who at the time was busy on *The Age of Improvement,* a wonderful and much used university textbook which certainly related political history to society, and society to the economy, in an integrated structure that was on a different historiographical planet from the prewar Oxford Histories, but it was still essentially a new style of political history. It was also the product of a new style of writing, unfortunately not easily reproduced. At supervisions I would be placed in the sitting room at Worcester College and Asa would station himself in the doorway communicating to his secretary's office and alternately dictate a paragraph of *Improvement* to her and a rapid fire comment to myself. The method gave him a high productivity rate and me an introduction to the politics of landownership and a technique of university teaching which I never managed to learn. The politics of landownership was a different matter. It led me to appreciate my good fortune a few years later when I stumbled on some excellent electioneering material from the 1840s in the Fitzwilliam MSS, which otherwise I might have overlooked since I was actually looking for evidence on estate management and the exploitation of coal - this supplied an article on 'Whigs and Liberals in the West Riding' which helped establish my credentials as a socio-political historian with some aspirations to being concerned with the 'total history' of landowners and not just with their narrowly economic functions or dysfunctions, and incidentally cleared the hurdle of getting published in the *English Historical Review*, which in the 1950s was still regarded by the academic establishment as an indispensable step towards recognition as a 'proper' historian. Perhaps more to the point Asa's idea of how to get started on landownership research was to get immersed in early Victorian contemporary opinion on landed issues; thus I acquired a store of research capital from a mass of pamphlet literature dealing not only with obvious topics like the Corn Laws or high farming, but also with conveyancers' criticisms of the laws of real property and attacks and defences of primogeniture. At the time this struck me as having a somewhat oblique connection with what I wanted to investigate, the basis of the strength of the landed interest; but it did show that the vested interests of specialist lawyers in the impenetrable mysteries of the existing land laws were an enormously strong first line of defence of the established landed regime, and it did supply a stock of research notes whose usefulness has not yet been exhausted, precisely because of its tangential nature. Although not unfamiliar with the PRO and with county record offices, Asa was keenly aware of the value of printed sources, especially local and national newspapers, and the immense body of parliamentary papers; he pointed my nose in those directions, and one of my paths into economic history was through the property press, and taxation records, which could be made to illuminate the operations of the land market.

It was, however, the arrival of Hrothgar Habakkuk in Oxford which showed me what economic history was all about and which converted me from a kind of jejune socio-political historian into a kind of socio-economic historian. He quickly recruited me to act as the secretary of the seminar he started, which functioned like a more civilised and specialised version of Oxford's Stubbs Society (a club ostensibly managed by undergraduate historians and in reality controlled largely by the Prestwiches and their allies, notorious for its intellectual savagery in demolishing papers given by Veronica Wedgwood, Laurence Stone, Joel Hurstfield, and other unacceptable figures) in the sense that it was like a club. Papers were delivered, and the secretary's job was to keep a record in a set of minutes. This rapidly forced me to become familiar with the terminology of Kitchin, Jugler, Kondratiev, Schumpeter, take-off, GNP, gross and net capital formation, income elasticities of demand, savings ratios, risk aversion, and all the rest of the vocabulary and concepts protecting the special mysteries of the professional academic. Moreover Habakkuk rapidly persuaded me to act as the local organising secretary for the first residential conference of the Economic History Society, which was held in Worcester College in 1951. This was memorable for the select attendance, perhaps a dozen or so, and the austere conditions - residents had to cross open quads to reach bathrooms, and Tawney wrapped himself in a blanket to try to keep warm during conference sessions, raining sparks from the bonfire mixture he smoked in his pipe. Eric Hobsbawm launched 'Economic Fluctuations and some Social Movements since

1800' at this conference; and I acquired institutional endorsement as an accredited economic historian. The rest, as they say, is (economic) history.

F.M.L. (Michael) **Thompson** (b. 13. 8. 1925) was an undergraduate at Queen's College, Oxford, and postgraduate at Merton College. He taught at University College 1951-68 before becoming Professor of Modern History at Bedford College (1968-77) and Director of the Institute of Historical Research 1977-90. His research has focused on landownership and society in Britain but his most recent book is *Gentrification and the Enterprise Culture 1780-1980* (2001).

Speaking Social History

Janet Tierney

'No other generation have ever known such a change. I mean things is changed out of all recognition
.... It went for years and years, it never changed, then all of a sudden, since the war ended, it went
haywire, as you might say.'. (Harry Dennis, retired farm labourer, East Yorkshire)

J.H. Plumb, writing in the late 1960s, felt that the strength of the past in all aspects of life was
infinitely weaker than it had been even a generation previously – 'few societies' as he put it,
'have ever had a past in such galloping dissolution as this'.[1] But then, by 1969, we had the
full sixties experience - the decade of the sweep-it-all-away mould-breakers, full of exciting
new things for the generation which sprang from the never-had-it-so-good 1950s to savour -
rock and roll, an ever-expanding range of mood-enhancing substances, skirts of increasingly
microscopic dimensions. Art became Op, music became metallic, architects developed a keen
interest in the possibilities of reinforced concrete and plate glass. The relics of the past either
were becoming quaintly trendy, in a Sergeant Pepper-ish sort of way, or, more often, were
being thrust ruthlessly away in the ceaseless quest for the new and original. In retrospect, it
was hardly surprising that Plumb should have considered the past to be suffering its death
throes; suggesting that it was taking rather too long about its decease, though, might arguably
have aroused some suspicions about the diagnosis.

The Swinging Sixties have given way in the last decade or so of the twentieth century to the
altogether more serious cult of self-improvement through 'lifelong learning'. One of the
more interesting phenomena which has grown out of this has been the explosion of interest in
local history. At a time when society generally has become far less 'clubbable' – where
people with an interest in, say, cameras or postage stamps no longer find it necessary to
gather together on a regular basis to discuss such things – the spell of the past regularly
entices people in large numbers to sit in draughty Church Rooms or village halls. Local
History societies have developed from rather earnest and predominantly middle-class
organisations, much given to field trips to ancient earthworks and pre-Reformation churches,
to altogether more socially diverse groups whose interests lie in the chronicling of their own
local, social histories. Talking about local history is not, however, enough. Sooner or later,
the call comes for a museum to house the tangible evidence of this bewitching Past
.....Museums over the years have had a bad press, even from their own practitioners, from
whom one would have hoped to expect a little sympathy and understanding for what they
were about. As early as 1876, Professor W. Boyd Dawkins[2] (Curator of the Manchester
Museum) described museums in Britain as '... a sort of advertising bazaar, or a receptacle
for miscellaneous curiosities unfitted for a private house' or else '... composed of an
accumulation of objects, valuable in themselves but valueless for all practical purpose,
because they are crowded together or stowed away for want of room.' Rather over a century

later, David Lowenthal, while admitting that museums are much more lively these days, still refers to objects as being 'mummified in a museum', depriving the past of life.[3] There is a certain justice in this viewpoint, as a visit to the British Museum, or some National Trust properties would confirm. Fortunately, there has been an increasing trend for Local Authority museums to tap into all this enthusiasm for the local past and to develop Social History collections.

From the point of view of a museum-based social historian, Economic and Social History means not just the study of a society within a quite tightly-defined local area, but increasingly, working with local people to develop collections and mount exhibitions which are of the community as much as they are about it. At the end of 1998, the East Riding of Yorkshire Museum Service was awarded two separate grants from the Heritage Lottery Fund to redevelop two of its museum sites – Goole Museum, and Skidby Windmill, just south of Beverley. The two sites could not be more different. Goole was a Company Town, created in 1826 by the Aire and Calder Navigation Company as the outport for their canal, and intended to rival Hull - which it did, quite successfully, for much of the nineteenth century. Two World Wars, depression, recession all took their toll of the town's prosperity, leaving it at the end of the twentieth century with a serious unemployment problem and the unenviable status as one of the most deprived areas in the East Riding. Despite all these difficulties, it remained a socially vibrant little town (even though known throughout the East Riding by the sobriquet of 'Sleepy Hollow'!) passionately interested in its own history and with an exceptionally strong Local History society. Skidby Windmill, on the other hand, despite its proximity to Hull, is uncompromisingly rural, dominating the landscape to the extent that it universally recognised as the symbol of East Yorkshire. Like Goole Museum, the mill had rather languished in the years leading up to Local Government Reorganisation, lacking any professional direction to its fortunes, and like Goole, the main plank in the strategy to revitalise it was to absorb the local community in the process of its regeneration.

Methodologically, the Museum Service was strongly influenced by the philosophy of the 'Leicester School', in particular the notion of the 'societal group' articulated by Charles Phythian-Adams – the 'complex group of families extending over a number of parishes and cemented by tradition and movement within a limited area.[4] 'In Goole, much of the population was born either there or in the small settlements along the Ouse and Humber nearby; those who have moved away, even decades previously, still have a strong emotional attachment to the town. This became very apparent when the members of the Local History Society and the (surprisingly far-flung) readership of the Goole Times were enlisted to provide their memories as the foundation on which the new museum displays were to be constructed.

At Skidby Windmill, the 'societal group' which the Museum Service identified was somewhat different, and the means by which 'the community' were drawn into the museum's development potentially more problematic. When the new museum service was formed after Reorganisation, it was decided that Skidby Windmill, then described, rather meaninglessly, as a 'Rural Heritage Centre', should be developed as the Museum of East Riding Rural Life. The regional shape of the (overwhelmingly rural) East Riding is effectively defined by its farming and sociological patterns, the Wold uplands largely given over to the production of grain, the Holderness plain to a more pastoral economy; a region of small, dispersed settlements, few towns, and an ideal breeding ground for both non-conformity and self-help. The 'societal group' for Skidby Windmill was thus, somewhat dauntingly, the entire rural population of the East Riding.

While there were a number of very active local history groups working in small market towns, such as Driffield and Pocklington, they did not have the homogeneity of community experience nor focused group memory that existed in the case of Goole. To gather together a 'history' of the rural East Riding, these groups were used in a rather different way. Their members generated a network of contacts within the wider community often through elderly relatives who were willing to contribute to the museum not by writing their memories, as in the case of Goole, but by speaking them. Thus for 10 months, a project officer on a temporary contract enlisted the help of the various local history groups, Men's Fellowships, Women's Institutes and many others. Over 60 recordings were made, and several hundred photographs of village life over the first 60 years of the twentieth century were collected to supplement them.

The object of the project was not to collect a random assortment of memories of East Riding rural life, but to build up a structured picture of life and work in the area which would be used as the basis for text panels in the new displays, using quotes to reinforce the more general statements made. A longer-term aim was the use of recordings (or edited versions of them) as primary source material for schools, and the use of extracts to construct information sheets, booklets and teaching materials. Transcripts and copies of the original recordings would also be lodged in the museum's study centre, for use by researchers and students.

Because of the geographical isolation of the East Riding, and the continued dominance of arable farming, many aspects of what might be considered a nineteenth century way of life continued there well into the twentieth century. From leaving school (at as early an age as was possible, for many) boys and young men continued to be hired onto farms as farm servants to work with the horses, long after the practice of hiring live-in farm servants had declined to virtual extinction in other parts of the country. As interviewees made clear, the expectation that young teenagers should leave home and find work was often expressed quite bluntly:

> 'Father said: "Now look lads: its time thy was getting thar feet under somebody else's table." I knew what he meant cause he told my elder brother that and he'd gone ... and so I had to look for a job.' (Alf Adamson, South Newbold)

The peculiar East Yorkshire 'horse lads' system survived longer because it was successfully modified to suit the particular needs of local agriculture. As several of the surviving 'horse lads' testified, the work was highly structured, and every boy and man had his particular place in the hierarchy. This is emphasised with great clarity by one interviewee, George Nellist:

> 'Every man was in his place, and you hadn't to go out of that place. There was Foreman, Wag, Thod, Fowat, Fiver and further down you had other lads. When you went in the field – Foreman first, Wag, Thod, Fowat and Fiver, all in that rotation.'

Structure in all things was clearly apparent in all aspects of working life. George Nellist, again, described the correct procedure for drying corn:

> 'Massey Harris self-binder chucked sheaves out. Then you stooked 'em, stood 'em up on end in field, facing North and South, so they got sun at both sides. You went in a field and just stuck a stook up anyhow, like, and didn't get it right, somebody shouted: "Which is North?" You had to poke 'em to North.'

Ploughing a straight furrow was equally obsessive:

'It was who could plough the straightest furrow … If anyone had a crooked furrow, they were in for it right. It was : "My God, lad, you've made a mess of it there, I saw an o'd hare with her leg broken, she'd broken it running round the bends in thar furrows!"'. (Norman Creaser)

'When you were drilling corn or turnips … you had to have 'em dead straight … 'cause everyone was looking: "By, he's been bloody p----d when he put that one in."' (Harry Dennis)

While reminiscing into a tape recorder about the days of one's youth and vigour may well lead to a certain golden patina developing on the memory, the personal recollections collected in this project in general were remarkably unsentimental. The way of life they described was one of hard work, badly paid. Agricultural workers who were interviewed expressed their views on the hardships of farm-work with considerable robustness. Ex-farm worker John Harrison's severely matter-of-fact description of helping the local shepherd out is enough to make the eyes water!

'When they was castrating lambs, I've held lambs up while the chap cuts 'em ..... and squeezes it out and then pulls 'em out with his teeth. They don't bleed as much.'

One of the great institutions in the East Riding was the Village Friendly Society, a movement which had started in the industrial towns of the West Riding and Lancashire, and which reached east Yorkshire during the 1830s. Until the passing of Lloyd George's national Insurance Act in 1911, they were effectively the only way that farm labourers and other working men could hope to provide for themselves or their families should they become incapable of work. Apart from the 'mutual aid' aspect, the Friendly Societies provided an important social outlet. The Club Feast, usually held in June or early July in the quiet lull before harvest, was a holiday and celebration for the whole village. Quite how important this was to East Riding villagers was described by Audrey Thompson of Middleton on the Wolds, where their lodge of Foresters held the last Friendly Society Club Feast in East Yorkshire in 1939. Audrey's father, uncle and grandfather were all members of the Club during the 1920s and 1930s:

'What we called the Middleton Feast when I was a kid was the highlight of the year... on the Friday morning, all the Foresters used to meet at the Robin Hood, and they all had staves to walk around the village with and follow the band. The flag preceded the parade, it was definitely the thing was the flag. And it took four men to hold it, it was a terrific thing.'

'All the young farm lads that were on the farms they used to come from miles away. I had cousins and uncles and, you know, they all used to come, that was the family gathering was Middleton Feast, it was bigger than Christmas…. Friday afternoon. That was when the Feast started up, as soon as you heard the music you knew that was it and then you were all down in the field, and that's when the celebrations begun really'.

Perhaps one of the most satisfying results of the entire project was not just the breadth of experiential evidence that was generated, nor even the extraordinary and unconscious vividness of language and memory which was recorded; it was the fact that ordinary, often poorly-educated elderly working people felt that they had something of great value to contribute, especially for 'young people', and revelled in it.

For Local History, or perhaps more accurately, Community Museums, social history and economic history are both about the way that society works and is experienced. Museums deal with the past, not in the manner of Boyd Dawkins's 'receptacle for miscellaneous curiosities unfitted for a private house', but as bearers of meaning for their communities. What our 10 month project has hopefully demonstrated is that the objects we collect, however totemic, are not in themselves sufficient. It is when people are encouraged to present their pasts themselves, in their own words, that the past truly lives.

Janet Tierney (b. 1. 7. 1953) was educated at Girton College, Cambridge and at the University of Leicester. She is currently Curator of Goole Museum & Skidby Windmill (Museum of East Riding Rural Life); Museums Education Officer, East Riding of Yorkshire Museums Service. Her research interests are nineteenth century social and agricultural history in north Lincolnshire and east Yorkshire.

---

[1] J.H. Plumb, *The Death of the Past* (1969).
[2] Quoted in Geoffrey Lewis, For Instruction and Recreation: A Centenary History of the Museums Association (1989).
[3] David Lowenthal, *The Past is a Foreign Country* (1985).
[4] Charles Phythian-Adams, *Rethinking English Local History* (1987).

Economic History: A Continuing Exercise in Interdisciplinarity

Richard Tilly

Economic history is to me an ongoing interdisciplinary project. It represents a marvellous compromise between the disciplines of economics and history. How and why I came to see it in that light calls for a few autobiographical observations. These are followed by some comments on how the disciplines have made themselves felt in my own special fields of research and teaching.

As a boy I made the discovery that history could be great fun, at once entertaining and edifying. It seemed to offer an intellectual escape from the prison of the drab present, a way of envisioning alternatives. As my formal education progressed, however, I found that history could also disappoint. Partly, no doubt, this followed from the oft-repeated tedium of having to memorise long lists of dates, Great Events and Great Men. Looking back, though, I now see those tedious exercises themselves as a response to a deeper malaise: history's lack of a general organising principle other than chronology. In those days, at my midwestern U.S. university in the early 1950s, history tended to be either political history, dominated by great men and ideas, or intellectual history, dominated by great thinkers, and marked by a profusion of 'explanations' at least as numerous as the number of periods observed.[1] Entrée Economics 1a: Principles of Economics. What an eye-opener! Armed with the vision of a 'competitive economy', I soon found myself able to realise that a large part of what went on in a country such as my own could do so independently of the great (and not-so-great) ideas of statesmen, generals and philosophers and independently of a government willing the results. Here, I sensed, was an important field of study, one with practical implications for contemporary problems. This first exposure, however, did not suggest to me that economics could have anything to do with history. How that connection came about is a story of its own.

Enter Rondo Cameron. To round out my undergraduate history major, I needed a few more course credits in the sub field of modern European history. And there it was: Economic History, more specifically, as I recall, the history of European industrialisation. This was a great new experience. 'Europe' became something other than just the checkerboard of different languages, diplomatic intrigues and wars it had been to me. It was now the seat of dynamic economic forces which were to transform the world. One result was that European history without those economic forces quickly became a terribly incomplete, virtually irrelevant, project. Another had to do with economics. For the idea of an economy radically transforming itself and growing in size was mind boggling. And it was an idea, I must add, that economics had not prepared me for. Was it consonant, I asked myself, with the Principles of Economics I had learned? When I and my fellow students posed such questions to Rondo C., he tended to light up his pipe, briefly disappear behind a cloud of smoke, and then reappear with delphic pronouncements containing references, if memory serves, to differences between 'static' and 'dynamic' views of the world and such like. What came across though was our mentor's evident belief that such questions were important, too important for quick, syllogistic responses; and also that if economic history did not harmonise with economic doctrine, the dissonance *could* reflect unfavourably on the latter. That stuck.

On to graduate school. Here economics took centre stage; and the roles of economics and history reversed themselves. The key question became: is history relevant for economics? As budding economic historians, we began to feel that economics was too formalised and in need of the stronger empirical foundations that history could supply. But did economists think so? At that time, perhaps fortunately, the answer tended to be 'yes'; for the problem of economic development (or of 'underdevelopment' as the topic was then unsentimentally called), stood high on the economics agenda. These were the heydays of W. W. Rostow, Simon Kuznets, Alexander Gerschenkron, Walther Hoffmann, Alexander Cairncross, John Habakkuk, Phyllis Deane and others whose work suggested considerable overlap between contemporary and historical problems of economic growth and development.[2] Important works emerged from this general context: Rondo Cameron's *France and the Economic Development of Europe*, David Landes' contribution to volume six of the *Cambridge Economic History of Europe* (in a later variant known as *The Unbound Prometheus*), in the U.S. field, Doug North's *The Economic Growth of the United States*, or Bob Fogel's book on railroads and U. S. growth.[3] Also in the U.S. about this time cliometrics was born. Economics and economic history had never seemed closer.

What emerged from the experience just sketched out was, methodologically speaking, a belief in economic history's dual mission: (a) as a means for understanding, perhaps helping to solve, contemporary economic problems by carrying on a dialogue with economics and demonstrating the value of a historical perspective; and (b) as a vehicle for interacting with historians and providing their work with the benefits of an economically informed history. In my own professional career this belief was to be sorely tested, I admit. But as I look back, I do not see grounds for total disillusionment.

In my adopted country, Germany, I enjoyed working the interdisciplinary angle in both directions. At first, to be sure, I found little room for manoeuvre on the economics side. German economics (in the mid-1960s) was less mathematical, more policy oriented and more open to an historical approach than its American counterpart. And German economic historians, possibly for that reason, showed little interest in the more explicit use of economic theory and quantitative techniques in their work that already characterised American cliometrics. In German economic history the dominant theme was industrialisation, a broader and 'softer' variant of the same growth paradigm that also held sway elsewhere (and especially in the U.S. and Great Britain). The principle addressee appeared to be history, rather than economics. In fact, the German field eschewed the use of economics to such a degree that in a survey (Tilly (1969) I felt obliged to characterise it as 'playing Hamlet without the prince'. In my own work (Tilly (1966 and 1968) I tried to show my economist colleagues that history contained some useful economics, for example by suggesting how government restraints on certain types of banking could call forth efficient institutional alternatives; and some of my students, with other topics and examples, did the same (Holtfrerich (1973); Fremdling (1975)).[4] As time went on, German economic history came to contain more economics, though much less so than did the Anglo-American historiography.[5] There have been exceptions, of course. But were we to view economic history as a martini cocktail, and economics as its input of gin, then we would find very few dry martinis in Germany's historiography, and many more in the Anglo-American one.

In the mid-1960s, historians proved more receptive to economic economic history. Thus early on, I could gain the impression that fruitful interactions were possible vis-à-vis German history. Whereas an older historiography had stressed the role of the German (and Prussian) state in shaping economic development since the late-eighteenth century, more recent work involving regional differentiation, including some of my own, showed that market forces were in general a more powerful factor than had been acknowledged, and that state-driven initiatives produced, or threatened to produce, economic 'solutions' clearly inferior to market-driven results. The tendency to associate economic change with state action also led the older historiography to ignore the extent to which the German economy of the early nineteenth century was an 'open' one, thus downplaying the extent to which it could (and did) realise significant gains from foreign trade, in particular from trade with Great Britain.[6] But the important point I wish to make here is that such findings were taken up by German historians and put to use in reinterpreting modern German history, e.g., by Hans-Ulrich Wehler, by Jürgen Kocka, and by others. For these historians, initially at least, were fighting on two fronts: against the old guard, with its emphasis on ideas, the state and the nation, on the one hand, and against the background of student revolt and a threatened politicisation of research, on the other. An important aim was to upgrade the importance of economic and social conditions as determinants of historical change without giving in to dogmatic Marxist-Leninist demands.[7] This applies to the statemaking era of the nineteenth century (Wehler (1987) and (1995)); but it also applies to later periods, for example to the analysis of World War One and its aftermath, where economic history has contributed to new perceptions of the overall achievements and limitations of the Weimar Republic.[8]

By emphasising economic history's interdisciplinary achievements I do not mean to suggest that our field does not face some serious problems today. The propitious conditions of the golden age of the 1960s are no longer with us. Times have obviously changed. Mainstream economics has become more and more mathematical. True, econometrics has also grown; and many economic historians have kept abreast of the changes. But overall there is no denying that, say, by the 1970s, a gap on the empirical and historical flank of economics had emerged and was visibly widening. It still is. That is to say, there were and are ample grounds for worrying and wondering about the relations between economic history and economics. The old question of the relevance of economic history for economics and its converse is still with us. Perhaps the fault lies with economics and its preoccupation with mathematical scholasticism, as some economists themselves say (Frey (2000)). Even then, however, as Larry Neal has recently pointed out (in Neal (2000)), a strategy of persuasion is needed if we, as economic historians, are to go on doing our interdisciplinary job.[9] But we need the historians too! And they have also begun to pose a problem, for in recent times their discipline has seemed to be travelling along a culturalist plane, with little interest in what economic history has to offer. Once again, however, this is a challenge to which our field must respond, perhaps along the lines of the 'New Institutional Economics', as one economic historian – who has recognised this very challenge – has suggested.[10]

Richard Tilly (b. Chicago, 17. 10. 1932) is Emeritus Professor of Economic and Social History, University of Münster, Germany. He was educated at the University of Wisconsin, Madison. Since 1966 he has been Director of Institut für Wirtschafts- und Sozialgeschichte, University of Münster.

[1] Along with dull recitations of facts and figures, I also experienced brilliant lecturers, and was thus able to retain the impression that history could be fascinating; but whereas the former type of performance deadened interest, brilliant history tended, thanks to its virtual non-replicability, to be frustrating.

[2] A sign of the times was the conference held in Konstanz, Germany, in 1960 to discuss Rostow's 'Stages of Economic Growth', for we find here a stellar cast of economists and historians locked in a debate about growth and development, and never a doubt about the utility of combining theoretical and historical economics. See W. W. Rostow (Ed), *The Economics of Take-off into Sustained Growth* (London: MacMillan, 1963)

[3] Apologies are perhaps due to those authors of important works who remain unnamed here; but I intended the list to be indicative, not exhaustive. Rondo Cameron, *France and the Economic Development of Europe* (Princeton: Princeton UP, 1961); David Landes, 'Technological Change and Industrialisation in Western Europe, 1750-1914', *CEHE*, Vol. 6 (Cambridge, 1965); Douglass North, *Economic Growth of the United States, 1790-1860* (New York, 1961); Robert Fogel, *Railroads and Economic Growth. Essays in Econometric History* (Baltimore, 1964).

[4] Tilly, Richard, `Soll und Haben: Recent German Economic History and the Problem of Economic Development,' *Journal of Economic History*, XXIX (1969), 298-319; *idem, Financial Institutions and Industrialisation in the Rhineland, 1815-1870* (Madison, 1966); idem, `Finanzielle Aspekte der preussischen Industrialisierung, 1815-1870,' in: Wolfram Fischer (Ed.), *Wirtschafts- und sozialgeschichtliche Probleme der frühen Industrialisierung* (Berlin, 1968); Carl-Ludwig Holtfrerich, *Quantitative Wirtschaftsgeschichte des Ruhrkohlenbergbaus im 19. Jahrhundert* (Dortmund, 1973); Rainer Fremdling, *Eisenbahnen und deutsches Wirtschaftswachstum, 1840-1879* (Dortmund, 1975).

[5] In 1980 I published a sequel to my 1969 'Soll und Haben' survey of German economic historiography which attempted to show how the field had been changing; and in 1996 I made still another attempt. Tilly, Richard, `Soll und Haben II. Wiederbegegnung mit der deutschen Wirtschafts- und Sozialgeschichte,' in: *idem, Kapital, Staat und sozialer Protest in der deutschen Industrialisierung* (Göttingen, 1980); idem, `Wirtschaftsgeschichte als Disziplin,' in: Gerold Ambrosius, Dietmar Petzina and Werner Plumpe (Eds.), *Moderne Wirtschaftsgeschichte. Eine Einführung für Historiker und Ökonomen* (Munich, 1996).

[6] Tilly, *Financial Institutions*; *idem,* `Los von England. Probleme des Nationalismus in der deutschen Wirtschaftsgeschichte,' *Zeitschrift für die gesamte Staatswissenschaft*, 124 (1968), 178-96; Herbert Kisch, *From Domestic Manufacture to Industrial Revolution. The Case of the Rhenish Textile Districts* (New York, 1989). Some of Kisch's essays were published in German in the 1960s, thus having some impact on the historiography long before 1989.

[7] The first major publication directed against the „old guard" was Fritz Fischer's book on World War One, *Griff nach der Weltmacht* (Düsseldorf, 1961), but though it drew much more on social and economic history than had the historiography it was attacking, its performance in this respect was, I would say, far from optimal. The group which organised around Wehler (the „Bielefeld School" and its journal, *Geschichte und Gesellschaft. Zeitschrift für historische Sozialwissenschaft*) went much further here. Unsurprisingly, once the research program of these historians had been launched, it took on a life of its own, continuing on its course long after the 'student revolt' had played out.

[8] Hans-Ulrich Wehler, *Deutsche Gesellschaftsgeschichte.* II: *Von der Reformära bis zur Industriellen und politischen 'deutschen Doppelrevolution', 1815-1848/9* (Munich, 1987); *idem,* III, *1850-1914* (Munich, 1995); Carl-Ludwig Holtfrerich, *Die deutsche Inflation, 1914-1923* (Berlin, 1980); Gerald Feldman, *The Great Disorder* (New York, 1993); Knut Borchardt, `Zwangslagen und Handlungsspielräume in der grossen Wirtschaftskrise der dreissiger Jahre: Zur Revision des überlieferten Geschichtsbildes,' in: *idem, Wachstum, Krisen, Handlungsspielräume der Wirtschaftspolitik* (Göttingen, 1982)

[9] Bruno Frey, `Was bewirkt die Volkswirtschaftslehre?' *Perspektiven der Wirtschaftspolitik*, I (2000), esp. Pp. 25-6; Larry Neal, `A Shocking View of Economic History,' *Journal of Economic History*, 60 (2000), 317-334.

[10] Hansjörg Siegenthaler, `Geschichte und Ökonomie nach der kulturalistischen Wende,' *Geschichte und Gesellschaft*, 25 (1999), 276-301.

Boundaries? Theories? Directions? Thinking About Economic and Business History

Steven Tolliday

Sometimes it is hard to see through the rain. In 2001, British academics hunker down in their beleaguered departments. They contemplate the consequences of rising workloads, proliferating administrative burdens and cheese-pared resources. They prepare to deal with the interminable demands of the national surveillance regimes (HEFCE, RAE, QAA) with their insistent demands for paper trails, self-policing, and measurable outcomes (under erratic and obscure rules). A historian in the future may well conclude that all this has constituted a sustained assault on quality, reflection and creativity in the arts and social sciences: - a current historian simply has to endure it. Yet despite these travails, economic historians (and many others in the arts and social sciences) are living in interesting times: times of intellectual flux. Old boundaries and frameworks are unwinding: new contenders are pressing in and staking claims. Economic history is engaging with the social, the cultural, even the linguistic, in new and exciting ways. When the future economic historian comes to write the history of the universities in 2001, she will draw on an increasingly wide range of approaches in analysing our plight. She will no doubt construe it partly in familiar 'economic' terms and identify the power of tightly drawn incentive systems (play the game or lose the cash). But she may also (in less familiar vein) be far more aware than past practitioners of the inseparability and interpenetratation of these themes with issues such as social construction, the power of surveillance and language, and the dilemmas of strategic choices and politics.

Twenty years ago, this would not have been the case. In the 1970s, the agendas of economic and business history were decisively reshaped under the influence of social-science based theories and quantitative methodologies. In some respects, this was a tonic and a revelation. Although economic and business history had a substantial pedigree in the universities, and had contributed numerous methods and approaches to the study of history (think of Tawney, Briggs, Habakkuk, or Laslett), the scope of these sub-disciplines had narrowed in the 1960s, and their institutional status in history departments had diminished. Against this background, the new social science methodologies and discourses were not only intrinsically interesting, but also offered paths to an improved identity and legitimacy for these sub-disciplines (especially in an era of expanding higher education when new territories could still be carved out). They also offered a route away from the confining orthodoxies of many history departments which were hostile to theory, focused almost exclusively on political and diplomatic history, and treated economic and social history as 'noises-off'.

By the early 1980s, the New Economic History (NEH) and Chandlerian business history had helped to create a measure of autonomy for the sub-disciplines, as well as exercising an impressive degree of hegemony over ideas inside them. Of course, neither NEH nor Chandlerian business history ever became totally dominant. But NEH achieved substantial institutional power in terms of appointments, and an ability to define core subjects and expertises. This went furthest in the USA where NEH carried economic history by and large out of history departments and into economics departments. In Britain, economic history retained a more varied methodological base, much closer links to social history, and more diversity in its departmental location. In both cases, however, NEH for a considerable time, set the agenda both through its prominence in the high profile debates of the time, and through its missionary zeal and its intimidating culture of expertise.

Chandler's 'institutional synthesis' was not totally dominant either – although for me, teaching at Harvard Business School in the late 1980s and editing the *Business History Review,* it looked like it at times. Without disparaging either the importance or achievement of Chandler's work, it was still frustrating to receive so many articles for *BHR* aiming to 'confirm', 'extend', or 'fill gaps' in Chandler's model, when (even with more or less the same material), so many of them could have been pursuing more interesting or more innovative questions. Chandler himself has always been extremely careful to define the parameters of his research and methodology. He has used a tight and narrow focus to explore a carefully defined set of questions about the dynamics of big business. In doing so, he found a way of effectively using social science methods to provide a set of analytical tools to explore the strategies and structures of corporations. Chandler himself was never a neo-classicist, and his approach did not itself arise out of neo-classical theory. It had roots in Weber and Schumpeter, and it drew on the important contributions of Coase, Simon and Penrose on the theory of the firm. But in its later stages it co-evolved with Oliver Williamson's transaction cost economics. Transaction costs economists found inspiration in Chandler's model and material, harnessed it to their theory, and carried it into economics departments (at times in a fairly reductive form).

This had implications for both the institutional and intellectual development of business history. Business history in the USA was able to move away from the previously dominant models of business history there - the corporate biography tradition and the more political and humanistic approach epitomised by Thomas Cochran. The subject was without doubt transformed and enriched. Yet, in some respects, Chandler's new approach was almost too successful. In the hands of less sophisticated followers, his ideas were used formulaically, and his insights transformed into universalistic precepts rather than stimulating hypotheses, with profound effects for the selection of subjects for study, the identification of what is significant, and modes of explanation.

In retrospect, these developments both gave and took away. Chandler's synthesis had a powerful logic that mesmerized many practitioners in his wake. Notwithstanding some notable achievements within this paradigm, it also induced researchers to narrow their horizons in order to concentrate on those areas where the paradigm worked best. The range and agenda of the subject became impoverished. NEH also narrowed, and I would argue misdirected, the focus of economic history. Institutionally, it turned economic history in the USA into a sub-discipline of economics and tied its practice to particular technical expertises of the economist. In doing so, it moved away from the potentially more nourishing mainstream of history, in a way that business history, because of its more heterodox methodological roots, never did. In the UK, economic history, continued awkwardly, but probably productively, to straddle the disciplinary divide between economics and history.

Theories
Since the 1980s, there has been an unwinding of these hegemonies. The limits of the earlier 'big ideas' have been highlighted, and in the process, alternatives have been sought. Greater pluralism has emerged. Economic historians can now draw relatively freely on diverse schools and approaches, ranging from ecology to anthropology, from game theory to linguistics, though none are dominant.

The New Economic History had numerous virtues. It produced brilliant historians and fascinating debates. It raised provocative questions. It emphasised the importance of carefully counting and quantifying, it opened up new sources, and it gave a new impetus to areas like historical demography. It also allowed stimulating procedures such as the use of counterfactuals and thought experiments (hitherto frowned on) into the pantheon of legitimate historical methods. But, it had crucial vices. It was always tied to the ideological baggage of neo-classical theory, at a time when economists' themselves were beginning to distance themselves from its simplifying assumptions. Also, at its worst, it came to fetishise technical expertise over substance. Statistical significance was raised above, or even confused with, historical significance.

One issue, perhaps above all others, epitomised its limits. Crudely speaking, it can be labelled 'the quest for the optimising outcome'. All actors are postulated to be in rational pursuit of an optimal outcome. This is a world with an impoverished range of choices and largely predetermined outcomes. Perhaps the most exquisite exposition can be found in McCloskey's rejection of the hypothesis of Victorian failure. He shows the entrepreneurs making rational, maximising choices along a primrose path to long-term unavoidable decline. Despite its dense information and flashes of colourful storytelling, however, this version of history becomes little more than a tableau in which the underlying laws of economic life can be illustrated.

Is there ever just one optimising outcome? Outside the neo-classical paradigm, things look different. Over different time frames, for different actors, within different external contexts, the 'optimising' outcome will be different. The historian above all is aware that contexts and interests are inherently ambiguous. An optimal solution to one problem, defined in one way today, may be a road to disaster if the problem is defined differently or the time horizon adjusted. There may be multiple 'rational' solutions, or no solutions at all.

The neo-classicists sometimes rejected the idea of multiple solutions. At other times, they attempted to incorporate a limited range of choice into their models. Most commonly, they posited single optimal outcomes, but the possibility of failure to achieve them due to informational imperfections. This reinserted capable human actors and the possibility of choice. For example, even though a mass market for cars in early 20th century America potentially existed, it required the inspiration of Henry Ford to dramatically seize the previously unperceived opportunity and turn it into reality. The winners were those actors who most successfully adapted to their constraints and contexts.

Over time, economic theory has moved even further to try to escape dependence on assumptions of perfect competition. In particular, much work has been done to theorise the role and function of informational imperfections. On this basis, mainstream economics purports to be able to deal with non-market factors like institutions and trust (for instance in rational choice theories). But the underlying reliance on the notion of economic behaviour based on individual maximising choices (subject to limits of information) remains the same.

Thus, such theory accepts 'bounded rationality', but not socially constructed and multiple logics/illogics of action. It takes as given the conditions within which optimising individuals determine their imperfectly informed decisions: but it does not accept that contexts can be ambiguous, indeterminate, or even fundamentally unknowable. Thus, exciting notions of free-riding, opportunism, agency costs, positional values, trust, and games, may be raised, but they are then quickly disciplined into a sophisticated but ultimately rigid neo-classical calculus. The black box is tantalisingly opened, but everything is pushed back into it again, and the lid slammed firmly shut.

Directions

Economic and business historians, while properly sceptical of the claims of failed overarching methodologies, can make creative and innovative use of the rich range of questions that mainstream economics and other theories have opened up. The theories can act as 'sensitising devices' to alert historians to ways of looking at issues or highlighting avenues for exploration. Peter Burke put this point nicely: "Some historians have accepted a particular theory and have attempted to follow it in their work.....Other historians are interested in theories rather than committed to them. They use them to become aware of problems, in other words, to find questions rather than answers". [Peter Burke, *History and Social Theory* (Ithaca New York, 1993 p. 19-20]

Much of this essay has criticised mainstream economists and their counterparts in economic history for trying to fit issues of context, culture and power into their assumptions by reducing them to 'information'. As a result, they cannot embrace paradox, irreconcilability, multiple and contradictory goals, or the thrilling uncertainty of strategic action – near misses, wrong turnings, the triumphs of folly and the failures of rationality. These are the very stuff that economic and business historians are embroiled with in their day to day research. But the impulse to find order in chaos is powerful, and ordering on the basis of reductionist social science can be a seductive solution. Yet economic historians can find other forms of order too, that are less formal and more challenging, and I will end with a couple of brief suggestions on some directions in which this may take us.

Firstly, economic historians should not fall into an undue modesty that history can do no more than provide material for theory. We need to be more confident in the role of rooted historical analysis in shaping thought, theory, assumptions, and research questions. Many of us accept (perhaps too easily) that models from the present provide us with scientific tools to illuminate the past. Yet historical study of context and contingency in the past can equally illuminate unsuspected elements in the present, and it can warn and guard against the pitfalls of ahistoric assumptions. The 'present-minded' idea fits well with ideas of linear progress, resulting in the continuous evolution and improvement of forms of organisation, technology or the division of labour. But 'historical-minded' ideas deal better with permanent change, fragility, and transition. They bring to bear a heightened awareness of complexity and contingency. To take an example from business history, new ways of organising economic activity in the future will be different and frequently unanticipated, but they will almost certainly embody historical elements combined in new ways, or older forms interpenetrating original elements. Principles of organisation and economic structures that economists have presumed to be internally superior in efficiency and logic have turned out to be highly context-dependent. Thus, institutional designs involving trust, information sharing, and network structures were once defined as economic solecisms. But economic historians were long aware of the properties and potential of such systems before Silicon Valley and Japanese subcontracting, or customised mass production and flexible specialisation, drew a wider audience to look again at the history of hybridisation or the interpenetration of organizational opposites.

And secondly, economic historians need to start to compare, counterpose, and pull together the insights they are generating from the diverse toolkit of methodologies that they now severally employ. This will involve a project of communicating across sub-disciplinary firewalls and moving from a plurality of legitimate approaches to the reconciliation or even confrontation of alternative approaches. One glaring need is to find ways to put politics more centrally back into economic history and to insist on the inescapability of economic history for good political history. But more generally there is a need to get to grips with the multiple aspects of economic 'moments'. A single example can perhaps illustrate the multiplicity of approaches running in parallel that yet have to talk fully to each other. A defining moment for business historians is the emergence of big business around the railroads and the industries of the mid-West hinterlands in the mid nineteenth century. Through Chandler's work, this has been seen as a matter of both organisational innovation and transaction cost economies. But now other histories of that moment have come forward. It has been seen as a vortex of an ecological revolution (Cronon[1]); a radical break in discourses of power and discipline (Macve[2]); as socially constructed technology (Misa[3]); as a trigger to new cultural and personal identities (Zunz[4]); and as a stimulus for the restructuring of American regulation and political economy (Berk[5]). The dissolution of old hegemonic frameworks has allowed plurality to emerge, now perhaps, we can look forward to the provocative interaction of multiple approaches.

Steven Tolliday (b.15. 5. 1951) is Professor of Economic and Social History in the School of History, University of Leeds, UK. His previous posts were at Kings' College, Cambridge and the Graduate School of Business Administration, Harvard University. He is past editor of *Business History Review*, and a founding editor and current editor of *Enterprise & Society*. His research areas include twentieth century British business and economic history; the world automobile industry; and the economic and social history of postwar Japan.

---

1. William Cronon, *Nature's Metropolis: Chicago and the Great West* (New York, W. W. Norton & Co, 1991)
2. Richard Macve and Keith Hoskin, 'Knowing more as knowing less? Alternative histories of cost and management accounting in the US and UK' *Accounting Historians Journal* 27, 1, June 2000
3. Thomas Misa, A nation of steel: the making of modern America, 1865-1925 (Baltimore, Johns Hopkins UP, 1995)
4. Olivier Zunz, *Making America Corporate* (Chicago, University of Chicago Press, 1990)
5. Gerald Berk, *Alternative Tracks: the constitution of the American industrial order, 1865-1917* (Baltimore, Johns Hopkins University Press, 1994)

Me, Myself and Economic History

B.R. Tomlinson

As part of a tutorial exercise in historical theory, I often ask students to prepare a short history of their life; these are then shuffled and dealt out to groups, who consider what such mass biography can tell us about the nature of historical sources, and the way in which we choose to present ourselves to the world. I have approached this exercise in the same spirit.

I first became aware of the importance of economic history when, at the age of 19, I was stopped by Customs officials on the dockside at Dover while hitch-hiking to Greece in the summer of 1967. The purpose of the interrogation was to ensure that no-one was smuggling more than £50 out of the country - and thus contributing to the capital flight undermining Harold Wilson's attempts to save the pound. Had I realised it, many of the themes with which my academic life has been concerned were encapsulated in that moment.

The pull of India, rather than the attraction of economic history, determined my early career. My doctoral research in Cambridge on the high politics of the Indian nationalist movement in the 1930s (published as *The Indian National Congress and the Raj, 1929-42* in 1976) showed the emptiness of the political rhetoric used by both the colonial state and its nationalist critics. But political history seemed to provide no fundamental explanation of what was happening, only the justifications that politicians and others produced for the actions that they took. Since I did not feel in charge of my own life, it was tempting to look for hidden forces that determined the lives of others, especially the apparently powerful, but culturally alien, proconsuls of the British Empire. What stuffed the stuffed shirts? The presence of both Ronald Robinson and Jack Gallagher in Cambridge, and the lively expanding literature sparked of by the 'Imperialism of Free Trade' provided a way to find the answer.

The events of the 1970s made economic history important. The problems of the international monetary system, and its implications for national economic policy and the viability of nation-states, remained a minor irritant rather than a major obsession for a few years - but the economic climate of the times made them inescapable. With the collapse of the Bretton Woods institutions and the long post-war boom that had fuelled the cultural confidence of the 1960s, into the chaos of the floating currency regimes and the OPEC crisis of 1971-3, such issues became impossible to ignore. These were good times for economic history - the 'decline of Britain' debate, the systemic crises in Britain's relationship to the international economy, and the demand by Third World governments for a 'New Economic Order' to redistribute global wealth, all required fresh research on the nature of the imperial economy, and the links between British business and colonial markets. The release of massive quantities of British government documents with the relaxation of the 50 year access rule provided a great deal of new material to be processed. Against this background I completed the research project on colonial financial and monetary history that was published in 1979 as *The Political Economy of the Raj, 1914-1947*.

This sort of economic history was never exactly main-stream. Monetary history remained an somewhat obscure subject and a minority taste. India was never enough of a Cold War battlefield, strategic threat, moral burden, or economic opportunity to figure largely in the priorities of funding councils or university curricula. Imperial history, too, was still largely concerned with constitutional questions, or fragmenting into a multiplicity of local histories and area studies that sought to capture the voice of the colonised in the history of the Empire. Yet distaste for the hypocrisy of the rhetoric of decolonisation and nation-building still inspired a number of scholars to seek to uncover the implicit calculations of profit and power that underlay the history of the British Empire. Thus my work on India was greatly helped by fruitful inter-disciplinary discussions and wide comparative perspectives.

Teaching in Birmingham University in the 1980s and early 1990s expanded my horizons still further. In a city that bore the scars of deindustrialisation, exacerbated by the hectoring short-term economic logic of Thatcherism, and made more complex by a vigorous multi-racial culture, it was easy to escape the siege mentality that afflicted much of the profession. In Sparkbrook or Handsworth, at least, those who are half in love with India can feel at home. At the University the theory of 'gentlemanly capitalism' was being hammered out by Tony Hopkins and Peter Cain, and there were opportunities for interdisciplinary teaching with economists and political scientists. The course that I taught with Peter Cain, on the international economic system in the twentieth century (to over 50 students each year drawn from six different degree programmes), was especially rewarding. It incorporated concepts drawn from a range of writers from David Hume to Jagdish Bhagwati, and historical examples drawn from California to Calcutta. Spells at the University of Washington (Seattle), Jawaharlal Nehru University (New Delhi) and the University of Melbourne also broadened my horizons, and showed the skeleton of common concerns that lay under the skin of students in other parts of the world.

By the 1980s there were new questions to be addressed, arising from conditions in Britain and elsewhere. Harry Johnson once remarked, with typical provocative simplicity, that economics is the science of rational choice. If that is the case, then economic history can explore why rational choices were not made, or why people did not maximise their opportunities through the exercise of an apparently free will. Issues of poverty and the unequal distribution of resources can be studied as well, or better, in India as anywhere else in the world. The rise of the new institutional economics suggested that answers to these questions should be sought in the study of market failure, institutional structures and imperfect information. These concerns provided the backbone of my *Economy of Modern India, 1870-1960*, published in 1993. The switch-back of boom and bust in many African and Asian economies in the 1980s and early 1990s also stimulated historians of the international economy to consider the broader constraints on economic growth and development - which can best, perhaps, be explained by considering long-term environmental and technological issues, rather than simple questions of political control and exploitation, or 'traditional' value systems.

Moving to Glasgow as Professor of Economic History at Strathclyde in 1994 has provided a fresh set of perspectives. In a society where notions of culture and identity have long been rooted in a sense of economic function, and in which rapid political change has led to a reassessment of notions of nationhood and citizenship, it seems all the more important to understand the history of material life that underlies the changing rhetoric that people use to explain or justify their circumstances. There is also a creative tension between the inward-looking romance of the kailyard and the opportunities and threats provided by global reach. For an imperial economic historian, working in the erstwhile 'Second City of the British Empire' has huge rewards, not least the local archives that contain the records of international trading companies, plantation-owning city magnates, East India captains and bankers, and soldiers turned colonial contractors. Family networks and kinship groupings provide a link between the local and the global, and connect the history of particular societies with larger events across the world as a whole. As oil prices rise, the Middle East explodes, and the mind-games between OPEC producers and Western governments begin again, economic historians should take heart. Economic depression brings intellectual opportunities, provided we know where to look for them. Just keep in mind the motto of Lola Montez: 'Courage, and shuffle the cards'.

B.R. (Tom) **Tomlinson** (b. 10. 6. 1948) is Professor of Economic History, University of Strathclyde. He has held research and teaching posts at the University of Washington, University of Melbourne and the Jawaharlal Nehru University. His research interests are Indian and imperial economic history and Scottish business networks in eighteenth-century Asia. He is currently working on projects investigating education and the diffusion of technology in colonial India.

Twentieth Century Economic and Social History: A Case for Convergence?

Jim Tomlinson

The intrinsic worth of a subject does not depend on institutional arrangements, so we should not regard as wholly tragic the institutional weakening of economic history in higher education, which has so obviously accelerated in the last decade. Some of the reasons for this are clearly unrelated to the academic value of what we do and beyond the control of the discipline. For example, the search for (spurious?) economies of scale in university departmental organisation is clearly a trend driven by national pressures. Yet there are undoubtedly demand side problems which, at least in principle, might be the result of our discipline's failings in making what we do appear congenial to potential students. These failings will arguably also affect our ability to defend our corner in arguments within universities.

From the point of view of those of us who work on the twentieth century, mainly on Britain, one of the features of much work which may be off-putting is the extent to which 'economic' and 'social' history remain so far apart. The social versus economic distinction, successfully broken down in many accounts of the seventeenth, eighteenth and nineteenth centuries, remains powerful for the last hundred years. This is nicely illustrated if one compares the organisation and content of the first and third volumes of the second edition of Floud and McCloskey.[1] In the1700-1860 volume it is hard to allocate many of the chapters to one or other of 'economic' or 'social' history. In the 1939-92 volume it is clear that all the chapters, bar that by Paul Johnson on the welfare state, are 'economic'. We can, in current jargon, talk of two quite dissimilar 'projects' at work in many of the economic and social accounts of this later period, projects which are defined by their background assumptions and methods as much as by subject matter.

On the one hand is the work of the economic historians who see their activity framed largely by economic theory, the use of quantified economic models, and explicit hypothesis testing. In an important sense this approach reverses adjective and noun to turn economic history into historical economics—economics provides the arguments, history the large data sets. This approach is embedded in a broader, basically positivist understanding of knowledge, which is in many ways still reminiscent of Popperian dicta about the nature of science, however much explicit reference to Popper's work has become unfashionable.[2] Such a methodological stance is plainly at odds with much recent social history which has taken a linguistic, 'relativistic' turn, displacing concern from the irreducible 'material' realities of class, state and power onto attempts to understand how these notions were socially and politically constructed at various points in the past, and how social identities were forged out of these constructions.[3]

This separation of approaches serves us twentieth century historians badly. It is intellectually flawed, in that it obstructs rather than helps our understanding of the past. It is also bad for our discipline, splitting us into factions who appear to have little to say to each other, and who therefore have been subject to the old adage 'united we stand, divided we fall'. Are there grounds for reconciliation? The argument here is a perhaps optimistic 'yes', based on a belief that both sides of this divide have much to learn from the other, and that our understanding of the past as well as our coherence as a discipline would gain from a greater willingness to converge or at least 'cross-fertilise'. To encourage such cross – fertilisation we need to recognise the limits of both existing approaches.

On the economic side the key term of the dominant discourse is economic *growth*. Since Ashton in *The Industrial Revolution* defended the effects of that episode in allowing escape from 'Asiatic standards' and 'unmechanised horrors' economic historians have re-defined that revolution in terms of an episode of (slow?) economic growth but retained Ashton's high moral ground of belief that improvements in aggregate human welfare can be equated with economic expansion, measured by the rate of growth of GDP.[4] In the 1950s and 1960s this idea of growth created a standard which has been applied to economic history across the centuries, but most comprehensively and unchallenged to the twentieth century. Thus, the central debate in twentieth century British and much other economic history has been about the causes and consequences of varying rates of growth (and, obsessively in the British case, its obverse, 'decline').

It is hardly original to point out that the concepts of national income and GDP which underlie notions of growth are in many respects both arbitrary and poor measures of economic welfare. From Tobin and Nordhaus's advocacy of measurable economic welfare, which takes into account changes in leisure and the impact of pollution, through feminist critiques of the treatment of household labour and through to Sen's profound re-conceptualisations of the meaning of 'welfare' and the at least partial embodiment of his ideas in the Human Development Index, GDP has been powerfully 'deconstructed'.[5] In addition, concerns with equality as integral to welfare have been re-emphasised in economics, as in recent work by A.B. Atkinson.[6] Yet despite all this, GDP and its growth retain their hold in the economic history literature, as well as beyond in the political and popular imagination.

Is the answer to the problem of the lack of a secure basis for measuring economic growth to give up trying to measure economic welfare? Should we in this area abandon the 'how many, how often, how representative?' question which many economic historians have made their watchword? Emphatically not. Economic statistics are vital to our understanding of economic welfare and the economic past. But it is the status and understanding of these statistics that in my view needs to be revised, taking more of the approach of at least some of the 'new' social history to the issue of how we can best understand the past.

In this social history social class has been shifted from an irreducible, 'material' fact to a socially and politically constructed phenomenon in which the 'language of class' plays a key role.[7] The argument here is that significant benefits would flow if we treated economic categories ('growth', 'decline/modernisation') as equally 'constructed' realities, with statistics a 'language' which usually underpins these categories. The logic of this would be, at its grandest, a 'social (including political) history of the economic', which would treat the economy not as brute material fact but as a product of socially-constructed understandings, often statistical, understandings, which can never achieve the status of Truth, but which equally are not to be dismissed as mere 'ideology'. Rather, accounts of the economy would be seen as always contingent but nevertheless significant 'stories' which have influenced behaviour and policy.

Such an approach, it has clearly to be recognised, challenges the centrality of orthodox economics to economic history. This is not because it dismisses economics as of no account, but rather sees it as one framework among many which help us to understand the economic past. It would be absurd to attempt to understand twentieth century Britain without knowing something of the economic theories that have been deployed for this purpose. Wholesale dismissal of economics is an understandable reaction to the discipline's imperialist ambitions, but is self- defeating. Recognition of the fragility of much economic argument (recognised, it should be noted, by many of the discipline's luminaries) should lead us to reflect on the fragility of *all* human knowledge, rather than to the belief that economics is unique in its ambition out-running its achievements. Knowledge of economics is important also because beliefs about 'the economy' have underpinned so much of the intellectual and political development of the twentieth century. But the status of economics in our attempts to understand that period should be akin to a nineteenth century historian's relationship to Evangelical religion. Such an influential set of ideas has to be understood because it was so vital to the world view of the period studied, but it does not have to be believed in; it does not, indeed must not, be treated as revealed Truth.

On the other side of this plea for 'convergence' is the belief that notwithstanding the inherently 'constructed' nature of statistics, they should still be central to social as well as economic history. Because we reject the idea of statistics as capable of ever being simply a measurement of an external reality does *not* mean we must discard them as an instrument of understanding. Rather, statistics can be seen as always constructing reality as they measure it. Such a view is well-established in some accounts of social statistics, for example in the work of Szreter,[8] but infrequently accepted on the economic side. So we can strongly agree with the late Alec Cairncross when he wrote that 'Why is there no history of economic statistics? Why has one of the most important changes in human affairs passed almost without comment and analysis?[9] However, that history has to be more than a technical discussion, based on a teleological account of a growing approximation to reality. It has to be grounded in an attempt to understand the political and social context which shaped the development of those economic statistics.

Much of the unease with some versions of the 'linguistic turn' reflects a legitimate worry that the issue of representativeness, for example in accounts of the construction of identities, has simply been ignored. Too much of this literature seems to rely on fascinating but possibly highly atypical case studies. The issues of 'how many, how often, how representative?' should not be consigned to a dustbin labelled 'positivist world view', but can be seen as applicable to many of the concerns of 'new' social history, even if the inherently constructed nature of the metrics is accepted.

Does such a case for convergence represent a collapse of judgement in the face of the insistent clamour from post-modernism? Here one should note that to some extent post-modernism is a term used to frighten the children, suggesting that if we disregard some (crude) positivist tenets we must collapse into 'relativism', which is only one step away from intellectual (and moral?) collapse. Yet, as Richard Evans[10] has pointed out, though much of post-modernism may be illogical and overblown, its more sober advocates present a real challenge to how history is often done. One positive way to rise to that challenge is to seek the kind of convergence that this brief essay has suggested.

Jim Tomlinson (b. 22. 10. 1951). Lecturer, Senior Lecturer, Reader in Economics Department at Brunel University (1977-96); Reader then Professor of Economic History (from 1997) Government Department. Research focus – economic and social policy in twentieth-century Britain, history of the Labour Party. Most recent book: *The Politics of Decline: Understanding Post-war Britain* (2000).

[1] Floud, R. and   McCloskey, D. (eds), *The economic history of Britain since 1700*   (2nd ed) 3 volumes (Cambridge, 1994). As Bob Milward notes in an unpublished paper: 'it is striking that the earlier a period the less do historians treat economic issues separately from social and political matters'.

[2] Popper, K., *The logic of scientific discovery* (London, 1959).

[3] Stedman Jones, G., Languages of class: studies in English working-class history, 1839-1982 (Cambridge, 1983).

[4] Ashton, T.S., *The industrial revolution, 1760-1830* (London, 1948).

[5] For a brief survey of these arguments see Tomlinson, J., *The Politics of decline: understanding post war Britain* (London, 2000).

[6] Atkinson, A. B., 'Bringing income distribution in from the cold' *Economic Journal* 107 (1997), pp.297-321.

[7] e.g. Lawrence, J., *Speaking for the people: party, language and popular politics in England, 1867-1914* (Cambridge, 1998).

[8] Szreter, S., *Fertility, class, and gender in Britain, 1860-1940* (Cambridge, 1996).

[9] Cairncross, A., 'The development of economic statistics as an influence on theory and policy' in Ironmonger, D., Hoa, T., and Perkins, J.O.N. (eds), *National income and economic progress: essays in honour of Colin Clark*(London, 1988), pp.10-25.

[10] Evans, R.J., *In defence of history* (London, 1997), ch.8.

The Education of an Economic Historian

Gabriel Tortella

Since the brief to which I am writing implies a rather subjective focus, I will approach the topic from an autobiographical point of view. I started studying economic history in my early twenties because I thought it would provide the answers to the political problems that preoccupied me at the time. I grew up in Spain under Franco's dictatorship, a political regime that was abhorrent to me and against which I rebelled as a student. I became a leader in the democratic student movement, and was detained several times by the police in the 1950s.While in jail I reflected that I had acted from ethical and emotional impulses but that I had very foggy ideas about what the profound causes of the dictatorship were and about what kind of society I was fighting for. At the time I was vaguely a Marxist, had learned some economics at the University of Madrid Law School, and had liked what I had learned, which was some basic elements of price theory. So it was while in jail that I decided to study economic history to better understand society. The problems of underdevelopment were the ones that preoccupied me most; at that time I already held the opinion that the Spanish civil war and the dictatorship were related to economic backwardness.

I was never tried for 'illegal association and propaganda', of which I was accused and which was a crime in Franco's Spain. Holding trial against a group of middle class university students under such brief was embarrassing even for the Franco regime, which at the time was attempting to gain some acceptance in the recently created European Community. When my detention ended I finished my Law degree and went to the U.S. (University of Wisconsin) to study economic history under Rondo Cameron. There I discovered that economic history could be not only a way of better understanding history but also of better understanding economics. At the time, in the mid-1960s, what today is called *cliometrics* was in its infancy, but was preached almost as the gospel by some, mostly young, professors. Jeffrey Williamson and Jan Kmenta were at Wisconsin at the time and it was by them that I was introduced to econometric history. For somebody who already had some training in economics and who had been fascinated by the beauties of economic theory, the 'new economic history', as Clio was called in those times, seemed rather natural. The problem I was privately grappling with then was how 'bourgeois' and 'Marxist' economic theory could be made compatible.

Research in economic history changed my views considerably, not only regarding the general theory of society but also regarding many other viewpoints I held at the time. For instance, I started out with the belief that competition was dangerous because it produced inequality, although I could not articulate precisely why (this is a widely held opinion today). The only answer I could give to explain *unfair* inequality was the Marxian 'primitive accumulation.' I emphasise *unfair* because

401

inequalities derived from different abilities (i.e., meritocratic inequalities) have never seemed wrong to me. Unfair inequality was a consequence of inherited or ill-acquired wealth, and this is what Marx called primitive accumulation. In the course of my research on nineteenth-century Spanish banks, however, I could see that competition was more dynamic and produced more egalitarian results than monopoly: exactly what Cournot's theory predicted. Later on, when studying the Spanish explosives industry in the late nineteenth and early twentieth centuries, I could confirm these results: Schumpeterian theories of innovation and profit perfectly predicted the industry's behaviour and the evolution of the profit rate. Later on, of course, my readings taught me that economic development tends to diminish inequality in the long run.

Earlier on, while writing a seminar paper on the economic origins of the Cuban war of independence, my Leninist-Hobsonian ideas on imperialism were also shattered. It was not the 'imperialist' U.S. that wanted to annex Cuba, it was rather the Cuban planters who wanted to be annexed by the U.S., in order to have access to the North American market without tariff barriers. Whatever happened to the *Maine*, American intervention was due more to political than to economic motives. The U.S. was afraid of a British intervention if the war in Cuba got out of hand. Imperialist rivalries were due more to geo-political antagonisms that to economic interests. Again, Schumpeter seemed to be closer to the mark than the Marxists.

Did economic history then convert me from Marxism to *laissez-faire* economics? Yes, but, first, I had never rejected conventional or bourgeois economic theory and, second, I have never totally rejected Marxism. I feel that one still has to give Adam Smith what is his own and Marx what is his. 'Historical materialism' still is a powerful conceptual tool to understand historical evolution: there are no iron laws in history, but economic interests still play a vital role in shaping political decisions. To say, as the *Communist manifesto* does in its opening sentence, that 'The history of all hitherto existing society is the history of class struggles' is a little bit exaggerated, but not altogether false. Again, going back to my own research, I have worked for many years on the causes of Spain's economic, social, and political retardation, and find that its economic backwardness explains the twists and turns of its political history better than the other way around. I also feel that the best all-encompassing long-term theories of economic history, which we have available - those of John R. Hicks and Douglass C. North - are heavily dependent upon those of Marx, and their authors have acknowledged it.

I think that social science, while having certain advantages over the physical sciences, still has some very serious problems. One advantage is, as Milton Friedman and Albert Einstein have pointed out, that the social scientist understands his subject in a way the physical scientist will never understand his, because the ultimate object of study in social science is the human being, whose behaviour and motivations are understandable to the observer, unlike the ultimate causes of the behaviour of the physical entities. One of the disadvantages of social science, however, is that partial equilibrium is an unsatisfactory way of studying social reality (unlike in the physical sciences, where experimenting is much easier). In other words, dividing society into different sciences (economics, sociology, anthropology, etc.) may make the study manageable, but it does violence to reality. After all, the ultimate aim of science is to predict, and the social sciences have been very mediocre (or rather terrible) predictors. This is one of the advantages of economic history broadly understood. Taking the long view blurs the details, but also permits one to understand phenomena that partial analysis cannot handle. And perhaps economic history, being, as Hicks said, a crossroads of social sciences, may be the best provider of evidence for theory, and therefore for accurate prediction. In fact, the best economists have had recourse to history to demonstrate their theories, from Adam Smith to Milton Friedman, through Jevons, Marshall, Keynes, Schumpeter, Heckscher, etc.

Economic history is undergoing some difficulties, especially in the Anglo-Saxon countries. The end of communism has brought about a fall of popular interest in Marxism and in economic history. Furthermore, cliometrics, while having excellent scientific credentials, discourages many historians educated in the humanities from venturing into what seems to them a dry and dismal science. Other, more exciting and titillating historical approaches, such as the cultural, anthropological, gender, etc., although much less solid and rewarding scientifically, attract them. It is a pity. Economic history can be a key social science but in order to show it we must make it attractive to the non-specialist reader. No matter how technical and econometric our methods, we must be willing and able to communicate them in an accessible language to the general reader and to reach out into dialogue with political and social historians. Otherwise we will confine ourselves to a shrinking ivory tower.

Gabriel Tortella (b. 24. 11. 1936) was educated at the University of Wisconsin and the University of Madrid. Since 1980 he has been Professor of Economic History at the University of Alcala but he has been visiting scholar at several US universities including Harvard. He was President of the International Economic History Association 1994-98. His research field is the economic development of Spain including banking, railroads and the state.

In Praise of Seamless Webs: The Making of a Social Historian

Rick Trainor

This is a historical account. It must be because my approach to economic and social history reflects so clearly my own experiences, especially as a student.

My route to economic and social history has been through history far more than through economics. As an undergraduate (at Brown) in the United States in the late 1960s I took only a single course in the latter - one more, perhaps, than some of my subsequent colleagues detected! But neither was I a focused student of history. My 'concentration' was in 'American Civilisation', an interdisciplinary combination of literature and political science with history. The American - and, to a much lesser extent, European - history I did was intellectually exciting, focused on the interpretation of primary sources in the context of broad debates. But, while much of what excited me was social, it was categorised as 'social and intellectual': my fellow students and I hadn't yet heard about the 'new social history' as such. Meanwhile, economic history barely penetrated our consciousness - it seemed a dull, old-fashioned 'background' to more exciting topics.

Thus my entry to economic and social history as such came later, in Oxford in the early 1970s. In some ways this, too, was an unlikely incubator for an economic and social historian. The core papers of the Oxford Modern History School - which I did, in what was then the traditional fashion for Rhodes Scholars, as a shortened second undergraduate degree - were very political in focus. Even the paper which might have been thought of as methodological - though no one called it that! - was 'Political Thought'. Absorbing another intellectual tradition, profiting from the personal attention of the finely honed tutorial system at Merton, and concentrating on the novel territory of English (and they meant English!) and General (meaning Continental European) history, I found this a highly enjoyable intellectual diet. But it was hardly economic and social history.

The latter entered my Oxford curriculum when, starting to develop an inclination to specialise in British history, I chose for my 'further subject' British Economic History 1700-1870 and for my special subject Peel's Government of 1841-6. The latter, for whom I had Angus Macintyre as a tutor of very broad interests, blended meaty economic subjects like the Bank Charter Act of 1844 with social topics such as public health reform and provided a rounded view of hybrid phenomena such as Chartism. Contrary to the stereotype of learning and teaching at Oxford, the relevant classes were lively affairs, involving spirited debates among students and tutors alike. Meanwhile, a more general introduction to social as well as economic history came through the 'further subject' which ranged from the transport revolution to the famous standard of living debate. Here I had four-stranded good fortune: a highly perceptive tutor (Philip Waller), an engaging guide to the historical uses of economic theory (Patrick O'Brien), the most unstuffy of class leaders (Max Hartwell, choreographing with great relish a voluble group of students largely well to his left) and an extremely incisive lecturer (Peter Mathias) who made topics like agricultural reform and country banking not only intellectually fascinating but also entertaining. For me, starved of the material base in my early studies, learning to relate it to other aspects of history - not excluding cultural and intellectual trends - was a liberating revelation.

Through these experiences I became an economic and social historian without ever defining the subdiscipline and without considering the possibility that the two strands within it could ever be profitably separated - or divorced from political history. These inclinations were reinforced when, after deciding to go into history as a career, I did the first phase of my doctorate at Princeton, completing the 'general examination' after coursework in British and European history. There, under the virtuoso tutelage of Lawrence Stone, I took for granted the intellectual vitality of the 'new social history' which was flourishing at Princeton, attempting to blend social with cultural, economic and political factors, using relevant concepts and methods from the social sciences. The ambitious objective was to understand the forces that shaped society as a whole, with special emphasis (reflecting the atmosphere of the time) on the factors of production and the exercise of power.[1]

This wide-ranging approach to social history inclined me toward geographically specific studies which allowed the investigation of a variety of inter-related topics over a long period. An exciting example of this genre appeared at just the right time: John Foster's study of militancy and its absence in three mid-nineteenth century British towns.[2] Whatever the merits of Foster's Leninist interpretative framework, his book demonstrated the value of linking, within the practicable framework of comparatively analysed urban case studies, economic and social structures with attitudes and behaviour. I discovered in the bowels of Princeton's Firestone Library a primary source ripe for such treatment: the Midland Mining Commission.[3] This was a 'blue book' investigation - full of first-hand testimony from witnesses rich and poor - of disorders, and their economic and social background, in the Black Country during the 'plug riots' of the early 1840s. Once I learned that in this district the period was a brief exception to supposed quiescence - contrasting with the apparently more enduring 'militancy' of the textile Lancashire on which Foster's book focused - the comparative social analysis of towns in the Victorian Black Country emerged as the subject for my thesis.

Returning to Oxford in 1974 to research and write the latter, I found at Nuffield College an environment which completed my evolution into an economic and social historian - or, more accurately, a social and economic historian - allied both to history and the social sciences. As Nuffield had been founded by self-styled social scientists in rebellion against the dominance of the old school of Oxford history, historians - students and fellows alike - had to find a home in the economics, politics or sociology groups. (The warden, Norman Chester, believed that the College's tolerance of 'recent economic, political and social history' excluded topics prior to 1832, which for him was the dividing line between the medieval and the modern eras!) As a budding social historian I was attached to sociology, where I had the great advantage of tutorials on sociological concepts, and constructively robust critiques of my emerging thesis, from my college supervisor, John Goldthorpe, who had read history as an undergraduate at UCL. In those encounters, in the common room and in rambles in the College's superb library (which included the priceless historical collection of G.D.H. Cole as well as hot-off-the-press titles in the social sciences), I began to think of myself as a historian who was also a social scientist.

Meanwhile, my formal supervision on the history side came at first from Max Hartwell, who enthused about topics and approaches far from his own pursuits. Apart from challenging fashionable left-wing interpretations, Max provided a recurrent reminder of the importance of economic theory and factors. These were reinforced by a stimulating class - long in advance of ESRC-enforced 'research training' -which he led with Stanley Engerman in 1975 on the quantitative approach to British economic history. Meanwhile, Brian Harrison had taken over my university supervision. Investing in me an amount of time and concentration which even then I found remarkable, Brian forced me to consider the broadest range of relevant issues and sources in what had become, at his invaluable suggestion, a study of authority and the elite which wielded it rather than a less focused 'histoire totale'. We never discussed what 'type' of history I was pursuing but - following his own distinguished example - it was clearly social history, informed by economic and (to a lesser extent) political history and by relevant sociological (and economic) issues and methods. This entailed an analysis of the exercise of authority 'in the round', including voluntary societies, industrial relations and party politics as well as local government and the Poor Law.[4] It was symptomatic of this broad approach that the teaching I did while at Nuffield - and subsequently while a research fellow at Wolfson and, briefly, a lecturer at Balliol - ranged across economic, social and political topics.

Thus when I was successfully interviewed in 1979 for a post in Glasgow's Department of Economic History I could portray myself with good conscience as a social historian who believed that, in teaching as well as in research, the social should be pursued in conjunction with the economic. This was just as well because in those days the chronologically broad first year course on which I cut my teeth concentrated heavily on the latter. At times, admittedly, the social focus of my special option on 'elites in 19th century British society' made senior colleagues such as Sydney Checkland wonder if I taught any economic history at all! But gradually my own teaching in British and (with Anne Crowther) European history struck a balance between the two tendencies. This became increasingly characteristic of the department as a whole, as reflected in the modification of its name to 'economic and social' in the late 1980s. The department's location in the social sciences faculty also suited my Nuffield background.

Yet I could hardly forget my broad training as a historian. This emerged in analysis of political and governmental factors in my research and teaching - and in persistent contacts, then unusual, with members of those Glasgow history departments which were in the arts faculty. These links bore fruit in 1985 in the externally funded interdepartmental DISH (Design and Implementation of Software in History) project of which I was the first director.[5] Historical computing often uses the sources and methods of economic and social history - notably extracts from the enumerators' returns of 19th century censuses. Yet by definition it transcends the subdisciplines of history. Thus increasing involvement in historical computing helped to re-connect me to the body of history without divorcing me from my home in social and economic history.

The latter, with an urban slant, remained the focus of my publications, which increasingly concerned themselves with the middle-class elites of the industrial provinces and their role in British society more generally. Through the Economic History Society - latterly as secretary - social and economic history also remained the focus of my wider professional role. Particularly in its 'new researcher' sessions at the annual conferences, the Society has remained faithful to its coverage of social as well as economic history - a dual role symbolised by the Economic History Review's adoption of the subtitle 'a journal of economic and social history' during the 1980s. From the late 1990s the renewal of links to the revived Urban History Group[6], increasing contacts with the Social History Society and (adapting to the declining numbers of discrete departments of economic and social history) the emergence of the Standing Conference of Heads of Economic and Social History promised an even fuller realisation of its long-standing dual mandate.

As a product of my own history, therefore, I am a social historian who retains active ties both to economic history and, to a lesser but still important extent, history as a whole. I am uncomfortable with the term 'economic history' unless it is used to encompass social history as well. Likewise I am uncomfortable with any suggestion that economic and social history should be divorced either from other social sciences or from history more broadly. Also, as someone whose own studies began partly in literature and who was trained as an undergraduate on both sides of the Atlantic to pay close attention to the provenance and language of texts, I regret finding myself occasionally in apparent conflict with 'postmodernist' analysts of 'discourse'. Extremists in both camps aside, there should be no dichotomy between that approach, on the one hand, and economic and social history as I understand it, on the other. The subdiscipline has shown itself capable of taking on board increasing enthusiasm for the study of consumption and of culture, and it should be able to cope with greater sensitivity to the form and content of evidence. In these respects, as more generally, I believe that economic and social history prospers intellectually insofar as it is broadminded in terms of its methods as well as its thematic coverage. The more that economic and social history displays such characteristics, the more it will be appreciated fully by - and interact productively with - scholars and students in cognate areas.

Richard H. (Rick) **Trainor** (b. New Jersey, 31. 12. 1948) holds degrees from Brown, Princeton and Oxford - where he took his doctorate. At the University of Glasgow he was Lecturer, then Senior Lecturer, in Economic (and Social) History between 1979 and 1995, when he was awarded a personal chair in social history. He was Dean of Social Sciences at Glasgow 1992-6 and Vice Principal there 1996-2000. Since September 2000 he has been Vice-Chancellor and Professor of Social History at the University of Greenwich. He is married to his Princeton, Oxford and Glasgow colleague Marguerite Dupree. He is the author of *Black Country Elites: The Exercise of Authority in an Industrialised Area 1830-1900* (Oxford: Clarendon Press, 1993) and - with Forbes Munro and Michael Moss - of *University, City and State: The University of Glasgow since 1870* (Edinburgh: Edinburgh University Press, 2000). He is currently writing a social history of the British middle class 1850-1950.

---

[1] E. Hobsbawm, 'From Social History to the History of Society', in M.W. Flinn & T.C. Smout, eds., *Essays in Social History, Oxford, Clarendon Press*, 1974, 1-22.

[2] *Class Struggle and the Industrial Revolution: Early Industrial Capitalism in Three English Towns*, London, Weidenfeld and Nicolson, 1974.

[3] Parliamentary Papers 1843, xiii (508).

[4] Lawrence Stone, whose historical sympathies knew neither thematic nor chronological boundaries, also continued to read and inspire my work.

[5] In 1989 Glasgow became host to the national Computers in Teaching Initiative Centre for History, Archaeology and Art History (CTICH) - and, after broadening in 2000 to all types of teaching, to the inter-university Subject Centre for History, Classics and Archaeology, part of the UK Learning and Teaching Support Network (LTSN).

[6] The Group, in which I found a congenial base complementary to the Society, began life in the 1960s as an offshoot of it.

Economics, History and Complexity

G. N. von Tunzelmann

The struggle for the soul of economic history has often been represented as one between economics and economists on the one side against history and historians on the other. Moreover, this contest has sometimes been seen as one between simplification through using economists' toolkits against factual detail as deployed by historians.[1] It is easy to criticise either of these tendencies when taken to extremes. It is more interesting, though, to weigh up the benefits of the two approaches and seek some reconciliation. As a former economic historian now working mostly in the emerging field of innovation studies, I have come to appreciate more deeply both the benefits and the costs of one or other approach, and to take on a more pragmatic as well as analytical view of the virtues of getting the best of both worlds.

At first blush it seems surprising to describe the economics approach as simplification. The fact that it has failed to take root in British economic history to the extent I would have expected when I began my research career has much to do, I believe, with the view of most of its practitioners that economic approaches were too complicated, too difficult. To appreciate this perspective, we have to inquire more deeply into what is simplicity and conversely what is complexity. An obvious response, and a reasonable one, is that economics uses relatively complex methods which allow it to produce relatively simple results, while history uses relatively simple methods to produce relatively complex results. This makes the situation remarkably similar to many contrasting industrial production systems of the kind I nowadays analyse in innovation studies. But this is also something of a sleight-of-hand, in using the key words with rather different meanings.

Deeper insight can be attained by having resort to the fashionable field of 'complexity theory'. Often highly complex in the methods it has adopted, complexity theory more simply teaches us that complexity is of at least two main kinds. On the one side is the analytical complexity involved in pursuing intellectually demanding areas - the years of study just as preparation and undoubted intellectual gifts required to produce ultimately satisfying results. Seemingly paradoxically, those ultimate results are often distinguished by their very simplicity. Here one thinks of the fundamental sub-atomic constituents of matter, the 'double helix' in genetics, the attempt to unify scientific fields of inquiry by Einstein. This sort of complexity has been referred to as 'cognitive complexity';[2] more crudely I have called it 'complexity in depth'.[3]

On the other side there is the complexity that arises from pursuing multiple areas. This too can be intellectually demanding, in the need to become a jack of all trades but master of at least some. The demands here may, however, be as much 'managerial' as intellectual - the prime requisite is often the ability to integrate the multiple modes of investigation as seamlessly as possible, so that again a rather 'simple', or at least internally consistent, story evolves as the end product. Boisot and Child refer to this as 'relational complexity' - the complexity that comes from multiplying interrelationships while again maintaining coherence. Again more crudely, I have called this 'complexity in breadth'.

The two perspectives of complexity permeate differences of approach throughout the natural as well as the social sciences, well summarised in the theme of Murray Gell-Mann's book, *The quark and the jaguar*, where the quark portrays the cognitively demanding search for the (simple) building blocks of the universe, whereas the jaguar represents the search for why such a complex and impressive creature should have emerged. Gell-Mann's objective is to reconcile these two - how quarks assemble themselves into jaguars - but despite the author's undoubted genius it is not apparent to me that he succeeds. That one approach is more dominant in physics while the other is perhaps more dominant in biology does not facilitate the integration between them.

This now gives us a handle on the difference between economists' and historians' approaches to economic history. The economist here functions more like the physicist in search of the quark - it is no accident that economics has long modelled its methodology on physics, though the conception that many economists have of physics is often woefully misguided.[4] The guiding force is 'cognitive complexity'; the quest is often for 'simple' axioms that are analytically robust. But even at this level there is some relational complexity: the three fundamental particles are drawn together by probably four fundamental forces. The historian instead generally functions more like the evolutionary biologist in search of the jaguar, guided by 'relational complexity'. However the two need to be combined in order to produce work that I find compelling, which is no doubt why what I see as good history - of any kind: political, social, economic, etc. - is so difficult to accomplish.

This brings me back to economic history. One way of thinking about economic history is as a study of how economic phenomena in historical time 'self-organise'. Out of the zillions of possibilities that arise out of the few fundamental particles and forces, it looks implicitly at one (or more) particular possibility that has in actuality emerged - just as the jaguar emerged from a very complex genomic structure (this falls into the area of what complexity theory calls the 'emergent properties' of the system). Out of the myriad of complex relations that might have ensued, this one at least did do so. What drives the observed one to emerge rather than the countless feasible alternatives is seen as being driven by 'strange attractors', often far from equilibrium states. Translating this into economic history, the latter observes the emergent properties of a particular historical context and the economic or other attractors which caused it to take this specific form.

The up-side of this perspective is the justification for studying any particular relevant phenomenon as a system, which the atomistic approach of conventional economics finds it problematic to do. To be sure, the latter has from the times of Adam Smith fallen back on the 'simplicity' of the 'invisible hand' to explain how market systems self-organise, but this is only a modest help in situations where the hand is made 'visible', through the exercise of power by either corporations or governments. Moreover, the invisible hand becomes more complex when the attractors change and when the forces holding the system together are seen to differ. Above all, economic history has to grapple with the conundrum of how the invisible hand, i.e. market system, emerges - for sure it cannot always be taken as already in existence.

The classic 'standard of living debate' is one in which such issues have never really been resolved, for all the excellent historical work that has gone into improving available estimates of wages and prices. The issue, as I have argued elsewhere,[5] boils down to a question of what is the appropriate counterfactual. Unless there is a counterfactual, there is little point in entering a debate. What is the observed industrial world of Britain circa 1850 being compared with in order to establish what might otherwise have happened to living standards? The more economic of the economic historians tend to compare *industrialised* Britain circa 1850 with a *non-industrialised* counterfactual, implicitly subject to slow productivity growth, diminishing returns and the like. Not surprisingly, this view almost invariably yields an 'optimist' view of the standard of living. The more political of the economic historians instead compare *capitalistic* Britain circa 1850 with a *non-capitalistic* alternative. As I have tried to show, this perspective unites the Hammonds, E.P. Thompson, and many other well-known 'pessimists'. For here the outcome is less immediately apparent - it is more plausible to come up with a counterfactual system of government and governance that could have generated much greater benefits for the working classes of industrialising Britain, always assuming that the industrialisation would have taken place regardless. Although Joel Mokyr, in an otherwise generous summary of this view, calls it a 'hypercounterfactual',[6] I do not see this to be the case. As it is, it comes as no surprise that the two sides of the debate have failed to come to any resolution, as they are simply talking past each other.

Little has however been done to specify what the counterfactual world would have looked like, in either of the standard-of-living contexts. The same cannot be said for the more overtly counterfactual studies of the contributions of specific innovations, such as the classic studies of the railways by Robert Fogel, Albert Fishlow and others in the USA, and by Gary Hawke for the UK.[7] Though criticised in many quarters for being ahistorical, indeed veering into science fiction, these studies in fact required the most demanding exercise of historical as well as theoretical capabilities. By going back to what I have said above about complex systems, it soon becomes evident why this should be so. The construction of 'possible worlds' requires assembling the elements and integrating forces of another complex system. Economic theory provides some of the toolkit for undertaking this massive exercise, but little guidance as to what the alternative world would actually look like. Even a brief reconsideration of Fogel's notorious effort to build a hypothetical canal system for the USA in 1890, deprived of the invention of the railroad, shows the extent to which it draws on historical skills in putting this hypothetical system back together. This is the kind of reason why I would assert that the two approaches need to be better integrated.

For all their historical as well as economic innovativeness, these studies have nevertheless been criticised for over-simplification, especially in regard to alternative technologies. My own work on the stationary steam engine has been criticised in similar terms, for not taking account of 'forward linkages' from the new technologies.[8] I am bound to say that the criticism was one that was anticipated; hence my consideration of whether the steam engine led to major breakthroughs in machinery, just as Fogel considered the possibility of earlier invention of the internal combustion engine. Equally I have to recognise from my present standpoint that more needs to be done about 'possible worlds' in the context of technology. I took on the study of the steam engine quite deliberately as investigating a 'general purpose technology', though of course the term itself is much more recent.[9] The complexity of the relations between the engine, the machinery it drove, and the people who worked with it, emerged from historical acquaintance with the subject matter. As the study progressed this indeed became more important than the initial focus on the 'social savings'. But nowadays the theory and evidence for developing such views are both much stronger.

This leads me to a final point, which is that British economic history seems to me to have lost much of its momentum. This cannot be for lack of opportunity. On the side of economic theory, the emergence not just of 'general purpose technologies' but of the whole area of the so-called 'new growth theory' has been a major stimulus to economic history and evaluations of its significance in North America. On this side of the Atlantic, there seems little reflection of that - even the praiseworthy attempts to apply 'new growth theory' here tend to do so in a passive way, rather than seriously questioning it (for it deserves to be questioned, in my view). But this is not the only missed opportunity. Douglass North has reaffirmed the 'new institutional economics',[10] and like Fogel won a Nobel Prize for doing so - here surely there is a role for historical values. North has always been explicit about how systems organise, both market and non-market; yet there is little evidence in recent times of British economic historians engaging with this approach, let alone disagreeing with it. Alfred Chandler's magisterial work on business history has, by contrast, generated some interesting, and probably merited, criticism in relation to its categorisation of the UK.[11] Yet business history and mainstream UK economic history do not seem to have integrated well with each other, even today as business and management studies boom. Of course, as an editor, I am totally biased but in my view the intellectually and historically interesting developments in Britain are taking place in such journals as *Industrial and Corporate Change*, rather than in standard British economic history. Among other things, innovation studies scholars are in the forefront of developing 'history-friendly' simulation models of industrial growth, and generating counterfactual industrial worlds.[12]

More than ever, economic history has much to offer, not just as a passive user of theories developed elsewhere, but as a nurturing ground for new ways of theorising. Many of the criticisms traditionally levelled by economists, which amount to its lack of micro-foundations, may be misplaced. Above all, economic history can provide so much of the basic material for understanding 'complex systems', for which there is so much demand. But in practice, at least in the UK, it does seem to be in danger of ignoring the possibilities and drifting, rudder-less, into a quiet backwater.

G. N. von Tunzelmann (19. 11. 1943) was educated at the University of Canterbury, New Zealand and Nuffield College, Oxford. He was Lecturer in Economic History at Cambridge, 1970-84 and is currently Professor of the Economics of Science and Technology, University of Sussex. His research focuses upon technological change and innovation.

---

[1] Crafts, 'Industrial Revolution'.
[2] Boisot and Child, 'Organisations as adaptive systems'.
[3] Wang and von Tunzelmann, 'Complexity and the functions'.
[4] Mirowski, *More heat than light*.
[5] von Tunzelmann, 'The standard of living debate'.
[6] Mokyr, *British Industrial Revolution*, pp. 119-21.
[7] For a summary see O'Brien, *Economic history*, and von Tunzelmann, 'Cliometrics'.
[8] Ayres, 'Technological transformations'.
[9] Helpman, *General purpose technologies*.
[10] North, *Institutions*.
[11] Chandler, *Scale and scope*, Cassis, *Big business*, Hannah, *Rise of the corporate economy*.
[12] Malerba et al., '"History-friendly" models'.

Works cited
Ayres, R.U., 'Technological transformations and long waves; part I', *Technol. Forecasting and Soc. Change*, 37 (1990), pp. 1-38.
Boisot, M., and Child, J., 'Organizations as adaptive systems in complex environments: the case of China', *Org. Science*, 10 (1999), pp. 237-52.

Cassis, Y., *Big business: the European experience in the twentieth century* (Oxford, 1997).

Chandler, A.D. jr., *Scale and scope: the dynamics of industrial capitalism* (Cambridge MA, 1990).

Crafts, N.F.R., 'Industrial Revolution in Britain and France: some thoughts on the question 'why was England first?'', *Econ. Hist. Rev.*, 30 (1977), pp. 429-41.

Fishlow, A.L., *American railroads and the transformation of the ante-bellum economy* (Cambridge MA, 1965).

Fogel, R.W., *Railroads and American economic growth: essays in econometric history* (Baltimore, 1964).

Gell-Mann, M., *The quark and the jaguar: adventures in the simple and the complex* (London, 1994).

Hannah, L., *The rise of the corporate economy* (London, 1976).

Hawke, G.R., *Railways and economic growth in England and Wales, 1840-1870* (Oxford, 1970).

Helpman, E. (ed.), *General purpose technologies and economic growth* (Cambridge MA, 1998).

Malerba, F., Nelson, R., Orsenigo, L., and Winter, S., ''History-friendly' models of industry evolution: the computer industry', *Ind. and Corp. Change*, 8 (1999), pp. 3-40.

Mirowski, P., *More heat than light: economics as social physics; physics as nature's economics* (Cambridge, 1989).

Mokyr, J. (ed.), *The British Industrial Revolution: an economic perspective* (Boulder, 1993).

O'Brien, P., *The economic history of the railways* (London, 1977).

North, D.C., *Institutions, institutional change and economic performance* (Cambridge, 1990).

von Tunzelmann, G.N., 'The standard of living debate and optimal economic growth', in J. Mokyr (ed.), *The economics of the Industrial Revolution*, (Totowa NJ, 1985), pp. 207-26.

von Tunzelmann, G.N., 'Cliometrics and technology', *Struct. Change and Econ. Dynamics*, 1 (1990), pp. 291-310.

Wang, Q., and von Tunzelmann, N., 'Complexity and the functions of the firm: breadth and depth', *Research Policy*, 29 (2000), pp. 805-18.

The Messiness of Life

Hans-Joachim Voth

Economic history is about the messiness of life. The phrase is Lawrence Stone's. In the Princeton tenure case of David Abraham – accused by Gerald D. Feldman and Henry A. Turner of falsifying evidence – Stone tried to defend certain differences between Abraham's translations and the original documents by reference to the 'messiness of life'. What he meant was the struggle to preserve the unique nature of the source against the various direct and indirect pressures to come up with supporting evidence for a hypothesis and the difficulty of working in an archive, often in a foreign language. Messiness of this sort will be familiar to most of us.

This is only partly the sense I have in mind. I first financed a good part of my education as an economic historian working as a management consultant during the summer vacations. Eventually, my experience as a consultant became an important source of income when I returned to academia. It was during those periods when I was working side-by-side with business analysts and economists at McKinsey that I think I partly learned what is unique about economic history. To make evidence speak – or, more precisely, to distil a plausible, even likely story out of a plethora of incomplete, partly contradictory, often highly confusing snippets of evidence goes to the very core of the discipline. This task seems to be markedly easier for economic historians than for graduates of some neighbouring social sciences and arts subjects. And coping with the 'messiness of life' – and not just our own lives, but of life in general, is crucial. It implies a willingness to look for indirect evidence, to interpret material collected for entirely different purposes to answer questions; and to do so where others have long given up because 'the data just isn't out there'.

One underlying assumption, clearly, is that there is such a thing as an outer world, that reality is not simply a social, linguistic and cultural construct. Meaning and significance do not, as our friends from the ever-growing loony-linguistic fringe in humanities departments tell us, only come out of the tip of fountain pens and ink cartridges. We can find out why America became a technological leader, why we type on keyboards reading QWERTY, or if wages in Britain increased markedly during the Industrial Revolution. These are difficult questions, to be sure, but there is no *epistemological reason* why they could not be answered. Perhaps even more importantly, economic historians believe that they should be answered, that the answers matter. Empirical positivism is essential to the field; unfortunately, this also means that at the tender age of 32, I hear myself sounding hopelessly out of touch in the ears of some of my students.

This is not to say that the empiricism of the subject is its most defining characteristic. Other fields – medieval history, archaeology, to name just two of the most obvious examples – are certainly in a similar league. What good economic history – or, what is to my mind synonymous with it – 'new' economic history does at its best is to organise the fragmented, partial, and often misleading evidence in such a way as to answer explicit questions. Deriving testable hypotheses is as much part of the equation as the skill to find and interpret sources that answer the question. Probably no other discipline has as many articles and even books with titles in the form of questions. 'Did monetary forces cause the Great Depression?' 'Seedcorn or chaff?' 'Did Victorian Britain Fail?' 'Is There Still Life in the Pessimist Case?' It might even be possible to write a history of the entire discipline, referring only to the contributions ending in a question mark.

To ask questions and to try to answer them by using empirical evidence with all the care of the historical profession, are essential elements of economic history. These may seem like trivial statements. My colleagues in the economics department at Pompeu Fabra in Barcelona would almost certainly not think this unusual. Attending history seminars at various universities, however, quickly makes it clear how distinguishing a feature this is. Especially in the areas of history most affected by the linguistic turn, the desire to *answer* a question seems passé, outdated, possibly even part of a repressive attitude. Talks often start with the presenter defining his or her aim as 'raising a number of interesting questions' – and leaving it precisely at that.

The attempt to answer questions is also important in rectifying one of the larger misunderstandings that affects economic history. Many of the students that join graduate degree programs in social and economic history seem deliberately 'innumerate', in McCloskey's phrase – proud of their unwillingness to master quantitative techniques, and inclined to focus exclusively on the social end of the spectrum. It is common enough not just with students, but in the perception of other historians as well, to emphasise the quantitative side of 'new economic history'. The Cambridge M.Phil. student that, at the end of my methodology class declared 'I just hate all this stuff', had nothing more elaborate in mind than a handful of regressions and simulation exercises. Certainly, some of the contributions in *Explorations*, the EcHR and the JEH seem to have required more number-crunching than the average Apollo mission to the moon. To my mind, emphasis upon quantitative techniques nonetheless misses the essential side of the discipline (or at least the part of the discipline I feel I belong to). Old-hat economic history was never unempirical. Some of the most conscientious (and mind-numbingly dull) data-gathering exercises were carried out in old-style economic history. The use of high-powered econometrics adds a new dimension, but is hardly crucial in methodological terms.

Much more central is the explicit use of theory to derive testable hypotheses. The most common examples, of course, rely on economic theory. This can take the form of important stylised facts. Did the 'take-off' into self-sustaining growth really require a doubling of the investment ratio, as Rostow assumed? The work by Feinstein and other national accounting exercises provide direct answers, and they do so within the framework established by Kuznets and others in 1940s and 1950s. Temin's work on the origins of the Great Depression is not just looking for the root cause of the greatest economic catastrophe in the 20th century; it also stands out for deriving clear implications from monetarist theory, the diligent datawork that allows such implications, and the wider implications for theory that can be drawn from his analysis.

Many of the more exciting developments in recent years have seen the application of theoretically based reasoning, from fields other than economics, to problems in economic and social history. Without the advances in demographic theory – on, say, how to partition infant mortality into endogenous and exogenous factors – some of the work of the Cambridge Group of Population Studies would have been inconceivable. Other notable examples have seen the application of insights from psychology and experimental economics to political history. Offer's work on bounded rationality and war, and on consumption and myopic choice, point us towards the unexploited potential of the discipline.

One could argue that this is simply a form of arbitrage; little more than what a bond trader does when he exploits minute differences in the pricing of assets with similar risk characteristics. To start with a historical problem, shop around for the latest insights of the various social sciences, and then derive hypotheses that can be confronted with the evidence is similar in that we further knowledge by applying insights produced by other fields. Rickert and Windelband, two German Neo-Kantians at the turn of the last century drew a distinction between nomothetic and ideographic sciences. Whereas the former aimed at formulating covering laws of widest applicability, the latter focused on describing as exactly as possible the detailed characteristics of their object of study. If physics is the paradigmatic nomothetic science, and history the most typical of ideographic disciplines, what is economic history?

When Descartes and Leibniz thought of a universal science, composed of arithmetic, geometry, mechanics and logic, they used the term *mathesis universalis.* Derived from the Greek root for learning, this was defined as a universal set of rules for the derivation of knowledge. Things, of course, are no longer quite so simple. Abstract principles and deductive reasoning alone are harder to sell as the model for universal science. Confronting theory with empirical facts, however, with the full range of the 'messiness of life', is a function that few other disciplines perform as well as economic history does. Of course, the field is not a *mathesis universalis* in disguise. Rather, it is that stretch of territory connecting the social sciences on the one hand and the humanities on the other, using explicit theoretical modelling and the full range of empirical techniques to ultimately explain phenomena that are specific to a time and place. Perhaps that is why the territory sometimes feels like no-man's land between C.P. Snow's 'two cultures'.

Hans-Joachim Voth (b. 1968 in Lübeck, West Germany). Studied history and economics in Bonn, Freiburg and St. Antony's College, Oxford. He pursued doctoral research at EUI, Florence and Nuffield College, Oxford, receiving the EHA's Alexander Gerschenkron Prize for his thesis in 1996. He is currently the Associate Director of the Centre for History and Economics, King's College, a Research Fellow at Robinson College, and an Assistant Professor at the Economics Department, Universitat Pompeu Fabra, Barcelona. He has written in the economic history of the British Industrial Revolution, on the history of smallpox and on inter-war Germany.

Confessions of a Card-Carrying Economic Historian

Jan de Vries

The ongoing appeal to me of economic history as an intellectual practice is located in a cluster of interrelated characteristics. This is an academic practice that is truly part of history and truly part of economics, and it links these identities in a 'middle kingdom' that is at once recognisable and porous, with its own tradition but open to syncretic adaptations of all sorts.

Interdisciplinarity - We hear a great deal about interdisciplinary and multidisciplinary studies. Sometimes it appears that the interstices between every disciplinary boundary have been colonised by bands of academic pioneers, exiles, squatters, etc. Not many of these enterprises flourish for long, and still fewer possess the characteristic that gives economic history its strength and appeal. That is, our field of study, at its best, is not an *escape* from discipline but entails an *embrace* of two disciplines - two demanding and very different disciplines. The economic historian joins an inductive and a deductive, an idiographic and a nomothetic discipline in what necessarily must be a difficult embrace. This is the source of its interest to me, and, I would add, of its value, not least to the two disciplines with which economic history must remain in continual dialogue.

Understanding the past - There are, of course, many mansions in Clio's house, and more than a few provide valuable historical knowledge. And, only a naïf of the first rank would now propose that a historian of any sort can uncover the plain and unvarnished truth about the past, to know *Wie es eigentlich gewezen*. But economic history – its undeserved reputation for unrepentant positivism notwithstanding – recognised long before most types of history the futility of supposing that research into the past could yield unmediated historical knowledge. It was, indeed, the engagement with economics that trained historians to seek out repeated and patterned behaviours, make comparisons and measure. Because economic life is so evidently the joint and often unexpected product of many people, the economic historian has long known that one cannot embark on research without first being equipped with organising concepts, measurement tools, and theory. We do not all cast our work in the 'hypothetico-deductive models' that the New Economic Historians had called for in their Young Turk phase, but more than in other fields, the reader of our work is informed of the assumptions and given the means to replicate and test the findings. Does this 'scientific' apparatus mark the economic historian as a deluded positivist or is it the attribute of a scholar acutely aware of the contested nature of all historical claims, as someone eager to engage in the debate rather than painfully to construct a terrain of exclusivity, accessible to no one but the author?

The unavoidably 'constructed' character of most economic history offers what for me is a highly satisfactory sort of knowledge. At its best it reveals how (a bit of) the world works. Three aspects of research in the field come to mind that, I believe, contribute to this satisfaction.

First, it is *intended* to be tested, challenged, and improved upon. Most historians today deny the notion that knowledge in their field is cumulative. The current weakness of the impulse to empirical refinement undercuts the basic motivation for maintaining a broadly-based discourse, leaving historians isolated, talking only to their closest soul-mates. Economic history remains an 'open' discipline, seeing this as the guarantor of improved historical understanding.

Second, it is an inherently inclusive field of study. The theoretical material most of us bring to economic history does not readily allow for a discourse of 'otherness.' and a sentimental savouring of the impossibility of understanding the behaviour of distant peoples, past times, or other genders or races. Our personal biases can limit the field, to be sure, but the intellectual foundations of the field must lead us, sooner or later, to overcome such limitations. There are, of course, those who suppose economic historians are unavoidably apologists for the rich and powerful. Perhaps we are more inclined than other historians to seek to understand the challenges they face, but the same should apply as we approach inventors, workers, peasants, housewives, pensioners, slaves, and all the other socio-economic categories of historical humankind with which we are concerned.

Third, and finally, economic history leads to the creation of complex reconstructions of the past. Rarely can we come to grips with a problem by focusing on an individual or by presenting a simple chronological narration of events. Our field recognises the importance of what Fernand Braudel called the 'plurality of social time', if only in a consciousness of the distinction between short-run and long-run processes, and it is inclined to reject the 'pernicious humanism' that limits so much historical research to a sterile anthropocentrism. These holistic impulses and the capacity to develop complex models of historical change release us from the banality of the narrative form that is the conspicuous mark of the larger discipline's failure of nerve in this generation.

Understanding economics - The interdisciplinary and social scientific character of economic history gives it a special place in the discipline of history, and thus far I have emphasised the role it can play in returning that errant discipline to its full vocation. It has a role no less important to play in dialogue with the discipline of economics.

For many years this role was defined by the New Economic Historians who emerged in the 1960s and quickly came to dominate the field in the United States. Economic History was destined to be a type of applied economics, testing with historical data models founded on neoclassical theory. The challenge to history was clear: replace stories and narration with testable hypotheses and analysis; reveal all assumptions and biases. However, these bold, reforming claims went yoked with a major weakness: reliance on an ahistorical theory whose impressive power is restricted to tests of market rationality, efficient allocation, and similar static concepts. Dynamic models could incorporate locomotion, but not irreversible, contingent change. In short, ahistorical theory can give convincing answers only to relatively minor historical questions. And what, in fact, does such work contribute to economic theory? Robert Solow may have been unduly severe when he answered 'It gives back to the theorist the same routine gruel that the economic theorist gives to the historian. Why should I believe, when it is applied to thin eighteenth century data, something that carries no conviction when it is done with more ample twentieth century data?'[1] In fact, imaginative use of these limited tests have often supported arguments concerning larger issues of dynamic economic change. But an economic history limited to neoclassical theory remains a tethered beast.

This New Economic History, tethered or not, has gained adherents internationally and remains influential today. Indeed, I am enough a child of this movement to view its achievements with respect and admiration. But from its earliest days there were critics who urged a restoration of focus on long-term economic change. Instead of a social scientific history, we should aspire to develop an historical social science. This impulse has led in various direction, ranging from the new institutionalism of Douglass North, to the 'total history' concept of Fernand Braudel, with its aim of crowning history as the 'queen of the social sciences'.

A history equipped to give depth and meaning to the superficial, event-focused disciplines remains a dream as noble as it is distant, but there is an unmistakable growth of interest in concepts that seek to restore time and space – history and geography – to economic theory. The new growth theory, the concept of path dependence, and models of *homo œconomicus* that add fear and love to the familiar impulse toward greed, all act to convince the economist that 'history matters'. Indeed, the more general drift away from Newtonian toward biological metaphors opens new possibilities for fruitful interaction between history and theories of complexity.

Boundaries - The appeal of economic history to me lies primarily in the satisfaction that comes from the special effort required to join two different and demanding disciplines. If the cost-benefit ratio seems attractive to me, perhaps this reflects a taste for boundary crossing. And this, in turn, may explain why I find the most attractive current areas of research to be those that also feature boundary issues. They are general historical issues, but I believe that economic history can play a leading role in their exploration. Let me mention the two most general: the boundaries between 'early modern' and 'late modern' history, and the (multiple) boundaries that limit deployment of a world history perspective.

Longevity has given Western history's conventions of periodisation a venerability that will prevent their speedy dismantling. But there are unmistakable trends toward a 'deconstruction' of the historiographical assumptions that under-girded the boundaries between ancient and medieval, and between late medieval and early modern. Economic historians have played, at best, ancillary roles in these developments. Now it is the great eighteenth century revolutions that guard the portals to modernity that are under discussion. They form a monument of periodisation that, more than the others, is implicated in the most important models of economics, political science, and sociology. There is little doubt in my mind that our current reassessments of what the future might look like will force a continued re-examination of the concept of 'modern history' that was so deeply implicated in the justification of a future that has now vanished from view. The French Revolution, as it was cultivated for over a century, is over; the British Industrial Revolution is also on its way to becoming something other than what we have known for most of the twentieth century. Undoubtedly, new principles will be advanced for the compartmentalisation and analysis of historical time; I suspect the years around 1800 will fade as a boundary, and that this will allow fruitful new questions to emerge, especially in economic history.

The second boundary issue concerns the effort to construct a foundation for a non-Eurocentric world history. Economic history, because of its long interest in comparative method, has much to offer this project, but much of what passes for world history is still transparently a form of

418

colonial and imperial history. Without wishing to minimise the difficulties ahead, I believe that economic history has real opportunities to lead in the development of suitable models for integrated and comparative studies that transcend historiographical traditions.

A useful example is found in current debates about the concept of 'early modern' as a world -- rather than a European – historical category. Some specialists in the field, such as Thomas Brady, argue that the very fact that most traditional European claims for the modernity of the Renaissance and Reformation have been decanted from the term 'early modern', it is now suitable as a vehicle to explore intercontinental—at least Eurasian – commonalities in the first era of continuous and direct commercial and political interaction.[2] Others, most recently and vigorously Jack Goldstone, remain concerned by the 'Eurocentric' baggage that unavoidably is carried by the term.[3] He advocates a new label, but shares the view that European and Asian societies in some 'pre-modern' era yet to be given a name can be studied with a common tool kit. At present these useful conceptual contributions and some rich, substantive studies of comparative history are mingled with no small amount of politically-charged rhetoric. But I am inclined to the view that all of it together constitutes a sign that our 'inter-discipline' has much to contribute at these boundaries.

Jan de Vries (b. 14. 11. 1943). A.B., Columbia University; Ph.D., Yale University, is currently Professor of History and Economics at the University of California at Berkeley and Co-editor of the *Journal of Economic History*. Author of major works on the Dutch and European economies in the early modern period including *The Dutch Rural Economy in the Golden Age, 1500-1700* (1974) and *European Urbanisation, 1500-1800* (1984).

---

[1] Robert Solow, 'Economic History and Economics', *American Economic Review* 75 (1985), p. 330.

[2] Thomas A. Brady, Jr., 'Introduction: Renaissance and Reformation, Late Middle Ages and Early Modern Era', in Thomas A. Brady, Jr., Heiko Oberman, and James Tracy, eds., *Handbook of Early Modern European History*, (Leiden, Brill Publishers, 1995), Vol 1, p. xxi.

[3] Jack A. Goldstone, 'The Problem of the "Early Modern" World,' *Journal for the Economic and Social History of the Orient* 41 (1999), 249-84.

Economic History in My Curriculum

Immanuel Wallerstein

I have often been accused of being an economic historian. One somewhat unfriendly critic once wrote that world-systems analysis, which is what I claim to do, is just an excuse for sociologists to do economic history. Unfriendly critics often are insightful, and perhaps he was right.

I was trained as a sociologist, have been a professor of sociology all my university life, and indeed have been president of the International Sociological Association. On the other hand, I was the pest who constantly wrote to the secretaries-general of the International Sociological Association and the International Association of Economic History that they should not hold their congresses at the identical time (which in fact in the end only occurred once, in 1982). And about the few scholarly journals that I regularly read are several that assert that they are journals of economic history. So I clearly have some affinity for the field, perhaps a love that dares not speak its name.

I guess the attraction that I have for economic history is that it seems to me that much of it contains writing about the real world as it really happens. I wouldn't say this is true of everything that calls itself economic history (and the new economic history seems to me in general a giant step away from this virtue). And it is surely not the case that only works of economic history describe the real world as it really happens. But the percentage has been higher in this 'field' than in most in social science. I find I get 'aha' experiences much more frequently when reading this material.

There are two different ways in which the practitioners of the field have defined it. For some, it is simply a specialty (dare I call it, a narrow specialty) in which they happen to be interested and to which they have dedicated their scholarly energy. They collect data on 'economic' variables that concern some particular problem in a particular place and period. They seek, in the best Ranke-ian tradition, to discover what 'really' happened.

These practitioners have two principal obstacles in their quest. The data for which they search is often, perhaps almost always, incomplete, especially if one wants accurately quantified data in periods of yesteryear. The second great obstacle is translating the quantities. Since economic variables have been historically noted using measuring rods that are relatively local, and since there was little standardisation before the nineteenth century (and a substantial degree of standardisation only as of the second half of the twentieth century), how to interpret weights and measures that are found in the archives has been a recurrent puzzle. Competent scholars work hard to overcome these obstacles, but they can never be entirely erased.

The second definition of what economic historians are trying to do is that they are seeking to determine the underlying or basic or continuing realities of social life by describing cycles and trends over long periods of time. This of course was the program of the *Annales*. This group of scholars sees economic history not as a specialty but as a way into a larger picture, sometimes called 'total' history. It is Fernand Braudel among recent economic historians who pushed this program furthest and most vigorously. And much of the reaction against Braudel is a reaction against such an intellectual program.

Economic historians are under great pressure from two different guilds, that of the 'historians' and that of the 'economists'. Both of these guilds have great authority and organisational strength within the world academy of knowledge. In general, most economic historians feel they have to 'choose' between these pressures, if only because they tend to have a Ph.D. in one or the other discipline, and are members of one or the other university department.

In the late nineteenth and early twentieth centuries, economic history was an orphan, more or less rejected by both guilds. The historians were dubious about anything that was not political or diplomatic history, and economic historians seemed to them to be pursuing a minor and not very important track. And economists rejected history. Alfred Marshall made this very clear in the organisation of the first department at Cambridge.

After the First World War however, economic history began to find acceptance as a legitimate sub-field within history departments. This is what we tend to call today the 'old economic history.' But economists remained however hostile. As late as the 1960's, when I was teaching at Columbia University, the Department of Economics decided that, after L. Carrington Goodrich retired, they would not replace him with another economic historian, since economic history didn't have a place within economics.

We have to talk about this different attitude of the two disciplines. History has tended to be a somewhat ecumenical discipline. Provided only that practitioners were willing to work with archives and utilise a Ranke-ian orientation, they were tolerated. Bit by bit any locus of historical research came to be seen as permissible. Economics on the other hand established itself originally as an 'isolationist' discipline. It used the famous *ceteris paribus* clause. Holding everything else constant, economics told the story of what happened in the market. Other scholars could deal with 'everything else'; it was of no concern to economists.

Something happened around the 1960s to economists. They began a shift from being an 'isolationist' discipline to being an 'imperialist' discipline. The premises and methods of economists were seen to be the only valid ones in social science. Economists could do political science and sociology better than political scientists or sociologists, or at least the economists insisted that the latter adopt their premises and methods. The same thing happened to economic history. Economists redefined it as testing their theoretical propositions with less good data about earlier moments in historical time. They told the economic historians that, if they did this, they were grudgingly welcome within the fraternity. This is the 'new economic history.' Indeed, as we know, the Nobel Prize for Economics, carefully controlled by the guild, actually awarded two economic historians the prize.

The problem today is not to continue the debate between the two modes of doing economic history,

421

but to reflect on what has been happening within the historical social sciences as a whole. I will not repeat here the arguments that are to be found in *Open the Social Sciences*,[1] the report of the Gulbenkian Commission on the Restructuring of the Social Sciences, which I chaired (and which had one 'economic historian' among the ten members). I merely want to point to one of its findings. The report recounts the degree to which there has come to be 'blurring' between the historic disciplines since 1945. My personal itinerary illustrates this widespread reality. It also discusses the problem of the parochiality of most research. This is an issue insufficiently discussed by economic historians, but is coming to the fore these days, as we are beginning to have more serious work done on the 'economic history' of the non-Western world, and therefore are beginning to question the validity of generalisations that we have facilely made from a study of European and North American data.

But the most important message of the Gulbenkian Report for economic historians is to be found in a statement on page 98:

> What seems to be called for is less an attempt to transform organisational frontiers than to amplify the organisation of intellectual activity without attention to current disciplinary boundaries. To be historical is after all not the exclusive purview of persons called historians. It is an obligation of all social scientists. To be sociological is not the exclusive purview of persons called sociologists. It is an obligation of all social scientists. Economic issues are not the exclusive purview of economists. Economic questions are central to any and all social scientific analyses. Nor is it absolutely sure that professional historians necessarily know more about historical explanations, sociologists more about social issues, economists more about economic fluctuations than other working social scientists. In short, we do not believe that there are monopolies of wisdom, nor zones of knowledge reserved to persons with particular university degrees.

I believe that people who do economic history will progress most in our common work if they bear this admonition in mind, and join in the task of reconstructing a reunified historical social science in the twenty-first century.

Immanuel Wallerstein (b. 28. 9. 1930) was educated at Columbia University and is currently Distinguished Professor of Sociology and Director of the Fernand Braudel Centre, Binghampton. He was President of the International Sociological Association 1994-98 and has published on world trade, geopolitics and historical capitalism.

---

[1] Stanford: Stanford University Press, 1996

Am I or am I not an Economic Historian?

Malcolm Wanklyn

One aspect of my professional life which has never caused me any concern is what kind of historian I am. For most of my professional life I have described myself as a regional historian, having drunk deeply at John Marshall's well when I was at an impressionable age. Bearing this badge I had been able to immerse myself in the land of my ancestors, the counties that bordered Wales, flitting from one type of history to another seemingly as the whim took me - industrial history, agrarian history, military history, urban history, transport history. As a result my CV, instead of showing a logical and steady development over 30 or more years, like that of my colleague John Benson, looks more like a scatter diagram in which the only common feature has been a preoccupation with the west of England in the period 1560 to 1760. Moreover, as time passed, my publications have become less focused in a chronological and geographical sense. By the late nineteen-nineties I had managed to escape from my early modern shell. Two of my four outputs since 1998 are firmly fixed in the nineteenth century. I also now wear with pride the distinction of being one of the few historians, and possibly the only one, to have published articles in Northern History, Southern History, and Midland History.

However, the brief for this essay collection has caused me to think deeply about what I am. Has my career been merely a reflection of the wilfulness of a child of a one parent family who had not acquired the self-discipline that comes with maturity, or was there some underlying thread? Was the central weakness of my career that I had failed to make up my mind as to whether I was a military historian or an economic historian? Had I not been most comfortable when able to incorporate both, as in my doctorate on the allegiance of Cheshire and Shropshire landowners in the English Civil War, and in the book Kevin Down and I are currently writing on a thousand years of Welsh borderland history? My immediate thoughts were that there was some form of unresolved conflict. After all, I seemed unable to decide on my next major research project. Should I return to my interest in internal trade which had resulted in the Gloucester Port Book database, or should I travel further back in my biological time line and write a book on strategy and tactics in the Civil War with my former research student Frank Jones? Was it to be the path of duty, a thanks offering to all those colleagues and local historians with whom I had worked on the Portbook Programme in the eighties and early nineties, or was I to seize the chance to let off steam by telling the political historians that they had failed to do justice to the most important outcome of the English Civil War, Parliament's victory and the king's defeat?

I began to look for a guiding thread by thinking backwards over my life as an historian. I had certainly graduated from a course that was designed to create economic historians, but I had not chosen to take Modern History with Economics and Politics at Manchester because I was particularly interested in economic history. The family view had been that courses which included economics were more likely to lead to a job, a curiously modern concept but not all that surprising as I was likely to be the sole breadwinner. Whilst at Manchester I was certainly inspired by the teaching of Bill Chaloner to conduct research into blue books and other primary sources on nineteenth century economic history mouldering away in the underground corridor that led from one wing of the Arts library to the other, but in my final year I refused to join his special subject because it was too modern. I had found nothing to stimulate me in the secondary sources on the inter-war economy, and I could not key into a family history of unemployment as my grandfather had kept his job as a clicker in the boot and shoe trade throughout the nineteen-thirties. Indeed in 1931 he had taken out a mortgage on the house in which I had been brought up for the first ten years of my life. The choice of special subject lay between T.S. Willan on Tudor Economic History or Donald Pennington on the English Civil War, but wilfulness prevailed when Willan would not allow me to write a dissertation on the Knightleys, a Northamptonshire landowning family heavily involved in depopulating enclosures whose park at Fawsley was criss-crossed with grassed over ridge and furrow.

The Civil War then had my undivided attention for the next three years until my masters dissertation on the king's armies in the west of England had been completed and I arrived at Wolverhampton, then a college of technology but teaching University of London arts and social science degrees to what now seem tiny groups of students. Here I was persuaded by one of the founding fathers of industrial archaeology, the metallurgist Reg. Morton, to become involved in the career of Dud Dudley, a local ironmaster who had also served as a Royalist officer. But this led not into economic history but back into the Civil War in terms of a doctorate on the allegiance of the landed gentry in 1642. Nevertheless I could not escape the influence of economic history. The first chapter I wrote for Brian Manning was over 10000 words on the landed gentry and technological breakthrough in the Cheshire salt industry (1620-1642). He raised his eyebrows, muttered in his beard that if I was not careful my thesis would be twice or three times the length it ought to be, and gently steered me in a different direction. As a result what could be described as economic history, a section on landowners and enterprise, took up no more than a twelfth of the final thesis. The study of the salt industry never saw the light of day.

Economic history tendencies, repressed during my doctoral research, burst forth in a post-doctoral investigation of industry in the Ironbridge Gorge before Abraham Darby, funded by ESRC. The Civil War fought back in terms of two articles on Royalist strategy published in the early eighties and a number of reviews. Then the port books took over for fifteen years. I owe the inspiration for that project not to Professor Willan but to Peter Edwards, the agrarian historian, who, on a train journey back from the P.R.O. to Wolverhampton, when asked about what sources he had used which he thought I ought to look at when I next travelled to London, mentioned that large quantities of cheese were travelling down the river Severn through Gloucester and that I might also find some iron. The result was the establishment of one of the first research teams in historical research modelled on what pertained in applied sciences in what was by then Wolverhampton Polytechnic. Enough has been written about the (River Severn) portbook programme elsewhere by myself and other members of the team.[1] All I need to add is that managing a project with inadequate resources (at times) and immense ambitions (at others) may have caused me to lose my hair, but it did not put me off economic history for good. Nevertheless in 1996 I declared a five year moratorium on the river, rejecting the blandishments of Chris Dyer and the Gloucestershire county archivist to turn parts of it into record society publications.

Instead I took up a neglected strand from my Ph.D. studies: investigating the economic interests of landowners through their probate inventories. At the same time a wider interest in their possessions emerged, possibly the awakening of an inherited interest as another grandfather had been a dealer in antiques. This opened up an encouraging new research seam on a segment of the population that had been curiously neglected by the cottage industry in probate inventory analysis inspired by Joan Thirsk and Francis Steer. Research for the regional history volume, however, obliged me to write a chapter on political development in the sixteenth and seventeenth century, of which the longest section was on the civil war. Writing my part of the book has been very much a labour of love. Not only did it enable me to bring together almost all the strands of my research including urban elites and non-elite Catholics of town and countryside as well as those noted above, it has also served in a more diffuse way as a homage to my ancestors. I put the draft to one side for the first half of 2000 because of the difficulty of keeping two balls in the air at the same time (head of history and chair of the faculty research committee) and the need to write my inaugural lecture. I resumed work on the draft by reading it through from beginning to end. The experience was like a shaft of light in terms of self-knowledge. Underpinning the whole of the argument was an historical mind for whom economic development was fundamental. The history of the Welsh borderland over five hundred years was merely the working out of economic trends. There was no escaping from it: at root I was an economic historian. Everything else was conditional and subordinate.

However, the surprise was not totally unexpected. Whilst working on my inaugural lecture on what constitutes historical knowledge, I had reached a similar realisation, but via a more conscious and less complicated road to Damascus. In the early hours of the morning throughout my professional career I have repeatedly run over in my mind such fundamental questions as how can historians justify teaching history at tertiary level to students who do not want to teach history themselves, and what do we really know about the past. The first question leads into a discussion of academic leadership and programme planning, elements of my professional career which are not appropriate in the context of this assignment. However, historical knowledge is a different matter. Soon after finishing my doctorate I had been invited to give an open lecture at the polytechnic in defence of quantification in history in the course of which, almost as an aside, I had drawn a distinction between that information which survives from the past which is opinion, and that which is fact, fact being the only type that was potentially susceptible to quantification. In 1977 we were almost all of the opinion that the objective of academic research and scholarship in history was to increase our knowledge of the past, and to try to impose some order on it with each generation building on what had gone before and, by howsoever a tortuous path, getting closer to an understanding of what happened in the past and why. There was scarcely a whisper about the linguistic turn.

Since then, of course, what historians do and the claims they make about the results of their research have been in the firing line, and in some respects rightly so. In my opinion the post-modernist critique has been salutary in the extreme. It should not and cannot be ignored, but in one respect it has gone too far. It has been alleged that we cannot know anything about the past because there is no such thing as historical fact, or that it is at such a superficial level as to be almost trite.[2] In my inaugural I revised and elaborated the opinion/fact dichotomy endeavouring to show that certain types of data from the past are factual and can be structured in such a way as to produce conclusions that are themselves statements of fact. These make it possible to contrast the past with the present. In the process differences can be identified and, if these cannot be fully explained, some explanations can be shown to be invalid. In my opinion it is no accident that all the examples I used came from economic history or from areas on the borderline between economic and social history, the most extended being data on family structure and child mortality.

Thus my debt to economic history is now very apparent to me. It has been the dominant theme of my professional life, even though I have only recently become aware of the scope of its influence. It has also reassured me that behind some types of historical study there lies a skeleton of factual knowledge which is sufficiently robust to support statements about the past that embody an element of truth.

Malcolm Wanklyn (b. 24. 4. 1942) is a graduate of the University of Manchester. History tutor at Wolverhampton University and its predecessors 1965-2000. Head of the Portbook/Dictionary of Traded Goods Research Programme from 1982. Professor of Regional History Wolverhampton, since 1999.

---

[1] e.g. Wanklyn, M.. 'The Severn navigation in the seventeenth century', *Midland History,* XIII (1988), pp. 34-58; Cox, N. and Wakelin, A. P., 'The innovation and imagination of an industrial pioneer: Abraham Darby I', *Industrial Archaeology Review*, XII (1990), pp. 127-44; Wanklyn, M., ' The impact of water transport on the economies of English river ports 1660-1760', *Economic History Review*, 2nd ser., XLIX (1998), pp. 20-34; Hussey, D., Milne, G. and Cox, N., *The Gloucester Port Book 1576-1765 CD-ROM* (Marlborough, 1998); Hussey, D., *Coastal and River Trade in Pre-industrial England; Bristol and its Region 1680-1730* (Exeter. 2000).
[2] Berkhofer, R., *Beyond the Great Story: History as Text and Discourse* (Cambridge, Mass., 1995); Jenkins, K. *Rethinking History* (London, 1991); Munslow, A., *The Routledge Guide to Historical Studies* (London, 2000)

The Day the World Fell Down and a Butterfly Flapped its Wings

Ron Weir

One attraction of economic history is that its practitioners are not afraid to think about the long run and, contrary to Keynes's famous dictum, death may not be only outcome; much may be learned en route about the enduring and fundamental processes of socio-economic change. Unlike economists however, historians are not generally required to project their thoughts into the future. On this occasion there is a compelling reason for doing so. Assuming that the Economic History Society, and the subject which it represents, survive for another 75 years what aspects of the discipline's past are likely to be of interest to our heirs and successors when they celebrate the Society's sesquicentennial in 2076? When the Society comes to commission the obligatory, commemorative essay what will the unfortunate recipient of the task find useful by way of sources? Will it be our publications, abundant or meagre as these may be? Possibly, but historical writing becomes dated with remarkable rapidity as interests re-focus and methods of discourse change. Will it be the content and methods of teaching? Again, possibly, but if we are to believe the predictions of the technologically foresighted, by then most students, regardless of subject, will be engaged in distance learning and able to download material prepared by a handful of the world's best teachers. Our current syllabi and methods may seem so obsolete and distant as to be of antiquarian interest only.

On the even more improbable assumption that the past is still considered a fit subject for investigation in 75 years time what might interest our future historian are the methods of recruitment of economic historians in the new, that is, post-Robbins universities. What follows is a memoire, a fragmentary recollection, of one newly appointed assistant-lecturer in Economic and Social History at the University of York. Like much historical evidence it is entirely subjective, unrepresentative of anything other than a particular time and set of circumstances.

Despite repeated petitions from York's leading citizens - the first in 1617 - that the city merited a university, it was not until 1960 that the government gave its approval in principle[1]. In April 1960 York - and East Anglia - were officially designated. York received its Charter in October 1963. With expansion in higher education East Anglia and York were both advertising in 1969 for new staff in economic history. Searching with some urgency would be a more apt description, for there was considered to be a shortage of suitably qualified applicants. Contemporary quantitative evidence makes this shortage something of a puzzle, at least as far as the further particulars for two assistant lecturers at York were concerned, for these stated that 'there will be approximately 40 students enrolled in the Department of Economics in 1969/70....(and) .. it is expected that the Department will have a staff of 22'.[2] Just in case this staff-student ratio appeared less than generous, it was pointed out that extra specialist help was forthcoming from the Institute of Social and Economic Research and, for tutorials, from suitably qualified Junior Research Fellows and graduates. One piece of the puzzle may be resolved by the fact that both

Economics and Economic & Social History were taught under the rubric of the B.A. in Social Sciences and thus read during the four terms of Part One by intending specialists in Politics and Sociology. York also had a high proportion of graduates: of the 600 students enrolled in Social Sciences 'approximately 100 will be graduate students'.[3] Staff-student ratios were generous, though less so than a narrow departmental perspective suggested. The rest of the explanation could be found in the prospectus which included, under the names of the existing staff in each department, the number of additional appointments still to be made. In a world where university funding was determined five years in advance and where public expenditure on higher education was under-written by continuous economic growth - notwithstanding the increasing realisation of better performing economies - perpetual expansion was an underlying assumption.

The staff shortage meant that it was not unusual to obtain an appointment without a doctorate and certainly without a long list of publications. Moreover, full employment gave the newly qualified graduate a wide range of choice in the job market. At this point frankness is in order. In 1969 I was a post-graduate in Edinburgh University and had not completed my doctorate nor decided to be an academic. On one of several trips to London, where multiple job applications made a nice vacation 'earner' by the simple expedient of arranging half a dozen interviews and recouping expenses from each potential employer, a common practice amongst 1960s Scottish graduates, I had made a provisional commitment to join the Bank of London and South America. This was after a mildly unusual interview which consisted of three opening questions: 'Did I play golf?', 'Did I play tennis?' and 'Did I intend to get married in the next six months?' to which the answers were 'not any more', 'yes', and 'possibly but unlikely' - in that order. These were followed by a fascinating discussion of the pleasures of home grown tobacco, a crop both the interviewer and I grew and of which I possessed more knowledge than the monetary economics that I had taken the trouble to revise for the interview. Like much else in British industry, selection processes were quite relaxed and certainly less rigorous than in the universities though these, as we shall see, were far from demanding.

It was not then lack of economic opportunity which guided me towards the groves of academe. Economic necessity did, however, play a contributory role coupled with a curiosity about economic history. I had been an undergraduate at Edinburgh from 1963 to 1967 in what began as the Department of Political Economy but was mysteriously re-branded as the Department of Economic Science without, it has to be said, making any obvious difference to the product. In the long tradition of Scottish universities, all students embarked on a three-year ordinary degree during which they were required to read a number of 'outside' subjects, amongst which was Economic History. Admission to the four year honours degree required an average mark of sixty per cent in the second year and opened up the opportunity of reading additional courses in Economic History. In the absence of external assessment, no league tables are available for the 1960s but there can be little doubt that the Economic History department at Edinburgh was then amongst the strongest, if not the strongest, in the UK. The attractions of Economics, whilst never wholly extinguished, were swiftly overshadowed by a series of superb courses and brilliant lecturers: Alan Milward and Berrick Saul with their veritable Cook's tour of modern industrialisation which embraced France, Germany, Austro-Hungary, Denmark, Japan, and North America; Michael Flinn on the industrial revolution; Chris Smout on Scotland since the Union - an Englishman who taught Scots how to re-interpret their own history - and Bill Fletcher, fresh from re-interpreting agriculture during the Great Depression. It was not just that these courses were well taught, it was that, by comparison with Economics, they dealt with topics which had a wider relevance than the nations whose histories were covered: the relationship between population and economic growth, the roles of capital formation and the state, the contribution of social values and institutions. Economic History seemed to possess a wider relevance, intellectual vitality, and application that Economics lacked. This strikes me now as an odd state

428

of affairs. Was it a question of personnel or of curriculum? The former seems unlikely for there were good lecturers amongst the Economics staff, though one tutor declined to take Keynesian economics seriously on the grounds that it was 'a passing fashion' - an accurate prediction as it turned out - but less than helpful for those who needed to know sufficient to get through the exam. The latter is the more likely suspect: is there a tutor anywhere who can make indifference curves exciting? It was not just the excessive doses of 'technique' but the lack of 'big questions'. By contrast, Economic History abounded with these. Moreover, lecturers were not afraid to admit that certain questions, in the current state of knowledge, were unanswered whilst at the same whetting the appetite by indicating that there was abundant scope for future research. There was, in other words, an optimism, an openness of enquiry, a missionary zeal, a confidence about Economic History that was missing in Economics.

Two years full-time research on the Scotch whisky industry followed, an extraordinarily enjoyable experience. This was funded by a postgraduate award from the Scottish Education Department which came with no strings attached and provided sufficient expenses to allow for prolonged visits to the archives of the malt distillers, the whisky industry's trade associations, the Distillers Company and its subsidiaries, the Public Record Office, and the Customs & Excise library. There was a generosity in Britain to youth and their higher education now sadly lost. There were no obligatory graduate 'training courses', though post-graduates were encouraged to take optional courses. One of these, which ran for two years, was econometrics. I enrolled for this following an assurance from the newly arrived Professor of Economics, J. N. Wolfe, that without econometrics my future would be 'as bleak as the handloom weaver'. At least the handloom weaver never had to master matrices or to plough through Johnston's, *Introductory Econometrics*. What there was in abundance was the constant encouragement, enthusiasm, and assistance of one's supervisors. In retrospect, it was an incredibly liberal system, a freedom to pursue and fashion a topic that subsequent interventionist funding agencies have eroded.

Having uncovered far more archival material than had been anticipated, little of the thesis had been written by the end of two years and so, in February 1969, advertisements by East Anglia and York for assistant lecturers were particularly attractive; they would provide a livelihood while 'writing-up'. The first interview was at Norwich with splendid overnight accommodation in the Royal Norfolk Hotel but favourable impressions dipped slightly the next morning when I asked an elderly woman if I was at the right bus stop for the University and was told: 'Oh, no, you bain got the wrong one. You want the bus for Cambridge - over there'. If that was the impact that U.E.A. had made on the local citizens, what sort of institution was it? The interview was rigorous and concluded with a full toss from Roy Campbell: 'Are you going to calculate in your thesis the enormous social costs of excessive alcohol consumption?'. Answer: 'No, but another graduate at Edinburgh is writing a history of the Scottish temperance movement'. Pause. Silence. Broken by long 'H'mmm' from Roy Campbell. The candidate emerged from the interview feeling that all had not gone as planned.

In fact East Anglia offered a two year appointment. The offer arrived at the same time as an invitation to attend for interview at York on 13 February 1969. With the charming tight-fistedness that pervades Yorkshire the letter stated: 'As it will be necessary for you to spend one night in York, the University will refund up to 35/- of your accommodation expenses and you may take a taxi out to Heslington. I enclose a leaflet listing the local hotels.' Not knowing York, I chose a city centre hotel. On arrival, a heavy snowfall covered the city and the temperature was well below freezing. Ushered to the bedroom by mine host, I was advised that, should the room feel cold, heating was available by means of a coin-operated one-bar electric fire; first impressions of York dipped even lower than East Anglia. The weather was no better and 'hotel' no warmer in the morning. Slipping and sliding down to the bus stop, I caught the number 19 for

Heslington for 9.30 interview. A local, the only other passenger, on hearing me ask for Heslington asks if I'm going to the university. In contrast to Norwich, she not only knows where the University is but seems to know everyone in it and maintains a non-stop conversation all the way to Heslington whilst I try to anticipate the questions at interview.

At Heslington Hall there is a friendly welcome from one of the many decorous secretaries who grace the upper floor. A warm smell of fresh coffee pervades the building. At 9.30 precisely the Registrar appears, ushers me into the Vice-Chancellor's office, and introduces Lord James, Alan Peacock, Eric Sigsworth, and Ed Cooney. It is difficult not to be impressed by the presence of the Vice-Chancellor at interviews for the most junior staff. Introductions are followed by a few relaxing questions about the current state of Economics at Edinburgh from Alan Peacock, then a long exchange with Ed Cooney about the Distillers Company (in which I learn more about industrial organisation than I ever explain), and next some questions from Eric Sigsworth about the courses I would be interested in developing. Finally, Alan Peacock says that he is surprised to see that I have taken graduate courses in econometrics - this is unusual for an economic historian - why did I do it? Forgetting about the fate of the handloom weaver, I mumble 'Masochism'. Peacock, Sigsworth, Cooney and the Registrar find this much to their amusement but Lord James has obviously not heard for he bellows, 'What did the man say!' 'Masochism', I repeat, louder this time, and Lord James joins in the merriment.

That was it, the selection process. No mini-lectures, no presentations of profound research findings to potential colleagues with the departmental teaching zealot indicating by body language that the candidate should *never* be let near students. No personnel officer to ensure that the candidate understands his contractual obligations to the university. Just a group of friendly, experienced scholars who seemed genuinely interested in your work and what you might offer the university.

Had I said the right thing? Apparently so, for a week later when I am in Elgin working on the records of Scottish Malt Distillers the company secretary comes in. He looks a bit embarrassed and apologises for opening a letter addressed to me. It offers a lectureship, commencing on 1 October 1969 at a salary of £1,355, rather than the advertised salary of £1,105. Masochism clearly pays. Other offers from East Anglia and the Bank of London and South America can now be declined. In October I joined the Department of Economics. Eric Sigsworth introduces the other economic historians; the first is Tony Harrison who greets me with 'Oh God, not another bloody Scot. Welcome to York'.

Ron Weir (b. 1. 5. 1944) is Provost of Derwent College at the University of York and Senior Lecturer in Economic History in the Department of Economics and Related Studies. His publications include *The History of Malt Distillers' Association of Scotland 1874-1974* (1974), (with Alan Peacock), *The Composer in the Market Place* (1975), and *The History of the Distillers' Company of Scotland 1877-1939* (1995). He is currently writing a second volume on the Distillers Company from 1939 to 1986. Teaching interests include computing and quantitative methods, economic and social history of Ireland, and business history.

---

[1] For a full account of the University's foundation see C. C. Storm-Clark, 'The Foundation of York University', in C. H. Feinstein (ed.), *York 1831-1981: 150 Years of Scientific Endeavour and Social Change* (York, 1981).
[2] Information to candidates, Assistant Lectureships, Department of Economics, University of York, 4 December 1968.
[3] *Idem.*

Looking Back on My Encounters with Economic History

Chris Wrigley

I went to university with the eager anticipation of someone venturing into an unknown land of fabulous intellectual riches. Neither of my parents had stayed at school much beyond the minimum school leaving age – my father had left at 13, I think my mother (five years younger) had left at 14. None of my home friends went to university. I arrived in Norwich in autumn 1965 to study history and english in the School of English Studies. The number of students at UEA in 1965 was well under 1000 I think. I had never heard of economic history when I arrived. I heard of it from female friends in the School of Social Science. I was interested to hear talk of essays on economic imperialism and also on the standard of living in the industrial revolution. I saw them carrying about library copies of the *Economic History Review*. When it came to choosing options from the other Schools I had no hesitation in choosing economic history.

Roy Campbell was very much the dominating figure in economic history, often appearing with Michael Miller, a fellow Scot, in tow. I had some contact with Michael Sanderson, then a quiet bachelor who ran a hall of residence. He was considerate. I had seminars with the newly appointed Richard Wilson, who was mostly patient and good humoured. I came to like and respect him After I had finished economic history there, Gerald Crompton arrived, a lively young figure. I was Treasurer of the University Labour Club in 1967 and Gerald and I talked at several of the Labour Club political meetings.

After I left Norwich I went to Birkbeck College, London University. I began research under Dr Mary Cumpston on 'Disraeli and the Empire', but after two months worked on 'Lloyd George and the Labour Movement' under Dr Eric Hobsbawm. I had been much influenced by his side of the Hartwell-Hobsbawm standard of living debate and by his essays in *Labouring Men*. I was interested in the history of British industrial relations. Strikes appeared in the textbooks like Halley's Comet. They received little attention, other aspects of industrial relations even less. I had read Henry Phelps Brown's book on 1906-1914. I was keen to study 1914-22, linked to that part of the career of David Lloyd George. Why Lloyd George? He was a key player in this area and in Radical politics. Moreover in 1967 his papers were opened to researchers when the 50 year closure rule on PRO documents became 30 – opening archives from 1917-36. As I began, James Hinton was finishing. Geoff Crossick was one year ahead. I saw much of Geoff early on – more confident and earnest than me. Also, through Eric's seminars at the Institute of Historical Research, I saw Pat Thane frequently. I met Eric Hobsbawm's postgrads Anna Davin, Logie Barrow, Virginia Berridge and John Shepherd. Of these I remember most Anna Davin, who regularly came to Eric's seminars and often sat cross-legged on the seat of her chair during them.

In these years, 1968-71, Eric Hobsbawm was very much economic history as far as I was concerned. I was nervous when I went to see him as my supervisor. Eric's questions soon made me realise that I needed to think more, to come up with more general ideas derived from my research. Thereafter, I spent much time thinking hard about what might he ask, as well as presenting more incisively my ideas. To my study of British history he brought me to think of other countries and their experiences beyond my narrow horizon. At the time I began research under him his *Industry and Empire* (1968) had just been published. I was delighted to help him revise *Industry and Empire* for a second edition (published in January 1999), and so pleased that he liked the chapter I wrote for the new edition. He is one of the economic and social historians whose work has excited me, making me eager to write economic history and read widely in the subject. I was also stimulated by A. J. P. Taylor Through the Beaverbrook Library I came to know him and I much enjoyed his research seminars. I shared something of his immense fascination with history and passion for it. History without frontiers.

In the summer of 1971, I was interviewed by Bob (R. Collison) Black, Cyril Ehrlich and Leslie Clarkson for a one year temporary lectureship at Queen's University, Belfast. I learnt a great deal about economic history and about teaching from my new colleagues (and from our students). Leslie Clarkson was lucid and enthusiastic. He gave me a copy of his *Pre-Industrial Economy in Britain* when it was published. I read that eagerly. Leslie's enthusiasm was contagious. I was fascinated by the period and read most of the major works on it during the year.

In the first meetings of the First Year seminar groups I was very taken by the attitudes of some of the Ulster students. They were quite clearly eyeing some of the others as if they were from another planet. They were uneasy with their presence for at least two or three sessions. Thereafter, they became more relaxed. Later, I asked two or three about this. I was told 'It's the first time I'd ever been in the company of Taigs . . . They were not as bad as I'd been led to expect'. Or a similar comment with 'Prods' not 'Taigs'. I said surely you had mixed with Catholics or Protestants before? – but was told they had not. This seemed to be a root cause of the tribal hostilities – a genuine lack of meetings, with each community building on a tradition of hatred unsullied by the realities of human contact.

I was made especially welcome in the Department by Max and Lorna Goldstrom. Max was (and is) a very effervescent person – full of enthusiasms and causes. He was hostile to the religious bigotry of Ulster. He loved to tell the story of when he went to hospital, he was confronted by people demanding to know if he was a Protestant or a Catholic. When he said he was an atheist, they demanded was he a Catholic or Protestant atheist! He eventually replied that he was a Jewish atheist!

I was also especially friendly with Ken Brown. He later became a key figure in his protestant group, conducting marriage and funeral services. Ken used to bring sandwiches to lunch. I was trying to lose weight and most days went to the staff club for an ox-tongue salad. Ken frequently joined me for this. So I saw as much of Ken as anyone else in the Department and came to appreciate his careful scholarship and his consistent hard work. At work I found him to be an encouraging and very pleasant colleague, one of the nicest people I've known in academic life. He and John Othick were putting on a special subject on the Great War and Britain 1910-21 and invited me to join them. Ken was always well prepared. I was mightily impressed when he wrote a lengthy seminar paper for one of the first sessions. John Othick who also gave a seminar, made a typically reflective and brilliant economic assessment. John was one of the most brilliant of the Queen's lecturers in economic history. He was fascinated by the big questions of international and comparative economic history. He was greatly impressed by the writings of Immanuel Wallerstein. He was also interesting on the then much neglected issue of the consumer sector and was knowledgeable about the chocolate industry.

I also liked Alan Davies the US economic historian. His main research at that time was in US trade fairs. Leslie Clarkson told me that Alan had all aspects of trade fairs referenced and cross-referenced in an elaborate filing system, but unfortunately was slow to write-up his thoughts on them. This sadly was true. Alan proudly showed me his filing cabinet and record cards. Little ever came of all this effort. Later he turned to writing about clocks and time, impressing David Landes. I was also friendly with the other member of the Department, Miriam Daly. She was out on a limb in the Department – a radical Republican and a woman among English and Welsh Protestants, mostly of a conservative hue. She was a little above medium height, usually well dressed and self-confident. She was very committed to the Republican cause and to Irish history. She was quite interested in me, as a socialist with some clear sympathies for Irish nationalism. Several times she invited me to join her and her husband for evenings in the Republican Clubs. I declined, with warm thanks. I was not keen to be linked to the nationalist nor the Protestant extremes, seeing myself more in tune with the Northern Ireland Labour Party (which was in fact disintegrating fast, or with the SDLP). I did baby-sit for her and James (her husband). They had adopted twins. I was very taken-aback in mid-1980 to learn that she had been tied up and shot in that house. The 'word on the street', apparently, was that the British Army had connived at the shootings that day, carried out by Protestant militaries. Whether this was true or false I doubt I shall ever know.

The other notable figure was Professor Ken Connell. He had fallen out with the Department and was in his own unit for Irish Economic and Social History. He was a friend of Eric Hobsbawm. Eric told me to make contact, which I did. He had periodic phases of very irrational action. In these he went to the Department late at night and left his colleagues odd memos accusing them of various laxities. After a while the university authorities responded to the department's requests to move him out. I was told that you could tell when Ken was in one of his odd phases. He would cycle around the campus in a great coat which very nearly reached his ankles. I was very taken aback the first time I saw him in such apparel, looking agitated and cycling to the university library. I was sorry to learn later that he had committed suicide. I greatly admired his Irish economic history works, very bright lights in a then under-researched area.

Cyril Ehrlich and his wife were great music buffs. When I was there they were immensely proud of their daughters, one or both were in the Northern Ireland Youth Orchestra. They were stalwarts of all high cultural events at Queen's and in Belfast. Someone told Cyril that I had come over with my record collection. However, they had not said that it was 90% rock 'n' roll, with only a few classical LPs. So Ken Brown, Leslie Clarkson and others were much amused when Cyril often spoke of me as a rare cultural Economic Historian and treated me as almost an arbiter of classical music taste.

In 1972 I was appointed to a lectureship at Loughborough. The senior economic historian there was Ian Keil, one of the kindest men I have known. Ian had been at Bristol University where he had completed a medieval history thesis on Glastonbury Abbey and its land holdings. He had been on one year contracts at Liverpool, ahead of John Harris and had moved into studying Leicestershire local history and Victorian social history. He was a little handicapped by the loss of sight in one eye but was indefatigable in serving the department by going on all manner of committees and, on occasion, he was acting head of the Economics Department. He was very much a respected figure throughout the university.

Older – in his high 50s – was John Angus, a man I greatly respected. John was in a precarious state of health. He had a very weak chest. Later I learned he had half his lungs removed after being badly injured in the Spanish Civil War. He did not help this by smoking Capstan's Full Strength cigarettes and drinking double gin and martinis at lunchtime and stiff whiskeys in evenings. But I felt then, and now, this kept him going. He had been close to his wife, Barbara, who had died before I arrived. John was tall, lean, held himself erect, had a small moustache and appeared the military man. An obvious right-wing Tory. In fact he had joined the CPGB when in Spain, had sold the *Daily Worker* before going to work after the Second World War, and had studied economic history as a mature student at Birkbeck College, where he had been much impressed by Eric Hobsbawm.

Back from Northern Ireland, I went to most Economic History conferences. The Dover Castle trip from the Kent conference in 1973 was memorable for the guided tour. The guide was an elderly working man, very much a 'Cor blimey gov, they got up to weird things in those days' style of guide. He also seemed to feel the more colourful accounts he gave that greater the tips that would come his way. In our party were some distinguished medieval economic historians. Professor Le Patourel was one, I think. Fixing them firmly with his eyes, he launched into the most extraordinary accounts of what happened in Dover Castle and in the Middle Ages. They, quiet gentlemen, nodded as he looked at them for approval of his powers in recounting medieval history. At one point I was having silent near hysterics out of sight behind a large pillar.

I think the first 'New Researcher' session was held at Kent in 1973. The sensation of the first batch was one given by Philip Cottrell, chaired by the then President, Richard Sayers. Phil gave his paper in a rather loud and emphatic manner – not in the genteel, understated way of some others. Sayers gave a rather pompous 'great scholar to newest of new beginners' response to Phil's paper before inviting questions. Phil replied to Sayers's august comments with words which came near to 'You have no idea of what you are talking about. My comments are based on the archives as footnoted . . . 'and so on. There was a real frission of horror among the old guard at such irreverent behaviour.

There was a famous occasion in the later 1960s or very early 1970s when Michael Postan chaired a session at which a very distinguished European economic historians gave an unintelligible lecture. When he asked for questions and there was silence, Postan in a very loud stage whisper, called to Eric Hobsbawm in the front row, 'Ask a question, 'obsbawm'. To his credit Eric Hobsbawm responded immediately with a good question. Postan was regarded by many as the Grand Old Man of Economic History in the early 1970s. He thrust himself centre stage, marching vigorously like an elderly 'Mr Toad' and holding forth in a guttural, central European accent.

A figure, venerated by Leslie Clarkson (and many others) was Jack Fisher. He was the lower end of medium height, with a game leg and he wore old sports jackets. He was a charismatic chair of conference sessions, his dynamism held everybody's attention and his witty but shrewd introductions upstaged the speaker he was introducing. He was the leading London University figure.

Miss E. M. Carus Wilson was a distinguished presence – tall, learned, pleasant but almost the epitome of an ageing blue-stocking. She was also a notable supporter of the Historical Association. Dr W. H. Chaloner was also a regular fixture of Economic History events. He was large, very full of himself, and tended to bulldoze forward in conversation. This was because he was very hard of hearing, or at least partly so. He had a rather old fashioned air about him – and so did his history.

Maurice Beresford was also a regular attender at the conferences. When it was held at Leeds, we were all amused to see Maurice striding in countryside clothes across the campus, almost being taken for a walk by a large dog. Walter Minchinton from Exeter was ubiquitous at conferences. He liked to lounge at the bar, awaiting people to come and buy him drinks. He was quite pleasant to talk to but I always felt he had a predatory air to him. The stories about him are legion. Walter went as a distinguished visitor to an Australian university. When he arrived he made a major fuss as there were twin beds. He was invited with his wife to the homes of leading academics. However, in the second term, after Christmas when he was invited round a second time, to the outrage of many, the 'Mrs Minchinton' this time was a different woman to the one before Christmas!

There were some older figures who went their own way. D. C. Coleman was often present but was scathing about the Society. Years later John Hatcher and Sidney Checkland were asked to sound him out about becoming president. They met in Hall at Cambridge and over much wine Coleman denounced the Society and its leading figures. Theo Barker and not Donald Coleman became the next President! The Society then seemed to be firmly controlled by a small group. Very few got on to Council who were not backed by the inner circle. In 1983 Phil Cottrell and I felt we would stand, regardless of not being so invited (and probably not wanted?). To our pleasant surprise we were both elected. On Council I was surprised at how marginalised Eric Hobsbawm and Sidney Pollard were, often treated brusquely by those at the front table of meetings. As a consequence, I suspect, both soon declined further nomination to the Council.

My main crusade early on, as a Council member was to open up Council so it was less of an oligarchy. It was very difficult to dislodge any of the old boys on Council, and humiliating for them when it happened. So I pressed for an enforced break in service: up to two three year terms (unless an officer) and then a two year break. It was a great struggle to get this agreed, and I only succeeded by ensuring the officers did not feel threatened. But when it came in it did help to transform Council, with several older figures bowing out gracefully and a range of younger academics from a wider pool of institutions coming on to it.

However, it should be said that Theo Barker and his friends did care about the Economic History Society and he in particular worked very hard for it. For many years he almost personified it. For the most part he was a benevolent oligarch. The Society did attract to itself most of the ablest figures in the profession. In my view the conferences always contained much of high quality. I returned from them with my batteries recharged and my enthusiasm bubbling over. I was stimulated by the better papers, by talking to leading practitioners and by buying the latest new economic history books from the publishers' stalls.

In the 1970s the more dynamic figures on Council, in terms of new ideas, had been people such as Leslie Clarkson, Barry Supple and Michael Rose. In the 1980s and 1990s those 'making waves' including several of the women – Maxine Berg, Pat Hudson, Maggie Walsh, Pam Sharpe, Pat Thane – and younger men such as Paul Johnson. Patrick O'Brien, as President, took particular pains to see that the society, and Council, was more inclusive – that people were not marginalised, that there were less grounds for feeling all stemmed from an inner clique. This process had begun somewhat when Richard Wilson was secretary, was accelerated by David Jenkins, and continued by Rick Trainor and Oliver Westall. Hence I felt Council was much more healthy when I came off in 2000 than it was in 1983, or – more generally – ten years earlier.

As for the Society generally, I feel it missed many opportunities during the 1970s and 1980s through the rather conservative and exclusive attitudes prevalent. Earlier, the Society for the Study of Labour History (with Eric Hobsbawm, John Saville, Royden Harrison, Asa Briggs, John F. C. Harrison, E. P. Thompson, Philip Bagwell and others) had gone its own way. More damaging, social history practitioners felt the Economic History Society did not cater for them – and so the Social History Society went its own way (with Michael Rose and others transferring their energies to it). Business History also broke off. Others stayed linked – with the Urban History Society from the beginning meeting immediately before the Economic

History conferences, and the Agricultural History Society meeting after them. Perhaps such fragmentation was inevitable, but perhaps not (in particular in the case of Social History). Yet at the same time the Society's Council has gained strength from the wider range of people being elected to it, including those from the new universities.

For me, the subject has repeatedly renewed itself. It advanced beyond the rather drab, consensual, often descriptive works of the pre-mid 1960s. After a range of livelier work, which included the best econometric studies, some of the work became reader unfriendly, with the statistical and other outcomes not lucidly explained. As a result general readers were lost and so also were students. This was extremely damaging to the viability of economic history courses. At its worst it was a handful of specialists writing for each other. At its best, of course, it reinvigorated the subject. In recent years several of the best practitioners of econometric history have acknowledged the need to take account of public policy, politics and other matters that others had long seen as important. Alongside this, publishers have been insisting on marketable books which are not monographs for a very few. So, again, economic history writing is rigorous and literate, with now a higher concern for also being numerate and sensitive to economic theories.

Such work in essence is what economic history means to me. It is satisfyingly more rigorous and more precise (or can be) than many other types of history. It encourages analytic comparative studies of the past. It deals often with large numbers of past people, not only generals, kings, queens and other such rogues (as William Morris put it), and with economic change or, at least, some economic history does. A lucid, quality work of economic history is a very satisfying book to read.

Chris Wrigley (b. 18. 8. 1947) was educated at the Universities of East Anglia and London. He is currently head of the School of History and Art History at Nottingham University. He was President of the Historical Association 1996-99, Vice-President of the Royal Historical Society 1997-2001, and Chair of the Society for the study of Labour History 1997-2001. His research interests are the history of British industrial relations; twentieth-century British history; Europe during and after the First World War.

Editor's note
Chris Wrigley's essay was distilled from a much longer hand-written notebook memoir which will be deposited in the Society's archive alongside other papers generated in the production of this volume.

APPENDICES

Appendix 1

ECONOMIC AND SOCIAL HISTORY

A note
Compiled by Douglas Farnie and Pat Hudson

The term economic history seems first to have entered the English Language (in print) in the 1860s. In 1861 the *Journal of the Society of Arts*, vol. 9 (p.295ff), reported upon a paper delivered to the Society in March that year entitled 'The Economic History of Paraffine' by Charles Tomlinson, Lecturer in Science, Kings College School, London. (Charles Tomlinson, 1808-97, DNB vol.19, 945, E. J. Carlyle; Boase, author of *Modern English Biography*, vol. 3, 983). A further reference occurred in *Macmillan's Magazine* on 7th March 1863 with 'Oysters: a gossip about their natural and economic history' by James G. Bertram. James Glass Bertram (1824-92) was a Scot, a sportsman and author of 30 articles (1861-91), especially on fishing, as well as other books which he wrote under three pseudonyms. (Boase, vol. 4, 383). His beautifully illustrated *The Harvest of the Sea.. A contribution to the natural and economic history of the British food fishes* appeared two years later (London 1865), with further editions in 1869, 1873 and 1885. These early mentions appear a decade before economic history entered the title of an examination paper (History Tripos Cambridge, 1876) and some two decades before the major debates between William Cunningham and Alfred Marshall in this country and before the *Methodenstreit* characterised by the positions of Carl Menger in Austria and Gustav von Schmoller in Germany, at which time analyses of the emergence of economic history as an academic discipline generally commence. A continuing close affinity between economic history and natural history can be traced in the works of Weber and in writings of the Annales 'School', amongst others. For most economic historians, economic history automatically includes social and cultural concerns at its very core. However, since the rise of formalism in economics in the second half of the twentieth century, the growth of econometric history and the expanding popularity of social history, in Britain at least, the term social history has often been joined to economic history firmly to signal the broad church nature of the subject and its concern with material life in the round.

Appendix 2

Biographies and autobiographies relating to economic historians

Compiled by Douglas Farnie

Note: The place of publication of all sources cited is London, unless otherwise indicated.

Biographies

Ashley, Anne, *William James Ashley: A Life* (1932).

Harris, José, *William Beveridge: A Biography* (1977, 2000).

Fink, C., *Marc Bloch. A Life History* (Cambridge and New York, 1989).

Alice Clark of C. & J. Clark Ltd., Street, Somerset, 1874-1934 (Oxford, 1934).

Cole, Margaret I., *The Life of G.D.H. Cole* (1971).

Carpenter, L.P., *G.D.H. Cole* (1973).

Wright, A.W., *G.D.H. Cole and Social Democracy* (1979).

Cunningham, Audrey, *William Cunningham, Teacher & Priest* (1950).

Henderson, W.O., *The Life of Friedrich Engels*, 2 vols. (1976).

Boughey, J., *Charles Hadfield. Canal Man and More* (1998).

Weaver, S.A., *The Hammonds. A Marriage in History* (1997).

Creighton, D.G., *Harold Adams Innis: Portrait of a Scholar* (Toronto, 1957).

Blumberg, Dorothy R., *Florence Kelley*, (New York 1966).

Chickering, R., *Karl Lamprecht: A German Academic Life* (1856-1915) (Atlantic Highlands; N.J., 1993).

Miller, D.L., *Lewis Mumford: A Life* (New York, 1989).

Hughes, T.P. and Hughes, Agatha C. (eds), *Lewis Mumford: Public Intellectual* (New York 1990).

Goldsmith, M., *Joseph Needham, Twentieth-Century Renaissance Man*, (Paris, 1995).

Owsley, Harriet C., *Frank Lawrence Owsley: Historian of the Old South: A Memoir* (Nashville, 1990).

Lyon, B.D., *Henri Pirenne: A Biography and Intellectual Study* (Ghent, 1974).

Polanyi-Levitt, Kari (ed), *The Life and Works of Karl Polanyi* (New York, 1990).

McRobbie, K. (ed), *Humanity, Society and Commitment: On Karl Polanyi* (Montreal, 1994)

Berg, Maxine, *A Woman in History. Eileen Power 1889-1940* (Cambridge, 1996).

Wes, M.A., *Michael Rostovtzeff, Historian in Exile. Russian Roots in an American Context* (Stuttgart, 1990)

Allen, R.M., *Opening Doors: The Life and Work of Joseph Schumpeter*, 2 vols. (New Brunswick, N.J., 1991)

Mitzman, A., *Sociology and Estrangement. Three Sociologists of Imperial Germany* [Tönnies, Sombart and Michels] (New York, 1973)

Terrill, R., *R.H. Tawney and his Times: Socialism as Fellowship* (1973)

Wright, A., *R.H. Tawney* (1987)

Kadish, A., *Apostle Arnold: The Life and Death of Arnold Toynbee. 1852-1883* (Durham, N.C., 1988).

Cannadine, D., *G.M. Trevelyan. A Life in History* (1992)

Billington, R.A., *Frederick Jackson Turner: Historian, Scholar, Teacher* (New York, 1973).

Weber, Marianne, *Max Weber: A Biography* (1975)

Ulmen, G.L., *The Science of Society: Toward an Understanding of the Life and Work of Karl August Wittfogel* (1978).

Cantor, N.J., *Inventing the Middle Ages: Lives, Works and Ideas of the Great Medievalists of the 20th Century* (Cambridge, 1992).

Autobiographies

Allen, G.C, *Appointment in Japan. Memories of Sixty Years* (1983).

Beveridge, W., *Power and Influence* (1953).

M.J. Bonn, *Wandering Scholar* (1949).

Boyson, R., *Speaking my Mind* (1994).

Clough, S.B., *The Life I've Lived. The Formation, Career and Retirement of an Historian* (Washington D.C., 1981).

J.R. Commons, *Myself* (New York, 1934).

Denman, D.R., *A Half and Half Affair. Chronicles of a Hybrid Don* (1993).

Fong, H.D., *Reminiscences of a Chinese Economist at 70* (Singapore, 1975).

Hancock, W.K., *Country and Calling* (1954).

Hewins, W.A.S ., *The Apologia of an Imperialist*, 2 vols. (1929)

Hurst, G.B., *Closed Chapters* (1942)

Nef, J.U., *Search for Meaning. The Autobiography of a Nonconformist* (Washington
    D.C.,1973).

Sigsworth, E.M., *A Respectable Life: Leeds in the 1930s* (Beverley, 1995).

Thistlethwaite, F., *A Lancashire Family Inheritance* (Cambridge 1996).

Utley, Freda, *Lost Illusion* (1948); *Odyssey of a Liberal. Memoirs* (Washington D.C., 1970).

Webb, Beatrice, *My Apprenticeship* (1926); *Our Partnership* (1948).

Eric Williams, *Inward Hunger: The Education of a Prime Minister* (1969, Chicago, 1971).

Woodruff, W., *Billy Boy* (Wakefield, 1993), reprinted as *The Road to Nab End. A
    Lancashire Childhood* (2000).

Zinsser, H., *As I Remember Him: The Biography of R.S.* (Boston, 1940).

Appendix 3

A Bio-Bibliography of Economic and Social History

Compiled by Douglas Farnie

Preface

The following list of some 700 names seeks to fill a gap in historiography. It is intended to throw light upon the lives of the men and women who have contributed to the literature of economic history, the literature which Negley Harte in 1977 aptly termed 'the gross fixed capital stock' of the profession. It also reaffirms a truism, to the effect that history is written by people, irrespective of the sources or the methods used. Most entries include not only biographical but also bibliographical and archival information: festschriften invariably include a full bibliography of the subject's works.

The sources used have been the standard biographical dictionaries published in the English language, supplemented by obituaries and memoirs. The willing cooperation of several colleagues must be gratefully acknowledged, including Peter Davies and Rory Miller of Liverpool, Michael Rose of Manchester, Pat Hudson of Cardiff, John Latham of Swansea, Stephen Fisher of Exeter, Lee Craig of Raleigh, NC, Yoshiteru Takei of Shizuoka and, above all, Harry Horton of Oldham.

The list covers some 140 years from the 1860s when the concept of 'economic history' seems first to have entered the English language (see Appendix 1). Throughout the aim has been to be as inclusive as possible and to embrace all aspects of a subject in constant evolution. As far as the founders of economic history are concerned the list is reasonably comprehensive. Inevitably it remains more selective in relation to living scholars. Apologies must be extended to all those whose names have been omitted. In many cases no biographical information has yet come to light upon such persons. Any additions or amendments will be gratefully received either by D.A. Farnie (31, Parksway, Swinton, Manchester M27 4JN), or by Pat Hudson (HudsonP@cardiff.ac.uk). The updated list will be published on the Society's website: http://www.ehs.org.uk

Key to Abbreviations

Note: The place of publication of all sources cited is London, unless otherwise indicated.
*Contains additional references

ANB	*American National Biography*, edited by J.A. Garraty and M.C. Carnes (New York, 1999, 24 vols.).
APU	*Architects and Craftsmen in History.* Festschrift für Abbot Payton Usher, edited by J.T. Lambie (Tübingen, 1956).
BDH	*The Blackwell Dictionary of Historians*, (1988), edited by J. Cannon, R.H.C. Davis, W. Doyle and J. P. Greene
BD	*Francis X, Gannon, Biographical Dictionary* . . (Boston, 3 vols., 1969, 1971, 1972).
BES	*Some Historians of Modern Europe*, edited by B. E. Schmitt (Chicago, 1942).
CA/CAP/CANR	*Contemporary Authors/Permanent Series/New Revision Series* (Detroit, 1967-99, 248 vols.).
CSN	*Newsletter of the Cliometric Society*, 15 vols, 1990-2000
DLB	*Dictionary of Literary Biography*, vol. 17, Twentieth Century American Historians (Detroit, 1983).
DNB	*Dictionary of National Biography* (1885-1996)
DPE	*Palgrave's Dictionary of Political Economy*, edited by Henry Higgs (1925, 3 vols.).
DWE	*A Biographical Dictionary of Women Economists*, edited by R.W. Dimand, Mary A. Dimand and Evelyn L. Forget (Cheltenham, 2000).
EHR	*Economic History Review.*
ESS	*Encyclopaedia of the Social Sciences*, edited by E.R.A. Seligman (1930-35, 15 vols.), listing 36 names.
GHT	*Guide to the History of Technology in Europe* (Science Museum, 1992, 1994, 1996, 2000).
HJK	*The British Marxist Historians. An Introductory Analysis*, edited by Harvey J. Kaye (Cambridge, 1984).
HSLC	*Transactions of the Historic Society of Lancashire and Cheshire.*
IDBH	*An International Dictionary of Business Historians*, edited by David J. Jeremy (Aldershot, 1994), listing 750 names.

IESS	*International Encyclopaedia of the Social Sciences*, edited by David L. Sills (New York, 1968, 18 vols.), including a Bibliographical Supplement as vol. 18 (1979).
JEEH	*Journal of European Economic History*
KB	*Encyclopaedia of Historians and Historical Writing*, edited by Kelly Boyd (Chicago,1999, 2 vols.).
LCAS	*Transactions of the Lancashire and Cheshire Antiquarian Society.*
MB	Maxine Berg, 'The First Women Economic Historians', *EHR*, NS. 45, 1992, 308-29.
MS	Tessa Morris-Suzuki, *A History of Japanese Economic Thought* (1989).
PBA	*Proceedings of the British Academy*, 1903-1998, 101 vols.
RCR	*The Study of History. A Bibliographical Guide* compiled by R.C. Richardson (Manchester, 2nd edn., 2000).
SLH	*Bulletin of the Society for the Study of Labour History*, 1960-2000.
TH	*Textile History,* 1968-2000.
TNS	*Transactions of the Newcomen Society, 1920-1994*, 65 vols.
WW	*Who's Who 2000.*
WWB	*Who's Who in British Economics. A Directory* . . . edited by Paul and Claire Sturges (Aldershot, 1990), listing 111 names
WWE	*Who's Who in Economics. A Bibliographical Dictionary of Major Economists 1700-1986*, edited by Mark Blaug (Brighton, 1983, 2nd edn.., 1986; 3rd edn., 1999), listing 34 names.
WWW	*Who Was Who, 1897-1990,* 8 vols.
WWWA	*Who Was Who in America* (Chicago, 1897-1985, 8 vols.).

A Bio-Bibliography of Economic and Social History

Abe, Etsuo, 1949. IDBH, 1.

Abe, Takeshi, 1952. IDBH, 1.

Abramovitz, Moses, CSN, 8:2, July 1993, 3-6, 23-26, A. Field.

Acsady, Ignac, 1845-1906. ESS, 1, 423, Julius Szekfü.

Adams, Henry Carter, 1851-1921. DPE, I, 799, J.H. Hollander.

Adelman, Irma, 1930. WWE 1999, 10.

Adelmann, Gerhard, 1925. IDBH, 3.

Aftalion, Albert, 1874 –1956. WWE 1999, 12.

Aldcroft, Derek H., 1936. IDBH, 4; CANR 55 (1997), 6.

Alford, Bernard William, 1937. CA, 101 (1981), 14.

Allen, George Cyril, 1900-1982.
 G.C. Allen, *Appointment in Japan. Memories of Sixty Years* (1983) PBA, 71 (1985), 473-92, Margaret Gowing.

Armstrong, John, 1944. IDBH, 9.

Armstrong, W.A., 1936. WWB, 10.

Anstey, Roger Thomas, 1927. CA, 13-16 (1975), 25.

Anstey, Vera Powell, 1889-1976. CAP, 1 (1975), 24; WWW, 7, 22.

Aries, Philippe, 1914-1984. KB, 50, P. Rushton.

Arkin, Marcus, 1926. CA 53-55 (1975), 23.

Arnold, Wilhelm, 1826-1883. ESS, 2, 220, C. Brinkman.

Asajima, Shoichi, 1931. IDBH, 10.

Ashley, Maurice Percy, 1907-1994. CA 41-44 R (1979), 30; WW 1995, 58.

Ashley, William James, 1860-1927.
 Anne Ashley, *William James Ashley: A Life* (1932), EHR, I:2, 1927, 319, W.R. Scott; ESS, 2, 268, A.P. Usher; BES, 20-44, Janet L. Macdonald; IESS, 1, 411, B. Semmel.

Ashmore, Owen. 1920-1995. LCAS, 90 (1994), 121-26, John Smith.

Ashton, Thomas Southcliffe, 1889-1968.
EHR, NS. 21:3, December 1968, iii, A.H. John; PBA, 56 (1970), 163-82, R.S. Sayers; L.S. Pressnell (ed), *Studies in the Industrial Revolution. Presented to T.S. Ashton* (1960), iii-iv, 328-33.

Ashworth, William, 1920-1991. CA 5-8 (1969).

Aylmer, Gerald Edward, 1926-2000. CANR 5 (1982), 32. *Independent*, 30 December 2000, Barrie Dobson.

Babelon, Ernest, 1854-1924. ESS, 2, 374, A.R. Burns.

Bailyn, Bernard, 1922. DLB, 19-26, A.R. Ekvich; KB, 67, D.R. Palm.

Baines, Dudley, 1939. WWB, 18.

Baines, Sir Edward, 1800-1890. DPE, I, 83, J. Bonar.

Bairoch, Paul, 1930-1999. JEEH, 29:I, Spring 2000, 203-08, A.M. Piuz.

Balderston, Theodore, 1949. WWB, 19.

Bamberg, James H., 1951. IDBH, 12.

Barker, Theodore Cardwell, 1923.
WW, 106; WWB, 22; *Journal of Transport History*, 3rd ser. 19:2, September 1998. 92-102, M. Daunton.

Barnes, Harry Elmer, 1889-1968.
L. Goodard (ed), *Harry Elmer Barnes. Learned Crusader. The New History in Action* (Colorado Springs, 1968). IESS, 2, 14-16, F.H. Hankins; ANB, 2, 189-92, J.D. Doenecke.

Beales, H. Lancelot ('Lance'), 1889-1988.
WWW, 8, 50: CA, 125 (1989), 20; *Social History Society Newsletter*, 14:I, Spring 1989, 3-5, Lord McGregor, W. Ashworth, J. Burrows, T.C. Barker, D.G. MacRae.

Beaver, Stanley Henry, 1907-1984. CA 114 (1985), 53.

Below, Georg Anton Hugo von, 1858-1927. ESS, 2, 508, C. Brinkmann.

Bennett, Henry Stanley, 1889-1972. PBA, 58 (1972), 551-67, B. Willey; WWW, 7, 61.

Beresford, Maurice Warwick, 1920. CA, 12-16 (1975), 68.

Berle, Adolf Augustus, Jr., 1895-1971. BD, I, 236; WWWA, 5, 56.

Berrill, Sir Kenneth, 1920. WW, 164.

Berry, Thomas S. CSN, 12:2 July 1997, 3-6, W. J. Hausman & Marilyn Gerriets

Beveridge, William Henry, Baron, 1879-1963.
W. Beveridge, *Power and Influence* (1953). José Harris, William Beveridge. A Biography (1977, 2000), PBA, 49 (1963), 417-29, Lord Salter.

Bindoff, S.T., 1908-1980.
E.W. Ives, R.J. Knecht & J.J. Scarisbrick (eds), *Wealth and Power in Tudor England. Essays Presented to S.T. Bindoff* (1978), xv-xxi, R.F. Leslie & A.G. Dickens. WWW, 7, 71.

Blainey, Geoffrey, 1930. KB, 93, G. Bolton.

Blaug, Mark, 1927. WW, 191; WWB, 40.

Blicksilver, Jack. 1926, IDBH, 23.

Bloch, Marc, 1886-1944.
Carol Fink, *Marc Bloch. A Life History* (Cambridge and New York, 1989). EHR, XIV:2, 1944, 161, M.M. Postan; APU, 75-84, L. Febvre; IESS, 2, 92-95, F. Braudel.

Blum, Jerome, 1913-1983. KB, 96, B. Thompson.

Bogue, Alan George Britton, 1921. CA 107 (1983), 54

Bonar, James, 1852-1941. PBA, 27 (1941), 359-76, E. Findly Shirras; WWW, 4, 118.

Bonn, Moritz Julius, 1873-1965. M.J. Bonn, *Wandering Scholar* (1949).

Booth, Alan, 1949. WWB, 44.

Booth, Charles, 1840-1916. DPE, I, 826, Clara E. Collett.

Borah, Woodrow, 1912. KB, 107, C. Perez.

Bordo, Michael David, 1942. WWE 1999, 136

Bowden, Sue, 1951. IDBH, 27.

Bowley, Sir Arthur Lionel, 1869-1957. DNB, R.G.D. Allen.

Boyson, Sir Rhodes, 1925.
R. Boyson, *Speaking My Mind* (1994). WW, 230; *Mont-Pelerin Society Newsletter*, May 1988, 23.

Boyns, Trevor, 1953. WWB, 46.

Bracegirdle, Brian, 1933. CA 101 (1981), 68.

Brady, Alexander, 1896-1985. CA 117 (1986) 59.

Braudel, Fernand, 1902-1985.
P. Burke, *The French Historical Revolution. The Annales School 1929-89* (1990), 32-56; IESS, 69, I. Wallerstein; J.H. Hexter, 'Fernand Braudel and the Monde Braudellien . . .', *Journal of Modern History*, 44, 1972, 480-539, reprinted in *On Historians. Reappraisals of some of the Makers of Modern History* (1979), 61-145.

Brenner, Robert, 1943. KB, 124, B. Thompson.

Brenner, Yehojachin Simon, 1926. CANR, 11 (1984), 89.

Bridenbaugh, Carl, 1903-1992. CANR 4 (1981), 90.

Briggs, Baron Asa, 1921.
D. Fraser (ed), *Cities, Class and Communication. Essays in Honour of Asa Briggs* (1990), 10-21, Godfrey Smith; CANR 7 (1982), 70; KB, 125, M. Hewitt; WW, 248.

Broadberry, Stephen N., 1956. WWB, 53.

Brown, Arthur Joseph, 1914. WWB, 54; WW 2001, 267.

Brown, Ernest Henry Phelps, 1906-1994. PBA, 90 (1995), 319-46, D. Worswick.

Brown, Kenneth D., 1943. IDBH, 29.

Bruland, Kristine, GHT.

Brunner, Otto, 1898-1982. KB, 147, S.K. Chenault.

Buchanan, Robert Angus, 1930. WW, 282.

Bücher, Karl, 1847-1930. IESS, 2, 163, Karl Polanyi.

Burke, Peter, 1937. KB, 152, P.C. Adamo

Burnett, John, 1925. CA 57-60 (1976), 97.

Burns, Arthur F., 1904 -1987. BD, ii, 258.

Buxton, Neil Keith, 1940. WW, 310.

Cain, Louis P., 1941. IDBH, 35.

Cain, Peter J., 1941. WWB, 65.

Cairncross, Sir Alexander Kirkland, 1926-1998. WW 1999, 312.

Callender, Guy Stephen S., 1865-1915. ESS, 3, 150, Helen R. Wright.

Cameron, Rondo Emmett, 1925. WWE, 139.

Cannan, Edwin, 1861-1935.
Economic Journal, June 1935, T.E. Gregory; *Economic Record*, June 1937, C.R. Fay.

Capie, Forrest H., 1940. IDBH, 37.

Cardoso, Fernando Henrique, 1931. KB, 176, C. Perez.

Cardwell, Donald Stephen Lowell, 1919-1998. CA, 101 (1981), 102.

Carpenter, Kenneth Edward, 1936. CA, 137 (1992), 56.

Carus-Wilson, Eleanora Mary, 1897-1977.
N.B. Harte & K.G. Ponting (eds), *Cloth and Clothing in Medieval Europe: Essays in Memory of Professor E.M. Carus-Wilson* (1980), 1-13, N.B. Harte, K.G. Ponting, Olive Coleman, PBA, 68 (1982), 503-20, Marjorie Chibnall.

Chaloner, William Henry, 1914-1987.
D.A. Farnie & W.O. Henderson (eds), *Industry and Innovation. Selected Essays* (1990), 5-12, B. Drewery & W.O. Henderson; LCAS, 85, 1988, 105pp.

Chambers, Jonathan David, 1898-1970.
E.L. Jones & G.E. Mingay (eds), *Land, Labour and Population in the Industrial Revolution. Essays Presented to J.D. Chambers* (1967), ix-xvii; WWW, 6, 193.

Chandler, Alfred Du Pont, Jr., 1918. KB, 195, Priscilla M. Roberts; KB, 195.

Chandler, George, 1915-1992. HSLC, 142, 1992, 226, N. Carrick.

Chapman, Stanley David, 1935. CANR, 9 (1983), 93; IDBH, 41.

Chapman, Sir Sydney John, 1871-1951.
D.A. Farnie, 'Three Historians of the Cotton Industry', TH, 9, 1978, 83-89; DNB, 210, E.R. Streat.

Chassagne, Serge, 1941. IDBH, 41.

Chaudhuri, Kirti Narayan, 1934. KB, 198, W.T. Johnson; WW, 371.

Checkland, Sydney George, 1916-1986.
A. Slaven & D.H. Aldcroft (eds), *Business, Banking and Urban History. Essays in Honour of S.G. Checkland* (1982), vii-xi, A.K. Cairncross; EHR, NS. 39:4, November 1986,v, P.L. Payne; PBA, 73 (1987), 411-24, A.K. Cairncross; WWW, 8, 134.

Chick, Martin J., 1958. WWB, 78; IDBH, 44.

Childe, Vere Gordon, 1892-1957. PBA 48, 1958, 305-12, S. Piggott.

Church, Roy A., 1935. CA, 124 (1988), 83.

Cipolla, Carlo Maria, 1922-2000. KB, 230, Kathleen Comerford.

Clapham, Sir John Harold, 1873-1946.
PBA, 32 (1946), 339-52, G. N. Clark; APU, 147-55, W.H.B. Court, reprinted in *Scarcity and Choice in History* (1970), 140-50; A.P. Usher, 'The Application of the Quantitative Method to Economic History', *Journal of Political Economy*, 40 (1932), 186; R. Floud, 'Words not Numbers: J.H. Clapham', *History Today*, 39 (1989), 42-47.

Clapp, Brian W., 1927. WWB, 82.

Clark, Alice, 1874-1934.
A. Clark, *The Working Life of Women in the Seventeenth Century* (1982, 1992), vii-xii, Amy L. Erickson. KB, 233, Amy L. Erickson; *MB.

Clark, Colin Grant, 1905-1989. IESS, 121, H.W. Arndt.

Clark, Sir George Norman (James), 1890-1979.
CA, 65-68 (1977), 121; PBA, 66 (1980), 407-26, G. Parker.

Clark, John Grahame Douglas, 1907-1995.
CA, 65-68 (1977), 122; PBA, 94 (1996), 337-90, J. Coles.

Clarke, Peter Frederick, 1942. CA 73-76 (1978), 122.

Clarkson, Leslie Albert, 1933. CA 73-76 (1978),123.

Clough, Shephard Bancroft, 1901-1990.
S.B. Clough, *The Life I've Lived. The Formation, Career and Retirement of an Historian* (Washington D.C., 1978). CANR 4 (1981), 141; CA 131 (1991), 113; JEEH, 21:2, Summer 1992, 389, The Jeeh.

Cochran, Thomas C., 1902. DLB, 109-16, S.P. Gietschier; IESS, 127, G. Porter.

Cognetti De Martiis, Salvatore, 1844-1901. ESS, 3, 620, P. Jannacone

Cohn, Gustav, 1840-1919. DPE, I, 840, E.L. Hargreaves; ESS, 3, 621, ERA. Seligman.

Cole, Charles Woolsey, 1906-1978. BD, 2, 282; CA 77-80 (1979), 94; CANR 22 (1988), 81.

Cole, George Douglas Howard, 1889- 1959.
Margaret I. Cole, *The Life of G.D.H. Cole* (1971). L.P. Carpenter, *G.D.H. Cole* (1973). A.W. Wright, *G.D.H. Cole and Social Democracy* (1979). A. Briggs & J. Saville (eds), *Essays in Labour History. In Memory of G.D.H. Cole* (1960), 3-40, J. Brown, H. Gaitskell, S.K. Bailey, G.D.N. Worswick.

Cole, W.A. ('Max'), 1926. CSN 13:2, July 1998, 3-6, 21-22, A.J.H. Latham.

Coleman, Donald Cuthbert, 1920-1995.
N. McKendrick & R.B. Outhwaite (eds), *Business Life and Public Policy. Essays in Honour of D.C. Coleman* (1986), vii-xii. CA, 13-16 (1975), 171; *Independent*, 9 September 1995, N.B. Harte.

Collett, Clara Elizabeth, 1860-1948. DWE, P. Groenewegen; WWW, 4, 236.

Collier, Frances, 1889-1962.
F. Collier, *The Family Economy of the Working Classes in the Cotton Industry, 1784-1853*, edited by R.S. Fitton (Manchester, 1965), v-viii, T.S. Ashton.

Collins, Henry, 1917-1969. SLH, 20, Spring 1970, 9, H.J. Fyrth.

Collins, Michael, 1946. WWB, 89.

Colmeiro, Manuel, 1818-1894. ESS, 3, 638, Fernando de los Rios.

Commons, John Rogers, 1862-1945.
J.R. Commons, *Myself* (New York, 1934). KB, 241, D.R. Palm.

Connell, Kenneth Hugh, 1917-1973. CAP 2 (1978), 131

Conze, Werner, 1910-1986. KB, 251, B. Stucktey

Cooper, John P., 1920-1978.
G.E. Aylmer & J.S Morrill (eds), *Land, Men and Beliefs. Studies in Early Modern History* (1983), ix-xviii.

Copeland, Melvin Thomas, 1884-1975. WWWA, 6, 90; 7, 125.

Coquéry-Vidrovitch, Catherine, 1935. KB, 253, Toyin Falola & J. E. Tishken.

Corley, T.A.B., 1923. WWB, 95; IDBH, 50.

Cossons, Sir Neil, 1939. WW, 48.

Court, William Henry Bassano, 1904-1971.
W.H.B. Court, *Scarcity and Choice in History* (1970), 1-61, 'Growing Up in an Age of Anxiety' (1904-1939); EHR, NS., 25:I, February 1972, v, S.B. Saul; PBA, 68 (1982), 521-36, P.J. Cain.

Crafts, Nicholas Francis Robert, 1949. WW, 461.

Creighton, Donald Grant, 1902-1979.
John S. Moir (ed), *Character and Circumstance. Essays in Honour of D.G. Creighton* (Toronto, 1970), 1-7; KB, 258, J. F. Vance.

Crouzet, François Marie-Joseph, 1922. CANR, 42 (1994), 106.

Cunningham, William, 1849-1919.
Audrey Cunningham, *William Cunningham, Teacher and Priest* (1950). PBA, 9 (1919-20), 465-74, W.R. Scott; *Economic Journal*, 29 (1919), 382-93, H.S. Foxwell & L.C.A. Knowles; DPE, I, 858, W.R. Scott; ESS, 4, 648, M.M. Knight.

Curtin, Philip D., 1922. KB, 281, J.C. Miller.

Daito, Eisuke, 1940. IDBH, 51.

Dangerfield, George B., 1904. BD, 111, 300.

Daniels, George William, 1878-1937.
Manchester School, ix, 1938, 67-77, S.J. Chapman, Henry Clay, Frances Collier.

Danielson, Nikolay Frantsevich, 1844-1918. ESS, 4, 707, P. Struve.

Darby, Henry Clifford, 1909-1992. PBA, 87 (1994), 289-308, M. Williams.

Daunton, Martin James, 1949. CANR, 52 (1996), 107; WW, 502.

David, Paul Allan, 1935. CA, 97-100 (1981), 131; WWE, 201. CSN, 14:2, July 1999, Susan B. Carter.

Davies, Peter Neville, 1927. IDBH, 52.

Davies, R.W., 1925. WWB, 114.

Davis, Lance Edwin, 1928. CA, 53-56 (1975), 139. CSN, 5:2, Feb. 1990, 3-10, J. Lyons

Davis, Ralph, 1915-1978. PBA, 65 (1979), 633-40.

Day, Clive, 1871-1951. WWWA, 5, 175.

Deane, Phyllis Mary, 1918. CSN, 11:2, July 1996, 3-32, N. Crafts. WW, 527; WWE, 204

Decker, Leslie Edward, 1930. CANR 30 (1990), 199.

De Canio, Stephen J., 1942. WWE, 207.

De Vries, Jan, 1943. KB, 306, C. Strikwerda.

Denman, Donald Robert, 1911-1999.
 D.R. Denman, *A Half and Half Affair. Chronicles of a Hybrid Don* (1993). WW 1999, 529.

Diaz-Alejandro, Carlos F., 1937-85. WWE, 216.

Dickinson, Henry Winram ('Dickie'), 1870-1952.
 TNS, 32, 1960, 111, C.E. Lee, L.E. Harris, S.B. Hamilton.

Dobb, Maurice, 1900-1976.
 M. Dobb, 'Random Biographical Notes', Cambridge Journal of Economics, 2:2, June 1978, 115-20. C.H. Feinstein (ed), *Socialism, Capitalism and Economic Growth. Essays Presented to Maurice Dobb* (Cambridge, 1967), 1-9, 351-60, E. J. Hobsbawm. PBA, 63 (1977), 333-44, R.L. Meek; IESS, 142, J. Eatwell; HJK, 26-29.

Dodd, Arthur Herbert, 1891-1975.
 Welsh History Review, 8, 1976-77, 94-96, J. Gwynn Williams.

Dopsch, Alfons, 1848-1953. KB, 319, R.F. Forrest.

Douglas, Paul Howard, 1892-1976.
 P.H. Douglas, *In The Fullness Of Time. The Memoirs Of Paul H. Douglas* (New York, 1972). BD, ii, 323; WWWA, 7, 161; IESS, 153-57, G.G. Cain.

Dowell, Stephen, 1833-1898. DPE, I, 867.

Dubofsky, Melvyn, 1934. BD, 111, 332.

Duby, Georges, 1919-1996. KB, 327, Helen J. Nicholson.

Dupree, Marguerite W., 1950. IDBH, 59.

Dutt, Romesh Chunder, 1848-1909. DNB, 536-38, F.H. Brown.

Dyer, Christopher Charles, 1944. WW, 598.

Dyos, Herbert J., 1921-1978. KB, 331, S. Gilley.

Easterlin, Richard Ainley, 1926. CA 109 (1983), 11; CSN, 8:1, Feb. 1993, 3-6, 15-18, K. Sokoloff

Edgerton, David Edward Herbert, 1959. IDBH, 61; GHT.

Efimenko, Alexandra Yakovlevna, 1848-1919. ESS, 5, 439, Y. Miakotin.

Ehrenberg, Richard, 1857-1921. ESS, 5, 444, R. Passow; IESS, 4, 539, F. Redlich.

Ehrlich, Cyril, 1925. CA, 103 (1982), 134.

Einaudi, Luigi, 1874-1961. IESS, 4, 542, U. Pappi.

Elliott, Anthony, 1921-1976. Joyce M. Bellamy & J. Saville (eds), *Dictionary of Labour Biography*, v (1979), ix; *Times*, 13 September 1976.

Elton, Sir Arthur Hallam Rice, 1906-1973. TNS, 45, 1973, 234; WWW, 7, 246.

Elvin, Mark, 1938. CA, 73-76 (1978), 187.

Engels, Friedrich, 1820-1895. W.O. Henderson, *The Life of Friedrich Engels* (1976, 2 vols.); *Economic Journal*, 5, 1895, 490-92, J. Bonar.

Engerman, Stanley Lewis. CA, 53-56 (1975), 180; WWE, 252. CSN, 15:1, Spring 2000, 3-9,T. O'Brien

Ennen, Edith, 1907-1999. KB, 359, Rita Gudermann.

Eucken, Walter, 1891-1950. APU, 28-38, F.C. Lane.

Evans, Eric, 1932. WWB, 146.

Everitt, Alan Milner, 1926. CANR, 11 (1984), 193.

Eversley, David Edward Charles (William Small), 1921. CANR 1 (1981), 182.

Fairbank, John K., 1907. BD, I, 317-21.

Falkus, Malcolm Edward, 1940. IDBH, 66.

Farnie, Douglas Antony, 1926.
    Social Scientists Specialising in African Studies (UNESCO, Paris, 1963, 1971), 161; CANR 12 (1984), 175; IDBH, 67; *Who's Who in the World* (New Providence, N.J., 14th edn., 1997).

Faucher, Léon, 1803-1854. DPE, ii, 40, A. de Foville.

Faulkner, Harold Underwood, 1890-1968. CA, 1-4 (1967), 307; WWWA, 5, 226.

Fay, Charles Ryle, 1884-1961. WWW, 6, 368.

Fearon, Peter Shawn, 1942. CA, 29-32 (1978), 200.

Febvre, Lucien, 1878-1956.
      S.W. Halperin (ed), *Some Twentieth Century Historians* (Chicago, 1961), 277-98, P.H. Throop; IESS, 5, 349, F. Braudel.

Feinstein, Charles Hilliard, 1932. WW, 665.

Feldenkirchen, Wilfried, 1947. IDBH, 68.

Ferguson, Niall Campbell, 1964.
      WW, 570 (Douglas Ferguson); *Sunday Telegraph Magazine*, 11 Feb. 2001, 17-21, N. Farndale

Finberg, Herbert Patrick Reginald, 1900-1974.
      Joan Thirsk (ed), *Land, Church and People. Essays Presented to Professor H.P.R. Finberg* (British Agricultural History Society, 1970), vii-xii, M.W. Beresford. WWW, 7, 264.

Finley, Moses, 1912-1986. PBA, 94 (1996), 459-74, C.R. Whittaker.

Fisher, Frederick Jack, 1908-1988.
      P.J. Corfield & N.B. Harte (eds), *London and the English Economy, 1500-1700* (1990), 23-39, P. Earle, Penelope J. Corfield, N.B. Harte, Lord McGregor of Durris, W. Elkan, C. Ehrlich, B. Supple, H.E.S. Fisher, P. Holwell, M.J. Wise. EHR, NS 41:i, August 1988, 343-5.

Fishlow, Albert. CSN, 13:3, Oct. 1998, 3-6, 24-5, E.White.

Fitton, Robert Sucksmith, 1925-1987.
      R.S. Fitton, *The Arkwrights. Spinners of Fortune* (Manchester, 1989), xi-xiv, P. Mathias.

Flinn Michael W., 1917-1983.
      T.C. Smout (ed), *The Search for Wealth and Stability. Essays in Economic and Social History Presented to M.W. Flinn* (1979), xiii-xx.

Floud, Roderick Castle, 1942. CANR, 1 (1981), 197; WW, 689.

Flux, Sir Alfred William, 1867-1942. WWW, 4, 295.

Fogel, Robert William, 1926. KB, 289, D.R. Palm; WW, 692. CSN, 5:3, July 1990, 3-8, 20-29, J. Lyons

Fohlen, Claude, 1922. IDBH, 71.

Foner, Philip S., 1910-1994. KB, 391, C. Phelps.

Fong, Hsien Ding (Hsien-Ting Fang).
    H.D. Fong. *Reminiscences of A Chinese Economist at Seventy* (Singapore, 1975).

Forbes, Robert James, 1900-1973. TNS, 45, 1973, 233.

Ford, Alec George, 1926. WWE, 280.

Foreman-Peck, James, 1948. WWB, 155.

Foster, John, 1940. WWB, 156.

Foxwell, Herbert Somerton, 1849-1936. PBA, 23 (1937), 470-86, J.M. Keynes.

French, M.J., 1956. WWB, 161.

Freudenberger, Herman, 1922. CA, 13-16 (1975), 288.

Freyre, Gilberto, 1900-1989. KB, 419, Virginia R. Bainbridge.

Frow, Edmund, 1906-1997.
    Guardian, 21 May 1997; *Manchester Region History Review*, XII, 1998, 2,
    Eric Taplin.

Furnivall, John Sydenham ('Furnivall of Burma'), 1878-1960.
    Times, 12 July 1960; 14 July, Dudley Stamp. IESS, 220, Frank N. Trager; KB, 427,
    E.A. Le Vos.

Furtado, Celso, 1920. WWE, 295.

Fussell, George Edwin, 1889. CANR, 3 (1981), 219.

Gallman, Robert E. CSN, 7:1, Feb. 1992, 3-9, B. Hutchinson

Garside, W.R., 1944. WWB, 164; IDBH, 78.

Gay, Edwin Francis, 1867-1946.
    Facts and Figures in Economic History, Articles by Former Students of E.F. Gay
    (Cambridge, Mass., 1932), v-vi, A.H. Cole, A.L. Dunham, N.S.B. Gras. WWWA, 2,
    206.

Geertz, Clifford, 1926. KB, 441, Inga Clendinnen.

Genovese, Eugene Dominick, 1926.
    DLB, 178-86, M. Bordelon; BD, ii, 371; KB, 443, J.D. Smith.

George, Anthony David, GHT.

George, M. Dorothy, 1878-1971. *Times*, 15 September 1971.

Gerschenkron, Alexander Pavlovich, 1904-1978.
    IESS, 228-32, A. Erlich; CANR, 1 (1978), 225.

Gibbins, Henry de Beltgens, 1965-1907.
DNB, 101, M. Epstein; DPE, ii, 877; ESS, 6, 652, J.F. Rees.

Gilbert, Keith Reginald, 1915-1973. TNS, 45, 1973, 233.

Gilboy, Elizabeth Waterman, DWE, J.J. Thomas.

Godley, Andrew C., 1963. IDBH, 82.

Gonner, Sir Edward Carter Kersey 1862-1922. WWW, 2, 417.

Gourvish, Terence R., 1943. IDBH, 85.

Gowing, Margaret May, 1921. CA, 81-81 (1979), 206.

Gras, Norman Scott Brien, 1884-1956.
Business History Review, 30:4, December 1956, 357-60, G.S. Gibb; IESS, 6, 252, F. Redlich.

Greasley, David, 1951. WWB, 180.

Gregory, Sir Theodore Emanuel Gugenheim, 1890-1970. WWW, 6, 458.

Gutman, Herbert G., 1928-1985. KB, 501, B.D. Palmer.

Habakkuk, Sir John Hrothgar, 1915.
CA, 151 (1996), 214; WW, 848; KB, 505, Pamela Sharpe. CSN, 12:3, Oct. 1997, 3-6, 28-31, M.Thomas

Hacker, Louis Morton, 1899-1987. CA, 17-20 (1976), 305; WWWA, 8, 317.

Hadfield, Ellis Charles Raymond, 1909.
J. Boughey, *Charles Hadfield: Canal Man and More* (1998). CA, 51 (1996), 205; RCR, 122.

Hallberg, Charles William, 1899. CAP, 1 (1975), 261.

Hamilton, Earl Jefferson, 1899-1989. CAP, 1 (1975), 262.

Hamilton, Henry, 1896-1964. WWW, 5, 482.

Hamilton, Stanley Baines, 1890-1977. TNS, 48, 1977, 143.

Hammond, John Le Breton, 1872-1949.
SA Weaver, *The Hammonds. A Marriage in History*, (1997). HA Schmidt (ed), *Historians of Modern Europe* (Baton Rouge La., 1971), 95-119, HR Winkler. PBA, 46 (1960), 267-94, R.H. Tawney; A.J. Toynbee, *Acquaintances* (Oxford, 1967), 95-107. P.F. Clarke, *Liberals and Social Democrats* (1978), 74-82.

Hancock, Sir William Keith, 1898-1988.
W.K. Hancock, *Country and Calling* (1954). PBA, 82 (1992), 399-414, A. Low; IESS, 262, J.D.B. Miller; CANR, 5 (1982); WWW, 8, 324.

Handlin, Oscar, 1915.
  DB, 191-7, Arnold Shankman; CANR 23 (1988), 166; KB, 514, Kathleen E Chamberlain; BD, ii, 401; WW, 874.

Hannah, Leslie, 1947. WW, 876; IDBH, 89.

Hanssen, Georg, 1809-1894.
  DPE, ii, 887; *Economic Journal*, 5, 1895, 141, G. Cohn; ESS, 7, 267.

Hara, Terushi, 1943. IDBH, 91.

Harley, Charles Knickerbocker, 1943. WWE 1999, 498.

Harris, John Raymond, 1923-1997.
  Times, 26 March 1997; *Independent*, 16 May 1997, W.R. Garside.

Harris, José, CA, 147 (1995), 260.

Harrison, Brian Howard, 1937. WW, 895.

Harte, Negley B., 1943. WWB, 296.

Hartwell, Ronald Max, 1921. CA, 25-28 (1977), 307.

Hasbach, Wilhelm, 1849-1920. ESS, 7, 278, H. Levy.

Hatcher, John, 1942. CA, 33-36 (1978), 383.

Hau, Michel, 1943. IDBH, 95.

Hausman, William J., 1949. IDBH, 95.

Havinden, Michael A., 1928. WWB, 210.

Hawke, Gary R., 1942. IDBH, 96.

Haxthausen, August von, 1792-1866.
  DPE, ii, 293, J.K. Ingram; ESS, 7, 283, K. Kocharovsky.

Hayek, Friedrich August von. 1899-1992.
  PBA, 84 (1993), 347-68, D. O'Brien; IESS, 274-82, F. Machlup.

Heaton, Herbert, 1890-1973. TH, 5, October 1974, 7-13, N.B. Harte.

Heckscher, Eli Filip, 1879-1952.
  Scandinavian Economic History Review, 1:i, 1953, 137-40, E.F. Soderlund; APU, 119-146, A. Montgomery; IESS, 6, 339-41, G. Ohlin.

Henderson, William Otto, 1904-1993.
  CANR, 4 (1981), 296; Downing College Association Newsletter, 1994, 33-34, P. Mathias; *Vierteljahrschrift für Sozial – und Wirtschaftsgeschichte*, 1994:2, 153-55, K.E. Born. B.M. Ratcliffe (ed), *Great Britain and her World, 1750-1914, Essays in Honour of W.O. Henderson* (Manchester, 1975), vii-xiv.

Henry, Louis, 1911-1991. KB, 526, Pamela Sharpe.

Hewins, William Albert Samuel, 1865-1931.
W.A.S. Hewins, *The Apologia of an Imperialist: Forty Years of Empire Policy, 1889-1929* (1929, 2 vols.). WWW, 3, 632; DNB, 17, 123.

Hewitt, Margaret, 1928-1991.
Daily Telegraph, 11 June 1991; *Times*, 12 June; *Guardian*, 18 June, Tom Sutcliffe; *Independent*, 18 June, J.R. Porter.

Heyd, Wilhelm von, 1823-1906. ESS, 7, 345, W. Stieda.

Heywood, Colin, 1947. WWB, 218.

Hicks, Sir John Richard, 1904-1989.
IESS, 300, G.C. Reid & J.N. Wolfe; *History of Political Economy*, 25:2, 1993, 351-74, Warren J. Samuels; *Times,* 22 May 1989.

Higgs, Henry, 1864-1940. WWE, 399.

Hill, John Edward Christopher, 1912. WW, 955; HJK, 101-07; KB, 531, R.J. Soderlund.

Hilton, George Woodman, 1925. CANR, 4 (1981), 301.

Hilton, Rodney Howard, 1916. WW, 959; HJK, 71; KB, 534, Virginia R. Bainbridge.

Hobsbawm, Eric John Ernest. 1917.
Henry Abelove et al. (eds), *Visions of History* (Manchester, 1983), 29-46. HJK, 132-45; CANR, 56 (1997), 209-13, F. Newton; WW, 965.

Hohenberg, Paul Marcel, 1933. CA, 25-28 (1977), 330.

Hollis of Heigham, Patricia Lesley, Baroness, 1941. WW, 979.

Holmes, Colin, 1938. CANR, 11 (1984), 266.

Honeyman, Katrina, 1950. IDBH, 106.

Hopkins, Antony Gerald, 1938. WW, 990.

Horn, Pamela Lucy Ray, 1936. CANR 30 (1990), 199.

Horrocks, Sally M., 1966. IDBH, 107.

Hoskins, William George, 1908-1992.
C.W. Chalklin& M.A. Havinden (eds), *Rural Change and Urban Growth: Essays in Regional History in Honour of W.G. Hoskins* (1974), xix-xxvi, 342-50. PBA, 87 (1994), 339-56, Joan Thirsk; * RCR, 123.

Hovell, Mark, 1888-1916.
M. Hovell, *The Chartist Movement*, (Manchester, 1918), xxi-xxxvii, T.F. Tout.

Huberman, Michael M., 1955. IDBH, 108.

Hudson, Patricia, 1948. WWB, 234.

Hufton, Olwen H., 1938. CA, 21-24 (1977), 429.

Hughes, Edward, 1899-1965. WWW, 6, 562.

Hughes, Jonathan Roberts Tyson, 1928-1992.
    CA 81-84 (1979), 254; CSN, 6:3, Oct. 1991, 3-6, 18-26, C. Calomiris

Huizinga, Johan, 1872-1945. IESS, 6, 533, Rosalie L. Cole.

Humphries, Jane, 1948. WWB, 239.

Hunt, Edward H., 1939. WWB, 240.

Hunter, Janet E., 1948. WWB, 240.

Hurst (Hertz), Sir Gerald Berkeley, 1871-1957.
    G.B. Hurst, *Closed Chapters* (1942). WW, 5, 563.

Hutchins, Barbara L., DWE, J.P. Henderson.

Hutt, William Harold, 1900-1988.
    WWW, 8, 370; *Guardian*, 23 June 1988, D.A. Farnie; *Daily Telegraph & Times*,
    25 June.

Hyde, Francis Edwin, 1908-1978.
    Sheila Marriner (ed), *Business and Businessmen. Studies in Business, Economic and
    Accounting History* (Liverpool, 1978), 3-12; WWW, 7, 398.

Inama-Sternegg, Karl Theodor von, 1843-1908. ESS, 7, 619, A. Dopsch.

Inkster, Ian, 1949. CA, 113 (1985), 237.

Innis, Harold Adams, 1894-1952.
    D.G. Creighton, *Harold Adams Innis: Portrait of a Scholar* (Toronto, 1957). DLB, *88
    Canadian Writers 1920-1959*, 2nd ser (1989), 124-32, W. Christian.

Ishii, Kanji, 1938. IDBH, 113.

Jackman, William T., 1871-1951. WWW, 5, 574.

Jackson, Gordon, 1934. WWB, 248.

James, Harold, 1956. CA, 127 (1989), 222.

Jarvis, Rupert Charles, 1899. CA, 103 (1982), 103.

Jenkins, David, T., 1944. WWB, 252.

Jequier, François, 1941. IDBH, 117.

Jeremy, David John, 1939. CA, 129 (1990), 231; IDBH, 118.

Jewkes, John, 1903-1988. WWW, 8, 396.

John, Angela V., 1948. CA, 125 (1989), 230.

Johnson, The Reverend Arthur Henry, 1845-1927. WWW, 2, 558.

Johnson, Paul, 1956. WWB, 257.

Jones, Eric. CSN, 7:3, Oct. 1992, 3-6, 23-24, Nancy Folbre & M. Huberman

Jones, Eric Lionel, 1936. CA, 104 (1982), 232.

Jones, Gareth Stedman, 1942. KB, 624, M. Hewitt.

Jones, Gwilym Peredur, 1892-1975. WWW, 3.

Jones, Stuart, 1933. IDBH, 124.

Josephson, Matthew, 1899-1978. BD, i, 385; WWWA, 7, 308.

Joslin, David Maelgwyn, 1925-1970.
    J.M. Winter (ed), *War and Economic Development. Essays in Memory of David Joslin* (1975), vii-viii, H.J. Habakkuk.

Joyce, Patrick, 1945. CA, 128 (1990), 214.

Judges, A.V., 1898-1973. Times, 15 February 1973, 19 February.

Kahan, Arcadius, 1920-1982. CA, 135 (1992), 247.

Kajimoto, Motonobu, 1948. IDBH, 127.

Katanka, Michael, 1922-1983. SLH, 47, Autumn 1983, 4.

Katoh, Kozaburo, 1930. IDBH, 128.

Katzenellenbogen, Simon E., 1939. WWB, 266.

Kautsky, Karl, 1854-1938. IESS, 8, 356, J.H. Kautsky.

Kelley (Wischnewetsky), Florence, 1859-1932.
    Dorothy R. Blumberg, *Florence Kelley* (New York, 1966).

Kiesewetter, Hubert, 1939. IDBH, 135.

Killick, John Roper, 1939. WWB, 271; IDBH, 136.

Kindleberger, Charles Poor, II, 1910. CANR, 36 (1992), 219.

King, Frank H.H., 1926. IDBH, 137.

Kipping, Matthias, 1961. IDBH, 137.

Kirby, Maurice W., 1946. WWB, 274.

Kita, Masami, 1945. IDBH, 138.

Klingender, Francis Donald, 1907-1955.
F.D. Klingender, *Art and the Industrial Revolution* (second revised edn, 1968), vii-xi, A. Elton.

Klugmann, James, 1912-1977. SLH, 36, Spring 1978, 7.

Knapp, Georg Friedrich, 1842-1926. IESS, 8, 241, A. Schweitzer.

Knoop, Douglas, 1883-1948. WWW, 4, 648.

Knowles, Lilian Charlotte Anne (Tomn), 1870-1926.
L.C.A. Knowles & C.M. Knowles, *The Economic Development of the British Overseas Empire*, i (1930), vii-xxii, C.M. Knowles. ESS, 8, 584, Eileen Power; *Economica*, 6 (1926), 119-22, W.H. Beveridge & G. Wallas. *MB, 328-29.

Kobayashi, Kesaji, 1951. IDBH, 142.

Kocka, Jűrgen, 1941. KB, 650, C. Lorenz; IDBH, 144.

Koenigsberger, Helmut Georg, 1918. CA, 33-36 (1987), 477; WW, 1161.

Kondratieff, Nikolai Dmitrievich, 1892-1937.
N.Jasny, *Soviet Economists of the Twenties* (Cambridge 1972), 158-78; WWE, 470.

Kuczynski, Jűrgen, 1904-1977. KB, 667, L. Blackwood.

Kula, Witold, 1916-1988. KB, 670.

Kuwahara, Tetsuya, 1947. IDBH, 152.

Kuznets, Simon, 1901-1985. IESS, 393-97, R.A.Easterlin.

Labrousse, Ernest, 1895-1988.
KB, 676, Martine B. Morris; H.A. Schmitt (ed), *Historians of Modern Europe* (1971), 235-54, P. Renouvin.

Lamprecht, Karl, 1856-1915.
Roger Chickering, *Karl Lamprecht: A German Academic Life* (Atlantic Highlands, N.J., 1993). BES, 217-39, Annie M. Popper; IESS, 8, 549, G. Diesener.

Landes, David Saul, 1924. CANR, 22 (1988), 257, M. Mueller; KB, 682, C. Strikwerda

Lane, Frederic Chapin, 1900-1984. JEEH, 17:i, Spring 1988, 159-84, H. Kellenbenz.

Larson, Henrietta Melia, 1894-1983. CAP, 2 (1978), 304; CA, 110 (1984), 305.

Latham, A.J.H. (John), 1940.
WWB, 284; IDBH, 156; *Who's Who in the World* (Wilmette, Ill., 8th edn, 1987-88), 596.

Lazonick, William Harold, 1945.
Warren J. Samuels (ed), *American Economists of the Late Twentieth Century* (Cheltenham, 1990), 159-73, F. Carstensen; IDBH, 156; WWE, 502.

Leadam, Isaac Saunders, 1848?-1913. WWW, 1, 418.

Lebergott, Stanley, 1918. CA 103, (1982), 288; CSN, 7:2, July 1992, 3-6, 17-21, F. Carstensen

Lee, Clive Howard, 1942. WWB, 290.

Le Play, Pierre G.F., 1806-1882. ESS, 9, 411, G. Salomon.

Le Roy Ladurie, Emmanuel, 1929. KB, 711, S. Carroll.

Levasseur, Pierre Emile ('the father of modern economic history in France'), 1828-1911. ESS, 9, 421, H. Hauser; IESS, 9, 261, C. Fohlen.

Levett, Ada Elizabeth, 1881-1932.
A.E. Levett, *Studies In Manorial History* (Oxford, 1938), i-xix, E.M. Jamison.

Levi, Leone,1821- 1888. DPE, ii, 598, G.B. Smith.

Lewis, Colin M., 1944. WWB, 294.

Lindenlaub, Dieter, 1937. IDBH, 159.

Lindert, Peter Harrison, 1940. WWE, 530; WWE (1999), 192.

Lipson, Ephraim, 1888-1960. DNB, 645-7, H. Heaton.

Lockwood, William W., 1906- 1978. BD, 111, 490; WWWA, 7, 355.

Lopez, Robert Sabatino, 1910-1986. CA, 119 (1987), 216; KB, 732, Felice Lifschitz.

Lower, A.R.M., 1889-1988. KB, 739, J.F. Vance.

Luchitsky, Ivan Vasilevich, 1845-1918. ESS, 9, 625, H. Sée.

Lynd, Helen Merrell, 1896- 1982. BD i, 4278; ANB, 14, 171-2.

Lyons, John S., 1944. IDBH, 163.

Lythe, S.G. Edgar. J. Butt and J.T Ward (eds), *Scottish Themes* (Edinburgh, 1976), xi-xvi.

McArthur, Ellen Annette, 1862-1927. MB, 327, citing *Girton Review* 75 (1927), 2-4.

McCloskey, Donald/Deirdre Nansen, 1942. WWE, 581.

MacPherson, W.J., 1924. WWB, 310.

Maddison, Angus, 1926. WWE, 553; WWE (1999), 719.

Malin, James C., 1893-1979. KB, 757, G. Cunfer.

Mann, Julia de Lacy, 1891-1985.
TH, 17:i, Spring 1986, 3-6, N.B. Harte. N.B. Harte & K.G. Ponting (eds), *Textile History and Economic History. Essays in Honour of Miss Julia de Lacy Mann* (Manchester, 1973), x-xvi.

Mantoux, Paul Joseph, 1877-1956. WWW, 5, 730; *Times*, 18 December 1956.

Marriner, Sheila, 1925-1998.
IDBH, 166. *Recorder, The University of Liverpool Alumni Magazine.*, 119, October 1993, P.N. Davies.

Marshall, Alfred, 1842-1924.
A.C. Pigou (ed), *Memorials of Alfred Marshall* (1956). PBA, 11 (1924-25), 446-57, W.R. Scott.

Marshall, Dorothy, 1900-1994. Times, 17 February 1994.

Marshall, John Duncan, 1919. *Regional Identity* (Manchester, 1998), 226-47, Elizabeth Roberts & O.M. Westall.

Mathias, Peter, 1928.
K. Bruland & P. O'Brien (eds), *From Family Firms to Corporate Capitalism. Essays in Business and Industrial History in Honour of Peter Mathias* (Oxford, 1998), vii-xi, 1-18. WW, 1381.

Matthews, Robert Charles Oliver, 1927. WWE, 577.

Mavor, James, 1854-1925. ESS, 10, 234, J.B. Brebner.

Meek, Ronald Lindley, 1917-1978.
J. Bradley & M. Howard (eds), *Classical and Marxian Political Economy, Essays in Honour of Ronald L. Meek* (1982), v-xiv, G. Houston, *History of Political Economy*, 11:i, 1979, i-iii, A. Skinner.

Meitzen, August, 1822-1910. ESS, 10, 302, A. Skalweit.

Melis, Federigo. JEEH, 10:iv, 1981, 709-42.

Mendenhall, Thomas C. II, 1910. BD, iii, 5111; CA, 115 (1985), 313.

Meredith, Hugh Owen, 1878-1964.
N.B. Harte (ed), *The Study of Economic History* (1971), xxv, xxxv. WWW, 6, 776.

Merger, Michèle, 1947. IDBH, 180.

Meyer, John Robert, 1927. WWE, 595. CSN, 10:1, Feb. 1995, 3-6, 20-24, J. Brown.

Meuvret, Jan, 1901-1971. BDH, 277, R. Bonney

Middleton, Roger, 1955. WWB, 335.

Miller, Edward, 1915-2001. *Daily Telegraph*, 11 January 2001.

Millward, Robert, 1939. WWB, 337.

Milward, Alan S., 1935. CANR, 45 (1995), 292; WW, 1423.

Minchinton, Walter Edward, 1921-1996. CANR, 29 (1990), 302; WW, 1996, 1344.

Mingay, Gordon Edmund, 1923. CANR, 45 (1995), 293.

Mishima, Yasuo, 1926. IDBH, 184.

Mitchell, Brian Redman, 1929. CA, 49-52 (1975, 378; WWB, 340.

Mitchell, Broadus, 1892-1988. CANR, 5 (1982), 375 *New York Times*, 30 April 1988.

Mitchison, Rosalind Mary, 1919. CA, 33-36 R (1978), 577.

Miyamoto, Matao, 1943. IDBH, 185.

Mokyr, Joel, 1946. CA, 136 (1992), 286.

Mollat Du Jourdin, Michel, 1911-1996. JEEH, 27:3, Winter 1998, 6478, J.J. Bergier.

Moore, Barrington Jr., 1913. KB, 835, B. Thompson.

Moore, Lynden (L.M. Briscoe), 1935. WWB, 344.

Morikawa, Hidemasa, 1930. IDBH, 187.

Morris, Cynthia Taft, 1928. WWE, 618.

Morris-Suzuki, Tessa, 1951. CA, 123 (1998), 267.

Mumford, Lewis, 1895-1990.
>D.Miller, *Lewis Mumford: A Life* (New York, 1989). T.P. Hughes & Agatha C. Hughes (eds), *Lewis Mumford: Public Intellectual* (New York, 1990). ANB, 16, 86-88, R. Casillo; IESS, 551, D.L. Foley; *KB, 845, C.M. Scribner; BD, i, 467.

Munro, J.E.C., 1849-1896. *Economic Journal*, 6, December 1896, 660, E.C.K. Gonnor.

Munro, J. Forbes, 1940. WWB, 354.

Munro, John Henry Alexander, 1938. CA, 41-44 (1979), 494.

Myrdal, Karl Gunnar, 1898-1987. CANR, 4 (1981), 447; IESS, 571-8, P. Streeten.

Nakagawa, Keiichiro, 1920. IDBH, 192.

Nash, R.C. (Norris), 1950. WWB, 359.

Nawa, Toichi, 1906-1978.
Journal of Contemporary History, 32:2, April 1997, 159-80, Kaoru Sugihara; MS, 114-16.

Neal, Frank, 1936(?). WWB, 359.

Neal, Larry D., 1941. IDBH, 194. CSN, 14:1, Feb. 1999

Needham, Noel Joseph Terence Montgomery, 1900-1995.
M. Goldsmith, *Joseph Needham. Twentieth Century Renaissance Man* (Paris, 1995). G. Werskey, *The Visible College. A Collective Biography of British Scientists and Socialists of the 1930s* (1978, 1988), 67-80, 167-69. CANR, 34 (1991), 321-23.

Nef, John Ulric, 1899-1988.
J.U. Nef, *Search for Meaning. The Autobiography of a Nonconformist* (Washington D.C., 1973). CA, 127 (1989) 321; WWWA for his father (1862-1915).

Neilson, Nellie, 1873-1947.
Journal of British Studies, 18, 1979, 142-52, Margaret Hastings & Elizabeth G. Kimball.

Nettels, Curtis Putnam, 1898. CA, 1-4 (1967), 706.

Nevins, Allan, 1890-1971.
R.A. Billington (comp.), *Allan Nevins on History* (New York, 2975), ix-xxvii. DLB, 315-27, R.M. McMurry; ANB, 16, 316-19, J.F. Wall.

Newmarch, William, 1820-1882. DPE,3, 17, F. Hendricks.

Nicholson, Joseph Shield, 1850-1927. PBA, 13 (1927), 346-67, W.R. Scott.

Nieboer, Herman Jeremias, 1873-1920. ESS, 11, 372, S.R. Steinmetz.

Nishimura, Shizuya, 1929. IDBH, 198.

Noro, Eitaro, 1900-1934. MS, 81-83.

North, Douglass Cecil, 1920. WWE, 642. CSN, 8:3, Oct.1993, 7-12, 24-28, G. Libecap

Nove, Alec, 1915-1994. PBA, 94 (1996), 627-44, A. Brown & A. Cairncross.

O'Brien, Patrick Karl, 1932. WW, 1529.

O'Connor, Harvey, 1897-1987. CA, 5-8 (1969), 841; BD, iii, 533.

Odling-Smee, John C., 1943. WWB, 371.

Offer, Avner, 1944. WW, 2001, 1556.

Okochi, Akio, 1932. IDBH, 204.

Ollerenshaw, Philip G., 1953. IDBH, 206.

Oser, Jacob, 1915. BD, 111, 536; CANR, 2 (1981), 515.

Otsuka, Hisao, 1907-1996. KB, 891, De-Min Tao.

Outhwaite, R.B., 1935. WWB, 377.

Overy, Richard James, 1947. CA, 119 (1987), 262.

Owsley, Frank Lawrence, 1890-1956.
 Harriet C. Owsley, *Frank Lawrence Owsley: Historian of the Old South: A Memoir* (Nashville, 1990). DLB, 336-42, M.E. Bradford; *KB, 897-98, Priscilla M. Roberts.

Palairet, Michael R., 1941. WWB, 381.

Palgrave, Sir Robert Inglis, 1827-1919. DPE, 111, 707-09, A.W. Kiddy.

Pares, Richard, 1902-1993. CANR, 59 (1998), 310-13; WW, 1993, 1448.

Parker, William N., 1919-2000.
 Newsletter of the Economic History Society, 23, February 2001, 30, J. Potter. CSN, 6:3, July 1991, 3-8, 19-25, P. Rhode

Patten, Simon Nelson, 1852-1922. DPE, 111, 714-16, B. Mitchell.

Payne, Peter L., 1929. WWB, 388.

Pearson, Robin, 1955. WWB, 391.

Peden, George C., 1943. WWB, 391.

Pelling, Henry Mathison, 1920.
 J. Winter (ed), *The Working Class in Modern British History. Essays in Honour of Henry Pelling* (1983), vii-xii. CA, 61-61 (1976), 421.

Perkin, Harold James, 1926. CANR, 14 (1985), 367.

Perren, Richard, 1943. WWB, 394.

Phillips, Alban William Housego, 1914-1975. IESS, 632, K. Lancaster,

Phillips, Ulrich Bonnell, 1877-1934. DLB, 350-64, K. Wood; KB, 916, J.D. Smith.

Pinchbeck, Ivy, 1898-1982. KB, 921, Margaret Shkimba.

Pirenne, Henri, 1862-1935.
 B.D. Lyon, *Henri Pirenne: A Biographical and Intellectual Study* (Ghent, 1974). S.W. Halperin (ed), *Some Twentieth Century Historians* (Chicago, 1961), 1-29, J.L. Cate; APU, 85-100, C. Verlinden; IESS, 12, 99, Hans van Werveke.

Platt, D.C.M. (Christopher), 1934-89.
 CA, 129 (1990), 344; *Bulletin of Latin American Research*, 9:1, 1990, 117-121, Rory Miller.

Plumb, John Harold, 1911.
N. McKendrick (ed), *Historical Perspectives. Studies in English Thought and Society* (1974), 1-18; WW, 1630.

Pohl, Hans, 1935. IDBH, 219.

Polanyi, Karl, 1886-1964.
Kari Polanyi-Levitt (ed), *The Life and works of Karl Polanyi*, (New York, 1990). K. McRobbie (ed), *Humanity, Society and Commitment: On Karl Polanyi* (Montreal, 1994). IESS, 12, 172, H. Zeisel; KB, 938, Pat Hudson.

Pollard, Sydney, 1925-1998.
JEEH, 28:2, Fall 1999, 411-15, P. Mathias. *Independent*, 10 December 1998, C. Holmes.

Ponting, Kenneth G. (Ken), 1913-1983. T.H. 14:2, 1983, 107-13, D.C. Coleman.

Pool, Arthur George, 1905- 1963. WWW, 6.

Porter, George R., 1792-1855. DPE, 111, 170, H.E. Egerton.

Porter, Glenn, 1944. CA, 73-76 (2978), 512.

Porter, J.H., 1943. WWB, 404.

Porter, Kenneth Wiggins, 1905. BD iii, 555; CANR, 2 (1981), 530.

Porter, Roy Sydney, 1946. WW, 1641.

Postan, Sir Michael Moissey (Munia), 1899-1981.
EHR, 35:i, February 1982, iv-vi, M.W. Flinn & P. Mathias; PBA, 69 (1983), 453-58, E. Miller.

Postgate, Raymond William, 1896-1971. SLH, 23, Autumn 1971, 4-5.

Potter, David M., 1910-1971. DLB, 953, Priscilla M. Roberts.

Potter, John, 1922. CA, 21-24 (1977), 690.

Pounds, Norman John Greville, 1912. CA, 1-4 (1967), 769.

Power, Eileen, 1889-1940.
*Maxine Berg, *A Woman in History. Eileen Power 1889-1940* (Cambridge, 1996), *KB, 954, Maxine Berg. WWW, 3, 1097; N.F. Cantor, *Inventing the Middle Ages* (1991), 381-95.

Press, Jon, 1953. IDBH, 222.

Pressnell, Leslie Sedden.
P.L. Cottrell & D.E. Moggridge (eds), *Money and Power. Essays in Honour of L.S. Pressnell* (1988), xvi-xvii.

Price, Jacob Myron, 1925. CANR, 1 (1981), 520.

Prothero, Rowland Edmund, Baron Ernle, 1851-1937.
Lord Ernle, *English Farming Past and Present* (6th edn, 1961), lxxix-cxlv, O.R. McGregor; WWW, 3, 418.

Pullan, Brian Sebastian, 1935. WW, 1666.

Putnam, Bertha Haven, 1872-1960.
Journal of British Studies, 18, 1979, 152-59, Margaret Hastings & Elizabeth G. Kimball.

Rae, John B., 1911-1988.
Journal of Transport History, 10:2, September 1989, 98, T.C. Barker.

Ramsay, George Daniel, 1909-1992. PBA, 87 (1994), 401-16, R.B. Wernham.

Ransom, Roger, 1938. CSN, 15:2, Summer 2000, 5-14, Kerry Odell.

Rau, Virginia, -1973. JEEH, 4:i, Spring 1995, 243-45, C. Verlinden.

Reader, William Joseph, 1920-1990.
CA, 132 (1991), 338; CANR, 39 (1992), 307; *Times*, 2 July 1990.

Redford, Arthur, 1896-1961.
A. Redford, *Labour Migration in England 1800-1850* (2nd edn. 1964), xv-xviii, W.H. Chaloner, reprinted in W.H. Chaloner, *Industry and Innovation*, edited by D.A. Farnie & W.O. Henderson (1990), 193-95.

Redlich, Fritz, 1892-1978.
F. Redlich, *Steeped in Two Cultures. A Selection of Essays* (1971), vii-xviii; JEEH, 11:2, Fall 1982, 447-72, H. Kellenbenz.

Rees, Sir James Frederick, 1883-1967. WWW, 6, 942.

Reynolds, Lloyd George, 1910. CANR, 15 (1985), 380; WWE, 715.

Reynolds, Robert Leonard, 1902-1966. CA, 1-4 (1967), 795; CA, 103 (1982), 423.

Richards, Eric, 1940. CA, 148 (1996), 379.

Robertson, Hector Menteith, 1905-1984. WWE, 720; CA, 113 (1985), 404.

Robinson, Eric, 1924. CA, 49-52 (1975), 460.

Rodney, Walter, 1942-1980. KB, 1001, Toyin Falola & J.E. Tishken.

Rogers, James Edwin Thorold, 1823-1890.
Political Science Quarterly, 4, 1889, 381; DPE, 111, 319, W.J. Ashley; ESS, 13, 417, J.F. Rees; IESS, 13, 542, A.W. Coats; DNB, W.A.S. Hewins; F. Boase, *Modern English Biography* (1900, 1965) 258.

Rogow, Arnold A., 1924. BD, iii, 563.

Roll, Eric (Erich), Baron Roll of Ipsden, 1907. CA, 102 (1981), 438; WW, 1761.

Rolt, Lionel Thomas Caswall, 1910-1974.
CANR, 1 (1981), 548; TNS, 46, 1974, 93; *Times*, 11 May 1974, 14 May, R.A. Buchanan.

Rooth, Tim, 1939. WWB, 433.

Roover, Raymond de, 1904-1972. JEEH, I:iv, 1972, 755-62, D. Herlihy.

Rörig, Fritz, 1882-1952. KB, 1013, P.A. Lambert.

Roscher, Wilhelm, 1817-1894.
DPE, 111, 323-7, A. Oncken; *Economic Journal*, 4, 1894, 558, G. Cohn

Rose, Mary B., 1953. WWB, 434.

Rose, Michael E., 1936. WWB, 434.

Rosenberg, Hans, 1904-1988. KB, 1016, R.F. Southard.

Rosenberg, Nathan,. CA 147 (1995), 385; CSN, 9:3, Oct. 1994, 3-6, 27-29, W. C. Sunderstrom.

Rosovsky, Henry, 1927. WWE, 732.

Rostovtzeff, Michael Ivanovitch, 1870-1952.
M.A. Wes, *Michael Rostovtzeff, Historian in Exile. Russian Roots in an American Context* (Stuttgart, 1990), cited by RCR, 126; PBA, 38 (1952), 347-61, A.H.M. James; APU, 55-73, C.B. Welles; A. Momigliano, *Studies in Historiography* (1966), 91-104; KB, 1017, J.A.S. Evans.

Rostow, Walt Whitman, 1916.
CANR, 8 (1983), 427-32, Deborah A. Straub & Jean W. Ross; BD, i, 508; WWE, 733; KB, 1019, Priscilla M. Roberts. CSN, 9:2, July 1994, 3-8, 26-32, J.V.C. Nye.

Rowbotham, Sheila, 1943.
H. Abelove et. Al. (eds), *Visions of History* (Manchester, 1983), 49-69; KB, 1020, Hera Cook; RCR, 123.

Rowe, D.J., 1940, WWB, 437.

Royle, Edward, 1944. CA, 61-61 (1976), 471.

Rubinstein, William David, 1946. CA, 114 (1985), 398.

Rudé, George, 1910-1993. KB, 1022, J. Friguglietti.

Rule, John, 1944. WWB, 438.

St Joseph, John Kenneth Sinclair, 1912-1994.
PBA, 87 (1994), 417-38, D.R. Wilson.

Salaman, Redcliffe Nathan, 1874-1955.
R.N. Salaman, *The History and Social Influence of the Potato* (Cambridge, 2nd edn 1985), xxix-xxxv; *Bibliographical Memoirs of Fellows of the Royal Society*, I, 1955, 239-45. K.M. Smith; *Transactions of the Jewish Historical Society*, 18, 1955, 296-98, the Reverend James W. Parkes; WWW, 5, 960.

Salvemini, Gaetano, 1873-1957. KB, 1045, R. Ranieri.

Salvioli, Giuseppe, 1857-1928. ESS, 13, 526, C. Barbagallo.

Samuel, Raphael, 1934-1996.
Oral History, 25, 1997, 30-37, P. Thompson; KB, 1047, R. McWilliam; RCR, 123.

Sandberg, Lars Gunnarsson, 1939. CA, 53-56 (1975), 501.

Sargent, Arthur John, 1871-1947. *Times*, 19 February 1947.

Saul, Samuel Berrick, 1924. WW, 1809.

Saville, John, 1916.
D.E. Martin & D. Rubinstein (eds), *Ideology and the Labour Movement. Essays presented to John Saville* (1979), 15-31, 258-63, R. Milliband & Joyce M. Bellamy.

Sawai, Minoru, 1953. IDBH, 238.

Sayers, Richard Sidney, 1908-1989. PBA, 76 (1990), 545, A.K. Cairncross.

Scherer, James Augustin Brown, 1870-1944. WWWA, 2, 470.

Schmitz, Christopher J., 1950. IDBH, 239.

Schmoller, Gustav, 1838-1917.
BES, 415-43, Pauline R. Anderson; APU, 9-14, 38-39, F.C. Lane; DPE 111, 751, B. Mitchell; ESS, 13, 576, H. Gehrig.

Schofield, Eunice, 1914-1992. HSLC, 142, 1992, M. Power.

Schofield, Maurice M., 1915-1989. HSLC, 139, 1989, 203, M.J. Power.

Schofield, Robert Edwin, 1923. CA, 162 (1998), 313.

Schofield, Roger Snowden, 1937. WW, 1819.

Schönert-Röhlk, Frauke, 1936. IDBH, 240.

Schulze-Gävernitz, Gerhart von, 1864-1943.
TH, 9, 1978, 79-83, D.A. Farnie, 'Three Historians of the Cotton Industry'.

Schumpeter, Elizabeth Boody, 1898-1953.
DWE; E.B. Schumpeter, *English Overseas Trade Statistics 1697 –1808* (Oxford, 1960), v-vii, E.W. Gilboy.

Schumpeter, Joseph Alois Julius, 1883-1950.
R.L. Allen, *Opening Doors: The Life and Work of Joseph Schumpeter* (New Brunswick, N.J., 1991, 2 vols.). APU, 22-27, F.C. Lane; ANB, 19, 443-45, M. Thornton.

Schwartz, Anna Jacobson, 1915. DWE; CA, 125 (1989), 406. CSN, 10:2, July 1995, 3-7, E.N. White.

Schwartz, Leonard, 1947. WWB, 447.

Scola, R, 1943-1988.
R. Scola, *Feeding the Victorian City. The Food Supply of Manchester,* 1770-1870 (Manchester, 1992), xvii-xix, Alan Armstrong.

Scott, William Robert, 1868-1940. PBA, 26 (1940), 479-88, J.H. Clapham.

Scoville, Warren Candler, 1913. CA, 1-4 (1967), 846.

Sée, Henri, 1864-1936.
BES, 444-76, H.T. Parker; APU, 107-18, M.M. Knight; IESS, 14, 143, A. Chabert.

Seebohm, Frederic, 1833-1912.
P. Vinogradoff, *Collected Papers* (1928), 272; DNB; DPE, iii, 754, W.H. Dawson; ESS, 13, 641, K. Smellie.

Semmel, Bernard, 1928. CA, 77-80 (1979), 486.

Shaw, William Arthur, 1865-1943. PBA, 29 (1943), 349-56, J.H. Clapham.

Silberling, Norman John, 1892-1942.

Sigerist, Henry E., 1891-1957. KB, 1091, R. Broer.

Sigsworth, Eric M., 1923-1992.
E.M. Sigsworth, *A Respectable Life. Leeds in the 1930s* (Beverley, 1994).

Simiand, François, 1873-1935. KB, 1095, J. Millhorn.

Simmons, Colin, 1948. WWB, 461.

Simmons, Jack, 1915-2000.
Daily Telegraph & Independent, 6 September 2000, M. Robbins & N. Scarfe; WW, 1870; *Journal of Transport History*, N.S. III, 1975-76, 133-44, H.J. Dyos.

Singer, Charles Joseph, 1876-1960. TNS, 32, 1960, 150; WWW, 5, 1005; DNB.

Singleton, John, 1960. IDBH, 249.

Slater, Gilbert, 1864-1938. WWW, 3, 1246.

Slaven, Anthony, 1937. IDBH, 250.

Slicher van Bath, Bernhard Hendrick, 1920. BDH, 381, CGA Clay.

Smart, William, 1853-1915. DPE, 111, 764-66, W.H. Dawson; ESS, 14, 111, T. Jones.

Smelser, Neil Joseph, 1930. CANR, 8 (1983), 470.

Smith, Merritt Roe, 1940. KB, 1105, Linda E. Endersby.

Smith, Sir Roland, 1928.
D.J. Jeremy & G. Tweedale (eds), *Dictionary of Twentieth Century Business Leaders* (1994), 195; WW, 1904; *Investors Chronicle*, 15 January 1988, 17, 'My Name is Legion'; *North West Business Insiders*, I, March 1991, 4-7, Martin Regan 'An Enigma within his own Lifetime'.

Smith, Robert Sydney, 1904-1969.
History of Political Economy, 1:i, 1969, 5-8, J.O. Blackburn, J.J. Spengler & C.D. Goodwin.

Soetbeer, Adolf Georg, 1814-1892. ESS, 14, 249, H. Moeller.

Sombart, Werner, 1863-1941.
A. Mitzman, *Sociology and Estrangement. Three Sociologists of Imperial Germany* (New York, 1973), including F. Tönnies (1855-1936) & R. Michels (1876-1936). APU, 14-16, F.C. Lane.

Soule, George Henry, 1887-1970. CAP, 2 (1978), 486.

Spiethoff, Arthur, 1873-1957. APU, 16-22, F.C. Lane.

Stamp of Shortlands, Lord, 1880-1941. PBA, 27 (1941), 453-65, J.H. Clapham.

Stampp, Kenneth M., 1912. BD, 111, 587; CA, 13-16 R (1975), 761.

Stark, Werner, 1909. CANR, 10 (1983), 435.

Staley, Alvah Eugene, 1906. BD, 11, 555; CA, 77-80 (1979), 517.

Stein, Stanley J., 1920. KB, 1148, B. Troyan.

Stone, Lawrence, 1919.
A.L. Beier, D. Cannadine & J.M. Rosenheim (eds), *The First Modern Society. Essays in English History In Honour of Lawrence Stone* (1989), 1-30, 575-611, J. Mitchell, C.S.L. Davies, Miriam Slater, J.M. Murrin, L. Stone.

Sugar, Peter F., 1919. KB, 1156, R.F. Forrest.

Sugihara, Kaoru, 1948. WWB, 490.

Sugiyama, Shinya, 1949. CA,, 132 (1991), 409; IDBH, 262.

Supple, Barry Emmanuel, 1930. WW, 1981.

Sutch, Richard Charles, 1942. CANR, 34 (1991), 439.

Suzuki, Toshio, 1948. IDBH, 264.

Suzuki, Yoshitaka, 1944. IDBH, 265.

Sweezy, Paul Marlor, 1910. CANR, 5 (1982), 514; BD, ii, 564.

Sykes, Joseph, 1899-1967. WWW, 6, 1097.

Sylla, Richard, 1940. IDBH, 267.

Tagány, Károly, 1858-1924. ESS, 14, 506, F. Eckhart.

Tann, Jennifer (pseudonym Geoffrey Booth), 1939. CA, 103 (1982), 503.

Taussig, Frank William, 1859-1940. ANB, 21, 342, Anne T. Keane.

Tawney, Richard Henry, 1880-1962.
R. Terrill, *R.H. Tawney and His Times: Socialism as Fellowship* (Cambridge, Mass., 1973). A. Wright, *R.H. Tawney* (1987). J.M. Winter (ed), *History and Society. Essays by R.H. Tawney* (1978), 1-40. 'Tawney the Historian'. PBA, 48 (1962), 461-82, T.S. Ashton; W.H.B. *Court, Scarcity and Choice in History* (1970), 127-40. J. Kenyon, *The History Men* (1983), 235-50; R. Dahrendorf, *The LSE 1895-1995* (Oxford, 1995), 232-42; IESS, 15, 518, L. Stone; DNB.

Temin, Peter, 1937. WWE, 829. CSN, 14:3, Oct. 1999, 3, 6.

Teuteberg, Hans Jürgen, 1929. IDBH, 271.

Thirsk, Irene Joan, 1922.
J. Thirsk, 'Nature versus Nurture', *History Workshop Journal*, 47, Spring 1999, 273-77; CA, 25-28 R (1977), 716. J. Chartres & D. Hey (eds), *English Rural Society 1500-1800. Essays in Honour of Joan Thirsk* (Oxford, 1990), 17-25, 369-82, A. Everitt & Margery Tranter.

Thistlethwaite, Frank, 1915.
F. Thistlethwaite, *A Lancashire Family Inheritance* (Cambridge, 1996); WW 2019.

Thomas of Swynnerton, Baron Hugh Swynnerton, 1931. WW, 2001, 2040.

Thomas, Brinley, 1906-1994. PBA, 90 (1995), 499-520, J.P. Lewis; WW, 1994, 1882.

Thomas, Sir Keith, 1933. CANR, 34 (1991), 449; WW, 2024.

Thompson, Edward Palmer, 1924-1993. .
J. Kaye & K. McLelland (eds), *E.P. Thompson. Critical Perspectives* (1990). H. Abelove et al. (eds), *Visions of History* (Manchester, 1983), 5-25; PBA, 90 (1995), 521-42, E.J. Hobsbawm; HJK, 169-71; *RCR, 124.

Thompson, Francis Michael Longstreth, 1925. KB, 1189, Christine S. Hallas; WW, 2029.

Thomson, James K.J., 1947. WWB, 507.

Tilly, Charles, 1929, and Louise A. Tilly, 1930. KB, 1194-97, C. Strikwerda.

Todd, John Alton, 1875-1954. WWW, 5, 1091.

Tolliday, Steven W., 1951. IDBH, 275.

Tomlinson, Jim, 1951. IDBH, 276.

Tooke, Thomas, 1774-1858. DPE, 111, 588, H.E. Egerton; ESS, 14, Lindley M. Fraser.

Tortella, Gabriel, 1936. IDBH, 278.

Toynbee, Arnold, 1852-1883.
   A. Kadish, *Apostle Arnold: The Life and Death of Arnold Toynbee 1852-1883* (Durham N.C., 1988). Johns Hopkins University Studies in History and Political Science, VII:i, 1889, 1-53, F.C. Montague. *The Academy*, 24 March 1883, 205, A. Milner; 26 July 1884, 54, Edith Simcox; ESS, 14, 666, J.L. Hammond.

Trainor, Richard Hughes (Rick), 1948. WW, 2001, 2090.

Trebilcock, Clive, 1942. WWB, 514.

Treble, John G., 1947. WWB, 514.

Tregonning, Kennedy Gordon, 1923. *CA 9-12 (1974), 903.

Trevelyan, George Macaulay, 1876-1962.
   D. Cannadine, *G.M. Trevelyan. A Life in History* (1992). *RCR, 124.

Tribe, Keith, 1949. WWB, 514.

Tsuchiya, Takeo, 1896-1988. MS, 85-87.

Tsunoyama, Sakae, 1921. IDBH, 279.

Tupling, George Henry, 1883-1962. LCAS, 72, 1962, 176-79, J.S. Roskell.

Turner, Frederick Jackson, 1861-1922.
   R.A. Billington, *Frederick Jackson Turner: Historian, Scholar, Teacher* (New York, 1973). DLB, 407-17, Odie B. Faulk.

Tweedale, Geoffrey, 1951. IDBH, 281.

Uchida, Hoshimi, 1926. IDBH, 281.

Unwin, George, 1870-1925.
   G.W. Daniels, *George Unwin: A Memorial Lecture* (Manchester, 1926). R.H. Tawney (ed), *Studies In Economic History: The Collected Papers of George Unwin* (1927, 1958), xi-lxxiv, 465-71. New DNB (Oxford, 2004), T.A.B. Corley.

Urquhart, Malcolm, C., CSN, 10:3, Oct., 1995, 3-6, 18-22, M. McInnis.

Usher, Abbot Payton, 1883-1965. APU, 157-66, W.N. Parker; IESS, 16, 221-24, J.H. Dales.

Utley, Freda (Winifred), 1889-1978.
   F. Utley, *Lost Illusion* (1948); *Odyssey of a Liberal. Memoirs* (Washington D.C., 1970); New DNB (Oxford, 2004), D.A. Farnie.

Vance, Rupert Bayless, 1899-1975. IESS, 781-83, R.L. Simpson.

Van Der Wee, Baron Herman, 1928. IDBH, 286.

Ville, Simon P., 1958. IDBH, 290.

Viner, Jacob, 1892-1970. IESS, 783-87, W.J. Baumol & Ellen Viner Seiler.

Vinogradoff, Sir Paul, 1854-1925.
P. Vinogradoff, *Collected Papers* (1928), i, 1-74; ii, 479-95, H.A.L. Fisher; PBA, 11 (1924-25), 486-501, W.S. Holdsworth; *English Historical Review*, 41, 1926, 236-43, F.M. Powicke, reprinted with corrections in *Modern Historians and the Study of History* (1955), 9-18; ESS, 15, 263, W. Seagle.

Vogel, Ezra F., 1930. CA, 13-16 91975), 824.

Von Mises, Ludwig Edler, 1881-1973. IESS, 16, 381, M.N. Rothbard.

Vries, Jan de, see entry under 'De Vries'.

Wada, Kazuo, 1949. IDBH, 293.

Wadsworth, Alfred Powell, 1891-1956.
Manchester Guardian, 5 November 1956; 15 November, R.H. Tawney; WWW, 5, 1124.

Wallerstein, Immanuel, 1930. CANR, 49 (1995), 431; KB, 1277, A.Y. So

Walsh, Margaret, 1942. IDBH, 294.

Ward, John Towers, 1930-1987. CANR, 7 (1982), 515; CANR, 122 (1988), 473.

Ward, J.R., 1946. WWB, 530.

Ware, Caroline Farrar, 1899-1990. DWE; CA, 131 (1991), 473.

Webb, Beatrice, 1858-1943.
B. Webb, *My Apprenticeship* (1926); *Our Partnership* (1948). PBA, 29 (1943), 285-312, R.H. Tawney; IESS, 16, 487-91, Margaret Cole.

Weber, Max, 1864-1920.
Marianne Weber, *Max Weber: A Biography* (1975). IESS, 16, 493-502., R. Bendix.

Weber, Wolfhard, 1940. IDBH, 297.

Wiener, Martin J., 1941. CA 85-88 (1980), 630.

Weir, Ronald B., 1944. WWB, 537.

White, Lynn Jr., 1907-1987. KB, 1295, T.F. Glick.

Whyman, John, 1939. WWB, 543.

Willan, Thomas Stuart, 1910-1994.
    Independent, 22 June 1994, C.B. Phillips; PBA, 101 (1998), 557-63, C.B. Phillips; WW, 1994, 2047.

Williams, Eric Eustace, 1911-1981.
    Eric Williams, Inward Hunger: The Education of a Prime Minister (1969, Chicago, 1971). KB, 1303, B. Schwarz. CA,125 (1989), 492.

Williams, John Henry, 1887-1980. CA, 105 (1982), 533.

Williams, Trevor Illtyd, 1921-1996. CA, 109 (1983), 528; CA, 154 (1997), 470.

Williamson, Jeffrey Gale, 1935. WWE, 888.

Williamson, Samuel H., CSN, 15:3, Fall 2000, 5-15, L. Craig & M. Haupert

Wilson, Charles Henry, 1914-1991.
    JEEH, 22:i, Spring 1993, 143-54, P. Mathias. D.C. Coleman & P. Mathias (eds), *Enterprise and History. Essays in Honour of Charles Wilson* (Cambridge, 1984), xii-ix, 278-80; WW, 1991, 1987.

Wilson, John F., 1955. IDBH, 302; WWB, 550.

Wilson, Richard G., 1938. IDBH, 303.

Winstanley, Michael J., 1949. CA, 129 (1990), 477.

Winter, Jay M., 1945. CA 73-76 (1978), 647

Wittfogel, Karl August, 1896-1988.
    G.L. Ulmen, *The Science of Society. Toward an Understanding of the Life and work of Karl August Wittfogel* (1978); IESS, 812-14, G.E. Taylor.

Wright, Chester Whitney, 1879-1966 WWWA, 4, 1036.

Wright, Quincy, 1890-1970. IESS, 814, M.B. Travis.

Wrigley, Christopher John, 1947. WW, 2258.

Wrigley, Sir Edward Anthony, 1931. WW, 2258; KB, 1340, Pamela Sharpe.

Woodruff, William, 1916.
    W. Woodruff, *Billy Boy* (Wakefield, 1993), reprinted as *The Road to Nab End. A Lancashire Childhood* (2000). CA, 101 (1981), 565.

Woodward, Donald, 1942. WWB, 556.

Worswick, George David Norman, 1916. WW, 2250.

Yamada, Moritaro, 1897-1980. MS, 83-87.

Yamamoto, Toru, 1946. IDBH, 308.

479

Yonekawa, Shin-ichi, 1931-1999.
>   Takeshi Yuzawa (ed), *Japanese Business Success.   The Evolution of a Strategy* (1994), xiii, G. Jones; IDBH, 312.

Yui, Tsunehiko, 1931. IDBH, 315.

Yunoki, Manabu, 1929. IDBH, 315.

Yuzawa, Takeshi, 1940. IDBH, 316.

Zamagni, Vera, 1943. IDBH, 317.

Zinsser, Hans (pseudonym R.S.), 1878-1940.
>   *As I Remember Him: The Biography of R.S.* (Boston, 1940); CA, 159 (1998), 449-51; WWWA, 1, 1396.